a Wolters Kluwer business

Governmental GAAP Guide

By Michael A. Crawford and D. Scot Loyd

Highlights

Financial professionals who work with state and local governments must stay current with emerging governmental standards or face some unfortunate consequences. This one-of-a-kind tool discusses all the promulgated accounting principles applicable to accounting and financial reporting by state and local governments. CCH's *Governmental GAAP Guide* delivers a thorough analysis of GASB Statements, GASB Interpretations, GASB Technical Bulletins, NCGA Statements, NCGA Interpretations, and certain AICPA Statements of Position and Audit and Accounting Guides. Everything has been analyzed and restated in plain English and is supported by timesaving examples and illustrations.

2008 Edition

The 2008 edition of *Governmental GAAP Guide* has been updated throughout with the very latest information on:

- *GASB Comprehensive Implementation Guide—2006 Questions and Answers*
- AICPA Audit and Accounting Guide *State and Local Governments—with conforming changes as of May 1, 2006*
- GASB-48 (Sales and Pledges of Receivables and Future Revenues and Intra-Entity Transfers of Assets and Future Revenues)
- GASB-49 (Accounting and Reporting of Pollution Remediation Obligations)

- GASB-50 (Pension Disclosures)
- GASB Technical Bulletin 2006-1 (Accounting and Financial Reporting by Employers and OPEB Plans for Payments from the Federal Government Pursuant to the Retiree Drug Subsidy Provisions of Medicare Part D)
- GASB Proposed Concepts Statement (Elements of Financial Statements)
- GASB Invitation to Comment (Fund Balance Reporting and Governmental Fund Type Definitions)
- GASB Proposed Statement (Accounting and Financial Reporting for Intangible Assets)
- GASB Proposed Statement (Land and Other Real Estate Held as Investments by Endowments)

In the 2008 edition, comprehensive examples have been added to provide practical guidance in the calculation of the invested in capital assets, net or related debt, and the restricted net assets components of net assets as reported in a statement of net assets.

In addition, the 2008 edition includes an updated Financial Statement Disclosures Checklist to assist financial statement preparers and attestors in meeting the disclosure requirements of generally accepted accounting principles.

Accounting Research Manager™

Accounting Research Manager is the accounting industry's largest and most comprehensive online database, providing easy access to objective and insightful government, accounting, auditing, and SEC information. While other research tools simply summarize the authoritative literature, leaving you to decipher often-complex information, Accounting Research Manager goes the extra mile to give you the clearest possible picture. We bring clarity to your government and financial reporting research.

The *Accounting Research Manager Government Library* provides one-stop access to governmental authoritative and proposal stage literature, including

- **GASB (Governmental Accounting Standards Board)** Statements & Interpretations, Technical Bulletins, Implementation Guides & related proposal stage literature

- **GAO (Government Accountability Office)** Governmental Auditing Standards, Financial Audit Manual
- **OMB (Office of Management and Budget)** Circulars, Compliance Supplements

The Government Library also offers in-depth, interpretive guidance. Users can access our government titles that include the ***Governmental GAAP Guide, Governmental GAAP Practice Manual, Local Government and Single Audits,*** and the ***Governmental GAAP Update Service***.

Learn more about Accounting Research Manager by visiting **www.accountingresearchmanager.com**.

CCH Learning Center

CCH's goal is to provide you with the clearest, most concise, and up-to-date accounting and auditing information to help further your professional development, as well as a convenient method to help you satisfy your continuing professional education requirements. The CCH Learning Center* offers a complete line of self-study courses covering complex and constantly evolving accounting and auditing issues. We are continually adding new courses to the library to help you stay current on all the latest developments. The CCH Learning

* CCH is registered with the National Association of State Boards of Accountancy (NASBA) as a sponsor of continuing professional education on the National Registry of CPE Sponsors. State boards of accountancy have final authority on the acceptance of individual courses for CPE credit. Complaints regarding registered sponsors may be addressed to the National Registry of CPE Sponsors, 150 Fourth Avenue North, Suite 700, Nashville, TN, 37219-2417. Telephone: 615-880-4200.

* CCH is registered with the National Association of State Boards of Accountancy (NASBA) as a Quality Assurance Service (QAS) sponsor of continuing professional education. Participating state boards of accountancy have final authority on the acceptance of individual courses for CPE credit. Complaints regarding QAS program sponsors may be addressed to NASBA, 150 Fourth Avenue North, Suite 700, Nashville, TN 37219-2417. Telephone: 615-880-4200.

Center courses are available 24 hours a day, seven days a week. You'll get immediate exam results and certification. To view our complete accounting and auditing course catalog, go to: **http://cch.learningcenter.com**.

11/07

For questions concerning this shipment, billing, or other customer service matters, call our Customer Service department at 1 800 248 3248.

2008

GOVERNMENTAL GAAP GUIDE

FOR STATE AND LOCAL GOVERNMENTS

MICHAEL A. CRAWFORD, CPA
D. SCOT LOYD, CGFM, CPA

This publication is designed to provide accurate and authoritative information in regard to the subject matter covered. It is sold with the understanding that the publisher is not engaged in rendering legal, accounting, or other professional services. If legal advice or other professional assistance is required, the services of a competent professional person should be sought.

—From a *Declaration of Principles* jointly adopted by a Committee of the American Bar Association and a Committee of Publishers and Associations

ISBN: 978-0-8080-9130-1

ISSN: 1088-9159

4025 W. Peterson Avenue
Chicago, IL 60646-6085
1 800 248 3248
http://CCHGroup.com

Portions of this work were published in a previous edition.

Printed in the United States of America

Contents

IV. Financial Reporting by General-Purpose Governments

V. Stand-Alone Financial Reporting by Special-Purpose Governments

Our Peer Review Policy

Thank you for ordering the 2008 *Governmental GAAP Guide*. Each year we bring you the best engagement guides available, with accompanying electronic workpapers and practice aids. To confirm the technical accuracy and quality control of our materials, CCH voluntarily submitted to a peer review of our publishing system and our publications (see the Peer Review Statement on the following page).

In addition to peer review, our publications undergo strict technical and content reviews by qualified practitioners. This ensures that our books, workpapers, and practice aids meet "real world" standards and applicability.

Our publications are reviewed every step of the way—from conception to production—to ensure that we bring you the finest guides on the market.

Updated annually, peer reviewed, technically accurate, convenient and practical—CCH's 2008 *Governmental GAAP Guide* shows our commitment to creating books and workpapers you can trust.

Peer Review Statement

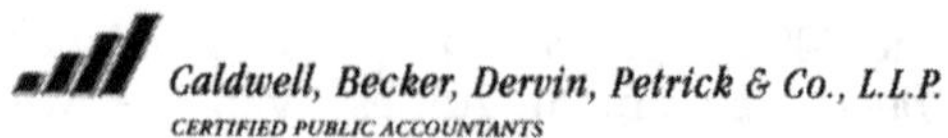

September 30, 2005

Executive Board
CCH INCORPORATED

We have reviewed the system of quality control for the development and maintenance of MILLER GOVERNMENTAL GAAP GUIDE (2006 Edition) of CCH INCORPORATED (the company) applicable to non-SEC issuers in effect for the year ended June 30, 2005, and the resultant materials in effect at June 30, 2005. The design of the system, and compliance with it, are the responsibilities of the company. Our responsibility is to express an opinion on the design of the system, and the company's compliance with that system based on our review.

Our review was conducted in accordance with the standards for reviews of quality control materials promulgated by the Peer Review Committee of the Center for Public Company Audit Firms of the American Institute of Certified Public Accountants. In performing our review, we have given consideration to the following general characteristics of a system of quality control. A company's system for the development and maintenance of quality control materials encompasses its organizational structure and the policies and procedures established to provide the users of its materials with reasonable assurance that the quality control materials are reliable aids to assist them in conforming with professional standards in conducting their accounting and auditing practices. The extent of a company's quality control policies and procedures for the development and maintenance of quality control materials and the manner in which they are implemented will depend upon a variety of factors, such as the size and organizational structure of the company and the nature of the materials provided to users. Variance in individual performance and professional interpretation affects the degree of compliance with prescribed quality control policies and procedures. Therefore, adherence to all policies and procedures in every case may not be possible.

Our review and tests were limited to the system of quality control for the development and maintenance of the aforementioned quality control materials of CCH INCORPORATED and to the materials themselves and did not extend to the application of these materials by users of the materials nor to the policies and procedures of individual users.

In our opinion, the system of quality control for the development and maintenance of the quality control materials of CCH INCORPORATED was suitably designed and was being complied with during the year ended June 30, 2005, to provide users of the materials with reasonable assurance that the materials are reliable aids to assist them in conforming with those professional standards in the United States of America applicable to non-SEC issuers. Also, in our opinion, the quality control materials referred to above are reliable aids at June 30, 2005.

CALDWELL, BECKER, DERVIN, PETRICK & CO., LLP.
CALDWELL, BECKER, DERVIN, PETRICK & CO., L.L.P.

20750 Ventura Boulevard, Suite 140 • Woodland Hills, CA 91364
(818) 704-1040 • FAX (818) 704-5536

Preface

Integrated Coverage of GASB-34 and GASB-35

Governmental Accounting Standards Board Statement No. 34 (GASB-34) (Basic Financial Statements—and Management's Discussion and Analysis—for State and Local Governments) and GASB-35 (Basic Financial Statements—and Management's Discussion and Analysis—for Public Colleges and Universities) serves as the primary guidance for those who prepare, audit, and use government financial reports. In addition, the GASB continues to work on the further development and clarification of accounting standards for state and local government entities.

New Pronouncements and Outstanding Exposure Drafts

Introduced in 2003 and updated annually, the *Comprehensive Implementation Guide—Questions and Answers* was developed by the GASB staff to assist financial statement preparers and attestors in the implementation and application of a number of GASB pronouncements. As of the publication date of this edition of CCH's *Governmental GAAP Guide,* the GASB has not issued its 2007 guide, *Comprehensive Implementation Guide—2007 Questions and Answers,* which was to be issued in the third quarter of 2007.

In 2004, the AICPA issued two updated guides that provide guidance for state and local governments and their auditors. The AICPA Audit and Accounting Guide *State and Local Governments—with conforming changes as of May 1, 2006,* presents recommendations of the AICPA State and Local Government Audit Guide Revision Task Force on the application of generally accepted auditing standards to audits of financial statements of state and local governments.

The second guide, AICPA Audit Guide *Government Auditing Standards and OMB Circular A-133—with conforming changes as of May 1, 2006,* presents recommendations of the AICPA State and Local Government Audit Guide Revision Task Force on the application of generally accepted government auditing standards (GAGAS) to audits of financial statements of state and local governments, and audits of compliance with major federal award programs under the Single Audit Act of 1996, as amended. As of the publication date of this edition of the *Governmental GAAP Guide,* the AICPA has not issued its audit and accounting guides with conforming changes as of May 1, 2007.

The following GASB pronouncements were issued in 2006 and, as of the publication date of this edition, 2007:

- GASB-48 (Sales and Pledges of Receivables and Future Revenues and Intra-Entity Transfers of Assets and Future Revenues) establishes accounting and financial reporting standards that (1) require enhanced disclosures pertaining to future revenues that have been pledged or sold; (2) provide guidance on sales of receivables, other assets, or future revenue within the same reporting entity; and (3) provide guidance on recognizing other assets and liabilities arising from the sale of specific receivables or future revenues.
- GASB-49 (Accounting and Reporting of Pollution Remediation Obligations) establishes accounting and financial reporting standards for governments that are faced with obligations to remediate or clean up pollution problems. The standard identifies the obligation triggers or events, the methods of estimating the obligation, the reporting of such obligations, and related note disclosure requirements.
- GASB-50 (Pension Disclosures) amends pension disclosures in GASB-25 (Financial Reporting for Defined Benefit Pension Plans and Note Disclosures for Defined Contribution Plans) and GASB-27 (Accounting for Pensions by State and Local Government Employers) to bring the current pension disclosure requirements in line with the disclosures recently required for governmental other postemployment benefit (OPEB) plans, including information about the funding status of the plan as of the most recent actuarial valuation.
- GASB Technical Bulletin No. 2006-1 (Accounting and Financial Reporting by Employers and OPEB Plans for Payments from the Federal Government Pursuant to the Retiree Drug Subsidy Provisions of Medicare Part D) clarifies the proper reporting of payments that an employer or defined-benefit other postemployment benefit (OPEB) plan receives from the federal government under the Medicare Part D prescription drug program.
- GASB Proposed Concepts Statement (Elements of Financial Statements) proposes new definitions for seven elements of historically based financial statements, including assets, liabilities, deferred outflow and inflow of resources, net assets, and inflow and outflow of resources. This proposed concepts statement focuses on the concept of measuring and reporting resources.
- GASB Invitation to Comment (Fund Balance Reporting and Governmental Fund Type Definitions) sought feedback from preparers, auditors, and users of governmental financial statements on possible solutions to current issues related to the reporting of fund balance reserves and designations, and the definition and use of governmental fund types.

- GASB Proposed Statement (Accounting and Financial Reporting for Intangible Assets) proposes to address the current inconsistencies in the accounting and financial reporting of intangible assets, particularly in the areas of recognition, initial measurement, and amortization.
- GASB Proposed Statement (Land and Other Real Estate Held as Investments by Endowments) proposes that land and other real estate held as investment by endowments be reported at fair value.

How to Use CCH's *Governmental GAAP Guide*

CCH's *Governmental GAAP Guide* is a single reference that discusses all of the promulgated accounting principles applicable to financial reporting by state and local governments that are in use today: GASB Statements, GASB Interpretations, GASB Technical Bulletins, NCGA Statements, and NCGA Interpretations. These original pronouncements have been analyzed and are restated in straightforward language to allow preparers and auditors of governmental financial statements to better understand the original promulgations. To facilitate research, major topics in the text are cross--referenced to the pertinent paragraphs of the original pronouncements. Illustrations, figures, and paragraphs called "Observations" demonstrate and clarify specific accounting principles.

The *Governmental GAAP Guide* alerts readers to and discusses financial accounting and reporting standards necessary to prepare the basic external financial statements of a governmental entity. A companion text, CCH's *Governmental GAAP Practice Manual: Including GASB 34 Guidance,* illustrates how governmental financial statements are prepared based on the standards established by GASB-34.

Acknowledgments

The preparation of this book was made possible by the efforts of a number of dedicated people. Sandy Miller, Courtney Crowder, and Scott M. Adair, CPA, provided thoughtful reviews for this new edition.

Although other individuals played an important role in the preparation of CCH's *Governmental GAAP Guide*, any errors or omissions are the responsibility of the authors. The *Governmental GAAP Guide* continues to evolve as new pronouncements are issued and as we strive to better explain governmental accounting and reporting standards. If you have suggestions you believe will improve the quality of the material, please send them to the publisher.

Mike A. Crawford
Oklahoma City, Oklahoma

D. Scot Loyd
McPherson, Kansas

About the Authors

Michael A. Crawford is Chairman of Crawford & Associates, P.C., a CPA firm headquartered in Oklahoma City, Oklahoma, that specializes in providing auditing, consulting, and accounting services solely to governmental entities. He is a past president of the Oklahoma Society of CPAs, an inductee into the Oklahoma Accounting Hall of Fame, the current Vice Chairman of the Governmental Accounting Standards Advisory Council (GASAC), and current Chair of the GASAC Agenda Committee. Mr. Crawford is recognized both nationally and internationally as a frequent lecturer at many national and state governmental conferences and has also authored various technical publications for the AICPA.

D. Scot Loyd is in the firm Swindoll, Janzen, Hawk & Loyd, LLC, a CPA firm headquartered in McPherson, Kansas. Mr. Loyd is partner in charge of a diversified governmental practice, including software development, relating to states, counties, cities, schools, and other miscellaneous government entities. As a member or Chair of several of the American Institute of Certified Public Accountants' (AICPA) Task Forces and Committees and the Mid-America Intergovernmental Audit Forum Committees such as the American Institute of Certified Public Accountants Government Performance and Accountability Committee (current), Professional Ethics Executive Committee (PEEC) (Past Member), Partnering for CPA Practice Success (PCPS) Technical Issues Committee (TIC) [Past Government A & A Zone Chairman], and AICPA Governmental Accounting and Auditing Committee, Mr. Loyd has been a contributor for all size firms to the standard-setting process. Mr. Loyd is also a frequent speaker at various AICPA and state society conferences.

I. BASIC GOVERNMENTAL ACCOUNTING CONCEPTS AND STANDARDS

CHAPTER 1
FOUNDATION AND OVERVIEW OF GOVERNMENTAL GENERALLY ACCEPTED ACCOUNTING PRINCIPLES

CONTENTS

INTRODUCTION

Accounting Principles Board Statement No. 4 (APB-4) (Basic Concepts and Accounting Principles Underlying Financial Statements of Business Enterprises) defines "generally accepted accounting principles" (GAAP) as conventions, rules, and procedures necessary to describe accepted accounting practice at a particular time. The importance of reporting entities following generally accepted accounting principles in the preparation of their financial statements is embodied in Rule 203 of the AICPA's Code of Professional Conduct, which states:

> A member shall not (1) express an opinion or state affirmatively that the financial statements or other financial data of any entity are presented in conformity with generally accepted accounting principles or (2) state that he or she is not aware of any material modifications that should be made to such statements or data in order for them to be in conformity with generally accepted accounting principles, if such statements or data contain any departure from an accounting principle promulgated by bodies designated by Council to establish such principles that has a material effect on the statements or data taken as a whole. If, however, the statements or data contain such a departure and the member can demonstrate that due to unusual circumstances the financial statements or data would otherwise have been misleading, the member can comply with the rule by describing the departure, its approximate effects, if practicable, and the reasons why compliance with the principle would result in a misleading statement.

The AICPA Council has designated the Financial Accounting Standards Board (FASB) as the body to establish accounting principles for both for-profit and not-for-profit organizations, the Governmental Accounting Standards Board (GASB) as the body to establish accounting principles for state and local governments, and the Federal Accounting Standards Advisory Board (FASAB) as the body to establish accounting principles for the federal government (APB-4, par. 138; AICPA Code of Professional Conduct, Rule 203).

The Financial Accounting Foundation (FAF) has agreed that the GASB has the authority to issue generally accepted accounting principles for state and local governmental units. Thus, the GASB establishes accounting principles for state and local governments, and the FASB establishes accounting principles for all other reporting entities, including not-for-profit organizations other than state and local governments.

Guidance for determining the applicability of specific accounting and reporting standards for governmental entities is established by the following pronouncements:

- SAS-69 (The Meaning of "Present Fairly in Conformity with Generally Accepted Accounting Principles")
- GASB-20 (Accounting and Financial Reporting for Proprietary Funds and Other Governmental Entities That Use Proprietary Fund Accounting)

The GASB has released a white paper entitled "Why Governmental Accounting and Financial Reporting is—and Should Be—Different." The central theme of the white paper is that the GASB's continued existence is vital to individuals and organizations who are interested in the financial performance of state and local governments, who have substantially different information needs than those who are interested in the financial performance of for-profit entities. For-profit entities, whose accounting standards are established by the Financial Accounting Standards Board (FASB), are environmentally different from government entities. According to the white paper, the primary purpose of governments is to enhance or maintain the well-being of citizens by providing services in accordance with public-policy goals. In contrast, for-profit business enterprises focus primarily on wealth creation, interacting principally with those segments of society that fulfill their mission of generating a financial return on investment for shareholders.

The white paper cites several other crucial differences that generate user demand for unique information from governments:

- Governments serve a broader group of stakeholders, including taxpayers, citizens, elected representatives, oversight groups, bondholders, and others in the financial community.
- Most government revenues are raised through involuntary taxes rather than a willing exchange of comparable value between two parties in a typical business transaction.
- Monitoring actual compliance with budgeted public-policy priorities is central to government public-accountability reporting.

- Governments exist longer than for-profit businesses and are not typically subject to bankruptcy and dissolution.

A governmental entity may be involved in a variety of activities that have characteristics similar to commercial enterprises and to not-for-profit entities, as well as to governmental activities. Determining which accounting standards should be observed to account for these varied activities has been confusing at times and somewhat complex. SAS-69 (AU 411) provides the fundamental guidance for determining which accounting standards governmental entities should observe to prepare their financial statements.

Even with the issuance of SAS-69 (AU 411) there was confusion about whether governmental activities that follow commercial accounting standards (proprietary fund activities) should continue to follow promulgations issued by the FASB. This problem was addressed with the issuance of GASB-20, which established two alternatives that could be used to account for proprietary fund activities.

GASB-20, discussed later in this chapter, establishes guidance for the incorporation of FASB pronouncements into funds that use proprietary fund accounting. Based on this guidance, either of two alternative methods can be used by an activity that follows proprietary fund accounting standards.

OBSERVATION: GASB-34 does not change the two alternatives established in GASB-20.

STATE AND LOCAL GOVERNMENT ACCOUNTING HIERARCHY (SAS-69)

Exhibit 1-1 shows the state and local government accounting hierarchy established by SAS-69 (AU 411). The hierarchy has five levels, each of which is subordinate to the level(s) directly above it. For example, if an accounting issue is addressed in both Level B and Level C, the guidance established in Level B must be followed because it is the highest source of accounting principles for the particular accounting issue (SAS-69, pars. 12 and 13).

EXHIBIT 1-1
STATE AND LOCAL GOVERNMENT ACCOUNTING HIERARCHY

Level A
- GASB Statements
- GASB Interpretations
- FASB pronouncements made applicable by a GASB Statement or GASB Interpretation

	• AICPA pronouncements made applicable by a GASB Statement or GASB Interpretation
Level B	• GASB Technical Bulletins • AICPA Audit and Accounting Guides made applicable by the AICPA and cleared by the GASB • AICPA Statements of Position made applicable by the AICPA and cleared by the GASB
Level C	• GASB Emerging Issues Task Force consensus positions (if created) • AICPA Practice Bulletins made applicable by the AICPA and cleared by the GASB
Level D	• GASB Implementation Guides • Practices widely recognized and prevalent
Level E	Other Accounting Literature (such as): • GASB Concepts Statements • Sources identified in Levels Athrough D in the private sector accounting hierarchy that have not been made applicable by the action of the GASB • APB Statements • FASB Concepts Statements • AICPA Issues Papers • International Accounting Standards of the International Accounting Standards Committee • Pronouncements of other professional associations or regulatory agencies • AICPA Technical Practice Aids • Accounting textbooks • Handbooks • Articles

Level A

The most authoritative sources of governmental GAAP are the pronouncements included in Level A of the state and local government accounting hierarchy, such as GASB Statements and Interpretations.

Under the accounting hierarchy established by SAS-69 (AU 411), only FASB pronouncements (Statements, Interpretations, and Technical Bulletins) that have been explicitly endorsed by the GASB establish governmental GAAP. In a similar fashion, only AICPA accounting pronouncements that have been made applicable to governmental accounting by a GASB Statement or Interpretation establish governmental GAAP. For example, AICPA Statements of Position, AICPA Practice Bulletins, and AICPA Accounting Interpretations would have to be endorsed by the GASB for them to be considered part of Level A of the state and local government accounting hierarchy (SAS-69, par. 12).

> **PRACTICE POINT:** As discussed later, the cutoff date for determining which FASB pronouncements apply to governmental entities is November 30, 1989. However, an amendment to a pronouncement that is issued after the cutoff date and applies to a FASB pronouncement that was issued before the cutoff date does not establish governmental GAAP. For example, FAS-13 (Accounting for Leases) was issued before the cutoff date and, therefore, should be applied by governmental entities, but any amendment to FAS-13 issued after November 30, 1989, does not have to be applied by governmental entities.

In the past, pronouncements of the FASB, the APB, and the Committee on Accounting Procedure have not, for the most part, been applied to information presented in governmental funds. The GASB decided that government-wide financial statements must be prepared by applying these pronouncements issued on or before November 30, 1989, (unless they conflict with GASB pronouncements) on a retroactive basis (with four exceptions discussed in GASB-34, par. 146). Pronouncements issued by the FASB after November 30, 1989, cannot be followed in the preparation of financial statements for governmental activities (GASB-34, par. 17).

Level B

The second most authoritative source of governmental accounting principles includes GASB Technical Bulletins. Technical Bulletins are prepared by the GASB staff and are issued as formal documents if a majority of the members of the GASB do not object to their issuance (SAS-69, par. 12).

Also included in Level B are AICPA Audit and Accounting Guides, and AICPA Statements of Position that have been made applicable by the AICPA and cleared by the GASB. SAS-69 (AU 411) states that the term "cleared" means that the GASB does not object to the issuance of the pronouncement proposed by the AICPA(SAS-69, par. 12).

> **PRACTICE POINT:** AICPA pronouncements specifically made applicable to state and local governments, as noted in the pronouncement, can be assumed to have been cleared by the GASB unless otherwise indicated.

Level C

The third level of the state and local government accounting hierarchy includes AICPA Practice Bulletins that have been made applicable by the AICPAand cleared by the GASB. AICPA Practice Bulletins are issued by the Accounting Standards Division based on the views of the AICPA's Accounting Standards Executive Committee. The accounting issues covered in Practice Bulletins are narrow in scope and are not on the agenda of either the FASB or the GASB (SAS-69, par. 12).

The third level of the hierarchy makes provisions for a future group of practicing accountants authorized by the GASB to reach consensus positions on governmental accounting issues. Although the GASB has not created such a body, its mission would be similar to the FASB's Emerging Issues Task Force (SAS-69, par. 12).

> **PRACTICE POINT:** Currently, there are no pronouncements that provide guidance in the Level C category unique to governmental entities.

Level D

The fourth level of the state and local government accounting hierarchy includes GASB Implementation Guides. These Guides are structured in a question and answer format, are developed by the GASB staff, and are subject to due process procedures, including the public announcement of the project and exposure to the GASB and an advisory group. An Implementation Guide is not formally voted on by the GASB, but a Guide will not be released if a majority of the Board members object to its issuance. GASB has issued its *Comprehensive Implementation Guide,* which consolidates previously issued guides for GASB-3, GASB-9, GASB-10, GASB-14, GASB-25, GASB-26, GASB-27, GASB-31, and GASB-34 (SAS-69, par. 12). Additionally, GASB has issued separate implementation guides on GASB-43, GASB-44, and GASB-45.

Also included in Level D of the hierarchy are accounting practices widely recognized and prevalent in the preparation of state and local governmental financial reports. Such practices can be identified by reading specific governmental financial statements and professional services that summarize governmental financial reporting practices (SAS-69, par. 12).

Level E

The final level is referred to as "other accounting literature" and is the least authoritative source of accounting principles. This category includes GASB Concepts Statements, which are broad in nature and, therefore, do not address specific governmental accounting principles, procedures, and methods. The GASB, in establishing future governmental accounting reporting standards, will be influenced by positions taken in Concepts Statements (SAS-69, par. 13).

The state and local government accounting hierarchy is not fully insulated from the private-sector hierarchy. The final level of the state and local government hierarchy includes sources identified in Levels A through D of the private-sector accounting hierarchy that have not been made applicable by actions of the GASB or the AICPA (SAS-69, par. 10).

Application Guidance

The structure established by SAS-69 (AU 411) is a hierarchy. Standards established in the highest level take precedent over those contained in a lower level. For example, accounting issues related to compensated absences are addressed in both GASB-16 (Accounting for Compensated Absences) and FAS-43 (Accounting for Compensated Absences). When preparing financial statements for a governmental entity, the accountant must observe the standards established in GASB-16 because GASB Statements are part of Level A of the hierarchy and FASB Statements are included in Level E, the other accounting literature level (SAS-69, pars. 12 and 13).

When an accounting issue is not addressed in a GASB Statement or Interpretation or other source listed in Level A of the hierarchy, the other levels of the hierarchy must be considered. For example, if a matter is addressed in an AICPA Audit and Accounting Guide that has been made applicable by the AICPA and cleared by the GASB, the guidance established in the publication should be used to prepare the financial statements of a state or local governmental entity (SAS-69, pars. 10, 12, and 13).

Accounting Principles Other Than GAAP

The establishment of generally accepted accounting principles for state and local governments is complicated by a factor not present in the promulgation of accounting principles for business enterprises. Some state and local laws do not recognize GASB or FASB pronouncements as the basis for preparing their governmental financial statements. For example, a governmental unit through a charter or constitution may require that a reporting entity prepare its budget and financial statements on a cash basis, modified cash basis, or regulatory basis of accounting. Although the governmental unit will probably maintain its accounting records on a non-GAAP basis for legal compliance purposes, it may still adopt a supplementary accounting system that will enable it to report on a GAAP basis (NCGA-1, par. 5).

HIERARCHY FOR PROPRIETARY FUND ACCOUNTING ACTIVITIES (GASB-20)

Since the inception of the GASB, there has been considerable confusion over the role of the GASB and the FASB in the promulgation of generally accepted accounting principles for entities that, in practice, can take the form of either a public entity or a private entity (i.e., colleges and universities).

Although the issuance of SAS-69 (AU 411) made it clear that FASB pronouncements would not automatically have to be followed in the preparation of financial statements for governmental funds, there was confusion about whether the guidance was applicable to proprietary funds.

In general, proprietary funds use the same measurement focus (flow of economic resources) and accounting basis (accrual) as commercial enterprises. Thus, governmental entities had to observe all FASB Statements and Interpretations in the preparation of financial statements for proprietary funds unless the GASB had specifically addressed the accounting issue involved in one of its own pronouncements. The issue that arose from SAS-69 (AU 411) was whether newly issued FASB pronouncements had to be observed in preparing proprietary fund financial statements, because proprietary fund accounting attempts to simulate commercial accounting.

That issue was not addressed in SAS-69 (AU 411), and in practice, some proprietary funds chose to follow all FASB pronouncements while other proprietary funds chose to ignore those FASB pronouncements that have not been made applicable to the public sector or cleared by the GASB. GASB-20 addresses this issue.

Enterprise Fund Activity Accounting and Financial Reporting Standards

GASB-20 allows for two distinct but acceptable alternatives for the reporting of Enterprise Funds.

> **PRACTICE POINT:** GASB-20 applies to proprietary funds and entities following proprietary fund accounting. However, Alternative 2 is only available to Enterprise Funds.

Alternative 1 Under Alternative 1, governmental entities using proprietary fund accounting must follow (1) all GASB pronouncements and (2) FASB Statements and Interpretations, APB Opinions, and Accounting Research Bulletins (ARBs) issued on or before November 30, 1989, except those that conflict with a GASB pronouncement (GASB-20, pars. 6–8).

OBSERVATION: The cutoff date of November 30, 1989, was chosen because it is the date when the Financial Accounting Foundation (FAF) Trustees reaffirmed the GASB's authority to promulgate accounting standards for state and local governmental entities. The action taken by the FAF was made in anticipation of the eventual issuance of SAS-69. The effective date of SAS-69 was March 15, 1992. However, the GASB believes that the 1989 date is a better date than the 1992 date for determining which FASB pronouncements are to be observed in the preparation of proprietary fund financial statements under Alternative 1.

Selecting the November 30, 1989, cutoff date means that all FASB Statements up to and including FAS-102 (Statement of Cash Flows—Exemption of Certain Enterprises and Classification of Cash Flows from Certain Securities Acquired for Resale) and FASB Interpretations up to and including FIN-38 (Determining the Measurement Date for Stock Option, Purchase, and Award Plans Involving Junior Stock) must be observed in preparing proprietary fund financial statements.

Under Alternative 1, if a FASB Statement or Interpretation issued after November 30, 1989, amends or supersedes a FASB Statement, FASB Interpretation, APB Opinion, or ARB issued on or before November 30, 1989, the newly issued FASB pronouncement does not apply to proprietary funds unless specifically adopted in a GASB pronouncement. If the GASB has not specifically adopted the FASB amendment or supersession, then the original FASB Statement, FASB Interpretation, APB Opinion, or ARB would continue to apply to the preparation of proprietary fund financial statements without modification (GASB-20, pars. 6–8).

Under Alternative 1, Level A of the state and local government accounting hierarchy for proprietary funds is expanded and includes the following sources of governmental generally accepted accounting principles (the additional authoritative sources in Level A are highlighted):

- GASB Statements
- GASB Interpretations
- FASB pronouncements made applicable by a GASB Statement or GASB Interpretation
- AICPA pronouncements that have been made applicable by a GASB Statement or GASB Interpretation
- **FASB Statements and Interpretations, APB Opinions, and ARBs issued on or before November 30, 1989, that do not conflict with GASB pronouncements**
- **FASB Statements and Interpretations that amend FASB Statements and Interpretations, APB Opinions, and ARBs**

issued on or before November 30, 1989, if specifically adopted in a GASB pronouncement

Alternative 2 Under Alternative 2, governmental entities using enterprise funds must follow (1) all GASB pronouncements and (2) all FASB Statements and Interpretations, APB Opinions, and ARBs, no matter when issued, except those that conflict with a GASB pronouncement. Unlike Alternative 1, Alternative 2 has no cutoff date for determining the applicability of FASB pronouncements (GASB-20, pars. 6–8).

> **OBSERVATION:** FAS-87, FAS-95, FAS-106, and FTB 85-3 are not applicable under Alternative 2, because they conflict with GASB pronouncements.

Under Alternative 2, if a newly issued FASB Statement or Interpretation amends or supersedes a FASB Statement, FASB Interpretation, APB Opinion, or ARB, the newly issued FASB pronouncement applies to the preparation of enterprise fund financial statements, assuming the amendment does not conflict with a GASB pronouncement (GASB-20, pars. 6–8).

Under Alternative 2, Level A of the state and local government accounting hierarchy for enterprise funds is expanded and includes the following sources of governmental generally accepted accounting principles (the additional authoritative sources in Level A are highlighted):

- GASB Statements
- GASB Interpretations
- **FASB Statements and Interpretations that do not conflict with GASB pronouncements (no action needed by the GASB)**
- AICPA pronouncements that have been made applicable by a GASB Statement or GASB Interpretation
- **FASB Statements and Interpretations that amend FASB Statements and Interpretations, APB Opinions, and ARBs (assuming the new guidance does not conflict with a GASB pronouncement) (GASB-20, pars. 6–8)**

The private-sector accounting hierarchy includes AICPA Industry Audit and Accounting Guides and Statements of Position that have been cleared by the FASB. If an AICPA Industry Audit and Accounting Guide or Statement of Position does not include governmental entities in its scope but has been cleared by the FASB, then the AICPA pronouncement is considered to be part of Level B authoritative support for enterprise funds under Alternative 2 (GASB-20, pars. 6–8).

PRACTICE POINT: If an AICPA Industry Audit and Accounting Guide (such as the *State and Local Governments Guide*) or Statement of Position has been made applicable by the AICPA to governmental entities, and cleared by the GASB, it is considered Level B guidance for state and local government entities under both alternatives.

In addition, if an AICPA Practice Bulletin does not include governmental entities in its scope but has been cleared by the FASB, the AICPApronouncement is considered to be part of Level C authoritative support (GASB-20, pars. 6–8).

PRACTICE POINT: If an AICPA Practice Bulletin has been made applicable by the AICPA to governmental entities, and cleared by the GASB, it would be considered Level C guidance for state and local government entities under both GASB-20 alternatives.

Prohibition of hybrid alternative GASB-20 prohibits the selective use of guidance established by Alternative 1 and Alternative 2. Thus, the preparer of financial statements for a proprietary fund must use either Alternative 1 or Alternative 2 and cannot use a combination of the two. For example, it would be inappropriate to reject the guidance established by a newly issued FASB Statement (guidance established in Alternative 1) and then incorporate the guidance established by another newly issued FASB Statement (guidance established in Alternative 2) (GASB-20, pars. 6–8).

Applicability of FAS-71 to Proprietary Fund Accounting

FAS-71 (Accounting for the Effects of Certain Types of Regulation) does not preclude the application of its standards to governmental entities. The guidance allows governmental entities to follow the standards established by FAS-71, but does not require them to do so. GASB-20 does not change the application guidance established in FAS-71. Thus, because FAS-71 was issued before November 30, 1989, the standards established by the Statement, and related pronouncements, may be used under Alternative 1 or Alternative 2 because application was made optional under FAS-71 (GASB-20, par. 9).

OBSERVATION: The pronouncements related to FAS-71 are FAS-90 (Regulated Enterprises—Accounting for Abandonments and Disallowances of Plant Costs), FAS-92 (Regulated Enterprises—Accounting for Phase-in Plans), and FAS-101 (Regulated Enterprises—Accounting for the Discontinuation of Application of FASB Statement No. 71).

Any pronouncements related to FAS-71 and issued after November 30, 1989, are subject to the guidance established by GASB-20. Thus, if a governmental entity followed Alternative 1 in the preparation of proprietary fund financial statements, and initially chose to apply FAS-71, any FASB Statement or Interpretation related to FAS-71 issued after November 30, 1989, would apply only if the Statement or Interpretation is adopted in a GASB pronouncement. If a governmental entity followed Alternative 2, and initially chose to apply FAS-71, any FASB Statement or Interpretation related to FAS-71 and issued after November 30, 1989, would apply (assuming the guidance does not conflict with a GASB pronouncement) because no action by the GASB is required (GASB-20, par. 9).

Applicability of FAS-116 and FAS-117

Alternative 2, established by GASB-20, allows proprietary funds to adopt all FASB pronouncements, including those issued after November 30, 1989, as long as those standards do not conflict with a GASB pronouncement. With the issuance of FAS-116 and FAS-117, which were directed to not-for-profit accounting and reporting issues, there was uncertainty about whether proprietary funds should incorporate the standards established by these two Statements. GASB-29 states that Alternative 2 should be interpreted to include only those FASB Statements and Interpretations that apply to commercial enterprises. Thus, the standards established by FAS-116 and FAS-117 are not incorporated into Alternative 2 (GASB-29, par. 7).

AICPA NOT-FOR-PROFIT MODEL (GASB-29)

GASB-29 (The Use of Not-for-Profit Accounting and Financial Reporting Principles by Governmental Entities) allowed some governmental entities to use the AICPA not-for-profit model as described in the AICPA's Statement of Position 78-10 (SOP 78-10) (Accounting Principles and Reporting Practices for Certain Nonprofit Organizations) or Industry Audit Guide, "Audits of Voluntary Health and Welfare Organizations." GASB-34 prohibits the use of that model but states that a governmental not-for-profit entity that reported as of June 30, 1999, using the not-for-profit model may report as a special-purpose government engaged only in business-type activities even if the entity does not satisfy the definition of an Enterprise Fund (GASB-34, par. 147).

IDENTIFYING A GOVERNMENTAL ENTITY

To determine whether the state and local government accounting hierarchy or the private-sector accounting hierarchy applies to a particular entity, the entity must be classified as a governmental or private entity. In most instances it is obvious how an entity should be classified, but there are occasions in which classification is not so obvious. These issues are addressed in the AICPAs *State and Local Governments* Guide.

The AICPA Audit Guide identifies the following as general categories of governmental entities:

- States, territories, and the District of Columbia
- Municipal corporations
- Other entities created by government

> **OBSERVATION:** The material in the AICPA *State and Local Government* Guide is based on a GASB staff paper titled "Applicability of GASB Standards," which was issued in November 1993. The staff paper is advisory and is not intended to "supersede decisions made by the courts or by any other duly constituted governmental body in determining whether a particular entity is a 'government' for any purpose whatsoever, including governmental audit or oversight."

States, Territories, and the District of Columbia

States and local governmental entities include all 50 states, tribal governments, all U.S. territories, and the District of Columbia. These governmental entities must observe the state and local government accounting hierarchy when preparing their financial statements.

> **PRACTICE POINT:** The state and local government accounting hierarchy does not apply to the federal government. Accounting standards for the federal government are established by the Federal Accounting Standards Advisory Board (FASAB).

Municipal Corporations

State governments create a variety of governmental entities to carry out the mission of the state. These entities may be general-purpose governmental entities (e.g., cities and counties) or special-purpose governmental entities (e.g., school districts and public authorities). Although special-purpose governments may or may not have the power to tax and borrow funds, or may have characteristics somewhat different from a general-purpose government in a particular state (such as being beyond the domain of the state civil service law), they are nonetheless governmental in nature and must observe the governmental accounting hierarchy.

Other Entities Created by Government

Entities included in the third category may or may not be considered governmental in nature. For example, some states provide colleges, universities, and hospitals with significant amounts of public funds. Because of a particular state's charter, however, it may be difficult to classify such institutions as public or nonpublic.

To address the issue, the GASB and the FASB jointly agreed to a definition of "government," which is presented as follows:

> Public corporations and bodies corporate and politic are governmental organizations. Other organizations are governmental organizations if they have one or more of the following characteristics:
>
> - Popular election of officers or appointment (or approval) of a controlling majority of members of the organization's governing body by officials of one or more state or local governments
> - The potential for unilateral dissolution by a government with the net assets reverting to a government
> - The power to enact and enforce a tax levy

In addition, the GASB's and FASB's definition of a "government" includes entities that have the authority to issue tax-exempt debt directly to other parties. However, an entity that has the authority to directly issue tax-exempt debt but has no other characteristics of a governmental entity (as defined above), may be considered a nongovernmental entity if the entity can offer "compelling, relevant evidence" that it is nongovernmental.

GASB RULE-MAKING PROCESS

The GASB has established a due process for the promulgation of governmental generally accepted accounting principles that encourages participation by parties interested in a particular accounting issue. Once a governmental accounting issue has been identified, the due process generally consists of the following potential stages:

- Preliminary Views
- Discussion Memorandum
- Exposure Draft
- Standard-setting

Preliminary Views Stage

A Preliminary Views document is issued by the GASB when they desire to solicit opinions from constituents on accounting and reporting alternatives and the preliminary views of the GASB members in the early stages of accounting standards setting.

Discussion Memorandum Stage

The GASB technical staff researches an issue and discusses the issue with a task force appointed often by the GASB chairman. The task force consists of individuals representing a variety of interested parties, including user groups, state and local governments, and academia. To provide a basis for broad discussion within the profession, a Discussion Memorandum may be issued by the GASB staff. The Discussion Memorandum identifies the issue, discusses possible solutions, and describes their advantages and disadvantages. At this stage, the GASB and its technical staff take no position regarding the preferred solution.

Exposure Draft Stage

The GASB technical staff receives responses from interested parties based on the description of the issue in the Discussion Memorandum or Preliminary Views Document. In addition, public hearings on the issue are usually held where participants can present their views orally and respond to questions raised by members of the GASB. When the GASB reaches its tentative solution to the issue, it issues an Exposure Draft for public comment.

> **PRACTICE POINT:** Copies of current Preliminary Views, Discussion Memorandums, and Exposure Drafts can be obtained from the GASB's Web site (www.gasb.org).

Standard-Setting Stage

After receiving comments on the Exposure Draft, the GASB may hold another public hearing. Once the GASB reaches a consensus on the accounting issue, it promulgates a standard that becomes part of generally accepted accounting principles for state and local governments. The GASB observes due process for major governmental accounting issues. If the issue is limited in scope, a Discussion Memorandum or Preliminary Views Document might not be prepared.

GASB Pronouncements

The GASB may express its position on a particular governmental accounting topic by issuing one or more of the following pronouncements:

- GASB Statement
- GASB Interpretation
- GASB Technical Bulletin

GASB Statement (Level A GAAP) The GASB addresses major governmental accounting issues by issuing a GASB Statement, but only after all aspects of the due process have occurred.

GASB Interpretation (Level A GAAP) The GASB addresses issues of lesser scope by issuing Interpretations. An Interpretation is subject to due process, although the procedures are not as formal as those for the promulgation of a Statement. Interpretations are directly voted on by the GASB and, if accepted by a majority of its members, become part of governmental generally accepted accounting principles.

GASB Technical Bulletin (Level A GAAP) The GASB recognizes that under certain circumstances it may not need to follow the due process used for issuing a Statement or an Interpretation. In 1984, the GASB authorized its staff to provide timely guidance on some governmental accounting issues by preparing a Technical Bulletin Series. The nature and purpose of GASB Technical Bulletins were addressed in GASB Technical Bulletin (GASB:TB) 84-1 (Purpose and Scope of GASB Technical Bulletins and Procedures for Issuance), which was issued in October 1984 (GASB:TB 84-1, par. 2).

GASB:TB 84-1 states that a Technical Bulletin, rather than a Statement or Interpretation, may be issued under the following general criteria:

- The guidance is not expected to cause a major change in accounting practice for a significant number of entities.
- The administrative cost involved in implementing the guidance is not expected to be significant for most affected entities.
- The guidance does not conflict with a broad fundamental principle or create a novel accounting practice (GASB:TB 84-1, par. 5).

The GASB follows due process before it issues a Technical Bulletin. Before the GASB releases an initial draft of a Technical Bulletin to the public for comment, members of the GASB are furnished with a copy. If a majority of the members do not object to the initial draft, the proposed Technical Bulletin is released to interested parties.

Responses from the interested parties are given to the GASB for its consideration at a public meeting. If a majority of the GASB members do not object to the proposed Technical Bulletin, the GASB will issue it as a formal Technical Bulletin. Each Technical Bulletin is published with a legend that reads, "The GASB has reviewed this Technical Bulletin and a majority of its members do not object to its issuance" (GASB:TB 84-1, pars. 6–12).

Governmental Accounting Standards Advisory Council (GASAC)

The GASB is assisted in its standards-setting process by the Governmental Accounting Standards Advisory Council (GASAC). The GASAC is responsible for consulting with the GASB on technical issues on the GASB's agenda, project priorities, matters likely to require the attention of the GASB, selection and organization of task forces, and such other matters as requested by the GASB or its chairman. The GASAC is also responsible for helping to develop the GASB's annual budget and aiding the Financial Accounting Foundation in raising funds for the GASB. The GASAC has 29 members who are broadly representative of preparers, attestors, and users of financial information.

OVERVIEW OF GOVERNMENTAL GENERALLY ACCEPTED ACCOUNTING PRINCIPLES

NCGA-1 (Governmental Accounting and Financial Reporting Principles), adopted by the GASB upon their establishment in 1984, states that financial statements of a state or local government should be prepared in accordance with generally accepted accounting principles. Certain governments may be required or permitted to prepare their financial statements on a regulatory basis of accounting or another comprehensive basis of accounting; however, generally accepted accounting principles continue to be the primary criteria for financial statements of states and local governments. Although generally accepted accounting principles for governments can be found primarily in the statements, interpretations, and other due-process documents of the NCGA, the GASB and, to some extent, the FASB and AICPA, the framework for such principles are established in Concepts Statements of the GASB.

Although not considered generally accepted accounting principles themselves, Concepts Statements are intended to provide a conceptual framework that can be used as a basis for establishing consistent financial reporting standards and serve multiple purposes, including

- dentifying the objectives and fundamental principles of financial reporting that can be applied to solve numerous financial accounting and reporting issues
- Providing the GASB with the basic conceptual foundation for considering the merits of alternative approaches to financial reporting and helping the GASB develop well-reasoned financial reporting standards
- Assisting preparers, auditors, and users in better understanding the fundamental concepts underlying financial reporting standards

Presently the GASB has issued three Concepts Statements and has on its current and future agenda two more. The issued Concepts Statements are as follows:

- *Concepts Statement No. 1* Objectives of Financial Reporting (GASB:CS-1)
- *Concepts Statement No. 2* Service Efforts and Accomplishments (GASB:CS-2)
- *Concepts Statement No. 3* Communication Methods in General Purpose External Financial Reports that Contain Basic Financial Statements (GASB:CS-3)

The Agenda Project Concepts Statements are as follows:

- Current Agenda: Proposed Concepts Statement (Elements of Financial Statements)
- Future Agenda: Concepts Statement (Measurement and Recognition)

The following discussion describes these Concepts Statements and their accounting and reporting framework objectives.

Objectives of Financial Reporting

The purpose of financial reporting by state and local governmental entities is to provide information to facilitate decision making by various user groups. GASB:CS-1 identifies the following primary user groups of governmental financial reports (GASB:CS-1, par. 30):

- Citizens of the governmental entity
- Direct representatives of the citizens (legislatures and oversight bodies)
- Investors, creditors, and others who are involved in the lending process

Although not specifically identified in the above listing, GASB: CS-1 states that intergovernmental grantors and other users have informational needs similar to the three primary user groups (GASB:CS-1, par. 31).

The financial reporting objectives identified by the GASB in GASB:CS-1 are to be used as a framework for establishing accounting and reporting standards for general purpose financial statements (GPFS); however, the framework may also be used by the GASB to establish standards for financial information presented outside of the GPFS. In addition, the financial reporting standards are applicable to general purpose financial information presented in special purpose financial reports prepared by state and local governmental entities (GASB:CS-1, pars. 8 and 9).

Although the governmental-type activities and business-type activities of a governmental entity can differ significantly, the GASB concluded that financial reporting objectives identified in GASB:CS-1 are applicable to both types of activities. Although financial reporting objectives are applicable to both governmental-type and business-type activities, the GASB does recognize that a specific objective may vary in its application to a particular reporting situation depending on the business-type activity and the user group that is evaluating the activity. For example, both creditors and a legislative body may be interested in a business-type activity, but creditors may be more concerned with the ability of the activity to generate cash flow from operations to service future debt requirements, whereas the legislature may be more concerned with the likelihood of future operations requiring subsidies from general revenues (GASB:CS-1, par. 43).

GASB:CS-1 identifies *accountability* as the paramount objective of financial reporting by state and local governments. Accountability is based on the transfer of responsibility for resources or actions from the citizenry to another party, such as the management of a governmental entity. Financial reporting should communicate adequate information to user groups to enable them to assess the performance of those parties empowered to act in the place of the citizenry (GASB:CS-1, pars. 56–58).

The GASB states (1) that accountability is a more important concept in governmental financial reporting than in business enterprise financial reporting and (2) that all governmental financial reporting objectives are derived from the accountability concept. The objectives of governmental financial reporting identified in GASB:CS-1 are summarized in Exhibit 1-2. In addition to the overall objective of accountability, GASB:CS-1 identified the following as objectives of governmental financial reporting (GASB:CS-1, pars. 56–58):

EXHIBIT 1-2

HIERARCHY OF OBJECTIVES

GASB Concepts Statement No. 1 (GASB:CS-1)

OVERALL GOAL:		Accountability	
BASIC OBJECTIVES:	Assist in fulfilling government's duty to be publicly accountable and enable users to assess that accountability	Assist users in evaluating the operating results of the governmental entity for the year	Assist users in assessing the level of services that can be provided by governmental entity and its ability to meet its obligations as they become due
COMPONENT OBJECTIVES:	• Sufficiency of current-year revenue • Compliance with budget and finance-related and contractual requirements • Assessment of governmental service efforts, costs, and accomplishments	• Sources and uses of financial resources • Financing of activities and sources of cash • Effect of current-year operations on financial position	• Financial position and condition • Information related to physical and other nonfinancial resources • Legal or contractual restrictions on resources and risk of loss of resources

- Financial reporting should assist in fulfilling a government's duty to be publicly accountable and should enable users to assess that accountability.
- Financial reporting should assist users in evaluating the operating results of the governmental entity for the year.
- Financial reporting should assist users in assessing the level of services that can be provided by the governmental entity and its ability to meet its obligations as they become due.

The GASB noted that although accountability is referred to only in the first objective, *accountability is implicit in all of the listed objectives.*

Assessment of accountability The assessment of accountability is fulfilled in part when financial reporting enables user groups to determine to what extent current-period expenses are financed by current-period revenues. This reporting objective is based on the concept of "interperiod equity," which argues that the citizenry that benefits from an expense should pay for the expenses. Financial reporting should provide a basis for determining whether, during a budgetary period, (1) a surplus was created (a benefit to the future citizenry), (2) a deficit was incurred (a burden to the future citizenry), (3) a surplus from a previous budgetary period was used to finance current expenditures (a benefit to the current citizenry), (4) a deficit from a previous budgetary period was satisfied with current revenues (a burden to the current citizenry), or (5) current and only current expenses were financed by using current and only current revenues (interperiod equity) (GASB:CS-1, pars. 59–61).

Financial reporting by a state or local government should provide a basis for user groups to determine whether (1) the governmental entity obtained and used resources consistent with the legally adopted budget and (2) finance-related legal or contractual requirements have been met. A budget reflects myriad public policies adopted by a legislative body and generally has the force of law as its basis for authority. The legally adopted budget is an important document in establishing and assessing the accountability of those responsible for the management of a governmental entity. While finance-related legal or contractual requirements are not as fundamental as the legally adopted budget, they nonetheless provide a basis for accountability, and financial reporting should demonstrate that accountability either has or has not been achieved with respect to the requirements (GASB:CS-1, pars. 39–41).

Assessing accountability of the management of a governmental entity encompasses qualitative analysis (economy, efficiency, and effectiveness) as well as quantitative analysis. GASB:CS-1 states that accountability relates to service efforts, costs, and accomplishments. Financial reporting, when combined with other information, may enable user groups, for example, to determine whether certain efforts should be funded or whether elected officials should be continued in office. The information used to measure the economy, efficiency, and effectiveness of a governmental entity should be based on objective criteria. Such information may be used to compare a governmental entity's current operating results with its prior-period operating results or with other governmental entities' current operating results (GASB:CS-1, par. 79).

Evaluation of operating results Financial reporting should enable user groups to evaluate the operations of a state or local governmental entity. One aspect of operations evaluation is concerned with presenting information about sources and uses of financial resources. With respect to financial resource outflows, financial information presentations should identify all outflows and classify them by function (public health, public safety, etc.) and purpose (adult education, crime prevention, etc.). All financial resource inflows should be presented and identified by source (grants, bond proceeds, etc.) and type (taxes, fees, etc.). Resource inflows and outflows should be presented in a manner that enables user groups to determine the extent to which inflows are sufficient to finance outflows. In addition, nonrecurring inflows and outflows of resources should be disclosed in the financial report (GASB:CS-1, par. 78).

GASB:CS-1 also states that to evaluate operating results, financial reporting should enable user groups to determine how a governmental entity financed its activities and met its cash requirements (GASB:CS-1, par. 78).

> **OBSERVATION:** To some extent, this component objective overlaps with the previous component objective (identification of sources and types of resource inflows). However, the objective of determining how cash requirements were met may require the preparation of a specific cash flow analysis.

Another element used in evaluating operations is the ability of the financial reporting to provide a basis for determining whether results of current operations improved or worsened the governmental entity's financial position as of the end of the current period (GASB:CS-1, par. 78).

Assessment of potential for providing services and ability to meet obligations Financial reporting should provide information concerning the financial position and condition of a state or local governmental entity. Resources should be described as current or noncurrent, and contingent liabilities should be disclosed. To assess the ability of an entity to raise resources from taxation, disclosure should include tax limitations, burdens, and sources. Likewise, the viability of issuing debt to raise revenues would require that an entity disclose debt limitations (GASB:CS-1, par. 79).

Disclosures in a financial report should enable user groups to assess current and long-term capital needs of the governmental entity. To this end, descriptions of physical and other nonfinancial resources with lives that extend beyond the current period should be included in the financial report. Such descriptions should include information that can be used to determine the service potential of such assets (GASB:CS-1, par. 79).

> **OBSERVATION:** Although the GASB endorsed disclosures concerning service potential of physical and other nonfinancial resources, it recognized that conventional financial reporting methods have not yet been adequately developed to satisfy this financial reporting objective.

Finally, to allow financial statement users to assess the ability of a governmental entity to meet its obligations, the legal and contractual restrictions on resources and the potential loss of an entity's resources should be disclosed in the financial report (GASB:CS-1, par. 79).

Service Efforts and Accomplishments

National Council on Governmental Accounting (NCGA) Concepts Statement 1 (Objectives of Accounting and Financial Reporting for Governmental Units) listed as one of its framework objectives "to provide information useful for evaluating managerial and organizational performance." The GASB was required by its 1984 structural agreement, which led in part to the Board's establishment, to recognize all NCGA statements until they were modified by the GASB. The GASB's Service Efforts and Accomplishments (SEA) reporting project has been a direct response to this mandated objective.

The GASB followed up the 1984 mandate to include in its accounting and financial reporting framework the objective "to provide information useful for evaluating managerial and organizational performance" with the issuance of Concepts Statement 2 (Service Efforts and Accomplishments) (GASB:CS-2) in 1994. GASB:CS-2 established the elements of SEA reporting, the objective and characteristics of SEA reporting, and the limitations of SEA information. The intent of GASB:CS-2 was to establish a framework for the development of "reporting standards" for performance measurement, not the establishment of the "performance standards."

SEA reporting guidance would encompass reporting categories, including

- Inputs
- Outputs

- Outcomes
- Efficiency
- Effectiveness
- Explanatory Factors

The desired end result of GASB SEA guidance is to provide guidelines on what might be reported with regard to the foregoing categories of information and how to present or report the information in general purpose external financial reports (for example, in a separate SEA report), if a government voluntarily elects to report such information.

OBSERVATION: Although the GASB has been conducting research and issuing documents regarding reporting for Service Efforts and Accomplishments (SEA) for over twenty years, several of the GASB's constituent groups have expressed their opposition to the GASB taking any official action on the SEA reporting project citing concern that the project would lead to the development of performance measurement standards by the GASB. One of the central issues in the SEA controversy is the contention by those in opposition that the GASB does not have the fundamental jurisdictional authority to provide guidance on SEA reporting, and that providing such guidance is contrary to the GASB's mission. In response to this concern, in November 2006, the Financial Accounting Foundation (FAF) Board of Trustees, which serves as the oversight body for both the GASB and FASB, reaffirmed that the GASB does have the jurisdictional authority to include SEA in its financial accounting and reporting standards-setting activities.

PRACTICE ALERT: At the time CCH's 2008 *Governmental GAAP Guide* went to press the GASB had added an SEA project to its current agenda. The objectives in this project are to (1) develop and propose principles-based guidelines that would help improve voluntary reporting of SEA performance information, (2) amend GASB:CS-2 based on knowledge obtained through GASB research, and (3) encourage more state and local governments to voluntarily report SEA information in order to enhance public accountability. These proposed revisions to GASB:CS-2 would incorporate the results of the significant research and experimentation that has occurred related to SEA reporting since the concepts statement was issued some time ago. In addition, in response to the comments received by the GASB in its due-process activities, the update to GASB:CS-2 proposes to include language to clarify the intent of GASB to propose "principles-based guidelines" for voluntary reporting SEA information.

Communication Methods in Financial Reporting

The GASB has issued Concepts Statement No. 3 (GASB:CS-3), "Communication Methods in General Purpose External Financial Reports That Contain Basic Financial Statements." GASB:CS-3 provides a conceptual basis for selecting communication methods to present items of information within general-purpose external financial reports that contain basic financial statements. These communication methods include reporting in basic financial statements, disclosure in notes to basic financial statements, presentation as required supplementary information (RSI), and presentation as supplementary information (SI).

GASB:CS-3 defines the communication methods commonly used in general purpose external financial reports, develops criteria for each communication method, and provides a hierarchy for their use. These definitions, criteria, and hierarchy should help the GASB and all government financial statement preparers determine the appropriate methods to use to communicate an item of information.

Once an item of information is considered appropriate for inclusion within general-purpose external financial reports, the appropriate communication method (placement) to be used to convey particular financial information should be determined. GASB:CS-3 states that this placement decision should be based on a hierarchy in the following order:

1. Recognition in basic financial statements
2. Disclosure in notes to basic financial statements
3. Presentation as required supplementary information (RSI)
4. Presentation as supplementary information (SI)

Recognition in the basic financial statements The financial statements provide a tabular presentation of amounts derived from the accounting records reflecting either the financial position of the reporting unit at a moment in time or inflows and outflows of resources during a period of time.

The criteria for financial information that is reported within the basic financial statements is as follows:

- Items are intended to provide reliable representation of the effects of transactions and other events
- Items are measurable with sufficient reliability

> **Example:** Reporting a government's revenues and receivables from taxable events or transactions

Disclosure in notes to basic financial statements The notes to the financial statements are an integral part of the financial statements and are essential to users' understanding of a reporting unit's financial position and inflows and outflows of resources.

The criteria for financial information that is reported within the notes to the financial statements is as follows:

- Information has a clear and demonstrable relationship to information in the financial statements
- Information is essential to users' understanding of the statements

> **Example:** Reporting the deposit and investment risks of the government that relate to the reported cash and investment balances and transactions

GASB:CS-3 states that the notes should not include either subjective assessments of the effects of reported information on the reporting unit's future financial position or predictions about the effects of future events on future financial position.

Presentation as required supplementary information Required supplementary information (RSI) is supporting information that the GASB has concluded is essential for placing basic financial statements and notes in an appropriate operational, economic, or historical context.

The criteria for financial information that is reported as required supplementary information is as follows:

- Information that has a clear and demonstrable relationship to information in the financial statements or the notes to the basic statements
- Information that provides a context that enhances the decision-usefulness of the basic statements or notes

> **Example:** Reporting the budgetary comparison information of the General Fund and major special revenue funds

As is the case for the notes to the financial statements, GASB:CS-3 states that RSI should not include either subjective assessments of the effects of reported information on the reporting unit's future financial position or predictions about the effects of future events on future financial position. GASB:CS-3 also states that RSI should not include information unrelated to the financial statements.

Presentation as supplementary information Supplementary information (SI) is information that is considered to be useful for placing the financial statements and notes in an appropriate context; however, the GASB does not require the information to be presented in a reporting unit's general-purpose external financial report.

The criteria for information that is reported as supplementary information is as follows:

- Information that is useful for placing basic financial statements and notes in an appropriate operational, economic, or historical context
- Information that is voluntarily included in a general-purpose external financial report

> **Example:** Reporting combining and individual fund financial statements for nonmajor funds

Elements of Financial Statements and Measurement and Recognition

The 2006 GASB white paper *Why Governmental Accounting and Financial Reporting Is—and Should Be—Different* makes a persuasive argument that public sector accounting is fundamentally different from accounting outside the public sector. For this reason the elements reported within the financial statements of states and local governments and their measurement and recognition criteria deserve different consideration. To provide the framework for establishing accounting principles related to the elements of financial statements and their measurement and recognition within the financial statements, the GASB has placed on its agenda two additional proposed Concepts Statements.

> **PRACTICE ALERT:** In August 2006, the GASB issued an exposure draft of a proposed Concepts Statement entitled "Elements of Financial Statements." As CCH's 2008 *Governmental GAAP Guide* went to press the GASB was redeliberating the proposed statement based on the responses to the exposure draft.

The proposed Concepts Statement "Elements of Financial Statements" would be the fourth issued by the GASB. It proposes new definitions for seven elements of historically based financial statements of state and local governments as follows:

- Elements of the statement of financial position

  1. Assets
  2. Liabilities
  3. Deferred Outflow of Resources
  4. Deferred Inflow of Resources

5. Net Position

- Elements of the Resources Flow Statements

6. Inflow of Resources
7. Outflow of Resources

The GASB-proposed definitions of the elements are based upon the inherent characteristics of each element, and they are linked by a common definition feature in that they are based on the concept of measuring and reporting *resources*. The proposed definitions of the elements apply to an entity that is a governmental unit (that is, a legal entity) and are applicable to any measurement focus under which financial statements may be prepared, for example, economic resources, current financial resources, and cash resources measurement focuses.

PRACTICE ALERT: Upon completing the current agenda project dealing with the proposed Concepts Statement, "Elements of Financial Statements," the GASB plans on turning its attention to another Concepts Statement, entitled "Measurement and Recognition." The objectives of this future agenda project are to develop framework criteria for when information should be reported in the financial statements of state and local governments and to focus on the conceptual role of measurement characteristics or attributes in financial reporting such as historical cost or fair value. As CCH's 2008 *Governmental GAAP Guide* went to press the GASB had not yet begun deliberating on the "Measurement and Recognition" proposed Concepts Statement.

SUMMARY OF BASIC GOVERNMENTAL ACCOUNTING PRINCIPLES

The objectives for governmental financial reporting discussed earlier in this chapter are the basis for determining specific accounting principles to be used by a governmental entity. There are 13 general principles of accounting and reporting applicable to governmental entities. These principles, which are established by NCGA-1 and GASB-34, provide a broad overview of financial reporting and are as follows:

1. Accounting and reporting capabilities
2. Fund accounting systems
3. Fund types
4. Number of funds
5. Reporting capital assets

6. Valuation of capital assets
7. Depreciation of capital assets
8. Reporting long-term liabilities
9. Measurement focus and basis of accounting
10. Budgeting, budgetary control, and budgetary reporting
11. Transfer, revenue, expenditure, and expense account classification
12. Common terminology and classification
13. Annual financial reports

Accounting and Reporting Capabilities

A governmental entity's accounting system should be designed to achieve the following:

- Present fairly and with full disclosure the funds and activities of the government in conformity with governmental generally accepted accounting principles
- Determine and demonstrate compliance with finance-related legal and contractual provisions

Fund Accounting Systems

NCGA-1 (as amended) defines a "fund" as follows:

> A fiscal and accounting entity with a self-balancing set of accounts recording cash and other financial resources, together with all related liabilities and residual equities or balances, and changes therein, which are segregated for the purpose of carrying on specific activities or attaining certain objectives in accordance with special regulations, restrictions, or limitations.

The detailed transactions and resulting balances of a governmental entity (the primary government as well as its blended component units) are generally recorded in individual funds; however, GASB-34 requires that only major funds be reported individually in a governmental entity's basic external financial statements.

Fund Types

Fund-based financial statements must be included in a governmental entity's financial report in order to demonstrate that restrictions imposed by statutes, regulations, or contracts have been followed.

GASB-34 identifies the following as fund types that are to be used to record a governmental entity's activities during an accounting period (GASB-34, par. 63):

- Governmental Funds (emphasizing major funds)
  —General Fund
  —Special Revenue Funds
  —Capital Projects Funds
  —Debt Service Funds
  —Permanent Funds
- Proprietary Funds
  —Enterprise Funds (emphasizing major funds)
  —Internal Service Funds
- Fiduciary Funds and Similar Component Units
  —Pension (and other employee benefit) Trust Funds
  —Investment Trust Funds
  —Private-Purpose Trust Funds
  —Agency Funds

> **OBSERVATION:** The fund classification scheme described in this section is for external reporting. The GASB does not direct how a governmental entity should construct its internal accounting structure to fulfill legal requirements or satisfy management strategies.

Governmental funds Financial statements for governmental funds have a short-term emphasis and generally measure and account for cash and "other assets that can easily be converted to cash." However, unlike current governmental financial reporting standards, GASB-34 requires fund reporting be restricted to a governmental entity's General Fund and its "major" funds (GASB-34, par. 64).

Generally, the fund types listed above are currently used in governmental financial reporting and are defined in NCGA-1 (as amended by GASB-34) as follows:

> *General Fund*—To account for all financial resources except those required to be reported in another fund.

> *Special Revenue Funds*—To account for the proceeds of specific revenue sources (other than trusts for individuals, private organizations, or other governments or for major capital projects) that are legally restricted to expenditure for specified purpose. (Resources restricted to expenditure for purpose normally financed from the General Fund may be accounted for through the General Fund provided that applicable

legal requirements can be appropriately satisfied, and use of Special Revenue Funds is not required unless they are legally mandated. The General Fund of a blended component unit should be reported as a Special Revenue Fund.)

Capital Projects Funds—To account for financial resources to be used for the acquisition or construction of major capital facilities (other than those financed by proprietary funds or in trust funds for individuals, private organizations, or other governments). (Capital outlays financed from general obligation bonds proceeds should be accounted for through a Capital Projects Fund.)

Debt Service Funds—To account for the accumulation of resources for, and the payment of, general long-term debt principal and interest. (Debt Service Funds are required if they are legally mandated and/or if financial resources are being accumulated for principal and interest payments maturing in future years. The debt service transactions of a special assessment issue for which the government is not obligated in any manner should be reported in an Agency Fund rather than a Debt Service Fund to reflect the fact that the government's duties are limited to acting as an agent for the assessed property owners and the bondholders.)

Permanent Funds—To account for resources that are legally restricted to the extent that only earnings, and not principal, may be used for the purposes that support the reporting government's programs—that is, for the benefit of the government or its citizenry.

PRACTICE ALERT: In October 2006, the GASB issued an Invitation to Comment (ITC) entitled "Fund Balance Reporting and Governmental Fund Type Definitions." Over recent years, GASB staff and consultants have been interviewing representatives from the financial statement user, preparer, and attestor communities on such issues as fund balance components, presentation, and usefulness of fund balance information. The preliminary results of the GASB research revealed that fund balance was one of the most widely used elements of financial information in state and local government financial statements but at the same time was one of the most misunderstood elements. It is likely that changes to the present fund balance presentation and definition of governmental fund types will result from this GASB project. At the time of the publication of CCH's 2008 *Governmental GAAP Guide,* the GASB was redeliberating the topics covered in the ITC. A final statement is anticipated by the third quarter of 2008.

Proprietary funds Financial statements for proprietary funds should be based on the flow of economic resources (measurement focus) and the accrual basis of accounting. The proprietary fund category includes Enterprise Funds and Internal Service Funds (GASB-34, par. 66).

Enterprise Funds This fund type may be used to "report any activity for which a fee is charged to external users for goods or services." GASB-34 states that an Enterprise Fund *must* be used to account for an activity if any one of the following three criteria is satisfied (GASB-34, par. 67):

1. The activity is financed with debt that is secured *solely* by a pledge of the net revenues from fees and charges of the activity.
2. Laws or regulations require that the activity's costs of providing services, including capital costs (such as depreciation or capital debt service), be recovered with fees and charges, rather than with taxes or similar revenues.
3. The pricing policies of the activity establish fees and charges designed to recover its costs, including capital costs (such as depreciation or debt service).

The first criterion refers to debt secured solely by fees and charges. If that debt is secured by a pledge of fees and charges from the activity and the full faith and credit of the primary government or component unit, this arrangement does not satisfy the "sole source of debt security" criterion and the activity does not have to be accounted for (assuming the other two criteria are not satisfied) in an Enterprise Fund. This conclusion is not changed even if it is anticipated that the primary government or component unit is not expected to make debt payments under the arrangement. On the other hand, debt that is secured partially by a portion of its own proceeds does satisfy the "sole source of debt security" criterion.

The second criterion could require that state unemployment compensation funds be reported in an Enterprise Fund.

The third criterion is similar to the previous standard for determining when an Enterprise Fund should be used to account for an activity except that the new standard is based on "established policies" rather than management's intent.

The three criteria should be applied to a governmental entity's principal revenue sources; however, the criteria do not have to be applied to "insignificant activities" of a governmental entity. If none of the criteria apply, the activity can be accounted for in a governmental fund.

> **PRACTICE POINT:** It should be noted that GASB-34 states that a fee-based activity can be accounted for in an Enterprise Fund even if the three criteria described above do not exist. The three criteria apply to fee-based activities that must be accounted for in an Enterprise Fund.

Internal Service Funds An Internal Service Fund may be used to account for activities that involve the governmental entity providing goods or services to (1) other funds or activities of the primary government or its component units, or other governments on a cost reimbursement basis and (2) the reporting entity is the *predominant* participant in the activity. If the reporting entity is not the predominant participant, the activity should be reported in an Enterprise Fund (GASB-34, par. 68)

Fiduciary funds Assets held by a governmental entity for other parties (either as a trustee or as an agent) and that cannot be used to finance the governmental entity's own operating programs should be reported in the fiduciary fund category, which includes (1) Pension (and other employee benefit) Trust Funds, (2) Investment Trust Funds, (3) Private Trust Funds, and (4) Agency Funds. The three trust funds are used to report resources and activities when the governmental entity is acting as a trustee (i.e., a fiduciary capacity) for individuals, private organizations, and other governments. GASB-34 states that the three trust funds are distinguished from an Agency Fund in that the trust funds are generally characterized "by the existence of a trust agreement that affects the degree of management involvement and the length of time that the resources are held" (GASB-34, par. 69).

Pension (or Other Employer Benefit) Trust Funds This fund type is used to account for resources held in trust for employees and their beneficiaries based on defined benefit pension agreements, defined contribution agreements, other postemployment benefit agreements, and other employee benefit arrangements (GASB-34, par. 70).

Investment Trust Funds An Investment Trust Fund is used by a governmental entity to report the external portion of an investment pool as defined in GASB-31 (Accounting and Financial Reporting for Certain Investments and for External Investment Pools), paragraph 18 (GASB-34, par. 71).

Private-Purpose Trust Funds This fund type is used to account for the principal and income for all other trust arrangements that benefit individuals, private organizations, or other governments. For example, a Private-Purpose Trust Fund would be used to account for escheat property as currently described in GASB-21 (Accounting for Escheat Property) (GASB-34, par. 72).

Agency Funds An Agency Fund is used by a governmental entity to report assets that are held in a custodial relationship. In a typical custodial relationship, a governmental entity receives assets, may temporarily invest those assets, and then remits those assets to individuals, private organizations, or other governments (GASB-34, par. 73).

PRACTICE POINT: Public-purpose funds that were previously classified as Expendable Trust Funds should be reclassified as Special Revenue Funds, and Nonexpendable Trust Funds should be reclassified as Permanent Funds.

Governmental and proprietary fund financial statements A governmental entity should report financial statements for its governmental and proprietary funds, but the basis for reporting these funds is not by fund type but rather by major funds (GASB-34, par. 74).

Focus on Major Governmental and Enterprise Funds A significant change in the focus of reporting governmental funds and enterprise funds is that major funds are reported for these funds; however, combined financial statements for fund types are not reported.

Fund financial statements must present in a separate column a (major) fund that satisfies both of the following criteria (GASB-34, pars. 75–76):

- Total assets, liabilities, revenues, or expenditures/expenses of the governmental (enterprise) fund are equal to or greater than 10% of the corresponding total (assets, liability, and so forth) for all funds that are considered governmental funds (enterprise funds).
- Total assets, liabilities, revenues, or expenditures/expenses of the governmental fund (enterprise fund) are equal to or greater than 5% of the corresponding total for all governmental and enterprise funds combined.

PRACTICE POINT: In determining total revenues and expenditures/expenses, extraordinary items are excluded.

The General Fund is always considered a major fund and therefore must be presented in a separate column. Major fund reporting requirements do not apply to Internal Service Funds or Fiduciary Funds.

If a fund does not satisfy the conditions described above, it can still be presented as a major fund if the governmental entity believes it is important to do so. All other funds that are not considered major funds must be combined in a separate column and labeled as nonmajor funds. Thus, there could be a nonmajor funds column for governmental funds and enterprise funds.

OBSERVATION: Based on research conducted by the GASB, it appears that major funds represent a significant percentage of a governmental entity's account balances and transactions. However, the major-fund concept is a minimum threshold. If a governmental entity believes that a fund that is not considered a major fund is important to readers of the financial statements, the entity should present that fund as a major fund in a separate column.

Number of Funds

A basic principle of governmental generally accepted accounting principles is that the actual number of funds used by a governmental entity should be kept to a minimum to avoid the creation of an inefficient financial system. In general, the number of funds established must be sufficient to meet operational needs and legal restrictions imposed on the organization. For example, only one General Fund should be maintained. In some circumstances it may be possible to account for restricted resources in the General Fund and still meet imposed legal requirements. Also, there may be no need to establish a Special Revenue Fund unless specifically required by law (NCGAI-9, par. 10, and NCGA-1, par. 29).

Reporting Capital Assets

At the fund-financial statement level, capital assets are not reported in governmental funds but are reported in proprietary funds and fiduciary funds (if any). All of a governmental entity's capital assets (with the exception of those of fiduciary funds) are reported in the government-wide financial statements and identified as related to either governmental activities or business-type activities (NCGA-1, par. 32, and GASB-34, pars. 6 and 80).

Valuation of Capital Assets

The governmental entity should report all of its capital assets, based on their original historical cost plus ancillary charges such as transportation, installation, and site preparation costs. Capital assets that have been donated to a governmental entity must be capitalized at their estimated fair value (plus any ancillary costs) at the date of receipt (GASB-34, par. 19).

> **PRACTICE POINT:** Under certain conditions works of art, historical treasures, and similar assets do not have to be capitalized. This exception is discussed in Chapter 18, "Expenses/Expenditures: Nonexchange and Exchange Transactions."

Depreciation of Capital Assets

The cost (net of estimated salvage value) of capital assets (except for certain infrastructure assets) should be depreciated over the estimated useful lives of the assets. Inexhaustible capital assets (such as land, land improvements, and certain infrastructure assets) should not be depreciated. Depreciation expenses should be reported in the government-wide financial statements (statement of activities), financial statements for proprietary funds (statement of revenues, expenses, and changes in fund net assets), and financial statements for fiduciary funds (statement of changes in fiduciary net assets). Depreciation expense is not reported in governmental funds (the General Fund, Special Revenue Funds, and so forth) (GASB-34, par. 21).

Reporting Long-Term Liabilities

There are three broad but distinct categories of long-term liabilities. Long-term liabilities related to proprietary funds should be reported both in government-wide financial statements and the fund financial statements. Long-term liabilities related to fiduciary funds should be reported only in the statement of fiduciary net assets. All other long-term liabilities that are not properly presented in either proprietary funds or fiduciary funds are general liabilities and should be reported only in the governmental activities column of the statement of net assets (a government-wide financial statement) (NCGA-1, pars. 32 and 42, and GASB-34, pars. 6 and 82).

Measurement Focus and Basis of Accounting

Government-wide financial statements have been established by GASB-34 in order to provide a basis for determining (1) the extent to which current services provided by the entity were financed with current revenues and (2) the degree to which a governmental entity's financial position has changed during the fiscal year. In order to achieve these objectives, government-wide financial statements should include a statement of net assets and a statement of activities.

Government-wide financial statements are based on a flow of all economic resources applied on the accrual basis of accounting. The flow of economic resources refers to all of the assets available to the governmental unit for the purpose of providing goods and services to the public. When the flow of economic resources and the accrual basis of accounting are combined, they provide the foundation for generally accepted accounting principles (GAAP) used by business enterprises in that essentially all assets and liabilities, both current and long-term, are presented in the statement of net assets.

The governmental entity's statement of activities includes all costs of providing goods and services during the period. These costs include depreciation, the cost of inventories consumed during the period, and other operating expenses. On the activity statement, revenues earned during the period are matched with the expenses incurred for exchange or exchange-like transactions. Nonexchange transactions are accounted for based on the standards established by GASB-33 (Accounting and Financial Reporting for Nonexchange Transactions).

Governmental fund-based financial statements must be included in a governmental entity's financial report in order to demonstrate that restrictions imposed by statutes, regulations, or contracts have been followed. These financial statements are based on the modified accrual accounting basis and the flow of current financial resources and therefore have a short-term emphasis and generally measure and account for cash and "other assets that can easily be converted to cash" (NCGA-1, par. 57 and GASB-34, pars. 15, 16, 92, and 107).

Financial statements of proprietary and fiduciary funds are based on the economic resources measurement focus and the accrual basis of accounting.

The GASB-34 financial statements require reconciliation between the government-wide and fund statements, which present financial information using different bases of accounting and measurement focuses. The process by which fund financial statements are converted to government-wide financial statements is illustrated in CCH's *Governmental GAAP Practice Manual: Including GASB 34 Guidance.*

Budgeting, Budgetary Control, and Budgetary Reporting

The following guidance should be followed as part of the budgetary process for a governmental entity (NCGA-1, pars. 76 and 123):

- An annual budget should be adopted by every governmental entity
- The accounting system should provide the basis for appropriate budgetary control
- A common terminology and classification scheme should be used for budgets, recording transactions, and preparing financial reports for each fund

Transfer, Revenue, Expenditure, and Expense Account Classification

The following guidance should be followed in the preparation of governmental financial reports (NCGA-1, par. 99, and GASB-34, pars. 6, 39, 53, 88, 100, and 112):

- Transfers should be reported separately from revenues and expenditures/expenses
- Proceeds from the issuance of general long-term debt should be recorded separately from revenues in the governmental fund financial statements

- Governmental fund revenues should be reported by fund and source at the fund-financial statement level
- Governmental expenditures should be reported by fund and at least by function
- Proprietary fund revenues should be reported by major sources, and expense should be classified in a manner like that used by similar business activities
- The statement of activities should report governmental activities at least at the level of detail required in the governmental fund statement of revenues, expenditures, and changes in fund balances
- Governments should present business-type activities at least by segment

Common Terminology and Classification

Governmental financial information is reported in budgets and external financial reports. NCGA-1 notes that it is advantageous to use common terminology and classification schemes throughout the "budget, the accounts, and the financial reports of each fund" (NCGA-1, par. 123).

Annual Financial Reports

The GASB recommends but does not require that a governmental entity prepare and publish a comprehensive annual financial report (CAFR) "as a matter of public record." The CAFR is discussed in Chapter 20, "Comprehensive Annual Financial Report." The financial reporting entity consists of (1) the primary government, (2) other entities for which the primary government is financial accountable, and (3) other entities that have a relationship with the primary government whose "exclusion would cause the reporting entity's basic financial statements to be misleading or incomplete." The reporting entity concept is discussed in Chapter 4, "Governmental Reporting Entity."

CHAPTER 2
BUDGETARY ACCOUNTING AND REPORTING

CONTENTS

INTRODUCTION

A budget is a plan of financial operations that provides a basis for the planning, controlling, and evaluating of governmental activities. The budget process is a political process that usually begins with the chief executive of a governmental unit submitting a budget to the unit's legislative branch for consideration. Ultimately, the legal authority for governmental expenditures is reflected in an appropriations bill(s) (NCGA-1, par. 77).

This chapter discusses the role of budgeting in governmental financial reporting. NCGA-1 (Governmental Accounting and Financial Reporting Principles) provides the basic guidance for reporting budgetary information and related information in a governmental entity's financial statements.

The budgetary process for governmental units is far more significant than it is for commercial enterprises because of the public nature of the process and the fiduciary responsibility of public officials. The importance of the budgetary process is emphasized by the fact that NCGA-1 states that every governmental unit should prepare an annual comprehensive budget. The statement further recommended that the annual budget serve as a basis for control and evaluation of a fund even if the fund was not legally required to adopt a budget (NCGA-1, pars. 77-78 and 80).

Budgetary Accounting System

Budgetary control is enhanced when the legally adopted budget is integrated into the governmental unit's formal accounting system. The integration of the budget and accounting system is referred to as the budgetary accounting system. Budgetary accounts are used in a budgetary accounting system (NCGA-1, par. 89).

A budgetary accounting system should be used by certain governmental fund types. NCGA-1 states that budgetary accounts should be used in the General Fund and Special Revenue Funds. Other governmental funds that should employ a budgetary accounting system are those subject to the controls of an annually adopted budget, and those processing numerous revenue, expenditure, and transfer transactions through the fund. For example, it may be appropriate to use budgetary accounts in a Capital Projects Fund when various construction projects are being currently financed through the fund (NCGA-1, par. 89).

Conversely, budgetary accounts are unnecessary in the following situations (NCGA-1, par. 89):

- *Debt Service Fund* Receipts and expenditures for a period are established by sinking fund provisions of a debt agreement, and few transactions are processed each period.
- *Capital Projects Fund* Various construction projects are under contract with independent contractors that are exclusively responsible for the progress of the project (turnkey projects).

Ultimately, professional judgment must be used to determine if a budgetary accounting system is necessary to provide adequate control over revenues and expenditures of a particular governmental fund (NCGA-1, par. 90).

Budgetary accounts are used exclusively for control and therefore do not affect the actual results of operations for the accounting period. Two important aspects of a budgetary accounting system are (1) accounting for the budget and (2) accounting for encumbrances (NCGA-1, pars. 91–93).

Accounting for the budget NCGA Interpretation No. 10 (NCGAI-10) (State and Local Government Budgetary Reporting) defines the "appropriated budget" as follows (NCGAI-10, par. 11):

> The expenditure authority created by the appropriation bills or ordinances that are signed into law and related estimated

> revenues . . . [including] all reserves, transfers, allocations, supplemental appropriations, and other legally authorized legislative and executive changes.

The appropriated budget for the current fiscal year may be recorded in the following manner:

Estimated Revenues (Control)	400,000,000	
Appropriations (Control)		390,000,000
Fund Balance (Budgetary)		10,000,000
To record operating budget.		

The estimated revenues account is a budgetary account that represents the total anticipated revenues expected to be available during the fiscal year on a budgetary basis. The estimated revenues account functions as an overall control account, and the specific revenue sources, such as property taxes, fines, and intergovernmental revenues, would be recorded in revenue subsidiary ledgers. Actual revenues are recorded in nonbudgetary accounts as they are recognized throughout the accounting period. Also, as actual revenues are recorded, similar postings are made to the subsidiary ledgers. The overall control account and the subsidiary ledgers provide a basis for the subsequent comparison of the estimated revenues with the actual revenues for the period. Thus, the estimated revenues account (a budgetary account) is used to compare estimated revenues with actual revenues for the period, but it does not function as a control account for revenues (NCGA-1, par. 93).

Appropriations is a budgetary account that represents the total authorized expenditures for a current fiscal period. The appropriations account is a control account with the details of the approved expenditures being recorded in appropriations subsidiary ledgers. During the year, expenditures are recorded both in (1) nonbudgetary accounts such as public safety and health and welfare expenditures and in (2) appropriations subsidiary ledger accounts. Throughout the fiscal year, the appropriations account and its subsidiary ledger accounts can be used to control the level of expenditures to avoid exceeding appropriated amounts. Thus, the appropriations account (a budgetary account) is used for both control and comparative purposes (NCGA-1, par. 93).

The difference between estimated revenues and appropriations as authorized in the budget is debited or credited to the fund's fund balance account (budgetary). The entry in the fund balance account reflects either an anticipated operating surplus (credit) or a deficit (debit) for the current budgetary period.

The use of budgetary accounts does not affect the actual revenues and expenditures recognized during the accounting period. This is accomplished by simply reversing, at the end of the period, the budgetary accounts created when the budget was initially recorded.

For example, the earlier entry used to illustrate the recording of the budget would be reversed as follows:

Fund Balance (Budgetary)	10,000,000	
Appropriations	390,000,000	
Estimated Revenues		400,000,000
To close budgetary accounts.		

The budgetary accounts can be grouped with related actual accounts as part of the closing to emphasize the comparative purpose of using the budgetary accounting system. The following example illustrates this type of closing, along with the use of other budgetary accounts:

Revenues	397,500,000	
Operating Transfers In	3,500,000	
Bond Proceeds	2,000,000	
Fund Balance	3,000,000	
Estimated Revenues		400,000,000
Estimated Operating Transfers In		4,000,000
Estimated Bond Proceeds		2,000,000
To close all revenue related budgetary and actual accounts.		

Appropriations	390,000,000	
Authorized Operating Transfers Out	6,000,000	
Expenditures		385,000,000
Operating Transfers Out		5,000,000
Fund Balance		6,000,000
To close all expenditure related budgetary and actual accounts.		

Accounting for encumbrances Encumbrances represent commitments related to contracts not yet performed (executory contracts), and are used to control expenditures for the year and to enhance cash management. A governmental unit often issues purchase orders or signs contracts for the purchase of goods and services to be received in the future. At the time these commitments are made, the following budgetary entry should be made for control purposes (NCGA-1, par. 91):

Encumbrances	100,000	
Reserve for Encumbrances		100,000
To record the issuance of a purchase order for supplies.		

The encumbrances account does not represent an expenditure for the period, only a commitment to expend resources. Likewise, the account reserve for encumbrances is not synonymous with a liability account since the liability is recognized only when the goods are received or the services performed (NCGA-1, par. 91).

When an executory contract is completed or virtually completed, the budgetary encumbrance accounts are eliminated and the actual expenditure and related liability are recorded, illustrated as follows:

Reserve for Encumbrances	100,000	
Encumbrances		100,000

To record the receipts of supplies and cancellation of the outstanding encumbrance.

Expenditures	97,000	
Vouchers Payable		97,000

To record the expenditure for supplies.

The original encumbrance entry is based on the estimated cost of goods and services and may differ from the eventual cost of the item.

During the budgetary period, the governmental unit can determine the remaining amount of the new commitments that can be signed by comparing the amount of appropriations to the sum of expenditures recognized and encumbrances outstanding.

At the end of the fiscal year, some encumbrances may be outstanding. NCGA-1 states that encumbrances outstanding at the end of the year are not expenditures for the year, and the reserve for encumbrances account is not to be treated as a liability. The treatment of the two budgetary accounts at the end of the year depends on whether appropriations, even if encumbered at the year-end, are allowed to lapse (NCGA-1, par. 91).

Lapsing appropriations When there are outstanding encumbrances at the end of the fiscal year, it is highly likely that the governmental unit will honor the open purchase orders or contracts that support the encumbrances. For reporting purposes, outstanding encumbrances are not considered expenditures for the fiscal year. If the governmental unit allows encumbrances to lapse, even though it plans to honor the encumbrances, the appropriations authority expires and the items represented by the encumbrances are usually reappropriated in the following year's budget.

NCGA-1 states that when outstanding encumbrances are allowed to lapse at year-end but the state or local government intends to honor the commitment, the encumbrances should be disclosed either as a reservation of the fund balance or in a note to the financial statements, and authorization for the eventual expenditure should be included in the following year's budget appropriations (NCGA-1, par. 92).

To illustrate the accounting necessary to comply with the NCGA-1 requirements, assume that encumbrances of $100,000 are outstanding at December 31, 20X5, but the governmental unit intends to honor the encumbrances and reappropriate funds to pay for the commitments in the 20X6 fiscal year. At the end of 20X5, the following entries should be made:

Reserve for Encumbrances	100,000	
Encumbrances		100,000

To close encumbrances outstanding at the end of the fiscal year.

Fund Balance	100,000	
Fund Balance—Reserve for Encumbrances		100,000

To reserve the fund balance by the estimated amount that will be reappropriated in 20X6 for outstanding encumbrances.

The first entry closes the encumbrances accounts because they are strictly budgetary accounts. The second entry meets the requirement of NCGA-1 in that the fund balance is reserved by the amount of the outstanding encumbrances.

At the beginning of the next fiscal year (January 1, 20X6), the following entries are made:

Encumbrances	100,000	
Reserve for Encumbrances		100,000

To recognize outstanding encumbrances from the prior year.

Fund Balance—Reserve for Encumbrances	100,000	
Fund Balance		100,000

To remove the restriction on the current fund balance based on outstanding encumbrances from the prior year.

The first entry reestablishes budgetary control over the outstanding encumbrances, while the next entry removes the fund balance restriction, which is no longer needed with the reestablishment of budgetary control. The appropriations control account created in the January 1, 20X6, budget will include the $100,000 since an expenditure for this amount is anticipated during 20X6.

From this point the normal entries for encumbrances and expenditures are followed. For example, if the goods or services are received on January 28, 20X6, the following entries would be made:

Expenditures	99,000	
Vouchers Payable		99,000

To record the receipts of goods or services.

Reserve for Encumbrances	100,000	
Encumbrances		100,000

To remove encumbrances on vouchered commitments.

The expenditures are reflected in the 20X6 financial statements as required by NCGA-1.

When lapsed encumbrances are reappropriated and treated in the manner described in the previous example, there are no differences between the budgetary accounting basis and the GAAP basis. The budgetary expenditures represented by the encumbrances are reflected in the budget in the same year that the expenditures are shown in the (GAAP) statement of operations.

Nonlapsing appropriations Appropriations for encumbrances that are outstanding at year-end and are nonlapsing do not require reappropriation the following year because the appropriation authority does not expire. NCGA-1 requires that outstanding encumbrances that are charged against nonlapsing appropriations be reported as a fund balance reserve. To illustrate, assume that encumbrances of $100,000 are outstanding as of December 31, 20X5. At the end of 20X5, the following entries would be made:

Fund Balance	100,000	
Encumbrances		100,000

To close encumbrances outstanding at the end of the fiscal year.

Reserve for Encumbrances	100,000	
Fund Balance—Reserve for Encumbrances		100,000

To reserve the fund balance by the estimated amount that represents outstanding encumbrances at the end of the fiscal year.

The two entries close the encumbrances accounts to avoid reporting budgetary accounts in the financial statements. The first entry closes the encumbrances account directly to the fund balance so that they are not shown as expenditures in the current fiscal year as required by GAAP. The second entry establishes a fund balance reserve as required by NCGA-1.

At the beginning of the next fiscal year (January 1, 20X6), the following entry would be made:

Fund Balance—Reserve for Encumbrances	100,000	
Reserve for Encumbrances—20X5		100,000

To recognize outstanding encumbrances from the prior year.

This entry reestablishes the reserve for encumbrances account (a budgetary account), but indicates that the reserve is applicable to amounts appropriated in the previous year's budget.

When goods or services are received, the following entry would be made during 20X6:

Expenditures—20X5	99,000	
Vouchers Payable		99,000
To record the receipt of goods or services.		

At the end of 20X6, the following closing entry would be made:

Reserve for Encumbrances—20X5	100,000	
Expenditures—20X5		99,000
Fund Balance		1,000
To close expenditures encumbered during the prior year.		

This closing entry enables 20X5 encumbered expenditures to be reported as an expenditure in 20X6 as required by GAAP.

When encumbrances are charged against nonlapsing appropriations in the manner illustrated, there are differences between the budgetary accounting amounts and the GAAP-basis amounts. The budget-based information reflects expenditures based on liabilities incurred and encumbrances outstanding, whereas the actual (GAAP-basis) financial statement does not include amounts encumbered at the end of the fiscal year. There must be a reconciliation between budgeted financial statements not prepared on a GAAP basis and the actual financial statements, which must be presented on a GAAP basis (NCGAI-10, pars. 15–17).

Once a method of accounting for encumbrances is established, it should be used on a consistent basis.

OBSERVATION: GASB-38 (Certain Financial Statement Note Disclosures) eliminated the disclosure requirement established by NCGA-1 to disclose the method used to account for encumbrances.

BUDGETARY ACCOUNTING BY FUND TYPE

Although the NCGA recommended that all funds adopt a budget for control purposes, the nature of budgeting is different for each of the three types of funds (NCGA-1, par. 78).

Budgeting for Governmental Funds

Governmental funds (General Fund, Special Revenue Funds, Capital Projects Funds, Debt Service Funds, and Permanent Funds) generally use a fixed budget, which reflects a specific estimate for revenues and expenditures. Once expenditures and revenues are incorporated into the budget, the total estimated expenditure appropriation amount becomes a limit for current expenditures, and the estimated revenue amount becomes the basis for comparison to actual revenues (NCGA-1, pars. 78 and 83–89).

Because the appropriated budget is used as the basis for control and comparison of budgeted and actual amounts, the basis for preparing the budget should be the same as the governmental fund's basis of accounting. The modified accrual basis is the recommended basis of accounting for governmental fund types, and the budget should reflect a similar basis for establishing expenditures and estimating revenues. When the budget basis and basis of accounting are different, a governmental unit usually maintains its records on the budget basis (legal basis) and uses supplementary information to convert the budget-based information to a modified accrual basis (generally accepted accounting principles) for financial reporting purposes. Also, to facilitate the comparison of budgeted amounts and actual expenditures and revenues, similar terms and classifications should be used in the preparation of the budget and the presentation of the financial report (NCGA-1, par. 90).

> **OBSERVATION:** From an accounting perspective, it is preferable that the budgetary system be on the same basis as the financial accounting system; namely, the modified accrual basis. However, some argue that a budget should be based on the cash basis, modified cash basis, or regulatory basis because those bases are more consistent with the statutory requirements and the financing of a governmental unit and are better understood by legislators. Financial reporting standards do not require that a budget be prepared on a GAAP basis.

Budgeting for Proprietary Funds

Generally, a proprietary fund should prepare a flexible budget, which changes as the activity level changes. In a proprietary fund, overall activity is measured in terms of revenues and expenses and fluctuates, in part, depending on the demand for goods and services by the public (Enterprise Fund) or by other governmental departments or agencies (Internal Service Fund). The flexible budget items are generally not considered appropriations but, rather, as an approved plan that can facilitate budgetary control and operational evaluations. A proprietary fund allows the governmental unit to prepare several budgets at different activity levels to establish an acceptable comparative basis for planned activity and actual results (NCGA-1, pars. 95–97).

> **OBSERVATION:** NCGA-1 discusses the preparation of several budgets based on anticipated activity levels. Even if several budgets are prepared, the budget ultimately used as a comparison with actual results should be based on the actual, not the anticipated, activity level. The preparation of the budget based on actual activity is feasible because the flexible budgeting approach can be expressed in terms of a formula (Total

Expenses = Fixed Expenses + Variable Expenses) and should be applicable at any activity level.

The basis of accounting used to prepare a budget for a proprietary fund should be the same as the basis used to record the results of actual transactions. It is not appropriate to integrate the budgetary system into the proprietary fund's accounting system when a flexible budget system is used. However, if a fixed budget is used, perhaps due to a legal requirement or preference, it may be useful to integrate the budgetary system into the fund's accounting system (NCGA-1, par. 94).

Budgeting for Fiduciary Funds

Fiduciary funds include Pension Trust Funds (and similar funds), Investment Trust Funds, Private-Purpose Trust Funds, and Agency Funds. The first three fund types are similar to proprietary funds and may use budgetary controls, although these resources are not available for governmental operations. Budgets are not appropriate for Agency Funds, because the government entity functions only as a custodial agent.

Budgeting by Program or Purpose

Since the release of GASB-34, issues have been raised about presenting budgetary comparisons when perspective differences exist. Perspective differences exist when the structure of financial information for budgetary purposes differs from the fund structure that is defined in GASB-34. In response to these issues, GASB issued GASB-41 (Budgetary Comparison Schedules—Perspective Difference—an amendment to GASB-34).

GASB-41 amends the first sentence of GASB-34, paragraph 130, including the footnote, to read as follows:

> Budgetary comparisons should be presented for the general fund and for each major special revenue fund that has a legally adopted annual budget. Governments are encouraged to present such budgetary comparison information in schedules as a part of RSI. However, a government with significant budgetary perspective differences that result in the government's not being able to present budgetary comparisons for the general fund and each major special revenue fund is required to present budgetary comparison schedules as RSI based on the fund, organization, or program structure that the government uses for its legally adopted budget.

Essentially, GASB-41 provides an alternative budgetary comparison presentation for governments that legally adopt a budget by program or purpose that may cross funds. (See an example presentation within the discussion of perspective differences for budgetary comparisons in Chapter 20, "Comprehensive Annual Financial Report.")

CHAPTER 3
BASIS OF ACCOUNTING AND MEASUREMENT FOCUS

CONTENTS

INTRODUCTION

The GASB states (1) that accountability is a more important concept in governmental financial reporting than in business enterprise financial reporting and (2) that all governmental financial reporting objectives are derived from the accountability concept. In addition to the overall objective of accountability, Governmental Accounting Standards Board Concepts Statement No. 1 (GASB: CS-1) (Objectives of Financial Reporting) identified the following as objectives of governmental financial reporting (GASB:CS-1, pars. 56–58):

- Financial reporting should fulfill a government's duty to be publicly accountable and should enable users of the financial statements to assess that accountability.
- Financial reporting should assist users in evaluating the operating results of the governmental entity for the year.
- Financial reporting should assist users in assessing the level of services that can be provided by the governmental entity and its ability to meet its obligations.

The GASB noted that although accountability is referred to only in the first objective, accountability is implicit in all of the listed objectives.

Although most interested observers may agree with the overall goal of financial reporting, implementing the goal is the subject of much debate. An important element in implementing the overall goal is selecting a basis of accounting and a measurement focus for governmental funds. The selection of a basis of accounting and measurement focus effects the establishment of specific accounting principles for state and local governments (NCGA:CS-1, par. 13).

An appreciation of the unique character of governmental financial reporting can be developed only when the concepts of basis of accounting and measurement focus are fully understood. For this reason, this chapter is a foundation chapter and does not discuss governmental generally accepted accounting principles (GAAP) except to illustrate basis of accounting and measurement focus.

PRACTICE ALERT: On the future GASB technical agenda is a proposed Concepts Statement entitled "Measurement and Recognition." The objectives of this future agenda project are to develop framework criteria for when information should be reported in the financial statements of state and local governments and to focus on the conceptual role of measurement characteristics or attributes in financial reporting such as historical cost or fair value. As CCH's 2008 *Governmental GAAP Guide* went to press the GASB had not yet begun deliberating on this proposed Concepts Statement. It is unknown at this time whether the results of the Concepts Statement project would dictate any changes to the current principles related to basis of accounting and measurement focus.

BASIS OF ACCOUNTING

An entity's accounting basis determines when transactions and economic events are reflected in its financial statements. NCGA-1 (Governmental Accounting and Financial Reporting Principles) states that basis of accounting refers to "when revenues, expenditures, expenses, and transfers—and the related assets and liabilities—are recognized in the accounts and reported in the financial statements." All operating transactions are the result of expected or unexpected resource flows (usually, but not exclusively, cash flows). Because of specific contractual agreements and accepted business practices, commitments that create eventual resource flows may not coincide with the actual flow of resources. For example, goods may be purchased on one date, consumed on another date, and paid for on still a third date. The accounting basis determines when the economic consequences of transactions and events are reflected in financial statements (NCGA-1, par. 58). Generally, accounting transactions and events may be recorded on an accrual basis, modified accrual basis, or an other comprehensive basis of accounting.

Accrual Basis

FASB Concepts Statement No. 1 (FASB:CS-1) (Objectives of Financial Reporting by Business Enterprises) describes accrual accounting in the following manner:

> Accrual accounting attempts to record the financial effects on an enterprise of transactions and other events and circumstances that have cash consequences for an enterprise in the periods in which those transactions, events, and circumstances occur rather than only in the periods in which cash is received or paid by the enterprise.

The essential elements of the accrual accounting method include the (1) deferral of expenditures and the subsequent amortization of the deferred costs (prepaid expenses, supplies, bond issue costs, etc.), (2) deferral of revenues until they are earned (grant proceeds received in advance), (3) capitalization of certain expenditures and the subsequent depreciation of the capitalized costs (depreciation of cost of equipment), and (4) accrual of revenues that have been earned and expenses that have been incurred (FASB:CS-1, par. 44, and NCGA-1, pars. 61 and 70).

Modified Accrual Basis

The modified accrual basis of accounting is a variation of the accrual basis that modifies the basis for cash flow considerations.

Revenues, including funds received from other governmental units and the issuance of debt, should be recorded when they are "susceptible to accrual." For revenue to be considered susceptible to accrual it must be both measurable and available to finance current expenditures of the fund. Revenue is considered available when it is collectible during the current period and the actual collection will occur either (1) during the current period or (2) after the end of the period but in time to pay current year-end liabilities (NCGA-1, pars. 62–63 and 69).

> **OBSERVATION:** There is no explicit definition of "measurable" in the pronouncements, but the term undoubtedly refers to the ability to quantify the amount of revenue expected to be collected. Thus, "measurable" can be interpreted as the ability to provide a reasonable estimate of actual cash flow.

Expenditures are recorded on a modified accrual basis when they are normally expected to be liquidated with current financial resources. Expenditures include salaries, wages, and other operating expenditures; payments for supplies; transfers to other funds; capital outlays; and payments for the service of debt. Although most expenditures are recorded on an accrual basis (timing emphasis), the measurement focus of a governmental fund significantly affects what items are to be considered expenditures in the governmental fund. Thus, expenditures for a governmental fund cannot be equated to expenses of a business enterprise (NCGA-1, par. 70).

Other Comprehensive Bases of Accounting (OCBOA)

Many small government entities account for transactions and prepare their financial statements on a comprehensive basis of accounting other than generally accepted accounting principles. The other comprehensive bases of accounting commonly used by smaller state and local governments include the following:

- Basis of cash receipts and disbursements (cash basis)
- Cash basis with modifications having substantial support (modified cash basis)
- Basis to comply with requirements of a regulatory agency whose jurisdiction the entity is subject to (regulatory basis)

Chapter 15 of the AICPA's *State and Local Governments* Guide provides guidance on the use of these bases of accounting for government entities.

> **PRACTICE POINT:** The AICPA has developed a Practice Aid entitled *Applying OCBOA in State and Local Government Financial Statements* that provides further nonauthoritative guidance on applying these other comprehensive bases of accounting. The Practice Aid provides practical examples on the financial statement presentation and form of auditor's reports for OCBOA financial statements of government entities.

MEASUREMENT FOCUS

The second critical element in the establishment of generally accepted accounting principles for governments is the selection of a measurement focus. Unlike the selection of an accounting basis, which is concerned with the timing of transactions and events, a measurement focus identifies what (and how) transactions and events should be recorded. The measurement focus is concerned with the inflow and outflow of resources that affect an entity. The balance sheet or statement of net assets should reflect those resources available to meet current obligations and to be used in the delivery of goods and services in subsequent periods. The activity statement for the period should summarize those resources received and those consumed during the current period. Although there are a number of measurement focuses, the two measurement focuses recognized as generally accepted for government transactions are as follows:

1. Flow of economic resources
2. Flow of current financial resources

Flow of Economic Resources (Applied on an Accrual Basis)

The flow of economic resources refers to all of the assets available to the governmental unit for the purpose of providing goods and services to the public. When the flow of economic resources and the accrual basis of accounting are combined, they provide the foundation for generally accepted accounting principles used by business enterprises. This approach recognizes the deferral and capitalization of expenditures and the deferral of revenues.

When the flow of economic resources is applied on an accrual basis for a fund, all assets and liabilities, both current and long-term, are presented in the fund's balance sheet or statement of net assets. The key differences between this approach and the current financial resources measurement focus as it applies to individual governmental funds are summarized as follows:

- Capital assets are recorded in the fund's balance sheet or statement of net assets net of accumulated depreciation.
- Long-term debts are recorded in the fund's balance sheet or statement of net assets.
- The fund's equity represents the net assets (total assets minus total liabilities) available to the fund.

The activity statement includes all costs of providing goods and services during the period. These costs include depreciation, the cost of inventories consumed during the period, and other operating expenses. On the activity statement, revenues during the period are recognized along with the total cost of the particular segment (function) of government. There is a smoothing effect on the activity statement. For example, expenses do not include the full cost of purchasing depreciable property during the period and revenues do not include the proceeds from the issuance of long-term debt.

Flow of Current Financial Resources (Applied on a Modified Accrual Basis)

The flow of current financial resources applied on a modified accrual basis is a narrow interpretation of what constitutes assets and liabilities for an accounting entity. Revenues, and the resulting assets, are accrued at the end of the year only if the revenues are earned and are expected to be collected in time to pay for liabilities in existence at the end of the period. Expenditures, and the related liabilities, are accrued when they are normally expected to be paid out of revenues recognized during the current period. To determine which revenues and expenditures should be accrued, an arbitrary date after the end of the year must be established. For example, revenues and expenditures may be accrued at the end of the year only if a cash flow occurs within forty-five, sixty, or some other number of days after the period end date (NCGA-1, par. 62).

Under the flow of current financial resources measurement focus, prepayments, purchases of supplies, and capital expenditures are not recorded as deferred costs but rather as current expenditures. Thus, the activity statement reflects only those expenditures that were made during the current period, and ignores cost allocations that might arise from expenditures incurred prior to the current period (NCGA-1, par. 70).

The balance sheet or statement of net assets under the flow of current financial resources approach reflects only those assets available to pay future expenditures or existing debts arising from operations (NCGA-1, pars. 61 and 70). The following table contrasts the two measurement focuses.

	Accounting Treatment	
	Flow of Economic Resources	*Flow of Current Financial Resources*
Supplies	Capitalized and amortized as goods are consumed	Treated as an expenditure when goods are acquired
Prepayments	Capitalized and amortized as goods are consumed or services are used	Treated as an expenditure when goods are acquired
Revenues and receivables arising from operations	Recorded when earned	Recorded when earned and realizable within an arbitrary number of days of the date of the balance sheet
Property, plant, and equipment	Capitalized and depreciated over economic life of asset	Treated as an expenditure when the asset is purchased
Expenditures, expenses, and liabilities arising from operations	Recorded when incurred	Recorded when incurred and payable within an specified number of days of the date of the balance sheet

Basis of Accounting/Measurement Focus Illustration

The differences and similarities of the flow of economic resources (accrual basis) and the flow of current financial resources (modified accrual basis) are illustrated in the following example, which uses the following assumptions:

Fiscal Year:	
Ended June 30, 20X5 (for simplicity it is assumed that this is the first year of operations for the fund)	-0-
Revenues:	
Billed during year	$30,000
Collected during year (one-half of the remaining balance is expected to be collected within 60 days of the year end and the remainder within 180 days)	26,000
Salaries:	
Paid during year	9,000
Payable at the end of year and expected to be paid within 30 days	1,000
Property, Plant, and Equipment:	
Purchased equipment on July 1, 20X4, at a cost of $20,000,estimated four-year life, no salvage value, straight-line method for depreciation	20,000
Noncurrent Note Payable:	
Equipment purchased was financed by issuing a 10% note whereby all interest and principal are paid four years from date of issuance	20,000
Supplies:	
Purchased during year	8,000
Consumed during year	6,000
Paid during year (balance to be paid 90 days after year-end date)	7,000
Pension:	
Annual required contribution	5,000
Amount funded during year	3,000

The financial statements for the governmental fund with the above financial information are presented in Exhibit 3-1.

EXHIBIT 3-1
FINANCIAL STATEMENTS

Fund Name
Statement of Revenues, Expenditures (Expenses), and Changes in Fund Balance (Net Assets) for Year Ended June 30, 20X5

	Flow of economic resources	*Flow of current financial resources (60-day assumption*)*
Revenues	$ 30,000	$ 28,000
Expenditures/Expenses		
Capital outlays	-0-	-0-
Salaries	10,000	10,000
Interest	2,000	-0-
Supplies	6,000	7,000
Pensions	5,000	3,000
Depreciation expense	5,000	-0-
Total	28,000	20,000
Excess of revenues over expenditures/ expenses	2,000	8,000
Net assets/Fund balance 7/1/X4	-0-	-0-
Net assets/Fund balance 6/30/X5	$ 2,000	$ 8,000

Fund Name
Statement of Net Assets/Balance Sheet June 30, 20X5

	Flow of economic resources	*Flow of current financial resources (60-day assumption*)*
Assets		
Current assets		
Cash	$ 7,000	$ 7,000
Receivables	4,000	2,000
Supplies	2,000	-0-
Total	13,000	9,000

* It is assumed that assets must be realizable in cash within 60 days of the end of the fiscal year to be considered available to finance current expenditures.

	Flow of economic resources	*Flow of current financial resources (60-day assumption*)*
Capital assets		
Equipment	20,000	-0-
Acc. depreciation	(5,000)	-0-
Net book value	15,000	-0-
Total assets	$ 28,000	$ 9,000
Liabilities and Net Assets/Fund Balance		
Current liabilities		
Accounts payable	$ 1,000	-0-
Salaries payable	1,000	$ 1,000
Total	2,000	1,000
Noncurrent liabilities		
Notes payable	22,000	-0-
Net pension obligation	2,000	-0-
Total	24,000	-0-
Total liabilities	26,000	1,000
Net Assets/Fund balance	2,000	8,000
Total liabilities and fund balance	$ 28,000	$ 9,000

* It is assumed that assets must be realizable in cash within 60 days of the end of the fiscal year to be considered available to finance current expenditures.

Conventional Accounting Basis and Measurement Focus

The governmental financial reporting model does not use a single basis of accounting and measurement focus in the preparation of government-wide financial statements and fund financial statements.

Government-wide financial statements Government-wide financial statements were established by GASB-34 (Basic Financial Statements—and Management's Discussion and Analysis—for State and

Local Governments) in order to provide a basis for determining (1) the extent to which current services provided by the entity were financed with current revenues and (2) the degree to which a governmental entity's overall financial position has changed during the fiscal year. In order to achieve these objectives, government-wide financial statements should include a statement of net assets and a statement of activities.

Government-wide financial statements are based on a flow of economic resources applied on the accrual basis of accounting. The flow of economic resources refers to all of the assets available to the governmental unit for the purpose of providing goods and services to the public. When the flow of economic resources and the accrual basis of accounting are combined, they provide a foundation for generally accepted accounting principles that is similar to that used by business enterprises. Businesses present essentially all assets and liabilities, both current and long-term, in their statement of net assets. A governmental entity's statement of activities includes all costs of providing goods and services during a period. These costs include depreciation, the cost of inventories consumed during the period, and other operating expenses. On the activity statement, revenues earned during the period are matched with the expenses incurred for exchange or exchange-like transactions. Nonexchange transactions are accounted for based on the standards established by GASB-33 (Accounting and Financial Reporting for Nonexchange Transactions).

Fund financial statements A governmental entity can use (and report) three broad categories of funds: governmental funds, proprietary funds, and fiduciary funds.

Governmental funds The governmental funds grouping includes five fund types (General Fund, Special Revenue Funds, Capital Projects Funds, Debt Service Funds, and Permanent Funds), which are used to record the more or less normal (non-business-like) operations of a governmental entity. The financial statements for these funds have a short-term emphasis and generally measure and account for cash and "other assets that can easily be converted to cash." These fund types are accounted for using the modified accrual accounting basis and the flow of current financial resources measurement focus.

Proprietary funds Financial statements for proprietary funds are based on the flow of economic resources measurement focus and the accrual basis of accounting. The proprietary fund category includes Enterprise Funds and Internal Service Funds. An Enterprise Fund is used to report any activity for which a fee is charged to external users for goods or services. An Internal Service Fund may be used to account for activities that involve the governmental entity providing goods or services to other funds or activities of the primary government or its component units, or other governments on a cost-reimbursement basis where the reporting entity is the *predominant* participant in the activity. If the reporting entity is not the predominant participant, the activity should be reported in an Enterprise Fund.

Fiduciary funds Assets held by a governmental entity for other parties (either as a trustee or as an agent) and that cannot be used to finance the governmental entity's own operating programs should be reported in the entity's fiduciary fund financial statements category. This fund grouping includes four fund types (Pension [and other employee benefit] Trust Funds, Investment Trust Funds, Private-Purpose Trust Funds, and Agency Funds). The financial statements for fiduciary funds should be based on the flow of economic resources measurement focus and the accrual basis of accounting (with the exception of certain liabilities of defined benefit pension plans and certain postemployment health care plans). Fiduciary fund financial statements are not reported by major fund (which is required for governmental funds and enterprise funds) but must be reported by fund type.

Exhibit 3-2 presents the basis of accounting and measurement focus that is required by generally accepted accounting principles for each fund category and type of government-wide activity.

EXHIBIT 3-2
Basis of Accounting and Measurement Focus

Fund Category/ Activity Type	Basis of Accounting	Measurement Focus
Governmental activities	Accrual basis	Economic resources
Business-type activities	Accrual basis	Economic resources
Governmental funds	Modified accrual basis	Current financial resources
Proprietary funds	Accrual basis	Economic resources
Fiduciary funds	Accrual basis	Economic resources

CHAPTER 4
GOVERNMENTAL REPORTING ENTITY

CONTENTS

INTRODUCTION

The fund is the basic unit for establishing accountability for activities specifically established by laws, regulations, and other governmental mandates. Each fund consists of self-balancing accounts, including accounts for the fund's assets, liabilities, and residual fund balance or net assets. A governmental unit's activities may be reflected in a number of governmental funds, proprietary funds, or fiduciary funds. In addition, agencies, authorities, and other governmental entities exist with their various funds that may be created by a state or local government. Ultimately, overall financial statements of the state or local government must be prepared, which raises the question of which funds should be included in these broad-based financial statements. The initial step in resolving this question is concerned with the conceptual definition of a financial reporting entity.

GASB-14 (The Financial Reporting Entity) establishes criteria for determining which organizations should be included in a governmental financial reporting entity.

The focal point for preparing financial statements of a financial reporting entity is the *primary government*. Primary governments include states, general-purpose local governments, and certain special-purpose governmental entities.

The identification of a financial reporting entity is built around the concept of financial accountability. If a primary government is financially accountable for another entity, that entity's financial statements should be included in the financial statements of

- The primary government and
- The primary government's component units

GASB-14 provides some flexibility in determining the components of the financial reporting entity. While financial accountability is central to the identification of component units, even if it does not exist, an entity will be considered a component unit if that entity's relationship with the primary government is such that its exclusion would create misleading or incomplete financial statements.

While GASB-14 is written from the perspective of a primary government, the standards established should be used to prepare the financial statements of governmental entities that are not primary governments. Thus, an entity that is not a primary government must assess its relationships with other entities to determine whether it is financially accountable for those entities. If financial accountability exists, a financial reporting entity should be constructed that includes the governmental entity and its component units.

In addition to establishing criteria for determining the scope of the financial reporting entity, GASB-14 addresses accounting and reporting standards for entities that are not component units.

These entities include governmental joint ventures, jointly governed organizations, and certain stand-alone governmental organizations.

> **NOTE:** The GASB addresses GASB-14 questions and answers in chapter 4 of the *GASB Comprehensive Implementation Guide.*

GASB-14 applies to financial reporting by all state and local governments. However, the basis for reporting is not necessarily the narrowly defined state or local government, but rather is the "financial reporting entity," as defined below (GASB-14, par. 9 and Glossary):

> A primary government, organizations for which the primary government is financially accountable, and other organizations for which the nature and significance of their relationships with the primary government are such that exclusion would cause the reporting entity's financial statements to be misleading or incomplete. The nucleus of a financial reporting entity usually is a primary government. However, a governmental organization other than a primary government (such as a component unit, a joint venture, a jointly governed organization, or other stand-alone government) serves as the nucleus for its own reporting entity when it issues separate financial statements [see later discussion in the section titled "The Financial Reporting Entity Concept"].

The focal point for defining the financial reporting entity begins with a "primary government," which is defined as follows:

> A state government or general purpose local government. Also, a special-purpose government that has a separately elected governing body, is legally separate, and is fiscally independent of other state or local governments.

Thus, states, cities, towns, municipalities, and similar general-purpose local governments, as well as certain special-purpose governmental entities, are primary governments (GASB-14, Glossary).

To prepare the financial statements of the financial reporting entity, the financial statements of a primary government are combined with the financial statements of its component units. "Component units" are defined as follows:

> Legally separate organizations for which the elected officials of the primary government are financially accountable. In addition, a component unit can be another organization for which the nature and significance of its relationship with a primary government is such that exclusion would cause the reporting entity's financial statements to be misleading or incomplete [see later discussion in section titled "Component Units"].

Although the standards GASB-14 establishes are discussed in the context of a primary government, GASB-14 recognizes that the focal point for defining a financial reporting entity may start with one of the following entities, rather than a primary government (GASB-14, Glossary):

> *Joint venture (governmental)*—Alegal entity or other organization that results from a contractual arrangement and that is owned, operated, or governed by two or more participants as a separate and specific activity subject to joint control, in which the participants retain (a) an ongoing financial interest or (b) an ongoing financial responsibility [see later discussion in section titled "Joint Ventures"].
>
> *Jointly governed organization*—A regional government or other multi-governmental arrangement that is governed by representatives from each of the governments that create the organization, but that is not a joint venture because the participants do not retain an ongoing financial interest or responsibility [see later discussion in section titled "Jointly Governed Organizations"].
>
> *Other stand-alone government*—A legally separate governmental organization that (a) does not have a separately elected governing body and (b) does not meet the definition of a component unit. Other stand-alone governments include some special-purpose governments, joint ventures, jointly governed organizations, and pools [see later discussion in section titled "Other Stand-Alone Government Financial Statements"].

The focal point for preparing a financial reporting entity's financial statements could be a component unit when the component unit issues separate financial statements (GASB-14, Glossary).

> **OBSERVATION:** The standards established in GASB-14 are based on the philosophy of building from the bottom up when preparing financial statements. This concept is discussed later in this chapter under the heading "Reporting Component Units."

The following are examples of governmental entities, in addition to primary governments, that must follow the standards established by GASB-14 (GASB-14, par. 9):

- Governmental enterprises
- Public benefit corporations
- Public authorities
- Public employee retirement systems

- Governmental utilities
- Governmental hospitals and other health care providers
- Governmental colleges and universities

The standards established by GASB-14 should be applied to all component units, both governmental and nongovernmental, when those units are part of the financial reporting entity (GASB-14, par. 9).

> **OBSERVATION:** Nongovernmental entities may be included in the definition of a governmental financial reporting entity. For example, a municipality may own a commercial concrete manufacturer. When the nongovernmental entity's financial information is included in a governmental financial reporting entity, the standards established by GASB-14 should be observed. The government's intent (operational or investment) has an impact on the accounting and financial reporting treatment of the nongovernmental entity within the government's financial statements.

THE FINANCIAL REPORTING ENTITY CONCEPT

GASB Concepts Statement No. 1 (GASB:CS-1) (Objectives of Financial Reporting) states that the basic foundation for governmental financial reporting is accountability. The Concepts Statement asserts that accountability "requires governments to answer to the citizenry—to justify the raising of public resources and the purposes for which they are used." In turn, the concept of accountability becomes the basis for defining the financial reporting entity. However, GASB-14 establishes a more operational definition by describing "accountability" (or accountable) as "the relationship that results from the appointment of a voting majority of an organization's governing board" (GASB-14, pars. 10–11).

At every level of government (local, state, and federal), all public resources are the responsibility of elected officials. In the context of financial reporting, once public officials are elected, the citizenry has a right to be informed as to how public resources were used during a period. To hold public officials responsible for an entity's financial affairs, care must be taken in defining the accounting entity. If the accounting entity is defined in a manner that does not represent the authority empowered in public officials, the objective of accountability cannot be achieved. Fundamentally, GASB-14 attempts to follow a basic rule of responsibility accounting, which reasons that one should not be held accountable for something that one cannot influence (GASB-14, pars. 10–11).

The reporting entity's financial statements should be structured so that a reader can differentiate between the primary government and its discretely presented component units. This is accomplished by formatting the government-wide financial statements so that balances and transactions of the primary government are presented separately from those of its discretely presented component units. In addition, the reporting entity's fund financial statements should include only the primary government's governmental, proprietary, and fiduciary funds, and the first two fund categories should be presented by major fund, with nonmajor funds being aggregated and presented in a single column. Fiduciary funds are presented by fund type (GASB-14, par. 11, as amended by GASB-34).

The two methods used to integrate the financial information of component units into the financial statements of the reporting entity are "discrete presentation" and "blending." GASB-14 defines these methods as follows (GASB-14, par. 11; GASB-34, pars. 6 and 126):

> *Discrete presentation method*—The method of reporting financial data of component units in a column(s) separate from the financial data of the primary government. An integral part of this method of presentation is that major component unit supporting information is required to be provided in the reporting entity's basic financial statements by (a) presenting each major component unit in a separate column in the reporting entity's statements of net assets and activities, (b) including combining statements of major component units in the reporting entity's basic statements after the fund financial statements, or (c) presenting condensed financial statements in the notes to the reporting entity's basic financial statements.

> *Blending method*—The method of reporting the financial data of a component unit that presents the component unit's balances and transactions in a manner similar to the presentation of the balances and transactions of the primary government [see later discussion in section titled "Blending Component Units"].

DEFINITION OF THE FINANCIAL REPORTING ENTITY

The financial reporting entity consists of the following (GASB-14, par. 12, as amended by GASB-34):

- The primary government (see later discussion in section titled "Primary Governments")
- Organizations for which the primary government is financially accountable (see later discussion in section titled "Financial Accountability")
- Other organizations for which the nature and significance of their relationship with the primary government are such that exclusion would cause the reporting entity's basic financial statements to be misleading or incomplete (see later discussion in section titled "Nature and Significance of Relationship")

GASB-14 defines "financial accountability" as follows:

> The level of accountability that exists if a primary government appoints a voting majority of an organization's governing board and is either able to impose its will on that organization or there is a potential for the organization to provide specific financial benefits to, or impose specific financial burdens on, the primary government. A primary government may also be financially accountable for governmental organizations with a separately elected governing board, a governing board appointed by another government, or a jointly appointed board that is fiscally dependent on the primary government [see later discussion in section titled "Financial Accountability"].

Although the focal point for defining the financial reporting entity is the primary government, other organizations that have a relationship with the primary government are evaluated to determine whether they should be included in the financial reporting entity (GASB-14, Glossary).

Although GASB-14 is written from the perspective of a primary government, other governmental entities that issue separate financial statements can be the focus for defining a financial reporting entity. For example, component units, joint ventures, jointly governed organizations, and stand-alone governmental entities should follow the guidance established in GASB-14 to determine which financial statements of other organizations should be combined with their statements to form a financial reporting entity (GASB-14, par. 12).

PRIMARY GOVERNMENTS

Definition of a Primary Government

The focal point in defining a financial reporting entity is the identification of a primary government. GASB-14 states that a primary government must have a separately elected governing body. States, including tribal governments, and general-purpose local governmental entities, such as counties and municipalities, are primary governments (GASB-14, Glossary).

In addition to states, tribal governments, and general-purpose local governmental entities, special-purpose governmental entities are considered primary governments if they satisfy all of the following criteria (GASB-14, par. 15):

- The entity has a separately elected governing body, elected by the citizenry in a general, popular election.

- The entity is legally separate from other entities (see later discussion in section titled "Determining Separate Legal Standing").
- The entity is fiscally independent of other state and local governmental entities (see later discussion in section titled "Determining Fiscal Independence or Dependence").

All governmental entities that are not legally separate from the primary government are part of the primary government. Thus, the primary government would be composed of various funds, departments, institutions, offices, and other governmental entities that do not have separate legal status. If a governmental entity is not legally separate from the primary government, its financial data should be merged with the financial data of the primary government (GASB-14, par. 14).

Determining separate legal standing GASB-14 provides the following definition of "separate legal standing":

> An organization created as a body corporate or a body corporate and politic or otherwise possessing similar corporate powers. An organization that has separate legal standing has an identity of its own as an "artificial person" with a personality and existence distinct from that of its creator and others.

An entity is a legally separate organization if it is given the powers that are generally held by an individual. In effect, a separate legal entity is an artificial person having such powers as a distinct separate name, the right to be a party in litigation, and the right to enter into legal contracts (GASB-14, Glossary).

Separate legal standing may be established in the corporate charter granted by a state or by the legislation passed to create the entity (GASB-14, par. 15).

For a special-purpose government to be a primary government, it must have separate legal standing. If it does not have such standing, it is part of the primary government that exercises the corporate powers related to its activities (GASB-14, par. 15).

Determining fiscal independence or dependence The third criterion that must be satisfied for a special-purpose government to be considered a primary government is fiscal independence. For an entity to be considered fiscally independent, it must have the authority, without substantive approval or modification of an other government, to do all of the following (GASB-14, par. 1):

- Establish a budget.
- Either levy taxes or set rates or charges.
- Issue bonded debt.

If a special-purpose government does not satisfy all three standards, the entity is fiscally dependent on the primary government that holds the power of approval or modification.

> **OBSERVATION:** Footnote 3 to GASB-14 acknowledges that a primary government may be temporarily subject to the financial control of another government. Usually this involves a state government taking control of a municipal government or a school district because of financial difficulties. When the financial control is temporary, the governmental entity subject to the control is considered fiscally independent for purposes of GASB-14.

Fiscal dependency does not require that the special-purpose government receive financial assistance from the primary government. Thus, a fiscally dependent relationship is not based on the existence of either a financial burden on or a financial benefit for the primary government. These terms are defined as follows in GASB-14:

> *Financial burden*—An obligation, legal or otherwise, to finance the deficits of, or provide financial support to, an organization; or an obligation in some manner for the debt of an organization [see later discussion in section titled "Financial Benefit to or Burden on a Primary Government"].

> *Financial benefit*—Legal entitlement to, or the ability to otherwise access, the resources of an organization [see later discussion in section titled "Financial Benefit to or Burden on a Primary Government"].

The authority of a primary government to approve or modify actions taken by a special-purpose government should be examined to determine whether that authority is procedural in nature or one of substantive evaluation. In many instances, a primary government has general oversight responsibility with respect to a special-purpose government, but that oversight is exercised within specific parameters that have been established. That is, the actions taken by the special-purpose government must comply with pre-established guidelines, limits, standards, or other parameters. Under this circumstance, the authority held by the primary government is considered procedural and not substantive. GASB-14 provides the following examples of authority that is procedural rather than substantive:

- State agency approves the issuance of debt based on a review to determine whether total debt issued by the special-purpose government does not exceed an established percentage of assessed property valuation.
- State department of education reviews a special-purpose government's budget to determine whether the special-purpose government qualifies for state funding based on pre-established conditions set by the state.
- Country clerk approves a special-purpose government's tax rate or levy to determine whether the rate or levy exceeds pre-established limits (GASB-14, Glossary).

On the other hand, if a special-purpose government's actions are subject to substantive approval or modification, the special-purpose government cannot be considered a primary government. For example, if a municipal government can review its public utility authority's budget and, based on that review, reduce the level of spending or require a change in rates, the special-purpose government (the utility authority) is not a primary government with respect to the definition of a financial reporting entity (GASB-14, par. 17).

Some special-purpose governments may be prohibited by law from issuing debt. Such prohibition in itself does not mean that a special-purpose government cannot be a primary government. The rationale for this conclusion is that another governmental entity cannot approve or modify the special-purpose government's ability to issue debt, because the ability does not exist (GASB-14, par. 18).

COMPONENT UNITS

Definition of Component Units

Component units can be governmental organizations, not-for-profit corporations, or even for-profit corporations. Acomponent unit cannot be a primary government (GASB-14, par. 20). GASB-14, as amended by GASB-39, requires that three separate criteria be applied to an organization to determine whether it is a component unit of the primary government. These three criteria are summarized as follows and in Exhibit 4-1:

1. Financial accountability
2. Nature and significance of relationship
3. Closely related or financially integrated

Financial Accountability

A primary government that is financially accountable for a legally separate entity should include the financial information of that entity with its own financial statements to form the financial reporting entity. Financial accountability exists if the primary government appoints a voting majority of the entity's governing body and if either one of the following conditions exists (GASB-14, par. 21):

- The primary government can impose its will on the other entity or
- The potential exists for the other entity to (1) provide specific financial benefits to or (2) impose specific financial burdens on the primary government.

EXHIBIT 4-1
DETERMINING WHETHER AN ORGANIZATION IS A COMPONENT UNIT OF A PRIMARY GOVERNMENT

Approach	Method of Integration	GASB Statement Reference
The primary government is financially accountable for the other organization.	Blending or discrete presentation	GASB-14, pars. 20–40
The nature and significance of the relationship between the primary government and the other organization.	Discrete presentation only	GASB-14, par. 40a (as amended by GASB-39)
The other organization is closely related to or financially integrated with the primary government.	Blending or discrete presentation	GASB-14, par. 41 (as amended by GASB-39)

OBSERVATION: The first criterion, financial accountability, is the primary objective benchmark that determines whether an entity is a component unit of the financial reporting entity. However, the other two criteria were added to allow for a greater degree of professional judgment in determining which entities are component units.

In addition, financial accountability may exist when another entity is fiscally dependent (see the earlier discussion in the section titled "Determining Fiscal Independence or Dependence") on the primary government, even if the primary government does not appoint a voting majority of the entity's governing body. Therefore, fiscal accountability could exist even when the entity's governing board is separately elected, appointed by a government higher than the primary government, or jointly appointed (see the later discussion in the section titled "Financial Accountability as a Result of Fiscal Dependency") (GASB-14, par. 21).

Appointment of a voting majority Financial accountability is dependent on whether a primary government appoints a voting majority of another entity's governing body. In most instances, the appointment of a simple majority is equivalent to a voting majority because the approval of financial issues is based on a simple majority vote. However, if more than a simple majority is required to approve financial issues, the appointment of a simple majority does not result in the primary government being financially accountable for the other entity (GASB-14, pars. 22–24).

PRACTICE POINT: Footnote 5 to GASB-14 states that in determining whether a majority of the entity's governing body has been appointed, the number of appointments by the primary government would include primary government officials who are serving on the entity's governing board as required by law.

GASB-14 defines "appoint" as follows:

> To select members of a governing board (as long as the ability to do so is not severely limited by a nomination process) or confirm appointments made by others (provided that the confirmation is more than a formality or part of a ministerial responsibility).

The above definition recognizes that the appointment process must be more than perfunctory in that the process must demonstrate substance rather than form. In determining whether the appointment process is substantive, the nomination and confirmation processes should be examined (GASB-14, Glossary).

Nomination process The appointment process should not be significantly restricted by the nomination process. If the primary government must appoint members of the other entity's governing body who are nominated by another entity or entities, financial accountability cannot exist. What constitutes substantive appointment authority by the primary government is subjective. However, in one example, GASB-14 characterizes a limiting nomination process as one where the primary government must select three appointees from a slate of five candidates. In practice, the nomination process should be carefully examined to determine the degree of involvement of the primary government in the nomination process (GASB-14, par. 23).

Confirmation process GASB-14 takes the position that the confirmation process is not a substitute for the appointment process. Thus, if prospective members of the other entity's governing body are nominated or appointed by parties other than the primary government's officials or appointees, the primary government's right to confirm the nomination or appointment may suggest the appointment process is not substantive (GASB-14, par. 23).

OBSERVATION: Based on the language of GASB-14, the appointment process could still be substantive even if the primary government's role in the appointment process is limited to confirmation. Although GASB-14 does not elaborate on this possibility, presumably the appointment process would be considered substantive if the primary government has the necessary prerequisites to conduct an effective confirmation hearing. These prerequisites could include the necessary legislative authority, sufficient staff to research issues, and a time frame that allows for sufficient investigation before nominations become effective.

Appointment authority is usually continuing and not limited to an initial appointment. Thus, the primary government may have the authority to make appointments as vacancies arise. In those circumstances where continuing authority for appointment does not exist, financial accountability between the primary government and the other entity will exist if the primary government has created the other entity (equivalent to appointing the governing body) and can unilaterally abolish the other entity (GASB-14, par. 24).

Imposition of will Imposition of will is evidenced by the primary government's ability to affect the day-to-day operations of the other entity. GASB-14 refers to this capability as "imposition of will," which is defined as

> The ability to significantly influence the programs, projects, activities, or level of services performed or provided by an organization.

The determination of whether imposition of will takes place is a matter of judgment, and the specific circumstances of each relationship must be carefully evaluated. In evaluating the imposition of will, the ability to affect day-to-day operations must be substantive and not merely procedural (see earlier discussion in the section titled "Determining Fiscal Independence or Dependence"). Although the determination of whether imposition of will takes place is a matter of judgment, GASB-14 states that existence of *any* of the following is a clear indication of the ability of the primary government to affect the day-to-day operations of another entity (GASB-14, Glossary):

- Appointed members can be removed at will by the primary government.
- The budget can be modified or approved by the primary government.
- Rate or fee changes that affect revenues can be modified or approved by the primary government.
- Decisions other than those related to the budget, rates, or fees may be vetoed, overruled, or modified by the primary government.
- Management personnel may be appointed, hired, reassigned, or dismissed by the primary government (GASB-14, pars. 25–26).

Financial benefit to or burden on a primary government GASB-14 states that financial benefit or financial burden is created if *any* of the following relationships exists (GASB-14, par. 27):

- The primary government has access to the other entity's resources.
- The primary government is legally required or has assumed the responsibility to finance the other entity's deficits or financially support the other entity.

- The primary government has responsibility for the other entity's debt.

In identifying financial benefits or financial burdens that create financial accountability, the benefits to or the burdens on the primary government can be either direct or indirect. For example, if the primary government is entitled to any surplus of another governmental entity, the effect is direct. On the other hand, if a component unit of the primary government is entitled to the surplus, the effect is indirect with respect to the primary government. Either direct or indirect financial burden or benefit implies financial accountability between a primary government and another entity (GASB-14, par. 28).

Governmental entities will enter into a variety of exchange transactions with other parties. Exchange transactions are characterized by each party giving up goods or services of approximately equivalent value. For example, a primary government may purchase used computer equipment from another governmental entity or a commercial enterprise. An exchange transaction does not create a financial benefit or financial burden relationship and therefore is not relevant in determining whether a primary government is financially accountable for another entity (GASB-14, par. 28).

Access to the other entity's resources Financial benefits arise when the primary government has the ability to use the resources of another entity. The ability need only exist—there need not be an actual transaction that has occurred during the period or during previous periods to demonstrate that the primary government has received assets from the other entity (GASB-14, par. 29).

A primary government may have a right to the residual assets of another entity if the other entity is liquidated or otherwise dissolved. An interest in the residual assets of another entity is not considered equivalent to access to the other entity's resources and therefore is not considered a benefit to the primary government for the purposes of determining financial accountability (GASB-14, par. 29).

Access to an entity's resources may be obvious because of the relationship between the primary government and the other entity. For example, an entity may be organized specifically to collect revenue that will be remitted to the primary government (for example, a state lottery) (GASB-14, par. 29).

Alternatively, access to an entity's resources may be based on a strategy that enables the other entity to charge a fee for its services that exceeds the amount needed to maintain its own capital, and then remit the excess to the primary government. Irrespective of the name used for such a remittance (payments in lieu of taxes, contributions, or amounts due the primary government), the relationship demonstrates that the primary government has access to the other entity's resources (GASB-14, par. 30).

Responsibility for deficits or support Specific financial burdens arise when the primary government is legally obligated or has assumed the responsibility to (1) finance an entity's deficit or (2) provide financial support to the entity. GASB-14 provides the following examples of this type of specific financial burden (GASB-14, par. 31):

- An entity charges an amount for its services that will not be sufficient to cover the total cost of providing such services, and a primary government, either by law or by public policy, assumes the responsibility for any deficit that may arise. Examples of this include operating subsidies for a public college or university and capital grants for urban mass transit systems.
- A primary government assumes the responsibility for any deficit that another entity may incur even though a deficit has never arisen and there is no expectation that one will arise.

A special arrangement may exist whereby an entity may be fully or partially funded through tax increment financing. A tax rate may be established at 7% by a primary government but another entity may receive 1% of the revenue raised to finance its operations. Tax increment financing is considered a form of financial burden irrespective of whether the incremental amount is collected by the primary government or directly by the other entity (GASB-14, par. 32).

Responsibility for debt The primary government may accept an obligation for the debt of another entity. The obligation may be expressed or implied. An expressed obligation could arise from legislation that specifically makes a state liable for another entity's debt, or covenants contained in a bond agreement that obligate the state in case of default by the other entity. In addition, the primary government may take explicit action by assuming responsibility for the debt of another entity. An implied obligation could be based on relevant legal precedents that have occurred in a particular state (GASB-14, par. 33).

GASB-14 lists the following as conditions that would obligate the primary government for the debt of another entity (GASB-14, par. 33):

1. The primary government is legally responsible for debt that is not paid after other default remedies have been pursued.
2. The primary government is required to provide funds to cover temporary deficiencies that will eventually be paid by primary repayment sources or by other default remedies.
3. The primary government is required either to fund reserves maintained by the other entity or to create its own reserve fund.
4. The primary government is authorized either to fund reserves maintained by the other entity or to create its own reserve fund

and has established such a fund (see 6 and 7 below for guidance that is relevant when the primary entity has not established a fund).

5. The primary government is authorized either to provide financing for a fund reserve maintained by the other entity for the purpose of repurchasing outstanding debt or to create its own reserve fund and has established such a fund (see 6 and 7 below for guidance that is relevant when the primary entity has not established a fund).
6. The debt contract states that the primary government may cover defaults, although it is not required to do so.
7. Legal precedents within a state, or actions taken by a primary government, related to actual or potential defaults make it probable that the primary government will be responsible for the other entity's defaulted debt.

NOTE: GASB-14 does not define the term *probable,* but the term is defined in FAS-5 (Accounting for Contingencies) as "the future event or events are likely to occur."

Financial accountability as a result of fiscal dependency A primary government is financially accountable for another entity when the other entity is fiscally dependent on the primary government. Under this circumstance, financial accountability can arise even when the other entity has a separately elected governing board, a board appointed by another government, or a jointly appointed board (GASB-14, par. 34).

Fiscal independence was discussed earlier in the context of a special-purpose government considered a primary government for financial reporting purposes. An entity that is not fiscally independent must be considered fiscally dependent. More specifically, fiscal dependency arises if one or more of the following activities cannot be performed by the entity without substantive approval or modification by a primary government (GASB-14, pars. 16–18):

- Establish a budget.
- Either levy taxes or set rates or charges.
- Issue bonded debt.

Special-purpose governments with separately elected governing boards Numerous governmental entities that have been established for special purposes and have separately elected governing boards are fiscally dependent on a primary government. For example, school districts often have separately elected boards but their fiscal activities are subject to approval or modification by the municipality or county in which they serve. Entities of this nature should be presented as component units of the primary government (GASB-14, par. 35).

Governmental organizations with boards appointed by another government More than one primary government may control to some degree the activities of another governmental entity. Specifically, the governing board of a governmental entity may be appointed by the state (a higher-level government) while a local government (lower-level government) is financially accountable for the governmental entity. GASB-14 takes the position that even though the local government does not appoint the voting majority of the entity's governing body, that governmental entity should be considered a component unit of the local government and not the state government. In this instance the fiscal dependency factor is considered more relevant in defining the financial reporting entity than the appointment power (GASB-14, par. 36). (See also the later discussion in the section titled "Potential for Dual Inclusion.")

Governing entities with jointly appointed boards Various primary governments may participate jointly in the appointment of the governing boards of a governmental entity. For example, two or more states may agree to create a port authority, or a state and several local communities may agree to create a mass transit authority. In these circumstances, no one primary government may have the authority to appoint a voting majority of the entity's governing body. When this occurs, the entity should be considered a component unit of the primary government to which it is fiscally dependent, unless the entity meets the criteria to be reported as a joint venture (discussed later in this chapter).

Potential for Dual Inclusion

It is possible that an entity could satisfy the GASB-14 criteria in a manner that would suggest that it is a component unit of more than one primary government. GASB-14 recognizes the anomaly but states that an entity can be a component unit for only one primary government. Professional judgment should be exercised to determine which primary government should report the entity as a component unit (GASB-14, par. 38).

The potential for dual inclusion generally occurs when (1) the state government appoints the governing board of an entity and (2) the state government and a local government provide funding for the entity. If the funding by the state is based on legislation which directs resources to the governmental entity using various state formulas, it is likely that the governmental entity is a component unit of the local government and not the state government (GASB-14, par. 38).

OBSERVATION: In those situations where state funding is more discretionary (not based on predetermined formulas) the question of which government, state government or local government, is financially accountable for the other entity becomes more difficult. The state and local governments should communicate with one another to determine which one of them is the most appropriate primary government for the entity.

Nature and Significance of Relationship

GASB-39 states that the financial statements of governmental and nongovernmental organizations for which a primary government (or the primary government's component units) is not financially accountable should still, under certain circumstances, be included in the primary government's financial statements. This determination is based on "the nature and significance of the relationship between the primary government and the potential component unit, including the latter's ongoing financial support of the primary government and its other component units." While that concept is broad, GASB-39 states that a legally separate, tax-exempt organization's financial statements are to be included in the primary government's financial statements if *all* of the following conditions exist (GASB-14, par. 40a, as amended by GASB-39):

- The economic resources received or held by the separate organization are entirely or almost entirely for the direct benefit of the primary government, its component units, or its constituents.
- The primary government or its component units is entitled to, or has the ability to otherwise access, a majority of the economic resources received or held by the separate organization.
- The economic resources received or held by an individual organization that the specific primary government, or its component units, is entitled to, or has the ability to otherwise access, are significant to that primary government.

When these conditions are satisfied, the other organization's financial statements are presented as a (discrete) component unit in the primary government's external financial statements.

Direct benefit of economic resources There is direct economic benefit when the other organization "obtains, seeks to obtain, or holds and invests resources that will benefit the primary government, its component units, or its constituents." This condition does not imply that there must be an actual transfer from the other organization during the year but rather that "the resources obtained or held are required to ultimately be used for the benefit of a specific primary government, its component units, or its constituents."

The first condition generally means that an organization that provides resources to multiple constituent groups, for example a federated fund-raising organization, would not be considered a component unit of a primary government. Under this circumstance it is possible that a significant amount of resources may be provided to the primary government (or its component units or constituents) in one year but in other years other governmental or nongovernmental entities may receive a significant portion of the other organization's resources. This situation would not satisfy the requirement that all or almost all of the resources be available to the primary government.

Access to economic resources The second condition requires that the primary government either (1) be entitled to a majority of the economic resources received or held by the separate organization or (2) have the ability to otherwise access those resources. There is no difficulty in applying this condition when the primary government is entitled to the resources. For example, that entitlement may be based on the legal relationship between the primary government and the separate organization or the donations made to the separate organization may be legally restricted by donors to the benefit of the primary government.

Difficulties arise when the criterion is based on the ability to otherwise access the resources of the other organization. The concept "ability to otherwise access" is broad and is not based on the narrow idea of control. GASB-39 states that this broad concept can be demonstrated in several ways, including the following:

- The primary government or its component units in the past have received, directly or indirectly, a majority of the economic resources provided by the organization.
- The organization previously has received and honored requests to provide resources to the primary government.
- The other organization is financially interrelated with the primary government.

GASB-39 notes that "this criterion (access to economic resources) will further limit inclusion to organizations such as entity-specific fund-raising foundations" because these foundations (1) have a history of providing economic resources to the primary government or (2) honor requests for economic resources initiated by the primary government.

The third example (financially interrelated) is based on the belief that most of the "other organizations" that are evaluated in the context of the criteria established by GASB-39 are nongovernmental entities that follow the financial and accounting standards established fundamentally by FAS-117 (Financial Statements of Not-for-Profit Organizations) as well as other FASB pronouncements, such as FAS-136 (Transfers of Assets to a Not-for-Profit Organization or Charitable Trust That Raises or Holds Contributions for Others).

GASB-39 uses the guidance established in FAS-136 by stating that the two parties are "financially interrelated" when both of the following two conditions exist:

1. One organization has the ability to influence the operating and financial decisions of the other. The ability to exercise that influence may be demonstrated in several ways:
   - The organizations are affiliates.
   - One organization has considerable representation on the governing board of the other organization.
   - The charter or bylaws of one organization limit its activities to those that are beneficial to the other organization
   - An agreement between the organizations allows one organization to actively participate in policy-making processes of the other, such as setting organizational priorities, budgets, and management compensation.
2. One organization has an ongoing economic interest in the net assets of the other. If the specified beneficiary has an ongoing economic interest in the net assets of the recipient organization, the beneficiary's rights to the assets held by the recipient organization are residual rights; that is, the value of those rights increases or decreases as a result of the investment, fundraising, operating, and other activities of the recipient organization. Alternatively, but less commonly, a recipient organization may have an ongoing economic interest in the net assets of the specified beneficiary. If so, the recipient organization's rights are residual rights, and their value changes as a result of the operations of the beneficiary.

Significant economic support The final condition recognizes that some governmental entities receive resources from various support groups that are clearly component units, but the GASB does not intend to require support that is insignificant to trigger the inclusion of such groups in the primary government's financial statements. This criterion is a materiality threshold. The GASB concedes that this materiality threshold is higher than that used for component units that are included in the reporting entity based on the financial accountability established by GASB-14 for the following reasons:

- The importance of the financial support is relative to the entire primary government rather than an individual reporting unit.
- The criteria are applied to an individual organization rather than all organizations of a similar type (for example, parent-teacher associations).

For example, many public school athletic programs have separate support organizations that may pay for team trips and banquets, additional compensation for coaches, and similar items. Generally these support groups would not be presented as component units of the public school district because the economic support to the school (not to the specific program or activity) is insignificant.

The financial statements of other organizations that are considered to be component units because of the nature and significance of their relationship to the primary government are to be discretely presented (not blended) in the primary government's financial statements.

Closely Related or Financially Integrated

The GASB recognizes that the three conditions listed above may be too constricting in that certain organizations that might not satisfy the three conditions listed can nonetheless be an important component units of a primary government. For this reason, GASB-39 states that professional judgment should be used to identify those organizations that "are closely related to, or financially integrated with the primary government" and, therefore, those organizations should also be reported as component units by the primary government (GASB-14, par. 41, as amended by GASB-39).

GASB-39 points out that financial integration may be exhibited and documented through the policies, practices, or organizational documents of either the primary government or the organization being evaluated as a potential component unit. Financial integration could be demonstrated in a number of ways, including the following:

- Descriptions in charters and bylaws of the primary government or the other organizations (for example, the charter might state that the organization will lose its tax-exempt status if it fails to distribute its resources to the primary government)
- Participation by the other organization's employees in a primary government's programs or activities
- Representation in financial aid accountability systems of work study fellowship grants to students of a primary government for work performed for the other organization
- Participation by the primary government's employees in the other organization's research activities and inclusion of those activities in the service effort report of the primary government

- Sharing of office space and administrative services by the primary government and the other organization

> **OBSERVATION:** The GASB emphasizes that the above list is not all-inclusive and that professional judgment rather than a list of relationships is the basis for determining whether the exclusion of a potential component unit's financial statements might result in the primary government's financial statements being misleading or incomplete.

The financial statements of other organizations that are considered to be component units because they are closely related to or financially integrated with the primary government may be presented in the primary government's financial statements by either blending or discrete presentation.

> **OBSERVATION:** Professional judgment must be used to identify those relationships that justify the inclusion of an affiliated entity and a PERS. Primary governments must evaluate entities for which they are not financially accountable to determine whether those entities should be included in the financial reporting entity because of the nature and significance of the relationship between the entity and the primary government. In addition, some practitioners have raised the question as to whether the relationship between a primary government and its related PERS may be insufficient to include the PERS in the financial statements of the reporting entity. However, it is likely that a PERS would be included in the financial reporting entity because of the fiduciary relationship between the primary government and the PERS.

REPORTING COMPONENT UNITS

When an entity is considered a component unit, its financial information and the financial information of its primary government should be presented in the financial statements of the financial reporting entity. The presentation of the financial information is accomplished by use of either

- The discrete presentation method or
- The blending method

The presentation in the reporting entity's financial statements should be formatted so that a reader can distinguish between the financial position and financial activities of the primary government and those of its discretely presented component units.

It is possible that a component unit (CU #1) of a primary government may have its own component units (CU #2 and CU #3). Under this circumstance, the financial statements should be built from the bottom up. CU #1 should include in its financial statements, through either blending or discrete presentation, or combination of the two, the financial statements of its component units (CU #2 and CU #3). In turn, the primary government would create its reporting entity by combining the financial statements of the CU #1 financial reporting entity with its own financial statements through blending or discrete presentation. Although CU #2 and CU #3 are not technically component units of the primary government, their financial information is nonetheless incorporated into the higher-level financial report of the primary government (GASB-14, par. 43).

Discrete Presentation of Component Units

GASB-34 (Basic Financial Statements—and Management's Discussion and Analysis—for State and Local Governments) was written in a manner that satisfies the financial reporting entity standards originally established by GASB-14 with respect to component units. Relevant guidance established by GASB-14 in this regard is reproduced below (GASB-34, par. 124):

> The financial statements of the reporting entity should allow users to distinguish between the primary government and its component units by communicating information about the component units and their relationships with the primary government rather than creating the perception that the primary government and all of its component units are one legal entity.

In addition, GASB-14, paragraph 51, requires that information related to each major component unit be presented in the reporting entity's basic financial statements. To satisfy this standard, any one of the following approaches can be done (GASB-34, par. 126):

- Present each major component unit in a separate column in the government-wide financial statements
- Present combining statements within the basic financial statements
- Present condensed financial statements in a note to the financial statements

PRACTICE POINT: Each of these three presentation methods creates information that is part of the basic financial statements.

PRACTICE POINT: The requirement for major component unit information does not apply to component units that are fiduciary in nature.

OBSERVATION: The *GASB Comprehensive Implementation Guide* points out that the reporting governmental entity cannot combine as a single function (for example, higher education) related information of the primary government and a discretely presented component unit, because GASB-14 requires that the financial statements of the reporting entity distinguish between the accounts and transactions of the primary government and its discretely presented component units.

Separate column(s) in government-wide financial statements Under this presentation format, the government-wide financial statements (statement of net assets and statement of activities) have columns for (1) governmental activities, (2) business-type activities and (3) major component units. These financial statements should provide a total column for governmental activities and business-type activities (the primary government), but a total column for the reporting entity is optional.

Combining statements Rather than presenting a separate column in the government-wide financial statements for each major component unit, combining statements for component units may be presented. The combining financial statements should be based on the accrual basis of accounting and should include a statement of net assets and a statement of activities. A separate column should be used for each major component unit, and all nonmajor component units should be aggregated into a single column. A total column for all component units should be presented and those totals should be traceable to the "component unit" column in the government-wide financial statements. The combining statements should be placed after the fund financial statements.

PRACTICE POINT: If the combining-statement method is used, a combining statement for nonmajor component units may be presented as supplementary information (but this is not a requirement).

PRACTICE POINT: If the combining-statement approach is used, GASB-34, par. 126, requires that the aggregated total component unit information, as discussed in GASB-14, be the total for the component unit and all of its component units, even if the component unit does not present a total column for its reporting entity as a whole within its stand-alone financial statements (GASB-37, par. 18).

Condensed financial statements in notes If the note-disclosure method is used, the following disclosures must be made (GASB-34, par. 127):

- Condensed statement of net assets
  - *Total assets* Distinguishing between capital assets and other assets. Amounts receivable from the primary

government or from other component units of the same reporting entity should be reported separately.

— *Total liabilities* Distinguishing between long-term debt outstanding and other liabilities. Amounts payable to the primary government or to other component units of the same reporting entity should be reported separately.

— *Total net assets* Distinguishing between restricted, unrestricted, and amounts invested in capital assets, net of related debt.

- Condensed statement of activities
  — Expenses, with separate identification of depreciation expense and amortizations of long-lived assets
  — Program revenues (by type)
  — Net program (expense) revenue
  — Tax revenues
  — Other nontax general revenues
  — Contributions to endowments and permanent fund principal
  — Extraordinary and special items
  — Change in net assets
  — Beginning and ending net assets

The notes to the financial statements should also describe the nature and amount of significant transactions between major component units and the primary government and other component units (GASB-34, par. 128).

PRACTICE POINT: GASB-14 states that if a discretely presented component unit does not issue a separate financial report, the reporting entity's CAFR, if one is issued, must include fund financial statements for the component unit (major fund reporting format). This information is presented as required supplementary information. This requirement is based on GASB-14 (par. 50), except GASB-34 requires that the fund financial statements be focused on major funds of the component unit rather than its fund types. Furthermore, if a component unit does not issue separate financial statements and uses proprietary fund accounting, then the reporting entity must include in its CAFR (as supplementary information) a statement of cash flows for the unit.

PRACTICE POINT: The *GASB Comprehensive Implementation Guide* raises the question of whether a reporting entity that has a discretely presented component unit that is not fiduciary in nature but that has fiduciary funds should bring forward totals for the component unit that includes its fiduciary funds. When the discretely presented component unit's own government-wide financial statements do not include its fiduciary funds, the totals for the component unit brought to the reporting entity's governmentwide financial statements do not include the component unit's fiduciary funds.

Blending Component Units

A basic strategy of GASB-14 is to present financial information for component units separately from the financial information for the primary government. This strategy is achieved through the use of the discrete-presentation method. However, in some circumstances the GASB believes that although a component unit is legally separate from the primary government it may simply be an extension of the primary government. Under this condition, it is more appropriate to use the blending method to incorporate the financial information of a component unit into the reporting entity's financial statements (GASB-14, par. 52).

When the blending method is used, transactions of a component unit are presented as if they were executed directly by the primary government, normally through presentation as a fund within the primary government's fund financial statements. In a similar manner, balances in a component unit's financial statements are merged with similar balances of the primary government in the preparation of the government-wide financial statements so that there is no way to identify which balances relate to a component unit and which relate to the primary government (GASB-14, par. 52).

The only two circumstances that require the blending of a component unit's financial statements with those of the primary government relate to

- Similar governing bodies and
- Scope of services

Similar governing bodies If the component unit's governing body is substantively the same as the primary government's, then a component unit's financial statements should be blended with the primary government. The blending of financial statements should also occur when the governing body of the primary government has sufficient membership on the component unit's government body that the primary government controls the component unit's activities, because the two bodies are considered substantively the same. The term "substantively the same" is not defined in GASB-14, but in footnote 7 in GASB-14 the following examples are offered (GASB-14, par. 53):

- When a component unit's governing body is composed of *all* city council members, along with the mayor serving ex officio, the two governing bodies are considered substantively the same.

- When a component unit's governing body is composed of the mayor and only two of the ten members of the city council, the two governing bodies are *not* considered substantively the same.

Because of the relatively large number of members of the governing body of a state government, it is unlikely that a state government would meet the "substantively the same criterion" (GASB-14, par. 53).

> **OBSERVATION:** The concept of being "substantively the same" includes two elements. First, a majority of the members of the governing body of the primary government must serve on the governing body of the component unit. In addition, the number of primary government members on the component unit's board must be a voting majority. Thus, a situation could arise where all of the members of a city council serve on the board of a component unit but their numbers are less than half (or whatever it takes to represent a voting majority) and therefore the primary government does not control the component unit's activities.

Scope of services The second circumstance that requires the blending of a component unit's financial statements depends on the scope of the services provided by the unit. If the component unit provides, either directly or indirectly, services or benefits exclusively or almost exclusively to the primary government, then blending should be used. The idea of exclusive services to or benefits for the primary government is similar to the purpose of an Internal Service Fund. Thus, the component unit is created to provide services or benefits not to external parties but to the primary government (GASB-14, par. 53).

The component unit may provide similar services or benefits to governmental entities other than the primary government. If the services or benefits provided to the other entities are insignificant, the component unit's financial statements should be blended with those of the primary government (GASB-14, par. 53).

The services or benefits provided to the primary government by the component entity may be direct or indirect. In a direct relationship, the services or benefits are provided to the primary government. For example, a component unit may be created to finance the construction of buildings for various departments or agencies of the primary government. In an indirect relationship, the services or benefits are provided to employees of the primary government. For example, a component unit may be created to administer employee benefit programs (filing claims under health insurance contracts, approving health care providers, etc.) for the primary government (GASB-14, par. 53).

Investments in For-Profit Corporations

A primary government may own voting stock in a variety of for-profit entities. The intent of the primary government determines how the ownership interest will be presented in the financial reporting entity. If ownership interest was purchased for investment purposes, the interest should be accounted for as an investment. On the other hand, if the purpose of the ownership interest is to enhance or facilitate the primary government's ability to deliver services to its citizens, the interest should be accounted for as a component unit (GASB-14, par. 55).

For example, if a primary government purchases common stock of a corporation to obtain a return on excess resources, the interest in the corporation should be accounted for as an investment. Alternatively, if a primary government purchases all of the common stock of a landscaping company to maintain and care for its buildings and open spaces, the interest should be accounted for as a component unit (GASB-14, par. 55).

REPORTING PERIODS

The fiscal year of the financial reporting entity should be the same as the fiscal year of the primary government. Ideally, the primary government and its component units should have the same fiscal years, and the GASB encourages the adoption of the same fiscal year by all of the units that compose the financial reporting entity (GASB-14, par. 59).

If it is impractical for a component unit to have the same fiscal year as the primary government, a component unit's financial statements that have an ending date that occurs during the primary government's fiscal year should be incorporated into the financial statements of the reporting entity. For example, if the primary government's fiscal year ends on June 30 and a component unit's fiscal year ends on December 31, for the fiscal year ended June 30, 20X5, the financial reporting entity should include the component unit's financial statements ended December 31, 20X4 (GASB-14, par. 59).

GASB-14 does allow one exception to the inclusion of a component unit that has a fiscal year different from, or that does not end within, that of the primary government. If a component unit's fiscal year ends within the first quarter after the end of the primary government's fiscal year, then the component unit's financial statements subsequent to the primary government's fiscal year financial statements may be included in the statements of the financial reporting entity. For example, if the primary government's fiscal year ends on June 30, and a component unit's fiscal year ends on August 31, for the fiscal year ended June 30, 20X5, the financial reporting entity could include the component unit's financial statements ended August 31, 20X5 (GASB-14, par. 59).

When the financial statements of a component unit have a fiscal year different from that of the primary government, it is likely that intra-entity transactions and related balances will differ. When the amounts differ, the nature and amount of the intra-entity transactions and related balances should be disclosed in a note to the financial statements (GASB-14, par. 60).

Once a component unit adopts a fiscal year, that date should be used consistently from year to year. If the fiscal year-end changes, the change should be disclosed in a note to the financial statements (GASB-14, par. 50).

NOTE DISCLOSURES

The following should be disclosed in a note to the reporting entity's financial statements (GASB-14, par. 61):

- Brief description of the component units
- Relationship of the primary government with each component unit
- Discussion of criteria used for including the component units
- Identification of method(s) used (discrete presentation or blending) to incorporate the component unit in the financial reporting entity's financial statements
- Identification of how financial statements of each component unit may be obtained

Focus of the Reporting Entity's Note Disclosures and Required Supplementary Information

GASB-14 adopts the basic philosophy that the financial information pertaining to the primary government, including blended component units, and similar information pertaining to discretely presented component units should be distinguishable. This philosophy is extended to disclosures in notes and the presentation of required supplementary information in the financial statements of the financial reporting entity (GASB-14, par. 62).

Determining what should be disclosed in notes to the financial statements is a matter of professional judgment. The professional accountant must consider what disclosures are essential to the fair presentation of the basic financial statements. Because the financial reporting entity includes the primary government and perhaps one or more discretely presented component units, an additional dimension of professional judgment arises with regard to whether the notes related to the primary government, some of the component units, all of the component units, or none of the component units should be presented in the reporting entity's financial statements (GASB-14, par. 62).

Notes Related to the Primary Government

Chapter 20, "Comprehensive Annual Financial Report," identifies numerous types of disclosures that may be made in notes to the financial statements. The list of disclosures in that chapter is not meant to be all-inclusive. GASB-14, as amended by GASB-34, points out that determining the need for a note disclosure should be based on the primary government's (1) governmental and business activities as presented in the government-wide financial statements and (2) individually presented major funds and aggregated nonmajor funds as presented in the fund financial statements (GASB-14, par. 63).

Notes Related to Discretely Presented Component Units

GASB-14 states that only some of the disclosures related to discretely presented component units need be presented in the reporting entity's financial statements. The specific disclosures to be made should be based on (1) a component entity's significance in relationship to all discretely presented component units and (2) the nature and significance of a component's relationship with the primary government. Thus, each discretely presented component unit must be evaluated separately to determine its relative importance (GASB-14, par. 63).

Identification of a component unit as significant does not mean that all of the notes relative to that component unit must be presented in the financial statements of the reporting entity. Only the notes that relate to the basis used to justify a significant relationship should be presented. Thus, two component units could be classified as significant, but the specific disclosures made for each component unit could be different because the basis for determining significance is different (GASB-14, par. 63).

The following are two examples of how the significance of a component unit may be identified:

- *Considered significant relative to all discretely presented component units* The debt of one component unit represents 80% of the debt of all component units and thus a summary of debt service requirements to maturity for the component unit should be disclosed.
- *Considered significant based on the relationship to the primary government* The primary government is obligated for the debt of a component unit and thus a summary of debt service requirements to maturity for the component unit should be disclosed.

PRIMARY GOVERNMENT SEPARATE FINANCIAL STATEMENTS

A primary government may be requested or required to issue its separate financial statements that do not include financial information of component units. GASB-14 does not prohibit the issuance of separate financial statements by the primary government. However, such statements should acknowledge that the financial statements do not include financial information of component units necessary for reporting in conformity with GAAP (GASB-14, par. 64).

> **OBSERVATION:** The GASB does not specify a generally accepted practice for reporting the primary government only. The AICPA's *State and Local Governments* Guide states that the notes to the financial statements and auditor's report should clearly disclose that the presentation is that of only the primary government and does not include any component units.

COMPONENT UNIT FINANCIAL STATEMENTS

GASB-14 is written from the perspective of a primary government in that it considers the focal point for the preparation of the financial statements of a financial reporting entity to be a primary government. However, component units may be requested or required to distribute separate financial statements, and the guidance in GASB-14 should also be used to prepare those statements. In effect, the focal point for the preparation of a component unit's financial statements is the component unit. For example, to determine whether a component unit itself has component units, standards established in paragraphs 21 through 41 should be applied to the entity (GASB-14, par. 65).

As discussed in the section titled "Reporting Component Units," governmental financial statements should be built in layers from the lowest-level component unit to the highest-level component unit. The bottom-up concept is important in determining which component units at which levels should be included in separately issued financial statements. From a practical perspective, if one visualizes looking down from each level or layer, then every component unit under a particular level should be included in the separately issued financial statements of the component unit at that level. Thus, a primary government should include all levels of component units in its separately issued financial statements, while the lowest-level component unit should present only its own financial statements because there are no component units below it (GASB-14, par. 65).

When a component unit issues separate financial statements, there should be an acknowledgment that the governmental entity (the issuing component unit) is a component unit of another government. The other governmental entity could be a primary government or another component unit that is the focal point of separately issued financial statements. In addition, the following disclosures should be made in a note to the component unit's separately issued financial statements (GASB-14, par. 65):

- Identify the other (higher-level) governmental entity.
- Describe the relationship with the (higher-level) governmental entity.

> **OBSERVATION:** The GASB does not specify a generally accepted practice for reporting the primary government only. The AICPA's *State and Local Governments* Guide states that the notes to the financial statements and auditor's report should clearly disclose that the presentation is that of only the primary government and does not include any component units.

REPORTING RELATIONSHIPS WITH ORGANIZATIONS OTHER THAN COMPONENT UNITS

A primary government may appoint all or some of the members of the governing board of an entity that is not a component unit because it does not satisfy the criteria established in paragraphs 21 through 41 of GASB-14. These organizations are broadly classified by GASB-14 as (1) related organizations, (2) joint ventures and jointly governed organizations, and (3) component units of another government with the characteristics of a joint venture or jointly governed organization (GASB-14, par. 67).

Related Organizations

A "related organization" is defined as follows:

> An organization for which a primary government is not financially accountable (because it does not impose will or have a financial benefit or burden relationship) even though the primary government appoints a voting majority of the organization's governing board.

Thus, related organizations are not component units, yet there is some form of accountability, other than financial accountability, that exists between the primary government and the related organization because of the appointment authority. For this reason, the primary government should disclose in a note to the financial statements the nature of its relationship to the related organizations (GASB-14, Glossary).

Some primary governments, especially states, have a common relationship with a number of related organizations. Rather than identify each related organization, related organizations with a common relationship can be grouped together for disclosure purposes. For example, if a state government appoints all of the members of 20 local governing boards for highway beautification and there is no other relationship with the boards, a single disclosure could be made without specifically naming the 20 boards (GASB-14, par. 67).

Due to the nature of the relationship between the primary government and related organizations, the primary government should consider whether related party transactions should be disclosed in the financial statements of the reporting entity (GASB-14, par. 68).

Financial statements issued by a related organization should disclose the related primary government and describe the relationship between the two (GASB-14, par. 68).

Joint Ventures

Governments may enter into a joint venture agreement or arrangement to provide a service directly to the individual governments involved or the citizens served by the governments. For example, two municipalities may enter into a joint venture to operate a landfill. The creation of a joint venture rather than a sole venture may be based on a number of reasons, ranging from economies of scales to effective risk management (GASB-14, par. 69).

GASB-14 provides the following definition of a "joint venture" (GASB-14, Glossary):

> A legal entity or other organization that results from a contractual arrangement and that is owned, operated, or governed by two or more participants as a separate and specific activity subject to joint control in which the participants retain (a) an ongoing financial interest or (b) an ongoing financial responsibility.

Joint control One condition for a joint venture is that not one entity can unilaterally control the operational and financial policies of the commonly controlled entity. Thus, if two participating governments have created an entity, and each of those governments has an equal influence on the entity, the prerequisite condition for a joint venture exists.

If the joint control criterion is satisfied but there is no ongoing financial interest or ongoing financial responsibility, the entity is a jointly governed organization and not a joint venture (see section titled "Jointly Governed Organizations") (GASB-14, par. 69).

Ongoing financial interest GASB-14 defines the term "ongoing financial interest" as follows (GASB-14, Glossary):

> An equity interest or any other arrangement that allows a participating government to have access to a joint venture's resources.

In addition, the term "equity interest" is defined as follows:

> A financial interest in a joint venture evidenced by the ownership of shares of the joint venture's stock or by otherwise having an explicit, measurable right to the net resources of the joint venture that is usually based on an investment of financial or capital resources by a participating government.

The concept of ongoing financial interest is not limited to an existing equity interest (holding voting stock of the entity). There may be an arrangement represented by a separate contract, letter of agreement, or other document that specifically describes a participating government's right of access to the joint venture's resources (GASB-14, Glossary).

Access to the joint venture's resources may be direct or indirect. Direct access to resources would include the participating government's right to a share of profits or surpluses earned by the joint venture or to participate in gains realized through the disposition of operating assets. Indirect access to resources enables participating governments to persuade the joint venture to use its surplus resources so that citizens are benefited directly rather than through their participating governments. For example, a regional recreation joint venture may be persuaded to build tennis courts at participating governments' playgrounds (GASB-14, par. 70).

Ongoing financial responsibility GASB-14 defines the term "ongoing financial responsibility" as follows (GASB-14, Glossary):

> (1) When a participating government is obligated in some manner for the debts of a joint venture or (2) when the joint venture's existence depends on continued funding by the participating government.

For an analysis of what constitutes "obligated in some manner," see the discussion in the section titled "Financial Benefit to or Burden on a Primary Government." The other component of ongoing financial responsibility deals with a participating government's financial responsibility for the continued existence of the joint venture.

In most instances, the continued existence of the joint venture is dependent on the participating governments because the participating governments, or their citizens, have agreed to buy the goods or services created by the joint venture. However, GASB-14 relates responsibility for continued existence to a single participating government. If the number of participating governments is small (two or three), the withdrawal of any one of the three participating governments could mean the end for the joint venture. As the number of participating governments increases, it becomes more likely that no one participating government's action would mean the end of the joint venture. Of course, there is no specific guidance as to which number of participants would invalidate the continued existence concept. For this reason, professional judgment must be exercised (GASB-14, par. 71).

Equity interest Financial reporting standards for joint ventures depend on whether the joint venture is represented by an equity interest. If a joint venture is represented by an equity interest, a participating government should show the interest as an asset. If an equity interest is not apparent, only certain disclosures concerning the joint venture should be made in the participating government's financial statements (GASB-14, par. 72).

A joint venture with an equity interest is demonstrated by a participating government's interest in the resources of the joint venture that is explicit and measurable. The equity interest is usually based on the contribution of resources, either financial assets or capital assets, by the participating government (GASB-14, par. 72).

The most obvious demonstration of an explicit and measurable interest in a joint venture would be the ownership of voting stock by a participating government. For example, a participating government that has a 25% interest in a joint venture generally has a proportional interest in the net resources of the joint venture. However, the demonstration of an equity interest in a joint venture can also be based on an arrangement other than that represented by voting stock ownership. For example, the participating governments can enter into a contract whereby the joint venture is created. The contract must be written in such a manner that the participant's interest in the joint venture's net resources is explicit and measurable. A residual interest in the net resources of a joint venture upon dissolution, because there is no other equitable claimant, is not equivalent to an equity interest (GASB-14, par. 72).

Reporting participation in joint ventures in which there is an equity interest If the reporting entity's participation in a joint venture is represented by an equity interest in the net resources of the joint venture, an asset should be reported in the financial statements of the participating government. The manner of presenting the asset, which represents the net equity in the joint venture's net assets, depends on whether the participating government accounts for the investment in a proprietary fund or a governmental fund (GASB-14, par. 73).

Proprietary funds The initial investment of financial and/or capital resources in the joint venture should be recorded at cost. Whether the initial investment should be increased or decreased depends on the joint venture agreement. If the joint venture agreement states that a participating government is to share in the profits and losses of the joint venture, the investment account should be adjusted to reflect the joint venture's results of operations (GASB-14, par. 73).

The recognition of a proportional share of the joint venture's results of operations is not dependent on whether there is an actual remittance between the joint venture and a participating government. In determining the joint venture's results of operations for a period, profits or losses on transactions with the proprietary fund should be eliminated. Nonoperating transactions, such as additional equity contributions, loans, and dividends, should be reflected as an addition or decrease to the carrying amount of the net investment in the joint venture (GASB-14, par. 73).

The interest in the net assets of the joint venture should be reported as a single asset (account) in the proprietary fund. There should be no attempt to present on a participating government's balance sheet a proportional interest in the various assets and liabilities of the joint venture. In addition, the proportional shares of the joint venture's results of operations should be presented as a single operating account on the proprietary fund's operating statement. There should be no attempt to present a proportional interest in the various operating accounts of the joint venture (GASB-14, par. 73).

To illustrate the accounting for a joint venture in which there is an equity interest, assume that the City of Centerville enters into a joint venture agreement with two other municipalities. In the terms of the agreement, each municipality has a one-third interest in the net assets and profits/losses of the joint venture. If Centerville contributes $100,000 in cash and $200,000 in equipment, the following entry would be made (all entries are made in an Enterprise Fund):

Investment In Joint Venture	300,000	
Cash		100,000
Equipment		200,000

If after the first year of operations, the joint venture incurs an operating loss of $90,000, the following entry would be made:

Equity Interest In Joint Venture Operating Losses	30,000	
Investment In Joint Venture ($90,000 × 1/3)		30,000

Governmental funds The initial investment of financial and/or capital resources in the joint venture should be recorded at cost, but only to the extent the investment is evidenced by current financial resources. When the investment in the joint venture is recorded in a governmental fund, only the portion of the investment considered available and expendable should be recorded on the balance sheet. Usually this portion of the investment is limited to amounts due to and from the joint venture. The remaining investment or payments made to the joint venture should be reported as expenditures of the governmental fund.

Government-wide financial statements Joint ventures that are presented in proprietary funds and governmental funds should also be presented in the government-wide financial statements and should be accounted for at this level using the method described earlier for proprietary funds.

Disclosure requirements for joint venture participants For all joint ventures, a participating government should disclose in a note to its financial statements a general description of the joint venture, including the following (GASB-14, par. 75):

- Description of ongoing financial interest, including equity interest, if applicable, or ongoing financial responsibility
- Information that enables a reader to determine whether the joint venture is accumulating assets that may result in a financial benefit to the participating government or experiencing fiscal stress that may result in a financial burden on the participating government

In addition, a participating government should disclose information about the availability of the joint venture's separate financial statements (GASB-14, par. 75).

Finally, a participating government should disclose information concerning related party transactions between the participating governments and the joint venture (GASB-14, par. 75).

Joint building or finance authorities Participating governments may enter into a relationship whereby there is a formal joint venture but the substance of the relationship is an undivided-interest arrangement. An undivided-interest arrangement is "an ownership arrangement in which two or more parties own property in which title is held individually to the extent of each party's interest." Thus, for accounting purposes, even though a joint venture exists, the undivided interest in property acquired through the joint venture is recorded directly by each participating government (GASB-14, par. 76).

A joint building authority and a finance authority are examples of this type of arrangement. A joint building authority may be created to construct or acquire capital assets and in turn to lease the assets to a participating government. Under this arrangement, a participating government would have capitalized the lease based on standards discussed in Chapter 14, "Leases." For this reason, a participating government would reflect the effects of the lease on its financial statements.

Jointly Governed Organizations

A state may allow local governments to form regional governments or similar entities to provide goods or services to the citizens served by the local governments. Such arrangements should be evaluated to determine whether they meet the definition of a joint venture. If an arrangement of this type does not create an ongoing financial interest or responsibility for a participating government, the only disclosures that need to be made in a participating government's financial statements are those concerning related party transactions (GASB-14, par. 77).

Component Units and Related Organizations with Joint Venture Characteristics

The third type of reporting relationship with organizations other than component units concerns component units and related organizations with joint venture characteristics. Agovernment may participate with other governments to create an organization that is either a component unit or a related organization of another government. For example, governments #1, #2, and #3 create an organization, and assume that the organization is either a component unit or a related organization of government #1. Thus, the majority participating government (government #1) reports the organization in a manner consistent with the standards applicable to component units or related organizations. The minority participating governments (governments #2 and #3) should report their relationships with the organization based on the standards discussed in the previous sections titled "Joint Ventures" and "Jointly Governed Organizations" (GASB-14, par. 78).

The organization reported as a component unit in the statements of the reporting entity that includes the financial statements of the majority participating government should present any equity interest of the minority participating governments as part of its equity section. The minority interest may be described in a manner such as "fund balance reserved for minority interests" or "net assets restricted for minority interests" (GASB-14, par. 78).

When participating governments jointly control an organization and one of the organizations is fiscally dependent on one of the participating governments, the majority participating government should report the organization either as a component unit or as a related organization. The minority participating governments should report the jointly controlled organization in accordance with the standards discussed in the previous sections titled "Joint Ventures" and "Jointly Governed Organizations" (GASB-14, par. 78).

Pools

Although a pool is another example of an arrangement in which a number of governments jointly participate in a venture, GASB-14 states that a pool is different from a joint venture. Pools are characterized by the following (GASB-14, par. 79):

- Membership is open (participants are free to join, resign, or alter their level of participation at will).
- Equity interest is recognized in participant's financial statements.
- Limited disclosures are required.

An investment pool would likely give participants a higher degree of flexibility in determining to what extent each participant wants to participate in the venture. In addition, a pool arrangement results in an investment being presented directly in the financial statements of a participating government, and therefore there is no need to compute and present a separate equity interest in the pool. Furthermore, because of the flexibility that characterizes each pool, it is not necessary to make the type of disclosures required for joint venture participants (as discussed in paragraph 75) (GASB-14, par. 79).

Governmental entities that participate in an external investment pool should observe the standards established by GASB-31 (Accounting and Financial Reporting for Certain Investments and for External Investment Pools).

GASBI-4 (Accounting and Financial Reporting for Capitalization Contributions to Public Entity Risk Pools) states that governmental entities that make capital contributions to or participate in the activities of a public entity risk pool should *not* account for the investment and subsequent results of operations of the pool as a joint venture. This prohibition applies to contributions to public entity pools where risk is transferred as well as where risk is not transferred. In addition, if under a retrospectively rated policy the governmental entity's ultimate premium payments are based on the experience of the public entity risk pool, GASBI-4 states that this relationship does not create a joint venture relationship for financial reporting purposes (GASBI-4, par. 3).

Undivided Interests

Participating governments may join with one another in a type of joint venture in which no new joint entity is created. Such an arrangement results in an undivided interest (joint operation). An undivided interest arises when two or more parties own property that is held individually on the basis of each party's interest in the property. In addition, liabilities related to the operation of the undivided interest are obligations of each participating government (GASB-14, par. 80).

In an undivided interest, no separate entity is created and, therefore, accounts and transactions related to the operations of the undivided interest must be recorded in the records of the participating governments. For this reason, there is no requirement to make disclosures similar to those described in the section titled "Disclosure Requirements for Joint Venture Participants" (GASB-14, par. 80).

Governments may participate in arrangements that have characteristics of both a joint venture (separate entity) and an undivided interest. Under this arrangement, the undivided interest should be accounted for as described in the previous paragraph and the equity interest related to the joint venture should be accounted for as described in the section titled "Reporting Participation in Joint Ventures in Which There Is an Equity Interest" (GASB-14, par. 80).

Cost-Sharing Arrangements

GASB-14 states that cost-sharing projects, such as the financing of highway construction by the federal, state, and local governments, are not joint ventures, because there is no ongoing financial interest or responsibility by the participating governmental entities (GASB-14, par. 81).

In addition, joint purchasing agreements that commit participating governments to purchase a stated quantity of goods or services for a specified period of time are not joint ventures (GASB-14, par. 81).

OTHER STAND-ALONE GOVERNMENT FINANCIAL STATEMENTS

Other stand-alone governmental entities are legally separate governmental entities (see the section titled "Determining Separate Legal Standing") that have the following characteristics (GASB-14, par. 66):

- They do not have a separately elected governing body and
- They are not component units of another governmental entity (see section titled "Financial Accountability").

As previously discussed, examples of other stand-alone governmental entities include the following (GASB-14, par. 66):

- Certain special-purpose governments
- Joint ventures
- Jointly governed organizations
- Pools

When a stand-alone governmental entity issues financial statements, the standards established by GASB-14 should be observed. Thus, the other stand-alone governmental entity becomes the focal point for preparing the financial statements of the financial reporting entity. For example, the other stand-alone governmental entity should follow standards established in the sections titled "Financial Accountability" and "Nature and Significance of Relationship" to determine whether it has component units for which financial statements should be incorporated into the standards of the financial reporting entity (GASB-14, par. 66).

Other stand-alone governmental entities for which the governing board's voting majority is appointed by a primary government should disclose the accountability relationship in their separately issued financial statements (see the section titled "Related Organizations") (GASB-14, par. 66).

> **OBSERVATION:** The description of the relationship between the stand-alone governmental entity and the primary government should emphasize the general concept of accountability rather than the specific criteria for financial accountability. There can be no financial accountability, as defined by GASB-14, for a stand-alone governmental entity or, by definition, it would be a component unit.

CHAPTER 5
TERMINOLOGY AND CLASSIFICATION

CONTENTS

INTRODUCTION

A governmental reporting entity should use consistent terminology and classifications in its accounting system. From an internal perspective, the use of a common language and classification scheme enhances management's ability to evaluate and control operations. For financial reporting purposes, the consistent use of terms and classifications in the budgeting, accounting, and reporting systems facilitates the preparation of financial statements and makes those financial statements more understandable to user groups (NCGA-1, pars. 124 and 126).

This chapter discusses terminology and classification standards for governmental financial statements as set out in NCGA-1 (Governmental Accounting and Financial Reporting Principles), as amended by GASB-34 (Basic Financial Statements—and Management's Discussion and Analysis—for State and Local Governments).

Reporting Interfund Activity in Fund Financial Statements

In order to determine how interfund transfers within and among governmental funds, proprietary funds, and fiduciary funds should be presented in the fund financial statements, transfers must be categorized as follows (GASB-34, par. 112):

- Reciprocal interfund activity
  - —Interfund loans
  - —Interfund services provided and used

- Nonreciprocal interfund activity
  —Interfund transfers
  —Interfund reimbursements

"Reciprocal interfund activities" are interfund activities that have many of the same characteristics of exchange and exchange-like transactions that occur with external parties. "Nonreciprocal interfund activities" are interfund activities that have many of the same characteristics of nonexchange transactions that occur with external parties.

Interfund loans (reciprocal interfund activity) The concept of a loan as envisioned by GASB-34 is based on the expectation that the loan will be repaid at some point. Loans should be reported as interfund receivables by the lender fund and interfund payables by the borrower fund. That is, the interfund loan should not be eliminated in the preparation of financial statements at the fund level. Thus, the proceeds from interfund loans should not be reported as "other financing sources or uses" in the operating statements in the fund financial statements. If a loan or a portion of a loan is not expected to be repaid *within a reasonable time,* the interfund receivable/payable should be reduced by the amount not expected to be repaid and that amount should be reported as an interfund transfer by both funds that are a party to the transfer.

> **PRACTICE POINT:** Question 7.346 of the *GASB Comprehensive Implementation Guide* attempts to answer the question of what is meant by "paid within a reasonable time." The Q&A Guide's answer is as follows: "There is no precise definition of the provision. Professional judgment should be exercised in determining whether an interfund loan should be reclassified. The *expectation* aspect of the phrase means that the government intends to, and has the ability to, repay the amount loaned. For example, recurring payments made to reduce the interfund loan balance may provide evidence that 'repayment is expected.' What constitutes a *reasonable time* for repayment is again a matter of professional judgment, but the notion is not without precedent in financial reporting standards. GASB-10 invokes a 'reasonable time' consideration in paragraphs 66b and 68, as amended, with regard to recovery of the full cost of internal service fund expenses."

Interfund services provided and used (reciprocal interfund activity) Interfund receivables/payables may arise from an operating activity (that is, the sale of goods and services) between funds rather than in the form of a loan arrangement. If the interfund operating activity is recorded at an amount that approximates the fair value of the goods or services exchanged, the provider/seller fund should record the activity as revenue and the user/purchaser fund should record an expenditure/expense, not an interfund transfer. Any unpaid balance at the end of the period should be reported as an interfund receivable/payable in the fund balance sheet or statement of net assets.

> **PRACTICE POINT:** GASB-34 points that GASB-10 (Accounting and Financial Reporting for Risk Financing and Related Insurance Issues), paragraph 64, requires that when the General Fund is used to account for risk-financing activities, interfund charges to other funds must be accounted for as interfund reimbursements.

Interfund transfers (nonreciprocal interfund activity) This type of nonreciprocal transaction represents interfund activities whereby the two parties to the events do not receive equivalent cash, goods, or services. Governmental funds should report transfers of this nature in their activity statements as other financing uses and other financial sources of funds. Proprietary funds should report this type of transfer in their activity statements following net income (loss) before transfers.

> **PRACTICE POINT:** Based on the standards established by GASB-34, there is no differentiation between operating transfers and residual equity transfers. Thus, equity-type transfers can no longer be reported as adjustments to a fund's beginning equity balance.

> **OBSERVATION:** GASB-34 points out that most payments *in lieu of taxes* should be reported as interfund transfers, unless the payments and services received are equivalent in value based on the exchange of specific services or goods. If the two are equivalent in value, the disbursing fund may treat the payment as an expenditure (expense) and the receiving fund may record revenue.

Interfund reimbursements (nonreciprocal interfund activity) A fund may incur an expenditure or an expense that will subsequently be reimbursed by another fund. Reimbursements should not be reported in the governmental entity's financial statements in order to avoid "double counting" revenues and expense/expenditure items. To illustrate, assume that the General Fund pays a utility bill of $50,000 for an Enterprise Fund. The initial payment is recorded as follows in the General Fund:

Expenditures—Utilities	50,000	
Cash		50,000

When the Enterprise Fund reimburses the General Fund at a later date, the General Fund reverses its original entry:

Cash	50,000	
Expenditures—Utilities		50,000

Eliminations and Reclassifications in Government-Wide Financial Statements

The preparation of government-wide financial statements is based on a consolidating process (similar to corporate consolidations) rather than a combining process. These eliminations and reclassifications related to the consolidation process are based on (1) internal balances (statement of net assets), (2) internal activities (statement of activities), (3) intra-entity activity, and (4) Internal Service Fund balances (GASB-34, par. 57).

Internal balances (statement of net assets) The government-wide financial statements present the governmental entity and its blended component units as a single reporting entity. Based on this philosophy, most balances between funds that are initially recorded as interfund receivables and payables at the individual fund level should be eliminated in the preparation of the statement of net assets within each of the two major reporting groups of the primary government (the government activities and business-type activities). The purpose of the elimination is to avoid the "grossing-up" effect on assets and liabilities presented on the statement of net assets within the governmental and business-type activities columns.

For example, if there is an interfund receivable/payable between the General Fund and a Special Revenue Fund, those amounts would be eliminated in order to determine the balances that would appear in the governmental activities column. Likewise, if there is an interfund receivable/payable between two proprietary funds of the primary government, those amounts would also be eliminated in the business-type activities column. However, the net residual interfund receivable/payable between governmental and business-type activities should not be eliminated but should be presented in each column (government activities and business-type activities) and labeled as "internal balances" or a similar description. These amounts will be the same and, therefore, will cancel out when they are combined (horizontally) in the statement of net assets in order to form the column for total primary government activities (GASB-34, par. 58).

> **OBSERVATION:** Generally, a governmental entity will maintain its accounting transactions using the conventional-fund approach and convert this information to a government-wide basis using the flow of economic resources and accrual basis of accounting at the time the government-wide financial statements are prepared. Thus, at the fund level the internal balance between a government fund (reported on the modified accrual basis) may not equal the related balance with a proprietary fund (reported on the accrual basis); however, once the

government fund activity is adjusted to the government-wide presentation, those adjusted amounts will equal the amounts presented in the proprietary funds.

There also may be interfund receivables/payables that arise because of transactions between the primary government and its fiduciary funds. These amounts should not be eliminated, but rather should be reported on the statement of net assets similar to receivables from and payables to external parties. (GASB-34, par. 58).

> **NOTE:** The financial statements of fiduciary funds are not consolidated as part of the government-wide financial statements.

Interfund balances between fiduciary funds and other funds (governmental and proprietary funds) are reported in fund financial statements but, as noted above, are not part of the internal balance amount reported on the statement of net assets (governmentwide financial statement). The *GASB Comprehensive Implementation Guide* points out that there is no need to explain in a note to the financial statement that internal balances with fiduciary funds are not reported as part of the internal balance; however, a governmental entity may (but is not required to) add some clarity to this difference by using one or both of the following approaches:

- Include an explanation in the note required by GASB-38, paragraph 14, with respect to the identification of the amounts due from other funds by (1) individual major funds, (2) aggregated nonmajor governmental funds, (3) aggregated nonmajor Enterprise Funds, (4) aggregated Internal Service Funds, and (5) fiduciary fund types.
- Separately present in the fund financial statements the amounts due to/from fiduciary funds from amounts due to/from other funds.

Internal activities (statement of activities) In order to avoid the "doubling-up" effect of internal activities among funds, interfund transactions should be eliminated so that expenses and revenues are recorded only once. For example, a fund (generally the General Fund or an Internal Service Fund) may charge other funds for services provided (such as insurance coverage or allocation of overhead expenses) on an internal basis. When these funds are consolidated in order to present the functional expenses of governmental activities in the statement of activities, the double counting of the expense (with an offset to revenue recorded by the provider fund) should be eliminated in a manner so that "the allocated expenses are reported only by the function to which they were allocated" (GASB-34, par. 59).

Internal activities should not be eliminated when they are classified as "interfund services provided and used." For example, when a municipal water company charges a fee for services provided to the general government, the expense and revenues related to those activities should not be eliminated. (GASB-34, par. 60). (This type of internal activity is further discussed in Chapter 20, "Comprehensive Annual Financial Report.")

Intra-entity activity Transactions (and related balances) between the primary government and its blended component units should be reclassified based on the guidance discussed in Chapter 20, "Comprehensive Annual Financial Report." Transactions (and related balances) between the primary government and its discretely presented component units should not be eliminated in the government-wide financial statements. That is, the two parties to the transactions should report revenue and expense accounts as originally recorded in those respective funds. Amounts payable and receivable between the primary government and its discretely presented component units should be reported as separate line items on the statement of net assets. Likewise payables and receivables between discretely presented component units must also be reported separately (GASB-43, par. 61).

> **PRACTICE POINT:** GASB-48, issued in September 2006, provides financial statement users with consistent measurement, recognition, and disclosure across governments and within individual governments relating to the accounting for sales and pledges of receivables and future revenues and intra-entity transfers of assets and future revenues. GASB-48 is effective for periods beginning after December 15, 2006; however, early application is encouraged. See further discussion of accounting and reporting treatment for intra-entity transfers of assets and future revenues in Chapter 17, "Revenues: Exchange and Nonexchange Transactions."

Internal Service Fund balances As described above (in the section titled "Internal Activities (statement of activities)" internal services and similar activities should be eliminated to avoid doubling-up expenses and revenues when preparing the governmental-activities column of the statement of activities. The effect of this approach is to adjust activities in an Internal Service Fund to a break-even balance. That is, if the Internal Service Fund had a "net profit" for the year, there should be a pro rata reduction in the charges made to the funds that used the Internal Service Fund's services for the year. Likewise, a net loss would require a pro rata adjustment that would increase the charges made to the various participating funds. After making these eliminations, any residual balances related to the Internal Service Fund's assets and liabilities should be reported in the governmental activities column in the government-wide statement of net assets (GASB-34, par. 62).

> **OBSERVATION:** In some instances, an internal service may not be accounted for in an Internal Service Fund but rather accounted for in another governmental fund (generally the General Fund or a Special Revenue Fund). Furthermore, the internal-service transaction may not cut across functional expense categories. That is, there is a "billing" between different departments, but the expenses of those departments are all included in the same functional expenses. Conceptually, the same break-even approach as described above should be applied so as not to gross-up expenses and program revenues of a particular functional expense; however, the GASB does not require that an elimination be made (unless the amounts are material) because the result of this nonelimination is that direct expenses and program revenues are overstated by equal amounts but net (expense) revenue related to the function is not overstated.

> **PRACTICE POINT:** The GASB takes the position that activities conducted with an Internal Service Fund are generally reported as government activities rather than business-type activities, even though an Internal Service Fund uses the flow of economic resources and the accrual basis of accounting. However, when Enterprise Funds account for all or the predominant activities of an Internal Service Fund, the Internal Service Fund's residual assets and liabilities should be reported in the business-type activities column of the statement of net assets.

Terminology and Classification in Governmental Fund Financial Statements

General long-term debt issue proceeds In governmental funds the proceeds from the issuance of long-term debt is recorded not as a liability but as an other financing source on the statement of revenues, expenditures, and changes in fund balances, using such captions as "bond issue proceeds" and "proceeds from the issuance of long-term notes." Discounts and premiums and certain payments to escrow agents for bond refundings should also be reported as other financing sources and uses. Proceeds from the issuance of special assessment debt for which a government entity is "not obligated in any manner" should not be referred to as bond proceeds but instead titled as "contributions from property owners" (NCGA-1, par. 108; GASB-6, par. 19; and GASB-34, par. 88).

Resources received based on current and advance refundings related to the defeasance of general long-term debt should be reported as an other financing source and given a label similar to "proceeds of refunding bonds" to describe the transaction. Related payments to the escrow agent should be reported as an other financing use and identified as "payments to refunded bond escrow agent." However, when the payments made to an escrow agent using funds other than those related to the refunding, the repayment should be reported as debt service expenditures (GASB-7, par. 8; GASB-34, pars. 82 and 88).

Other general long-term debt transactions GASB-34 points out that debt issuance costs paid out of the proceeds of debt issuance should be reported as an expenditure in governmental funds rather than netted against the proceeds (and presented as an other financing source). Debt issuance costs paid from resources other than debt proceeds should also be recorded as an expenditure at the same time the related debt proceeds are recorded (GASB-34, par. 87).

Demand bonds Demand bonds may be reported as general longterm debt of a governmental fund or long-term debt of a proprietary fund when all of the following criteria are met (GASBI-1, par. 10):

- Before the financial statements are issued, the issuer has entered into an arm's-length financing (takeout) agreement to convert bonds "put" but not resold into some other form of long-term obligation.
- The takeout agreement does not expire within one year from the date of the issuer's balance sheet.
- The takeout agreement is not cancelable by the lender or the prospective lender during that year, and obligations incurred under the takeout agreement are not callable by the lender during that year.
- The lender or the prospective lender or investor is expected to be financially capable of honoring the takeout agreement.

When the conditions of GASB Interpretation No. 1 (GASBI-1) (Demand Bonds Issued by State and Local Governmental Entities) have not been met, demand bonds must be presented as a liability of the fund that received the proceeds from the issuance of the bonds, or as a current liability if the proceeds were received by a proprietary fund. If demand bonds are issued and no takeout agreement has been executed at their issuance date or at the balance sheet date, the bonds cannot be considered a long-term liability (GASBI-1, pars. 10 and 13).

If the demand bonds are presented for redemption, the redemption should be recorded as an expenditure of the fund from which debt service is normally paid.

Demand bonds that were originally classified as general longterm debt because a take-out agreement existed at the issuance date of the bonds would have to be reclassified if the original takeout agreement expires. Under this circumstance, it would be necessary to establish a liability in the fund that originally recorded the demand bond proceeds. Any actual bond redemption occurring after the debt is reclassified as the liability of a specific governmental fund should be recorded as an expenditure of the fund that accounts for the servicing of the debt (GASBI-1, par. 13).

Capital lease transactions Because general capital assets of a governmental fund do not represent current financial resources available for appropriation and expenditure, a capital lease transaction should not be reported as a capital asset and a liability of a governmental fund. NCGA-5 (Accounting and Financial Reporting Principles for Lease Agreements of State and Local Governments) states that when the capitalized lease represents the purchase or construction of general capital assets, the transaction should be shown as a capital outlay expenditure and other financing sources in a governmental fund (NCGA-5, pars. 13–14).

Capital asset sales When a governmental entity sells a capital asset of a governmental fund, the proceeds from the sale should be reported as an other financing source, unless the transactions meets the definition of a special item as defined by GASB-34 (GASB-34, par. 88)

Revenue and expenditure classification A governmental fund's results of operations are presented in a statement of revenues and expenditures and changes in fund balances. This statement should reflect the all-inclusive concept, and all financial transactions and events that affect the fund's operations for the period should be presented in the activity statement. A governmental fund's activity statement is not referred to as an income statement because the accounting basis for its preparation is the modified accrual basis, not the accrual basis. Similarly, net income is not an element presented in a governmental fund's activity statement for the same reason and also because the statement does not reflect allocations of various economic resources, such as the depreciation of capital assets (NCGA-1, par. 57).

Revenues For governmental funds, NCGA-1 defines "revenues" as an "increase in (sources of) fund financial resources other than from interfund transfers and debt issue proceeds." Revenues should be classified by fund and source. Revenues applicable to a particular fund should be reflected in the fund's activity statement and should not be attributed to another fund. NCGA-1 notes that major revenue sources include taxes, licenses and permits, intergovernmental revenues, charges for services, fines and forfeits, and miscellaneous items (NCGA-1, par. 109).

As a supplement to the accumulation of revenues by fund and source, revenues may be classified in various ways to facilitate management evaluation and preparation of special reports or analyses, or to aid in the audit or review of accounts. For example, revenues may be classified by the operating division or branch responsible for their actual collection (NCGA-1, par. 110).

> **OBSERVATION:** The GASB is in the process of developing a conceptual framework for elements of financial statements. This process will result in a Concepts Statement that may redefine elements such as assets, liabilities, revenues, and expenditures/expenses and new elements such as deferred resource inflows and outflows.

Expenditures Governmental fund expenditures represent decreases in or uses of fund financial resources, except for those transactions that result in transfers to other funds. Initially, expenditures should be classified according to the fund accountable for the disbursement. To facilitate both internal and external analysis and reporting, expenditures may be classified further by (1) function (or program), (2) organizational unit, (3) activity, (4) character, and (5) object class (NCGA-1, pars. 109 and 111).

Function (or program) classification Functions refer to major services provided by the governmental unit or responsibilities established by specific laws or regulations. Classifications included as functions are public safety, highways and streets, general governmental services, education, and health and welfare. Rather than use a functional classification, a governmental unit that employs program budgeting may group its expenditures by program classifications and sub classifications. A program classification scheme groups activities related to the achievement of a specific purpose or objective. Program groupings would include activities such as programs for the elderly, drug addiction, and adult education (NCGA-1, par. 112).

Organizational unit classification An accounting system should incorporate the concept of "responsibility accounting" so that information reflecting a unit's responsibility for activities and expenditures will be present in the system. When an organization is responsible for certain expenditures, but the expenditures are not coded so the disbursements can be associated with the organization, it becomes difficult to hold the organizational unit responsible for the activity. Organizational unit classification generally groups expenditures based on the operational structure (department, agencies, etc.) of the governmental unit. Often, functions or programs are administered by two or more organizational units. For example, the responsibility for the public safety function is shared by the police and fire departments (NCGA-1, par. 113).

Activity classification Function or program classifications are broad in nature and often do not provide a basis for adequately analyzing governmental operations. For this reason, expenditures may be associated with specific activities, thus allowing measurement standards to be established. These standards can be used (1) as a basis for evaluating the economy and efficiency of operations and (2) as a basis for budget preparation. Also, grouping expenditures by activity is an important part of management accounting in which decisions may require the development of accounting data different from the information presented in the external financial reports. For example, in a make-or-buy decision, it may be necessary to consider a depreciation factor in computing a per unit cost figure (for external reporting purposes, depreciation is not generally presented) (NCGA-1, par. 114).

Character classification Categorizing expenditures by character refers to the fiscal year that will benefit from the expenditure. Character classifications include the following (NCGA-1, par. 115):

Character	*Period(s) Benefited*
Current expenditures	Current period
Capital outlays	Current and future periods
Debt service	Current, future, and prior periods
Intergovernmental	Depends on the nature of the programs financed by the revenue

As discussed in the following section, object classes are subdivisions of expenditure character groupings.

Object class classification Object classes represent the specific items purchased or services acquired within the overall character classifications. For example, debt service expenditures can be further classified as payments for principal and interest, while current expenditures by object class may include the purchase of supplies and disbursements for payroll (NCGA-1, par. 116).

NCGA-1 recognizes that external reporting of expenditures by object class should be restrained because the user, on both an internal and an external basis, could be overwhelmed by voluminous information that does not enhance the decision-making process (NCGA-1, par. 116).

Terminology and Classification in Proprietary Fund Financial Statements

Revenues of a proprietary fund should be reported by major sources, and expenses should be classified in a manner similar to a business entity that is involved in the same activities as the proprietary fund. However, the presentation of information in a proprietary fund's financial statements cannot be inconsistent with guidance provided by the GASB, including pronouncements issued by its predecessor (NCGA-1, par. 117; GASB-20, par. 16; GASB-34, par. 100).

> **OBSERVATION:** For a discussion of the reporting standards that apply to businesslike activities see the Enterprise Funds section of Chapter 7, "Proprietary Funds."

Classification of Expenses and Revenues in Government-Wide Statement of Activities

The format for the government-wide statement of activities is significantly different from any operating statement used in fund financial reporting. The focus of the statement of activities is on the *net cost* of various activities provided by the governmental entity. The statement begins with a column that identifies the cost of each governmental activity. Another column identifies the revenues that are specifically related to the classified activities. The difference between the expenses and revenues related to specific activities computes the net cost or benefits of the activities, which "identifies the extent to which each function of the government draws from the general revenues of the government or is self-financing through fees and intergovernmental aid" (GASB-34, pars. 38–40).

> **OBSERVATION:** The GASB established the unique presentation format for the statement of activities in part because it believes that format provides an opportunity to provide feedback on a typical economic question that is asked when a program is adopted; namely, "What will the program cost and how will it be financed?"

The governmental entity must determine the level at which governmental activities are to be presented; however, the level of detail must be at least as detailed as that provided in the governmental fund financial statements (which are discussed later). Generally, activities would be aggregated and presented at the functional category level; however, entities are encouraged to present activities at a more detailed level, such as by programs.

> **OBSERVATION:** Due to the size and complexities of some governmental entities, it may be impractical to expand the level of detail beyond that of functional categories. The minimum level of detail at which governmental activities can be presented is discussed in paragraphs 111–116 of NCGA-1. Business-type activities should be reported at the level of segments, which is defined later in this chapter. The GASB encourages governmental entities to expand the detail level from functions (which is very broad) to more specific levels, such as programs and services. However, the GASB was

concerned about requiring a more detailed expense format presentation than is now required by current standards.

Once the level of detail is determined, the primary government's expenses for each governmental activity should be presented. It should be noted that these are expenses and not expenditures and are based on the concept of the flow of economic resources, which includes depreciation expense. As noted earlier, the minimum level of detail allowed by GASB-34 is functional program categories, such as general government, public safety, parks and recreation, and public works. At a minimum, each functional program should include direct expenses, which are defined as "those that are specifically associated with a service, program, or department and, thus, are clearly identifiable to a particular function" (GASB-34, par. 41).

Revenues and other resource inflows A fundamental concept in the formatting of the statement of activities, as described above, is the identification of resource inflows to the governmental entities that are related to specific programs and those that are general in nature. GASB-34 notes that specific governmental activities are generally financed from the following sources of resource inflows:

- Parties who purchase, use, or directly benefit from goods and services provided through the program (for example, fees for public transportation and licenses)
- Outside parties (other governments and nongovernmental entities or individuals) who provide resources to the governmental entity (for example, a grant to a local government from a state government)
- The reporting government's constituencies (for example, property taxes)
- The governmental entity (for example, investment income)

The first source of the resources listed above is always program revenue. The second source is program revenue if it is restricted to a specific program, otherwise the item is considered general revenue. The third source is always general revenue, even when restricted. The fourth source of resources is usually general revenue.

Using this classification scheme the governmental entity should format its statement of activities based on the following broad categories of resource inflows (GASB-34, par. 47):

- Program revenues
  —Charges for services
  —Operating grants and contributions

—Capital grants and contributions

- General revenues
- Contributions to permanent funds
- Extraordinary items
- Special items
- Transfers

Program revenues These revenues arise because the specific program with which they are identified exists, otherwise the revenues would not flow to the governmental entity. Program revenues are presented on the statement of activities as a subtraction from the related program expense in order to identify the net cost (or benefit) of a particular program. This formatting scheme enables a reader of a governmental entity's statements to identify those programs that are providing resources that may be used for other governmental functions or those that are being financed from general revenues and other resources. Program revenues should be segregated into (1) charges for services, (2) operating grants and contributions, and (3) capital grants and contributions (GASB-34, par. 48).

> **PRACTICE POINT:** Identifying revenues with a particular function does not mean that revenues must be allocated to a function. Revenues are related to a function only when they are directly related to the function. If no direct relationship is obvious, the revenue is a general revenue, not a program revenue.

Charges for services Revenues that are characterized as charges for services are based on exchange or exchange-like transactions and arise from charges for providing goods, services, and privileges to customers or applicants who acquire goods, services, or privileges directly from a governmental entity. Generally, these and similar charges are intended to cover, at least to some extent, the cost of goods and services provided to various parties. GASB-34 lists the following as examples of charges-for-services revenue (GASB-34, par. 49):

- Service charges (such as water usage fees and garbage collection fees)
- Licenses and permit fees (such as dog licenses, liquor licenses, and building permits)
- Operating special assessments (such as street-cleaning assessments or special-street lighting assessments)
- Intergovernmental charges that are based on exchange transactions (such as one county being charged by another that houses its prisoners)

Program-specific grants and contributions (operating and capital) Governmental entities may receive mandatory and voluntary grants or contributions (nonexchange transactions) from other governments or individuals that must be used for a particular governmental activity. For example, a state government may provide grants to localities that are to be used to reimburse costs related to adult literary programs. These and other similar sources of assets should be reported as program-specific grants and contributions in the statement of activities but they must be separated into those that are for operating purposes and those that are for capital purposes. If a grant or contribution can be used either for operating or capital purposes, at the discretion of the governmental entity, it should be reported as an operating contribution (GASB-34, par. 50).

> **NOTE:** Mandatory and voluntary nonexchange transactions are defined in GASB-33 (Accounting and Financial Reporting for Nonexchange Transactions) as amended (see Chapter 17, "Revenues: Nonexchange and Exchange Transactions").

Grants and contributions that are provided to finance more than one program (multipurpose grants) should be reported as program-specific grants "if the amounts restricted to each program are specifically identified in either the grant award or the grant application." (The grant application should be used in this manner only if the grant was based on the application.) If the amount of the multipurpose grants cannot be identified with particular programs, the revenue should be reported as general revenues rather than program-specific grants and contributions.

Earnings related to endowments or permanent fund investments are considered program revenues if those are restricted to a specific program use; however, the restriction must be based on either an explicit clause in the endowment agreement or contract. Likewise earnings on investments that do not represent endowments or permanent fund arrangements are considered program revenues if they are legally restricted to a specific program. Investment earnings on endowments or permanent fund investments that are not restricted, and therefore are available for general operating expenses, are not program revenues but rather should be reported general revenues in the "lower" section of the statement of activities.

Earnings on investments not related to permanent funds that are legally restricted for a particular purpose should be reported as program revenues. Also, earnings on "invested accumulated resources" of a specific program that are legally restricted to the specific program should be reported as program revenues (GASB-34, par. 51).

General revenues General revenue should be reported in the lower portion of the statement of activities. Such revenues include resource flows related to income taxes, sales taxes, franchise taxes, and property taxes, and they should be separately identified in the statement. Nontax sources of resources that are not reported as program revenues must be reported as general revenues. This latter group includes unrestricted grants, unrestricted contributions, and investment income (GASB-34, par. 52).

General revenues are used to offset the net (expense) revenue amounts computed in the upper portion of the presentation, and the resulting amounts are labeled as excess (deficiency) of revenues over expenses before extraordinary items and special items.

> **OBSERVATION:** All taxes, including dedicated taxes (for example, motor fuel taxes) are considered general revenues rather than program revenues. The GASB takes the position, that only charges to program customers or program-specific grants and contributions should be characterized as reducing the net cost of a particular governmental activity.

Contributions to permanent funds When a governmental entity receives contributions to its term and permanent endowments or to permanent fund principal, those contributions should be reported as separate items in the lower portion of the statement of activities. These receipts are not considered to be program revenues (such as program-specific grants) because, as in the case of term endowments, there is an uncertainty of the timing of the release of the resources from the term restriction and, as in the case of permanent contributions, the principal can never be expended (GASB-34, par. 53).

Extraordinary items The next section of the statement of activities includes the category where extraordinary items (gains or losses) are presented. GASB-34 incorporates the definition of "extraordinary items" (unusual in nature and infrequent in occurrence) as provided in APB Opinion No. 30 (APB-30) (Reporting the Results of Operations—Reporting the Effects of Disposal of a Segment of a Business, and Extraordinary, Unusual, and Infrequently Occurring Events and Transactions) (GASB-34, par. 55).

Special items Unlike APB-30, the GASB identifies a new classification, "special items," which are described as "significant transactions or other events within the control of management that are either unusual in nature or infrequent in occurrence." Special items should be reported separately and before extraordinary items. If a significant transaction or other event occurs but is not within the control of management and that item is either unusual or infrequent, the item is not reported as a special item but the nature of the item must be described in a note to the financial statements (GASB-34, par. 56).

Transfers Transfers should be reported in the lower portion of the statement of activities. (GASB-34, par. 53). (The standards that determine how transfers should be reported in the statement of activities were discussed earlier in this chapter.)

Reporting Extraordinary and Special Items in Fund Financial Statements

GASB-34 mandates that the following format be used for governmental funds (GASB-34, par. 86):

	Major Fund 1	Major Fund 2	Nonmajor Funds	Total
Revenues (detailed)	$XXX	$XXX	$XXX	$XXX
Expenditures (detailed)	XXX	XXX	XXX	XXX
Excess (deficiency) of revenues over (under) expenditures	XXX	XXX	XXX	XXX
Other financing sources and uses, including transfers (detailed)	XXX	XXX	XXX	XXX
Special and extraordinary items (detailed)	XXX	XXX	XXX	XXX
Net change in fund balance	XXX	XXX	XXX	XXX
Fund balances—beginning of period	XXX	XXX	XXX	XXX
Fund balances—end of period	$XXX	$XXX	$XXX	$XXX

Special and extraordinary items: Governmental funds This category includes special items and extraordinary items, as defined earlier, and would be presented after the category titled "other financing sources and uses." If a governmental entity has both special items and extraordinary items, they should be reported under the single heading labeled "special and extraordinary items." That is, there should not be separate broad headings for each item type (GASB-34, par. 89). (See Chapter 20, "Comprehensive Annual Financial Report," for further discussion of special and extraordinary items.)

When a significant transaction or other event occurs that is either unusual or infrequent but not both and is not under the control of management, that item should be reported in one of the following ways:

- Presented and identified as a separate line item in either the revenue or expenditures category
- Presented but not identified as a separate line item in either the revenue or expenditures category, and described in a note to the financial statements

> **PRACTICE POINT:** An extraordinary gain or loss related to the early extinguishment of debt cannot occur on a statement of revenues, expenditures, and changes in fund balances because this statement presents only the changes in current financial resources (as part of other financing sources and uses on the current financial resources measurement focus) and not gains and losses from economic events and transactions.

Special and extraordinary items: Proprietary funds The operating statement of a proprietary fund should be prepared based on the following guidance (GASB-34, par. 100):

- Revenues should be reported by major source.
- Revenues that are restricted for the payment of revenue bonds should be identified.
- Operating and nonoperating revenues should be reported separately.
- Operating and nonoperating expenses should be reported separately.
- Separate subtotals should be presented for operating revenues, operating expenses, and operating income.
- Nonoperating revenues and expenses should be reported after operating income.
- Capital contributions and additions to term and permanent endowments should be reported separately.
- Special and extraordinary items should be reported separately.
- Transfers should be reported separately.

> **PRACTICE POINT:** Revenues should be reported net of related discounts or allowances. The amount of the discounts or allowances must be presented on the operating statement (either parenthetically or as a subtraction from gross revenues) or in a note to the financial statements.

Reporting Net Assets in Government-Wide Financial Statements

Net assets represent the difference between a governmental entity's total assets and its total liabilities. The statement of net assets must identify the components of net assets (GASB-34, par. 32).

- Invested in capital assets, net of related debt
- Restricted net assets
- Unrestricted net assets

Invested in Capital Assets, Net of Related Debt

"Invested in capital assets" (net of related debt) is the difference between (1) capital assets, net of accumulated depreciation, and (2) liabilities "attributable to the acquisition, construction, or improvement of those assets." When debt has been used to finance the acquisition, construction, or improvement of capital assets but all or part of the cash has not been spent by the end of the fiscal year, the unspent portion of the debt should not be used to determine the amount of invested capital assets (net or related debt) amount. The portion of the unspent debt "should be included in the same net assets component as the unspent proceeds—for example, restricted for capital projects" (GASB-34, par. 33).

> **OBSERVATION:** The GASB concluded that if the unspent portion of the capital related debt was considered "capital related," the "invested in capital assets, net of related debt" component of net assets would be understated because there would be no capital assets to offset the debt. On the other hand, including the unspent proceeds with capital assets would not be appropriate. The GASB agreed that a practical solution would be to allocate that portion of the "capital related" debt to the component of net assets that includes the unspent proceeds to the net assets component that includes the unspent proceeds asset, for example, "restricted net assets—capital projects." The GASB stated that they did not believe that this implies that the debt is "payable" from restricted assets but, rather, is merely consistent with the philosophy of "net" assets.

Common errors made by financial statement preparers include the following:

- Failure to properly reduce the "related debt" amount by the balance of unspent capital debt proceeds before it is netted against capital assets

- Failure to include capital debt related accounts such as unamortized debt issuance costs and bond premiums and discounts in the computation
- Improper inclusion of net assets restricted for capital related debt service

In determining capital-related debt, governments are not expected to categorize all uses of bond proceeds to determine how much of the debt actually relates to assets that have been capitalized. Unless a significant portion of the debt proceeds is spent for non-capitalized purposes, the entire amount could be considered "capital related." In addition, if debt is issued to refund existing capital-related debt, the new debt is also considered capital-related because the replacement debt assumes the capital characteristics of the original issue.

Unamortized debt issue costs, bond premiums and discounts, and deferred amounts from debt refunding should "follow the debt" in calculating net asset components for the statement of net assets. That is, if debt is capital-related, the deferred amounts would be included in the calculation of invested in capital assets, net of related debt. If the debt is restricted for a specific purpose and the proceeds are unspent, the net proceeds would affect restricted net assets. Reporting both within the same element of net assets prevents one classification from being overstated while another is understated by the same amount. If the debt proceeds are not restricted for capital or other purposes, the unamortized costs would be included in the calculation of unrestricted net assets.

Example

Assume a local government has the following balances within its governmental activities' assets and liabilities:

- *Restricted Cash for Debt Service* $800,000 (debit balance that represents cash accumulated from property tax levies legally restricted for the debt service payments on capital-related general obligation bonds)
- *Restricted Cash for Capital Projects* $1,200,000 (debit balance that represents unspent proceeds from general obligation bonds to be used for capital projects)
- *Restricted Cash for Capital Replacement* $2,500,000 (debit balance that represents cash set aside from excess net revenues of years that is restricted by ordinance for use in replacing capital assets)
- *Capital Assets* $34,500,000 (debit balance that represents the historical cost of governmental activities capital assets including infrastructure)

- *Accumulated Depreciation* $9,500,000 (credit balance that represents the accumulated depreciation on depreciable capital assets)
- *Unamortized Bond Issuance Costs* $500,000 (debit balance that represents the unamortized bond issuance costs associated with capital-related debt)
- *Accrued Interest Payable* $300,000 (credit balance that represents the amount of accrued but unpaid interest on capital-related general obligation bonds)
- *General Obligation Bonds* $10,200,000 (credit balance that represents outstanding principal balance of capital-related general obligation bonds)
- *Unamortized Bond Discount* $200,000 (debit balance that represents unamortized discount from the sale of the capital-related general obligation bonds)
- *Capital Lease Obligations Payable* $1,000,000 (credit balance that represents outstanding principal balance of capital lease obligations)

Based on the above assumptions, the calculation of net assets invested in capital assets, net of related debt should be as follows:

Capital Related Assets:	
Capital assets	$34,500,000
Accumulated depreciation	(9,500,000)
Unamortized bond issuance costs	500,000
Subtotal—capital-related assets	25,500,000
Capital Related Debt:	
General obligation bonds	10,200,000
Capital lease obligations	1,000,000
Unamortized bond discount	(200,000)
Restricted cash for capital projects—unspent bond proceeds	(1,200,000)
Subtotal—capital-related debt	9,800,000
Net Assets Invested in Capital Assets, Net of Related Debt	$15,700,000

Note that in the above calculation the following account balances are not included:

- *Restricted Cash for Debt Service* $800,000: Excluded because the restricted cash is to be used for debt service on capital debt as opposed to the acquisition or construction of capital assets and does not represent unspent bond proceeds
- *Restricted Cash for Capital Replacement* $2,500,000: Excluded because the restricted cash has been accumulated for net resources of the entities' operations and does not represent unspent bond proceeds
- *Accrued Interest Payable* $300,000: Excluded because the liability is payable from restricted cash for debt service and the *GASB Comprehensive Implementation Guide* states that accrued interest on any capital-related debt, including deep-discount debt, generally should not be included in the computation of the invested in capital assets, net of related debt component of net assets. The amount of the borrowing attributable to the acquisition, construction, or improvement of a capital asset is the proceeds rather than the total amount, including interest, that will be paid at maturity.

> **PRACTICE POINT:** The answer to Question 7.136 of the *GASB Comprehensive Implementation Guide* states that if the outstanding capital debt exceeds the carrying value of capital assets, the caption "invested in capital assets net of related debt" should still be used and a negative amount reported. Also in Question 7.134 of the *Guide* the GASB staff states that if a government has capital assets but no related debt, the net assets component should be titled "invested in capital assets" and exclude the "net of related debt" wording because this might mislead financial statements users when there is no capital debt.

Restricted Net Assets

Restricted net assets arise if either of the following conditions exists (GASB-34, par. 34):

- Restrictions are externally imposed by creditor (such as through debt covenants), grantors, contributors, or laws or regulations of other governments
- Restrictions are imposed by law through constitutional provisions or enabling legislation

GASB-34 points out that enabling legalization "authorizes the government to assess, levy, charge, or otherwise mandate payment of resources (from external resource providers)" and includes a legally enforceable requirement that those resources be used only for the specific purposes stipulated in the legislation.

> **PRACTICE POINT:** In its definition of "legal enforceability," GASB-46 states that a government can be compelled by an external party (citizens, public interest groups, or the judiciary) to use resources created by enabling legislation only for the purposes specified by the legislation. However, enforceability cannot ultimately be proven unless it is tested through the judicial process; therefore professional judgment must be exercised.

Restricted net assets should be identified based on major categories that make up the restricted balance. These categories could include items such as net assets restricted for capital projects and net assets restricted for debt service.

In some instances net assets may be restricted on a permanent basis (in perpetuity). Under this circumstance, the restricted net assets must be subdivided into expendable and nonexpendable restricted net assets (GASB-34, par. 35).

> **PRACTICE POINT:** GASB-34 points out that, generally, the amount of net assets identified as restricted on the statement of net assets will not be the same as the amount of reserved fund balance or reserved net assets presented on the fund balance sheets/statement of net assets because (1) the financial statements are based on different measurement focuses and bases of accounting and (2) there are different definitions for restricted net assets and reserved fund balance. (Fund financial statements are discussed later.)

The basic concept of restricted net assets is that the restrictions are not unilaterally established by the reporting government itself and cannot be removed without consent of those imposing the restrictions (externally imposed restrictions) or though formal due process (internally imposed restrictions).

"Externally imposed restrictions" are commonly found in the form of

- Laws and regulations of another government that has jurisdiction over the reporting government
- Debt covenants of the government's creditors
- Requirements contained in grant agreements with grantors
- Contractual agreements with donors or other contributors

"Legally imposed restrictions" are commonly found in the form of

- The reporting government's constitution or similar document (such as a municipal charter)
- Enabling legislation (such as state laws for a state and municipal ordinances for a municipality) that creates a new resource and imposes legally enforceable restrictions on the use of the new resource

> **OBSERVATION:** It is important to note that the earmarking of an existing resource or revenue for a specific use by the reporting government does not result in the reporting of restricted net assets from the earmarking. Question 7.24.11 of the *GASB Implementation Guide* states that "earmarking existing revenue is not equivalent to enabling legislation." The earmarking of an existing resource is similar to a designation of the government's intent and is not the same as a legal restriction established at the time the revenue was created.

Common errors made by financial statement preparers related to reporting restricted net assets include the following:

- Inappropriately classifying all reserved fund balances of governmental funds as restricted net assets of governmental activities
- Inappropriately believing that all assets reported as restricted will also be reported as restricted net assets
- Failing to reduce restricted assets by the liabilities payable from those restricted assets or the liabilities that were incurred to generate the restricted assets

Example

Assume a local government has the following balances within its governmental activities' assets and liabilities:

- *Restricted Cash for Street Improvements* $500,000 (debit balance that represents the unspent portion of a state gas tax shared with the local government and restricted for street improvements pursuant to the state's enabling legislation)
- *Restricted Cash for Debt Service* $800,000 (debit balance that represents cash accumulated from property tax levies legally restricted for the debt service payments on capital-related general obligation bonds)
- *Restricted Cash for Bond Issue Capital Projects* $1,200,000 (debit balance that represents unspent proceeds from general obligation bonds to be used for capital projects)

- *Restricted Cash for Capital Replacement* $2,500,000 (debit balance that represents cash set aside and transferred to a capital replacement fund by the local government in the amount of 2% of annual revenues of each year that is restricted by local ordinance for use in replacing capital assets)
- *Restricted Investments for Museum* $1,000,000 (debit balance that represents the principal amount of a museum endowment that cannot be spent: only the interest earnings may be used for museum purposes)
- *Investment in Joint Venture* $1,200,000 (debit balance representing the carrying value of an investment in a joint venture with equity interest)
- *Accounts Payable from Restricted Assets—Streets* $200,000 (credit balance that represents the amount of open invoices to be paid from cash restricted for street improvements as noted above)
- *Accounts Payable from Restricted Assets—Bond Issue Capital Projects* $500,000 (credit balance that represents the amount of open invoices to be paid from cash restricted for the unspent proceeds of the capital general obligation bonds as noted above)
- *Accounts Payable from Restricted Assets—Capital Replacement* $700,000 (credit balance that represents the amount of open invoices to be paid from cash restricted for capital replacement as noted above)
- *Accrued Interest Payable on Bonds* $300,000 (credit balance that represents the amount of accrued but unpaid interest on capital-related general obligation bonds)
- *General Obligation Bonds Payable* $10,200,000 (credit balance that represents outstanding principal balance of capital-related general obligation bonds)

Based on the above assumptions, the calculation of restricted net assets should be as follows:

Assets:	
Restricted Cash for Street Improvements	$500,000
Restricted Cash for Debt Service	800,000
Restricted Cash for Bond Issue Capital Projects	1,200,000
Restricted Investments for Museum	1,000,000
Subtotal—Restricted Assets	3,500,000

Less Related Liabilities:	
Accounts Payable from Restricted Assets—Streets	200,000
Accrued Interest Payable on Bonds	300,000
General Obligation Bonds Payable (unspent proceeds portion)	1,200,000
Subtotal—related liabilities	1,700,000
Restricted Net Assets	$1,800,000

Note that in the above calculation the following account balances are not included:

- *Restricted Cash for Capital Replacement* $2,500,000: Excluded because the restricted cash is essentially the earmarking of existing resources and not the result of externally imposed restrictions or legal restrictions from constitutional law or enabling legislation
- *Investment in Joint Venture* $1,200,000: Question 7.25.1 of the *GASB Implementation Guide* states that an equity interest in a joint venture is generally not restricted (even though it may be comprised of equity in capital assets) and should be included in the computation of unrestricted net assets
- *Accounts Payable from Restricted Assets—Bond Issue Capital Projects* $500,000: Although these are liabilities payable from restricted cash, the restricted cash has already been reduced to zero by netting the portion of the bonds representing unspent proceeds against the restricted asset; further reduction would result in the reporting of negative net assets for this category

PRACTICE POINT: Question and answer 7.24.13 of the *GASB Implementation Guide* states that negative amounts should not be reported for any category of restricted net assets. Restricted net assets are intended to portray, as of a point in time, the extent to which the government has assets that can only be used for specific purposes. If liabilities that relate to specific restricted net assets exceed those assets, the net negative amount should reduce unrestricted net assets.

- *Accounts Payable from Restricted Assets—Capital Replacement* $700,000: Excluded because the related asset is the result of an earmarking and is not included in the computation of restricted net assets
- *General Obligation Bonds Payable* $9,000,000 ($10,200,000 less the portion related to unspent bond proceeds in restricted cash): Excluded because this remaining long-term debt balance is

considered in the computation of net assets, invested in capital assets net of related debt

The $1,800,000 of restricted net assets as determined in the above example should be displayed on the face of the statement of net assets in the following manner by category of restriction:

Restricted Net Assets:	
Restricted for street improvements	$ 300,000
Restricted for debt service	500,000
Restricted for permanent endowment—museum	1,000,000

Note that none of the above restricted net assets are required to be disclosed in the notes to the financial statements as being restricted by enabling legislation. Although the net assets restricted for street improvements represent the net assets resulting from resources restricted by the state's enabling legislation, it is not restricted by the enabling legislation of the reporting government, which would require note disclosure.

Unrestricted Net Assets

"Unrestricted net assets" are net assets that are not classified as invested in capital assets (net of related debt) or restricted net assets. Portions of the entity's net assets may be identified by management to reflect tentative plans or commitments of governmental resources. The *tentative* plans or commitments may be related to items such as plans to retire debt at some future date or to replace infrastructure or specified capital assets. Designated amounts are not the same as restricted amounts because designations represent planned actions, not actual commitments. For this reason, designated amounts should not be classified with restricted net assets but rather should be reported as part of the unrestricted net asset component. In addition, designations cannot be disclosed as such on the face of the statement of net assets (GASB-34, pars. 36–37).

Reporting Restrictions in Proprietary Funds

Assets and liabilities presented on the statement of net assets of a proprietary fund should be classified as current and long-term, based on the guidance established in ARB-43 (Restatement and Revision of Accounting Research Bulletins). The statement of net assets may be presented in either one of the following formats (GASB-34, pars. 97–98):

- *Net assets format* Assets less liabilities equal net assets
- *Balance sheet format* Assets equal liabilities plus net assets

Net assets should be identified as (1) invested in capital assets, net of related debt; (2) restricted; and (3) unrestricted. The guidance discussed earlier (in the context of government-wide financial statements) should be used to determine what amounts should be related to these three categories of net assets. GASB-34 notes that capital contributions should not be presented as a separate component of net assets. Also, similar to the guidance for government-wide financial statements, designations of net assets cannot be identified on the face of the proprietary fund statement of net assets.

> **PRACTICE POINT:** GASB-34 did not change the current standards used to account for capital assets of a proprietary fund; however, the modified approach to reporting infrastructure asset systems (as described in Chapter 10, "Capital Assets") can also be used to account for these capital assets when they are presented in a proprietary fund. For example, a highway reported under the modified approach that is part of a toll road system could be accounted for in an Enterprise Fund.

Reporting Reservations and Designations in Governmental Funds

Reservations The term "reserve" should be used only to identify that portion of the fund balance of governmental funds segregated for future purposes or not available to finance expenditures of the subsequent accounting period. Valuation accounts, such as the allowance for uncollectible property taxes, should not be referred to in the financial statements as a reserve. Likewise, estimated liabilities or deferred revenues should not be classified as reserves. Amounts properly classified as fund balance reserves should be reported as part of the fund balance section of the balance sheet and not placed somewhere between the liability section and the fund balance section (NCGA-1, pars. 118 and 119).

The AICPA's *State and Local Governments* Guide points out that a statutory requirement or contractual commitment to a third party that is not reported as a liability is an example of an amount that is legally segregated for a specific purpose and that nonappropriable amounts include balances related to "inventories, prepaid items, noncurrent receivables that are not offset by deferred revenue, and the noncurrent portion of interfund receivables."

PRACTICE POINT: GASB-34 points out "reserved fund balances of the combined nonmajor funds should be displayed in sufficient detail to disclose the purposes of the reservations (for example, reserved for debt service or reserved for encumbrances)." In addition, GASB-33 (Accounting and Financial Reporting for Nonexchange Transactions), footnote 13, states that a reservation should be reported for time restrictions (both permanent and for specific time periods) and purpose restrictions for as long as the restriction exists.

Designations Portions of the fund balance may be identified by management to reflect tentative plans or commitments of governmental resources. The tentative plans or commitments may be related to items such as debt retirement. Designated amounts are not the same as fund balance reserves because they represent planned actions, not actual commitments. A fund balance reserve arises from statutory requirements or actions already taken by the governmental unit. For this reason, designated amounts should not be classified with fund balance reserves but rather should be reported as part of the unreserved fund balance. The amount and nature of the designated amount should be explained in (1) a separate line in the balance sheet, (2) a parenthetical comment, or (3) a note to the financial statements (NCGA-1, pars. 120–122).

The undesignated fund balance is the difference between the total unreserved fund balance and the total amount of the designations; however, the AICPA's *State and Local Governments* Guide states that "designations should not result in reporting negative undesignated balances in the financial statements at year-end, regardless of the amount of undesignated fund balance at the time the designation was made."

PRACTICE ALERT: In October 2006, the GASB issued an Invitation to Comment (ITC) entitled "Fund Balance Reporting and Governmental Fund Type Definitions." Over recent years, GASB staff and consultants have been interviewing representatives from the financial statement user, preparer, and attestor communities on such issues as fund balance components, presentation, and usefulness of fund balance information. The preliminary results of the GASB research revealed that fund balance was one of the most widely used elements of financial information in state and local government financial statements but at the same time was one of the most misunderstood elements. It is likely that changes to the present fund balance presentation will result from this GASB project. As CCH's 2008 *Governmental GAAP Guide* went to press the GASB was redeliberating the topics covered in the ITC. A final statement is anticipated by the third quarter of 2008.

II. FUND ACCOUNTING

CHAPTER 6
GOVERNMENTAL FUNDS

CONTENTS

INTRODUCTION

This chapter discusses the financial accounting and reporting standards that apply to governmental funds, which comprise the following "fund" types:

- The General Fund
- Special Revenue Funds
- Capital Projects Funds
- Debt Service Funds
- Permanent Funds

Governmental funds primarily are used to account for the sources, uses, and balances of current financial resources and often have a budgetary orientation. Current financial resources are those assets that are expendable during a budgetary period and they are often segregated into a specific governmental fund based on restrictions imposed by outside authorities or parties, or strategies established by internal management. Liabilities, often referred to as "current liabilities," of a governmental fund are obligations that will be paid from resources held by that particular fund. The difference between a fund's assets and a fund's liabilities is the fund balance (fund equity).

PRACTICE ALERT: In October 2006, the GASB issued an Invitation to Comment (ITC) entitled "Fund Balance Reporting and Governmental Fund Type Definitions." Questions from preparers, auditors, and users of governmental financial statements have arisen regarding the appropriate use of governmental type funds as currently defined. It is likely that changes to the definition of governmental fund types will result from this GASB project. As CCH's 2008 *Governmental GAAP Guide* went to press the GASB was redeliberating the topics covered in the ITC. A final statement is anticipated by the third quarter of 2008.

THE GENERAL FUND

Every general-purpose state and local government must have a General Fund to account for all of the unit's financial resources except for those resources that must be accounted for in a special-purpose fund. The General Fund is used to account for the governmental unit's current operations by recording inflows and outflows of financial resources. Current inflows typically are from revenue sources such as property taxes, income taxes, sales taxes, fines, and penalties. Current outflows are usually related to the unit's provision for various governmental services such as health and welfare, streets, public safety, and general governmental administration. In addition to accounting for current operating revenues and expenditures, the General Fund accounts for other sources of financial resources, such as the issuance of long-term debt and transfers from other funds, and uses of financial resources such as transfers to other funds. Although a state or local government can maintain more than one fund in each fund type, it can report only one General Fund.

PRACTICE POINT: When a governmental entity has a component unit that is blended into its financial statements, the General Fund of the component unit must be reported as a Special Revenue Fund.

SPECIAL REVENUE FUNDS

NCGA-1 states that the purpose of a Special Revenue Fund is to account for the proceeds of specific revenue sources (other than sources for major capital projects) that are legally restricted to expenditures for specified purposes. An example of a Special Revenue Fund is a fund that accounts for a state gasoline tax for which distributions are made to local governments and expenditures are restricted to the maintenance of the local highway system. NCGA-1 makes the point that a Special Revenue Fund should be used only when it is legally mandated. In many instances, it may be possible to account for restricted resources directly in the General Fund if these restricted resources are used to support expenditures that are usually made from the General Fund.

> **OBSERVATION:** NCGA-1 states that a Special Revenue Fund should be used "to account for the proceeds of specific revenue sources (other than trusts for individuals, private organizations, or other governments or for major capital projects) that are legally restricted to expenditure for a specified purpose." Restricted net assets as reported in the government-wide financial statements would arise for all Special Revenue Funds that are created based on this guidance; however, in practice Special Revenue Funds are established for purposes other than that stipulated by NCGA-1. Thus, the nature of each Special Revenue Fund must be evaluated to determine how its net assets should be presented on the statement of net assets.

CAPITAL PROJECTS FUNDS

A governmental entity may be involved in a number of capital projects, ranging from the construction of schools and libraries to the construction of storm sewers and highways. The acquisition or construction of capital facilities other than those financed by proprietary fund activities may be accounted for in a Capital Projects Fund. A Capital Projects Fund is usually used to account for major capital expenditures, such as the construction of civic centers, libraries, and general administrative services buildings. The acquisition of other capital assets, such as machinery, furniture, and vehicles, is usually accounted for in the fund responsible for the financing of the expenditure. The purpose of a Capital Projects Fund, as defined by NCGA-1 (Governmental Accounting and Financial Reporting Principles) (as amended by GASB-34 [Basic Financial Statements—and Management's Discussion and Analysis—for State and Local Governments]) is

> To account for financial resources to be used for the acquisition or construction of major capital facilities (other than those financed by proprietary funds or in trust funds for individuals, private organizations, or other governments). (Capital outlays financed from general obligation bonds proceeds should be accounted for through a Capital Projects Fund.)

A separate Capital Projects Fund is usually established when the acquisition or construction of a capital project extends beyond a single fiscal year and the financing sources are provided by more than one fund, or a capital asset is financed by specifically designated resources. Specifically designated resources may arise from the issuance of general obligation bonds, receipts of grants from other governmental units, designation of a portion of tax receipts, or a combination of these and other financing sources. A Capital Projects Fund must be used when mandated by law or stipulated by regulations or covenants related to the financing source. For control purposes, it can also be advantageous to use a separate Capital Projects Fund even though one is not legally required. As with all funds in a governmental entity, the purpose of establishing a specific fund is to establish a basis of accountability for resources provided for a particular purpose.

DEBT SERVICE FUNDS

A Debt Service Fund is created to account for resources that will be accumulated and used to service general long-term debt. General long-term debt can include noncurrent bonds and notes, as well as other noncurrent liabilities that might arise from capitalized lease agreements and other long-term liabilities not created by the issuance of a specific debt instrument. The purpose of a Debt Service Fund, as defined by NCGA-1 (Governmental Accounting and Financial Reporting Principles) (as amended by GASB-34 [Basic Financial Statements—and Management's Discussion and Analysis—for State and Local Governments]) is

> To account for the accumulation of resources for, and the payment of, general long-term debt principal and interest. (Debt Service Funds are required if they are legally mandated and/or if financial resources are being accumulated for principal and interest payments maturing in future years. The debt service transactions of a special assessment bond issue for which the government is not obligated in any manner should be reported in an Agency Fund rather than a Debt Service Fund to reflect the fact that the government's duties are limited to acting as an agent for the assessed property owners and the bondholders.)

A Debt Service Fund is somewhat similar to a sinking fund used by a commercial enterprise in that resources are accumulated for the purpose of eventually retiring long-term obligations.

> **OBSERVATION:** Although separate Debt Service Funds can be established for long-term obligations that are not based on an outstanding debt instrument (such as compensated absences and special termination benefits), these obligations are generally accounted for in other funds such as the General Fund or Special Revenue Funds.

PERMANENT FUNDS

Governmental entities may receive resources from other parties, including individuals, private organizations, and other governments, whereby the use of the resources are according to NCGA-1, "legally restricted to the extent that only earnings, and not principal, may be used for purposes that support the reporting government's programs." Moreover the government itself may set aside general resources on a permanent basis whose earnings can be used only for a particular government program.

For example, a cemetery perpetual-care fund should be created when the earnings of the dedicated resources can be used only for the maintenance of a public cemetery and the principal of the fund is to remain intact. GASB-34 (Basic Financial Statements—and Management's Discussion and Analysis—for State and Local Governments) requires that a Permanent Fund be used to report this type of resource restriction.

OBSERVATION: Based on the standards established by GASB-34, public-purpose trust funds previously presented as Nonexpendable Trust Funds are now to be presented as a Permanent Funds. A Permanent Fund is a governmental fund and therefore is accounted for under the modified accrual basis of accounting. The GASB believes that even though a public-purpose trust fund might initially appear to be appropriately classified in the fiduciary fund category, these funds are created for the benefit of the governmental entity rather than for external parties. Thus, it is more appropriate for them to be considered governmental funds (at the fund financial statement reporting level) and governmental activities (at the government-wide financial statement reporting level).

PRACTICE POINT: In some instances the mandated purpose of specific resources to be accounted for in a separate fund may be such that it is not readily apparent which fund type should be used for financial reporting purposes. For example, the *GASB Comprehensive Implementation Guide* notes that a governmental entity may need to account for financial resources that are legally restricted by enabling legislation, but a minimum balance (unexpendable) is defined by the legislation and that balance must be maintained in the fund. The unexpendable portion of the fund description would suggest that a Permanent Fund should be used while the legal restriction characteristic would suggest that a Special Revenue Fund could be appropriate. The GASB's Guide notes that either fund type could be used under this circumstance. If a Permanent Fund is used, the portion of the fund that is expendable should be identified as unreserved; however, if a Special Revenue Fund is used, the portion of the fund that is not expendable should be identified as a reserved fund balance.

ACCOUNTING AND REPORTING

Basis of Accounting and Measurement Focus

The modified accrual basis of accounting and flow of current financial resources measurement focus are used to prepare the financial statements of governmental funds. These concepts are discussed in Chapter 3, "Basis of Accounting and Measurement Focus."

Budgetary System and Accounts

The General Fund and Special Revenue Funds often have an annual budget that serves as the plan of financial operations and establishes the basis for the financial and legal control and evaluation of activities financed through these Funds. The budgetary control process is most effective when a budgetary accounting system, including the use of budgetary accounts, is employed. GASB-34 requires that a budgetary comparison schedule be presented for the General Fund and each major Special Revenue Fund that has a legally adopted annual budget. The budgetary process is illustrated in Chapter 2, "Budgetary Accounting."

> **OBSERVATION:** The *GASB Comprehensive Implementation Guide* raises the question of whether a Special Revenue Fund that does not meet the percentage criteria in paragraph 76a and 76b of GASB-34 but is nonetheless considered a major fund is required to present a budgetary comparison schedule. The GASB's Guide states that if a fund is considered a major fund (for whatever reason), then all of the major fund reporting requirements must be satisfied, including those related to budgetary information. In order for the budgetary information to apply to a major Special Revenue Fund, that fund must have a legally adopted annual budget.

Unlike some governmental funds, a Capital Projects Fund is project-oriented rather than period-oriented, and for this reason it is often not necessary to record the fund's budget for control purposes. For example, the authorization of a bond ordinance by the legislature or the public will identify the specific purpose of the fund as well as the amount of resources that can be used to construct or purchase the capital asset. Subsequent action by the legislature will generally not be necessary.

Unless a Debt Service Fund budget is legally adopted, there is no requirement to record the fund's budget or to prepare financial statements that compare the results of operations for the period on a budget basis with those on an actual basis. Usually the loan or bond indenture provision that requires the establishment of a Debt Service Fund also controls expenditures to be made from the fund. NCGA-1 states that it is unlikely that budgetary accounts should be integrated into the financial accounting system of a Debt Service Fund when the receipts and expenditures (1) are controlled by bond indenture or sinking fund provisions and (2) occur infrequently during the budgetary period.

Revenues and Other Financing Sources

Revenues Revenues represent increases in current financial resources other than increases caused by the issuance of long-term debt or the receipt of transfers from other funds. General Fund revenues are recorded when they are susceptible to accrual, which means that the revenues must be both measurable and available.

Other financing sources "Other financing sources" is a classification of governmental fund resources other than those defined as "revenues." For example, when long-term debt is issued and the proceeds are available to a governmental fund the proceeds are recorded as other financing sources. The long-term debt is not recorded as a liability in the governmental fund but, rather, is reported as a liability only in the entity's statement of net assets (government-wide financial statement). Interfund transfers from other funds are also reported as "other financing sources."

> **PRACTICE POINT:** The face amount of the long-term debt and related discount or premium and debt-issuance costs should be separately reported in the governmental fund operating statement. The debt-issuance costs should be presented as an expenditure and the other items should be presented as other financing sources and uses. GASB-34, as amended, requires that the "face amount," and not the proceeds (net of any discount or premium) from the issuance of the debt, be presented as an other financing source.

Classification and disclosure Revenues should be presented in the governmental funds' statement of revenues and expenditures and identified by major source, such as property taxes, income taxes, and so on (see Chapter 5, "Terminology and Classification"). The revenue recognition methods used by the governmental funds should be explained in the summary of significant accounting policies.

Expenditures and Other Financing Uses

Expenditures NCGA-1 describes expenditures as decreases in fund financial resources other than through interfund transfers. Events that represent (1) a reduction of a governmental fund's expendable financial resources or (2) a claim at the end of the period that is normally expected to be liquidated by using current expendable financial resources are recorded as expenditures. Expenditures are accrued when incurred if the event or transaction results in a reduction of the governmental fund's current financial resources. If there is no reduction in the fund's current financial resources, no expenditure is recorded. For example, a governmental unit may incur an estimated liability for compensated absences, but if the actual payments to employees are not due at period end, the expenditure would not be reflected in the governmental fund. Instead, it is reported as a liability in the entity's statement of net assets (a government-wide financial statement).

Other financing uses Other financing uses may consist of transfers to other funds and expenditures related to the issuance of general obligation debt.

Classification and disclosure For internal and external analysis and reporting, governmental fund expenditures may be classified by (1) function or program, (2) organizational unit, (3) activity, (4) character, and (5) object class (see Chapter 5, "Terminology and Classification").

Assets

Assets of governmental funds include resources that are considered current expendable financial resources available for subsequent appropriation and expenditure. Assets other than those that are currently expendable, such as capital assets, are indeed assets, but they are not available to finance future expenditures that will be made from the governmental funds.

Current assets The governmental funds' balance sheet is unclassified in that current and noncurrent categories are not presented. However, it is implied that all assets presented in the governmental funds are current assets unless otherwise designated. In the governmental accounting model, a current asset is one that is currently available for expenditure. Thus, the governmental funds generally reflects only those assets that can be used to finance expenditures of the current budgetary period.

Current assets of the governmental funds may include items such as cash, temporary investments, various receivables, advances and loans, and amounts due from other funds.

> **OBSERVATION:** Certain noncurrent assets (not currently expendable) may be reported in governmental funds, but these assets result in the reservation of the fund balance. For example, if a long-term interfund note receivable is reported in the General Fund, the General Fund's fund balance should be reserved.

Investments The standards established by GASB-31 (Accounting and Financial Reporting for Certain Investments and for External Investment Pools) apply to most governmental fund investments. The accounting standards for investments are discussed in Chapter 9, "Deposits and Investments."

Noncurrent assets Governmental funds do not usually reflect assets that are not available to finance current expenditures. However, assets that are noncurrent, other than capital assets, may be presented in the governmental funds' balance sheets as long as the fund balance is reserved by an equal amount. To illustrate, if a $100,000 advance to a Special Revenue Fund will not be repaid during the subsequent budgetary period, the transaction would be recorded as follows in the General Fund:

Interfund Loans Receivable—	100,000	
General Fund Cash		100,000
Fund Balance	100,000	
Fund Balance—Reserved for Loans to Special Revenue Fund		100,000

Capital assets General capital assets, such as land, buildings, and equipment, purchased and used by governmental funds should be recorded as a capital outlay expenditure in the governmental funds and not reported as a fund asset. However, the capital asset is reported in the entity's statement of net assets (a government-wide financial statement).

The accounting for governmental funds' expenditures associated with the acquisition or construction of a capital asset is illustrated by the following transactions:

Transaction: Purchase orders and contracts of $400,000 related to the construction of an addition to a building are signed and the project is to be funded from a Capital Projects Fund:

Capital Projects Fund		
Encumbrances	400,000	
Reserve for Encumbrances		400,000

Transaction: Purchase orders and contracts that were encumbered for $150,000 are vouchered for $157,000 and paid:

Capital Projects Fund		
Reserve for Encumbrances	150,000	
Encumbrances		150,000
Expenditures—Capital Outlays	157,000	
Vouchers Payable/Cash		157,000

Transaction: Construction is completed and the remaining purchase orders and contracts are vouchered for $245,000 and paid:

Capital Projects Fund		
Reserve for Encumbrances	250,000	
Encumbrances		250,000
Expenditures—Capital Outlays	245,000	
Vouchers Payable/Cash		245,000

Classification and disclosure With respect to governmental funds' assets, the following disclosures should be made:

- Disclose valuation bases and significant or unusual accounting treatment for material account balances or transactions. (Disclosures should be described in the order of appearance in the balance sheet.)
- Disclose detail notes on the following, if appropriate:
  —Pooling of cash and investments
  —Investments by type
  —Disaggregation of receivables by type of receivable, if not presented on the face of the balance sheet

The assets that appear on the governmental funds' balance sheet are presented in an unclassified format.

Liabilities

Governmental fund liabilities are debts of the governmental unit that are to be met by using current appropriations and expenditures of the governmental fund's expendable financial resources. Liabilities that do not require the use of current expendable financial resources but will be retired at a later date by funds made available through governmental funds, are reported as an obligation on the statement of net assets (a government-wide financial statement).

Current liabilities Although the governmental funds' balance sheet is unclassified, a liability presented on the financial statement is considered to be a current liability. Current liabilities of governmental funds include items such as accounts and vouchers payable, short-term notes payable, accrued liabilities, interest payable, and payroll withholdings. These liabilities represent debts that will be paid within a few days or weeks after the close of the state or local government's fiscal year and are generally easy to identify as current rather than noncurrent liabilities. Liabilities must be evaluated to determine whether they are debts of governmental funds or are more appropriately reported on the entity's statement of net assets.

Bond, tax, and revenue anticipation notes Governmental units may issue bond, tax, or revenue anticipation notes that will be retired when specific taxes or other specified revenues are collected by the unit. For example, a local government may issue property tax anticipation notes a few weeks or months before the anticipated receipt of property tax installments are to be paid by taxpayers. Bond, tax, and revenue anticipation notes are discussed in Chapter 12, "Long-Term Debt."

Demand bonds A bond agreement may contain a clause that allows bondholders to require a governmental unit to redeem the debt during a specified period of time. The demand feature, or put, and related circumstances must be evaluated to determine whether the demand bonds should be reported as a debt obligation in the statement of net assets (a government-wide liability) or short-term debt (a governmental fund liability). This topic is discussed in Chapter 12, "Long-Term Debt."

Arbitrage Arbitrage involves the simultaneous purchase and sale of the same or essentially the same securities with the objective of making a profit on the spread between the two markets. In the context of governmental finance, this practice often occurs when a governmental entity issues tax-exempt debt and uses the proceeds to invest in debt securities that have a higher rate of return. Because of the spread between the debt securities interest rates and the tax-exempt interest rate, an entity can more effectively manage its financial resources. However, state and local governments must cautiously apply this indirect federal tax subsidy because the federal government has established arbitrage restrictions (requirements for how long the funds can be invested) and arbitrage rebate rules (the amount of arbitrage earnings that must be paid to the federal government).

The governmental entity must apply the rules and regulations established by the federal government in order to determine whether the entity has a liability that it should record in its financial statements. Such liabilities should be recorded using the general guidance established by FAS-5 (Accounting for Contingencies). If the governmental entity should accrue a liability, it should record the portion that represents the use of current financial resources as an expenditure (although some governmental entities offset the amount against interest income) and the balance of the liability as a liability in its government-wide financial statements.

Capital leases Rather than acquire capital assets by making current payments or issuing bonds or notes to finance the acquisition, a governmental unit may enter into a long-term lease agreement. Accounting for lease agreements in a governmental fund is based on whether the agreement is classified as a capital lease or operating lease. NCGA-5 (Accounting and Financial Reporting Principles for Lease Agreements of State and Local Governments) requires that governmental units apply the standards established by FAS-13 (Accounting for Leases), as amended, with appropriate modifications to reflect the measurement focus of government funds. Accounting for lease agreements is discussed in Chapter 14, "Leases."

General long-term debt The proceeds from the issuance of long-term debt not specifically assigned to a particular fund are recorded in the governmental funds; however, the liability itself is not reported as debt of the governmental funds but, rather, is reported as an obligation in the government-wide financial statements. For example, the issuance of general obligation serial bonds of $10,000,000 would be recorded as follows:

CAPITAL PROJECTS FUND		
Cash	10,000,000	
Proceeds From Issuance of Serial Bonds		10,000,000

Bonds issued between interest payment dates Long-term bonds may be issued on a date that does not coincide with an interest payment date. When this occurs, the proceeds from the bond issuance include an amount of accrued interest. The accrued interest does not represent other financing sources of a governmental fund, and it should be recorded as a payable to the governmental fund responsible for servicing the long-term debt. For example, assume that $10,000,000 of bonds carrying a 6% interest rate are issued for $10,100,000, including two months of interest ($100,000) and the proceeds are recorded in a Capital Projects Fund. The issuance of the bonds between interest payment dates would be recorded as follows, assuming a Debt Service Fund will accumulate resources to make interest and principal payments over the life of the bonds:

CAPITAL PROJECTS FUND		
Cash	10,100,000	
Long-Term Debt Issued		10,000,000
Due to Debt Service Fund		100,000
DEBT SERVICE FUND		
Due from Capital Projects Fund	100,000	
Accrued Interest Payable		100,000

Alternatively, the portion of the proceeds that represents the accrued interest may be recorded directly in the fund responsible for servicing the debt. If this approach were chosen, the previous illustration would be recorded as follows:

CAPITAL PROJECTS FUND		
Cash	10,000,000	
Long-Term Debt Issued		10,000,000
DEBT SERVICE FUND		
Cash	100,000	
Accrued Interest Payable		100,000

Bond premium, discount, and bond issuance costs The face amount of the long-term debt, any related discount or premiums, and debt issuance costs should be reported separately. The debt proceeds (based on the face amount of the debt), discount, and premium must be presented as other financing sources and uses. The debt issuance costs should be presented as an expenditure.

Unmatured principal and interest Under the modified accrual basis, expenditures of a governmental fund are recognized when the related liability is incurred. The one significant exception to this fundamental concept is the accounting treatment for unmatured principal and accrued interest. Unmatured principal and accrued interest are not recognized as a liability of a governmental fund until the amounts are due to be paid.

For example, if long-term debt was issued on October 1, 20X5, and the first interest payment was due on April 1, 20X5, there would be no accrual of interest as of December 30, 20X5 (end of fiscal year). Likewise, if a serial bond repayment was due on April 1, 20X5, the liability would not be recorded in the Debt Service Fund's balance sheet as of December 30, 20X5, even though the amount would be due the next day.

Current accounting standards provide for an exception to the basic concept that general long-term indebtedness is not reported as an expenditure until the amount becomes due and payable. When funds have been transferred to the Debt Service Fund during the fiscal year in anticipation of making debt service payments "shortly" after the end of the period, it is acceptable to accrue interest and debt in the Debt Service Fund as an expenditure in the year the transfer is made.

> **OBSERVATION:** Prior to the issuance of GASBI-6 (Recognition and Measurement of Certain Liabilities and Expenditures in Governmental Fund Financial Statements) there was a considerable amount of confusion about what was meant by "shortly." The Interpretation states that "shortly" means "early in the following year"; however, the period of time after the end of the year cannot be greater than one month (GASBI-6, pars. 9 and 13).

Debt extinguishments Scheduled debt retirements are accounted for as just described. In addition to scheduled retirements, general obligations of a governmental unit may be extinguished by (1) legal defeasance or (2) in-substance defeasance or debt refunding. These topics are discussed in Chapter 12, "Long-Term Debt."

Zero-interest-rate bonds Zero-interest-rate bonds are issued at a deep discount, and the difference between the initial price of the bonds and their maturity value represents interest. Interest is not accrued but, rather, is recognized as an expenditure when due and payable. The interest expenditure for zero-interest-rate bonds is recorded when the bonds mature. However, the accrued interest must be recognized as part of the general debt in the governmental entity's statement of net assets.

To illustrate the accounting for zero-interest-rate bonds, assume that $3,000,000 (maturity value) of non-interest-bearing term bonds are issued to yield a rate of return of 5%. The bonds mature in 10 years and are issued for $1,841,730 ($3,000,000 × 0.61391, where $i = 5\%$, $n = 10$ for the present value of an amount). The issuance of the bonds, assuming the proceeds are made available to the General Fund, is recorded as follows:

GENERAL FUND		
Cash	1,841,730	
Discount on Long-Term Debt Issued	1,158,270	
Other Financing Sources— Long-Term Debt Issued		3,000,000

At the end of the first fiscal year, the amount of accrued interest earned by investors on the bonds is $92,087 ($1,841,730 × 5%). Because the interest will not be paid by the Debt Service Fund until the bonds mature, the accrued interest is not recognized as an expenditure. The accrued interest must be included as part of general long-term debt in the government-wide statement of net assets.

When the bonds mature in 10 years, assuming that sufficient funds have been accumulated in the Debt Service Fund, the following entries are made:

DEBT SERVICE FUND		
Expenditures—Principal	1,841,730	
Expenditures—Interest	1,158,270	
Cash		3,000,000

Classification and disclosure With respect to governmental funds' liabilities, the following disclosures should be made:

- Description of general long-term debt and other obligations
- Changes in long-term debt balances
- Changes in short-term debt balances
- Disaggregation of payables by type, if not on the face of the balance sheet
- Debt service requirements to maturity (for debt serviced from the governmental funds)
- The amount of debt considered retired resulting from debt refunding or in-substance defeasance transactions and the cash flow and economic gains or losses from the transactions in the current period

Fund Equity

Reporting fund balance reservations and designations governmental funds' equity (the difference between "fund assets—current financial resources" and "fund liabilities—obligations payable from current financial resources") is reported as reserved, unreserved but designated, and/or unreserved-undesignated. This topic is discussed further in Chapter 5, "Terminology and Classification."

> **PRACTICE POINT:** If the entire fund balance of a governmental fund is expendable and is reserved or restricted for the purpose for which the fund was established, the entire fund balance of that fund should be reported as "unreserved" on the fund's balance sheet. The fact that a separate fund was established provides sufficient reporting of the restricted nature of the fund's equity.

Reporting a special revenue fund's net assets at the government-wide level NCGA-1 states that a Special Revenue Fund should be used "to account for the proceeds of specific revenue sources (other than trusts for individuals, private organizations, or other governments or for major capital projects) that are legally restricted to expenditure for specified purpose." Restricted net assets from the government-wide perspective would arise for all Special Revenue Funds that are created based on this guidance; however, in practice Special Revenue Funds are established for purposes other than that stipulated by NCGA-1. Thus, the nature of each Special Revenue Fund must be evaluated to determine how its net assets should be presented on the statement of net assets.

FUND FINANCIAL STATEMENTS

GASB-34 requires that the following financial statements be presented for governmental funds:

- Balance sheet
- Statement of revenues, expenditures, and changes in fund balances

Reporting standards require that a governmental fund be presented in a separate column in the fund financial statements if the fund is considered a major fund. All other governmental funds are considered nonmajor and are aggregated in a single column in the fund financial statements. See Chapter 1, "Foundation and Overview of Governmental Generally Accepted Accounting Principles," for discussion of the definition of "major funds."

(Exhibit 20-4 in Chapter 20, "Comprehensive Annual Financial Report," is an illustration of a balance sheet for governmental funds.

Exhibit 20-5 is an illustration of a statement of revenues, expenditures, and changes in fund balances for governmental funds.)

GOVERNMENT-WIDE FINANCIAL STATEMENTS

The information developed for the preparation of the fund statements for the five governmental fund types (on the modified accrual basis and current financial resources focus) is the starting point for converting the information in preparing the governmental activities column of the government-wide financial statements (on the accrual basis and economic resources focus). Government-wide financial statements are more fully discussed and illustrated in Chapter 20, "Comprehensive Annual Financial Report."

> **Note:** The process by which fund financial statements are converted to government-wide financial statements is comprehensively illustrated in Appendix 20A of this guide and in CCH's *Governmental GAAP Practice Manual: Including GASB-34 Guidance.*

CHAPTER 7
PROPRIETARY FUNDS

CONTENTS

INTRODUCTION

A proprietary fund is used to account for a state or local government's activities that are similar to activities that may be performed by a commercial enterprise. For example, a hospital may be operated by a governmental unit, such as a city, or by a profit-oriented corporation. The accounting and reporting standards used by a proprietary fund and a business enterprise are similar because the activities performed are basically the same.

Although a proprietary fund is accounted for in much the same manner as a commercial enterprise, a proprietary fund is nonetheless a fund used by governmental entities. NCGA-1 (Governmental Accounting and Financial Reporting Principles) defines a "fund" as

> A fiscal and accounting entity with a self-balancing set of accounts recording cash and other financial resources, together with all related liabilities and residual equities or balances, and changes therein, which are segregated for the purpose of carrying on specific activities or attaining certain objectives in accordance with special regulations, restrictions, or limitations.

The basic objective of a proprietary fund, as alluded to in the NCGA's definition, is different from the fundamental purpose of a commercial enterprise. The purpose of a proprietary fund is not to maximize its return on invested capital. Generally, the purpose of a proprietary fund is to provide a service or product to the public or other governmental entities at a reasonable cost. The objective is achieved by creating one of the following two types of proprietary funds: an Enterprise Fund or Internal Service Fund.

ENTERPRISE FUNDS

An Enterprise Fund may be used to "report any activity for which a fee is charged to external users for goods or services." GASB-34 states that an Enterprise Fund *must* be used to account for an activity if any one of the following criteria is satisfied (GASB-34, par. 67):

- The activity is financed with debt that is secured *solely* by a pledge of the net revenues from fees and charges of the activity.
- Laws or regulations require that the activity's costs of providing services, including capital costs (such as depreciation or capital debt service), be recovered with fees and charges, rather than with taxes or similar revenues.
- The pricing policies of the activity establish fees and charges designed to recover its costs, including capital costs (such as depreciation or debt service).

> **OBSERVATION:** Some financial statement preparers raised the question about whether the three criteria listed above apply to activities that are currently accounted for in Internal Service Funds. GASB-34 takes the position that an Enterprise Fund, not an Internal Service Fund, must be used when external users are the predominant participants in the fund. GASB-37 reemphasizes this point by adding a footnote to paragraph 67 that states, "the focus of these criteria is on fees charged to external users" (GASB-37, par. 14).

The first criterion refers to debt secured solely by fees and charges. If that debt is secured by a pledge of fees and charges from the activity and the full faith and credit of the primary government or component unit, this arrangement does not satisfy the "sole source of debt security" and the activity does not have to be accounted for (assuming the other two criteria are not satisfied) in an Enterprise Fund. This conclusion is not changed even if it is anticipated that the primary government or component unit is not expected to make debt payments under the arrangement. On the other hand, debt that is secured partially by a portion of its own proceeds does satisfy the "sole source of debt security" criterion.

The second and third criteria refer to the establishment of a pricing policy that recovers costs, including depreciation expense or debt service. In some situations the activity might be responsible for little or no debt. The *GASB Comprehensive Implementation Guide* states that in this circumstance, the criteria are still met when debt service requirements (if any) are used to establish the pricing policy. There is no assumption that there is equality between the deprecation expense and the debt service on capital debt for a particular activity.

The third criterion is similar to the previous standard for determining when an Enterprise Fund should be used to account for an activity except that the new standard in GASB-34 is based on "established policies" rather than management's intent.

> **OBSERVATION:** The criteria established by GASB-34 are different from those established by NCGA-1. The GASB believes that the establishment of the three criteria listed above will reduce the degree of subjectivity that is now used by governmental entities in determining when an Enterprise Fund should be used.

The three criteria should be applied to a governmental entity's principal revenue sources; however, the criteria do not have to be applied to "insignificant activities" of a governmental entity. If none of the criteria apply, the activity can be accounted for in a governmental fund.

> **OBSERVATION:** The *GASB Comprehensive Implementation Guide* points out that while professional judgment must be

used to determine what is an activity's principal revenue source, the focus should be on the relationship of a particular revenue source to an activity's total revenues.

PRACTICE POINT: It should be noted that GASB-34 (Basic Financial Statements—and Management's Discussion and Analysis—for State and Local Governments) states that a fee-based activity can be accounted for in an Enterprise Fund even if the three criteria described above do not exist. The three criteria apply to fee-based activities that must be accounted for in an Enterprise Fund.

Common Enterprise Funds

Activities commonly reported as Enterprise Funds of state and local governments include the following:

- Airport
- Electric, gas, water, wastewater, and sanitation/landfill
- Golf
- Hospital or other health care services
- Lotteries and gaming
- Parking and transit
- Unemployment insurance

INTERNAL SERVICE FUNDS

GASB-34 (Basic Financial Statements—and Management's Discussion and Analysis—for State and Local Governments) describes an Internal Service Fund as a proprietary fund that may be used to report "any activity that provides goods or services to other funds, departments, or agencies of the primary government and its component units, or to other governments, on a cost reimbursement basis." An Internal Service Fund should be used only when the reporting government itself is the predominant participant in the fund. When the transactions with the other governmental entities represent the predominant portion of the activity, an Enterprise Fund must be used.

There is no circumstance under which an Internal Service Fund *must* be used. For example, an activity may be centralized by a governmental entity whereby all departments, programs, and so forth within the reporting entity must use the centralized activity and be billed for the service provided. That activity could be accounted for in an Internal Service Fund, but it could also be accounted for in another governmental fund (probably the General Fund).

Common Internal Service Funds

Activities commonly reported as Internal Service Funds of state and local governments include the following:

- Central services, such as purchasing, warehousing, information systems, etc.
- Risk management/self-insurance
- Vehicle and equipment maintenance

ACCOUNTING AND REPORTING

Basis of Accounting and Measurement Focus

The accrual basis of accounting and the flow of economic resources are used to prepare the financial statements of a proprietary fund. These concepts are discussed in Chapter 3, "Basis of Accounting and Measurement Focus."

GASB-20 (Accounting and Financial Reporting for Proprietary Funds and Other Governmental Entities That Use Proprietary Fund Accounting) allows two distinct but acceptable alternatives for the reporting of Enterprise Funds or governmental accounting entities that use proprietary fund accounting. The two alternatives are discussed in Chapter 1, "Foundation and Overview of Governmental Generally Accepted Accounting Principles."

Budgetary System and Accounts

Although the National Council on Governmental Accounting recommended that all funds adopt a budget for control purposes, it recognized that the nature of budgeting is different for governmental funds and proprietary funds. Generally, a proprietary fund should prepare a flexible budget, which reflects changes in the activity level. A fixed budget is inappropriate for proprietary funds because, in a fixed budget, overall activity is measured in terms of revenues and expenses and will fluctuate, in part, depending on the demand for goods and services by the public or governmental agencies. The flexible budget does not provide a basis for appropriations. Rather it serves as an approved financial plan that can facilitate budgetary control and operational evaluations. A flexible budget approach allows the governmental unit to prepare several budgets at different activity levels to establish an acceptable comparative basis for planned activity and actual results.

The basis of accounting used to prepare a budget for a proprietary fund should be the same as the basis used to record the results of actual transactions. It is not appropriate to integrate the budgetary accounts into the proprietary fund's accounting system.

Because a proprietary fund is generally not subject to a legislatively adopted budget, governmental entities are normally not required to use an encumbrance system to control executory contracts and other commitments for such funds.

Revenues

FASB:CS-6 (Elements of Financial Statements) defines *revenues* as "inflows or other enhancements of assets of an entity or settlements of its liabilities (or a combination of both) during a period from delivering or producing goods, rendering services, or other activities that constitute the entity's ongoing major or central operations." A proprietary fund should recognize revenue on an accrual basis, meaning that revenue is considered realized when (1) the earning process is complete or virtually complete and (2) an exchange has taken place.

> **PRACTICE ALERT:** In August 2006, the Governmental Accounting Standards Board (GASB) issued an exposure draft on a proposed Concepts Statement entitled "Elements of Financial Statements." This proposed Concepts Statement would be the fourth issued by the GASB, and it proposes new definitions for seven elements of historically based financial statements of state and local governments as follows:
>
> - Elements of the statement of financial position:
>
>   1. Assets
>   2. Liabilities
>   3. Deferred Outflow of Resources
>   4. Deferred Inflow of Resources
>   5. Net Position
>
> - Elements of the resources flow statements:
>
>   6. Inflow of Resources
>   7. Outflow of Resources
>
> The GASB-proposed definitions of the elements are based upon the inherent characteristics of each element and are

linked by a common definition feature in that they are based on the concept of measuring and reporting *resources.* The proposed definitions of the elements apply to an entity that is a governmental unit (that is, a legal entity) and are applicable to any measurement focus under which financial statements may be prepared, for example, economic resources, current financial resources, and cash resources measurement focuses. As CCH's 2008 *Governmental GAAP Guide* went to press the GASB was redeliberating the proposed statement based on the responses to the exposure draft. However, the results of this project are likely to differ from the concepts in FASB:CS-6.

PRACTICE POINT: Proprietary funds, such as water and sewer Enterprise Funds, have unbilled revenue at the end of an accounting period. Whether revenue is billed or unbilled is not the critical issue in the recognition of revenue. When a service has been provided (for example, the consumption of a service by a customer), the related revenue should be recognized.

Uncollectible accounts related to revenue GASB-34, footnote 41, requires that revenues be reported net of related discounts or allowances. The amount of the discounts or allowances must be presented on the operating statement (either parenthetically or as a subtraction from gross revenues) or in a note to the financial statements. GASB-34 does not require that estimates of bad-debt expenses be reported as an offset to revenues, but the *GASB Comprehensive Implementation Guide* states that estimates of uncollectible accounts should be presented in a manner similar to discounts and allowances.

Capital contributions from governmental funds A proprietary fund must take into consideration the nature of a capital contribution received from another fund. The *GASB Comprehensive Implementation Guide* notes that when a transfer to a proprietary fund is from a governmental fund and consists of financial resources, both the governmental fund and the proprietary fund must record the transaction as a transfer. Transfers should also be presented in the governmental activities column (as a transfer out) and the business-type activities column (as a transfer in) in the statement of activities.

If the transfer consists of nonfinancial resources (such as a capital asset), the governmental fund will not record the transfer (because only financial resources are accounted for in a governmental fund); however, the proprietary fund will record the transaction not as a transfer but as capital contribution revenue in the lower portion of its operating statement. Even though the transfer is not presented in the governmental fund it must be presented as a transfer in the governmental activities column in the statement of activities; however, the inconsistency between the treatment of the transfer at the fund financial statement level and the government-wide financial statement level would generate a reconciling item for the governmental fund's operating statement.

Expenses

FASB:CS-6 defines "expenses" as outflows or other using up of assets or incurrences of liabilities (or a combination of both) during a period from delivering or producing goods, rendering services, or carrying out other activities that constitute the entity's ongoing major or central operations. For example, a proprietary fund would record a loss contingency as an expense irrespective of when the related liability is expected to be paid.

PRACTICE ALERT: In August 2006, the Governmental Accounting Standards Board (GASB) issued an exposure draft on a proposed Concepts Statement entitled "Elements of Financial Statements." This proposed Concepts Statement would be the fourth issued by the GASB, and it proposes new definitions for seven elements of historically based financial statements of state and local governments as follows:

- Elements of the statement of financial position:

  1. Assets
  2. Liabilities
  3. Deferred Outflow of Resources
  4. Deferred Inflow of Resources
  5. Net Position

- Elements of the resources flow statements:

  6. Inflow of Resources
  7. Outflow of Resources

The GASB-proposed definitions of the elements are based upon the inherent characteristics of each element and are linked by a common definition feature in that they are based on the concept of measuring and reporting *resources.* The proposed definitions of the elements apply to an entity that is a governmental unit (that is, a legal entity) and are applicable to any measurement focus under which financial statements may be prepared, for example, economic resources, current financial resources, and cash resources measurement focuses. As CCH's 2008 *Governmental GAAP Guide* went to press the GASB was redeliberating the proposed statement based on the responses to the exposure draft. However, the results of this project are likely to differ from the concepts in FASB:CS-6.

Depreciation expense All depreciable property of a proprietary fund must be depreciated in accordance with generally accepted accounting principles as applied by a commercial enterprise.

Uncollectible accounts related to nonrevenue transactions A governmental entity may make loans to other parties and subsequently have to write off those loans as uncollectible. A change in the allowance for uncollectible accounts not related to revenue transactions must be presented as an expense rather than netted against revenue, because there is no related revenue account.

Payments in lieu of taxes An Enterprise Fund may make a payment to a local government in lieu of the payment of property taxes. Prior to the issuance of GASB-34, such payments often were presented as quasi-external transactions, and therefore reported as an expense by an Enterprise Fund. However, GASB-34 eliminated the quasi-external transaction category and in order for a transaction to be presented as an expense by an Enterprise Fund, it must be considered an exchange or exchange-like transaction. An exchange transaction occurs when two parties exchange assets or commitments of approximate equal value. The GASB defines an exchange-like transaction as being "an identifiable exchange between the reporting government and another party, but the values exchanged may not be quite equal or the direct benefits of the exchange may not be exclusively for the parties to the exchange."

Assets

Assets, as defined in FASB:CS-6, are "probable future economic benefits obtained or controlled by a particular entity as a result of past transactions or events." The Concepts Statement also states that an asset has the following three characteristics (FASB:CS-6, par. 26):

It embodies probable future benefit that involves a capacity, singly or in combination with other assets, to contribute directly or indirectly to future net cash inflows.
A particular entity can obtain the benefit and control others' access to it.
The transaction or other event giving rise to the entity's right to or control of the benefit has already occurred.

Governmental funds, in contrast to proprietary funds, report only those assets available to finance current operations. For example, a General Fund could not accrue a gain arising from a settled lawsuit, even though the amount is known with certainty, if payments from the other party are to be received over several years. A proprietary fund's financial statements would reflect all assets related to the operations of the fund irrespective of when the asset is expected to be realized.

PRACTICE ALERT: In August 2006, the Governmental Accounting Standards Board (GASB) issued an exposure draft on a proposed Concepts Statement entitled "Elements of Financial Statements." This proposed Concepts Statement would be the fourth issued by the GASB, and it proposes new definitions for seven elements of historically based financial statements of state and local governments as follows:

- Elements of the statement of financial position:

  1. Assets
  2. Liabilities
  3. Deferred Outflow of Resources
  4. Deferred Inflow of Resources
  5. Net Position

- Elements of the resources flow statements:

  6. Inflow of Resources
  7. Outflow of Resources

The GASB-proposed definitions of the elements are based upon the inherent characteristics of each element and are linked by a common definition feature in that they are based on the concept of measuring and reporting *resources.* The proposed definitions of the elements apply to an entity that is a governmental unit (that is, a legal entity) and are applicable to any measurement focus under which financial statements may be prepared, for example, economic resources, current financial resources, and cash resources measurement focuses. As CCH's 2008 *Governmental GAAP Guide* went to press the GASB was redeliberating the proposed statement based on the responses to the exposure draft. However, the results of this project are likely to differ from the concepts in FASB:CS-6.

Reporting restrictions on asset use In a proprietary fund it is assumed that assets (especially current assets) are unrestricted in that there are no conditions that would prevent the governmental entity from using the resources to pay existing liabilities. If the name of the asset account does not adequately explain the normally perceived availability of that asset, the item should be identified as a restricted asset on the statement of net assets. For example, an amount of cash may be restricted to a specific type of expenditure and therefore it would be misleading to report the restricted cash with all other cash (classified as current asset). Under this circumstance, the cash should be reported as restricted cash in the financial statement category labeled noncurrent assets. On the other hand, equipment is not available to pay liabilities but the title of the account adequately describes the availability (or lack of liquidity) of the asset and therefore there is no need to identify the asset as restricted (GASB-34, par. 99).

Interest capitalization Interest cost incurred during the construction of the following assets of a proprietary fund should be capitalized:

- Assets that are constructed or otherwise produced for an enterprise's own use (including assets constructed or produced by others for the enterprise for which deposits or progress payments have been made)
- Assets intended for sale or lease that are constructed or otherwise produced as discrete projects (for example, real estate developments)
- Investments (equity, loans, and advances) accounted for by the equity method while the investee has activities in progress necessary to commence its planned principal operations provided that the investee's activities include the use of funds to acquire qualifying assets for its operations

On the other hand, the construction cost of the following assets related to a proprietary fund should not include an interest cost element:

- Inventories that are routinely manufactured or otherwise produced in large quantities on a repetitive basis
- Assets that are in use or ready for their intended use in the earning activities of the enterprise
- Investments accounted for by the equity method after the planned principal operations of the investee begin
- Investments in regulated investees that are capitalizing both the cost of debt and equity capital
- Assets acquired with gifts and grants that are restricted by the donor or grantor to acquisition of those assets to the extent that funds are available from such gifts and grants (interest earned from temporary investment of those funds that is similarly restricted shall be considered in addition to the gift or grant for this purpose)

Interest costs incurred by a proprietary fund are subject to capitalization based on the guidelines established by FAS-34 (Capitalization of Interest Cost). The interest capitalization period begins when the following conditions are present:

- Expenditures for the capital asset have been made.
- Activities that are necessary to get the capital asset ready for its intended use are in progress.
- Interest cost is being incurred.

To determine the amount of interest cost to be capitalized, the weighted-average amount of accumulated expenditures for the period is multiplied by the proprietary fund's average borrowing rate for the period. Rather than use the overall average borrowing rate, the following approach can be employed:

- The interest rate for the obligation incurred specifically to finance the construction of the capital asset may be used.
- The overall average borrowing rate of the proprietary fund would be used for any accumulated expenditures in excess of specific borrowings.

The amount of interest cost to be capitalized is limited to the actual amount of interest expense recognized for the period.

The *GASB Comprehensive Implementation Guide* points out that interest capitalization for proprietary funds should take into consideration only debt that is to be paid by a proprietary fund. In some instances, a self-constructed capital asset may be initially reported in a proprietary fund but later transferred to a governmental activity. The *GASB Q&A Guide* states that in this circumstance, interest capitalized as part of the cost basis of the capital asset should not be removed when the asset is reported as part of governmental activities.

PRACTICE POINT: FAS-62 (Capitalization of Interest Cost in Situations Involving Certain Tax-Exempt Borrowings and Certain Gifts and Grants) states that the amount of interest cost to be capitalized for assets constructed with tax-exempt borrowings is equal to the cost of the borrowing, less interest earned on related interest-bearing investments acquired with proceeds of the related tax-exempt borrowings.

Infrastructure assets The *GASB Comprehensive Implementation Guide* points out that the modified approach may be applied to eligible infrastructure assets accounted for as either governmental activities or business-type activities. For example, an Enterprise Fund that owns a toll road (which is an infrastructure asset) could use the modified approach. If the Enterprise Fund uses the modified approach, it should be used in the preparation of both the government-wide and proprietary fund financial statements. See Chapter 10, "Capital Assets," for further discussion of infrastructure assets and the modified approach.

> **PRACTICE POINT:** An Enterprise Fund that previously depreciated eligible infrastructure assets before the standards established by GASB-34 were adopted can use the modified approach for those assets. This adoption would not be accounted for as a change in an accounting principle; rather, the net book value of the infrastructure as of the date of adopting the method would be the starting point for implementing the modified approach.

Customer deposits for utility services Governmental entities that provide utility services, such as electric, water, sewer, and gas, may require deposits from customers, or a governmental entity may charge developers and/or customers system development fees (tap fees). A customer deposit is generally required to be paid before a service is turned on, and when the service is terminated, the deposit is returned to the customer. Utility services are generally accounted for as Enterprise Funds, and the *AICPA's State and Local Governments—Audit and Accounting Guide* points out that receipts of customer deposits should be recorded as a liability and continue to be reported as such until they are "applied against unpaid billings or refunded to customers." Generally, these customer deposits are reported as restricted assets and offset with a corresponding liability payable from restricted assets.

Customer system development fees The AICPA's *State and Local Governments* Guide also notes that the initial receipt of a customer system development fee should be recorded as a liability and recognized as revenue using the general guidance related to either an exchange transaction or a nonexchange transaction. In an exchange transaction the governmental entity and the other party to the transaction exchange cash, goods, or services that are essentially of the same value.

A nonexchange transaction arises when the transfer of goods or services between two parties is not of equal value. When a customer system development fee is considered to be a nonexchange transaction, it must be accounted for based on the guidance established by GASB-33. See Chapter 17, "Revenues: Nonexchange and Exchange Transactions," for a discussion of nonexchange revenues.

Liabilities

FASB:CS-6 defines "liabilities" as "probable future sacrifices of economic benefits arising from present obligations of a particular entity to transfer assets or provide services to other entities in the future as a result of past transactions or events."

Unlike governmental funds, a proprietary fund reports both current and noncurrent liabilities expected to be paid from the fund. A proprietary fund may receive the proceeds from the issuance of either general obligation bonds or revenue bonds.

> **PRACTICE ALERT:** In August 2006, the Governmental Accounting Standards Board (GASB) issued an exposure draft on a proposed Concepts Statement entitled "Elements of Financial Statements." This proposed Concepts Statement would be the fourth issued by the GASB, and it proposes new definitions for seven elements of historically based financial statements of state and local governments as follows:
>
> - Elements of the statement of financial position:
>
>   1. Assets
>   2. Liabilities
>   3. Deferred Outflow of Resources
>   4. Deferred Inflow of Resources
>   5. Net Position
>
> - Elements of the resources flow statements:
>
>   6. Inflow of Resources
>   7. Outflow of Resources
>
> The GASB-proposed definitions of the elements are based upon the inherent characteristics of each element and are linked by a common definition feature in that they are based on the concept of measuring and reporting *resources*. The proposed definitions of the elements apply to an entity that is a governmental unit (that is, a legal entity) and are applicable to any measurement focus under which financial statements may be prepared, for example, economic resources, current financial resources, and cash resources measurement focuses. As CCH's 2008 *Governmental GAAP Guide* went to press the GASB was redeliberating the proposed statement based on the responses to the exposure draft. However, the results of this project are likely to differ from the concepts in FASB:CS-6.

General obligation bonds A governmental entity may issue general obligation bonds whereby the proceeds are used to construct capital assets reported in a proprietary fund. If the debt is directly related to and expected to be paid from the proprietary fund, both the capital asset and the debt are reported in the proprietary fund financial statements and the business-type activities column of the government-wide statement of net assets. However, the *GASB Comprehensive Implementation Guide* points out that if the proprietary fund is not expected to service the debt, the debt is reported in the governmental activities column and the capital asset is reported in the business-type activities column of the statement of net assets.

Revenue bonds Principal and interest on revenue bonds are paid exclusively from the earnings of a proprietary fund. If the debt is also secured by specific fixed assets of the proprietary fund, they are referred to as mortgage revenue bonds. Revenue bonds are recorded as a liability of the Enterprise Fund.

> **PRACTICE POINT:** A proprietary fund's long-term liabilities may include obligations other than those that arise from the issuance of a security debt instrument. These other obligations may be created from capitalized leases, claims and judgments, special employee termination benefits, and pension obligations. These, as well as other liabilities of a proprietary fund, should be accounted for in a manner similar to the accounting and reporting standards applicable to a commercial enterprise.

Fund Equity

Proprietary fund net assets should be identified as (1) invested in capital assets, net of related debt; (2) restricted; and (3) unrestricted, similar to the presentation of net assets in the government-wide financial statements. GASB-34 notes that capital contributions should not be presented as a separate component of net assets. Also, similar to the guidance for government-wide financial statements, designations of net assets cannot be identified on the face of the proprietary fund statement of net assets. See Chapter 5, "Terminology and Classification," for discussion of the net assets components.

> **PRACTICE POINT:** Restricted net assets arise only when (1) externally imposed by creditors (such as through debt covenants), grantors, contributors, or laws or regulations of other governments or (2) imposed by law through constitutional provisions or enabling legislation.

FUND FINANCIAL STATEMENTS

Based on the fundamental concepts discussed above, the following financial statements must be prepared for Enterprise Funds and Internal Service Funds (GASB-34, par. 91):

- Statement of net assets (or balance sheet)
- Statement of revenues, expenses, and changes in fund net assets
- Statement of cash flows

Statement of Net Assets

Assets and liabilities presented on the statement of net assets of a proprietary fund should be classified as current and noncurrent, based on the guidance established in Chapter 3 of ARB-43 (Restatement and Revision of Accounting Research Bulletins). The statement of net assets may be presented in either one of the following formats (GASB-34, pars. 97–98):

- Net assets format: assets less liabilities equal net assets
- Balance sheet format: assets equal liabilities plus net assets

(Exhibit 20-6, "Comprehensive Annual Financial Report," in Chapter 20, illustrates a statement of net assets for proprietary funds that is consistent with the standards established by GASB-34.)

Statement of Revenues, Expenses, and Change Fund Net Assets The operating statement of a proprietary fund is the statement of revenues, expenses, and changes in fund net assets. In preparing this statement, the following standards should be observed (GASB-34, par. 100):

- Revenues should be reported by major source
- Revenues that are restricted for the payment of revenue bonds should be identified

(Exhibit 20-7, "Statement of Revenues, Expenses, and Changes in Net Assets: Proprietary Funds," in Chapter 20, illustrates a statement of revenues, expenses, and changes in net assets for proprietary funds that is consistent with the standards established by GASB-34.)

Reconciliations Although there must be a reconciliation between the government-wide financial statements (statement of net assets and statement of changes in net assets) and the governmental funds, generally there is no need for a similar reconciliation between the government-wide financial statements and proprietary fund financial statements because both sets of financial statements are based on the same measurement focus and basis of accounting (GASB-34, par. 104).

> **OBSERVATION:** In a circumstance where there are differences between the two sets of financial statements, the differences must be reconciled on the face of the proprietary fund financial statements. GASB-34 notes that a reconciling item could arise when the residual assets and liabilities of an Internal Service Fund is presented as part of the business-type activities column in the statement of net assets (a government-wide financial statement). This circumstance can arise only when "enterprise funds are the predominant or only participants in an Internal Service Fund."

Statement of Cash Flows

Proprietary funds should prepare a statement of cash flows based on the guidance established by GASB-9, except the statement of cash flows should be formatted based on the *direct method* in computing cash flows from operating activities. The statement of cash flows would be supplemented with a reconciliation of operating cash flows and operating income (the indirect method) (GASB-34, par. 105).

(Exhibit 20-8, "Statement of Cash Flows: Proprietary Funds," in Chapter 20, illustrates a statement of cash flows for enterprise funds that is consistent with the standards established by GASB-34.)

Segment Information: Enterprise Funds

Segment disclosures must be made by governmental entities that report Enterprise Funds or that use enterprise fund accounting and reporting standards to report activities. A segment is defined as follows (GASB-34, par. 122, as amended by GASB-37, par. 17):

> . . . an identifiable activity (or grouping of activities) reported as or within an Enterprise Fund or an other stand-alone entity that has one or more bonds or other debt instruments (such as certificates of participation) outstanding, with a revenue stream pledged in support of that debt. In addition, the activity's revenues, expenses, gains and losses, assets and liabilities are required to be accounted for separately.

The *GASB Comprehensive Implementation Guide* emphasizes that paragraph 122 of GASB-34 does not require that the pledged revenue stream be the only backing for the debt in order for the activity to be considered a segment. For example, the debt could also be backed by the full faith and credit of the governmental entity.

OBSERVATION: The original language used in GASB-34 was interpreted by some financial statement preparers as requiring disclosures for activities that were not intended to be covered by the GASB. The purpose of GASB-34 was to "provide separate financial statement information for *identifiable activities* that were combined in a single major Enterprise Fund or included in the nonmajor fund aggregation." In order to clarify this objective, GASB-37 revised paragraph 122 of GASB-34 by adding the following points: (1) A segment is an identifiable activity (or grouping of activities), as discussed in paragraph 39b, footnote c of GASB-34, reported by, as, or within an Enterprise Fund (or an other stand-alone entity) that has one or more bonds or other debt instruments (such as certificates of participation) outstanding, with a revenue stream pledged in support of that debt, and (2) based on the agreement between the governmental entity and an external party, there is a requirement that related revenues, expenses, gains and losses, assets, and liabilities be accounted for separately.

PRACTICE POINT: Segment disclosures do not apply to an activity that is solely related to conduit debt "for which the government has no obligation beyond the resources provided by related leases or loans." Also, segment disclosures do not apply when an activity is reported as a major fund.

The following segment disclosures should be made by providing condensed financial statements in a note(s) to the financial statements:

- A description of the goods or services provided by the segment.
- Condensed statement of net assets that includes the following:
  - Total assets: Distinguishing between current assets, capital assets, and other assets (Amounts receivable from other funds or component units should be reported separately.)
  - Total liabilities: Distinguishing between current and longterm amounts (Amounts payable to other funds or component units should be reported separately.)
  - Total fund net assets: Distinguishing between restricted, unrestricted, and amounts invested in capital assets (net of related debt), with separate identification of expendable and nonexpendable components for restricted net assets, if appropriate
- Condensed statement of revenues, expenses, and changes in net assets:
  - Operating revenues by major sources
  - Operating expenses, with separate identification of depreciation expense and amortizations of long-lived assets
  - Operating income (loss)

- — Nonoperating revenues (expenses), with separate reporting of major revenues and expenses
- — Capital contributions and additions to permanent and term endowments
- — Extraordinary and special items
- — Transfers
- — Changes in net assets
- — Beginning and ending net assets

- Condensed statement of cash flows:
  - — Net cash provided (used by):
    a. Operating activities
    b. Noncapital financing activities
    c. Capital and related financing activities
    d. Investing activities
  - — Beginning and ending balances of cash (or cash and cash equivalent balances)

The *GASB Comprehensive Implementation Guide* provides the following examples for determining when segment information is presented in a governmental entity's financial statements:

Fact Pattern	*Suggested Guidance*
A City uses a single Enterprise Fund to account for its water and sewer operations. Although both operations are accounted for in a single fund, the city maintains separate asset, liability, revenue and expense accounts for each. There are outstanding revenue bonds that pertain to the water reservoir and distribution lines. The sewer operation has no long-term debt attributable to it. What are the segment reporting requirements for the Water and Sewer Fund?	Segment information for the water activity must be disclosed in the notes to the financial statements because that activity has "one or more revenue bonds or other revenue-backed debt instruments" outstanding. The sewer activity has no such debt and therefore segment information related to this activity does not have to be presented.
A public university has fifteen residence halls on its campus ten of which have individual bond debt secured by the room fee revenues of the specific dorm. Is	As defined earlier a segment is an activity that has an identifiable revenue stream that is dedicated to support revenue bonds or other revenue-backed debt

Fact Pattern	*Suggested Guidance*
the "identifiable activity" the entire group of fifteen residence halls, or only those with revenue bonds outstanding?	and has identifiable expenses, gains and losses, assets, and liabilities that are related to its activities. Whether each dorm or the dorm system constitutes the segment depends on the breadth of the pledged revenue. If the pledged revenue of a specific dorm applies only to the debt of that particular dorm then each dorm is considered a separate segment (ten segments). On the other hand, if the pledged revenues from all of the ten dorms apply to the dorm debt as a whole, then there is one segment (the dorm segment).

Professional judgment must be used to determine whether segment information for discretely presented component units must be made in the notes to the financial statements. GASB-34 states that the decision should be based on the following factors:

- The significance of the individual component unit to all component units presented on a discrete basis
- The relationship between the individual component unit and the primary government

The *GASB Comprehensive Implementation Guide* states that a condensed statement of cash flows is not required when segment disclosures are made for major discretely presented component units.

Presentation of Internal Service Funds in the Fund Financial Statements

The major fund reporting requirement does not apply to Internal Service Funds even though they are proprietary funds. Instead, all Internal Service Funds should be combined into a single column and presented on the face of the proprietary funds' financial statements. This column must be presented to the right of the total column for all Enterprise Funds. The Internal Service Funds column and the Enterprise Funds total column should not be added together.

(An example of the presentation of the financial statements of Internal Service Funds can be found in Exhibit 20-6, Exhibit 20-7, and Exhibit 20-8, in Chapter 20, "Comprehensive Annual Financial Report.")

GOVERNMENT-WIDE FINANCIAL STATEMENTS

Enterprise fund financial statements generally serve as the basis for the business-type activities column presentation in the government-wide financial statements. There is usually no need for a reconciliation between the government-wide financial statements and proprietary fund financial statements, because both sets of financial statements are based on the same measurement focus and basis of accounting (GASB-34, par. 104). However, the treatment of internal service fund activity within the government-wide financial statements does require additional consideration.

Integrating Internal Service Funds into Government-Wide Financial Statements

Internal Service Funds and similar activities should be eliminated to avoid doubling-up expenses and revenues in preparing the government activities column of the statement of activities. The effect of this approach is to adjust activities in an Internal Service Fund to a breakeven balance. That is, if the Internal Service Fund had a "net profit" for the year there should be a pro rata reduction in the charges made to the funds that used the Internal Service Fund's services for the year. Likewise, a net loss would require a pro rata adjustment that would increase the charges made to the various participating funds. After making these eliminations, any residual balances related to the Internal Service Fund's assets, liabilities, and net assets should generally be reported in the governmental activities column in the statement of net assets.

To illustrate the merging of an Internal Service Fund's accounts in the government-wide financial statements, assume the following preclosing trial balances exist at the end of a governmental entity's fiscal year:

Preclosing Trial for Governmental Activities

	Dr.	Cr.
Assets	16,000	
Liabilities		6,000
Program Revenues		39,000
Program A Expenses	10,000	
Program B Expenses	20,000	
Interest Expense	4,000	
Investment Income		1,000
Net Assets		4,000
Totals	50,000	50,000

Note: These amounts include all governmental funds (General Fund, Special Revenue Funds, Capital Projects Funds, Debt Service Funds, and Permanent Funds) adjusted from a modified accrual basis (as presented in the fund-level financial statements) to an accrual basis (which is the basis required in the government-wide financial statements).

Preclosing Trial Balance for Internal Service Fund

	Dr.	Cr.
Assets	4,000	
Liabilities		2,000
Revenues		5,000
Expenses	4,500	
Net Assets		1,500
Totals	8,500	8,500

Note: The Internal Service Fund balances are reported on an accrual basis at the fund financial statement level.

The activities accounted for in the Internal Service Fund resulted in a "net profit" of $500 ($5,000 – $4,500), which means that the operating expenses listed in the preclosing trial balance of government activities are overstated by $500. In order to merge the residual amounts of the Internal Service Fund into the government-activities column of the reporting entity, the following worksheet adjustments are made:

	Preclosing Trial Balance for Governmental Activities		*Eliminations Based on Internal Service Residual Balances*		*Preclosing Trial Balance for Governmental Activities Including Internal Service Residual Balances*	
	Dr.	Cr.	Dr.	Cr.	Dr.	Cr.
Assets	16,000		4,000		20,000	
Liabilities		6,000		2,000		8,000
Program Revenues		39,000				39,000
Program A Expenses	10,000			300	9,700	
Program B Expenses	20,000			200	19,800	
Interest Expense	4,000				4,000	
Investment Income		1,000				1,000
Net Assets		4,000		1,500		5,500
	50,000	50,000	4,000	4,000	53,500	53,500

Note: It is assumed that during the year the Internal Service Funds activities were provided to Program A (60%) and Program B (40%), which were reported in governmental funds.

Once the government activities have been adjusted to include residual values (including assets, liabilities, net assets, and operating activities), the statement of net assets and statement of activities must be formatted to reflect the standards established by GASB-34.

The government-wide financial statements are divided into governmental activities and business-type activities. Generally, as illustrated above, the activities conducted by an Internal Service Fund are related to government activities and therefore the residual amounts of the Internal Service Fund should be consolidated with other governmental funds and presented in the governmental activities column of the government-wide financial statements. However, the activities of an Internal Service Fund must be analyzed to determine whether they are government- or businesstype in nature, or both. If the activities are business-type in nature, the residual amounts must be consolidated with the business-type activities in the government-wide financial statements. In addition, the operating accounts reported by the Internal Service Fund must be analyzed to determine whether they should be used to compute the "net profit or loss" that is the basis for allocation to the governmental or business-type activities.

> **NOTE:** For a discussion of government-wide financial statements see Chapter 20, "Comprehensive Annual Financial Report."

Activities That Are Exclusively Government Activities

When the activities conducted by an Internal Service Fund are related to governmental activities rather than business-type activities, the residual balances of the fund are allocated to the government activities columns in the government-wide financial statements. However, several accounts may appear on the Internal Service Fund's operating statement (namely, interest expense, investment income, depreciation expense, and interfund transfers in/out) that must be considered before the residual amounts of the Internal Service Fund are allocated to the governmental activities column that appears in the government-wide financial statements.

Interest expense Generally, interest expense on debt issued by an Internal Service Fund is considered an indirect expense and should not be allocated as a direct expense to specific functional categories that appear on the statement of activities; rather, it should be presented as a single line item, appropriately labeled. For this reason, when an Internal Service Fund has interest expense, only the profit or loss before interest charges should be allocated to the governmental operating programs. The interest expense should be combined with other interest expense related to governmental activities and the single amount should be presented on the statement of activities.

To illustrate the allocation of Internal Service Fund accounts when interest expense exists for the fund, assume that in the previous example the preclosing trial balance for the Internal Service Fund is as follows:

	Dr.	Cr.
Assets	4,000	
Liabilities		2,000
Revenues		5,000
Expenses	4,400	
Interest Expense	100	
Net Assets		1,500
Totals	8,500	8,500

The activities accounted for in the Internal Service Fund result in a "net profit before interest expense" of $600 ($5,000 – $4,400); that amount is the basis for allocation to the program expenses reported in the governmental activities column of the statement of net assets. The interest expense of $100 is directly allocated to the interest expense row that appears in the statement. The eliminating entry under this circumstance is illustrated as follows:

	Preclosing Trial Balance for Governmental Activities		*Eliminations Based on Internal Service Residual Balances*		*Preclosing Trial Balance for Governmental Activities Including Internal Service Residual Balances*	
	Dr.	**Cr.**	**Dr.**	**Cr.**	**Dr.**	**Cr.**
Assets	16,000		4,000		20,000	
Liabilities		6,000		2,000		8,000
Program Revenues		39,000				39,000
Program A Expenses	10,000			360	9,640	
Program B Expenses	20,000			240	19,760	
Interest Expense	4,000		100		4,100	
Investment Income		1,000				1,000
Net Assets		4,000		1,500		5,500
	50,000	50,000	4,100	4,100	53,500	53,500

Investment income A fundamental concept in the formatting of the statement of activities is the identification of resource inflows to the governmental entities that are related to specific programs and those that are general in nature.

Based on the nature of an Internal Service Fund, investment income will usually be considered general revenue and reported in the lower section of the statement of activities. Therefore, when an Internal Service Fund has investment income, only the net profit or loss before investment income should be allocated to the operating programs. The investment income should be combined with other unrestricted income and presented as a separate line item in the statement of activities.

To illustrate the allocation of Internal Service Fund accounts when investment income exists for the fund, assume that in the previous example the preclosing trial balance for the Internal Service Fund is as follows:

	Dr.	Cr.
Assets	4,000	
Liabilities		2,000
Revenues		4,800
Expenses	4,400	
Interest Expense	100	
Investment Income		200
Net Assets		1,500
Totals	8,500	8,500

The activities accounted for in the Internal Service Fund result in a "net profit before interest expense and investment income" of $400 ($4,800 – $4,400); that amount is the basis for allocation to the program expenses reported in the governmental activities column of the statement of activities. The investment income of $200, as illustrated below, is combined with the investment income of the other governmental funds and presented as a single amount, as follows:

	Preclosing Trial Balance for Governmental Activities		*Eliminations Based on Internal Service Residual Balances*		*Preclosing Trial Balance for Governmental Activities Including Internal Service Residual Balances*	
	Dr.	Cr.	Dr.	Cr.	Dr.	Cr.
Assets	16,000		4,000		20,000	
Liabilities		6,000		2,000		8,000
Program Revenues		39,000				39,000
Program A Expenses	10,000			240	9,760	

Program B Expenses	20,000			160	19,840	
Interest Expense	4,000		100		4,100	
Investment Income		1,000		200		1,200
Net Assets		4,000		1,500		5,500
	50,000	50,000	4,100	4,100	53,700	53,700

Depreciation expense GASB-34 requires that depreciation expense be reported on the statement of activities as a direct expense of specific functional categories if the related capital asset can be identified with the functional or program activities. Because an Internal Service Fund bills various operating departments, depreciation expenses on capital assets held by the fund are directly related to the functional categories (public safety, health and sanitation, etc.) that use the services of the Internal Service Fund. For this reason, depreciation expense should be included in the computation of the net profit or loss allocated to the various programs presented in the statement of activities.

> **PRACTICE POINT:** Depreciation expense related to capital assets that are not identified with a particular functional category (such as the depreciation on city hall) does not have to be reported as a direct expense of specific functions but, rather, may be presented as a separate line item in the statement of activities or included in the general governmental functional category. However, when unallocated depreciation expense is reported as a separate line in the statement of activities it should be indicated on the face of the statement that the amount reported as depreciation expense represents only unallocated depreciation expense and not total depreciation expense.

Interfund transfers (nonreciprocal interfund activity) GASB-34 states that interfund transfers are a type of nonreciprocal transaction that represents interfund activities whereby the two parties to the events do not receive equivalent cash, goods, or services. Governmental funds should report transfers of this nature in their fund operating statements as other financing uses and other financial sources of funds. Proprietary funds should report this type of transfer in their activity statements after nonoperating revenues and nonoperating expenses.

Based on the nature of transfers in/out as defined in GASB-34, these transfers should not be considered when determining the amount of net profit or loss that must be allocated back to the various programs reported on the statement of activities.

Activities That Are Exclusively Business-Type Activities

When activities conducted by an Internal Service Fund are related to business-type activities rather than governmental activities, the residual balances of the fund are allocated to the business-type activities column in the government-wide financial statements.

To illustrate the consolidation of an Internal Service Fund's accounts in the government-wide financial statements when its activities are exclusively related to business-type activities, assume the following preclosing trial balances exist at the end of the fiscal year:

Preclosing Trial Balance for Business-Type Activities

	Dr.	Cr.
Assets	20,000	
Liabilities		5,000
Operating Revenues		47,000
Operating Expenses	40,000	
Nonoperating Revenues		10,000
Nonoperating Expenses	5,000	
Interest Expense	2,000	
Investment Income		1,000
Net Assets		4,000
Totals	67,000	67,000

Note: These amounts include all Enterprise Funds. Because Enterprise Funds are presented at the fund financial statement level using the accrual basis of accounting, these totals are the basis for preparing the business-type activities columns in the government-wide financial statements.

Preclosing Trial Balance for Internal Service Fund

	Dr.	Cr.
Assets	1,500	
Liabilities		2,000
Revenues		5,000
Expenses	7,000	
Net Assets		1,500
Totals	8,500	8,500

The activities accounted for in the Internal Service Fund resulted in a "net loss" of $2,000 ($5,000 – $7,000), which means that the expenses listed in the preclosing trial balance of business-type activities are understated by $2,000. In order to merge the residual amounts of the Internal Service Fund into the business-type activities column of the reporting entity, the following worksheet adjustments are made:

	Preclosing Trial Balance for Business-Type Activities		*Eliminations Based on Internal Service Residual Balances*		*Preclosing Trial Balance for Business-Type Activities Including Internal Service Residual Balances*	
	Dr.	**Cr.**	**Dr.**	**Cr.**	**Dr.**	**Cr.**
Assets	20,000		1,500		21,500	
Liabilities		5,000		2,000		7,000
Operating Revenues		47,000				47,000
Operating Expenses	40,000		2,000		42,000	
Nonoperating Revenues		10,000				10,000
Nonoperating Expenses	5,000				5,000	
Interest Expense	2,000				2,000	
Investment Income		1,000				1,000
Net Assets		4,000		1,500		5,500
Totals	67,000	67,000	3,500	3,500	70,500	70,500

Because the Internal Service Fund's activities exclusively support the services provided by Enterprise Funds, the assets, liabilities, and net assets of the Internal Service Fund are presented as part in the businesstype activities column of the statement of net assets and the additional expense (the net loss of $2,000 incurred in the Internal Service Fund) increases the operating expenses reported in the statement of activities.

Interest expense When interest expense is incurred by an Internal Service Fund that services only Enterprise Funds, the interest is directly related to business-type activities. That is, the funds could have been borrowed by the Internal Service Fund or directly by the Enterprise Funds. For this reason, interest expense under this circumstance should be used in determining the amount of net profit or loss incurred by the Internal Service Fund that should be allocated to business-type activities.

Investment income As explained earlier, investment income earned by an Internal Service Fund would generally not be considered in determining the amount of net income or net loss to be allocated to governmental activities. This concept also applies to Internal Service Funds that exclusively service Enterprise Funds except the investment income is presented in the statement of activities as a business-type activity.

Depreciation expense Depreciation expense of an Internal Service Fund that exclusively services Enterprise Funds is directly related to the activities of the Enterprise Funds. For this reason the net profit or loss incurred by an Internal Service Fund under this circumstance should include the charge for depreciation.

Interfund transfers (nonreciprocal interfund activity) Based on the nature of transfers in/out as defined in GASB-34, these transfers should not be considered when determining the amount of net profit or loss that must be allocated back to business-type activities when an Internal Service Fund provides services only to Enterprise Funds. Transfers in/out by the Internal Service Fund are reported as a business-type activity in the lower section of the statement of activities.

Activities That Support Predominantly Governmental Funds

When activities conducted by an Internal Service Fund predominantly support governmental activities but also support Enterprise Funds, the residual balances of the Internal Service Funds are for the most part allocated to the governmental activities column of the government-wide financial statements. However, a portion of the net income or loss related to services provided to the Enterprise Funds is allocated to business-type activities.

To illustrate the consolidation of an Internal Service Fund's accounts in the government-wide financial statements when its activities are predominantly related to governmental activities, assume the following preclosing trial balances exist at the end of the fiscal year:

Preclosing Trial Balance for Governmental Activities

	Dr.	Cr.
Assets	16,000	
Liabilities		6,000
Program Revenues		39,000
Program A Expenses	10,000	
Program B Expenses	20,000	
Interest Expense	4,000	
Investment Income		1,000
Net Assets		4,000
Totals	50,000	50,000

Preclosing Trial Balance for Business-Type Activities

	Dr.	Cr.
Assets	20,000	
Liabilities		5,000

Operating Revenues		47,000
Operating Expenses	40,000	
Nonoperating Revenues		10,000
Nonoperating Expenses	5,000	
Interest Expense	2,000	
Investment Income		1,000
Net Assets		4,000
Totals	67,000	67,000

Preclosing Trial Balance for Internal Service Fund

	Dr.	Cr.
Assets	1,500	
Liabilities		2,000
Revenues		5,000
Expenses	7,000	
Net Assets		1,500
Totals	8,500	8,500

During the year the Internal Service Fund billed the operating department of the General Fund for 80% (Programs A and B) of its activities and the balance was billed to Enterprise Funds. The activities accounted for in the Internal Service Fund resulted in a *net loss* of $2,000 ($5,000 – $7,000), which means that the expenses listed in the preclosing trial balance of governmental activities and business-type activities are understated. In order to consolidate the residual amounts of the Internal Service Fund into the governmental activities and business-type activities columns of the government-wide financial statements, the following worksheet adjustments are made:

	Preclosing Trial Balance for Governmental Activities		*Eliminations Based on Internal Service Residual Balances*		*Preclosing Trial Balance for Governmental Activities Including Internal Service Residual Balances*	
	Dr.	**Cr.**	**Dr.**	**Cr.**	**Dr.**	**Cr.**
Governmental Activities:						
Assets	16,000		(a)1,500		17,500	
Internal Balances			(b) 400		400	
Liabilities		6,000		(a) 2,000		8,000
Program Revenues		39,000				39,000
Program A Expenses	10,000		(a) 960		10,960	

	Dr.	Cr.	Dr.	Cr.	Dr.	Cr.
Program B						
Expenses	20,000		(a) 640		20,640	
Interest Expense	4,000				4,000	
Investment Income		1,000				1,000
Net Assets		4,000		(a) 1,500		5,500
Totals	50,000	50,000	3,500	3,500	53,500	53,500

	Preclosing Trial Balance for Business-Type Activities		*Eliminations Based on Internal Service Residual Balances*		*Preclosing Trial Balance for Business-Type Activities Including Internal Service Residual Balances*	
	Dr.	**Cr.**	**Dr.**	**Cr.**	**Dr.**	**Cr.**
Business-Type Activities:						
Assets	20,000				20,000	
Liabilities		5,000				5,000
Internal Balances				(b) 400		400
Operating Revenues		47,000				47,000
Operating Expenses	40,000		(a) 400		40,400	
Nonoperating Revenues		10,000				10,000
Nonoperating Expenses	5,000				5,000	
Interest Expense	2,000				2,000	
Investment Income		1,000				1,000
Net Assets		4,000				4,000
Totals	67,000	67,000	400	400	67,400	67,400

The first entry, (a), allocates the net loss back to the funds that used the services during the period in a manner similar to entries discussed earlier in this section. The second entry, (b), arises because the governmental activities subsidized business-type activities through a deficit incurred in the Internal Service Fund. In effect, the governmental activities paid some of the expenses for the Enterprise Fund. This is treated as an internal transaction and a "receivable" is created for the governmental activities column and a "payable" is created for the business-type activities column of the government-wide financial statements. Internal balances are presented on the face of the statement of net assets for both the governmental activities and the business-type activities, but they offset (net to zero) when totals are extended to the "reporting entity column" on the statement.

Differentiating between governmental and business-type activities The activities of an Internal Service Fund must be analyzed to determine whether account balances and transactions of the fund must be reported as a governmental activity or a business-type activity on the government-wide financial statements. The *GASB Comprehensive Implementation Guide* raises the issue of how the activities of a state board (accounted for as an Internal Service Fund) that manages investments for several state funds (Pension Trust Funds, Internal Service Funds, Enterprise Funds, and various governmental funds) should be reported in the government-wide financial statements. The state board's activities are financed exclusively by a fee that is charged to each participant. The *GASB Comprehensive Implementation Guide* points out that the activities of the state board should be reported in the governmental activities column in the government-wide financial statements. The fact that a high percentage of the state board's activity involved pension funds is irrelevant even though fiduciary fund financial statements are not presented at the government-wide financial statement level. The criterion to determine where to include an Internal Service Fund's balances is based on whether the fund services governmental funds or Enterprise Funds. Only if Enterprise Funds are the predominant or only participants in the state board's activities should the balances be presented in the business-type activities column.

Activities with External Parties

GASB-34 states that an "Internal Service Fund should be used only if the reporting government is the predominant participant in the activity." When external parties are the predominant participants in the services offered by a governmental entity, an Enterprise Fund should be used.

A governmental entity may establish an Internal Service Fund that has its predominant activities with other units of the reporting entity but for simplicity purposes also makes sales (of a nonpredominant amount) to external parties. Under this circumstance, the external sales and related cost of sales should not be used to determine the net profit or loss amount that is the basis for adjusting the expenses incurred in the governmental column of the statement of activities.

To illustrate the consolidation of an Internal Service Fund's accounts in the government-wide financial statements when sales are made to an external party and the activities of the fund are predominantly governmental activities, assume the following preclosing trial balances exist at the end of the fiscal year:

Preclosing Trial Balance for Governmental Activities

	Dr.	Cr.
Assets	16,000	
Liabilities		6,000
Program Revenues—General Government		29,000
Program Expenses—General Government	21,000	
Program Revenues—Other		10,000
Program Expenses—Other	9,000	
Interest Expense	4,000	
Investment Income		1,000
Net Assets		4,000
Totals	50,000	50,000

Preclosing Trial Balance for Internal Service Fund

	Dr.	Cr.
Assets	1,500	
Liabilities		2,000
Revenues		4,520
Revenues—External Parties		480
Expenses	7,000	
Net Assets		1,500
Totals	8,500	8,500

The sales to external parties are billed at approximately 20% above the direct cost incurred by the Internal Service Fund.

The activities accounted for in the Internal Service Fund resulted in a net loss of $2,000 ($5,000 – $7,000); however, the revenue from external parties and the related cost ($400) is not part of the basis used to allocate the results of operations to governmental activities.

The net loss to be allocated to governmental activities is computed as follows:

	Total	*Related to External Activities*	*Related to Internal Activities*
Revenues	$5,000	($480)	$4,520
Expenses	7,000	(400)	6,600
Net loss to be allocated			$2,080

In order to consolidate the residual amounts of the Internal Service Fund into the governmental activities columns of the government-wide financial statements, the following worksheet adjustments are made:

	Preclosing Trial Balance for Governmental Activities		*Eliminations Based on Internal Service Residual Balances*		*Preclosing Trial Balance for Governmental Activities Including Internal Service Residual Balances*	
	Dr.	**Cr.**	**Dr.**	**Cr.**	**Dr.**	**Cr.**
Assets	16,000		1,500		17,500	
Liabilities		6,000		2,000		8,000
Program Revenues—General Government		29,000		480		29,480
Program Expenses—General Government	21,000		400		21,400	
Program Revenues—Other		10,000				10,000
Program Expenses—Other	9,000		2,080		11,080	
Interest Expense	4,000				4,000	
Investment Income		1,000				1,000
Net Assets		4,000		1,500		5,500
Totals	50,000	50,000	3,980	3,980	53,980	53,980

OBSERVATION: In the above example it is assumed that the activity performed by the Internal Service Fund should be classified as general governmental expenses. For example, the activity could be data processing. For this reason, the amount related to external sales ($400) is classified as program revenues from general government activities and the related expense ($480) is classified as general government expenses in the statement of activities. The balance of the adjustment ($2,080) is allocated to specific programs (for example, public safety), which for simplicity are identified as "other program expenses." If the activity of the Internal Service Fund were predominantly related to business-type activities rather than governmental activities, the residual balances of the Internal Service Fund would be merged with other business-type activities.

Activities with Fiduciary Funds

In some instances, an Internal Service Fund provides services or goods to fiduciary funds. The *GASB Comprehensive Implementation Guide* states that in determining whether the services are predominantly provided to internal parties (therefore an Internal Service

Fund is appropriate) or predominantly provided to external parties (therefore an Enterprise Fund is appropriate), the activities with fiduciary funds should be considered internal. However, in folding the activities into the government-wide financial statements, activities with fiduciary funds should be treated as external transactions. In this circumstance, the external sales and related cost of sales should not be used to determine the net profit or loss amount (the look-back adjustment) that is the basis for adjusting the expenses incurred in the governmental column of the statement of activities.

REPORTING CASH FLOWS OF PROPRIETARY FUNDS

In November 1987, the FASB issued FAS-95 (Statement of Cash Flows), superseding APB-19 (Reporting Changes in Financial Position). The issuance of FAS-95 raised the question of whether governmental entities using proprietary fund accounting would have to prepare a statement of cash flows rather than a statement of changes in financial position. In September 1989, GASB issued GASB-9 (Reporting Cash Flows of Proprietary and Nonexpendable Trust Funds and Governmental Entities That Use Proprietary Fund Accounting) to provide authoritative guidance in the preparation of cash flow statements for proprietary fund types. Proprietary funds cannot use the standards established by FAS-95 to prepare their cash flow statements.

GASB-9 essentially adopts the fundamental concepts established in FAS-95. The fundamental differences between GASB-9 and FAS-95 are as follows:

- GASB-9 requires the use of four categories, rather than three, to summarize cash activity of proprietary fund types.
- In GASB-9, cash flows from operating activities are more narrowly defined for proprietary fund types.

OBSERVATION: The standards adopted in GASB-9 deviate from the standards and the language established in FAS-95. The GASB did not wish to create a comparability issue by having two separate sets of reporting standards with respect to the preparation of the statement of cash flows: a set of standards for commercial enterprises and a set of standards for proprietary fund types. GASB-9 did not address all of the issues addressed in FAS-95 because the GASB believed that such issues seldom would be encountered in the governmental sector. When preparing the financial statements for a proprietary fund type, if the accountant encounters an accounting issue that is not addressed in GASB-9 but is addressed in FAS-95, the guidance established by FAS-95, as well as amendments to GASB-9, may be used.

GASB-9, as amended by GASB-34, establishes the requirement for presentation of a statement of cash flows for the following entities (GASB-9, par. 5):

- Proprietary funds
- All governmental entities that follow proprietary fund accounting standards

The second category of entities includes public benefit corporations and authorities, governmental utilities, and governmental hospitals. The category also includes governmental colleges and universities that follow accounting and reporting standards established by NCGA-1 (Governmental Accounting and Financial Reporting Principles). Thus, statements of cash flows must be presented for proprietary funds of governmental colleges and universities that follow standards established by NCGA-1 (GASB-9, par. 5).

The following entities are exempt from the standards established by GASB-9 (GASB-9, par. 5):

- Public employee retirement systems (PERS)
- Pension Trust Funds
- Investment Trust Funds

Basic Requirement and Purpose

GASB-9 establishes the statement of cash flows as a basic financial statement for proprietary fund types (GASB-9, par. 6).

FASB Concepts Statement No. (1) (FASB:CS-1) (Objectives of Financial Reporting by Business Enterprises) concludes that one of the purposes of financial reporting is to "help present and potential investors and creditors and other users in assessing the amounts, timing, and uncertainty of prospective cash receipts from dividends or interest and the proceeds from the sale, redemption, or maturity of securities or loans." Because proprietary fund accounting is essentially the same as commercial accounting, the GASB decided that the presentation of a statement of cash flows provides user groups with relevant information.

Specifically, GASB-9 notes that the statement of cash flows, along with related disclosures and information in other financial statements, can be useful in assessing the following (GASB-9, par. 7):

- Ability of an entity to generate future cash flows
- Ability of an entity to pay its debt as the debt matures
- Need to seek outside financing
- Reasons for differences between cash flows from operations and operating income (or net income if operating income

is not separately presented in the entity's statement of operations)

- Effect on an entity's financial position of cash and noncash transactions from investing, capital, and financing activities

These assessments can be made when a statement of cash flows is prepared in a manner that summarizes (1) cash flows from operations, (2) noncapital financing activities, (3) capital and related financing activities, and (4) investing activities. In addition, noncash transactions that have an effect on the entity's financial position should be presented. Finally, there should be a reconciliation between operating income (or net income if operating income is not presented) and net cash flow from operating activities (GASB-9, pars. 6–7).

> **OBSERVATION:** GASB-9 requires that the amounts per the statement of cash flows "be easily traceable to similarly titled line items or subtotals shown in the statement of financial position"; however, there is no requirement that a single amount identified on the statement of cash flows be exactly the same as a single amount on the statement of financial position. For example, the ending balance of cash and cash equivalents on the statement of cash flows could be traceable to two balances on the statement of financial position (unrestricted and restricted cash and cash equivalents). Because it is obvious to a reader that cash amounts include both restricted and unrestricted amounts, the requirements of GASB-9 are satisfied. It is, of course, a matter of professional judgment to determine what is "easily traceable" from one financial statement to another. If it is concluded that the information is not easily traceable, one option could be to include a reconciliation at the bottom of either financial statement that would easily tie the two financial statements together and therefore satisfy the reporting requirement established by GASB-9.

Focus of Statement

APB-19 allowed entities to use funds as the focal point in the preparation of the statement of changes in financial position. For example, some entities defined funds as working capital, others as cash, and still others used a combination of working capital accounts to define funds. Thus, there was no single definition of funds, and the result was a lack of comparability between different entities' financial statements (GASB-9, par. 8).

With the issuance of FAS-95, a more rigid focal point was constructed: a statement of cash flows must focus on summarizing activities that have an effect on cash, or cash and cash equivalents. GASB-9 uses the same focal point as FAS-95.

In addition to selecting a more definite focal point, the GASB requires that the information on the statement of cash flows be easily traceable to the information on the balance sheet. For example, if an entity selects cash and cash equivalents as the focal point of the statement of cash flows (GASB-9, par. 8):

- The statement of cash flows should show a reconciliation between the beginning and ending balances of cash and cash equivalents, and
- The same beginning and ending balances of cash and cash equivalents should be presented in the entity's balance sheets.

Cash includes amounts that are subject to immediate use by the entity. Examples are

- Cash on hand
- Cash on (demand) deposit with financial institutions that can be withdrawn without prior notice or penalty
- Other deposits or cash management pools that have characteristics similar to demand deposit accounts (for example, additional funds may be deposited to the account at any time and withdrawals can be made at any time without prior notice or penalty)

Cash equivalents are short-term, highly liquid investments that have both of the following characteristics:

- Readily convertible to known amounts of cash
- Mature in such a short period of time that their values are effectively immune from changes in interest rates

Examples of cash equivalents provided by GASB-9 include treasury bills, commercial paper, certificates of deposit, money market funds, and cash management pools (GASB-9, par. 10).

> **PRACTICE POINT:** To be considered a cash equivalent, amounts in cash management pools must be the equivalent of demand deposit accounts (free to deposit and free to withdraw). If amounts in cash management pools are not considered to be cash equivalents, transactions affecting those accounts should be classified as investing activities on the statement of cash flows.

For an investment to be considered a cash equivalent, it must mature no more than three months after the date it is purchased (GASB-9, par. 8).

The GASB allows the focal point of the statement of cash flows to include cash equivalents because cash equivalents generally are acquired as part of a governmental entity's cash management strategy.

Excess cash is invested because it is available, not because the strategy is part of the entity's investment or financing strategy (GASB-9, par. 10).

If an entity believes that cash equivalents are acquired for reasons other than cash management, cash equivalents (all or some of the cash equivalents) do not have to be part of the focus (analyzing the effect of activities on cash and cash equivalents) of the preparation of the statement of cash flows (GASB-9, par. 10).

An entity should establish and disclose its treatment of cash equivalents in the preparation of the statement of cash flows. The policy should be disclosed in the entity's summary of significant accounting policies. If the policy is subsequently altered, the alteration is considered a change in an accounting principle that must be accounted for by restating prior years' financial statements presented on a comparative basis (GASB-9, par. 11).

> **PRACTICE POINT:** Some proprietary fund types have restricted assets that include cash and cash equivalents. For cash flow reporting purposes, unrestricted cash and unrestricted cash equivalents should be included with restricted cash and restricted cash equivalents. As noted in GASB-9, a governmental entity may elect to treat its unrestricted cash equivalents as investments. The same election can be made for restricted cash equivalents. The method of defining cash equivalents should be disclosed in the entity's summary of significant accounting policies.

Cash Flow Amounts

A fundamental rule in financial reporting is that amounts and accounts should not be netted. For example, an amount due to a proprietary fund from a vendor and an amount due from the same vendor should not be netted for financial reporting purposes. This concept is maintained for the preparation of the statement of cash flows, except as explained in this section (GASB-9, par. 12).

GASB-9 states that gross amounts of related receipts and payments that have the following characteristics may be netted (GASB-9, par. 13):

- Transactions have a quick turnover rate.
- Transaction amounts are large.
- Transactions result in instruments with short maturities. (The instruments mature no more than three months after the date of purchase or due on demand.)

Such transactions include investments (other than cash equivalents), loans receivable, and debt (GASB-9, par. 13).

For example, if a proprietary fund type entered into transactions during the year that resulted in the (nonoperating) borrowing of $10,000,000 from other funds and the loaning of $12,000,000 to other funds, the net amount of $2,000,000 could be presented in the statement of cash flows for the year.

GASB-9 provides one other set of transactions that may be netted. Net purchases and sales of a governmental entity's highly liquid investments may be reported on a net basis under the following circumstances (GASB-9, par. 14):

- During the year, substantially all of the entity's assets consisted of highly liquid investments or other assets that are readily marketable.
- During the year, the entity had relatively no debt. "Relativity" is defined as the amount of average debt to the amount of average assets during the year.

Entities that would qualify for netting based on the previously listed criteria would function as investment accounts because there would be substantially no operating assets or debt.

> **OBSERVATION:** FAS-102 exempts certain common trust funds from the requirement to prepare a statement of cash flows. Some governmental entities are similar to the common trust funds exempted by FAS-102. However, the GASB stated that such governmental entities must prepare a statement of cash flows. GASB-9 does not allow such governmental entities to substitute a statement of changes in net assets for a statement of cash flows, but they may net the purchases and sales of highly liquid investments.

Classification of Cash Flows

The format of the statement of cash flows adopted by GASB-9 provides for four main categories of cash flows, unlike FAS-95, which requires three main categories. The categories to be used by a proprietary fund type are (1) cash flows from operating activities, (2) cash flows from noncapital financing activities, (3) cash flows from capital and related financing activities, and (4) cash flows from investing activities. Thus, the general format of a statement of cash flows for a proprietary fund type would appear as follows (GASB-9, par. 15):

Cash flows from operating activities	$X
Cash flows from noncapital financing activities	X
Cash flows from capital and related financing activities	X

Cash flows from investing activities	X
Net increase in cash (or cash and cash equivalents)	X
Cash (or cash and cash equivalents) at 6/30/X4	X
Cash (or cash and cash equivalents) at 6/30/X5	$X

The amount of cash related to each of the four categories includes transactions that increase cash as well as those that decrease cash. Furthermore, the net amount for each category should be described as either net cash provided or net cash used (GASB-9, par. 15).

Operating Cash Flows

All transactions that are not classified as capital and related financing activities, noncapital financing activities, or investing activities are classified as operating activities. Thus, operating activities are related to the governmental entity's delivery of its goods and/or services to its customers (operating revenues) and the use of resources related to the delivery of its goods and/or services (operating expenses). Cash flows related to these activities should be used to compute net cash flows from operations (GASB-9, par. 16).

The specific types of cash inflows and outflows from operations are presented in the summary below. Related cash inflows and outflows are paired (GASB-9, pars. 17–18).

In addition to the categories listed, GASB-9 identifies transactions related to *certain* loan programs that should be used to determine the net cash flows from operations. Conceptually, cash flows related to loans would be considered investing activities. However, some loan programs are established as part of the strategy to achieve social and educational goals of the governmental entity and should therefore be considered operating activities. For example, cash flows from student loan programs would be considered part of a governmental entity's operating activities and would be used to determine cash flows from operations for the year (GASB-9, par. 19).

Operating cash flows would include both cash payments to the recipients of these certain loan programs and repayments, including interest, from the recipients (GASB-9, par. 19).

If a governmental entity issues bonds to finance these certain loan programs, the proceeds and repayments, including interest, would be classified as noncapital financing activities (GASB-9, par. 19).

Cash flows from operations do not include some transactions and events, even though these transactions and events may be cash flows and may appear on the entity's statement of operations. These transactions and events include the following (the parenthetical comment describes where the item would be presented in the statement of cash flows):

- Interest payments on capital debt (cash flows from capital and related financing activities)

- Interest payments on noncapital debt (cash flows from noncapital financing activities)
- Interest receipts from investments (cash flows from investing activities)
- Subsidies to finance operating deficits (cash flows from noncapital financing activities)

Cash Inflows: Operating Activities	*Cash Outflows: Operating Activities*
Receipts from the sale of goods or services, including collections on trade accounts and short-term and long-term trade notes receivable	Payments for services and goods held for resale, including payments on trade accounts and short-term and long-term trade notes payable
	Payments for other goods or services
	Payments for employees services
Receipts from interfund services provided	Payments for interfund services used, including payments in lieu of taxes that are payments for, and reasonably equivalent in value to, service provided
Receipts from grants for specific activities that would be considered operating activities of the entity making the grant	Payments of grants for specific activities to other governmental entities or organizations that would be considered operating activities of the entity making the grant
Receipts from interfund reimbursements	Payments for taxes, duties, fines, and other fees or penalties
All other receipts that cannot be classified as capital and related financing, noncapital financing, or investing activities	All other payments that cannot be classified as capital and related financing, noncapital financing, or investing activities

Under FAS-95, the elements previously listed would be used to compute cash flows from operations. However, GASB-9 states that these activities should not be classified as operational cash flows.

The cash flows from operating activities is a residual category. That is, if a transaction cannot be classified into one of the other three categories discussed in the following section, the transaction is placed in the operating activities category by default.

Cash flows to/from component units GASB-9 requires that the direct method be used in formatting the cash flows from operating activities category and that there be a separate reporting of cash flows from interfund services provided and used; however, there is no requirement that there be a separate reporting for cash transactions with component units. The *GASB Comprehensive Implementation Guide* points out that while the latter category is not mandated, a governmental entity may, if it so desires, present such transactions in its operating activities section.

> **PRACTICE POINT:** GASB-34, paragraph 128, requires that the notes to the financial statements also describe the nature and amount of significant transactions between major component units and the primary government and other component units.

Noncapital Financing Cash Flows

GASB-9 created a classification of cash flows that was not established by FAS-95. Cash flows related to noncapital financing activities must be presented separately on a proprietary fund type's statement of cash flows. The noncapital financing category comprises transactions related to operating debt and subsidies. For example, borrowing and repaying funds (including interest) for purposes other than acquiring, constructing, or improving capital assets would be considered a noncapital financing activity (GASB-9, par. 20).

The specific types of cash inflows and outflows from noncapital financing activities are presented in the following summary. Where appropriate, related cash inflows and outflows are paired (GASB-9, pars. 21–22).

GASB-9 notes that in the previous classification, cash payments of grants to another government or organization are not considered to be noncapital financing activities when the specific activity that the grant is to be used for is considered to be an operating activity by the grantor. As noted in footnote 10, it is irrelevant whether the grantee actually uses the grant as an operating subsidy or for capital purposes (GASB-9, par. 22).

Capital and Related Financing Cash Flows

Cash flow expenditures for the acquisition of capital assets used in the entity's operations and the financing of those activities should be classified as cash flows from capital and related financing activities on the statement of cash flows. Also, repayments on debt issued to finance the acquisition, construction, or improvement of capital assets would be included in this category. Finally, the category would include payments for capital assets acquired from vendors on credit (GASB-9, par. 23).

The specific types of cash inflows and outflows from capital and related financing activities are presented in the following summary. Where appropriate, related cash inflows and outflows are paired (GASB-9, pars. 24–25).

Cash Inflows: Noncapital Financing Activities	*Cash Outflows: Noncapital Financing Activities*
Receipts from issuing bonds, notes, and other instruments not related to the acquisition, construction, or improvement of capital assets	Repayments of funds borrowed not related to the acquisition, construction, or improvement of capital assets
	Payments of interest on liabilities incurred for purposes other than acquiring, constructing, or improving capital assets
Receipts from grants or subsidies except (1) amounts restricted for capital purposes and (2) amounts considered to be operating activities by the governmental unit making the grant or providing the subsidy	Payments of grants or subsidies to other governmental entities or organizations except those that are considered to be for activities that would be considered operating unit activities by the governmental unit making the grant or providing the subsidy
Receipts from other funds except (1) those amounts that are clearly attributable to acquisition, construction, or improvement of capital assets, (2) interfund service provided, and (3) reimbursement for operating transactions	Payments to other funds, except for interfund services used
Receipts from property and other taxes collected for the entity and not restricted to capital purposes	

PRACTICE POINT: FAS-95 classifies the construction, acquisition, and improvement of capital assets as investing activities, while GASB-9 classifies them as capital and related financing cash flows activities. FAS-95 classifies all financing, capital and noncapital, as financing activities, while GASB-9 classifies them as capital and related financing cash flows activities or noncapital activities, depending on their character. Finally, FAS-95 classifies cash payments for interest expense as operating activities, while GASB-9 classifies (1) interest payments on capital debt as part of capital and related financing cash flows activities and (2) interest payments on noncapital debt as part of noncapital financing activities.

Cash Inflows: Capital and Related Financing Activities	*Cash Outflows: Capital and Related Financing Activities*
Receipts from the issuance or refunding of bonds, mortgages, notes, and other (short-term or long-term) borrowings that are clearly related to the acquisition, construction, or improvement of capital assets	Payments to retire or refunding of obligations specifically used to acquire, construct, or improve capital assets Payments to vendors who provided the financing for the acquisition, construction, or improvement of capital assets Payments for interest on obligations that were used to acquire, construct, or improve capital assets
	Payments to acquire, construct, or improve capital assets
Receipts from capital grants	
Receipts from other funds, other governments, and other organizations or individuals that are for the specific purpose of defraying the cost of acquiring, constructing, or improving capital assets	
Receipts from the sale of capital assets	
Receipts from an insurance policy that provides coverage against the theft or destruction of capital assets	
Receipts from special assessments, property taxes, or other taxes levied to specifically finance the acquisition, construction, or improvement of capital assets	

Investing Cash Flows

The fourth category of transactions on the statement of cash flows relates to investing activities. This category is narrowly defined and is limited to cash payments to other loans and the collection of cash receipts for those loans, and payments for acquiring debt and equity instruments and proceeds from the liquidation of debt and equity investments. The exception for the payment and subsequent receipt of loans in this category is that program loans are considered operating activities (GASB-9, par. 26).

The specific types of cash inflows and outflows from investing activities are presented in the following summary. Where appropriate, related cash inflows and outflows are paired (GASB-9, pars. 27–28).

> **PRACTICE POINT:** FAS-95 classifies investment earnings (dividends and interest) as an operating activity, whereas GASB-9 classifies such earnings as an investing activity.

Capital Distinguished from Noncapital Financing

In most debt transactions, it is apparent whether the debt has been issued to construct, acquire, or improve capital assets and therefore the proceeds and subsequent repayments of the principal and interest related to the debt should be classified as capital financing activities on the statement of cash flows (GASB-9, par. 29).

The GASB did recognize, however, that in some instances distinguishing capital financing from noncapital financing may not be obvious. Therefore, GASB-9 provides the following additional guidance (GASB-9, par. 29):

- When debt is issued and it is not clear that the purpose of issuing the debt was to construct, acquire, or improve capital assets, the issuance of the debt and the subsequent debt service payments (principal and interest) should be classified as noncapital financing activities on the statement of cash flows.
- When capital debt has been issued but the related capital asset has been sold, abandoned, etc., the debt service payments on the original capital debt should continue to be classified as capital financing activities on the statement of cash flows.

Cash Inflows: Investing Activities	*Cash Outflows: Investing Activities*
Receipts from loan collections, with the exception of program loans	Loans made to other parties, with the exception of program loans

Cash Inflows: Investing Activities	*Cash Outflows: Investing Activities*
Receipts from the sale of invest-in debt instruments instruments issued by other entities except for the sale of investments that are considered to be cash equivalents	Payments for investing in debt instruments issued by other entities except for purchases of investments that are considered to be cash equivalents
Receipts from the sale of investments in equity instruments	Payments for investments in instru-ments equity instruments
Receipts that represent the return of investments in equity instruments	
Receipts of interest and dividends on investments and loans, except for program loans	
Withdrawals from investment pools that are not used as demand deposits	Deposits to investment pools that are not used as demand deposits

- When capital debt is decreased through a refunding, the proceeds from the new debt and the payment to retire the old debt should be classified as capital financing activities. In addition, subsequent debt service payments on the new debt should be classified as capital financing activities on the statement of cash flows.

In the final guideline, debt may be issued to decrease capital debt but the proceeds from the refunding may exceed the amount needed to retire the capital debt. Under this circumstance, the use of the excess funds determines how the proceeds from the issuance of the debt and subsequent debt service payments should be classified. For example, assume that $1,000,000 of new debt (5-year, 10%, serial bonds) is issued to refund $980,000 of capital debt and the excess ($20,000) is used for operating purposes. The following example describes how the transaction would affect the statement of cash flows, assuming the transaction occurred on the last day of the governmental entity's fiscal year (GASB-9, par. 29):

	Year of Refunding	*Subsequent Years*
Cash flows from operating activities:		
Operating expense	$ (20,000)	
Cash flows from capital and related financing activities:		
Issuance of debt	980,000	
Retirement of debt	(980,000)	
Retirement of serial debt ($980,000/5 years)		$ (196,000)
Interest on serial debt ($980,000 × 10%)		(98,000)

Cash flows from noncapital financing activities:		
Issuance of operating debt	20,000	
Retirement of serial debt ($20,000/5 years)		(4,000)
Interest on serial debt ($20,000 10%)		(2,000)

OBSERVATION: The classification of capital and related financing activities is dependent on the definition of a capital asset. While GASB-9 does not attempt to define a capital asset, it is noted in Appendix A to the Statement that the accounting treatment for a particular transaction would provide guidance in determining whether an asset is a capital asset. For example, if a lease agreement is capitalized based on the guidelines established by FAS-13 (Accounting for Leases), as amended, cash flows related to the transaction would be classified as a cash flow from capital and related financing activities. In addition, transactions related to both tangible and intangible assets should be included in the capital and related financing activities grouping. For example, the acquisition of water rights would be considered a capital transaction.

Formatting the Statement of Cash Flows

The net amount of cash flows from each of the four categories should be shown on the statement of cash flows. In addition, the effects of those net amounts should be shown in a manner that reconciles the beginning balance of cash, or cash and cash equivalents, to the ending balance of cash, or cash and cash equivalents (GASB-9, par. 30).

Proprietary funds should prepare a statement of cash flows based on the guidance established by GASB-9, except the statement of cash flows should be formatted based on the *direct method* in computing cash flows from operating activities. The statement of cash flows would be supplemented with a reconciliation of operating cash flows and operating income (the indirect method) (GASB-9, par. 30; GASB-34, par. 105).

PRACTICE POINT: Before the issuance of GASB-34 (Basic Financial Statements—and Management's Discussion and Analysis—for State and Local Governments), a governmental entity could use either the direct method or the indirect method.

Under the direct method, cash flows from operating activities are presented by major categories. At a minimum, the following categories must be presented (GASB-9, par. 31):

- Receipts from customers
- Receipts from interfund services provided
- Receipts from other operating activities

- Payments to other suppliers of goods and/or services
- Payments to employees
- Payments for interfund services used, including payments in lieu of taxes that are payments for, and reasonably equivalent in value to, services provided
- Payments for other operating activities

The governmental entity is not limited to the categories listed, and additional categories should be used if the usefulness of the financial statements is enhanced (GASB-9, par. 31).

In computing amounts for operating activities under the direct method, the accrual amount on the statement of operations is converted to a cash amount by taking into consideration related accruals and deferrals on the balance sheet. For example, to compute cash receipts from customers, the accrual sales figure would be adjusted by the net change for the year in customer receivables and deferred customer revenues (GASB-9, par. 32).

Under the indirect method (supplemented presentation), net cash flow from operating activities would be determined by adjusting operating income. If the entity does not present operating income on its statement of operations, net cash flow from operating activities would be computed by adjusting net income.

Using the indirect method, the amount of net cash flows from operating activities is computed by adding or subtracting amounts that appear on the statement of operations but do not provide or use cash. For example, depreciation expense is presented on the statement of operations but depreciation is not a cash flow. Therefore depreciation expense is added to operating income. Thus, cost allocations (depreciation and amortization), deferrals, and accruals must be added or subtracted to operating income in order to convert operating income to net cash flow from operating activities (GASB-9, par. 32).

If the governmental entity does not present operating income on its statement of operations, the amounts that differentiate operating income and net income must be added to or subtracted from net income. Generally, transactions such as the following must be added to or subtracted from net income in order to compute operating income (loss) using net income as the starting point (GASB-9, par. 32):

- Interest income (subtract from net income)
- Interest expense (add to net income)
- Gain on sale of capital assets (subtract from net income)
- Loss on sale of capital assets (add to net income)
- Grants from other governments (subtract from net income)
- Grants to other governments (add to net income)

- Operating transfers in (subtract from net income)
- Operating transfers out (add to net income)

The reconciliation should include all major classes of reconciling items, including, at a minimum, the following (GASB-9, par. 33):

- Net change in receivables related to operations
- Net change in inventories
- Net change in payables related to operations

The governmental entity is not limited to the three categories, and additional categories should be used if the usefulness of the financial statements is enhanced (GASB-9, par. 33).

Except for the netting convention allowed, cash inflows and cash outflows in each major section of the statement of cash flows should be shown at gross amounts. For example, assume a governmental entity has borrowed $10,000,000 for capital expenditures during the year and has repaid $8,000,000 to reduce capital debt during the same year. In the section titled "Cash Flows from Capital and Related Financing Activities," an inflow of $10,000,000 and an outflow of $8,000,000 would be disclosed separately, rather than a single net cash inflow of $2,000,000 (GASB-9, par. 35).

In preparing a statement of cash flows for an individual proprietary fund type, the gross amounts of interfund cash transfers should be presented in the appropriate category. In preparing combined and combining statements of cash flows for all proprietary funds, interfund transfers may be eliminated under the following conditions (GASB-9, par. 36):

- Interfund transfers are eliminated in preparing other combined and combining financial statements.
- Interfund eliminations made as part of preparing combined or combining statements of cash flows should be apparent from the headings or disclosed in a note.

Combined or combining statements of cash flows should be prepared using only the direct method of presenting cash flows from operations.

Noncash Investing, Capital, and Financing Activities

Certain transactions may have a significant impact on the financial position of a governmental entity but may not affect, or may only partially affect, the entity's cash position. For example, a governmental entity may acquire equipment by issuing a long-term note. While the transaction does not affect cash, it does have an effect on the entity's balance sheet (GASB-9, par. 37).

GASB-9 states that such transactions should be adequately described in a separate schedule. The format of the schedule may be narrative or tabular. In addition, the schedule may be presented on the same page as the entity's statement of cash flows (GASB-9, par. 37).

Examples of transactions that should be presented in a governmental entity's schedule of noncash investing, capital, and financing activities include the following (GASB-9, par. 37):

- Acquiring property, plant, and equipment through deferred payment plans
- Acquiring property rights through lease contracts that must be capitalized as required by FAS-13
- Acquiring property through an exchange of property
- Retiring debt through the issuance of other debt
- Retiring debt by giving property to a debtor

OBSERVATION: The concept of reporting noncash investing, capital, and financing activities, commonly referred to as "the all financial resources approach," was established by APB-19.

Some transactions will have both a cash and a noncash component. Under this circumstance, only the cash portion of the transactions should be displayed in the statement of cash flows, and the noncash portion should be presented in the schedule of noncash investing, capital, and financing activities. For example, assume that an entity purchases $100,000 of equipment by making a down payment of $20,000 and signing a note for the balance. The $20,000 cash payment is classified on the statement of cash flows as a cash outflow in the capital and related financing activities category, and the longterm financing of $80,000 is presented in the schedule supporting the statement of cash flows (GASB-9, par. 37).

PRACTICE POINT: The *GASB Comprehensive Implementation Guide* notes that noncash transactions (and transactions that involve both cash and noncash elements) must be reported in a schedule that "clearly describes the cash and noncash aspects of transactions involving similar items" and that schedule may be reported on the face of the statement or on a separate page that references the statement. The schedule may be set up as a narrative format or a tabular format. Noncash transactions should not be reported only in a note to the financial statements.

Cash Overdraft Position

An overdraft position creates a presentation problem on the statement of cash flows because of the treatment of a negative cash position on an entity's balance sheet. On the balance sheet the cash overdraft must be presented as a current liability rather than as negative asset, because the negative asset concept has no meaning in financial reporting. That means that the change in cash for the period is determined by the difference between the beginning balance of cash and an assumed zero balance in cash at the end of the period. Unless there is an adjustment to the statement of cash flows, the net change (decrease) in cash for the period will be greater on the statement of cash flows than the implied change as interpreted on the comparative balance sheet.

This difference can be removed by making an adjustment (increase) to the noncapital financing activities on the statement of cash flows. The adjustment is based on the assumption that the cash overdraft is covered by the bank through a loan to the entity. The adjustment shown in the "cash flows from noncapital financing activities" category on the statement of cash flows should clearly explain the nature of the assumption. For example, the line item could be labeled "cash overdraft position assumed to be financed" or the adjustment could be cross-referenced to a note that would explain the entity's (negative) cash position and the nature of the financing assumption. In the following period, it would be assumed that the "loan" from the bank is repaid by showing an assumed loan repayment as a noncapital financing activity.

Illustration Exhibit 7-1 is an example of a statement of cash flows based on the requirements established by GASB-9, as amended. As required by GASB-34, the direct method is used to determine cash flows from operating activities.

EXHIBIT 7-1 ILLUSTRATION
Enterprise Fund
Statement of Cash Flows
For Year Ended June 30, 20X5

Cash flows from operating activities:		
Cash received from customers	$ 990,000	
Cash operating grants received from other governments	50,000	
Cash payments for goods and services	(270,000)	
Cash payments to employees	(620,000)	
Internal activity payments to other funds	(40,000)	
Net cash provided by operating activities		$ 110,000
Cash flows from noncapital financing activities:		
Proceeds from issuing long-term debt	$ 100,000	

Operating subsidies received from other governments	20,000	
Tax receipts collected by other governmental agencies	10,000	
Repayments of revenue bonds	(240,000)	
Interest paid	(30,000)	
Net cash used for noncapital financing activities		$ (140,000)
Cash flows from capital and related financing activities:		
Proceeds from issuing bonds	$ 100,000	
Receipts from capital grants	90,000	
Proceeds from sale of capital assets	30,000	
Payments for capital acquisitions	(150,000)	
Principal repayments	$ (50,000)	
Interest paid	(40,000)	
Net cash used for capital and related financing activities		$ (20,000)
Cash flows from investing activities:		
Proceeds from sale of investments	$ 90,000	
Receipts of interest and dividends	30,000	
Payments for investment	(40,000)	
Net cash provided from investing activities		$ 80,000
Net increase in cash and cash equivalents		30,000
Cash and cash equivalents 6/30/X4		20,000
Cash and cash equivalents 6/30/X5		$ 50,000
Reconciliation of operating income to net cash provided by operating activities:		
Operating income		$ 50,000
Adjustments to reconcile operating income to net cash provided by operating activities:		
Depreciation expense	$ 100,000	
Increase in customer receivables	(90,000)	
Decrease in inventories	10,000	
Increase in accounts payables	30,000	
Net decrease in other operating net assets	10,000	
Total adjustments		60,000
Net cash provided by operating activities		$ 110,000

CHAPTER 8
FIDUCIARY FUNDS

CONTENTS

INTRODUCTION

Fiduciary funds are used to account for assets held by a governmental entity for other parties (either as a trustee or as an agent) and that cannot be used to finance the governmental entity's own operating programs, which includes

- Pension (and other employee benefit) Trust Funds
- Investment Trust Funds

- Private Trust Funds
- Agency Funds

The three trust funds are used to report resources and activities when the governmental entity is acting as a trustee (i.e., in a fiduciary capacity) for individuals, private organizations, and other governments. GASB-34 states that the three trust funds are distinguished from an Agency Fund in that the trust funds are generally characterized "by the existence of a trust agreement that affects the degree of management involvement and the length of time that the resources are held" (GASB-34, par. 69).

PENSION (AND OTHER EMPLOYEE BENEFIT) TRUST FUNDS

Pension (and other employee benefit) Trust Funds are used to account for resources held in trust for employees and their beneficiaries based on defined benefit pension agreements, defined contribution agreements, other postemployment benefit agreements, and other employee benefit arrangements (GASB-34, par. 70).

Defined benefit pension plans are subject to the standards established by GASB-25 (Financial Reporting for Defined Benefit Pension Plans and Notes Disclosures for Defined Contribution Plans).

> **PRACTICE POINT:** Questions often arise as to when a government's pension or other postemployment benefit plans should be presented as Pension (or Other Benefit) Trust Funds within the government's financial statements. Such trust funds should be used when the government has the fiduciary responsibility for administering the plan. For example, a local government that maintains and administers its own sole-employer defined-benefit pension plan should report the plan as a Pension Trust Fund within its fiduciary fund financial statements. However, a local government that merely participates in an agent multiple-employer or cost-sharing plan administered and managed by another government or third party would not report the plan as a Trust Fund within its financial statements.

Assets held and benefits paid by pension plans generally are administered by a public employee retirement system (PERS) or by a trust fund (in practice, the terms PERS and Pension Trust Funds are used interchangeably along with defined benefit pension plans) established by a governmental employer or the plan sponsor. A PERS often administers several pension funds for various governmental entities located within a particular state. In addition, a PERS may administer defined contribution plans, deferred compensation plans, and postemployment health-care plans as well as other employee benefit plans. GASB-25 describes a PERS as "a state or local governmental fiduciary entity entrusted with administering a plan (or plans) and not to the plan itself." Thus, the standards established by GASB-25 do not address directly the financial reports prepared by a PERS but rather apply to the individual plans administered by the PERS. Thus, the standards must be applied to the PERS's combining financial statements on an individual plan basis.

The standards established by GASB-25 apply to all state and local governmental entities. They address measurement and reporting guidance for defined benefit pension plans and disclosure requirements for defined contribution plans. These plans are defined in GASB-25 as follows:

> *Defined benefit pension plan*—A pension plan having terms that specify the amount of pension benefits to be provided at a future date or after a certain period of time; the amount specified usually is a function of one or more factors such as age, years of service, and compensation.
>
> *Defined contribution plan*—A pension plan having terms that specify how contributions to a plan member's account are to be determined, rather than the amount of retirement income the member is to receive. The amounts received by a member will depend *only* on the amount contributed to the member's account, earnings on investments of those contributions, and forfeitures of contributions made for other members that may be allocated to the member's account.

NOTE: GASB-25 supersedes the note disclosures established by GASB-5 (Disclosure of Pension Information by Public Employee Retirement Systems and State and Local Governmental Employers) that apply to defined contribution plans. The disclosure requirements for defined contribution plans are discussed in Chapter 13, "Pension, Postemployment, and Other Employee Benefit Liabilities."

OBSERVATION: GASB-25 does not change the guidance established by NCGA-1 for defined contribution plans accounted for as pension trust funds. When a defined benefit pension plan is accounted for in a pension trust fund, the accounting and reporting standards established by GASB-25 must be observed. The measurement of a governmental employer's pension expenditures/expense is now based on the standards established by GASB-27 (Accounting for Pensions by State and Local Governmental Employers), which is discussed in Chapter 13, "Pension, Postemployment, and Other Employee Benefit Liabilities." GASB-25 defines a "pension trust fund" as "a fund held by a governmental entity in a trustee capacity for pension plan members; used to account for the accumulation of assets for the purpose of paying benefits when they become due in accordance with the terms of the plan; a pension plan included in the financial reporting entity of the plan sponsor or a participating employer."

In some instances, pension plans have characteristics of both defined benefit pension plans and defined contribution plans. GASB-25 states that "if the substance of the plan is to provide a defined benefit in some form, the provisions of this Statement for defined benefit pension plans apply."

> **NOTE:** GASB-25 does not apply to postemployment health-care plans or pension plans that do not provide retirement income. GASB-43 addresses other postemployment benefits, including health-care benefits.

The standards established by GASB-25 apply to defined pension benefit plans irrespective of how they are funded. The following defined benefit pension plans are included:

> *Single-employer plan*—A plan that covers the current and former employees, including beneficiaries, of only one employer.
>
> *Agent multiple-employer plan*—An aggregation of single-employer plans, with pooled administrative and investment functions. Separate accounts are maintained for each employer so that the employer's contributions provide benefits only for employees of that employer. Aseparate actuarial valuation is performed for each individual employer's plan to determine the employer's periodic contribution rate and other information for the individual plan, based on the benefit formula selected by the employer and the individual plan's proportionate share of the pooled assets. The results of the individual valuations are aggregated at the administrative level.
>
> *Cost-sharing multiple-employer plan*—Asingle plan with pooling (cost-sharing) arrangements for the participating employers. All risks, rewards, and costs, including benefit costs, are shared and are not attributed individually to the employers. Asingle actuarial valuation covers all plan members and the same contribution rate(s) applies for each employer.

The GASB-25 standards apply to plans reported as (1) stand-alone plans (the plan's financial statements are presented as separate reports by the plan or by a PERS) and (2) Pension Trust Funds or fiduciary component units in the statement of fiduciary net assets and statement of changes in fiduciary net assets of the plan sponsor or employer (GASB-25, par. 13, as amended by GASB-34).

> **NOTE:** The accounting and reporting requirements for stand-alone pension and other postemployment benefit plan financial

statements are discussed in Chapter 22, "Pension, Postemployment, and Other Benefit Plans."

INVESTMENT TRUST FUNDS

Investment Trust Funds are used by a governmental entity to report the external portion of an investment pool as defined in GASB-31 (Accounting and Financial Reporting for Certain Investments and for External Investment Pools). Governmental entities often pool resources for investment purposes. In some investment arrangements the participants in the pool may be restricted to only governmental units and departments that are part of a single governmental entity. This investment pooling strategy is referred to by GASB-31 (Accounting and Financial Reporting for Certain Investments and for External Investment Pools) as an "internal investment pool" and is described as follows:

> An arrangement that commingles (pools) the moneys of more than one fund or component unit of a reporting entity. (Investment pools that include participation by legally separate entities that are not part of the same reporting entity as the pool sponsor are not internal investments pools but rather are external investment pools.)

As suggested in the above description, the pooling participants may include external parties, in which case the strategy creates an "external investment pool," which is described as follows:

> An arrangement that commingles (pools) the moneys of more than one legally separate entity and invests, on the participant's behalf, in an investment portfolio; one or more of the participants is not part of the sponsor's reporting entity. An external investment pool can be sponsored by an individual government, jointly by more than one government, or by a nongovernmental entity. An investment pool that is sponsored by an individual state or local government is an external investment pool if it includes participation by a legally separate entity that is not part of the same reporting entity as the sponsoring government. If a government-sponsored pool includes only the primary government and its component units, it is an internal investment pool and not an external investment pool.

The primary activity of an Investment Trust Fund involves investing its resources in a variety of assets for the purpose of generating current income and capital appreciation. These investments may include investments in securities as well as other investments, such as real estate or limited partnerships. All investments held by Investment Trust Funds must observe the standards established by GASB-31, paragraph 7 (fair value) paragraph 8 (investment contracts), paragraph 10 (open-end mutual funds), paragraph 11 (non-SEC-registered pools), paragraph 12 (2a7-like pools), paragraph 13 and paragraph 14 (recognition and reporting), and paragraph 15 (disclosures).

Sponsoring Governments

GASB-34 (Basic Financial Statements—and Management's Discussion and Analysis—for State and Local Governments) states that the fiduciary fund category should be used to account for "assets held in a trustee or agency capacity for others and therefore cannot be used to support the government's own programs." When an external investment pool is created, a fiduciary relationship is created between the sponsoring government and the external parties that participate in the pool. An Investment Trust Fund (a fiduciary fund) is used when a governmental entity has an external investment pool.

Sponsoring governments may pool funds from governmental units that make up its financial reporting entity (internal portion of the pool) and from governmental units that are not part of its financial reporting entity (external portion of the pool). The internal portion of each governmental external investment pool should be allocated to the various funds and component units that make up the financial reporting entity, based on each fund's or component unit's equity interest in the investment pool.

> **NOTE:** The accounting for the internal portion of an investment pool is discussed in Chapter 9, "Deposits and Investments."

> **PRACTICE POINT:** A "sponsoring government" is defined as "a governmental entity that provides investment services—whether an external investment pool or individual investment accounts—to other entities and that therefore has a fiduciary responsibility for those investments."

A sponsoring government should report the external portion of each investment pool in an Investment Trust Fund. In the statement of fiduciary net assets, the difference between the fund's assets and its liabilities should be labeled as "net assets held in trust for pool participants."

When the governmental investment pool issues a separate financial report, the sponsoring government should describe in a note to its financial statements how to obtain the investment pool's annual report. When the governmental investment pool does not issue a separate financial report, the sponsoring government should make the following disclosures in its financial statements:

- The basic disclosures required for governmental investment pools (as described earlier)

- For each pool, separate presentation of disclosures required by GASB-3 and GASB-28 and "other cash and investment standards"
- Condensed statements of net assets and changes in net assets for each pool (if the pool includes participation by internal and external governmental entities, the condensed information should include totals for the combined internal and external portions; however, net equity of the pool should be apportioned between the amounts applicable to internal and external participants)

Individual Investment Accounts

In addition to organizing external investment pools, a governmental entity may create "individual investment accounts," which are defined as follows:

> An investment service provided by a governmental entity for other, legally separate entities that are not part of the same reporting entity. With individual investment accounts, specific investments are acquired for individual entities and the income from and changes in the value of those investments affect only the entity for which they were acquired.

Governmental entities that provide individual investment accounts should report those accounts in a separate Investment Trust Fund(s) in a manner similar to the presentation of the external portion of an investment pool as described earlier. However, note disclosures that apply to external investment pools do not apply to individual investment accounts.

When a governmental entity offers an entity an individual investment account service as an alternative (or supplement) to participation in an external investment pool, the individual investment account should be reported in a trust fund, separate from that used to report the investment pool.

PRIVATE-PURPOSE TRUST FUNDS

Private-Purpose Trust Funds are used to account for the principal and income for all other trust arrangements that benefit individuals, private organizations, or other governments.

When a fiduciary relationship between a governmental entity and another party is created and it is not appropriate to account for the related transactions in a Pension Trust Fund or Investment Trust Fund, a Private-Purpose Trust Fund should be used to account for the principal and income for all other trust arrangements that benefit individuals, private organizations, or other governments.

For example, a Private-Purpose Trust Fund would be used to account for escheat property as currently described in GASB-21 (Accounting for Escheat Property).

> **OBSERVATION:** The *GASB Comprehensive Implementation Guide* raises a question about a governmental unit (sheriff's department) that charges inmates to use a pay telephone and uses the proceeds to finance inmate expenditures, such as meals, uniforms, and so forth. The *GASB Q&A Guide* points out that this relationship is not one that would suggest that a Private-Purpose Trust Fund should be used to account for the receipts and the expenditures. Furthermore, if a separate fund is used, it should be a Special Revenue Fund.

> **PRACTICE POINT:** The *GASB Comprehensive Implementation Guide* states that when resources or an activity benefits both the government and private parties, two separate funds (Special Revenue Fund and Private-Purpose Trust Fund) should be used unless one of the two activities is a minor activity, in which case the predominant activity would determine which fund type would be used.

In some circumstances, a fund's principal or income may benefit a discretely presented component unit. The *GASB Comprehensive Implementation Guide* points out that a discretely presented component unit is part of the financial reporting entity, so it is not an "individual, private organization or other government" and, therefore, the resources should be reported in a Special Revenue Fund.

AGENCY FUNDS

Assets held by a governmental entity (either as a trustee or as an agent) for other parties and that cannot be used to finance the governmental entity's own operating programs should be reported in the entity's fiduciary fund financial statements as an Agency Fund.

Generally, an Agency Fund is created to act as a custodian for other funds, governmental entities, or private entities. Assets are recorded by the Agency Fund, held for a period of time as determined by a legal contract or circumstances, and then returned to their owners. For example, an Agency Fund may be used to account for taxes collected by one governmental entity for another governmental entity. When one entity collects taxes for the other governmental entity, the collecting entity would make the following entry in the Agency Fund:

Cash	xxx	
Due to Other Governmental Unit		xxx

When the taxes are remitted to the other governmental unit as determined by state law or local ordinance, the collecting entity would make the following entry in the Agency Fund:

Due to Other Governmental Unit	xxx	
Cash		xxx

Thus, the basic accounting procedures for an Agency Fund are simple.

In an Agency Fund, the measurement focus is custodial, because the fund is not involved with the performance of governmental services. An Agency Fund has no revenues or expenditures and, therefore, no fund balance or need to measure the results of operations for a period. The custodial nature of an Agency Fund means that there is no need to adopt a budgetary accounting system.

An Agency Fund should be established only when it is legally mandated or when the creation of the fund enhances the operational efficiency or effectiveness of the governmental entity. For example, payroll deductions from gross earnings of governmental employees may be accounted for in an Agency Fund, but unless legally prohibited, the withholdings may be shown as a liability of the fund that incurred the payroll expenditure.

A governmental entity may issue bonds that it is responsible to repay, but the proceeds are to be used to finance the construction of a capital asset for a component unit. If at the end of the accounting period there are unspent bond proceeds that will subsequently be transferred to the component unit to pay future construction costs, the unspent amount should not be reported in an Agency Fund. The *GASB Comprehensive Implementation Guide* states that the financial arrangement between the governmental entity and its component unit is similar to an expendituredriven grant whereby the amounts transferred during the year and the unreimbursed costs at the end of the year represent the amount of the grant for the year, whereas the unspent portion is the "unearned portion" of the grant and therefore should be reported as an asset of the governmental entity.

The *GASB Comprehensive Implementation Guide* provides the following examples for determining when an Agency Fund should be used:

Fact Pattern	*Suggested Guidance*
A county tax collector collects property taxes for all taxing bodies in the county, including the tax-levying funds of the county. The county uses an Agency Fund as a distribution	The $750,000 held for county funds must be allocated to the appropriate funds. That is, the reported cash balance (not the actual cash balance) in the Agency Fund must be

Fact Pattern	*Suggested Guidance*
mechanism for the taxes. At year-end, the collector is holding $3,450,000 in the tax distribution account.	reduced by $750,000 and the cash balances of other funds should be increased by the appropriate amounts.
Of that total, $750,000 will be distributed to the county funds, and the remaining $2,700,000 represents taxes collected for the other taxing bodies in the county. How does the county apply the "clearing account" provision in paragraph 111 for Agency Funds?	The amounts due to other funds should not be reported as receivable/payables in the county's financial statements. The $2,700,000 should continue to be reported in the Agency Fund since that amount is held in trust for amount is taxing bodies in the county.
If a government uses a central payroll system and reports all payroll deductions in an Agency Fund, should the unremitted balances in the Agency Fund at year-end be reclassified to the funds from which the payroll deductions arose?	No. The assets held by the Agency Fund will be distributed to outside parties, not to the government's funds.

Negative Cash Positions or Excess Liabilities in Agency Funds

Sometimes an Agency Fund distributes more cash than it has, or it has more liabilities than assets. The AICPA *State and Local Governments* Guide notes that if the governmental entity that reports the Agency Fund in its fund financial statements is responsible for the shortfall, an interfund payable should be established by the fund responsible for the shortfall and the Agency Fund should report an interfund receivable.

For example, assume that an Agency Fund has a cash position of $20,000 but expends $25,000 (a cash overdraft). If it is assumed that the General Fund is responsible for the overdraft, the following entries would be made by the two funds:

AGENCY FUND		
Amounts due to Other Parties	20,000	
Due from General Fund	5,000	
Cash		20,000
Cash Overdraft (liability)		5,000
GENERAL FUND		
Expenditures/Revenues	5,000	
Due to Agency Fund		5,000

Note: The charge in the General Fund could be either an expenditure or a reduction to revenue depending on the nature of the arrangement that gave rise to the General Fund liability. For example, if the liability arises from escheat property claims, the charge is generally made to revenue rather than expenditure.

The interfund loan would not be eliminated in the preparation of the fund financial statements and the government-wide financial statements. Agency Funds financial information is not incorporated into the government-wide financial statements.

ACCOUNTING AND REPORTING

Basis of Accounting and Measurement Focus

The accrual basis of accounting and the flow of economic resources are used to prepare the financial statements of fiduciary funds. These concepts are discussed in Chapter 3, "Basis of Accounting and Measurement Focus."

Budgetary System and Accounting

Pension Trust Funds (and similar employment or postemployment benefit trust funds), Investment Trust Funds, and Private-Purpose Trust Funds are accounted for in a manner similar to proprietary funds and may use budgetary controls. Budgets are not appropriate for Agency Funds, because the government entity functions only as a custodial agent and such funds do not record revenues or expenditures.

FUND FINANCIAL STATEMENTS

The following financial statements should be prepared for Fiduciary Funds:

- Statement of fiduciary net assets
- Statement of changes in fiduciary net assets

Fiduciary fund financial statements are not reported by major fund (which is required for governmental funds and proprietary funds) but must be reported based on the following fund types:

- Pension (and other employee benefit) Trust Funds
- Investment Trust Funds
- Private-Purpose Trusts
- Agency Funds

Statement of Fiduciary Net Assets

The assets, liabilities, and net assets of Fiduciary Funds should be presented in the statement of fiduciary net assets by type of fiduciary fund. There is no need to divide net assets into the three categories (invested in capital assets [net of related debt], restricted net assets, and unrestricted net assets) that must be used when preparing government-wide financial statements as described in GASB-34.

(Exhibit 20-9, in Chapter 20, "Comprehensive Annual Financial Report," is an illustration of a statement of fiduciary net assets.)

Statement of Changes in Fiduciary Net Assets

The statement of changes in fiduciary net assets should summarize the additions to, deductions from, and net increase or decrease in net assets for the year. In addition, GASB-34 requires that the statement provide information "about significant year-to-year changes in net assets."

(Exhibit 20-10, in Chapter 20, "Comprehensive Annual Financial Report," is an illustration of a statement of changes in fiduciary net assets.)

> **PRACTICE POINT:** Agency funds are not included in the Statement of Changes in Fiduciary Net Assets, because they do not report net assets.

REQUIRED SUPPLEMENTARY INFORMATION

Except as noted in the following paragraph, GASB-25 and GASB-43 requires two supplementary schedules to be presented in the government's financial statements:

- Schedule of funding progress and
- Schedule of employer contributions

This required supplementary information should be presented immediately after the notes to the financial statements.

> **OBSERVATION:** When a pension or other postemployment benefit plan uses the aggregate cost method, GASB-25 and GASB-43 requires that only a schedule of employer contributions be presented. However, the plan must disclose the fact that the aggregate cost method is used.

Required supplementary information is not required when the financial statements of a cost-sharing plan or an agent plan are included in the governmental employer's financial report if both of the following two conditions are satisfied:

1. The plan also separately presents its financial statements (which include the required supplementary information) in a publicly available, stand-alone financial report.
2. The governmental employer states in a note to its financial statements how the stand-alone financial statements may be obtained.

When the financial statements of a single-employer plan are included in the governmental employer's financial report, that financial report should include only the schedule of funding progress for the three most recent actuarial valuations; the schedule of employer contributions should not be presented. Also, the employer government should disclose the availability of the standalone plan report.

When a plan's financial statements are not publicly available in a stand-alone financial report, the governmental employer's financial report should include both the schedule of funding progress and the schedule of employer contributions for all years required by the standards established by GASB-25 and GASB-43.

> **PRACTICE POINT:** GASB-27 and GASB-45 establish the required supplementary information for pension and OPEB expenditures/expense that must be disclosed in an employer's financial statements.

Schedule of Funding Progress

The schedule of funding progress should contain the following information for at least the preceding six years (GASB-25, par. 37):

- Actuarial valuation date
- Actuarial value of plan assets
- Actuarial accrued liability
- Total unfunded actuarial liability
- Actuarial value of assets as a percentage of the actuarial accrued liability (funded ratio)
- Annual covered payroll (all elements included in compensation paid to active employees on which contributions to the pension plan are based)
- Ratio of unfunded actuarial liability to annual covered payroll

The actuarial information should be presented as of the actuarial valuation date, and it should be measured in accordance with the standards established by GASB-25 and GASB-43. However, plans that obtain biennial valuations do not have to repeat duplicate information.

> **PRACTICE POINT:** When a funding excess exists, the ratios should be computed in the same manner as when a funding deficiency exists.

(An example of a schedule of funding progress is reproduced in Exhibit 22-4, in Chapter 22, "Pension and Other Postemployment Benefit Plans.")

Schedule of Employer Contributions

The schedule of employer contributions should contain the following information for at least the past six years (GASB-25, pars. 38–39):

- Dollar amount of annual required contributions (ARC) of the employer(s)
- Percentage of ARC recognized as an employer contribution in the pension plan's statement of changes in plan net assets
- Dollar amount of required contributions (if any) from other than employers and plan members
- Percentage of required contributions (if any) from other than employers and plan members recognized in the pension plan's statement of changes in plan net assets

> **PRACTICE POINT:** If contributions are made by parties other than employers and plan members, the schedule should be titled "Schedule of Contributions from the Employer(s) and Other Contributing Entities."

(An example of a schedule of employer contributions is reproduced in Exhibit 22-5, in Chapter 22, "Pension and Other Postemployment Benefit Plans.")

GOVERNMENT-WIDE FINANCIAL STATEMENTS

The focus of government-wide financial statements is on the overall financial position and activities of the government as a whole. These financial statements are constructed around the concept of a primary government as defined by GASB-14 (The Financial Reporting Entity) and therefore encompass the primary government and its component units except for fiduciary funds of the primary government and component units that are fiduciary in nature. Financial statements of fiduciary funds are not presented in the government-wide financial statements but are included in the fund financial statements.

> **OBSERVATION:** The financial statements of Fiduciary Funds are excluded from government-wide financial statements because resources of these funds cannot be used to finance a governmental entity's activities. The financial statements are included in the fund financial statements because a governmental entity is financially accountable for those resources even though they belong to other parties.

III. SPECIFIC ACCOUNTING AND REPORTING ISSUES

CHAPTER 9
DEPOSITS AND INVESTMENTS

CONTENTS

INTRODUCTION

The accounting treatment of governmental deposits with financial institutions is essentially the same as accounting for deposits by private-sector businesses, with certain exceptions for unique considerations involving fund accounting. Guidance for most investments held by governmental entities is found in GASB-31 (Accounting and Financial Reporting for Certain Investments and for External Investment Pools). GASB-31 defines an "investment" as a security or other asset acquired primarily for the purpose of obtaining income or profit. The standards established by GASB-31 apply to (1) all investments held by governmental external investment pools and (2) other specified investments held by all other governmental entities (except external investment pools, defined benefit pension plans, and Internal Revenue Code Section 457 deferred compensation plans).

ACCOUNTING AND FINANCIAL REPORTING FOR INVESTMENTS

Accounting Basis and Measurement Focus

The standards established by GASB-31 apply to governmental funds, proprietary funds, government-wide financial statements, and fiduciary funds. That is, an entity must use fair value as the basis to present investments identified in GASB-31 in its various balance sheets and statements of operations.

Pooled Cash and Investments

Amounts of cash and temporary investments belonging to various funds of the government entity may be pooled with similar assets of other funds to maximize the return on invested resources. Adequate records must be maintained to provide a basis for identifying each fund's assets, including interest earned and receivable at the end of the period. Each fund's portion of the pooled assets may be designated "equity in pooled cash and temporary investments" or some other, similar designation. The method of allocating interest on pooled resources to each fund should be disclosed in the financial statements.

Scope of the Standards Established by GASB-31

The standards established by GASB-31 address the following (GASB-31, par. 2):

- *Interest-earning investment contracts* A direct contract, other than a mortgage or other loan, that a government enters into as a creditor of a financial institution, broker-dealer, investment company, insurance company, or other financial services company and for which it receives, directly or indirectly, interest payments. Interest-earning investment contracts include time deposits with financial institutions (such as certificates of deposit), repurchase agreements, and guaranteed and bank investment contracts (GICs and BICs).
- *External investment pools* An "external investment pool" is defined as

an arrangement that commingles (pools) the moneys of more than one legally separate entity and invests, on the participants' behalf, in an investment portfolio; one or more of the participants is not part of the sponsor's reporting entity. An external investment pool can be sponsored by an individual government, jointly by more than one government, or by a nongovernmental entity. An investment pool that is sponsored by an individual state or local government is an external investment pool if it includes participation by a legally separate entity that is not part of the same reporting entity as the sponsoring government. If a government-sponsored pool includes only the primary government and its component units, it is an internal investment pool and not an external investment pool.

- *Open-end mutual fund* An SEC-registered investment company that issues shares of its stock to investors, invests in an investment portfolio on the shareholders' behalf, and stands ready to redeem its shares for an amount based on its current share price. An open-end mutual fund creates new shares to meet investor demand, and the value of an investment in the fund depends directly on the value of the underlying portfolio. Open-end mutual funds include governmental external investment pools that are registered as investment companies with the SEC and that operate as open-end funds.
- *Debt securities* Any security representing a creditor relationship with an entity. It also includes (a) preferred stock that either is required to be redeemed by the issuing entity or is redeemable at the option of the investor and (b) a collateralized mortgage obligation (CMO) or other instrument that is issued in equity form but is accounted for as a nonequity instrument. However, it excludes option contracts, financial futures contracts, and forward contracts. Thus, the term debt security includes, among other items, U.S. Treasury securities, U.S. government agency securities, municipal securities, corporate bonds, convertible debt, commercial paper, negotiable certificates of deposit, securitized debt instruments [such as CMOs and real estate mortgage investment conduits (REMICs)], and interest-only and principal-only strips. Trade accounts receivable arising from sales on credit and loans receivable arising from real estate lending activities of proprietary activities are examples of receivables that do not meet the definition of a security; thus, those receivables are not debt securities. (However, if they have been securitized, they would then meet the definition.)
- *Equity securities (including unit investment trusts)* Any security that represents an ownership interest in an entity, including common, preferred, or other capital stock. However, the term equity security does not include convertible debt or preferred

stock that either is required to be redeemed by the issuing entity or is redeemable at the option of the investor. (Applies only when the instrument has a readily determinable fair value.)

- *Closed-end mutual funds* An SEC-registered investment company that issues a limited number of shares to investors that are then traded as an equity security on a stock exchange. (Applies only when the instrument has a readily determinable fair value.)
- *Options contracts* A contract giving the buyer (owner) the right, but not the obligation, to purchase from (call option) or sell to (put option) the seller (writer) of the contract a fixed number of items (such as shares of equity securities) at a fixed or determinable strike price on a given date or at any time on or before a given date. (Applies only when the instrument has a readily determinable fair value.)
- *Stock warrants* Certificates entitling the holder to acquire shares of stock at a certain price within a stated period. Warrants often are made part of the issuance of bonds or preferred or common stock. (Applies only when the instrument has a readily determinable fair value.)
- *Stock rights* Rights given to existing stockholders to purchase newly issued shares in proportion to their holdings at a specific date. (Applies only when the instrument has a readily determinable fair value.)

> **PRACTICE POINT:** GASB-31 applies to purchased put and call option contracts, but not to written option contracts. Written option contracts are not investments but rather obligations of the option writer.

The investments listed above (and all investments held by governmental external investment pools) should be accounted for at "fair value," which is defined as the amount at which a financial instrument could be exchanged in a current transaction between willing parties, other than in a forced or liquidation sale. Investments in equity securities, option contracts, stock warrants, and stock rights should be reported at fair value when the fair value of each instrument is readily determinable. The readily determinable condition is satisfied if sales prices or bid-and-asked quotations are currently available on a securities exchange registered with the Securities and Exchange Commission (SEC) or on the over-the-counter market. Those prices or quotations for the over-the-counter market must be publicly reported by the National Association of Securities Dealers Automated Quotations (NASDAQ) systems or the National Quotation Bureau. Equity securities, option contracts, stock warrants, and stock rights that are traded only in a foreign market satisfy the readily determinable condition when the foreign market has characteristics (breadth and scope) similar to the U.S. equity markets (GASB-31, par. 3).

> **OBSERVATION:** The GASB notes that quoted market prices are the most reliable and verifiable sources of measuring investments at fair value. For certain investments (such as debt instruments and participating interest-earning investment contracts), however, quoted market prices are not available and the governmental entity will need to estimate fair value based on techniques such as discounted future cash flows, fundamental analysis, and matrix pricing.

> **OBSERVATION:** "Investments" as defined by GASB-31 are restricted to instruments that are held primarily to earn income or a profit. For this reason, the standards established by the Statement do not apply to noninvestment transactions or to arrangements such as the holding of securities to guarantee acceptable performance by third-party contractors or to securities seized by the governmental entity. In addition, GASB-31 does not apply to an equity interest in a component unit; however, an equity interest in a for-profit corporation may be considered an investment if the purpose of the acquisition is not to provide governmental services [see paragraph 55 of GASB-14 (The Financial Reporting Entity)].

GASB-31 states that the value of restricted stock is not readily determinable. "Restricted stock" is defined as

> Equity securities whose sale is restricted at acquisition by legal or contractual provisions (other than in connection with being pledged as collateral) except if that restriction terminates within one year or if the holder has the power by contract or otherwise to cause the requirement to be met within on year. Any portion of the security that can reasonably be expected to qualify for sale within one year, such as may be the case under SEC Rule 144 (17 Code of Federal Regulations § 230.144) or similar rules of the SEC, is not considered restricted.

> **PRACTICE POINT:** The standard establishes fair value, rather than market value, as the basis for measuring assets. Market value implies that an asset can be measured on that basis only if there is an active market. Fair value, which is a much broader concept, encompasses a variety of measurement techniques, including appraisal value and present value of net future cash flows as well as market value.

> **OBSERVATION:** While the standards established by GASB-31 are similar to the accounting standards established by FAS-115, there are significant differences. GASB-31 standards require that investments in debt instruments be reported at fair value

in the governmental entity's statement of financial position and that unrealized gains and losses related to the valuation be reported on the entity's activity statement. FAS-115 requires that investments in debt instruments be classified as part of (1) the held-to-maturity portfolio, (2) the trading portfolio, or (3) the available-for-sale portfolio. Investments included in the held-to-maturity portfolio are reported at amortized cost, while investments in the trading and available-for-sale portfolios are reported at fair value, with unrealized gains or losses for the available-for-sale portfolio reported as an equity component and gains or losses for the trading portfolio reported on the commercial enterprise's statement of income. (FAS-124 requires that investments in debt securities be reported at fair value and unrealized gains and losses be reported on the entity's not-for-profit activity statement.)

OBSERVATION: The standards established by GASB-31 do not apply uniformly to all governmental entities. The fair value approach applies only to investments in certain securities held by most governmental entities; however, the fair value approach applies to all investments held by governmental external investment pools. Thus, governmental external investment pools must apply fair value to investments such as real estate interests, loans, limited partnerships, and futures contracts.

Valuation

Investments held by governmental entities, including governmental external investment pools, should be reported at fair value, except in the following situations (which are discussed later in this section):

- Participating interest-earning investment contracts
- Money market investments and certain participating interest-earning investment contracts
- Investment positions in 2a7-like pools

Ideally, the governmental entity's determination of fair value should be based on quoted market prices. When a governmental entity does not report an investment in a security at fair value (because market information is lacking) and the entity has invested in put option contracts or has written call option contracts on the same security, the put and call option contracts should be taken into consideration in determining the amount at which the investment in the security should be presented. For example, the GASB drew the following conclusions with respect to this issue (GASB-31, par. 7):

- If an entity has the right to sell securities under a put option, the combined measures of the security and the option contract should approximate the strike price if that price is above the security's market price. If the put option contract is not reported at fair value, the entity should consider the unrecorded value of the option contract in measuring the underlying security at fair value.

- If the strike price is less than the security's market price, the combined value of a security subject to sale under a call option and the call option liability should approximate the strike price. If the call option contract is not reported as a liability and is not reported at fair value, the quoted market price of the underlying security would need to be adjusted in order for the security's fair value to be properly reported.

Investments in open-end mutual funds should be reported at fair value, based on the current share price determined by the fund (GASB-31, par. 10).

Participating interest-earning investment contracts Interest-earning investment contracts include time deposits with financial institutions (such as certificates of deposit), repurchase agreements, and guaranteed and bank investment contracts. These contracts are considered participation contracts when they enable the investor to "capture market (interest rate) changes through the investment's negotiability or transferability, or redemption terms that consider market rates." Participating interest-earning investment contracts should be reported at fair value (except as explained in the following section) (GASB-31, par. 8).

When an interest-earning investment contract is not participating, the investor is exposed to interest rate risk (that is, a change in the market interest rate will result in a change in the value of the investment). However, the GASB points out that while the nonparticipating contract can result in changes in the value of the investment, the holder of the investment is unlikely to eventually realize any interim gain or loss. For example, if interest rates fall, the holder of a nonparticipating contract has an unrealized gain in the valuation of the investment, but in order to realize the gain, the holder would have to redeem the contract early and pay an early-redemption penalty and in fact may incur a realized loss from the redemption. For this reason, the GASB states that nonparticipating contracts (for example, certificates of deposit) should not be reported at fair value but rather should be reported at cost, assuming that the value of the investment is not affected by the financial institution's credit standing or other relevant factors.

Money market investments and certain participating interest-earning investment contracts A "money market investment" is defined by GASB-31 as "a short-term, highly liquid debt instrument, including commercial paper, banker's acceptances, and U.S. Treasury and agency obligations." Money market investments and participating interest-earning investment contracts that mature within one year or less of the date of their acquisition may be reported at amortized cost, assuming that the investment is not affected by the financial institution's credit standing or other relevant factors. The relevant date for determining the time period to maturity ("one year or less" criterion) is the date the investment was acquired rather than the date the investment was originally issued (GASB-31, par. 9).

> **OBSERVATION:** Based on a cost-benefit consideration, GASB-31 allows for money market investments to be reported at amortized cost rather than fair value. The GASB believes that reporting such investments at amortized cost will reasonably approximate fair value.

> **PRACTICE POINT:** Asset-backed securities, derivatives, and structured notes are not considered money market investments. "Asset-backed securities" are defined as "assets that are composed of, or collateralized by, loans or receivables." The collateralization can be based on "liens on real property, leases, or credit card debt." "Structured notes" are defined as "debt securities whose cash flow characteristics (coupon, redemption amount, or stated maturity) depend on one or more indexes, or that have embedded forwards or options."

Asset-backed securities, derivatives, and structured notes are not considered money market investments. "Asset-backed securities" are defined as "assets that are composed of, or collateralized by, loans or receivables." The collateralization can be based on "liens on real property, leases, or credit card debt."

Structured notes are defined as "debt securities whose cash flow characteristics (coupon, redemption amount, or stated maturity) depend on one or more indexes, or that have embedded forwards or options."

> **PRACTICE POINT:** GASB-31 notes that investments in money market investments and participating interest-earning investment contracts may be based on commingled funds from internal and external pool participants. In this circumstance, the investment should be reported based on the guidance discussed in Chapter 8, "Fiduciary Funds."

Investment positions in 2a7-like pools A governmental entity that holds an investment position in a 2a7-like pool should report the investment based on the pool's share price. A "2a7-like pool" is defined as follows (GASB-31, par. 12):

> An external investment pool that is not registered with the SEC as an investment company, but nevertheless has a policy

that it will, and does, operate in a manner consistent with the SEC's Rule 2a7 of the Investment Company Act of 1940 (17 Code of Federal Regulations § 270.2a-7). Rule 2a7 allows SEC-registered mutual funds to use amortized cost rather than market value to report net assets to compute share prices if certain conditions are met. Those conditions include restrictions on the types of investments held, restrictions on the term-to-maturity of individual investments and the dollar-weighted average of the portfolio, requirements for portfolio diversification, requirements for divestiture considerations in the event of security downgrades and defaults, and required actions if the market value of the portfolio deviates from amortized cost by a specified amount.

Investments in external investment pools Investments in external investment pools (both governmental pools and nongovernmental pools) that are not SEC-registered (except for 2a7-like pools) should be reported at fair value "based on the fair value per share of the pool's underlying portfolio." In determination of the fair value of the investment, legally binding promises given by the pool's sponsor that guarantee the unit value of the fund should be taken into consideration, along with the ability of the sponsor to successfully fulfill the guarantee. If the governmental entity cannot obtain sufficient information from the pool sponsor to determine the fair value of the investment in the pool, the best estimate of its fair value should be made and the basis for the estimate should be disclosed in a note to the financial statements (GASB-31, par. 11).

Recognition and Reporting

All investment income, including changes in the fair value of investments, must be reported as revenue on the governmental entity's operating statement. Investment income includes interest and dividend income, realized gains and losses on the sale of investments, and changes in the fair value of investments the governmental entity holds. If the governmental entity elects to separately identify (in a note to its financial statements) the change in the fair value of its investments, the change should be labeled as "net increase (decrease) in the fair value of investments," which is defined as "the difference between the fair value of investments at the beginning of the year and at the end of the year, taking into consideration investment purchases, sales, and redemptions" (GASB-31, par. 13).

PRACTICE POINT: GASB-20 (Accounting and Financial Reporting for Proprietary Funds and Other Governmental Entities That Use Proprietary Fund Accounting) states that standards established by FASB Statements issued before November 30, 1989, should be observed by governmental entities that follow proprietary fund accounting, assuming that the guidance is not inconsistent with Statements issued by the GASB. Thus, with respect to investment accounting guidance, proprietary activities should continue to observe the standards established by FAS-52 (Foreign Currency Translation) and FAS-80 (Accounting for Futures Contracts) when they are applicable.

Unrealized gains and losses (from the valuation of investments at the end of the period) and realized gains and losses (from the sale of investments during the period) must not be reported separately on the operating statement. Realized gains and losses may be presented separately in a note to the financial statements of the governmental entity if such gains and losses are measured as the difference between the sales price of the investment and the original cost of the investment. However, governmental external investment pools that prepare separate financial reports may report realized gains and losses separately from the net increase or decrease in the fair value of investments on the face of their operating statements. If a governmental external investment pool elects this option, the unrealized gains and losses should be labeled as net increase (decrease) in the fair value of investments, as noted in the previous paragraph.

The calculation of the increase or decrease in the fair value of investments is illustrated in Appendix C of GASB-31, part of which is reproduced in Exhibit 9-1.

EXHIBIT 9-1
CALCULATION OF CHANGE IN FAIR VALUE OF INVESTMENTS

Year 1

Specific Identification Method

		A	*B*	*C*	*D*	*E*	*F*
	Cost	Beginning fair value	Purchases	Sales	Subtotal*	Ending fair value	Change in fair value**
Security 1	$100	$100	—	—	$100	$120	$ 20
Security 2	520	540	—	—	540	510	(30)
Security 3	200	240	—	$250	(10)	0	10
Security 4	330	—	$330	—	330	315	(15)
		$880	$330	$250	$960	$945	$(15)

*Column D = Columns A + B – C.

**Column F = Column E – Column D.

Aggregate Method

Fair value at December 31, 20X1	$ 945
Add: Proceeds of investments sold in year 20X1	250
Less: Cost of investments purchased in year 20X1	(330)
Less: Fair value at December 31, 20X0	(880)
Change in fair value of investments	$ (15)

Year 2

Specific Identification Method

		A	*B*	*C*	*D*	*E*	*F*
	Cost	Beginning fair value	Purchases	Sales	Subtotal*	Ending fair value	Change in fair value**
Security 1	$100	$120	—	$110	$ 10	$ 0	$(10)
Security 2	520	510	—	—	510	550	40
Security 3	330	315	—	330	(15)	0	15
Security 4	310	—	310	—	310	300	(10)
		$945	$310	$440	$815	$850	$ 35

*Column D = Columns A + B − C.

**Column F = Column E − Column D.

Aggregate Method

Fair value at December 31, 20X2	$850
Add: Proceeds of investments sold in year 20X2	440
Less: Cost of investments purchased in year 20X2	(310)
Less: Fair value at December 31, 20X1	(945)
Change in fair value of investments	$ 35

OBSERVATION: The calculation of the change in the fair value of investments simplifies a difficult presentation problem that arises when assets are presented at fair value and some of the assets are held for more than two accounting periods before they are sold. Specifically, the question is how to present realized and unrealized gains and losses for the same investment. For example, assume that an investment purchased for $100 has a value of $150 at the end of the first year and is sold for $180 during the second year. The governmental entity has a $50 unrealized gain in year 1 ($150 − $100) and a $80 realized gain in year 2 ($180 − $100); however, the maximum amount of (economic) gain that can be reported on operating

> statements for the two years is $80. For this reason, the effect on the operating statement in the second year is $30, because the $50 unrealized gain must be netted against the $80 realized gain. The illustrated calculation of the net change in investments simplifies the computation by not separating unrealized and realized gains and losses. The standard prohibits the presentation of realized gains and losses on the income statement, because the presentation may detract from the reporting of the change in the fair value of investments and could be misinterpreted if the reader does not understand how a realized gain may not be an economic gain in the year the investment is sold if the investment had an unrealized gain (that was equal to the realized gain in the current period) in the previous period.

Investments in internal investment pools Some governmental entities combine resources from various funds and component units into one or more "internal investment pools," which GASB-31 defines as follows (GASB-31, par. 14):

> An arrangement that commingles (pools) the moneys of more than one fund or component unit of a reporting entity. Investment pools that include participation by legally separate entities that are not part of the same reporting entity as the pool sponsor are not internal investment pools, but rather are external investment pools.

Under this arrangement, for external financial reporting purposes the internal investment pool must allocate its investments to the various funds and component units based on the equity interest that each fund or component unit holds in the internal investment pool. Also, investment income and losses that the internal investment pool incurs must be allocated to the participating funds and component units based on their respective equity interests in the investment pool.

In some circumstances, a fund (the investing fund) may have an equity interest in an internal investment pool, while another fund (the income recipient fund) may receive the investment income from the investment pool. When the recipient fund's right to the investment income is based on "legal or contractual provisions," that language must be used as a basis for determining how each fund should record the allocation of investment income. If, based on the specific language in the provision, the investment income is considered to belong to the recipient fund, then the recipient fund should record the investment income. However, if the specific language is interpreted to mean that the investment income belongs to the investing fund, the investment income should be recorded in the investing fund—and subsequently (or perhaps concurrently) recorded as a transfer by the investing fund (transfers-out) and by the recipient fund (transfers-in). On the other hand, when a recipient fund's right to the investment income is based on other than "legal or contractual provisions" (i.e., management's discretion), the investment income should be recorded in the investing fund, with each of the funds involved in the transfer subsequently recording an interfund transfer.

Investments Not Subject to GASB-31

GASB-31 does not establish accounting standards for investments in securities not specifically listed in the Statement. The AICPA's *State and Local Governments* Guide states that generally those investments should be reported "at original cost when acquired and that any purchased discount or premium from the investment's face or maturity value [be] accreted or amortized to investment income over the life of the investment in a systematic and rational manner." For example, if a governmental entity acquires nonmarketable equity securities, the investment is recorded at cost in subsequent periods (irrespective of its change in fair value) unless there is a decline in its fair value that is other than temporary.

Other Investments

Investments that are not subject to the fair value standards established by GASB-31 should generally be accounted for based on the historical cost concept. Investments not subject to GASB-31 standards include the following:

- Investments in land and other real estate
- Investment in equity securities (equity method)
- Investments in nonpublic equity securities (cost method)
- Escheat property

Investments in land and other real estate A donee may transfer income-producing real estate (or a partial interest in such real estate) to a governmental entity for the benefit of an individual, a private organization, or other government. Such transfers should be recorded at estimated fair value at the date of receipt; however, historical cost (including amortized cost for long-lived assets) should be used to account for the donated assets in subsequent periods. For example, if the transferred asset is an apartment building, the Private-Purpose Trust Fund would generally report rental income (a receipt of resources) on an accrual basis and report various expenses (a reduction of resources) when incurred.

> **PRACTICE POINT:** Guidance provided in the AICPA's Audit and Accounting Guide *Use of Real Estate Appraisal Information* may be useful in determining the estimated fair value of land or improved real estate.

> **PRACTICE ALERT:** In March 2007, the GASB issued an Exposure Draft of a Proposed Statement entitled "Land and Other Real Estate Held as Investments by Endowments." The proposed Statement is in response to questions raised, especially within the college and university community, regarding the difference between permanent and term endowments in accounting for land and other real estate held as investments, including permanent funds and other governmental entities that exist for similar purposes having different accounting methods for the same transactions. Current accounting standards pertaining to the recording of land and other real estate held as investments with permanent and term endowments, including permanent funds, involves the reporting of such assets at historical cost. This proposed Statement would require that land and other real estate held as investments by endowments be reported at fair value at the reporting date. Any changes recorded in fair value during the period should be reported as investment income. This proposed Statement applies to all state and local governments.

Investments in equity securities (equity method) In some instances a governmental entity may be named as the trustee of an equity interest in a company where the interest represents 20% or more of the voting stock of a company. Under this circumstance the guidance established by APB-18 (The Equity Method of Accounting for Investments in Common Stock) should be followed. Per the standards established by APB-18, an asset should be reported in the financial statements of the Private-Purpose Trust Fund. The initial receipt of the securities from the donee should be recorded at fair value. The recognition of a proportional share of the investee company's results of operations is not dependent on whether there is an actual remittance between the investee and the Private-Purpose Trust Fund.

In determining the investee company's results of operations for a period, profits on transactions (if any) with the Private-Purpose Trust Fund should be eliminated. Nonoperating transactions, such as additional equity contributions, loans, and dividends, should be reflected as an addition or decrease to the carrying amount of the net investment in the investee company.

The interest in the net assets of the investee company should be reported as a single asset (account) in the Private-Purpose Trust Fund. There should be no attempt to present on the Private-Purpose Trust Fund's balance sheet a proportional interest in the various assets and liabilities of the investee company. In addition, the proportional share of the investee company's results of operations should be presented as a single operating account on the Private-Purpose Trust Fund's statement of changes in fiduciary net assets. Finally, a proportional interest in the various operating accounts of the investee company should not be presented.

Investments in nonpublic equity securities (cost method) When a donee transfers equity securities (where the fair value is not readily determinable) to a governmental entity to be used to benefit individuals, private organizations, or other governments, the securities should be recorded at fair value. However, once the investment is recorded, it should be accounted for based on the historical cost principle. Thus, the Private-Purpose Trust Fund would record dividend income (a receipt of resources) when the board of directors of the investee company declares the dividend.

Escheat property GASB-21 defines the "escheat process" as "the reversion of property to a governmental entity in the absence of legal claimants or heirs." Governmental entities that receive escheat property may manage the receipts in a number of ways, including using the funds to finance current operations or investing the funds and using only the investment income to finance governmental activities. GASB-37 requires that escheat property generally be reported in the governmental or proprietary fund that ultimately will receive the escheat property. Escheat property that is held for individuals, private organizations, or another government is reported either in (1) a Private-Purpose Trust Fund, (2) an Agency Fund, or (3) in the governmental or proprietary fund that reports escheat property. In the last case, the portion of the escheat property that is expected (likely to occur) to revert to an external party is reported as a liability (GASB-21, pars. 3–6, as amended by GASB-37, par. 3).

The *GASB Comprehensive Implementation Guide* provides additional insight into the issue by classifying escheat property in the following categories:

- Property that will be paid to heirs or beneficiaries
- Property temporarily held for other governments
- Property that will revert to the government itself in the absence of rightful heirs or claimants

The *GASB Comprehensive Implementation Guide* identifies two alternatives that could be used to account for escheat property. Under Alternative 1, all three categories of escheat property are accounted for in either a governmental fund or a proprietary fund and all estimated amounts due to other parties (other governments or claimants) are reported as a liability of the fund. Under Alternative 2, (1) the estimated portion of the amount of escheat property for all three categories that is expected to revert to the governmental entity is accounted for in either a governmental fund or a property fund and (2) the balance of the amount of the escheat property that is expected to be distributed to external parties is accounted for in an Agency Fund (for property temporarily held for other governments) or a Private-Purpose Trust Fund (for property expected to be distributed to claimants).

Escheat property that is reported in a Private-Purpose Trust Fund is reported as an "addition" in the statement of changes in fiduciary net assets and any balance remaining at the end of the accounting period is reported as "held in trust for trust beneficiaries" in the statement of fiduciary net assets. When the escheat property is reported in an Agency Fund only a statement of fiduciary net assets is prepared. Consistent with the basic standards established by GASB-34, escheat property reported in a Private-Purpose Trust Fund or an Agency Fund is not reported in the entity's government-wide financial statements.

When escheat property is reported in a governmental or proprietary fund, the total amount of escheat property received during the year is apportioned between an escheat liability account and an escheat revenue account. The amount of the liability recorded is the estimated amount expected to be paid to claimants, and the balance is recorded as revenue. Again, based on the standards originally established by GASB-34, escheat property reported in a governmental or proprietary fund is reported in the government-wide financial statements based accrual accounting principles.

PRACTICE POINT: Escheat property reported as revenue in a governmental fund must satisfy the criteria of measurability and availability.

Disclosures

GASB-31 establishes that a governmental entity must disclose in a note(s) to the financial statements the following information about its investments (GASB-31, par. 15):

- The methods and significant assumptions used to estimate the fair value of an investment, when fair value is not based on a quoted market price
- The policy used to identify investments that are reported at amortized cost
- For investments in external investment pools that are not SEC-registered, a description of regulatory oversight, if any, and a statement as to whether the fair value of the investment is the same as the value of the pool shares
- Description of involuntary participation (i.e., participation required by law) in an external investment pool
- For positions in external investments pools for which fair value information cannot be obtained from the pool sponsor, the methods and significant assumptions used to estimate the fair value and the reasons for having to use such an estimate
- Income from investments whereby the income from one fund has been assigned to another fund

PRACTICE POINT: In some instances, an external investment pool may not provide fair value information or timely information to participants in the pool. For example, the year-end date for the external investment pool may not be the same as the year-end date for the participant. Under these circumstances, the participant must estimate its fair value position in the pool, disclose (as noted above) the methods and significant assumptions used to compute the estimate, and disclose why an estimate must be made.

In addition, if (1) a governmental entity elects to disclose in its notes any realized gains and losses from investments or (2) an external investment pool elects to report on its operating statement any realized gains and losses from investments, the following must be disclosed:

- That the determination of realized gains and losses is independent of the determination of the net change in the fair value of investments
- That realized gains and losses on investments that were held by the governmental entity during a previous accounting period(s) but sold during the current period were used to compute the change in the fair value of investments for the previous year(s) as well as the current year

Summary of Investment Measurement Standards

Exhibit 9-2 summarizes the measurement standards established by GASB-31 for governmental entities (except external investment pools, defined benefit pension plans, and IRC § 457 deferred compensation plans).

EXHIBIT 9-2
SUMMARY OF MEASUREMENT STANDARDS FOR INVESTMENT SPECIFIED IN GASB-31

Investments held by governmental entities (except external investment pools, defined benefit pension plans, and IRC § 457 deferred compensation plans)	*Appropriate accounting method*
• Marketable equity securities (including unit investment trusts and closed-end mutual funds)	Report at fair value (paragraph 3).
• Marketable option contracts	
• Marketable stock warrants	
• Marketable stock rights	
• Interest-earning investment contracts	Nonparticipating contracts (for example, certificates of deposits) should be reported at cost rather than fair value, assuming the value of the

Investments held by governmental entities (except external investment pools, defined benefit pension plans, and IRC §457 deferred compensation plans)	*Appropriate accounting method*
	investment is not affected by the financial institution's credit standing or other relevant factors (GASB-31, par. 8).
	Participating interest-earning investment contracts that mature beyond one year of their acquisition date should be reported at fair value (GASB-31, par. 8).
	Participating interest-earning investment contracts that mature within one year or less at the date of their acquisition may be reported at amortized cost, assuming the investment is not affected by the financial institution's credit standing or other relevant factors (GASB-31, par. 9).
• Debt securities	Report at fair value. **Exception:** Money market investments that mature within one year or less at the date of their acquisition may be reported at amortized cost, assuming the investment is not affected by the financial institution's credit standing or other relevant factors (GASB-31, par. 9).
• Open-end mutual fund	Report at fair value based on the fund's current share price (GASB-31, par. 10).
• External investment pools are not SEC registered (including governmental pools and non-governmental pools, except 2a7-like pools)	Report at fair value based on the fair value per share of the pool's underlying portfolio. If the governmental entity cannot obtain sufficient information from the pool sponsor to determine the fair value of the investment in the pool, the best estimate of its fair value should be made and the basis for the estimate should be disclosed in a note to the financial statements (GASB-31, pars. 11 and 15e).
• 2a7-like pools	Report the investment based on the pool's share price (GASB-31, par.12).

DISCLOSURE REQUIREMENTS FOR DERIVATIVES NOT PRESENTED AT FAIR VALUE ON THE STATEMENT OF NET ASSETS

Overview

In June 2003, GASB issued Technical Bulletin 2003-1 (GASB:TB 2003-1) ("Disclosure Requirements for Derivatives Not Presented at Fair Value on the Statement of Net Assets"), which supersedes GASB: TB 94-1. However, the GASB continues to research the issues related to derivatives, and additional guidance is expected in future years.

> **PRACTICE ALERT:** In May 2006, the GASB issued a Preliminary Views (PV) document to improve the accounting and financial reporting of derivatives by state and local governments. The proposal would require that the fair value of derivatives be reported in the financial statements as well as the change in the fair value. If, however, a derivative is effectively hedging (reducing) the risk it was created to address, then the annual changes in the derivative's fair value would be deferred and reported in a government's balance sheet. Governments would also disclose additional information about their derivatives in the notes to the financial statements.

Scope of Technical Bulletin 2003-1

The scope of GASB:TB 2003-1 is limited in that it establishes only disclosure requirements for derivatives that are not currently reported at fair value in the statement of net assets (balance sheet). Currently, the following standards, although not specifically referring to investments in derivatives, nonetheless require that derivatives be reported at fair value in the statement of net assets:

- GASB-31 (Accounting and Financial Reporting for Certain Investments and for External Investment Pools) requires that investments in (1) interest-earning investment contracts, (2) external investment pools, (3) open-end mutual funds, (4) debt securities, and (5) equity securities be reported at fair value; furthermore, any embedded derivatives in these investments must also be reported at fair value.
- GASB-25 (Financial Reporting for Defined Benefit Pension Plans and Note Disclosures for Defined Contribution Plans) and GASB-43 (Financial Reporting for Postemployment Benefit Plans Other Than Pension Plans) requires that all investments (excluding insurance contracts) held by defined benefit plans be reported at fair value.

In some instances, a derivative may be reported in the financial statements, but not at fair value. For example, a governmental entity might have made a premium payment in order to enter into a derivative contract and even though the premium cost may be reported in the statement of net assets, the reported amount is not equivalent to reporting the derivative at fair value.

Definition of Derivatives

GASB:TB 2003-1 incorporates the definition of a "derivative" found in FAS-133 (Accounting for Derivative Instruments and Hedging Activities), as amended:

> A derivative instrument is a financial instrument or other contract with all three of the following characteristics:
>
> a. It has (1) one or more underlyings and (2) one or more notional amounts or payment provisions or both. Those terms determine the amount of the settlement or settlements, and, in some cases, whether or not a settlement is required.
> b. It requires no initial net investment or an initial net investment that is smaller than would be required for other types of contracts that would be expected to have a similar response to changes in market factors.
> c. Its terms require or permit net settlement, it can readily be settled net by a means outside the contract, or it provides for delivery of an asset that puts the recipient in a position not substantially different from net settlement.

PRACTICE POINT: FAS-133 notes that the term "notional amounts" may be referred to by other names such as "face amount."

PRACTICE POINT: GASB:TB 2003-1 incorporates the definition of a derivative established by FAS-133 but it does not incorporate all of the standards established by FAS-133 as amended. FAS-133 requires that all derivatives be reported at fair value as assets or liabilities in the statement of net assets. GASB:TB 2003-1 establishes only disclosure requirements for certain derivatives. As CCH's 2008 *Governmental GAAP Guide* went to press the GASB was developing an Exposure Draft of a Statement on reporting derivatives at fair value.

Underlyings Aderivative's value is based on the value of the item (the underlying) that it is related to. For example, a foreign currency option is a derivative whose value is based on the movement of a particular foreign currency in relationship to the dollar. A governmental entity might have an investment in a debt security that is denominated in a foreign currency, such as the euro, and in order to protect itself from foreign currency risk it could acquire a derivative based on the movement of the euro in relationship to the dollar. Other underlyings relate to items such as interest rates, commodity prices, and stock market indexes.

Notional amount Because a derivative's value is based on the related underlying, there must be some way to determine how the derivative contract will eventually be settled. That amount or quantity is referred to as the "notional amount." For example, in a foreign currency option, the notional amount is the specified amount of foreign currency identified in the contract. The foreign currency contract could identify <1,000,000 as the notional amount, and if at the date of the contract settlement the exchange rate is $1 is equal to <1.1, the basis for settling the contract is $909,091 [=1,000,000 × (1.0/1.1)].

> **PRACTICE POINT:** As explained below, the notional amount is used as the basis for determining how the contract will be settled; however, the actual settlement is generally on a net, not a gross, basis.

Small or no initial investment One of the attractions of investing in a derivative is that the investment strategy allows an investor to employ leverage. That is, a derivative "does not require an initial net investment in the contract that is equal to the notional amount (or the notional amount plus a premium or minus a discount) or that is determined by applying the notional amount to the underlying." For example, an option to buy 1,000 shares of a particular company's common stock does not require an investment equal the number of shares times the current market price of the stock; however, it puts the investor in the same position to earn a profit as if the shares had actually been acquired.

Net settlement Investors in derivatives are generally not interested in delivering or receiving the item that underlies the derivative contract. For example, a futures contract that involves 1,000 troy ounces of gold would meet the net settlement condition if the parties are required to settle the contract by a payment based on the change in the price of gold from the date the derivative contract was executed through the date it is settled. If the derivative contract does not allow for a net settlement, it is not considered a derivative as defined by FAS-133.

Required Disclosures

GASB:TB 2003-1 requires that the following disclosures be made for derivatives that exist as of the date of the statement of net assets but are not reported at fair value in the statement:

- Objective of the derivative
- Significant terms of the derivative
- Fair value of the derivative
- Risks related to the derivative
- Associated debt

Objective of the derivative Derivative transactions are often complex. GASB:TB 2003-1 requires that the governmental entity provide context for understanding the purpose of the derivative. Items to be disclosed include strategies related to the reason for entering into the derivative transaction, the type of derivative, and options purchased or sold. For example, the following disclosure illustrates the objective of a municipal utility that entered into a commodity swap in order to mitigate its exposure to price changes for the fuel oil it uses to generate electricity:

> The municipal utility uses fuel oil in order to generate electricity and is therefore exposed to market price fluctuations of this raw material. In order to reduce this exposure, a commodity swap (a derivative) is entered into during the year.

Significant terms of the derivative In order to provide insight into the significance of the derivative strategy, the governmental entity should disclose its significant terms, which include the notional amount and the initial date of the contract, and its expiration or maturity date. In addition, depending on the type of derivative, other terms might include interest rates, embedded options, and other terms unique to the particular derivative. The significant terms of the commodity swap in the example disclosure paragraph above could be described as follows:

> The commodity swap was entered into by the municipal utility on October 1, 20X5, and expires in one year. Payments are made at the end of each quarter, beginning on December 31, 20X5, and are based on the commodity spot price as of that date and the notional amount of 10 million gallons of fuel oil.

Fair value of the derivative The disclosure should include the fair value of the derivative as of the date of the statement of net assets. If the valuation is not based on quoted market prices, the disclosure should describe the method used to estimate the fair value and the significant assumptions that the method is based on.

GASB:TB 2003-1 adopts the description of fair value offered in paragraph 24 of GASB-25:

> Fair value should be measured by the market price if there is an active market for the investment. If there is not an active market for an investment but there is an active market for similar investments, selling prices in that market may be helpful in estimating fair value. If a market price is not available, a forecast of expected cash flows may aid in estimating fair value, provided that the expected cash flows are discounted at a rate commensurate with the risk involved.

In many instances there will not be a quoted market price to determine the fair value of a derivative; however, GASB:TB 2003-1 provides guidance for estimating the fair value of investments when market quotations are not available. Specifically, GASB:TB 2003-1 points out that these valuation approaches should be formula-based and that the method used should be disclosed.

Risks related to the derivative Although the purpose of entering into a derivative contract is to reduce or mitigate risks, the derivative transaction itself might expose or increase the entity's exposure to specific risks. GASB:TB 2003-1 requires that an entity disclose its exposure to the following types of risks related to derivative contracts that exist as of the date of the statement of net assets:

- *Credit risk* The risk that a counterparty will not fulfill its obligations under the terms of the derivative contract. Credit risk related to the counterparty can be conveyed by information such as credit quality ratings established by rating agencies, the maximum loss that could arise in the case of nonperformance by the counterparty (exclusive of collateral or other security, if any), the amount, nature, and description of collateral or other securities available under the terms of the contract, description of any master netting arrangement that mitigates credit risk, and the extent of diversification among counterparties.
- *Interest rate risk* The risk that changes in interest rates will adversely affect the fair values of financial instruments held by the governmental entity or change its cash flows. Interest rate risk related to derivatives should be described based on the terms of the contract. For example, a governmental entity involved in an interest rate swap that under certain conditions

will require it to increase its net cash payments must disclose that fact.

- *Basis risk* The risk that "arises when variable interest rates on a derivative and an associated bond or other interest-paying financial instrument are based on different indexes." Basis risk should be conveyed by disclosing the payment terms under the contract and any payment terms of the government's associated debt.
- *Termination risk* The risk that arises should the counterparty to the derivative contract be unable to perform. Termination risk disclosures include, when applicable, (1) termination dates identified in the contract, (2) events that have occurred that could terminate the contract, and (3) out-of-the-ordinary termination events included in the contract or covered by other regulations that govern the particular derivative contract.
- *Rollover risk* The risk that arises when a government has a variable-rate bond outstanding but the length of the related derivative does not extend to the maturity date of the bond. Rollover risk is described by disclosing the maturity date of the derivative and the maturity date of the related debt.
- *Market-access risk* The risk related to a strategy that assumes that the governmental entity will be financially able to enter credit markets at a future date and execute its plan that is part of the derivative strategy, or that the cost of entering the credit market will be too costly to execute the plan. When a governmental entity is exposed to market-access risk, that possibility should be disclosed and explained.

Associated debt A governmental entity may enter into a derivative contract in order to change the nature of interest payments. For example, a governmental entity could execute an interest rate swap in order to change the interest rate from a variable rate to a fixed rate or vice versa. GASB:TB 2003-1 states that when interest rate swaps (and other derivatives that effectively change the contract interest rate to a synthetic interest rate) exist, the derivative's net cash flow should be disclosed as part of the debt service requirements of the associated debt. Specifically, GASB-38 (Certain Financial Statement Note Disclosures) requires that a governmental entity disclose debt service requirements to maturity with separate presentations for each of the five years following the date of the statement of net assets and in five-year increments thereafter through the year of maturity. The disclosure must identify the principal and interest components of debt service. Following is an illustration of the disclosure requirements established by GASB-38 and GASB:TB 2003-1 with respect to associated debt related to an interest rate swap:

Variable-Rate Bonds

Year Ended June 30	Principal	Interest	Interest Rate Swap, Net (A)	Total
20X1		$ 2,400,000	$ 500,000	$ 2,900,000
20X2		2,400,000	500,000	2,900,000
20X3		2,400,000	500,000	2,900,000
20X4	$100,000,000	2,400,000	500,000	2,900,000
20X5	100,000,000	1,920,000	400,000	2,320,000
20X6–20X8	300,000,000	2,880,000	600,000	3,480,000
Total	$500,000,000	$14,400,000	$3,000,000	$17,400,000

(A) This amount represents the cash that was paid or due to the counterparty for the year ended June 30, 20X1, based on the terms of the variable-to-fixed interest rate swap derivative. The amounts for the subsequent years are based on the assumption that interest rate conditions that existed during 20X1 will be the same over the term of the derivative contract.

DEPOSIT AND INVESTMENT RISK DISCLOSURES

Guidance for disclosures related to deposits, investments, and reverse repurchase agreements is established in GASB-3 [Deposits with Financial Institutions, Investments (Including Repurchase Agreements), and Reverse Repurchase Agreements], as amended by GASB-40 (Deposit and Investment Risk Disclosures).

The purpose of GASB-3 and GASB-40 is to provide users of financial statements with information to assess the risk related to a governmental entity's investments, including repurchase agreements, deposits with financial institutions, and reverse repurchase agreements. GASB-3 requires that the following disclosures related to investment risk be made in notes to the governmental entity's financial statements (GASB-3, par. 63):

- Legal or contractual provisions for deposits and investments, including repurchase agreements
- Deposits and investments, including repurchase agreements, as of the balance sheet date
- Legal or contractual provisions for reverse repurchase agreements
- Reverse repurchase agreements as of the balance sheet date

GASB-40 amends GASB-3 to require the following additional disclosures related to deposit and investment risks:

- Credit risk, including custodial credit risk and concentrations of credit risk
- Interest rate risk
- Foreign currency risk
- Deposit and investment policies related to the applicable risks

> **PRACTICE POINT:** The additional risk disclosures required by GASB-40 should generally be made for the primary government, including its blended component units. The disclosures should be made for the governmental activities, business-type activities, individual major funds, nonmajor funds in the aggregate, and fiduciary fund types when the risk exposures are significantly greater for these units than for the primary government as a whole.

Legal or Contractual Provisions for Deposits and Investments

The governmental entity should disclose the types of investments that can be acquired by the primary government based on legal and contractual restrictions. There may be significantly different restrictions for component units, or the restrictions may vary significantly among funds or fund types. Under both of these circumstances, the different investment restrictions should be disclosed when investment activities for the component unit's individual funds or individual fund types are material in relationship to the reporting entity's investment activities. Violation of these and other investment restrictions should be disclosed in notes to the financial statements (GASB-3, pars. 65–66).

The following is an example of a note that describes legal or contractual provisions for deposits and investments, including repurchase agreements:

> The City follows the practice of pooling cash and investments of all funds with the City Treasurer except for restricted funds generally held by outside custodians on behalf of Enterprise Funds, investments of the Employees' Retirement Fund held by trustees, and other similar funds. Each fund's portion of total cash and investments is summarized by fund type in the balance sheet or statement of net assets as equity in pooled cash and investments.
>
> Various restrictions on deposits and investments, including repurchase agreements, are imposed by statutes. These restrictions are summarized below.
>
> *Deposits* All deposits with financial institutions must be collateralized in an amount equal to 110% of uninsured deposits. The collateral must be held by the pledging financial institution's trust department. Briefly during the year, the

value of the collateralized property fell to 103% of uninsured deposits.

Investments The City is authorized to make direct investments in U.S. government, federal agency, and instrumentality obligations. In addition, the City may invest in investment-grade bonds, commercial paper rated A-1 by Standard and Poor's Corporation or P-1 by Moody's Commercial Paper Record, repurchase agreements, and the state treasurer's investment pool. When repurchase agreements are executed, the fair value of the securities must be equal to 105% of the cost of the repurchase agreement. On two occasions during the year, which represented 13% of all repurchase agreement transactions, the fair value of securities were equal to 103% and 104% of the cost of the repurchase agreement.

Disclosures Related to Cash Deposits with Financial Institutions

When deposits with financial institutions are fully insured or collateralized by securities held by the governmental entity or its agent in the governmental entity's name, the only disclosure necessary is a statement that deposits with financial institutions are fully insured or collateralized by securities held in the government's name. On the other hand, when deposits are not fully insured or collateralized, the governmental entity is exposed to "custodial credit risk," which is defined as "the risk that a government will not be able to recover deposits if the depository financial institution fails or will not be able to recover collateral securities that are in the possession of an outside party."

Specifically, deposits with financial institutions are subject to custodial credit risk (and must be disclosed) when they are not covered by depository insurance and have one of the three following characteristics (GASB-40, par. 8):

1. Uncollateralized (no securities are pledged to the depositor government)
2. Collateralized with securities held by the pledging financial institution in the depositor government's name
3. Collateralized with securities held by the pledging financial institution, or by its trust department or agent, but not in the depositor government's name

Depository insurance includes the following:

- Federal depository insurance funds, such as those maintained by the Federal Deposit Insurance Corporation (FDIC)

- State depository insurance funds
- Multiple financial institution collateral pools that insure public deposits. (In such a pool, a group of financial institutions holding public funds pledge collateral to a common pool.)

When a governmental entity has deposits in financial institutions at the end of the year that are subject to any one of the three custodial risks described above, the disclosure should include (1) the amount of the bank balance, (2) a statement that the balance is uninsured, and (3) the nature of the custodial credit risk for each uninsured deposit (category 1, 2, or 3, as listed above).

In addition, the governmental entity should disclose deposit policies that are related to custodial credit risks. If a governmental entity has no deposit policy that addresses custodial credit risk to which it is exposed, that fact must nonetheless be disclosed (GASB-40, par. 6).

The following is an example of a disclosure related to deposits with financial institutions whereby some of the deposits are uninsured:

> **NOTE X. Custodial Credit Risk Related to Deposits** Custodial credit risk is the risk that, in the event of a bank failure, the City's deposits might not be recovered. Neither the state nor the City has a deposit policy for custodial credit risk. As of June 30, 20X1, $500,000 of the City's bank balances of $10,400,000 were exposed to custodial credit risk as follows:

Uninsured and uncollateralized	$200,000
Uninsured and collateralized with securities held by pledging financial institutions	180,000
Uninsured and collateralized with securities held by the pledging bank's trust department but not in the City's name	120,000
Total	$500,000

> **PRACTICE POINT:** The disclosure is based on the deposited amount as reported by the bank rather than the amount reported in the financial statements because the former identifies the amount of the deposit subject to custodial credit risk.

Deposits in foreign financial institutions denominated in a foreign currency are subject to foreign currency risk (the risk that changes in exchange rates will adversely affect the fair value of a deposit). When a governmental entity is exposed to foreign currency risk, GASB-40 requires that the U.S. dollar amount of the deposit and the currency used to denominate the deposit be disclosed (GASB-40, par. 17).

If the governmental entity has suffered losses from defaults by counterparties to deposit transactions or has recovered amounts reported as losses in previous years, those amounts should be disclosed in the financial statements (GASB-3, par. 75).

Level of detail Disclosure requirements for deposits with financial institutions focus on the primary government (including blended component units) and also on deposits reflected in (1) governmental activities, (2) business-type activities, (3) major funds, (4) nonmajor governmental funds and enterprise funds in the aggregate, and (5) fiduciary fund types (GASB-40, par. 5).

> **OBSERVATION:** The standards established by GASB-40 do not change the disclosure requirements for deposits of discretely presented component units, which are described in GASB-3 (par. 64) as amended by GASB-14 (The Financial Reporting Entity) and GASB-34. (Basic Financial Statements—and Management's Discussion and Analysis—for State and Local Governments).

Disclosures Related to Investments

Deposits and investments generally are two of the largest asset classifications reported in a governmental entity's financial statements. Their importance was emphasized by the issuance of GASB-3 to provide users of financial statements with disclosures sufficient to assess risks related to a governmental entity's investments, including repurchase agreements, deposits with financial institutions, and reverse repurchase agreements. The disclosures in GASB-3 concentrated on describing credit risk and especially custodial credit risk, which are defined as follows:

- *Credit risk* The risk that an issuer or other counterparty to an investment will not fulfill its obligations.
- *Custodial credit risk* The custodial credit risk for investments is the risk that a government will not be able to recover the value of investment or collateral securities that are in the possession of an outside party if the counterparty to the transaction fails.

GASB-40 was issued in order to modify custodial credit risk disclosures and to "establish more comprehensive disclosure requirements addressing other common risks of the deposits and investments of state and local governments."

> **OBSERVATION:** GASB-40 focuses on what the GASB considers to be the most common risks related to deposits and

investments; however, the Board encourages preparers of governmental financial statements to disclose other risks that are not specifically mandated in GASB-40.

Investment Types

Generally, disclosures related to investments should be formatted based on investment types, such as investments in U.S. treasuries, corporate bonds, and equities. Professional judgment must be used in order not to aggregate dissimilar investments for disclosure purposes. For example (for disclosure purposes), investments in mutual funds that predominantly invest in equities should generally not be aggregated with direct equity securities held by the governmental entity (GASB-40, par. 4).

Level of Disclosure

Investment disclosures should focus separately on (1) governmental activities, (2) business-type activities, (3) individual major funds, (4) aggregated nonmajor funds, and (5) fiduciary fund types of the primary government when the risk is significantly greater for one of the five categories than for the primary government as a whole. For example, GASB-40 points out that concentration of credit risk may not be great for the overall primary government but it could be for an individual major fund because that particular fund invests most of its resources in the securities of a single issuer (GASB-40, par. 5).

Investment Policies

GASB-40 requires that a governmental entity disclose investment policies that are related to investment risks. For example, if the entity holds investments denominated in a foreign currency, it should disclose its investment policy with respect to foreign currency risk. For example, a governmental entity may have an investment policy that limits investments denominated in foreign currencies to 5% of total investments. If the entity has adopted no policy with respect to a particular risk, that fact should be part of the disclosure (GASB-40, par. 6). Specifically, GASB-40 addresses disclosure issues related to the following investment risks:

- Concentration of credit risk
- Credit risk
- Custodial credit risk

- Foreign currency risk
- Interest rate risk

Credit Risk

GASB-40 requires a governmental entity to make disclosures related to investments in debt instruments about the credit risk (the risk that an issuer or other counterparty to an investment will not fulfill its obligations). Credit risk disclosure is accomplished by classifying debt investments as of the entity's balance sheet date by debt type and by credit quality ratings assigned by nationally recognized rating agencies (Standard & Poor's, Moody's Investors Service, and Fitch). For example, investments in commercial paper could be rated as A1 by Standard & Poor's, Aaa by Moody's Investors Service, and F-1 by Fitch. If the investment grade of a governmental entity's investment in commercial paper varies, the investment categories must be expanded to disclose the different quality of ratings by dollar amount (GASB-40, par. 7).

The disclosure for debt investments applies to external investment pools, money market funds, bond mutual funds, and other pooled investments for fixed-income securities. If credit ratings for any of these investments are not available, the disclosure should indicate which investments are unrated.

> **PRACTICE POINT:** Unless there is evidence to the contrary, investments in U.S. government debt or debt guaranteed by the U.S. government is considered to have no credit risk and therefore the credit rating for these investments does not have to be disclosed.

Custodial credit risk GASB-40 points out that a governmental entity's investments are exposed to custodial credit risk when they are uninsured, unregistered, and are held by either (1) the counterparty or (2) the counterparty's trust department or agent, but not in the government's name. When investments held as of the date of the balance sheet are exposed to custodial credit risk the following proposed disclosures should be made:

- The type of investment
- The reported amount
- How the investments are held

> **OBSERVATION:** The GASB reiterates the point made in GASB-3 (par. 69) that generally, investments in external investment pools and in open-end mutual funds are not subject to custodial credit risk because "their existence is not evidenced by securities that exist in physical or book entry form." Also,

securities for reverse repurchase agreements are not exposed to custodial credit risk, because those securities are held by the buyer-lender.

GASB-3 established the following three categories of disclosure requirements for investments (and deposits):

Category	*Investments*	*Deposits*
1	Insured or registered or securities held by the entity or its agent in the entity's name	Insured or collateralized, with securities held by the entity or by its agent in the entity's name
2	Uninsured and unregistered, with securities held by the counterparty's trust department or agent in the entity's name	Collateralized, with securities held by the pledging financial institution's trust department or agent in the entity's name
3	Uninsured and unregistered, with securities held by the counterparty or by its trust department or agent but not in the entity's name (this includes the portion of the carrying amount of any repurchase agreement that exceeds the market value of the underlying securities)	Uncollateralized (this includes any bank balance that is collateralized with securities held by the pledging financial institution, or by its trust department or agent but not in the entity's name)

Because of new federal statutes since the issuance of GASB-3 (especially the passage of the Government Securities Act), GASB-40 limits custodial credit disclosures for investments (and deposits) to category 3. That is not to say that custodial risk does not continue for the other two categories; however, the GASB believes that "given the experience of the financial community and the current regulatory environment, the Board now believes an exception-based disclosure is justified."

OBSERVATION: GASB-40 limits disclosures to investment and deposit positions as of the date of the balance sheet, while GASB-3 had a broader scope. For example, paragraph 73 of GASB-3 required that when the amount of uninsured and unregistered securities held during the year by the counterparty, its trust department, or its agent but not held in the governmental entity's name (the third category of custodial credit risk) significantly exceeded the amount of the securities held as of the balance sheet date, the reason for this situation should be briefly described in a note to the financial statements. Also, paragraph 74 of GASB-3 required the disclosure of types of investments held during the period but not held as of the balance sheet date. GASB-40 eliminates these requirements in order to avoid window dressing as of the balance sheet date; however, the Board "acknowledges that there may be a valid concern and notes that this was of concern during the development of Statement 3, but does not believe it rises to the level of an essential disclosure."

Financial Institutions and Brokers-Dealers as Counterparties

GASB Technical Bulletin (GASB:TB) 87-1 (Applying Paragraph 68 of GASB Statement 3) addressed the question of whether a financial institution or broker-dealer that purchases securities on behalf of a governmental entity is considered a counterparty to the transaction. Classifying a financial institution or broker-dealer (that purchases securities for a governmental entity) as a counterparty is important in determining how investments are categorized under paragraph 68 of GASB-3. Uninsured or unregistered securities (including repurchase agreements) may be classified in one of the following three categories (GASB:TB 87-1, pars. 2–4):

Category A Uninsured and unregistered investments held by the governmental entity or held by the governmental entity's agent in the name of the governmental entity.

Category B Uninsured or unregistered investments held in the name of the governmental entity but held by the counterparty's trust department or the counterparty's agent.

Category C Uninsured and unregistered investments held by the counterparty, the counterparty's trust department, or the counterparty's agent, but not held in the governmental entity's name.

OBSERVATION: Although GASB-40 reduces the scope of disclosures with respect to custodial credit risk related to investments, the guidance established by GASB:TB 87-1 is still relevant in determining when a financial institution or broker-dealer that purchases securities on behalf of a governmental entity is considered a counterparty to the transaction.

A financial institution or broker-dealer may act as the governmental entity's custodial agent, in which case the investment would be classified in Category A. On the other hand, a financial institution or broker may be a counterparty to an investment transaction, in which case the investment would be classified in either Category B or Category C. When the financial institution or broker-dealer fills both roles (custodial agent and counterparty), the role of the counterparty must prevail with respect to classifying the investment; therefore, the investment would be classified in Category B or Category C but not in Category A(GASB:TB 87-1, par. 4).

GASB:TB 87-1 also addresses the definition of a *trust department* with respect to the dual role (custodial agent and counterparty) of a broker-dealer. A trust department is authorized and registered under state or federal laws and is part of a financial institution such as a commercial bank or savings and loan association. An important characteristic of a trust department is its fiduciary role; it holds assets for other parties, and those assets are legally separate from the assets of the financial institution of which it is a part (GASB:TB 87-1, par. 5).

Based on this description, GASB:TB 87-1 states that nonfinancial institution broker-dealers cannot have a trust department. A nonfinancial institution broker-dealer could, through its trust department, be the governmental entity's custodial agent. However, if the broker-dealer is also a counterparty to the investment transaction, the investment could not be classified in either Category B because GASB:TB 87-1 does not consider the broker-dealer's trust department to be a legal trust department) or Category A(because the broker-dealer would be considered both the custodial agent and the counterparty, and as noted earlier, the role as the counterparty would prevail in categorizing the investment as required by GASB-3) (GASB:TB 87-1, par. 5).

GASB:TB 87-1 presents two examples to illustrate the classification of investments whereby a financial institution or broker-dealer is a counterparty to an investment transaction.

Example 1 A governmental entity instructs a broker to purchase $800,000 of U.S. government securities, and the broker holds the investment but identifies the securities as owned by the governmental entity in its internal records. Since the broker is a member of the Securities Investor Protection Corporation (SIPC), its customer's account is insured to $500,000. Part of the investment ($500,000) should be classified as insured (Category A) and the balance ($300,000) should be classified as uninsured or unregistered and held by a counterparty (Category C) (GASB:TB 87-1, par. 6).

Example 2 A governmental entity instructs a financial institution to purchase $800,000 of U.S. government securities. The financial institution's trade department executes the transaction and the securities are held by the financial institution's trust department. The financial institution is not a member of the SIPC. The trust department identifies the securities as owned by the governmental entity in its internal records. The entire investment should be classified as uninsured and unregistered and held by the counterparty's trust department (Category B) (GASB:TB 87-1, par. 7).

If it were assumed that the trade department of the financial institution held the securities, then the investment would be classified as uninsured and unregistered and held by the counterparty (Category C).

Book entry systems GASB:TB 87-1 provides guidance in determining how the use of a book entry system affects the credit risk of securities that are owned by a governmental entity or securities that are related to a repurchase agreement entered into by a governmental entity. For the most part, only financial institutions and brokerdealers can be members of the Federal Reserve or participants in the Depository Trust Company (DTC). Governmental entities may have accounts in the Federal Reserve book entry system, but those accounts are not similar to Federal Reserve member accounts because of their lack of flexibility. Additionally, governmental entities may have access to the Federal Reserve or DTC book entry system through a Federal Reserve member or a DTC participant, but this is not equivalent to having an account directly with those organizations (GASB: TB 87-1, pars. 8–9).

The Federal Reserve or DTC book entry system is not a critical issue in determining how investments should be categorized under GASB-3. The Federal Reserve or DTC generally should not be considered an agent of the governmental entity, a counterparty's trust department or agent, or a counterparty. As described below, the characteristics of the investment transactions must be evaluated to identify which party "holds" the governmental entity's securities (GASB:TB 87-1, pars. 8–9).

Entity's agent For securities to be classified in Category A, there must be an agency relationship between the governmental entity and the party holding the securities. The agency relationship should have the following characteristics (GASB:TB 87-1, par. 10):

- There is a contractual relationship between the governmental entity and the custodial agent.
- The contract names the custodial agent as the governmental entity's agent.
- The securities held by the custodial agent are held in the name of the governmental entity.

To satisfy the condition that a custodial agent holds securities in the name of a governmental entity, the governmental entity must have unconditional rights and claims to the securities held by the agent. For securities that are part of a repurchase agreement, the governmental entity must have unconditional rights and claims to the securities if the counterparty defaults on the repurchase agreement. For securities to be considered held in the name of a governmental entity in the Federal Reserve or DTC book entry system, the following conditions must be satisfied (GASB:TB 87-1, par. 10):

- Securities must be held in a separate custodial or fiduciary account (a custodial or fiduciary account is an account that is separate from the account in which the custodian's own securities are held).
- The custodian's internal control records must identify the securities as being owned by or pledged to the governmental entity.

The custodial or fiduciary account does not have to specifically identify the governmental entity that owns the securities or the entity to which the securities are pledged (GASB:TB 87-1, par. 10).

Counterparty's trust department or agent When the governmental entity's uninsured and unregistered securities are held by a counterparty's trust department or counterparty's agent, the classification of the securities into Category B or Category C depends on whether the securities are held in the name of the governmental entity. The following factors suggest that the securities are held in the name of the governmental entity (GASB:TB 87-1, par. 11):

- The counterparty's trust department or agent uses a separate custodial or fiduciary Federal Reserve or DTC account.
- The counterparty's trust department or agent identifies the securities in its internal accounting records as belonging to the governmental entity.
- The counterparty's trust department or agent recognizes the governmental entity's rights to the securities.

If it is concluded that the counterparty's trust department or agent holds the securities in the name of the governmental entity, the securities should be classified in Category B. Category C should be used to classify the securities if it is concluded that the securities are not held in the name of the governmental entity (GASB:TB 87-1, par. 11).

Counterparty In the following circumstances, uninsured and unregistered securities should be classified in Category C even though the securities are held by a custodian (GASB:TB 87-1, par. 12):

- The custodian of the securities keeps the securities in its Federal Reserve account and the custodian is a counterparty to the sale or the pledging of the securities.
- The custodian of the securities keeps the securities in its DTC account and the custodian is a counterparty to the sale.

The circumstances surrounding an investment transaction must be evaluated to determine how uninsured and unregistered securities should be classified when the securities are pledged through the DTC. There must be a written agreement between a pledgee and the DTC in order to pledge securities through the DTC book entry system. A pledgee must be a DTC participant, and for this reason, a governmental entity must have a participant act as a pledgee for the entity. Securities should be considered under the control of the pledgee if the DTC procedures and the written agreement give the pledgee the following rights (GASB:TB 87-1, par. 13):

- Right to have the securities moved from the pledger's account to the pledgee's account
- Right to approve any release of the pledge on the securities

When these conditions are satisfied, the securities are classified in Category A, B, or C depending on (1) who fills the role of the pledgee (the governmental entity's agent, the counterparty's trust department, or the counterparty's agent) and (2) in whose name the securities are held (the governmental entity or some other party) (GASB:TB 87-1, par. 13).

Concentration of credit risk GASB-40 recognizes that there is an additional dimension to credit risk that relates to the amount of investment in any one entity. For this reason GASB-40 requires that a governmental entity disclose the amount invested in a separate issuer (except investments held in the U.S. government or investments guaranteed by the U.S. government) when that amount is at least 5% of total investments. The base (total investments) to be used to determine the 5% threshold must be selected consistent with the "level of disclosure criterion" required by GASB-40 (the level of disclosure was discussed earlier) (GASB-40, par. 11).

Interest rate risk Interest rate risk arises from investments in debt instruments and is defined as "the risk that changes in interest rates will adversely affect the fair value of an investment." The amount of loss in the fair value of a fixed-income security increases as the current market interest rate related to the investment rises (GASB-40, pars. 14–16).

GASB-40 requires that a governmental entity provide information about debt investments so that a reader can assess to some degree the entity's exposure to interest rate risk. This disclosure is achieved by grouping investments into investment types and using one of the following methods to inform users of the level of interest rate sensitivity for debt investments:

- Segmented time distributions
- Specific identification
- Weighted average maturity

- Duration
- Simulation model

The disclosure method selected to demonstrate interest rate risk should be the one that the governmental entity uses to identify and manage its interest rate risk. Assumptions that are necessary to describe interest rate risk, such as the timing of cash flows (for example, when an investment has a call provision) and changes in interest rates, should also be disclosed.

GASB-40 requires additional disclosures for investments in debt instruments whose fair values are "highly sensitive" to changes in interest rates. For example, a debt investment may have a variable-interest rate that is 1.3 times the three-month London Interbank Offered Rate (LIBOR). For debt investments that are highly sensitive to changes in interest rates, the governmental entity must provide (1) a description of the interest rate sensitivity and (2) contract terms (such as multipliers and benchmark indexes).

Segmented time distributions The segmented time distributions method of disclosing interest rate risk is simple because it groups "investment cash flows into sequential time periods in tabular form." For example, investment types could be categorized as those that mature in less than one year, between one and five years, and so on.

Specific identification The specific identification method does not compute a disclosure measure but presents a list of the individual investments, their carrying amounts, maturity dates, and any call options.

Weighted average maturity When the weighted average maturity method is used to describe a governmental entity's exposure to interest rate risk, the disclosure "expresses investment time horizons—the time when investments become due and payable—in years or months, weighted to reflect the dollar size of individual investments." For example, assume that a debt investment type comprises the following two specific investments (A and B):

Investment	*Months to Maturity*	*Maturity Amount*	*Weighted Months*
A	50	$100,000	16.7*
B	90	200,000	60.0
Total		$300,000	76.7

*50 × ($100,000/$300,000) = 16.7 months

Based on the above facts, the governmental entity would disclose (in tabular form, along with similar information for other investment types) that this particular investment type had a fair value of $300,000 and a weighted average maturity of 76.7 months.

Duration GASB-40 defines "duration" as follows:

> A measure of a debt investment's exposure to fair value changes arising from changing interest rates. It uses the present value of cash flows, weighted for those cash flows as a percentage of the investment's full price. Effective duration makes assumptions regarding the most likely timing and amounts of variable cash flows arising from such investments as callable bonds, prepayments, and variable-rate debt.

A variety of methods can be used to compute the effective duration of an investment. GASB-40 does not mandate the use of a specific technique. The following example is based on the Macaulay duration approach that is illustrated in Appendix C (Illustration 4) of GASB-40. To illustrate this approach, assume that a governmental entity as of June 30, 20X5, has an investment in a bond that has an 8% coupon rate (semiannual payments), $1,000 maturity value, and a maturing date of two years. The cash flows from the investments are summarized as follows:

CASH FLOWS					(A)	(B)	(C)
				Present Value Factor	*Present Value*	*Periods Before Cash*	*(A) X*
12/31/X5	*6/30/X6*	*12/31/X6*	*6/30/X7*	*@ 4%*	*@ 6/30/X5*	*Flows*	*(B)*
40	—	—	—	.96154	$38.46	.5	19.23
—	40	—	—	.92456	36.98	1.0	36.98
—	—	40	—	.88900	35.56	1.5	53.34
—	—	—	1,040	.85480	889.00	2.0	1,778.00
					$1,000.00		1,887.55

The Macaulay duration is computed by dividing the total present values (column C) by the bond price, as follows:

$1,887.55/$1,000 = 1.8876 years

Next, the effective duration is computed by dividing the Macaulay duration (as computed above) by 1 + the coupon rate per payment period. Thus, the effective duration, which is to be disclosed by investment type, is 1.82 years, as follows:

1.8876/1.04 = 1.815 years

Simulation model Finally, a governmental entity can use various simulation models to describe its exposure to interest rate risk, which "estimate changes in an investment's or a portfolio's fair value, given hypothetical changes in interest rates." For example, an investment type's fair value could be presented as of the balance sheet date along with estimated fair values of the same investments assuming that there is a 100-point, 200-point, and so forth increase in the current market interest rate.

Foreign currency risk Investments (as well as deposits in foreign financial institutions) denominated in a foreign currency are subject to "the risk that changes in exchange rates will adversely affect the fair value of an investment." When a governmental entity is exposed to foreign currency risk, GASB-40 requires that the U.S. dollar amount of the investment (classified by investment type) and the currency used to denominate the investment be disclosed (GASB-40, par. 17).

If the governmental entity has suffered losses from defaults by counterparties to investments or has recovered amounts reported as losses in previous years, those amounts should also be disclosed in the financial statements (GASB-3, par. 75).

ACCOUNTING AND REPORTING FOR REPURCHASE/REVERSE REPURCHASE AGREEMENTS

In addition to requiring certain disclosures for investments, and deposits with financial institutions, GASB-3 established accounting, reporting, and disclosure guidelines for repurchase and reverse repurchase agreements. Descriptions of the accounting and reporting standards follow for each specific type of agreement (GASB-3, pars. 78–83).

Repurchase Agreements

In a repurchase agreement transaction, the governmental entity (buyer-lender) transfers cash to a broker-dealer or financial institution (seller-borrower); the broker-dealer or financial institution transfers securities to the governmental entity and promises to repay the cash plus interest in exchange for the return of the *same* securities.

The governmental entity should report income from repurchase agreements as interest income (GASB-3, par. 82).

Reverse Repurchase Agreements

Governmental entities sometimes enter into reverse repurchase agreements when they want to temporarily convert securities in their portfolios to cash. In these transactions, the governmental entity is the seller-borrower, transfers securities to the buyer-lender for cash, and promises to repay cash plus interest in exchange for the return of the *same* securities. The cash obtained in these transactions is often used for operating or capital purposes or is invested in other securities to improve yield.

The governmental entity should report assets and liabilities arising from reverse repurchase agreements as separate line items in its balance sheet. The liability account should be reported as a debt of a governmental fund and identified as obligations under reverse repurchase agreements. The assets should be reported as investments (GASB-3, par. 81).

Dollar Fixed Coupon Repurchase Agreements

The governmental entity should report income from dollar fixed coupon repurchase agreements as interest income (GASB-3, par. 81).

Dollar Yield Maintenance Repurchase Agreements

When a governmental entity enters into a dollar yield maintenance repurchase agreement, the transaction should be accounted for as a purchase and sale of securities with an appropriate recognition of a gain or loss at the time of the sale of the securities (GASB-3, par. 83).

Dollar Fixed Coupon Reverse Repurchase Agreements

The governmental entity should report assets and liabilities arising from dollar fixed coupon reverse repurchase agreements as separate line items in its balance sheet. The liability account should be reported as a debt of a governmental fund and identified as obligations under reverse repurchase agreements. The assets should be reported as investments (GASB-3, par. 82).

Dollar Yield Maintenance Reverse Repurchase Agreements

When a governmental entity enters into a dollar yield maintenance reverse repurchase agreement, the transaction should be accounted for as a sale and purchase of securities with an appropriate recognition of a gain or loss at the time of the sale of the securities (GASB-3, par. 83).

Legal or Contractual Provisions for Reverse Repurchase Agreements

If reverse repurchase agreements were used during the period, the governmental entity should disclose the source of legal or contractual authorization for such transactions. Also, significant violations of restrictions related to reverse repurchase agreements should be disclosed (GASB-3, pars. 76–77).

The following is an example of a note that describes the legal or contractual provisions for reverse repurchase agreements:

> The City, under state statute, is allowed to enter into reverse repurchase agreements. Areverse repurchase agreement is a transaction in which a broker-dealer or financial institution transfers cash to the City and the City transfers securities to the broker-dealer or financial institution and promises to repay the cash plus interest in exchange for the same or similar securities. By state statute, proceeds from reverse repurchase agreements are to be used only for investment purposes; however, on several occasions during the period, the City used the proceeds to temporarily finance current operations.

Reverse Repurchase Agreements

Disclosures for reverse repurchase agreements as of the balance sheet date depend on whether the transaction is based on a yield maintenance agreement (GASB-3, pars. 78–79).

Yield maintenance agreement In a yield maintenance agreement, the securities to be returned to the governmental entity provide a yield specified in the agreement. The following disclosures should be made for commitments to repurchase securities based on yield maintenance reverse repurchase agreements as of the balance sheet date (GASB-3, par. 79):

- The fair value of securities to be repurchased at the balance sheet date
- A description of the terms of the agreement

Other agreements For all reverse repurchase agreements outstanding as of the balance sheet date, other than yield maintenance agreements, the total amounts of the obligation under the agreements (including accrued interest) and the total fair value of the securities related to the agreements should be disclosed. The difference between the two amounts is a measure of the credit risk exposure for the governmental entity in reverse repurchase agreements (GASB-3, pars. 78–79).

Losses from reverse repurchase agreements because of defaults by counterparties, and subsequent recovery of such losses, should be disclosed either in the governmental entity's operating statement or in notes to the financial statements (GASB-3, par. 80).

GASBI-3 requires that a governmental entity disclose whether the maturity dates of investments made with proceeds from reverse repurchase agreements are generally matched with the maturity dates of the related reverse repurchase agreements during the accounting period. The degree to which such matching occurs as of the balance sheet date also must be disclosed (GASBI-3, par. 6).

Also, GASBI-3 notes that disclosures made by pension plans relative to paragraph 80 of GASB-3 are no substitute for the disclosure requirements established by paragraph 29 of GASB-25 (GASBI-3, par. 5).

The following is an example of a note that illustrates disclosure requirements for reverse repurchase agreements:

> The City was obligated under certain reverse repurchase agreements as of the balance sheet date. Credit risk exposure for the City arises when a broker-dealer or financial institution does not return the securities or their value at the conclusion of the reverse repurchase agreement. The amount of the potential economic loss is the difference between the fair value of the securities related to the reverse repurchase agreements, including accrued interest, and the amount of the obligation, including accrued interest, under the reverse repurchase agreement. As of the balance sheet date, the City is exposed to potential economic losses of $5,000. The City of Centerville's investment strategy is to match maturity dates of investments made from the proceeds of reverse repurchase agreements with the maturity dates of the related reverse repurchase agreements. As of June 30, 20X5, the maturity dates of investments coincide with the maturity dates of the related reverse repurchase agreements.

Reverse Repurchase Agreements and Investment Pools

Some governmental entities may combine their resources from various funds into one investment pool, and that investment pool in turn may enter into reverse repurchase agreements. Under this circumstance, the investment pool must allocate the assets and liabilities that arise from the reverse repurchase agreement to the individual funds based on each fund's equity in the pool. In addition, cost incurred and income earned based on reverse repurchase agreements made by the investment pool should be allocated to the participating funds' operating statements based on their respective equity interest in the investment pool.

> **PRACTICE POINT:** Although GASBI-3 refers specifically to balance sheets and operating statements, the standards established also apply to statements of plan net assets and statements of changes in plan net assets as described in GASB-25 (Financial Reporting for Defined Benefit Pension Plans) and GASB-43 (Financial Reporting for Postemployment Benefit Plans Other Than Pension Plans).

SECURITIES LENDING TRANSACTIONS

As part of the management of its cash and investments, a governmental entity may enter into a "securities lending transaction," which the GASB defines as follows:

> Transactions in which governmental entities transfer their securities to broker/dealers and other entities for collateral—which may be cash, securities, or letters of credit—and simultaneously agree to return the collateral for the same securities in the future.

The accounting standards for securities lending transactions apply to (1) governmental funds, (2) proprietary funds, (3) government-wide financial statements, and (4) fiduciary funds. These standards are applied without modification to these four financial reporting circumstances.

Securities lending transactions are generally entered into by large governmental entities, such as pension funds and investment pools, that have significant resources to invest for extended periods.

In a securities lending transaction, the governmental entity (lender) transfers its investments in securities, referred to as the underlying securities, to a broker/dealer (borrower), and the entity receives cash, other securities, or letters of credit. The purpose of the transaction is to enhance the return on the governmental entity's portfolio. For example, cash collateral may be received by the entity and subsequently invested. If the investment income exceeds the amount paid (interest) to the broker/dealer, the governmental entity will earn a net profit on the transaction; however, if the return is less than the amount paid, a net loss will occur. From the broker/dealer perspective, the securities are borrowed to cover short positions in specific securities.

At the end of the securities lending transaction, the governmental entity will return the collateral (the cash, securities or similar securities, or letter of credit) to the broker/dealer, and the broker/dealer will return the underlying securities (or similar securities) to the entity. Although the governmental entity can deal directly with a broker/ dealer, securities lending transactions are usually executed through a "securities lending agent," which GASB-28 (Accounting and Financial Reporting for Securities Lending Transactions) defines as "an entity that arranges the terms and conditions of loans, monitors the fair values of the securities lent and the collateral received, and often directs the investment of cash collateral."

Securities lending transactions raise the fundamental question of whether the governmental entity has incurred a liability that should be presented on its balance sheet. GASB-28 addresses that fundamental question, along with disclosure requirements.

> **PRACTICE POINT:** GASB-28 notes that although no current accounting standard exists that addresses securities lending transactions, the prevailing practice is not to report such transactions as liabilities.

The standards established by GASB-28 apply to all governmental entities that have entered into securities lending transactions during the accounting period for which financial statements are being prepared.

The disclosure requirements established by GASB-28 apply to the primary government and its blended component units. For component units that are discretely presented, the disclosure guidance established by GASB-14 (The Financial Reporting Entity) must be observed (GASB-28, par. 4).

Accounting Standards

For all securities lending transactions, the governmental entity should report the underlying securities (the securities loaned to the broker/dealer) as assets in its balance sheet. Although the underlying securities are transferred to the broker/dealer, they are nonetheless reported as an asset of the governmental entity. Additional accounting treatment for the transaction depends on whether the governmental entity receives (1) cash, (2) securities that can be pledged or sold, (3) securities that cannot be pledged or sold, or (4) letters of credit (GASB-28, par. 5).

Receipt of cash When a governmental entity transfers securities to a broker/dealer or other entity and receives cash as collateral, the securities lending transaction should be recorded as a secured loan. A liability should be recognized, and the transferred securities should not be removed from the governmental entity's balance sheet (GASB-28, par. 6).

In transactions that involve cash collateral, the broker/dealer is paid interest (borrower rebate) on the amount it advances to the governmental entity. The government uses the cash to earn investment income by depositing the funds with a financial institution or by purchasing securities. The profitability of the transaction from the governmental entity's perspective depends on the rate of return on the collateral invested and the interest paid to the broker/dealer.

> **OBSERVATION:** GASB-3 (Deposits with Financial Institutions, Investments [Including Repurchase Agreements], and Reverse Repurchase Agreements) defines a "reverse repurchase agreement" as "an agreement in which a broker/dealer or financial institution (buyer/lender) transfers cash to a governmental entity (seller/borrower); the entity transfers securities to the broker/dealer or financial institution and promises to repay the cash plus interest in exchange for the same securities." On the basis of this definition, the GASB states that a reverse repurchase agreement is essentially the same (from an economic perspective, not a legal and tax perspective) as a securities lending transaction in which cash collateral is received by the governmental entity. GASB-3 requires that reverse repurchase agreements be accounted for as secured loans and not as sales of the securities that are the basis for the transaction. Thus, the accounting and disclosure standards established by GASB-28 for securities lending transactions involving cash collateral are similar to those established by GASB-3 for reverse repurchase agreement transactions.

To illustrate securities lending transactions that involve cash collateral, assume a governmental entity holds investments in U.S. governmental securities that have a cost and fair value basis of $900,000. These securities are transferred to a broker/dealer for cash of $927,000, with the requirement that the securities be returned to the governmental entity at the end of five days. The entity would make the following entry to record the securities lending transaction:

	Debit	Credit
Cash	927,000	
Liability under Securities Lending Transaction		927,000

The securities transferred to the broker/dealer remain on the balance sheet of the governmental entity. As illustrated in the example, the governmental entity records the cash collateral received from the broker/dealer and will subsequently record any securities or deposits acquired or made using the cash collateral as an asset.

> **PRACTICE POINT:** In note 4, GASB-28 points out that the governmental entity may receive cash (collateral) from a

broker/dealer that cannot be invested in securities (only deposited). When this restriction is imposed, the securities lending transactions "should be accounted for as involving securities collateral rather than cash collateral." Accounting for the receipt of securities collateral is discussed in the following section.

Receipt of securities that can be pledged or sold When a governmental entity transfers securities to a broker/dealer and receives securities that can be pledged or sold, even if the borrower has not defaulted on the transaction, the securities lending transaction should be recorded as a secured loan in a manner similar to a collateral transaction previously illustrated (asset and liability accounts are created). The broker/dealer pays the governmental entity a loan premium or fee for the loan of the securities (GASB-28, par. 6).

PRACTICE POINT: In note 5, GASB-28 states that the right to pledge or sell collateral securities without a borrower default must be stated in the securities lending transaction. However, that right could exist for purposes of GASB-28, if the right has been previously demonstrated by pledging or selling securities under a previous contract that did not contain the explicit right. Also, the right could exist if "there is some other indication of the ability to pledge or sell the collateral securities." A borrower default would include "failure to return underlying securities, pay income distributions, or make margin calls; acts of insolvency; and suspension by the Securities and Exchange Commission, an exchange, or a self-regulatory association."

In a securities lending transaction that involves securities as collateral, the broker/dealer receives certain incidents of ownership over the underlying securities during the term of the transaction, including the right to sell or pledge the securities. The governmental entity also receives certain incidents of ownership over the collateral securities. Although both parties have certain ownership rights over the securities they hold (the underlying securities and the collateral securities), each has income distribution rights as described by GASB-28 as follows:

> Interest, dividends, stock splits, and other distributions made by an issuer of securities. Income distributions on underlying securities are payable from the borrower to the lender, and income distributions on collateral securities are payable from the lender to the borrower.

Thus, the governmental entity has distribution rights on the underlying securities and the broker/dealer has distribution rights on the collateral securities.

To illustrate this type of securities lending transaction, assume that in the previous example the governmental entity received investments in corporate fixed-income securities that have a fair value of $927,000, with the requirement that the underlying securities be returned to the governmental entity at the end of five days. The governmental entity would make the following entry to record the securities lending transaction:

Investments in Corporate Fixed-Income Securities	927,000	
Liability under Securities Lending Transaction		927,000

PRACTICE POINT: Both the securities transferred to the broker/dealer (underlying securities) and the securities received from the broker/dealer (collateral securities) are reported on the balance sheet of the governmental entity. The reporting of underlying securities on the balance sheet of the governmental entity is necessary because the securities lending transaction is considered to be a loan of securities and not a sale. At the termination date of the transaction, the governmental entity receives the same or similar securities from the broker/dealer. The reporting of the collateral securities is necessary because the governmental entity is entitled to the risk and rewards of these securities during the term of the contract. The governmental entity can sell or pledge the securities, but at the end of the transaction it must return similar securities to the broker/dealer. If, for example, the collateral securities are sold at one price and their value rises before the governmental entity must return similar securities to the broker/dealer, the governmental entity will have an economic loss on the investment.

Receipt of securities that cannot be pledged or sold When a governmental entity transfers securities to a broker/dealer and receives securities that cannot be pledged or sold unless the borrower defaults, the securities lending transaction is not recorded in the general ledger by the governmental entity. Thus, investment and liability accounts are not created by the transaction. In this type of securities lending transaction, the GASB has concluded that the government's control over the collateral securities is so limited that it would be inappropriate to record the transaction as a secured loan (GASB-28, par. 7).

Receipt of letters of credit In a letter of credit, a financial institution guarantees specified payments of a customer's draft for a designated period of time. When a governmental entity transfers securities to a broker/dealer and receives a letter of credit, the securities lending transaction is not recorded by the governmental entity (GASB-28, par. 7).

Transaction Costs

Costs incurred by a governmental entity in executing a securities lending transaction should be reported as an expenditure/expense in the governmental entity's operating statement. GASB-28 states that such costs include the following (GASB-28, par. 8):

- *Borrower rebates* Payments from the lender to the borrower as compensation for the use of the cash collateral provided by the borrower. [Borrower rebates are to be reported as interest expenditure/expense.]
- *Agent fees* Amounts paid by a lender to its securities lending agent as compensation for managing its securities lending transactions.

Transaction costs should not be netted against income (interest income, investment income, loan premiums or fees, or any other income that arises from the securities lending transaction). GASB-28 provides the following definition of "loan premiums or fees":

> Payments from the borrower to the lender as compensation for the use of the underlying securities when the borrower provides securities or letters of credit as collateral.

> **PRACTICE POINT:** GASB-28 does not change the requirement established by GASB-25 that investment expenses be reported in the additions section (as a reduction to the total of contributions and investment income) of the statement of changes in plan net assets of a defined benefit pension plan.

Governmental Investment Pools

Some governmental entities combine resources from their various funds into an investment pool, and the investment pool in turn may enter into securities lending transactions as defined by GASB-28. Thus, such transactions may create assets and liabilities that must be reported by the governmental entity (when cash or securities that may be sold or pledged with a borrower default are received as collateral). Under this circumstance, the investment pool must allocate the assets and liabilities that arise from the securities lending transactions to the individual funds based on each fund's equity in the pool (GASB-28, par. 9).

> **PRACTICE POINT:** GASB-28 requires such an allocation because an internal investment pool usually is not reported as a separate fund in a governmental entity's financial statements. Thus, the investment pool must observe the

standards established by GASB-28 so that it has sufficient information to make the allocation to the various funds based on the relative equity position of each participating fund. Under this approach, the fund "that has the risk of loss on the collateral assets" will report its appropriate share of assets and liabilities related to securities lending transactions entered into by the governmental investment pool.

Costs incurred and income earned based on securities lending transactions made by the investment pool should be recorded by the investment pool based on the standards established by GASB-28. In turn, those cost and income amounts should be allocated to the participating funds based on their respective equity interest in the investment pool (GASB, par. 10).

PRACTICE POINT: The standards established by GASB-28 apply only to the entities that make up the governmental reporting entity (the primary government and its components) and not to legally separate (outside) entities that participate in the investment pool.

Disclosure Standards

Generally, governmental entities are restricted as to how resources may be invested. Restrictions may be based on legal or contractual provisions. GASB-28 requires that the following be disclosed with respect to securities lending transactions (GASB-28, pars. 11–16):

- Basis of authorization (legal or contractual authorization) for entering into securities lending transactions
- Significant violations of the basis of authorization because securities lending transactions were executed during the accounting period
- General description of securities lending transactions including:
  - — Types of securities loaned by the governmental entity
  - — Types of collateral received by the governmental entity
  - — Whether the governmental entity has the right to sell or pledge securities received as collateral without a borrower default
  - — Amount by which the value of the securities received as collateral exceeds the value of the securities loaned by the governmental entity
  - — Restrictions on the amount of securities that can be loaned

— Carrying value and fair value of the underlying securities (the securities loaned by the governmental entity to the broker/dealer) at the balance sheet date

- Description of loss indemnification (a securities lending agent's guarantee that it will protect the lender from certain losses) provided by the securities lending agent (an entity that arranges the terms and conditions of loans, monitors the fair value of the securities lent and the collateral received, and often directs the invest of cash collateral)
- Statement of whether the maturity dates of investments made with cash collateral received from broker/dealers match the maturity dates of the related securities loans
- The extent to which maturity dates of investments made with cash collateral received from broker/dealers match the maturity date of the related securities loans as of the balance sheet date
- Amount of losses from default of a borrower or lending agent for the year related to securities lending transactions
- Amount of losses recovered from defaults in previous periods
- Amount of credit risk (if any) as of the date of the balance sheet (if no credit risk exists, that fact should be stated in the disclosure)

The disclosure requirement relating to the matching of maturing dates can be a general description rather than a detailed listing of maturity dates. The following are three illustrative general descriptions provided in GASB-28:

- The policy is to match the maturities of the collateral investments and the securities loans and that at year end all securities loans could be terminated on demand by either the entity or the borrower and that substantially all cash collateral was invested in overnight or on-demand investments. (Disclosure explains how maturities are matched.)
- Substantially all securities loans can be terminated on demand either by the entity or by the borrower, although generally the average term of these loans is one week; cash collateral is invested in securities of a longer term, generally with maturities between one week and three months. (Disclosure explains how maturities are not matched.)
- At year end, 50% of the collateral investments were in maturities of less than one week, and the weighted-average term to maturity of all collateral investments was 35 days. (Disclosure explains how maturities are not matched.)

GASB-28, as amended by GASB-40, defines "credit risk" as "the risk that an insurer or other counter party to an investment will not fill its obligations." For securities lending, credit risk is the aggregate of the lender's exposures to the borrowers of its securities. Thus, the governmental entity has credit risk with respect to the broker/dealer when the amount the broker/dealer owes the governmental entity exceeds the amount the governmental entity owes the broker/dealer. To calculate credit risk, the governmental entity must consider the extent, if any, to which the right of offset exists in the case of the broker/dealer, where "offset" refers to the legal right a party has to offset amounts due to and due from another party in the case of default.

To compute the amount owed to the governmental entity, the following must be considered: (1) the fair value of the underlying securities (including accrued interest), (2) unpaid income distributions on the underlying securities, and (3) accrued loan premiums or fees due from the broker/dealer. To compute the amount owed the broker/dealer, the following must be considered: (1) the cash collateral received, (2) the fair value of collateral securities received (including accrued interest), (3) the face value of letters of credit, (4) unpaid income distributions on collateral securities held by the governmental entity, and (5) accrued borrower rebates payable to the broker/dealer.

Generally, the governmental entity initially does not have a credit risk because the fair value of collateral received from the broker/dealer is usually a few percentage points greater than the value of the underlying securities loaned to the broker/dealer. For purposes of the transaction (not for financial reporting), the underlying securities and the collateral securities (but not the securities purchased by cash collateral) are marked-to-market each day and the agreement may require that the broker/dealer provide additional collateral if the fair value of the collateral falls below the fair value of the underlying securities. When the governmental entity is not exposed to credit risk at the end of the year, GASB-28 simply requires that that fact be disclosed by using language such as, "The governmental entity has no credit risk exposure at year end because amounts owed to borrowers exceed amounts borrowers owe the governmental entity."

Collateral securities and underlying securities The carrying amounts and fair values of both collateral securities reported on the governmental entity's balance sheet and underlying securities that are the basis for securities lending transactions should be disclosed (based on the requirements of paragraph 9 of GASB-40). Also, collateral securities reported on the governmental entity's balance sheet should be classified, as required by GASB-3, as amended by GASB-40, paragraph 9.

Collateral securities arising from securities lending transactions should be classified according to the current scheme, unless the collateral securities are part of a "collateral investment pool," which is defined as follows by GASB-28:

> An agent-managed pool that for investment purposes commingles the cash collateral provided on the securities lending transactions of more than one lender.

Underlying securities are not subject to custodial credit risk if the related custodial securities are presented in the governmental entity's balance sheet (and therefore the related custodial securities are evaluated to determine whether they are subject to custodial credit risk as defined in GASB-40). However, underlying securities are subject to custodial risk when the related custodial securities are not presented in the governmental entity's balance sheet (and therefore are not subject to custodial risk disclosures), in which case the determination of whether they are subject to custodial risk is based on the type of collateral that supports the underlying securities.

Cash collateral held as deposits Deposits with financial institutions (including cash collateral held as deposits) must be evaluated for the possible need for custodial credit risk disclosures based on the guidance established by paragraph 8 of GASB-40.

CHAPTER 10
CAPITAL ASSETS

CONTENTS

INTRODUCTION

Capital assets include the following items (GASB-34, par. 19):

- Land and land improvements
- Easements
- Buildings and building improvements
- Vehicles
- Equipment
- Property rights related to capitalized leases
- Works of art, historical treasures, and other similar assets
- Infrastructure assets
- All other tangible or intangible assets used in operations

PRACTICE POINT: The *GASB Comprehensive Implementation Guide* defines land improvements as "betterments, other than buildings, that ready land for its intended use." Examples include the excavation of the land, utility installations, parking lots, and landscaping.

The accounting standards that are used to determine which assets should be presented in a governmental entity's financial statements vary depending on whether an asset is presented in (1) governmental funds, (2) proprietary and fiduciary funds, (3) the government-wide financial statements.

GOVERNMENTAL FUNDS

The modified accrual basis of accounting and the current financial resources measurement focus should be used in accounting for assets within governmental funds. On the balance sheet of a governmental fund, assets are not classified as current or noncurrent. However, when assets are presented on a governmental fund's balance sheet, it is implied that they are current. In governmental accounting, current assets represent current financial resources that are available for appropriation and expenditure. Financial resources are considered current when they are available for subsequent appropriation and expenditure. Examples of current financial resources include cash, various receivables, and short-term investments (NCGA-1, par. 39).

Capital assets represent past expenditures, not financial resources available to finance current governmental activities. For this reason, general capital assets (assets not related to a proprietary fund or fiduciary fund) of a governmental entity are not presented in a specific governmental fund but, rather, are reported in the entity's government-wide financial statements (as discussed later in this chapter). Capital assets that are acquired through the use of resources from a governmental fund should be recorded as an expenditure for the period. For example, if a governmental entity uses resources from the General Fund to purchase equipment that has a cost of $10,000, the following entry would be made.

Expenditures—Capital Outlays	10,000	
Cash		10,000

PROPRIETARY AND FIDUCIARY FUNDS AND THE GOVERNMENT-WIDE FINANCIAL STATEMENTS

The accrual basis of accounting and economic resources measurement focus should be used to determine which assets should be presented in the proprietary and fiduciary funds and the government-wide entity's statement of net assets.

Inexhaustible capital assets should be presented in the proprietary and fiduciary funds and government-wide statements of net assets at historical cost less accumulated depreciation. For depreciable capital assets, a single amount (net of accumulated depreciation) may be presented on the face of the financial statements, in which case accumulated depreciation and the major categories of capital assets (land, buildings, equipment, infrastructure, etc.) must be reported in a note. Capital assets that are inexhaustible and not subject to depreciation (such as land, construction in progress, and certain infrastructure assets described below) must be presented as a separate line item on the face of the statement of net assets if these assets are significant (GASB-34, par. 20).

PRACTICE POINT: The *GASB Comprehensive Implementation Guide* defines an inexhaustible capital asset as one "whose economic benefit or service potential is used up so slowly that its estimated useful life is extraordinarily long." Examples of inexhaustible capital assets are land and some land improvements (for example, landscaping).

PRACTICE POINT: The *GASB Comprehensive Implementation Guide* notes that construction in progress is a capital asset and should be reported in the statement of net assets with other assets that are not depreciated, such as land.

PRACTICE POINT: The *GASB Comprehensive Implementation Guide* points out that land improvements must be evaluated to determine whether they are subject to depreciation. That is, costs that are permanent in nature are not subject depreciation. For example, grading cost incurred to prepare a site for the construction of a building is generally considered a permanent improvement and is reported as part of the carrying value (historical cost) of the land and, therefore, is not depreciated. Costs that are not permanent should be depreciated. For example, paving a parking lot is not permanent and is reported as a land improvement subject to depreciation.

ACCOUNTING AND FINANCIAL REPORTING

Capitalization Policies

A governmental entity may establish a policy whereby capital acquisitions that are less than an established amount are accounted for as an expense rather than capitalized. The *GASB Q&A Guide* addresses the question of whether the threshold amount applies to the purchase of a group of assets (such as the acquisition of 100 computers) as well as to an individual asset (such as the acquisition of a single computer). There is no pronouncement that addresses this issue, but the general rule of materiality should apply. That is, it is acceptable to expense capital assets acquired as a group as long as the financial statements are not materially misstated and any policy established is applied in a consistent manner.

Valuation of Capital Assets

The governmental entity should report its capital assets in the various statements of net assets, based on their original historical cost (including capitalized interest costs, if applicable) plus ancillary charges such as transportation, installation, and site preparation costs, and then depreciated if they are exhaustible. Capital assets that have been donated to a governmental entity must be capitalized at their estimated fair value (plus any ancillary costs) at the date of receipt.

Reporting Capital Assets Where Ownership Is Unclear

All of a governmental entity's capital assets are reported in the government-wide financial statements. Footnote 64 to GASB-34 notes that a government that has the primary responsibility for maintaining a particular infrastructure asset should report the asset in its financial statements. The *GASB Comprehensive Implementation Guide* makes it clear that the footnote applies only to situations in which it is unclear who owns a particular asset. For example, ambiguity of ownership may arise for infrastructure assets such as highways.

Some localities require homeowners to repair and maintain sidewalks adjacent to their properties, and localities establish regulations to determine when and how those sidewalks are to be maintained. The GASB's *Guide* states that because the property owners, under this arrangement, are responsible for the maintenance of the sidewalks, the sidewalks should not be reported as assets by the government. The establishment of minimum maintenance standards by the governmental entity is not the same as accepting responsibility for the maintenance of the asset itself.

There may be an arrangement whereby one governmental entity maintains an asset but another governmental entity is responsible for the replacement of the asset. The GASB's *Guide* states that under this arrangement, and when ownership is unclear, the government that is responsible for maintaining the capital asset should report the asset in its financial statements.

The GASB's *Guide* also addresses whether title and ownership are one and the same. Public assets are unique in that while title is held by the governmental entity, citizens and numerous other parties and entities have the right to use the property. Nonetheless, the governmental entity that holds title to an asset generally should report the asset in its financial statements. The GASB's *Guide* notes that one exception to this generalization occurs when a lessee reports a capitalized leased based on the standards established by NCGA-5 (Accounting and Financial Reporting Principles for Lease Agreements of State and Local Governments).

In many instances capital assets purchased by state or local government are financed or partially financed by federal awards, and the federal government can retain a reversionary interest in the asset. The *GASB Comprehensive Implementation Guide* states that such assets (even though the federal government retains a reversionary interest in the asset's salvage value) should be reported by the state or local government because "the state or local government is the party that uses the assets in its activities and makes the decisions regarding when and how the assets will be used and managed." Except in the case of certain infrastructure assets (where the modified approach is used), depreciation expense should be recorded for these assets.

Gifted Capital Assets

Often a governmental entity, as part of the agreement to allow the construction of residential or commercial property, requires that a real estate developer construct an asset (such as a street or park) that will be given to a local government. If the governmental entity is informed of the construction cost of the asset, that estimate could be used as a basis of capitalizing the public asset. On the other hand, if the developer does not or cannot provide the information to the governmental entity, the estimated fair value of the asset must be determined and used as the basis for capitalization. The *GASB Comprehensive Implementation Guide* notes that one acceptable way to determine fair value is an estimate made by the entity's public works department.

The *GASB Comprehensive Implementation Guide* notes that when a developer builds streets and donates those streets and the related right-of-way or land, the recipient government should record the right-of-way as well as the streets as capital assets based on their fair value at the date of donation.

Works of Art, Historical Treasures, and Similar Assets

Works of art, historical treasures, and similar assets generally have to be capitalized at their historical cost (or estimated fair value at the date of donation), "whether they are held as individual items or in a collection." However, such assets do not have to be capitalized if they are part of a collection and all of the following conditions are satisfied (GASB-34, par. 27):

- They are held for public exhibition, education, or research in furtherance of public service rather than financial gain.
- They are protected, kept unencumbered, cared for, and preserved.

- They are subject to an organizational policy that requires the proceeds from sales of collection items to be used to acquire other items for collections.

> **PRACTICE POINT:** The *GASB Comprehensive Implementation Guide* points out that when a governmental entity has multiple collections, works of art, and historical treasures, the recognition provisions of paragraph 27 of GASB-34 may be applied for the entire entity or on a collection-by-collection basis. Also, the GASB's *Guide* states that GASB-34 does not require that the organizational policy referred to in paragraph 27c of GASB-34 be formal; however, there should be some evidence to verify its existence.

> **PRACTICE POINT:** If a governmental entity had capitalized collections as of June 30, 1999, those collections must remain capitalized and subsequent additions to the collections must be capitalized even if they satisfy the three conditions listed above.

The *GASB Comprehensive Implementation Guide* notes that FAS-116 (Accounting for Contributions Received and Contributions Made) describes collections of works of art and historical treasures as "generally . . . held by museums, botanical gardens, libraries, aquariums, arboretums, historic sites, planetariums, zoos, art galleries, nature, science and technology centers, and similar educational, research and public service organizations that have those divisions; however, the definition is not limited to those entities nor does it apply to all items held by those entities." For example, animals in a zoo are capital assets, and they could be considered a collection; however, the *GASB Q&A Guide* notes that "only successful breeding colonies of zoo animals would likely meet the requirements of paragraph 27b that collections be preserved."

In some instances items in a collection are permanently attached to a structure and removing them might damage them or significantly reduced their value. The *GASB Q&A Guide* states that such items do not have to be subject to a written policy in order for them not to be capitalized, because the nature of how the items are displayed "demonstrates a commitment and probability that they will be maintained."

If a governmental entity capitalizes a collection that previously had not been reported at the date that GASB-34 was implemented, the capitalization should be reported as a change in an accounting principle (prior-period adjustment) and not as a correction of an error.

Works of art, historical treasures, and similar assets that were given to a governmental entity before the implementation of GASB-34 should be reported at the fair value of the asset at the date of gift and not at the date of implementation.

> **PRACTICE POINT:** The *GASB Comprehensive Implementation Guide* points out that GASB-34 does not provide a

definition of inexhaustible collections or individual works of art or historical treasures; however, the GASB's *Guide* provides the following description of the items: "Those items with extraordinarily long useful lives that because of their cultural, aesthetic, or historical value, the hold of the asset (or assets) applies effort to protect and preserve the asset in a manner greater than that for similar assets without such cultural, aesthetic, or historical value."

Works of art, historical treasures, and similar assets that are received as donations must be recorded as revenue based on the standards established by GASB-33 (Accounting and Financial Reporting for Nonexchange Transactions). If these donated items are added to a noncapitalized collection, the governmental entity must simultaneously record a program expense equal to the amount of the donation recorded as revenue (GASB-34, par. 28).

Works of art, historical treasures, and similar assets that are "inexhaustible" do not have to be depreciated. All other capitalized items must be depreciated (GASB-34, par. 29).

NOTE: Depreciation methods and reporting of depreciation expense is discussed in detail in Chapter 18, "Expenses/ Expenditures: Nonexchange and Exchange Transactions."

PRACTICE ALERT: In December 2006, the GASB issued an Exposure Draft on a proposed Statement entitled, "Accounting and Financial Reporting for Intangible Assets." This proposed Statement is in response to questions raised regarding the accounting and financial reporting treatment for intangible assets and the inclusion of these intangible assets as capital assets. In current practice, inconsistencies exist regarding the accounting and financial reporting for intangible assets, particularly in the areas of recognition, initial measurement, and amortization. The proposed Statement describes an intangible asset as an asset that possesses all of the following characteristics: (1) lack of physical substance, (2) non-financial nature, and (3) initial useful life extending beyond a single reporting period. In addition, the proposed Statement proposes the following:

- That all intangible assets subject to the provisions of the proposed Statement be classified as capital assets and all existing authoritative guidance related to the accounting and financial reporting for capital assets be applied to these intangible assets, as applicable
- That outlays incurred related to an internally generated intangible asset that is considered identifiable be capitalized only upon the occurrence of specific events or circumstances
- The circumstances in which intangible assets should be considered to have indefinite useful lives, and that intangible assets with indefinite useful lives not be amortized unless their useful lives become finite.

ACCOUNTING FOR GENERAL INFRASTRUCTURE ASSETS

"Infrastructure assets" are defined by GASB-34 as "long-lived capital assets that normally are stationary in nature and normally can be preserved for a significantly greater number of years than most capital assets" and include the following (GASB-34, par. 19):

- Bridges
- Dams
- Drainage systems
- Lighting systems
- Roads
- Tunnels
- Water and sewer systems

Buildings are generally not considered infrastructure assets unless they "are an ancillary part of a network of infrastructure assets."

Infrastructure Assets Transition Period

The GASB recognizes that one of the major problems in implementing the standards established by GASB-34 is the reporting of infrastructure assets and has decided to issue transition standards that provide governmental entities with relief in reporting these assets. The transition standards apply only to general infrastructure assets (those that are reported as governmental activities, not business-type activities).

GASB-34 requires that governmental entities capitalize all acquisitions of general infrastructure assets made after GASB-34 is implemented. There were three implementation dates (so-called Phase 1, 2, and 3 governmental entities) identified in GASB-34 as follows:

Primary Government's Annual Revenues	*Required Implementation Date for GASB-34*
Equal to or greater than $100 million (Phase 1 government)	For periods beginning after June 15, 2001
Between $10 million and $100 million (Phase 2 government)	For periods beginning after June 15, 2002
Less than $10 million (Phase 3 government)	For periods beginning after June 15, 2003

GASB-34 does not require that all major general infrastructure assets be reported at the date the standards established by GASB-34 are implemented. Specifically paragraph 154 of GASB-34 states that "at the applicable general infrastructure transition date, Phase 1 and

Phase 2 governments are required to capitalize and report major general infrastructure assets that were acquired (purchased, constructed, or donated) in fiscal years ending after June 30, 1980, or that received major renovations, restorations, or improvements during that period." GASB encourages governmental entities to report all general infrastructure assets on the appropriate implementation date; however, as described in the following tabulation, the GASB-34 provides compliance relief (depending on the size of the entity) for the reporting of major general infrastructure assets at the effective date of the standard:

Size of Entity	*Infrastructure Reporting Transition Option*
Phase 1 governments	Must retroactively report all major general infrastructure assets for fiscal years beginning after June 15, 2005
Phase 2 governments	Must retroactively report all major general infrastructure assets for fiscal years beginning after June 15, 2006
Phase 3 governments	Retroactive reporting of all major general infrastructure assets is encouraged but not required

Major general infrastructure assets are defined later in this chapter.

In some instances it will not be practical to determine the historical cost of major general infrastructure assets that have to be capitalized on a retroactive basis. Under this circumstance, "governments should report the estimated historical cost for major general infrastructure assets that were acquired or significantly reconstructed, or that received significant improvements, in fiscal years ending after June 30, 1980." The reporting of nonmajor networks is encouraged but is not required.

GASB-34 notes that during the transition period, capitalization information might not be available for all networks of infrastructure assets. Under this circumstance the governmental entity may report capital assets for those networks for which information is available (GASB-34, par. 150).

Governmental entities that apply the transition guidance for reporting general infrastructure assets must make the following disclosures in their financial statements (GASB-34, par. 151):

- A description of the infrastructure assets that are reported in the statement of net assets and those that are not reported

- A description of eligible infrastructure assets that are reported based on the modified approach described in paragraphs 23–25 of GASB-34

The transition guidance established by GASB-34 is summarized in Exhibit 10-1.

Summary of GASB-34 Capitalization Guidance for General Infrastructure Assets

Reporting portions of major infrastructure assets The *GASB Comprehensive Implementation Guide* raises the issue of whether a governmental entity can report portions of infrastructure networks that were acquired prior to the July 1, 1980. The *GASB Q&A Guide* points out that infrastructure networks should be reported on a network-by-network basis and not as a portion of a network; however, the reporting of infrastructure cost incurred prior to July 1, 1980, for one network does not mean that similar costs for all other networks must also be presented. It should be remembered that the selective reporting of network costs is available only when it is not practical to determine or reasonably estimate the cost of infrastructure assets acquired prior to the implementation of the standards established by GASB-34.

Transition for noninfrastructure assets The *GASB Comprehensive Implementation Guide* points out that the transition option established by paragraphs 148–151 of GASB-34 does not apply to noninfrastructure capital assets such as land and buildings.

Reporting construction-in-progress (CIP) for infrastructure assets The *GASB Comprehensive Implementation Guide* states that although CIP infrastructure assets are subject to the transition guidance described above, from a practical perspective it is likely that their cost would be reported at the implementation date for GASB-34 rather than the later transition date provided for infrastructure assets.

Estimating infrastructure asset cost If governmental entities have not maintained historical cost information for general infrastructure assets, it will be necessary to estimate their costs (as described later in this chapter). The GASB does not identify a single estimation method to be used to make this determination but it does illustrate in paragraph 158 of GASB-34 the current replacement cost method. The *GASB Comprehensive Implementation Guide* points out that the illustration would have to be modified if "changes in construction methods or specifications have changed significantly from the original acquisition date of the infrastructure asset."

EXHIBIT 10-1
GASB-34 ACCOUNTING FOR CAPITAL ASSETS

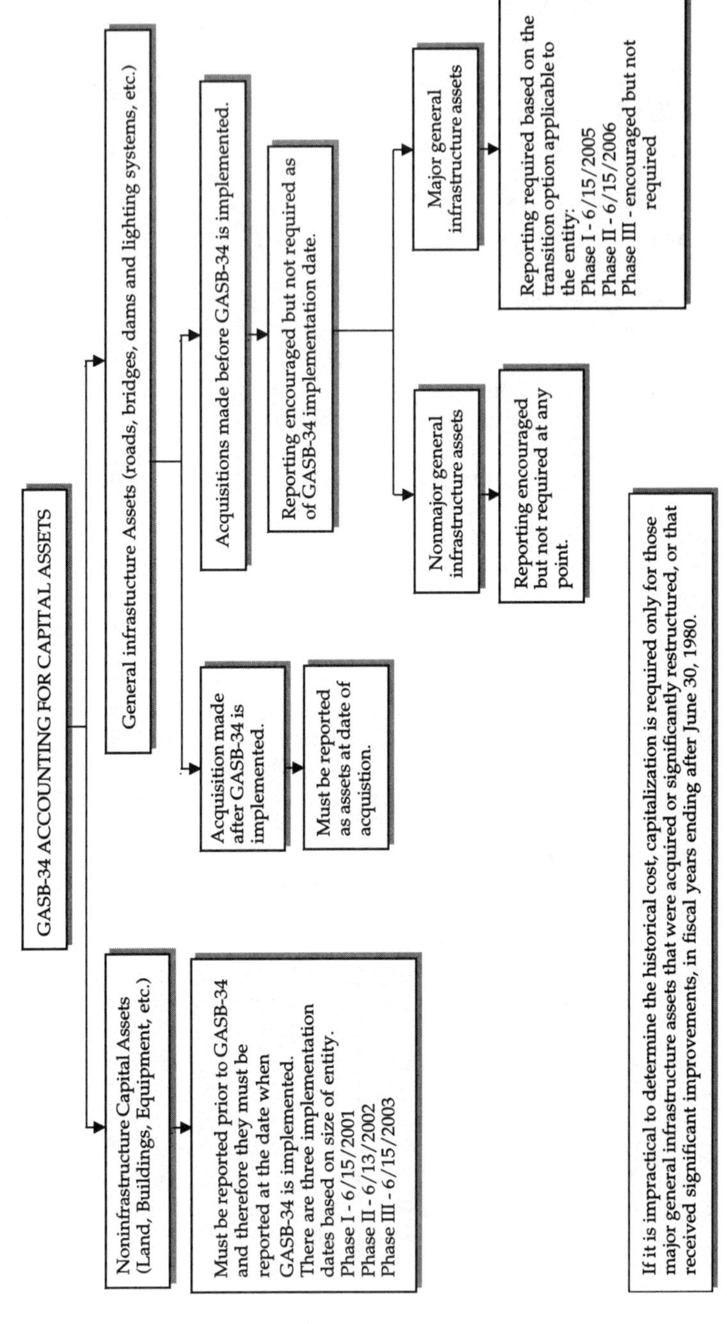

GASB-34 ACCOUNTING FOR CAPITAL ASSETS
Noninfrastructure Capital Assets (Land, Buildings, Equipment, etc.)
Must be reported prior to GASB-34 and therefore they must be reported at the date when GASB-34 is implemented.
There are three implementation dates based on size of entity.
Phase I - 6/15/2001
Phase II - 6/13/2002
Phase III - 6/15/2003
General infrastucture Assets (roads, bridges, dams and lighting systems, etc.)
Acquisition made after GASB-34 is implemented.
Must be reported as assets at date of acquistion.
Acquisitions made before GASB-34 is implemented.
Reporting encouraged but not required as of GASB-34 implementation date.
Nonmajor general infrastructure assets
Reporting encouraged but not required at any point.
Major general infrastructure assets
Reporting required based on the transition option applicable to the entity:
Phase I - 6/15/2005
Phase II - 6/15/2006
Phase III - encouraged but not required
If it is impractical to determine the historical cost, capitalization is required only for those major general infrastructure assets that were acquired or significantly restructured, or that received significant improvements, in fiscal years ending after June 30, 1980.

Determining the net carrying value of infrastructure assets In determining the net carrying value of infrastructure assets at the date they are initially reported in the statement of net assets, accumulated depreciation should be based on the current estimated total life of the asset and not the original estimated total life. Therefore any infrastructure assets that are still in use could not be reported at a zero net carrying value.

Presenting the net carrying value of infrastructure assets Like other capital assets, infrastructure assets should be presented in the statement of net assets at historical cost (or estimated cost) less accumulated depreciation. A single amount (net of accumulated depreciation) may be presented on the face of the financial statement, in which case accumulated depreciation and the major categories of capital assets (land, buildings, equipment, infrastructure etc.), must be reported in a note.

Initial Capitalization of General Infrastructure Assets

Determining major general infrastructure assets As noted earlier, a governmental entity may have to estimate the cost of major general infrastructure assets. Although the GASB describes some methods that can be used to estimate historical cost under these circumstances, "governments may use any approach that complies with the intent of this Statement" (GASB-34, pars. 154–155).

> **PRACTICE POINT:** The governmental entity that has the primary responsibility for maintaining a particular infrastructure asset should report the asset in its financial statements. Infrastructure assets that are maintained through a contract with a third party must nonetheless be reported by a governmental entity.

In order to identify major general infrastructure assets, the evaluation should be targeted at the network or subsystem level and must satisfy one of the following criteria (GASB-34, par. 156):

- The cost/estimated cost of the subsystem is expected to be equal to or greater than 5% of the total cost of all general capital assets reported in the first fiscal year ending after June 15, 1999
- The cost/estimated cost of the network is expected to be equal to or greater than 10% of the total cost of all general capital assets reported in the first fiscal year ending after June 15, 1999

The reporting of nonmajor networks is encouraged but it is not required by GASB-34.

Establishing capitalization at transition Ideally, the capitalization of general infrastructure assets at the transition date will be based on historical cost; however, GASB-34 defines how current replacement cost could be used to make a reasonable estimate of the historical cost of such assets (GASB-34, par. 157).

Estimated historical cost from current replacement cost Under this method, the cost of the existing infrastructure asset is estimated by referring to the current replacement cost of a similar asset and deflating that cost by the use of an appropriate price-level index (GASB-34, pars. 158–159).

For an illustration of one method of estimating the historical cost of look-back infrastructure assets, assume the following facts:

- Look-back infrastructure assets—1,500 miles of residential streets
- Estimated weighted-average age of streets—10 years
- Current standard cost to construct one mile of residential street: $75,000
- Price index position at the end of the current year: 100
- Price index position 10 years ago: 60

Based on the above facts developed by the governmental entity, the estimated historical cost of the general infrastructure assets (1,500 miles of residential streets) is computed as $67,500,000, as follows:

Miles of residential streets (infrastructure assets)	1,500
Current standard cost per mile to construct a mile of residential street	× $75,000
Total estimated current replacement cost	$112,500,000
Relationship of current index position to historical index position (60/100 = 60%)	× 60%
Total estimated cost of infrastructure assets	$67,500,000

The infrastructure assets would be reported in the statement of net assets at $67,500,000 less accumulated depreciation (depending on the method of depreciation method used).

Estimated historical cost from existing information Documents created at the time of construction may provide sufficient information to estimate the historical of infrastructure assets. For example, information related to the bond issuance that financed the construction of the asset could be relevant in estimating the historical cost of the asset (GASB-34, par. 160).

Methods of Calculating Depreciation

In order to compute depreciation expense on infrastructure assets, a governmental entity may use "any established depreciation method." There is no list of acceptable depreciation methods. In order for a depreciation method to be acceptable, it must meet the general conditions of being both *systematic* and *rational*. The systematic criterion requires that an established set of computational procedures be defined (essentially a formula) so that the application of the depreciation method results in the same pattern of depreciation expense under a specific set of circumstances (cost, salvage value, estimated life, etc.). The rationality criterion is poorly defined but it is generally interpreted to mean that the pattern of depreciation expense is based on a reasonable objective(s). For example, the objective might be to reflect more depreciation expense in the early life of the asset based on the assumption that the infrastructure asset will deteriorate more in its earlier life (GASB-34, pars. 161–162).

> **OBSERVATION:** Depreciation methods that might be used by governmental entities to account for infrastructure assets include the straight-line method, sum-of-the-years' digits method, and a variety of declining balance methods, such as the 150% declining method. The most common method used by governmental entities is the straight-line method.

Composite methods For some infrastructure assets a group life depreciation method may be appropriate to track asset costs and to compute depreciation expense. Under a composite method, similar (all interstate highways in a state) or dissimilar infrastructure assets (such as roads, bridges, or tunnels) are combined in order to form a single historical cost basis for computing depreciation and accounting for the disposition of infrastructure assets. The composite method requires that an annual depreciation rate be determined for the collection of assets based on the relationship of depreciation expense to the total capitalized cost of the infrastructure assets that make up the group (GASB-34, par. 163).

There is no single set of procedures for employing composite depreciation methods. The GASB makes the following observations as to how the methods could be implemented (GASB-34, par. 164):

- The composite life could be based on a simple average or weighted average life of the group assets.

- The composite depreciation rate could be based on an assessment of the useful lives of the grouping of assets.

Once a composite depreciation rate is determined, it should be used throughout the life of the group assets. However, it may be necessary to change the rate if the composition of the group assets changes (assets are replaced) or the estimated composite life of the remaining assets changes significantly. The change in the composite depreciation rate under these circumstances would be accounted for as a change in an accounting estimate as defined in APB-20 (Accounting Changes) (GASB-34, pars. 165–166).

Modified Approach for Infrastructure Assets

The GASB does not require that infrastructure assets that are part of a network or subsystem of a network (referred to as eligible infrastructure assets) be depreciated if the following conditions are satisfied (GASB-34, par. 23):

- An asset management system is employed that:
  - Has an up-to-date inventory of eligible infrastructure assets
  - Performs condition assessments of the assets and summarizes the results using a "measurable scale"
  - Estimates, on an annual basis, the annual amount needed to "maintain and preserve the eligible infrastructure assets at the condition level established and disclosed by the government"
- The government documents that the eligible infrastructure assets are being "preserved approximately at (or above) a condition level established and disclosed by the government"

OBSERVATION: The documentation of condition assessments must be carefully done so that their results can be replicated. GASB-34 describes results as being subject to replication as "those that are based on sufficiently understandable and complete measurement methods such that different measurers using the same methods would reach substantially similar results."

PRACTICE POINT: The *GASB Comprehensive Implementation Guide* identifies the following as buildings that may be an ancillary part of a network or subsystem: (1) turnpike rest areas, (2) road maintenance buildings related to a highway system, and (3) water pumping buildings related to a water system.

PRACTICE POINT: The *GASB Comprehensive Implementation Guide* states that a subsystem makes up a part of a network (a collection of related assets). For example, a sewer system (the network) could comprise storm drains and retention ponds.

The condition level must be established and documented by governmental policy or legislative action, and the assessment itself may be made either by the governmental entity directly or by external parties. Professional judgment and good faith are the basis for determining what constitutes acceptable and accurate documentation of the condition of eligible infrastructure assets. However, GASB-34 states that governmental entities should document the following (GASB-34, par. 24):

- Complete condition assessments of eligible infrastructure assets are performed in a consistent manner at least every three years
- The results of the three most recent complete condition assessments provide reasonable assurance that the eligible infrastructure assets are being preserved approximately at (or above) the condition level established and disclosed by the government

PRACTICE POINT: GASB-34 points out that the condition level could be applied to a group of assets by using a condition index or "as the percentage of a network of infrastructure assets in good or poor condition."

PRACTICE POINT: If a governmental entity identifies a subsystem of infrastructure assets as "eligible" (and therefore the computation of depreciation is optional), the documentary requirements apply only to the subsystem and not to the entire network of infrastructure assets.

PRACTICE POINT: The *GASB Comprehensive Implementation Guide* points out that GASB-34 requires that the modified approach be applied to all assets in the network or subsystem; however, a governmental entity could decide to use the modified approach for one network but not for another network. On the other hand, if the eligible infrastructure assets are reported by two or more different departments, either all or none of the assets in the network or subsystem must be subjected to the modified approach.

PRACTICE POINT: The *GASB Comprehensive Implementation Guide* recognizes that numerous asset management systems are available to governmental entities. The GASB does not sanction management systems. It is the responsibility of

> the management of a governmental entity to assess a management system and determine whether that system can satisfy the standards established by paragraphs 23 and 24 of GASB-34.

A governmental entity may perform the condition assessment annually or may use a cycle basis. If a cyclical basis is used for networks or subsystems, all assets of these groups must be assessed during the cycle. However, rather than apply the condition assessment to all assets, a statistical sample approach may be employed in the annual approach or in the cycle approach.

Because eligible infrastructure assets do not have to be depreciated, all expenditures related to their maintenance should be recognized as a current expense when incurred. Expenditures that are capital in nature (additions and improvements) should be capitalized as part of the eligible infrastructure assets because they, by definition, increase the capacity or efficiency of the related infrastructure asset (GASB-34, par. 25).

The adequate maintenance of the condition of eligible infrastructure assets is a continuous process and if the conditions established by GASB-34 are initially satisfied but subsequently are not, the infrastructure assets are not considered "eligible" and depreciation expense must be computed for them and reported in the statement of activities. The change in accounting for depreciation expense should be reported as a change in an accounting estimate (GASB-34, par. 26).

> **OBSERVATION:** The nonrecognition of depreciation expense for eligible infrastructure assets is optional. A governmental entity can decide to depreciate all infrastructure assets that are exhaustible rather than carve out and identify "eligible infrastructure assets."

The *GASB Comprehensive Implementation Guide* points out that parks are considered land and therefore are not infrastructure assets; however, a subsystem within a park (such as roads and trails) could be considered an infrastructure asset and therefore eligible for the modified approach.

When an infrastructure asset is subject to the modified approach, the transfer of the asset from one governmental entity to another is recorded by the transferring government as a functional expense, depending on the nature of the asset transferred.

Electing the Modified Approach for Reporting Infrastructure Assets

A governmental entity can begin to use the modified approach to account for eligible infrastructure assets if both of the following conditions are satisfied (GASB-34, par. 152):

- One complete condition assessment is available.
- The governmental entity documents that the eligible infrastructure assets are being preserved approximately at (or above) the condition level identified.

GASB-34 points out that initially the three most recent complete condition assessments and the estimated and actual amounts to maintain and preserve the assets for the previous five reporting periods (as required by GASB-34, paragraph 132) may not be available. Under this circumstance, the governmental entity should present the information that is available (GASB-34, par. 153).

Reporting Infrastructure under the Modified Approach

Governmental entities that use the modified (depreciation) approach for certain eligible infrastructure assets must present the following schedules as required supplementary information (RSI) (GASB-34, pars. 132–133):

- The assessed condition of infrastructure assets (for at least the three most recent complete condition assessments) along with the date of the assessments
- A comparison of (1) the estimated annual required amount at the beginning of the year needed to maintain and preserve the condition level established and disclosed in the financial statements and (2) the amount actually expensed for each of the past five reporting periods

The schedules described above must be accompanied by the following related disclosures:

- The basis for the condition measurement and the measurement scale used to assess and report the condition.
- The condition level at which the government intends to preserve the eligible infrastructure assets.
- Factors that have a significant effect on trends related to the information presented in the schedules described above, including changes in the measurement scale, the basis for the condition measurement, or the condition assessment methods used.
- If there is a change in the condition level established by the governmental entity, the estimate of the effect of the change on the estimated annual amount needed to maintain and preserve the assets for the current period.

OBSERVATION: The GASB encourages governments that gather information that must be disclosed when they use the modified approach to disclose such information even if they do not use the modified approach.

The *GASB Comprehensive Implementation Guide* provides the following guidance for the modified approach for reporting infrastructure assets:

- In performing the condition assessment, a governmental entity should use the same method, basis, and scale for the complete assessment period. If a three-year cycle is used, the consistency standard applies to the three-year period. The method, basis, or scale may be changed before an assessment period begins, but all changes must be disclosed in the notes to the RSI.
- The methods used to perform a condition assessment will change over time and new methods may be adopted before the beginning of the condition assessment period.

ACCOUNTING AND FINANCIAL REPORTING FOR IMPAIRMENT OF CAPITAL ASSETS AND FOR INSURANCE RECOVERIES

Unlike commercial accounting [FAS-144 (Accounting for the Impairment or Disposal of Long-Lived Assets)], until the issuance of GASB-42 (Accounting and Financial Reporting for Impairment of Capital Assets and for Insurance Recoveries) there had been no guidance on how to measure or report the impairment of these assets for a governmental entity. Although GASB-42 applies to proprietary fund and government-wide financial statements, those standards do not apply to governmental funds. GASB-42 defines capital assets consistent with paragraph 19 of GASB-34.

OBSERVATION: For the purposes of GASB-42, land is considered a capital asset that is separate from buildings and depreciable improvements and therefore should be evaluated separately for impairment.

Definition of Capital Asset Impairment

GASB-42 describes the impairment of a capital asset as "a significant, unexpected decline in the service utility of a capital asset." The significant and unexpected decline is based on events or changes in circumstances that were not anticipated when the capital asset was placed into service. "Service utility" is the "usable capacity that at acquisition was expected to be used to provide service, as distinguished from the level of utilization, which is the portion of the usable capacity currently being used."

GASB-42 identifies the following five indicators of an impairment of a governmental capital asset:

1. Evidence of physical damage, such as, for a building, damage by fire or flood, to the degree that restoration efforts are needed to restore service utility
2. Change in legal or environmental factors, such as a water treatment plant that cannot meet (and cannot be modified to meet) new water quality standards
3. Technological developments or evidence of obsolescence, such as that related to diagnostic equipment that is rarely used because new equipment is better
4. A change in the manner or expected duration of usage of a capital asset, such as closure of a school prior to the end of its useful life
5. Construction stoppage, such as stoppage of construction of a building due to lack of funding

OBSERVATION: The five examples listed above are identified as common indicators of impairment. The GASB recognizes that the list is not all-inclusive. Professional judgment must be used to identify other events and changes that give rise to capital asset impairments.

Impairment Test: Two-Step Process

The five common capital asset impairment indicators (and other events and changes as described above) do not have to be applied every time they arise. Such an approach would be prohibitively expensive to apply and the resulting financial reporting benefits would be marginal. For this reason, GASB-42 provides for the testing of capital asset impairment by determining whether both of the following factors are present:

1. The magnitude of the decline in service utility is significant
2. The decline in service utility is unexpected

The magnitude of the decline in service utility is significant GASB-42 considers a significant decline to be evidenced by the continuing operating expenses related to the use of the impaired capital asset or the costs to restore the asset are significant in relationship to the current service utility.

The decline in service utility is unexpected All capital assets subject to depreciation generally reflect a decline in utility with age or usage; however, asset impairment arises when that decline is unexpected. For example, restoration costs are generally not part of a capital asset's normal life cycle and if they were later contemplated because of an event or change, that development would suggest an unexpected decline in the service utility of the capital asset. On the other hand, the incurrence of normal maintenance costs or preservation costs does not suggest the impairment of a capital asset.

Temporary Impairments

The impairment of a capital asset should generally be considered permanent. If an impairment of a capital asset is considered temporary, the historical cost of the capital asset should not be written down. However, impairments can be considered temporary only when there is evidence to support such a conclusion. The following illustrates an example of a temporary impairment:

> A middle school that is not being used due to declining enrollment should not be written down if future middle school enrollment projections substantiated by current elementary school enrollment demonstrate that the middle school will be needed in a few years.

> **PRACTICE POINT:** The carrying amount of impaired capital assets that are idle at year-end should be disclosed, regardless of whether the impairment is considered permanent or temporary.

Measuring the Impairment of Capital Assets

When a capital asset is considered to be impaired based on the criteria in GASB-42, the amount of the impairment loss (based on historical cost) should be determined by using one of the following measurement approaches:

- Restoration cost approach (generally used to measure impairment losses from physical damage from fire, wind, and the like)
- Service units approach (generally used to measure impairment losses from environmental factors, technological changes, obsolescence, or change in the manner or duration of use)

- Deflated depreciated replacement cost approach (generally used to measure impairment losses from change in the manner or duration of use)

> **OBSERVATION:** GASB-42 suggests that impairment losses from construction stoppages be determined based on the lower of the carrying value or fair value of the impaired asset.

The specific method to be used should be the approach "that best reflects the decline in service utility of the capital asset." Once an approach has been used, that approach should also be used to measure subsequent impairment write-downs with similar characteristics.

Restoration Cost Approach

Under the restoration cost approach, the write-down is based on the proportion of the capital asset impaired as expressed in current restoration cost. The current restoration cost is then converted to a historical cost basis under either a cost index or a ratio approach. The following steps are used for the ratio approach:

- *Step 1* Determine the restoration cost in current dollars.
- *Step 2* Determine the replacement cost in current dollars for the capital asset.
- *Step 3* Determine the carrying value of the impaired capital asset before adjustment (historical cost less accumulated depreciation).
- *Step 4* Determine the relationship between the restoration cost in current dollars and the replacement cost in current dollars for the capital asset.
- *Step 5* Determine the impairment lost by multiplying the carrying value of the asset by the percentage computed in Step 4.

> **OBSERVATION:** The restoration cost approach can also be implemented by using an appropriate cost index.

The estimate of the restoration cost should be based on the amount of the impairment caused by the change or event and should exclude costs related to demolition, cleanup, additions, and improvements.

To illustrate the restoration cost approach, assume that a building originally cost $10,000,000, had an estimated useful life of 40 years (with a nominal residual value), and was 30% depreciated, when it was discovered that ceilings had been partially insulated with asbestos. The cost of restoring the ceilings is $3,000,000. The estimated current replacement cost for the building is $13,000,000. The computation of the impairment write-down is as follows:

Step 1	$3,000,000
Step 2	$13,000,000
Step 3 ($10,000,000–$3,000,000)	$7,000,000
Step 4 ($3,000,000/$13,000,000)	23%
Impairment write-down	$1,610,000

If it is assumed that the event that caused the impairment was considered unusual in nature but not infrequent in occurrence and was not within the control of management, it would be considered a "special item" as defined in GASB-34 and would be recorded in proprietary fund or government-wide financial statements as follows:

Special Item—Impairment Loss	1,610,000	
Accumulated Depreciation—Building		1,610,000

An impairment loss would not be recognized in a governmental fund, because the capital assets are not reported in such funds and because the event does not reduce current financial resources of the entity.

Service Units Approach

Under the service units approach, the write-down is based on the proportion of the capital asset, as expressed in service units, that has been lost due to the event or change that created the impairment. The total service units can be based on the maximum service units or total service units throughout the life of the capital asset and can be expressed in a variety of measurement units, including years of service, number of citizens benefited, and various outputs.

To illustrate the service units approach, assume that waste treatment equipment costs $1,000,000, and originally had an estimated useful life of 40 years (with a nominal residual value). After ten years of use, new environmental regulations are established and the equipment can be used for only five more years before new equipment must be acquired. The amount of the service units lost, expressed in years, is 25 years, and the amount of the impairment loss is $625,000 [=$1,000,000 × (25/40)].

Deflated Depreciated Replacement Cost Approach

The computation of the impairment loss using the deflated depreciated replacement cost approach is based on determining the current cost of an asset needed for the current level of service. Based on the assumed carrying value (cost minus accumulated depreciation) of the theoretical asset, that carrying value is deflated to the historical cost basis for when the original asset was acquired. For example, assume that a building had an original cost of $5,000,000 and was 40% depreciated. The building was to be used originally as a clinic but because of the construction of a new clinic, the building will be used instead as a warehouse. The cost of a suitable (based on the new usage) warehouse is approximately $1,500,000 and the replacement cost of the clinic is $7,000,000. The amount of the impairment loss is computed as follows:

Deflator ($7,000,000/$5,000,000)	1.4
Assumed carrying amount of a new warehouse ($1,500,000 × 60%)	$900,000
Carrying amount of old building ($5,000,000 × 60%)	$3,000,000
Deflated assumed carrying amount of a new warehouse ($900,000/1.4)	642,857
Impairment loss	$2,357,143

Insurance Recoveries

GASB-42 provides the following presentation guidance for insurance recoveries related to impairments of capital assets:

- Restoration or replacement costs should be reported separately (as an expenditure) from any insurance recovery (as an other financing source or extraordinary item) in the financial statements of a governmental fund.
- Restoration or replacement costs should be reported separately from the impairment loss and associated insurance recovery in the government-wide and proprietary fund financial statements.
- The impairment loss should be reported net of any insurance recovery when the recovery is realized or realizable in the same year as the impairment loss.
- Insurance recovery proceeds that are realized or realizable in a period subsequent to the recognition of the impairment loss should be reported as program revenue, nonoperating revenue, or an extraordinary item.

Reporting Impairment Write-Down

When a permanent capital asset impairment is determined, the amount of the write-down must be evaluated and classified in the financial statements in one of the following categories as established by GASB-34:

- Program expense based on the guidance established by paragraphs 41–46 of GASB-34
- Extraordinary item based on the guidance established by paragraph 55 of GASB-34 or paragraphs 19–24 of APB-16
- Special item based on the guidance established by paragraph 56 of GASB-34
- Operating expense based on guidance established by paragraphs 101–102 of GASB-34

> **OBSERVATION:** If the impairment write-down is related to a proprietary fund capital asset, the write-down would be classified either as (1) an operating expense, (2) an extraordinary item, or (3) a special item. If the impairment is related to a governmental fund capital asset, no write-down is reported, because the write-down does not consume current financial resources of the governmental fund.

CHAPTER 11
OTHER ASSETS

CONTENTS

INTRODUCTION

The accounting standards that are used to determine which assets should be presented in a governmental entity's financial statements and how they should be presented vary depending on whether an asset is presented in (1) governmental funds, (2) proprietary funds and fiduciary funds, or (3) the government-wide financial statements.

> **NOTE:** For a discussion of how cash deposits and investments and capital assets should be presented, see Chapter 9, "Deposits and Investments," and Chapter 10, "Capital Assets."

GOVERNMENTAL FUNDS

The modified accrual basis of accounting and the current financial resources measurement focus should be used in accounting for assets within governmental funds.

> **PRACTICE POINT:** Governmental fund assets that are not considered current financial resources (e.g., capital assets) are presented only in the governmental entity's government-wide financial statements and not in the fund financial statements.

Materials and Supplies

Materials and supplies in inventory are current assets of a governmental fund, but they are not considered current financial resources. As discussed in Chapter 3, "Basis of Accounting and Measurement Focus," governmental funds, for the most part, measure the flow of current financial resources. However, one of the exceptions to this generalization is the accounting for inventories. Inventories may be accounted for by using either the consumption method (flow of economic resources) or the purchase method (flow of current financial resources). National Council on Governmental Accounting Statement No. 1 (NCGA-1) (General Accounting and Financial Reporting Principles) states that when the inventory amount is significant, that amount must be reported in the governmental fund's balance sheet (NCGA-1, par. 73).

Consumption method The consumption method of accounting for inventories is not consistent with the fundamental governmental fund concept that only expendable financial resources should be presented in a fund's balance sheet. Under the consumption method, a governmental expenditure is recognized only when the inventory items are used. For example, if a governmental unit purchased $100,000 of supplies, the following entry would be made (NCGA-1, par. 73):

Supplies Inventory	100,000	
Vouchers Payable		100,000

At the end of the period, an inventory of supplies would be made, and the amount of inventory consumed would be recognized as a current expenditure. To continue with the example, assume that supplies worth $25,000 remain at the end of the accounting period. The current period's expenditure for supplies would be recorded in the following manner:

Expenditures—Supplies	75,000	
Supplies Inventory		75,000

Because inventories are reported as an asset (even though they do not represent expendable financial resources), it is necessary to reserve the fund balance by an amount equal to the carrying value of the inventory. Thus, in the above example, the following entry would be made at the end of the accounting period:

Fund Balance—Unreserved	25,000	
Fund Balance—Reserved for Supplies Inventory		25,000

PRACTICE POINT: NCGA-1, Appendix A, points out that "an equity reserve for inventories need not be established unless minimum amounts of inventory must be maintained."

Purchase method The purchase method of accounting for inventories is consistent with the governmental fund concept of reporting only expendable financial resources. Under the purchase method, purchases of inventories are recognized as expenditures when the goods are received and the transaction is vouchered. To illustrate, assume the same facts as those used in the consumption method example presented earlier. When the supplies are acquired, the transaction would be recorded as follows (NCGA-1, par. 73):

Expenditures—Supplies	100,000	
Vouchers Payable		100,000

At the end of the period, no adjustment is made to the expenditures account even though only $75,000 of goods was consumed. However, NCGA-1 requires that an inventory item must be presented on the balance sheet if the amount of inventory is considered significant. If it were concluded that the ending inventory of supplies was significant, the following entry would be made at the end of the accounting period:

Supplies Inventory	25,000	
Fund Balance—Reserved for Supplies Inventory		25,000

Under both the consumption method and the purchase method, the reserved fund balance would be presented under the broad caption of fund balance in a manner similar to the following illustration:

Fund Balance	
Fund Balance—Reserved for Supplies Inventory	$25,000
Fund Balance—Unreserved	400,000
Total	$425,000

Materials and supplies reported at the lower of cost or market A governmental entity may (but is not required to) account for inventories of materials and supplies based on the guidance established by ARB-43 (Restatement and Revision of Accounting Research Bulletins, Chapter 4, Inventory Pricing). ARB-43 requires that inventories or supplies be subjected to the lower of cost or market test for possible write-down. That is, if the replacement cost of inventories or supplies is less than the cost of the items (using FIFO, LIFO, or the average cost method) a write-down is required.

The AICPA's *State and Local Governments* Guide points out that if a governmental entity does not choose to follow ARB-43 with respect to the lower of cost or market method, it should nonetheless write down inventories or supplies if they are affected by physical deterioration or obsolescence. This requirement applies to the use of either the consumption method or the purchase method. The purchase method could be affected by the need for a write-down because NCGA-1, paragraph 73, requires that a governmental fund record inventories or supplies when a significant amount of inventories or supplies exist at the end of the year. Under this circumstance, a write-down would require a reduction both in the asset balance and the reserve fund balance for inventory or supplies.

Prepayments and Deferrals

Prepaid items and deferrals may include items such as prepaid expenses, deposits, and deferred charges. Like inventory items, prepayments and deferrals do not represent expendable financial resources. However, NCGA-1 states that these items may be accounted for by using either the allocation method or the nonallocation method (NCGA-1, par. 73).

> **PRACTICE POINT:** NCGA-1 does not specifically refer to an allocation method and a nonallocation method but rather describes the process of allocation.

Allocation method When the allocation method is used to account for prepayments and deferrals, an asset is established at the date of payment and subsequently amortized over the accounting periods that are expected to benefit from the initial payment. For example, if a state or local government purchased a three-year insurance policy for $45,000, the transaction would be recorded as follows under the allocation method (NCGA-1, par. 73):

Prepaid Insurance	45,000	
Vouchers Payable		45,000

At the end of each year, the partial expiration of the insurance coverage would be recorded as follows:

Expenditures—Insurance	15,000	
Prepaid Insurance		15,000

Prepayments and deferrals are reported as assets of the specific governmental fund that will derive future benefits from the expenditure. In the above example, the governmental unit's fund would report prepaid insurance as an asset of $30,000 at the end of the first year of the insurance coverage.

Because prepayments and deferrals are not current financial resources, the fund's fund balance should be reserved by the amount presented in the asset balance. Thus, at the end of the first year in the current example, the following entry would be made:

Fund Balance—Unreserved	30,000	
Fund Balance—Reserved for Prepaid Insurance		30,000

The balance in the reserved fund balance would fluctuate each year as a result of changes in the carrying value of the prepayment and deferral accounts.

The allocation method is not consistent with the basic governmental fund concept that only current financial resources should be presented in the fund's balance sheet.

Nonallocation method The nonallocation method of accounting for prepayments and deferrals is consistent with the basic governmental fund concept that only expendable financial resources are reported by a specific fund. Payments for the prepaid items or deferrals are fully recognized as an expenditure in the year of payment. Under the nonallocation method no asset for the prepayment or deferral is created, and no expenditure allocation to future accounting periods is required. To continue with the previous example, the only entry that will be made if the nonallocation method is used is to recognize the expenditure in the year of payment as shown in the following illustration (NCGA-1, par. 73):

Expenditures—Insurance	45,000	
Vouchers Payable		45,000

OBSERVATION: Although NCGA-1 requires that significant amounts of inventories be recorded in the balance sheet no matter which accounting method is used, no similar requirement is extended to significant amounts of prepayments and deferrals. It can be assumed that significant amounts of prepayments and deferrals should also be reported in a fund's balance sheet.

If the expenditure account is closed to the fund balance account and no asset is recognized, there is no need to establish a fund balance reserve for prepaid insurance when the nonallocation method is used. However, if the nonallocation method is used and the decision is made to report significant amounts of prepayments and deferrals at period end, a fund balance reserve should be recognized.

Escheat Property

Under certain conditions, state laws allow governmental entities to receive title to property without compensation to other parties. The assets received by the governmental entity are referred to as escheat property. One common example of the receipt of escheat property is when a deposit with a financial institution is inactive for a stated period of time. After certain procedures followed by the financial institution are performed, the balance in the account reverts to a governmental entity. Another circumstance under which a governmental entity receives escheat property is when an individual dies without a will and with no known heirs.

When property escheats to a governmental entity, state laws generally establish procedures under which claimants can assert their ownership of the property. In some states, potential claimants must assert their rights to property within a stated period of time. In other states, time restrictions are not imposed by the state.

The circumstances under which escheat property is received and held by a governmental entity create a number of accounting issues, which were addressed by the issuance of GASB-21 (Accounting for Escheat Property). GASB-21 defines the "escheat process" as "the reversion of property to a governmental entity in the absence of legal claimants or heirs." Governmental entities that receive escheat property may manage the receipts in a number of ways, including using the funds to finance current operations or investing the funds and using only the investment income to finance governmental activities (GASB-21, par. 3).

Appropriate fund type When escheat property is received, it generally should be reported in the governmental fund or proprietary fund to which the property escheats; however, escheat property held for other parties (individuals, private organizations, or another governmental entity) should be reported in a fiduciary fund (Private-Purpose Trust Fund) or the governmental or proprietary fund that is normally used to account for escheat property, offset by a liability to the other party.

> **NOTE:** Accounting for escheat property in proprietary funds, government-wide financial statements, and fiduciary funds is discussed later in this chapter (GASB-21, par. 4, and GASB-34, par. 72).

Accounting and reporting standards When escheat property is received during the year, the total amount received is apportioned between an escheat liability account and an escheat revenue account. The amount of the liability recorded is the estimated amount expected to be paid to claimants, and the balance is recorded as revenue. As it would do in any accounting estimate, the governmental entity uses relevant information and current circumstances to make its best estimate of total future payments to claimants. Generally, the estimated liability is based on the governmental entity's historical relationship between escheat property received and amounts paid to claimants, taking into consideration current conditions and recent trends. The estimated liability is based on projected payments to claimants and not on the amount that by law must be retained by the governmental entity for possible payment to claimants. Payments made to claimants reduce the escheat liability (GASB-21, par. 5).

To illustrate the accounting for escheat property in a General Fund, assume that a governmental entity receives $50,000 of escheat property during the year, pays out claims of $10,000, and estimates additional payments to claimants of $5,000 after the year. To record the activity for the year, are made the following entries in the governmental entity's General Fund (GASB-21, pars. 4-6):

Cash	50,000	
Revenues—Escheat		50,000
To record the receipt of escheat property.		
Revenues—Escheat	10,000	
Cash		10,000
To record payments to claimants.		

Revenues—Escheat	5,000	
Claimant Liability		5,000

To record estimated future payments to claimants.

Payments and estimated payments to claimants are recorded as reductions to revenue rather than as expenditures. This approach is similar to recording property tax revenue at a net amount (expected amount to be received), rather than using a bad debts expense account (GASB-21, pars. 4-6).

PROPRIETARY AND FIDUCIARY FUNDS AND THE GOVERNMENT-WIDE FINANCIAL STATEMENTS

The accrual basis of accounting and economic resources measurement focus should be used to determine which assets should be presented on the balance sheet or statement of net assets of a proprietary or fiduciary fund and in the statement of net assets within the government-wide financial statements.

GASB-20 (Accounting and Financial Reporting for Proprietary Funds and Other Governmental Entities that Use Proprietary Fund Accounting) allows for two distinct but acceptable alternatives for the reporting of Enterprise Funds.

> **NOTE:** The guidance established by GASB-20 is discussed in Chapter 1, "Foundation and Overview of Governmental Generally Accepted Accounting Principles."

> **PRACTICE POINT:** The two alternatives are not applicable to Internal Service Funds.

Materials and Supplies

Materials and supplies in inventory are current assets of proprietary and fiduciary funds and the government-wide financial statements under the accrual basis of accounting and economic resources measurement focus. Only the consumption method of accounting for inventories is consistent with the fundamental concept of the economic resources measurement focus. Under the consumption method, an expense is recognized only when the inventory items are used.

Prepayments and Deferrals

Prepaid items and deferrals may include items such as prepaid expenses and deferred charges, such as unamortized bond issuance costs. As is the case for inventory items, prepayments and deferrals represent economic resources in proprietary and fiduciary funds and in the government-wide financial statements. Only the allocation method is used to account for prepayments and deferrals, with an asset established at the date of payment and subsequently amortized over the accounting periods that are expected to benefit from the initial payment.

Escheat Property

In order to prepare proprietary or fiduciary fund and government-wide financial statements, escheat property should be accounted for using the accrual basis of accounting and the economic resources measurement focus.

When a Private-Purpose Trust fund is used to account for escheat property, there may be transfers from that fund and a governmental fund or proprietary fund. Such transfers are recorded as transfers out by the Private-Purpose Trust Fund and transfers in by the governmental fund. During a period that has transfers, the remaining assets held by the Private-Purpose Trust Fund at the end of the year may be greater or less than the escheat liability account. If the amount of assets is greater than the liability, the Private-Purpose Trust Fund reports the difference as fund balance. If the amount of assets is less than the liability, the fund reports the difference as an asset (Advance to Governmental Fund), and the governmental fund reports the same amount as a liability (Advance from the Private-Purpose Trust Fund). Thus, a Private-Purpose Trust Fund used to account for escheat property can never show a deficit fund balance amount (GASB-21, pars. 5-6).

ALL FUNDS AND FINANCIAL STATEMENTS

Interfund Receivables/Payables

Governmental entities are generally involved in a variety of interfund transactions that may give rise to an interfund receivable or payable. For a discussion of the standards that apply to the reporting of interfund receivables and payables, see Chapter 5, "Terminology and Classification."

Overdrafts in Internal Investment Pools

When a fund overdraws its position in an internal investment pool, the AICPA's *State and Local Governments* Guide requires that the fund that overdrew its position report an interfund payable and the fund that is assumed (based on management's discretion) to have funded the overdraft report an interfund receivable.

For example, assume that a Capital Projects Fund participates in an internal investment pool and withdraws $900,000 from the pool to pay for capital assets even though its equity position at the time of withdrawal is $850,000. If it is assumed that management deems the excess withdrawal to have been provided by the General Fund, the following entries would be made by the two funds:

CAPITAL PROJECTS FUND		
Capital Expenditures	900,000	
Interest in Investment Pool		850,000
Due to General Fund		50,000
GENERAL FUND		
Due from Capital Projects Fund	50,000	
Interest in Investment Pool		50,000

The accounting for the overdraft and assumed coverage of the overdraft is the same no matter which fund types are involved. For example, an overdraft between two funds of the governmental fund category (as shown above) would be treated in the same way as an overdraft between funds that do not belong to the same fund category (for example, the General Fund may fund an overdraft by an Enterprise Fund).

The interfund loan would not be eliminated when the fund financial statements are prepared; however, the treatment of the interfund loan at the government-wide financial statement level would depend on the fund categories involved. For example, if the interfund loan was between two governmental funds, the interfund loan would be eliminated; however, if the interfund loan was between a governmental fund and an Enterprise Fund, the amounts would be reported as part of the internal balance presented on the statement of net assets.

Disclosure: Disaggregation of Receivables and Payables

Much of the information contained in governmental as well as corporate financial statements is highly aggregated in that a single balance often represents a host of individual account balances. In many instances the aggregation does not obscure the nature of the reported balance, but in some cases a reader of the financial statement may be misinformed because of the aggregation.

In a limited way, current governmental reporting standards address the aggregation issue. For example, GASB-3 (Deposits with Financial Institutions, Investments [Including Repurchase Agreements], and Reverse Repurchase Agreements) requires reporting by investment type, and GASB-34 requires reporting capital asset and long-term liabilities by class and type.

GASB-38 requires that a governmental entity present in the notes to its financial statements the details of receivables and payables reported on the statements of net assets and balance sheets "when significant components have been obscured by aggregation." In addition, significant receivable balances that are not expected to be collected within one year of the date of the financial statements should be disclosed.

The disclosure format depends on the complexity of the financial operations of a particular governmental entity and the amount of detail that it displays on the face of its financial statements. In some instances, there may be enough detail presented directly in the financial statements and the disclosure may simply be limited to identifying receivables that are not expected to be collected within one year, if any. In other situations it may be necessary to present a fairly involved disclosure such as the following illustration, which assumes that the governmental entity presents three major governmental funds (General Fund, Route 30 Construction Fund, Gas Tax Fund), aggregated nonmajor governmental funds, two major Enterprise Funds, and Internal Service Funds. See Exhibit 11-1.

EXHIBIT 11-1
ILLUSTRATION OF DISCLOSURE

NOTE—Receivables and Payables

The major components of receivables as of June 30, 20X5, were as follows:

	Various Taxes	Accounts	Due from Other Governments	Other	Total Receivables
Governmental Activities:					
General Fund	$4,000,000	$6,700,000	$1,350,000	$1,900,000	$13,950,000
Route 30 Construction Fund	1,000,000				1,000,000
Gas Tax Fund		1,300,000	2,800,000		4,100,000
Other governmental funds	2,300,000	800,000	250,000	120,000	3,470,000
Internal Service Funds		1,200,000			1,200,000
Total-governmental activities	$7,300,000	$10,000,000	$4,400,000	$2,020,000	$23,720,000

	Various Taxes	Accounts	Due from Other Govern-ments	Other	Total Receivables
Business-Type Activities:					
Parking Authority	—	$350,000		$260,000	$610,000
Municipal Airport	—	7,800,000	$570,000	710,000	9,080,000
Other proprietary funds	—	1,400,000	450,000	330,000	2,180,000
Total-business type activities	—	$9,550,000	$1,020,000	$1,300,000	$11,870,000

The only receivable not expected to be collected within one year is $400,000 due the Municipal Airport from a vendor.

The major components of payables as of June 30, 20X5, were as follows:

	Suppliers	Wages and Salaries	Other	Total Payables
Governmental Activities:				
General Fund	$1,200,000	$1,800,000	$660,000	$3,660,000
Route 30 Construction Fund	950,000		120,000	1,070,000
Gas Tax Fund	450,000		90,000	540,000
Other governmental funds	990,000	145,000	75,000	1,210,000
Internal Service Funds	820,000	122,000	105,000	1,047,000
Total governmental activities	$4,410,000	$2,067,000	$1,050,000	$7,527,000
Business-Type Activities:				
Parking Authority	$125,000	$75,000	$122,000	$322,000
Municipal Airport	420,000	130,000	202,000	752,000
Other proprietary funds	195,000	125,000	220,000	540,000
Total-business type activities	$740,000	$330,000	$544,000	$1,614,000

CHAPTER 12
LONG-TERM DEBT

CONTENTS

INTRODUCTION

The accounting standards that are used to determine which long-term liabilities should be presented in a governmental entity's financial statements and how they should be presented vary depending on whether a liability is presented in (1) governmental funds, (2) proprietary or fiduciary funds, or (3) the government-wide financial statements.

This chapter discusses the accounting and reporting treatment for certain long-term obligations of state and local governments, including

- Bonds and notes
- Bond, tax, and revenue anticipation notes
- Demand bonds
- Conduit debt obligations
- Arbitrage liability
- Extinguishment of debt and debt refunding/defeasance

Certain long-term obligations are discussed in other chapters as follows:

- Accrued compensated absences, employer pension, and other postemployment benefit obligations (see Chapter 13, "Pension, Postemployment, and Other Employee Benefit Liabilities")
- Capital lease obligations (see Chapter 14, "Leases")

- Claims and judgments (see Chapter 15, "Risk Management, Claims, and Judgments")
- Landfill closure and postclosure obligations (see Chapter 16, "Other Liabilities")
- Pollution remediation obligation (see Chapter 16, "Other Liabilities")

TYPE OF LONG-TERM DEBT

Bonds and Notes

State and local governments generally issue long-term obligations in two forms:

1. General obligation bonds
2. Revenue bonds and notes

General obligation bonds General obligation bonds represent bonded indebtedness of the government entity to which repayment is supported by the full faith and credit of the government in the form of its taxing ability. General obligation bonds normally require voter approval and are typically repaid with property or other taxes levied for such purpose.

Revenue bonds and notes Revenue bonds and notes are obligations evidenced in the form of bonds or notes to which repayment is supported by specific revenue sources other than property taxes, such as utility revenues, hospital revenues, and other business-type activity revenue.

Bond, Tax, and Revenue Anticipation Notes

NCGAI-9 (Certain Fund Classifications and Balance Sheet Accounts) addresses the issue of accounting for bond, tax, and revenue anticipation notes. Anticipation notes are issued with the expectation that the government will receive specific resources in the near future and that these resources will be used to retire the liability. Tax anticipation notes are often issued as part of a cash management strategy that recognizes that certain taxes (such as property taxes) will not be collected evenly over the fiscal year. Bond anticipation notes may be issued with the understanding that as soon as the proceeds from the issuance of specific long-term bonds are received, the bond anticipation notes will be extinguished (NCGAI-9, par. 12).

Demand Bonds

Demand bonds allow bondholders to require a governmental entity to redeem bonds on the basis of terms specified in the bond agreement. For example, the bond agreement may allow the bonds, based on action taken by bondholders, to be retired five years after their issuance (NCGAI-9, pars. 1–5).

When demand bonds are issued, should the governmental unit treat the debt as current or long-term? That is, (1) should a governmental fund account for the demand bonds in a specific fund, or classify the debt as a general long-term liability (and reported only in the entity's government-wide financial statements), or (2) should a proprietary fund classify the debt as a current liability or long-term liability? GASBI-1 (Demand Bonds Issued by State and Local Governmental Entities) addresses the issue (NCGAI-9, pars. 1–5).

When demand bonds are redeemed, the funds needed to retire the debt may come from the governmental entity's available cash, proceeds from the resale of the redeemed bonds by remarketing agents, short-term credit arrangements, or long-term credit arrangements. A short-term credit agreement may be based on standby liquidity agreements or other arrangements entered into by the governmental unit. In instances where the redeemed bonds are not readily resold, there may be a take-out agreement whereby a financial institution agrees to convert the bond to long-term debt, such as installment notes. A key factor in determining the appropriate accounting for demand bonds is the existence of a take-out agreement (NCGAI-9, par. 10).

GASBI-1 concludes that the issues surrounding the accounting for demand bonds are similar to the issues associated with bond anticipation notes as discussed in NCGAI-9. NCGAI-9 states that bond anticipation notes should be classified as general long-term debt "if all legal steps have been taken to refinance the bond anticipation notes and the intent is supported by an ability to consummate refinancing the short-term note on a long-term basis in accordance with the criteria set forth in the Statement of Financial Accounting Standards No. 6" (NCGAI-9, par. 12).

GASBI-1 is applicable to demand bonds that have an exercisable provision for redemption at or within one year of the governmental unit's balance sheet date. Such bonds may be reported as a general long-term liability in the government-wide financial statements when all of the following criteria are met (GASBI-1, par. 10, and GASB-34, pars. 6, 82, and 97):

- Before the financial statements are issued, the issuer has entered into an arm's-length financing (take-out) agreement to convert bonds "put" but not resold into some other form of long-term obligation.
- The take-out agreement does not expire within one year from the date of the issuer's balance sheet.
- The take-out agreement is not cancelable by the lender or the prospective lender during that year, and obligations incurred under the take-out agreement are not callable by the lender during that year.

- The lender or the prospective lender or investor is expected to be financially capable of honoring the take-out agreement.

Even when a take-out agreement is cancelable or the obligation created by the take-out agreement is callable during the year, the demand bonds may be considered long-term debt if (1) violations can be objectively determined and (2) no violations have occurred prior to the issuance of the financial statements. However, if violations have occurred and a waiver from the take-out agreement lender has been obtained, the debt should be considered long-term for financial reporting purposes (GASBI-1, par. 10).

When the conditions of GASBI-1 have not been met, demand bonds must be presented as a liability of the fund that received the proceeds from the issuance of the bonds. If demand bonds are issued and no take-out agreement has been executed at their issuance date or at the balance sheet date, the bonds cannot be considered a long-term liability (GASBI-1, pars. 10 and 13).

Conduit Debt Obligations

In August 1995, the GASB issued GASBI-2 (Disclosure of Conduit Debt Obligations). Governmental entities may enter into arrangements whereby a nongovernmental entity is able to finance the acquisition of facilities by the governmental entity issuing "conduit debt obligations," which the GASB describes as follows:

> Certain limited-obligation revenue bonds, certificates of participation, or similar debt instruments issued by a state or local governmental entity for the express purpose of providing capital financing for a specific third party that is not a part of the issuer's financial reporting entity.

For example, a governmental entity may issue revenue bonds for the purpose of financing the construction of an industrial plant by a private enterprise. In a conduit debt arrangement, the governmental entity issues the debt, debt proceeds are used to construct the facility, and the private enterprise signs a mortgage note or lease with the governmental entity. In the transaction, the governmental entity serves as a debtor (for the original issuance of the debt), and a lender or lessor (for the receipt of the mortgage note or lease from the nongovernmental entity). In the arrangement, even though the obligation bears the name of the governmental entity, the governmental entity is not responsible for the payment of the original debt but rather that debt is secured only by the cash payments agreed to be paid by the nongovernmental entity under the terms of the mortgage note or lease agreement.

Generally, the conduit debt transaction is arranged so that payments required by the nongovernmental entity (mortgage or lease payments) are equal to the mortgage payment schedule related to the original debt (entered into by the governmental entity). The nongovernmental entity benefits from the conduit debt transaction because interest rates are lower on the original loan entered into by the governmental entity, and the lower financing cost is the basis for arranging the mortgage or lease schedule payments to be made by the nongovernmental entity.

Generally the governmental entity should disclose the amount of the conduit debt outstanding as of its balance sheet date; however, if that amount is not determinable, the amount of the original balance of the debt may be disclosed for conduit debt issued prior to the effective date of the Interpretation. When the outstanding balance of conduit debt is composed of current balances and original issuance balances, the two amounts must be segregated for disclosure purposes.

> **PRACTICE POINT:** For conduit debt issued after the effective date of GASBI-2, the governmental entity must make arrangements (generally, by having access to the nongovernmental entity's debt amortization schedule and confirmation of subsequent payments) to track payments passed through by the nongovernmental entity to the original creditor.

The GASB states that conduit debt does not create a liability and therefore does not have to be presented on the governmental entity's financial statements. However, the Interpretation notes that some governmental entities report conduit debt, along with related capital assets, on their balance sheet. The Interpretation does not require those governmental entities to cease such presentation, and they can continue to report future conduit debt obligations in a similar fashion, if those new agreements are "substantially the same as those already reported" on the balance sheet.

> **PRACTICE POINT:** When conduit debt is presented on the governmental entity's balance sheet, debt disclosure requirements (such as debt service requirements until the debt matures) must be observed. However, no such disclosure requirements apply to conduit debt that is only disclosed in the financial statements.

The GASB established the exception so that governmental entities that are currently accounting for conduit debt as an obligation will not remove the debt from their balance sheet as the result of the Interpretation.

> **OBSERVATION:** The Interpretation is an interim solution and the GASB currently has a research project on its agenda that focuses on the definition of elements (such as assets, revenues, and liabilities) of governmental financial statements. Once that research project is completed, the GASB is expected to address

the issue of conduit debt. An interim solution to the issue was deemed appropriate because of the current inconsistent treatment of conduit debt by governmental entities.

Arbitrage Liability

Arbitrage involves the simultaneous purchase and sale of the same or essentially the same securities with the object of making a profit on the spread between two markets. In the context of governmental finance, arbitrage describes the strategy of issuing tax-exempt debt and investing the proceeds in debt securities that have a higher rate of return; however, state and local governments are subject to rules and regulations established by the Internal Revenue Code and the U.S. Treasury that under certain conditions create an arbitrage rebate to be paid to the federal government.

In general, state and local governments should use the guidance established by FAS-5 (Accounting for Contingencies) to determine whether an arbitrage liability must be recognized. The AICPA's *State and Local Governments* Guide requires that the arbitrage analysis be made annually "to determine whether it is material and thus should be reported in the financial statements."

GOVERNMENTAL FUNDS

The measurement focus for governmental funds is generally the flow of current financial resources. Liabilities that will consume current financial resources of the fund responsible for payment during the fiscal period are presented in that fund's balance sheet. No explicit current liability classification exists on a fund's balance sheet (the financial statement is unclassified). However, the mere presentation of the liability in the balance sheet of the government's fund implies that the debt is current and will require the use of expendable financial resources (NCGA par. 18).

OBSERVATION: The definition of "current liabilities" differs significantly between a governmental entity and a commercial enterprise. ARB-43 (Restatement and Revision of Accounting Research Bulletins) describes "current liabilities" as those items that will be liquidated through the use of current assets. "Current assets" are defined as resources expected to be realized or consumed within the entity's operating cycle. Thus, the term to maturity of a current liability of a commercial enterprise could be a year or longer, depending on the entity's operating cycle. A liability of a governmental suit is considered current when it is expected to be liquidated with current financial resources. The term to maturity for a government's current liability is much shorter than that for a commercial enterprise.

See Chapter 16, "Other Liabilities," for a discussion of the definition of and accounting treatment for fund liabilities of governmental funds.

Anticipation Notes

Tax and revenue anticipation notes For governmental funds, notes issued in anticipation of the receipt of taxes or revenues should be presented as a liability of the fund that will actually receive the proceeds from the issuance of the notes. The tax or revenue anticipation note represents a governmental fund liability that will be extinguished through the use of expendable available resources of the fund (NCGAI-9, par. 12).

Bond anticipation notes Notes issued in anticipation of proceeds from the subsequent sale of bonds may be classified as general long-term obligations (and therefore presented only in the government-wide financial statements) when the conditions surrounding the notes satisfy the requirements established in FAS-6 (Classification of Short-Term Obligations Expected to Be Refinanced). FAS-6 states that what is typically considered a current liability may be treated as a long-term liability when (1) the intention is to refinance the debt on a long-term basis and (2) the intention can be substantiated through a post-balance-sheet issuance of the long-term debt or by an acceptable financing agreement (NCGAI-9, par. 12).

The actual issuance of the bonds must occur after the balance sheet date but before the balance sheet is issued to satisfy the post-balance-sheet condition for a governmental unit. The amount of the bond anticipation notes that is included as general long-term debt and presented in the government-wide financial statements cannot be greater than the proceeds of the actual bond sale. In addition, the maturity date of the newly issued bonds (or serial bonds) must be sufficiently later than the balance sheet date so as not to require the use of a fund's available expendable resources to retire the maturing bonds (NCGAI-9, par. 12).

When the intent to refinance the bond anticipation notes is substantiated by a financing agreement, the maximum amount of the notes that can be presented as a general long-term obligation in the entity's government-wide financial statements is the amount of the estimated bond proceeds expected to be realized under the agreement. If a portion of the actual bond proceeds is restricted for purposes other than the extinguishment of the bond anticipation notes, the restricted portion must be classified as a governmental fund liability. For example, if the bond anticipation notes total $10,000,000 and the actual bonds when sold under the financing agreement are expected to yield $12,000,000, but $4,000,000 of the proceeds are restricted for other purposes, only $8,000,000 of the $10,000,000 bond anticipation notes can be classified as a general long-term liability. If the amount available under the financing agreement fluctuates depending on some measurable factor, the amount of the notes to be classified as long-term is based on a reasonable estimate of the minimum amount that will be available under the agreement. When a reasonable estimate cannot be made, none of the bond anticipation notes can be classified as long-term debt (NCGAI-9, par. 12, and GASB-34, par. 82).

When a liability for bond anticipation notes meets the criteria for classification as a general long-term liability, a note to the financial statements must contain (1) a general description of the financing agreement and (2) the terms of any new debt incurred or expected to be incurred as a result of the agreement. If the criteria established by FAS-6 have not been satisfied, bond anticipation notes must be presented as a liability in the financial statements of the governmental fund that recorded the proceeds from the issuance of the notes (NCGAI-9, par. 12).

To illustrate the accounting for bond anticipation notes, assume that $10,000,000 of bond anticipation notes is issued and the proceeds are recorded in the Capital Projects Fund. If the criteria established in FAS-6 are met, the following entries woud be made.

Capital Projects Fund		
Cash	10,000,000	
Proceeds From Issuance Of Bond Anticipation Notes		10,000,000

Note: The debt is shown as a long-term liability in the government-wide financial statements.

If the FAS-6 criteria are not satisfied, the following entry would be made:

Capital Projects Fund		
Cash	10,000,000	
Bond Anticipation Notes Payable		10,000,000

Note: The debt is not shown as a long-term liability in the government-wide financial statements.

Demand Bonds

To illustrate the accounting for demand bonds in governmental funds, assume that $4,000,000 of demand bonds is issued and the proceeds are to be used by a Capital Projects Fund. When the criteria established by GASBI-1 are met (a general long-term liability exists), the following entries are made:

CAPITAL PROJECTS FUND		
Cash	4,000,000	
Proceeds From Issuance Of Demand Bonds		4,000,000

Note: The debt is shown as a long-term liability in the government-wide financial statements.

When the demand bonds are issued and the criteria established in GASBI-1 are not met, the following entry would be made:

CAPITAL PROJECTS FUND		
Cash	4,000,000	
Bonds Payable On Demand		4,000,000

Note: The debt is not shown as a long-term liability in the government-wide financial statements.

If the demand bonds are presented for redemption, the redemption should be recorded as an expenditure of the fund from which debt service is normally paid. To illustrate, assume that the $4,000,000 demand bonds are redeemed and paid out of the Debt Service Fund from funds transferred from the General Fund. The following entries would be made if the demand bonds were originally classified as general long-term debt, and the debt is converted to long-term installment notes as determined under the terms of a take-out agreement:

GENERAL FUND		
Cash	4,000,000	
Proceeds From Issuance of Long-Term Installment Notes to Finance Redemption of Demand Bonds		4,000,000
Transfers out (to Debt Service Fund)	4,000,000	
Cash		4,000,000
DEBT SERVICE FUND		
Cash	4,000,000	
Transfers in (from General Fund)		4,000,000
Expenditures (for Redemption of Demand Bonds)	4,000,000	
Cash		4,000,000

Note: The debt would be removed from the government-wide financial statements since it has been liquidated.

If the demand bonds redeemed were originally recorded as a liability of the Capital Projects Fund (no take-out agreement), the following entries would be made to redeem the demand bonds:

General Fund

Transfers out (to Debt Service Fund)	4,000,000	
Cash		4,000,000

Debt Service Fund

Cash	4,000,000	
Transfers in (from General Fund)		4,000,000
Expenditures (for Redemption of Demand Bonds)	4,000,000	
Cash		4,000,000

Capital Projects Fund

Bonds Payable on Demand	4,000,000	
Other Financing Sources (Retirement of Fund Liabilities by Payments Made by Other Funds)		4,000,000

The liability of the Capital Projects Fund is reduced by simultaneously crediting "Other Financing Sources." That account would appear on the Capital Projects Fund's statement of revenues and expenditures.

Demand bonds that were originally classified as a general long-term liability because a take-out agreement existed at the issuance date of the bonds would have to be reclassified if the original take-out agreement expires. Under this circumstance, it would be necessary to establish a liability in the fund that originally recorded the demand bond proceeds. For example, if the $4,000,000 demand bonds illustrated earlier were originally recorded as a long-term liability (in the government-wide financial statements), the following entries would be made if the take-out agreement expires (GASBI-1, par. 10):

Capital Projects Fund

Other Financing Uses (Reclassification of General Long-Term Debt as a Fund Liability)	4,000,000	
Bonds Payable (on Demand)		4,000,000

Note: The debt is reported as a governmental fund liability and as an obligation in the government-wide financial statements.

Any actual bond redemption occurring after the debt is reclassified as the liability of a specific governmental fund should be recorded as an expenditure of the fund that accounts for the servicing of the debt (GASBI-1, par. 13).

PRACTICE POINT: The date of reclassification is not the date the take-out agreement expires. If the take-out agreement expires within one year of the date of the balance sheet, the debt must be reclassified as the liability of a specific governmental fund.

PROPRIETARY AND FIDUCIARY FUNDS

The accrual basis of accounting and economic resources measurement focus is used to determine which liabilities should be presented on the balance sheet/statement of net assets of a proprietary or fiduciary fund. In general, a proprietary or fiduciary fund should report liabilities in a similar manner that a commercial enterprise does assuming that the presentation is not inconsistent with standards established by the GASB.

GASB-20 allows for two distinct but acceptable alternatives for the reporting of Enterprise Funds. Under Alternative 1, governmental entities using proprietary fund accounting must follow (1) all GASB pronouncements and (2) FASB Statements and Interpretations, APB Opinions, and Accounting Research Bulletins (ARBs) issued on or before November 30, 1989, except those that conflict with a GASB pronouncement (GASB-20, pars. 6–8).

Under Alternative 2, governmental entities using proprietary fund accounting must follow (1) all GASB pronouncements and (2) all FASB Statements and Interpretations, APB Opinions, and ARBs, no matter when issued, except those that conflict with a GASB pronouncement. Unlike Alternative 1, Alternative 2 has no cutoff date for determining the applicability of FASB pronouncements (GASB-20, pars. 6–8).

NOTE: The guidance established by GASB-20 is discussed in Chapter 1, "The Foundation and Overview of Governmental Generally Accepted Accounting Principles."

PRACTICE POINT: The two alternatives are not applicable to Internal Service Funds.

Bond, Tax, and Revenue Anticipation Notes

A proprietary or fiduciary fund must apply FAS-6 to determine whether bond, tax and revenue anticipation notes should be presented on the proprietary fund's balance sheet as a current or long-term liability (NCGAI-9, par. 12).

Demand Bonds

GASBI-1 is applicable to demand bonds accounted for in a proprietary fund that have an exercisable provision for redemption at or within one year of the fund's balance sheet date. Such bonds may be reported as a long-term liability in the proprietary fund when all of the criteria of GASBI-1 are met (GASBI-1, par. 10, and GASB-34, pars. 6, 82, and 97). When the conditions of GASBI-1 have not been met, demand bonds must be presented as a current liability if the proceeds were received by a proprietary fund. If demand bonds are issued and no take-out agreement has been executed at their issuance date or at the balance sheet date, the bonds cannot be considered a long-term liability (GASBI-1, pars. 10 and 13 and GASB-34, par. 82).

GOVERNMENT-WIDE FINANCIAL STATEMENTS

The accrual basis of accounting and the economic resources measurement focus is used to determine which liabilities should be presented in a governmental entity's statement of net assets. Liabilities should be presented in the statement of net assets based on their relative liquidity. The liquidity of liabilities is based on maturity dates or expected payment dates. Because of the significant degree of aggregation used in the preparation of government-wide financial statements, the GASB notes that the liquidity of an asset or liability account presented in the statement of net assets should be determined by assessing the average liquidity of the class of assets or liabilities to which it belongs, "even though individual balances may be significantly more or less liquid than others in the same class and some items may have both current and long-term elements" (GASB-34, par. 31).

Both governmental activities and business-type activities should be presented in the statement of net assets.

Governmental activities should be accounted for and reported based on all applicable GASB pronouncements, NCGA pronouncements, and the following pronouncements issued on or before November 30, 1989, unless they conflict with GASB or NCGA pronouncements (GASB-34, par. 17):

- Financial Accounting Standards Board (FASB) Statement and Interpretations
- Accounting Principles Board (APB) Opinions
- Accounting Research Bulletins (ARBs) of the Committee on Accounting Procedure

> **OBSERVATION:** In the past, pronouncements of the FASB, the APB, and the Committee on Accounting Procedure have not, for the most part, been applied to information presented in governmental funds. The GASB decided that government-wide financial statements must be prepared by applying these pronouncements issued on or before November 30, 1989 (unless they conflict with GASB pronouncements), on a retroactive basis (with four exceptions discussed in paragraph 146 of GASB-34). Pronouncements issued by the FASB after November 30, 1989, cannot be followed in the preparation of financial statements for governmental activities.

Business-type activities must follow either Alternative 1 or Alternative 2 of GASB-20 (Accounting and Financial Reporting for Proprietary Funds and Other Governmental Entities That Use Proprietary Fund Accounting) as discussed in the previous section for proprietary funds.

Bond, Tax, and Revenue Anticipation Notes

Bond, tax, and revenue anticipation notes should be presented in the government-wide financial statements. To determine the liquidity of these debts the criteria established by NCGAI-9 must be used to determine whether bond anticipation notes are current or noncurrent (due in more than one year). Tax and revenue anticipation notes are considered current liabilities (liabilities due within one year).

Demand Bonds

Demand bonds should also be presented in the government-wide financial statement. To determine the liquidity of this type of debt the criteria established by GASBI-1 must be used to determine whether the demand bonds are current or noncurrent (due in more than one year).

EXTINGUISHMENT OF DEBT AND DEBT REFUNDING/DEFEASANCE

A governmental unit may extinguish debt in a manner whereby the unit (1) has no further legal responsibilities under the original debt agreement or (2) continues to be legally responsible for the debt but the extinguishment is considered an in-substance defeasance (retirement).

Debt is considered to be extinguished under the following circumstances (FAS-76, pars. 3–6):

- The debtor pays the creditor and is relieved of all its obligations with respect to the debt. This concludes the debtor's reacquisition of its outstanding debt securities in the public securities market, regardless of whether the securities are canceled or held as treasury bonds.
- The debtor is legally released from being the primary obligor under the debt either judicially or by the creditor and it is probable (as defined in FAS-5 [Accounting for Contingencies]) that the debtor will not be required to make future payments with respect to the debt under any guarantees.

- The debtor irrevocably places cash or other assets in a trust to be used solely for satisfying scheduled payments of both interest and principal of a specific obligation and the possibility that the debtor will be required to make future payments with respect to that debt is remote. In this circumstance, debt is extinguished even though the debtor is not legally released from being the primary obligor under the debt obligation (in-substance defeasance).

When debt is extinguished as an in-substance defeasance transaction, only monetary assets can be contributed to the irrevocable trust. The monetary assets must be (1) denominated in the same currency in which the debt is payable, and (2) essentially risk free with respect to the timing, amount, and collection of principal and interest. GASB-7 (Advanced Refundings Resulting in Defeasance of Debt) lists the following as examples of essentially risk free assets denominated in U.S. dollars (GASB-7, par. 4):

- Direct obligations of the U.S. government
- Obligations guaranteed by the U.S. government
- Securities backed by U.S. government obligations as collateral under an arrangement by which the interest and principal payments on the collateral generally flow immediately through to the holder of security

The monetary assets must generate cash flows that approximate the debt service requirements of the original debt. That is, cash must be available from the trust to pay interest and make principal repayments as they become due. The cash flows must be sufficient to meet trustee fees and similar administrative expenditures if these expenditures are expected to be made from the assets of the trust. If the administrative expenditures are to be paid directly by the governmental unit, a liability for the total expected administrative expenditures should be recognized in the period in which the debt is considered extinguished (GASB-7, par. 4).

> **PRACTICE POINT:** The liability recognized based on the expected administrative expenditures financed by the governmental unit may be classified as general long-term debt and therefore presented only in the government-wide financial statements if the expenditures do not require current appropriation and expenditure of governmental fund financial resources.

The concept of in-substance defeasance was established by FAS-76 (Extinguishment of Debt). Under that Statement debt could be removed from an entity's financial statements (even though it is not legally retired) by creating an irrevocable trust and transferring certain types of assets to the fund that will be used to meet debt service requirements of the obligation over it remaining life. GASB-7 essentially incorporated the standards established by FAS-76 with respect to in-substance defeasance and thus enabled governmental entities to remove debt from their financial statements even when the debt instrument is not legally surrendered by an investor.

In 1997, FAS-125 (Accounting for Transfers and Servicing of Financial Assets and Extinguishments of Liabilities) superseded the standards established by FAS-76 and prohibited the use of in-substance defeasance to remove debt from an entity's financial statements. However, the action by the FASB does not invalidate the standards established by GASB-7. For this reason, governmental entities can continue to execute an in-substance defeasance of outstanding debt.

The amount of the debt considered to be retired based on an in-substance defeasance transaction must be disclosed as long as the debt remains legally outstanding. In addition, disclosures should include a general description of the in-substance defeasance transaction (GASB-7, par. 11).

When market interest rates decrease, governmental and commercial entities must decide if it is feasible to change their debt structure, thus reducing future debt service payments. When an entity uses the proceeds from the issuance of new debt to retire old debt before its maturity date, the process is referred to as a "refunding."

Current and Advance Refundings

The refunding of old debt (defeasance) can be accomplished as either a current refunding or an advance refunding. Debt is defeased when either legal requirements (current refunding) or accounting requirements (advance refunding) are satisfied. Legal requirements are met and debt is defeased when debt holders are paid at the maturity date or at a call date stipulated in the debt agreement. When debt is paid before its maturity date (at a call date or retired by repurchasing the debt in the secondary market) and the retirement is financed by issuing new debt, the process is referred to as a current refunding of debt. Accounting requirements are met when debt is in-substance defeased based on conditions established by FAS-76. Essentially, FAS-76 states that an in-substance defeasance occurs when cash and other assets are placed in an irrevocable trust that is to be used exclusively to service the future debt requirements of the (old) debt. When an in-substance defeasance is financed by issuing new bonds, the process is referred to as an "advance refunding of debt."

GASB-7 establishes both accounting standards and disclosure standards for advance refundings of debt. The accounting standards apply to funds whose measurement focus is the flow of current financial resources. Funds included in this category are the General Fund, Special Revenue Funds, Debt Service Funds, Capital Projects Funds, and Permanent Funds. An advance refunding of debt would be recorded in one of these funds and the related debt (both the new debt and the old debt) would be presented only in the governmental entity's government-wide financial statements (GASB-7, par. 7, as amended by GASB-34).

The disclosure standards established by GASB-7 apply to all governmental entities and include state and local governments as well as public benefit corporations, public authorities, public employee retirement systems, governmental utilities, governmental hospitals, and public colleges and universities (GASB-7, par. 7).

Advance Refundings in Governmental Funds

When general long-term debt that is reported in the government-wide financial statements but not a government fund is defeased through an advance refunding, the proceeds from the issuance of the new debt should be recorded as "Other Financing Source—Proceeds of Refunding Debt" in the governmental fund that receives the proceeds from the issuance of the new debt. The newly issued debt should also be recorded as a liability in the governmental unit's government-wide financial statements. When payments to the escrow agent to defease the old debt are made from the proceeds of the newly issued debt, the payments should be recorded as "Other Financing Use—Payment to Refunded Debt Escrow Agent." The defeased debt should be removed from the governmental unit's government-wide financial statements (GASB-7, pars. 8–9, and GASB-34, par. 16).

> **NOTE:** GASB-7 uses the term "bond" instead of the more general term *debt* in its account titles when referring to advance refundings resulting in defeasance of debt. The defeasance of the old debt could be accomplished through refinancing other than issuing bonds. Therefore, the general term debt is used for the term bond throughout this analysis and explanation.

For example, if a governmental unit defeased $500,000 of long-term notes by issuing $500,000 of long-term bonds and placed the proceeds in an irrevocable escrow, the following entries would be made assuming that the proceeds from the issuance of the new debt were recorded in the Debt Service Fund:

DEBT SERVICE FUND		
Cash	500,000	
Other Financing Source—Proceeds of Refunding Debt		500,000

To record the issuance of long-term bonds.

Other Financing Use—Payment to Refunded Debt Escrow Agent	500,000	
Cash		500,000

To record the payment to the escrow agent for debt defeasance.

Note: In the government-wide financial statements, long-term notes payable would be removed and bonds payable would be presented.

> **NOTE:** If the cash is never deposited to the governmental entity's accounts, the first two entries may be combined to show only the source and use of the proceeds.

When payments made to the escrow agent to defease the debt are made from the governmental unit's resources and not from proceeds generated from the issuance of new debt, the payments should be recorded as a debt service expenditure and not as an other financing use. For example, if it is assumed in the previous illustration that the $500,000 debt was defeased by issuing $400,000 of bonds and using $100,000 from the General Fund, the following entries would be made (GASB-7, par. 8):

Debt Service Fund		
Cash	400,000	
Other Financing Source—Proceeds of Refunding Debt		400,000
Other Financing Use—Payment to Refunded Debt Escrow Agent	400,000	
Cash		400,000
General Fund		
Expenditures—Principal	100,000	
Cash		100,000

Note: In the government-wide financial statements, long-term notes of $500,000 would be removed and bonds payable of $400,000 would be presented.

Payments made to the escrow agent from current governmental resources that represent accrued interest on the defeased debt should be recorded as a debt service expenditure (interest) and not as an other financing use (GASB-7, par. 8).

Advance Refundings in Proprietary Funds

Accounting standards for advance refundings of debt for proprietary funds were originally established by APB-26 (Early Extinguishment of Debt). Proprietary funds had to account for (advance) refunded debt as required by APB-26, but they also had to make the note disclosures required by GASB-7. The accounting standards established by APB-26 required that any gain or loss on the early extinguishment of debt be reported on a proprietary fund's statement of operations. Because current refundings and advance refundings are considered early extinguishments of debt, any related gain or loss had to be used to compute the net income of a proprietary fund.

In December 1993, the GASB revised the accounting standards related to the refunding of debt by proprietary funds with the issuance of GASB-23 (Accounting and Financial Reporting for Refundings of Debt Reported by Proprietary Activities).

The standards established by GASB-23 apply to all funds maintained by state and local governmental entities that use proprietary fund accounting. This includes not only all states and municipalities, but also public benefit corporations and authorities, public utilities, and public hospitals and other public healthcare providers.

> **PRACTICE POINT:** GASB-23 applies to both current refundings and advance refundings of debt. GASB-23 supersedes paragraphs 13 and 14 of NCGAI-9. Those paragraphs required that any gain or loss arising from a current refunding or an advance refunding be reported on a proprietary fund's operating statement as an extraordinary item.

When a governmental entity that uses proprietary fund accounting refunds debt (either a current refunding or an advance refunding), the difference between (1) the book value of the refunded (old) debt and (2) the amount required to retire the debt should be accounted for as a deferral and should not be reported as a gain or loss on the fund's operating statement.

The book value of the retired debt includes its maturity value, any related unamortized discount or premium, and any unamortized bond issuance costs. The amount required to retire the old debt (reacquisition price) depends on whether the transaction is a current refunding or an advance refunding. For current refundings, the reacquisition price is the amount paid to debt holders (face value of the debt plus the premium amount, if any). For advance refundings, the reacquisition price is the amount of assets that must be placed in escrow to satisfy the in-substance defeasance criteria established by FAS-76 (FAS-76, pars. 3–5).

Transaction costs related to the issuance of the new debt that is the basis for the refunding are not considered when determining the difference between the book value of the old debt and the reacquisition price.

> **PRACTICE POINT:** For an advance refunding, FAS-76 states that if "it is expected that trust assets will be used to pay related costs, such as trustee fees, as well as to satisfy scheduled interest and principal payments of a specific debt, those costs shall be considered in determining the amount of funds required by

the trust. On the other hand, if the debt incurs an obligation to pay any related costs, the debt shall accrue a liability for those probable future payments in the period that the debt is recognized as extinguished" (paragraph 5). In the latter circumstance (accrual of future payments), the amount accrued should be used to determine the amount of the (GASB-23) deferral, but not reported as a current expense.

The amount deferred (difference between the book value of the debt and the reacquisition price) is reported on the proprietary fund's balance sheet as a decrease (contra liability) or increase (valuation account) to the book value of the new debt issued to finance the refunding and is commonly referred to as unamortized or deferred gain (loss) on refunding. The deferral and the book value of the new debt may be presented as (two) separate line items on the proprietary fund's balance sheet, or the two amounts may be netted and presented as a single line item. If the two amounts are presented on a net basis, the amount of the deferral should be reported parenthetically or in a note to the financial statements.

Subsequently, the deferral is amortized over the original remaining life of the old debt or the life of the new debt, whichever is less. The amount is amortized in a "systematic and rational manner" as a component of interest expense. If the amount deferred is a deferred loss, interest expense is increased because of the periodic amortization. If the amount deferred is a deferred gain, interest expense is decreased.

PRACTICE POINT: Amortization methods that satisfy the systematic and rational guideline include (1) the effective interest method, (2) the straight-line method for term bonds, and (3) the bonds outstanding method for serial bonds. In financial accounting, it is generally accepted that periodic interest expense should be determined on the basis of the effective interest method or the straight-line method if the results from applying the latter method are not materially different from the use of the effective interest method. GASB-23 does not use the effective interest method as the benchmark for determining the acceptability of periodic amortization.

PRACTICE POINT: The standards established by GASB-23 for accounting for gains or losses that arise from refundings are significantly different from the standards applicable to similar transactions in the private sector (APB-26). For government entities, any loss will be deferred, while in the private sector, a loss must be reported immediately on an entity's statement of operations.

Refunding Debt Previously Refunded

Debt that is used to refund previously issued debt may also be subsequently refunded. Any gain or loss from the subsequent refunding should be deferred and combined with any unamortized deferred gain or loss related to the original refunding. The combined deferral should be amortized over the shorter of (1) the remaining amortization period that was used in the original refunding or (2) the life of the newly issued debt. The standard applies to current refundings as well as to advance refundings.

To illustrate, assume that Debt A was issued on January 1, 20X1, with a maturity date in 7 years. On January 1, 20X3, Debt A is refunded by issuing Debt B with a maturity date in 10 years. If a deferred loss (contra liability account) of $300,000 is created by the refunding, the deferral is amortized over 5 years (the lesser of the 5 years remaining in the original life of Debt A and the 10-year life of Debt B). Further, assume that on January 1, 20X5, Debt B is refunded by issuing Debt C with a maturity date in 2 years. If a deferred loss of $600,000 is created by the second refunding, that amount is combined with the unamortized deferred loss related to the original refunding ($300,000 – $120,000), and the combined amount of $780,000 ($600,000 + $180,000) is amortized over 2 years (the lesser of the 3 years remaining in the amortization period for the first refunding and the 2-year life of Debt C).

EXHIBIT 12-1
COMPREHENSIVE ILLUSTRATION: CURRENT REFUNDING

In a current refunding, proceeds from the newly issued debt are used to immediately retire the old debt. For proprietary funds, the computation of the loss (deferred) arising from a current refunding is shown in Illustration 1 of Appendix B of GASB-23. That illustration is presented below in a modified form to demonstrate additional aspects of a current refunding. The illustration is based on the following facts:

- The refunding (both the retirement and the issuance of debt) occurs on January 1, 20X3.
- The book value of the old debt, which was originally issued at par, is:

10% bonds payable	$35,000,000
Less unamortized bond issuance costs	250,000
Book value	$34,750,000

To determine the book value of the debt, subtract the unamortized bond issuance costs from the amount of the debt. For financial reporting purposes, however, the unamortized bond issuance costs must be reported as an asset.

- The refunded bonds are serial bonds that mature at the rate of $7,000,000 per year with a final payment date of January 1, 20X8. The bonds are callable on 1/1/X3 at a 3% call premium.

EXHIBIT 12-1
COMPREHENSIVE ILLUSTRATION: CURRENT REFUNDING (cont'd)

- The balance in the bond sinking fund as of January 1, 20X3, is $3,550,000. The call premium is paid using cash in the bond sinking fund, and the balance in the fund is transferred to a sinking fund for the new debt.
- New debt (par value of $35,000,000) is sold at par with a stated interest rate of 5%. The newly issued bonds are serial bonds that mature at the rate of $5,000,000 per year, with the final payment date 7 years from January 1, 20X3.

To record the current refunding, the following entries would be made in the proprietary fund on January 1, 20X3:

Cash	35,000,000	
Bonds Payable (New Issuance)		35,000,000
Bonds Payable (Old Issuance)	35,000,000*	
Deferred Loss On Early Retirement Of Debt	1,300,000	
Unamortized Bond Issuance Cost (Old Issuance)		250,000
Cash—Sinking Fund		1,050,000
Cash		35,000,000

*Reacquisition price ($35,000,000 × 1.03%)	$36,050,000
Book value	34,750,000
Deferred loss on early retirement of debt	$ 1,300,000

Based on the above analysis, the deferred loss arising from the early retirement of debt is $1,300,000. Under APB Opinion No. 26 (APB-26), that amount would be reported as a loss (extraordinary) on the statement of operations for the proprietary fund. However, GASB-23 requires that the amount be capitalized as a contra liability account (offset against bonds payable) and be amortized in a systematic and rational manner over the lesser of the original remaining life of the old bonds (5 years) or the life of the new bonds (7 years). Thus, in the illustration, the amortization period is 5 years.

If the deferred amount is amortized using the straight-line method, the annual amortization is $260,000 ($1,300,000/5 years).The amortization would be part of the interest expense the proprietary fund recognizes each year.

If the deferred amount is amortized using the effective interest method, the effective interest rate must be computed. The effective interest rate is the discount rate that, when applied to future principal and interest payments of the new debt, equals the book value of the new debt ($33,700,000 = $35,000,000 − $1,300,000). The effective interest rate is 6.213%.

OBSERVATION: The effective interest rate can be determined by using various computer software packages or a financial calculator. In the illustration, the last two principal payments ($10,000,000) must be assumed to have been made on January 1, 20X8, even though they were actually made on January 1, 20X9, and January 1, 20Y0. This assumption is necessary because the remaining life of the old bonds (five years) is less than the life of the new bonds (seven years).

The following amortization schedule can be prepared to facilitate the annual entries that must be made to account for the newly issued debt over its life.

Date	(A) *Principal and Interest Payments*	(B) *Interest Expense*	(C) *Amortization of Deferred Loss*	(D) *Book Value of Debt*
1/1/X3				33,700,000
1/1/X4	6,750,000	2,093,781	343,781	29,043,781
1/1/X5	6,500,000	1,804,490	304,490	24,348,271
1/1/X6	6,250,000	1,512,758	262,758	19,611,029
1/1/X7	6,000,000	1,218,433	218,433	14,829,462
1/1/X8	15,750,000*	920,538[R]	170,538	-0-
	41,250,000	7,550,000	1,300,000	

Column (B) = Column (D) × 6.213%

Column (C) = Column (A) – $5,000,000 – Column (B)

Column (D) = Column (D) (previous year)+Column (C) – $5,000,000 (except for 1/1/X8 see explanation below).

*Includes $5,000,000 for the actual principal payment for 1/1/X8, and $10,000,000 for the assumed principal payments on 1/1/X9 and 1/1/Y0, and actual interest payment due as of 1/1/X8.

[R] Rounding error

According to the information developed in the amortization schedule, the following entry would be made as of December 31, 20X3:

Bond Interest Expense	2,093,781	
Deferred Loss on Early Retirement of Debt		343,781
Bond Interest Payable (35,000,000×5%)		1,750,000

On January 1, 20X4, the following entry would be made to record the payment of the interest and the repayment of part of the principal:

Bond Interest Payable	1,750,000	
Bonds Payable	5,000,000	
Cash		6,750,000

DISCLOSURES

Long-Term Debt Disclosures

NCGAI-6 requires that a governmental entity disclose debt service requirements to maturity but does not specify the detail information that should be included in the disclosure. GASB-38 (Certain Financial Statement Note Disclosures) requires that the NCGAI-6 disclosure be continued but with separate presentations for each of the five years following the date of the balance sheet and in five-year increments thereafter through the year of maturity. The disclosure must identify the principal and interest components of debt service.

The disclosure requirement also applies to the minimum lease payments for capital leases and noncancelable operating leases, as described in Chapter 14, "Leases."

An illustration of the disclosure requirement for debt for the year ended June 30, 20X5, is presented as follows:

Note—Debt Service Requirements to Maturity—Primary Government

Year Ended	Governmental Activities				Business-Type Activities	
	General Obligation Bonds		Notes Payable		Revenue Bonds	
June 30	Principal	Interest	Principal	Interest	Principal	Interest
20X1	$ 1,200,000	$ 2,400,000	$ 450,000	$ 220,000	$ 900,000	$ 820,000
20X2	2,300,000	2,500,000	420,000	210,000	850,000	800,000
20X4	2,600,000	2,700,000	400,000	200,000	850,000	600,000
20X5	2,400,000	2,600,000	400,000	195,000	825,000	420,000
20X6–X0	6,500,000	2,350,000	350,000	170,000	800,000	400,000
20Y1–Y5	15,500,000	7,300,000	1,200,000	650,000	2,500,000	920,000
20Y6–Y0	7,300,000	3,900,000	800,000	240,000	2,000,000	640,000
20Z1–Z5	6,200,000	2,750,000	—	—	500,000	230,000
20Z6–Z0	12,900,000	2,150,000	—	—	650,000	125,000
20A1–A5	4,100,000	700,000	—	—	—	—
Total	$61,000,000	$29,350,000	$4,020,000	$1,885,000	$9,875,000	$4,955,000

(Other debt disclosure requirements are discussed in Chapter 20, "Comprehensive Annual Financial Report.")

If a governmental entity has debt that carries a variable interest rate, the debt service disclosures should be based on the interest rate in effect as of the date of the current balance sheet. In addition, the conditions that affect the determination of the variable interest rate should be disclosed.

PRACTICE POINT: The notes to the financial statements should focus on the primary government (which includes its blended component units) and support the information included in the government-wide financial statements and the fund financial statements. Note disclosures related to discretely presented component units should be presented based on the requirements established by GASB-14, paragraph 63.

Short-Term Debt Disclosures

GASB-34 requires that the activity in long-term debt presented in the statement of net assets be summarized in a note to the financial statements, but there was no similar requirement for short-term debt. GASB-38 extends the analysis to the statement of net assets and balance sheet for short-term debt outstanding during the year "even if no short-term debt is outstanding at year-end." GASB-38 does define short-term debt but notes that short-term debt "results from borrowings characterized by anticipation notes, use of lines of credit, and similar loans."

The schedule of changes in short-term debt is presented in a note to the financial statements and includes the following components:

- Beginning balance
- Increases for the year
- Decreases for the year
- Ending balance

In addition, the disclosure should include the reason the short-term debt was issued during the year. An example of the disclosure is presented as follows:

NOTE—Short Term Debt

During the year, the City issued bond anticipation notes in order to begin the reconstruction of a major bridge that had been heavily damaged by floodwaters. The proceeds from the short-term debt were needed immediately to begin the project, and these notes were paid off approximately three months later, when long-term bonds were issued to finance the capital project. Short-term debt activity for the year ended June 30, 20X5, is summarized as follows:

	Beginning Balance	**Proceeds**	**Repayment**	**Ending Balance**
Bond anticipation notes	$0	$12,000,000	$(12,000,000)	$0

Demand Bond Disclosures

When a governmental entity has demand bonds outstanding, irrespective of the exercisable date of the demand provision, GASBI-1 requires that the following information be disclosed (GASBI-1, par. 11):

- General description of the demand bond program
- Terms of any letters of credit or other standby liquidity agreements outstanding
- Commitment fees to obtain the letters of credit
- Any amounts drawn on the letters of credit as of the balance sheet date
- A description of the take-out agreement (expiration date, commitment fees to obtain the agreement, and terms of any new obligation under the take-out agreement)
- Debt service requirements if the take-out agreement is exercised

If installment notes arise from the exercise of the take-out agreement, the amount of the installment loan should be part of the schedule of debt service requirements (GASBI-1, par. 14).

The disclosures are in addition to the general long-term debt disclosures as required by NCGA-1 and NCGAI-6 (Notes to the Financial Statements Disclosure). These general disclosure requirements are discussed later in this chapter (GASBI-1, par. 11).

Conduit Debt Disclosures

The following information should be disclosed in the financial statements of the issuing entity related to conduit debt obligations:

- Description of the conduit debt transaction
- Total amount of outstanding conduit debt as of the date of the balance sheet
- Statement that the governmental entity has no responsibility for the payment of the debt except for the payments received on the underlying lease or loan agreement

Refunding Disclosures

GASB-7 established disclosure standards for advance refundings by all governmental entities but did not address disclosure requirements for current refundings. GASB-23 requires that the disclosure requirements established in GASB-7 be extended to current refundings.

GASB-7 disclosure standards are applicable to all advance refundings resulting in the defeasance of debt irrespective of whether the defeased debt is presented only as general long-term debt or as a liability of a specific fund (GASB-7, pars. 11–14, as amended by GASB-34).

A note to the financial statements should provide a general description of an advance refunding that results in debt defeasance. At a minimum, the note should contain the following disclosures (GASB-7, par. 11):

1. The difference between (a) the cash flow requirements necessary to service the old debt over its life and (b) the cash flow requirements necessary to service the new debt and other payments necessary to complete the advance refunding
2. The economic gain or loss that arises because of the advance refunding

The life of the old debt is based on its stated maturity date and not on its call date, if any (GASB-7, par. 11).

> **OBSERVATION:** The two disclosures described above are the only disclosure requirements for advance refunding mandated by GASB-7; however, Appendix A (paragraph 22) of GASB-7 notes that the GASB believes that, generally, disclosures should include (1) amounts of the old and new debt, (2) additional amounts paid to the escrow agent, and (3) management's explanation for an advance refunding that results in an economic loss. The GASB also states that ultimately the specific disclosures by a particular governmental entity are dependent on "such things as the number and relative size of the entity's advance refunding transactions, the fund structure of the reporting entity, and the number and type of refundings of its component units."

Difference in cash flow requirements The cash flow requirements of the old debt are simply the sum of all future interest and principal payments that would have to be paid by the governmental entity if the debt remained outstanding until its maturity date. The cash flow requirements of the new debt are the sum of all future interest and principal payments that will have to be paid to service the new debt in the future, and other payments that are made from the governmental entity's current resources rather than from proceeds from the issuance of the new debt. Any proceeds from the issuance of the new debt that represent accrued interest (when the bonds are sold between interest payment dates) should not be included as cash flow requirements related to the new debt (GASB-7, par. 11).

When new debt is issued in an amount that exceeds the amount needed to defease the old debt, only the portion of the new debt needed to defease the old debt should be included as cash flow requirements related to the new debt (GASB-7, par. 11).

Economic gain or loss The economic gain or loss is computed by determining the difference between the present value of cash flow requirements of the old debt and the present value of cash flow requirements of the new debt. The interest or discount rate used to determine the present value of the cash flows is a rate that generally must be computed through trial and error, either manually or by using a computer software package. The objective is to identify an interest rate that, when applied to the cash flow requirements for the new debt, produces an amount equal to the sum of the (1) proceeds of the new debt (net of premium or discount) and (2) accrued interest, less the (a) underwriting spread and (b) nonrecoverable issuance costs (GASB-7, par. 11).

Issuance costs related to the advance refunding may include such transaction costs as insurance, legal, administrative, and trustee costs. These costs may be recoverable through the yield in the escrow fund or nonrecoverable. Treasury Department regulations establish the maximum allowable yield of the escrow fund, and certain issuance costs (allowable costs) may be used to reduce the amount defined as proceeds from the issuance of the new debt. The effect of the Treasury Department regulations is to increase the allowable amount that can be legally earned in the escrow fund. Although issuance costs may be allowable under the Treasury Department regulations, they may not be recoverable through the escrow fund because (1) the interest rate on U.S. securities purchased by the escrow fund may be less than the legal maximum rate allowed by the Treasury Department or (2) the escrow fund may be used to liquidate the old debt on a call date and the investment period may be too short to allow for the full recovery of the allowable costs through escrow earnings. When issuance costs are considered allowable costs by the Treasury Department and they are recovered through the escrow fund, the result is that such costs are not an actual cost to the governmental entity. These are referred to as recoverable costs and are not used to compute the interest or discount rate used to determine the present value of the cash flow requirements related to the old debt and new debt (GASB-7, par. 12).

COMPUTING THE REQUIRED REFUNDING DISCLOSURES

To clarify the computation of the differences in cash flow requirements and the economic gain or loss arising from an advance refunding, GASB-7 presented three examples in an appendix. The following sections present the steps that may be followed to compute the required disclosures. After a general description of the steps, Example II from GASB-7 is used to demonstrate how the following suggested four steps can be applied to a specific set of circumstances.

Step 1

Compute the amount of resources that will be required to (1) make a payment to the escrow agent in order to defease the debt and (2) pay issuance costs. The resources may be generated entirely from the issuance of new debt, or the refunding may be partially financed by using other resources of the governmental unit.

> **OBSERVATION:** If the old debt is defeased entirely by using other resources of the governmental unit (no new debt is issued), the transaction is not subject to the accounting and disclosure standards established by GASB-7 because it does not satisfy the definition of an advance refunding. Although this method of financing the defeasance is not discussed in GASB-7, it would appear that the accounting standards established by GASB-7 would be appropriate—that is, funding of the irrevocable trust would be treated as a debt service expenditure. The disclosure standards established by GASB-7 would not be appropriate because there would be no new debt service requirements. On the other hand, if a governmental entity accumulates sufficient funds internally to pay off all or part of a debt, the debt would not be considered defeased because an irrevocable trust, as described in GASB-7, would not be established.

The payment to the escrow agent must be large enough to make all interest payments and the principal payment based on either the call date or maturity date of the old debt. Either the call date or the maturity date is used, depending on which is specified as the retirement date in the escrow fund agreement. The amount of the required payment to the escrow agent is also dependent on the rate of return that can be earned in the escrow fund. The escrow rate of return is determined by the market investment conditions and the allowable yield on the escrow investment as determined by Treasury Department regulations.

The amount of the issuance costs must be added to the amount paid to the escrow agent to determine the total amount of resources required to defease the debt.

Step 2

Compute the effective interest rate target amount. The effective interest rate target amount is computed by subtracting the amount of nonrecoverable issuance costs from the amount of the resources required to defease the old debt and to pay issuance costs (computed in Step 1). By reducing the amount required to defease the old debt (and to pay issuance costs) by the nonrecoverable issuance costs, the effective interest rate (to be computed in Step 3) will be decreased. If all issuance costs are recoverable and the new debt is sold at par, the coupon rate on the new debt will be the same as the effective interest rate.

Step 3

Compute the effective interest rate. The effective interest rate is the interest rate used to discount the debt service requirements on the new debt so that it is exactly equal to the effective interest rate target amount (computed in Step 2). The computation of the effective interest rate is relatively easy if you have access to a computer and a software program. If you do not have access to a computer, the computation of the effective interest rate is tedious because it must be determined through trial and error and by using interpolation.

Step 4

Compute (1) the difference between the cash flow required to service the old debt and the cash flow required to service the new debt and (2) the economic gain or loss resulting from the advance refunding. The difference between the cash flow requirements can be computed as follows:

Total interest payments on old debt (using the maturity date of the old debt)	$X	
Principal payment to retire old debt	X	
Total cash flow requirements to service old debt		$X
Total interest payments on new debt	$X	
Principal payments to retire new debt	X	
Other resources used to defease old debt	X	
Less: Accrued interest on new debt at date of issuance	–X	
Total cash flow requirements to service new debt		–X
Difference in cash flow requirements		$X

The economic gain or loss on the advance refunding can be computed as follows:

Present value of cash flow requirements to service old debt		$X
Present value of cash flow requirements to service new debt	$X	
Other resources used to defease old debt	X	
Less: Accrued interest on new debt at date of issuance	–X	–X
Economic gain (loss) on advance refunding		$X

EXHIBIT 12-2
COMPREHENSIVE ILLUSTRATION: DISCLOSURE COMPUTATIONS

Step 1: Compute the amount of resources that will be required to (1) make a payment to the escrow agent and (2) pay issuance costs.

Debt service requirements on old debt (to call date)		
Interest on 12/31/X2	$20.00	
Principal on 12/31/X2	100.00	
Total debt service requirements	120.00	
Present value factor	×	.887*
Required payment to escrow agent		$106.44
Issuance costs		5.00
Amount of new debt		$111.44

Step 2: Compute the effective interest rate target amount.

Resources required to defease the old debt	$106.44
Issuance costs	5.00
Less: Nonrecoverable issuance costs ($5.00 − $2.65)	−2.35
Effective interest rate target amount	$109.09

Step 3: Compute the effective interest rate.

Initially, you must make a reasonable estimate of what the effective interest rate will be. Since the escrow fund yield rate is 12.74% and the effective interest rate target amount ($109.09) is less than the amount of the new debt ($111.44), the effective interest rate must be less than 12.74%. Therefore, you may estimate that the rate is 12% and then compute the present value of the new debt service cash flow requirements as follows:

	Present Value of New Debt Service Cash Flow Requirements at 12%	
Interest payment made on new debt on 12/31/X2 ($111.44 × 10%)	$ 11.14	
Present value factor for an amount at an interest rate of 12% for 1 period	× .89286	$ 9.95
Interest payment made on new debt on 12/31/X3 ($111.44 × 10%)	$ 11.14	

Present value factor for escrow fund assuming a yield (i) of 12.74% for 1 year (n), where the present value factor = $1/(1+i)^n$ $1/(1+1.1274)^1$ = .887

Present value factor for an amount at an interest rate of 12% for 2 periods	× .79719	8.88
Principal payment made to retire new debt on 12/31/X2	$111.44	
Present value factor for an amount at an interest rate of 12% for 2 periods	× .79719	88.84
Present value of debt service on new debt		$107.67

Because the present value of the debt service payments ($107.67) is less than the effective interest rate target amount ($109.09), the effective interest rate must be less than 12%.Therefore, you may estimate that the rate is 11% and then compute the present value of the new debt service cash flow requirements as follows:

Present Value of New Debt Service Cash Flow Requirements at 11%

Interest payment made on new debt on 12/31/X2 ($111.44×10%)	$ 11.14	
Present value factor for an amount at an interest rate of 11% for 1 period	× .90090	$ 10.03
Interest payment made on new debt on 12/31/X3 ($111.44×10%)	$ 11.14	
Present value factor for an amount at an interest rate of 11% for 2 periods	× .81162	9.04
Principal payment made to retire new debt on 12/31/X2	$ 111.44	
Present value factor for an amount at an interest rate of 11% for 2 periods	× .81162	90.45
Present value of debt service on new debt		$109.52

Because the present value of debt service payments ($109.52) is greater than the effective interest rate target amount ($109.09), the effective interest rate must be greater than 11%.

At this point, it is known that the approximate effective interest rate is between 11% and 12%. Interpolation must be used to compute the approximate effective interest rate, using the following equation:

$$\text{Effective Interest Rate} = \frac{\text{Present value of debt service payments on new debt at 11\%} \;\textbf{minus}\; \text{Effective interest rate target amount}}{\text{Present value of debt service payments on new debt at 11\%} \;\textbf{minus}\; \text{Present value of debt service payments on new debt at 12\%}}$$

$$= \frac{\$109.52 - \$109.09}{\$109.52 - \$107.67}$$

$$= \frac{.43}{1.85}$$

$= .23$ of 1%

$= .23\%$

Thus, the effective interest rate is approximately 11.23% (11% + .23%) and the present value factors can be computed as follows:

Present value factor for an amount at an interest rate of 11.23% for 1 period $= \frac{1}{(1.1123)^1} = .89905$

Present value factor for an amount at an interest rate of 11.23% for 2 periods $= \frac{1}{(1.1123)^2} = .80830$

Step 4: Compute difference in cash flow requirements and the economic gain or loss on the refunding.

Cash Flow Requirements

Total interest payment on old debt ($20+$20)	$ 40.00	
Principal payment to retire old debt	100.00	
Total cash flow requirements to service old debt		$140.00
Total interest payments on new debt ($11.14+$11.14)	22.28	
Principal payment to retire new debt	111.44	
Other resources used to defease old debt	-0-	
Less: Accrued interest on new debt at date of issuance	-0-	
Total cash flow requirements to service new debt		133.72
Difference in cash flow requirements		$6.28

Computation of Economic Gain or Loss

Present value of cash flow requirements to service old debt:		
Interest payment 12/31/X2 ($20×.89905)	$17.98	
Interest payment 12/31/X3 ($20×.80830)	16.17	
Principal payment 12/31/X3 ($100×.80830)	80.83	$114.98

Present value of cash flow requirements to service new debt:		
Interest payment 12/31/X2 ($11.14×.89905)	10.01	
Interest payment 12/31/X3 ($11.14×.80830)	9.00	
Principal payment 12/31/X3 ($111.44×.80830)	90.08	
Other resources used to defease old debt	-0-	
Less: Accrued interest on new debt at date of issuance	-0-	109.09
Economic gain on advance refunding		$5.89

Thus, the difference between the cash flow requirements is $6.28, and the economic gain is $5.89.

Generally, the advance refunding disclosures required by paragraph 11 of GASB-7 should focus on the primary government, including its blended component units. Thus, disclosures related to governmental activities, business-type activities, major funds, and aggregated nonmajor funds (GASB-7, par. 13, and GASB-34, par. 113).

For periods after an in-substance debt defeasance has occurred, the amount of the defeased debt outstanding should be disclosed with a distinction between amounts that apply to the primary government (including blended component units) and discretely presented component units (GASB-7, par. 14, as amended by GASB-14, par. 42).

> **PRACTICE POINT:** The required disclosures for defeased debt outstanding are applicable only to in-substance defeased debt and not to legally defeased debt.

The following are examples of notes to a financial statement that provide disclosures for (1) an advance refunding resulting in defeased debt and (2) prior-year defeasance of debt outstanding.

Note X—Defeased Debt

On December 31, 20X1, the City of Centerville issued general obligation bonds of $111.44 (par value) with an interest rate of 10% to advance refund term bonds with an interest rate of 20% and a par value of $100. The term bonds mature on December 31, 20X3, and are callable on December 31, 20X2. The general obligation bonds were issued at par and, after paying issuance costs of $5.00, the net proceeds were $106.44. The net proceeds from the issuance of the general obligation bonds were used to purchase U.S. government securities and those securities were deposited in an irrevocable trust with an escrow agent to provide debt service payments until the term bonds are called on December 31, 20X2. The advance refunding met the requirements of an in-substance debt defeasance and the term bonds were removed from the City's government-wide financial statements.

As a result of the advance refunding, the City reduced its total debt service requirements by $6.28, which resulted in an economic gain (difference between the present value of the debt service payments on the old and new debt) of $5.89.

Note Y—Prior Years' Debt Defeasance

In prior years, the City has defeased various bond issues by creating separate irrevocable trust funds. New debt has been issued and the proceeds have been used to purchase U.S. government securities that were placed in the trust funds. The investments and fixed earnings from the investments are sufficient to fully service the defeased debt until the debt is called or matures. For financial reporting purposes, the debt has been considered defeased and therefore removed as a liability from the City's government-wide financial statements. As of December 31, 20X1, the amount of defeased debt outstanding amounted to $795.

CHAPTER 13
PENSION, POSTEMPLOYMENT, AND OTHER EMPLOYEE BENEFIT LIABILITIES

CONTENTS

INTRODUCTION

A state or local government often provides a number of pension, postemployment, and other employee benefits to its employees including the following:

- Termination benefits
- Compensated absences benefits
- Pension and retirement benefits
- Postemployment health-care and other benefits

A common theme among the accounting requirements of these types of benefits is the measurement and recognition of the costs of the benefits at the time the employee works and earns them rather than when they are paid. This chapter addresses the accounting and financial reporting issues related to these types of benefits.

TERMINATION BENEFITS

In June 2005, the GASB issued GASB-47 (Accounting for Termination Benefits), which provides for the accounting and reporting of all forms of employment termination benefits for state and local governments, such as early-retirement incentives, severance pay, and other voluntary or involuntary benefits.

Prior to GASB-47, guidance on governmental employer accounting and reporting for termination benefits was limited to only one form of termination benefits: voluntary short-term benefits. As a result, there has been significant variation among state and local governments in the accounting for termination benefits. In order to enhance both consistency of reporting of termination benefits and the comparability of financial statements, GASB-47 expands the guidance to address all forms of termination benefits, whether voluntary or involuntary, and requires that similar forms of termination benefits be accounted for in the same manner.

Termination benefits could be provided in a number of ways to departing employees. For example, employees could be offered extended health-care-related termination benefits for a specified period of time or enhanced defined pension benefits in exchange for early retirement.

PRACTICE POINT: GASB-47 makes a distinction between "voluntary" and "involuntary" termination benefits. However, the scope of GASB-47 does not include unemployment compensation, for which accounting requirements are established in NCGA-4 (Accounting and Financial Reporting Principles for Claims and Judgments and Compensated Absences). Excluded from the scope of GASB-47 are postemployment benefits (pensions and OPEB), which are part of the compensation that employers offer in exchange for services received.

Voluntary Termination Benefits

Voluntary termination benefits are defined as benefits provided by employers to employees as an inducement to hasten the termination of services or as a result of a voluntary early termination. Examples of voluntary termination benefits include the following:

- Cash payments (one-time or installments)
- Health-care coverage when none would otherwise be provided

Involuntary Termination Benefits

Involuntary termination benefits are defined as benefits arising as a consequence of the involuntary early termination of services, such as layoffs. Examples of voluntary termination benefits include the following:

- Career counseling
- Continued access to health insurance through the employer's group plan
- Outplacement services
- Severance pay

Other benefits, such as health-care continuation under the Consolidated Omnibus Budget Reconciliation Act (COBRA), are provided as a result of voluntary and involuntary terminations, in certain circumstances.

Measurement and Recognition of Termination Benefits

In general terms, the employer should account for termination benefits in accordance with the measurement and recognition requirements laid out in GASB-47, paragraphs 9 through 16, which are summarized below.

Measurement: Health-care-related termination benefits Generally, the measurement criteria requires the employer to measure the cost of termination benefits by calculating the discounted present value of expected future benefit payments in accordance with the following requirements, as applicable: (1) projection of benefits, (2) health-care trend rate, and (3) discount rate. In certain circumstances the benefit costs may be based on unadjusted premiums.

Measurement: Non-health-care-related termination benefits If the benefit terms establish an obligation to pay specific amounts on fixed or determinable dates, the cost of the benefits are required to be measured at the discounted present value of expected future payments. However, if the terms do not establish such an obligation to pay on fixed or determinable dates, the benefit cost may, alternatively, be measured at the undiscounted total of estimated future payments at current cost levels.

Recognition in accrual-basis financial statements An employer is required to recognize a liability and expense for *voluntary* termination benefits, on the accrual basis of accounting, when the employees accept an offer and the amount can be estimated.

An employer is required to recognize a liability and expense for *involuntary* termination benefits, on the accrual basis of accounting, when a plan of termination has been approved by those in authority to commit the employer to the plan, the plan has been communicated to the employees, and the amount can be estimated.

Recognition in modified accrual basis financial statements In governmental fund financial statements prepared on the modified accrual basis of accounting, termination benefit liabilities and expenditures are recognized to the extent that the liabilities are normally expected to be liquidated with expendable available financial resources similar to other governmental fund liabilities.

> **PRACTICE POINT:** If a health-care-related termination benefit affects the employer's obligation to provide defined-benefit postemployment health-care benefits (OPEB), the effects of the termination benefits on the employer's OPEB obligations should be accounted for and reported under the requirements of GASB-27 or GASB-45, as applicable.

Disclosures

GASB-47 requires the footnotes to include a description of the termination benefits arrangements, the costs of termination benefits in the period in which the employer becomes obligated if that information is not otherwise identifiable from information displayed on the face of the financial statements, and significant methods and assumptions used in determining the termination benefit liabilities and expenses.

Effective Date

The requirements of GASB-47 are effective for financial statements in two parts. For termination benefits provided through an existing defined-benefit OPEB plan, the provisions of GASB-47 should be implemented simultaneously with the requirements of GASB-45. For all other termination benefits, GASB-47 is effective for financial statements for periods beginning after June 15, 2005. Earlier application is encouraged.

COMPENSATED ABSENCES

Many governmental and business entities provide a variety of compensated absences, such as paid vacations, paid holidays, sick pay, and sabbatical leaves, for their employees. Because of the nature of these commitments, compensated absences plans generally create an economic liability for a governmental entity.

Accounting issues related to compensated absences were initially addressed in FAS-43 (Accounting for Compensated Absences). National Council on Governmental Accounting Statement No. 4 (NCGA-4) (Accounting and Financial Reporting Principles for Claims and Judgments and Compensated Absences) required that governmental entities follow the standards established by FAS-43, but apply those standards in the context of the governmental accounting model.

In November 1992, however, the Governmental Accounting Standards Board (GASB) superseded portions of NCGA-4 by issuing GASB-16 (Accounting for Compensated Absences). The standards established by GASB-16 apply to all governmental entities without exception. Thus, the standards must be observed by governmental funds, proprietary funds, and fiduciary funds.

The accounting standards that are used to account for compensated absences depend on whether the liability is presented in a (1) governmental fund, (2) proprietary or fiduciary fund, or (3) the government-wide financial statements.

Recognition and measurement criteria GASB-16 establishes the basic concept that a liability for compensated absences should be recorded when future payments for such absences have been earned by employees. Thus, GASB-16 establishes the basic principle that there should be no accrual for compensated absences that are dependent on the performance of future services by employees, or when payments are dependent on future events that are outside the control of the employer and employees (GASB-16, par. 6).

> **OBSERVATION:** The basic measurement standard established by GASB-16 is different from the standard established by FAS-43. That difference relates to the accounting for sick leave and other compensated absences with characteristics similar to sick leave. GASB-16 takes the position that most sick-leave plans are based on the occurrence of a specific future event that is not controlled by the employer or the employee. The future event is sickness. Even though an employee has earned sick leave benefits, the benefits will not be paid (paid time off) unless the employee is sick. Due to the need for the occurrence of a future event, sick-leave benefits would generally not be accrued, but rather would be recorded as an expenditure/expense when sick leave is taken.

GASB-16 applies the accrual concept in the context of the following compensated absences (GASB-16, par. 6):

- Vacation leave and other compensated absences with similar characteristics
- Sick leave and other compensated absences with similar characteristics
- Sabbatical leave

Vacation leave and other compensated absences with similar characteristics Compensated absences for vacation leave and benefits with similar characteristics should be recorded as a liability when earned by employees if the following conditions are satisfied (GASB-16, par. 7):

- Compensated absence is earned on the basis of services already performed by employees.
- It is probable that the compensated absence will be paid (payment may be in the form of paid time off, cash payments at termination or retirement, or some other means) in a future period.

Fringe-benefit arrangements may allow employees to earn compensated absences, but employees may not be entitled to benefits until certain minimum conditions (such as minimum time of employment) are met. Under this arrangement, a governmental entity should accrue for compensated absences that are probable (that is, likely to take place). Thus, a governmental entity must determine whether it is likely that benefits earned, but not payable until certain conditions are met, will be paid. On the other hand, benefits related to compensated absences that have been earned, but are expected to lapse, should not be accrued. For example, some benefits may lapse because there is a cap on the number of vacation days that can be carried forward from period to period (GASB-16, par. 7).

Although the standards established in GASB-16 are discussed in the context of vacation leave, those standards are equally applicable to compensated absences that have characteristics similar to vacation leave. Thus, any compensated-absence benefit that is not dependent on an event outside of the control of the employer or the employee should be accounted for in a manner similar to vacation leave benefits. Generally, these types of benefits are granted to employees solely on the basis of the length of their employment. For example, a governmental entity that provides its employees with one personal day for each six months worked is providing a compensated absence benefit that should be accrued, because it is based on length of employment. On the other hand, an entity that provides its employees with military-leave benefits should not accrue this compensated absence, because the benefit will be paid only if an employee serves in the military at a future date (GASB-16, par. 7). See Exhibit 13-1.

EXHIBIT 13-1
ILLUSTRATION: VACATION LEAVE

To illustrate the use of compensated absences for vacation leave, assume the following:

- Each employee earns one day of vacation for each month worked starting with the hire date.
- An employee is entitled to use vacation leave after one year of employment.
- If an employee is terminated, all earned (but unused) vacation leave is paid at the employee's current pay rate. (Employees with less than one year of service receive no payment.)
- The estimated liability for vacation leave is based on the following information:

Number of current employees by length of service:

Category 1—Employees who have worked for more than one year	70
Category 2—Employees who have worked for less than one year	30

Characteristics of employee-categories:

	Category 1	*Category 2*
Current average daily pay rate	$135	$75
Average number of vacation days accumulated	25	7

Based on prior experience, it is estimated that approximately 30% of employees with less than one year of experience will work at least one year and therefore be entitled to termination pay for accumulated vacation days.

The estimated liability for compensated absences liability for vacation leave is computed below:

Category	*Number of Employees*		*Average Pay Rate*		*Average Vacation Days Accumulated*		*Probability Factor*		*Extended Amounts*
1	70	×	$135	×	25	×	100%	=	$236,250
2	30	×	75	×	7	×	30%	=	4,725
Estimated liability for vacation leave									$240,975*

* Estimate should also include a provision for additional salary-related payments (see the section entitled "Liability Calculation").

OBSERVATION: The accrual of compensated absences for vacation leave is usually straightforward. Most governmental entities impose few, if any, restrictions on an employee's right to take vacation days earned or to receive accumulated vacation pay when termination occurs. Thus, in most instances the number of vacation days earned to date should be the basis for the accrual for compensated absences for vacation leave. However, in some cases, the right to receive vacation leave may depend on some unfulfilled condition. For example, a new employee may have to work a minimum of six months before vacation days are earned. In this case, the governmental entity must determine whether it is probable that newly hired employees eventually will meet the minimum work criterion. If so, the entity must include these employees' past work experience in the calculation of the compensated-absence accrual. Including this type of work experience could be seen as a violation of GASB-16's basic premise that accrual is appropriate only when payments do not depend on events outside the control of the employer and employee. GASB-16 states that future employment is a condition controlled by the employer and employee—the employer could fire the employee or the employee could quit.

Sick leave and other compensated absences with similar characteristics Sick-leave benefits often differ from other compensated absences in that sick-pay benefits are dependent on employee illness (a future event). However, sick-leave programs often allow employees to accumulate sick days, and if they are not used, employees may be paid for all or perhaps a maximum number of the accumulated sick days on termination or retirement, referred to as termination payments (GASB-16, par. 8).

Due to the unique characteristics of sick-leave programs, the GASB addressed the issue separately. Thus, compensated absences for sick leave and other compensated absences with similar characteristics should be accrued only when it is probable that the employer will have to make termination payments. Sick-pay benefits that have been earned, but probably will be used only for sick leave, should not be accrued, but rather recorded as an expenditure/expense when employees are paid for days not worked due to illness (GASB-16, par. 8).

PRACTICE POINT: Other compensated absences are considered similar to sick leave when the benefit is based on a specific future event that is not subject to control by the employer and employees. Examples of other compensated absences with this characteristic include leaves for military service, jury duty, and close-family funerals.

GASB-16 established two methods, the termination payment method and the vesting method, that can be used to calculate the liability related to compensated absences for sick leave. Neither method allows for the accrual of nonvesting (rights that cannot or will not vest) sick leave (GASB-16, par. 8).

Termination payment method Under the termination payment method, a governmental entity generally estimates its sick pay liability based on past history, adjusted for changes in pay rates, administrative policies, and other relevant factors. Thus, the accrual applies historical information or trends to a governmental entity's current workforce (GASB-16, par. 8). See Exhibit 13-2.

EXHIBIT 13-2
ILLUSTRATION: SICK LEAVE
(TERMINATION PAYMENT METHOD)

To illustrate the termination payment method, assume the following:

- Sick leave can be used only for personal sickness or close-family sickness.

- Sick leave accumulates with no limit, and sick leave not taken before termination or retirement will be paid to an employee at the rate of 80% of the employee's current pay rate if the employee has ten years or more of service.
- Each employee earns one day of sick leave for each month worked, and when sick leave is taken, the employee is paid at his or her current rate of pay.
- The estimated liability for sick leave is based on the following governmental entity's experience over the past five years:

— Number of employees terminated or retired during past five years	10 employees
— Number of sick days paid on termination or retirement for employees during past five years	90 sick days
— Total number of years worked by all employees terminated or retired during past five years	180 years
— Current average daily pay rate	$100

- Currently the governmental entity's active labor force includes 100 employees who have accumulated 1,200 years of work.

The estimated liability for sick leave compensated absences is computed below:

Sick days paid	90 days
Multiply by average current pay rate	× $ 100
	$ 9,000
Multiply by final payment percentage	× 80%
	$ 7,200
Divide by number of years worked by retired/terminated employees	÷ 180 years
	$ 40
Multiply by number of years worked by current labor force	× 1,200
Estimated liability for sick leave	$ 48,000*

*Estimate should also include a provision for additional salary-related payments.

PRACTICE POINT: Although termination payments for sick leave are usually paid in cash to employees, some governmental entities allow an employee to forego direct payments for additional service credit in determining the amount of pension benefits due to the employee. Such arrangements are not termination payments, but they should be considered in determining the actuarial valuation of the governmental entity's pension obligations.

OBSERVATION: The estimation methodology is based on an example presented in Appendix C to GASB-16. However, there is no prescribed method that must be used to compute the estimate. A governmental entity must determine the most appropriate method to compute the estimate. For example, GASB-16 notes that a governmental entity could estimate the liability by "developing a ratio based on historical data of sick leave paid at termination compared with sick leave accumulated and by applying that ratio to the sick leave accumulated by current employees as of the balance sheet date."

Vesting method The termination payment method may be difficult for some governmental entities to apply. For example, in some instances relevant historical information may not be available or the workforce may be too small to successfully apply historical ratios or trends. The vesting method focuses on vesting sick leave. Vesting sick-leave rights include vested rights and those rights that will eventually vest, generally after a minimum number of years have been worked. The vesting method differs in the termination payment method in the following ways (GASB-16, par. 8) (see Exhibit 13-3):

EXHIBIT 13-3
ILLUSTRATION: SICK LEAVE (VESTING METHOD)

To illustrate the vesting method, assume the following:

- Sick leave can be used only for personal sickness or close-family sickness.
- Sick leave accumulates with no limit, and any sick leave not taken at termination or retirement will be paid to an employee at the rate of 80% of the employee's current pay rate if the employee has ten years or more of service.
- Each employee earns one day of sick leave for each month worked, and when sick leave is taken, the employee is paid at his or her current rate of pay.
- The estimated liability for sick leave is based on the following estimates:

Number of current employees by classification:

Category 1—Administrative/professional	10
Category 2—Uniformed	20

Category 3—Clerical/secretarial	70
Total	100

Characteristics of employee-categories:

	Category 1	*Category 2*	*Category 3*
Current average daily pay rate	$150	$130	$60
Average number of sick days accumulated	13	16	8
Probability employee will work at least 10 years	90%	95%	25%

The estimated liability for compensated absences liability for sick leave is computed below:

Category	*Number of Employees*		*Average Pay Rate*		*Average Sick Days Accumulated*		*Probability Factor*		*Extended Amounts*
1	10	×	$150	×	13	×	90%	=	$17,550
2	20	×	$130	×	16	×	95%	=	39,520
3	70	×	$60	×	8	×	25%	=	8,400
									65,470
Multiply by percentage of final payment									80%
Estimated liability for sick leave									$52,376*

*Estimate should also include a provision for additional salary-related payments (see the section entitled "Liability Calculation").

- The vesting method includes all vesting sick leave amounts for which payment is probable, not just the vesting amounts that will result in terminal payments.
- The vesting method is based on accumulated benefits as of a balance sheet date, not on amounts accruing over expected periods of service.

OBSERVATION: Although the termination payment method is more consistent with the termination payment concept used to account for sick leave, the GASB believes that "the vesting method also provides a reasonable estimate of anticipated termination payments."

OBSERVATION: The vesting method is somewhat deficient in that the liability may include a provision for sick leave that will be satisfied by employee absences because of sickness rather than amounts paid at termination or retirement. GASB-16 recognizes the deficiency but states that the approach is acceptable "because of concerns about the cost-benefit of trying to estimate the extent to which such use might occur."

Sabbatical leave Governmental fringe benefits may include earning sabbatical leaves. In determining whether compensated absences for sabbatical leaves should be accrued, the criteria discussed earlier must be satisfied (see discussion in section titled "Vacation Leave and Other Compensated Absences with Similar Characteristics"). In applying those criteria, the purpose of the leave must be evaluated. If sabbatical leave provides employees with unrestricted time off, a liability for compensated absences should be accrued. The amount of the accrual should be based on the periods during which the rights to sabbatical leaves are earned and the probable amounts that will be paid (through paid time off or by other means) to employees under the sabbatical program (GASB-16, par. 9).

Some sabbatical-leave benefits provide restricted leaves. The nature of the duties performed by governmental personnel change, but the governmental entity dictates the services or activities to be performed by employees on sabbatical. For example, employees may be required to perform research or participate in continuing professional education programs. Compensated-absences liability for sabbatical-leave programs based on restricted leaves should not be accrued. Instead, it should be reported as a current expenditure/expense during periods that employees perform their directed duties as required under sabbatical programs (GASB-16, par. 9).

Liability calculation The accrual of compensated absences should be based on pay rates that are in effect as of the balance sheet date, unless a specific rate is established by contract, regulation, or policy. For example, some governmental contract agreements may entitle employees to sick-pay termination settlements at one-half of employees' current pay rates (GASB-16, par. 9).

In addition to the basic pay rate, the accrual of compensated absences should include estimated employer payments related to the payroll. GASB-16 describes these payments as items for which a government is "liable to make a payment directly and incrementally associated with payments made for compensated absences on termination" (incremental salary-related payments). To meet the standard of being directly and incrementally associated with payment of termination payments for compensated absences, the related payroll payments must be (1) a function of the employee's salary amount and (2) payable as part of salary for compensated-absences balances at the date an employee takes time off, retires, or is terminated (GASB-16, par. 11).

Salary-related payments include the employer's share of Social Security and Medicare payroll taxes because those taxes are a function of an employee's level of salary and are also paid to the federal government when employees receive payments for compensated absences. However, all of an employee's salary may not be subject to payroll taxes, a fact the employer should take into consideration when estimating the compensated absences accrual (GASB-16, par. 11).

Another salary-related payment is the employer's share of contributions to pension plans. When the pension plan is a defined contribution plan or a cost-sharing, multiple-employer defined benefit pension plan, the employer's share of the contribution should be part of the accrual for compensated absences if the employer is liable for contributions to the plan based on termination payments made to employees for compensated absences. The salary-related pension contribution must be part of the accrual, because it is included in the base used to determine the employer's share of contributions to the pension plan. On the other hand, the accrual should not include contributions to single-employer plans and agent multiple-employer defined benefit plans, in which case the actuarial computation for employer contributions takes into consideration termination payments for compensated absences (GASB-16, par. 11).

> **PRACTICE POINT:** Other fringe benefits should be evaluated to determine whether they are directly and incrementally related to the payment of salaries at termination. For example, healthcare insurance fringe benefits are generally based on the governmental entity's claims experience and characteristics of its labor force rather than on the salary level of an employee. Therefore, the compensated absences accrual should not include an estimate for healthcare insurance costs. Additionally, life insurance benefits should not be part of the accrual unless (1) the insurance benefit is a function of the salary earned by an employee and (2) the life insurance premium for the last month of employment (termination date) is based on the total amount paid rather than on a normal salary amount.

The amount accrued for salary-related payments should be based on rates in effect as of the balance sheet date and should be applied to the total accrual for compensated absences. For example, salary related payments applicable to the accrual of vacation leave should apply to the total accrual for vacation leave even though most of the earned leave will usually be satisfied as paid time off rather than as termination pay (GASB-16, par. 10).

> **PRACTICE POINT:** GASB-16 does not attempt to address all compensated absences that might be part of a governmental entity's fringe-benefit package. If a governmental entity has

such fringe benefits, those benefits should be accounted for using the broad concepts established in the Statement. Also, each compensated absence benefit should be accounted for on the basis of the substance of the benefit plan, not on its name. For example, a fringe benefit may be labeled as sick leave when in fact employees can be absent from work for reasons other than illness. In this case, standards related to vacation-leave absences should be observed rather than the standards related to sick leave.

Governmental Funds

Recognition of expenditure While GASB-16 establishes standards for the measurement of the compensated absences liability, the amount that should be reported as an expenditure in a governmental fund is based on the modified accrual basis of accounting and current financial resources measurement focus. Thus, only the portion of the estimated future payments for compensated absences that will use current expendable resources should be reported as a liability of a governmental fund; however, the entire amount would be presented in the governmental entity's statement of net assets. (NCGA-1, pars. 70–71, as amended by GASB-34).

Proprietary and Fiduciary Funds

The accrual basis of accounting should be used to determine the amount of the liability related to compensated absences that should be presented on the balance sheet of a proprietary or fiduciary fund. In determining the amount of the liability the guidance discussed earlier in the context of governmental funds should be followed, except the total amount of the estimated debt should be presented as a liability (not just the portion of the debt that will use expendable financial resources).

Government-Wide Financial Statements

The accrual basis of accounting and the economic resources measurement focus should also be used to determine the amount of the liability related to compensated absences that should be presented in a governmental entity's statement of net assets. Liabilities should be presented in the statement of net assets based on their relative liquidity. In determining the amount of the liability the guidance discussed earlier in the context of governmental funds should be followed, except the total amount of the estimated debt should be presented as a liability (not just the portion of the debt that will use expendable financial resources).

EMPLOYER PENSION OBLIGATIONS

GASB-27 (Accounting for Pensions by State and Local Government Employers) addresses accounting and reporting issues related to pension information presented in the financial statements of state and local governmental employers. Governmental employers may provide pension benefits through either a defined benefit pension plan or a defined contribution plan. For the most part, the standards address issues related to defined benefit pension plans, which is a common type of pension plan adopted by state or local governmental employers.

> **OBSERVATION:** GASB-27 provides limited guidance for defined contribution plans. In a defined contribution plan, future pension payments to a particular employee are based on the amounts contributed to the plan, earnings on those investments, and forfeitures allocated to an employee's account. A defined contribution plan does not create the difficult accounting and reporting issues raised by a defined benefit pension plan.

The standards established by GASB-27 relate to the (1) measurement of pension expenditures/expense, (2) the presentation of the related pension liability or asset, (3) appropriate note disclosures in the financial statements, and (4) required supplementary information. The standards are structured to satisfy the following broad objectives considered critical by the GASB (GASB-27, pars. 3–7):

- The measurement of pension expenditures/expense should be similar to the governmental employer's required contributions for the period, assuming the contributions are based on actuarially sound funding policies.
- The consistent measurement of pension information reported by the employer and the pension plan.

The standards established by GASB-27 apply to all state and local governmental employers, irrespective of the type of governmental fund (government fund type or proprietary fund type) that is used to report the pension expenditures/expense. In addition, the standards apply to all governmental employers' financial statements whether they are reported as (1) stand-alone financial statements or (2) part of another governmental entity's financial report (GASB-27, pars. 3–7).

The standards established by GASB-27 (as they apply to the measurement and reporting of pension expenditures/expense and related pension information) supersede the following pronouncements (GASB-27, pars. 3–7):

- NCGA-1 (Governmental Accounting and Financial Reporting Principles)
- NCGA-6 (Pension Accounting and Financial Reporting: Public Employee Retirement Systems and State and Local Governments)
- NCGA Interpretation No. 8 (NCGAI-8) (Certain Pension Matters) (except the requirements for special termination benefits, as amended by paragraph 6 of GASB-27)
- GASB-4 (Applicability of FASB Statement No. 87, "Employers' Accounting for Pensions," to State and Local Governmental Employers)
- GASB-5 (Disclosure of Pension Information by Public Employee Retirement Systems and State and Local Governmental Employers)
- GASB-12, paragraph 11 (Disclosure of Information on Postemployment Benefits Other Than Pension Benefits by State and Local Governmental Employers)

GASB-27 applies to all pension benefits administered in a defined benefit pension plan except postemployment health-care benefits. In addition, the standards do not apply to other postemployment benefits that are administered through a plan that does not provide retirement income (GASB-27, pars. 3–7).

> **OBSERVATION:** The GASB addresses other postemployment benefits for employers (including health-care benefits) in GASB-45 (see the appendix in this chapter). Pending implementation of GASB-45, the disclosure requirements established by GASB-12 (as amended by GASB-27) should be observed. In addition, interim guidance for the financial statement presentation of postemployment health-care plans administered by defined benefit pension plans are addressed in GASB-26 (Financial Reporting for Postemployment Healthcare Plans Administered by Defined Benefit Pension Plans). GASB-43 provides guidance for accounting and financial reporting for other postemployment benefit plans.

Employers that Participate in Defined Benefit Pension Plans

Sole and agent employers: Measurement of annual pension cost and net pension obligation Defined benefit pension plans may be administered in a variety of forms, including a single-employer plan. Governmental employers whose defined benefit pension plans are administered as single-employer or agent multiple-employer plans should determine their pension cost by first calculating the annual required contribution (ARC). The "ARC" is defined as "the employer's periodic required contributions to a defined benefit pension plan, calculated in accordance with the parameters." The "parameters" are defined as "the set of requirements for calculating actuarially determined pension information included in financial reports" and are more fully described in paragraphs 9–10 of GASB-27. If an employer has a net pension obligation (NPO), the ARC must be adjusted to reflect a possible amortization of the NPO. The NPO adjustment is discussed in paragraphs 11–13 of GASB-27.

The annual pension cost differs from the pension expenditures/expense reported in a governmental employer's financial statements. The annual pension cost "measures the period cost of an employer's participation in a defined benefit pension plan," whereas the pension expenditures/expense is "the amount recognized by an employer in each accounting period for contributions to a pension plan." Also, the NPO differs from the pension liability reported in a governmental employer's financial statements. GASB-27 defines the *NPO* as follows (GASB-27, pars. 8–13):

> The cumulative difference since the effective date of this Statement between annual pension cost and the employer's contributions to the plan, including the pension liability (asset) at transition, and excluding (a) short-term differences and (b) unpaid contributions that have been converted to pension-related debt.

Conversely, the pension liability is the amount recognized by an employer for contributions to a pension plan less than pension expenditures/expense.

The ARC and the required employer contribution should be based on the same covered payroll amount. The covered payroll amount (which is the basis for measuring the ARC and the employer's contribution) may be based on projected payroll, budgeted covered payroll, or actual covered payroll, as long as the measurement is consistently applied from period to period. The ARC is the basis for computing the annual pension cost and the NPO, if any. Thus, the comparison of the ARC and the required employer contribution should be based on the same definition of covered payroll. Also, the ARC does not include pension-related debt. GASB-27 defines "pension-related debt" as follows (GASB-27, pars. 8–13):

> All long-term liabilities of an employer to a pension plan, the payment of which is not included in the annual required contributions of a sole or agent employer (ARC) or the actuarially determined required contributions of a cost-sharing employer. Payments generally are made in accordance with installment contracts that usually include interest. Examples include contractually deferred contributions and amounts

assessed to an employer upon joining a multiple-employer plan.

Because pension-related debt is not part of the ARC, it also is not part of the annual pension cost.

Calculation of the ARC (the parameters) The measurement of pension plan information should be based on an actuarial valuation that is performed at least biennially; however, the actuarial valuation date does not have to coincide with the governmental entity's year-end date (GASB-27, pars. 9–10).

When a defined benefit pension plan has experienced significant changes related to the computation of pension cost, a new actuarial valuation should be performed on a current basis, rather than waiting for the next scheduled valuation date.

The ARC used by the governmental employer or sponsor to compute its pension expenditure/expense must be based on an actuarial valuation that is "not more than 24 months before the beginning of the employer's fiscal year (first fiscal year if actuarial valuations are biennial)."

> **OBSERVATION:** Different timing periods were established for GASB-25 and GASB-27 because of two different objectives considered relevant by the GASB. Because GASB-25 (which is discussed in Chapter 22, "Pension, Postemployment, and Other Benefit Plans") is concerned with reporting by the pension plan as a separate entity or separate governmental fund, one objective was concerned with the timeliness of the information. The GASB believed that the actuarial information used to compute the plan's actuarial liability and related funding progress should be based on an actuarial analysis that is no more than 12 months old. On the other hand, GASB-27 addresses the issue of employer expenditure/expense, and the measurement of the annual required contribution, which has budgetary implication for governmental entities. Based on research conducted by the GASB prior to the issuance of GASB-27, it identified delays between the development of actuarial information by the pension plan and the communication of the information to governmental employers. Initially, the GASB proposed 18 months as the maximum difference between the actuarial evaluation date and the date of the financial statement, after receiving comments from interested parties the timing period was extended to 24 months.

Each year's most recent financial statements should reflect actuarially computed pension information that is based on an actuarial valuation date that is no more than one year (two years for plans that use a biennial valuation approach) before the date of the most current financial statements.

All actuarial computations (including the ARC) reflected in the employer's financial statements must be based on the parameters established by GASB-27. Generally, that means the computation of the actuarial information presented in the financial statements must be based on the same actuarial methods and assumptions used to determine the employer's pension plan contributions. However, if the employer's pension plan contributions are not based on certain broad criteria established by GASB-27, the actuarial methods and assumptions used to compute the actuarial information included in the employer's financial statements must be modified (GASB-27, pars. 9–10).

> **PRACTICE POINT:** The GASB established consistent pension accounting and reporting standards for pension plans (GASB-25 [Financial Reporting for Defined Benefit Pension Plans and Note Disclosures for Defined Contribution Plans]) and pension expenditures/expense for governmental employers (GASB-27). A pension plan's schedule of funding progress and schedule of employer contributions contain actuarial elements that must be calculated by the related governmental employer and presented in its financial statements. The basis for the computation for each entity is the definition of the "parameters," which is found in both GASB-25 and GASB-27.

The computation of the parameters is based on the following components (GASB-27, pars. 9–10):

- Benefits to be included
- Actuarial assumptions
- Economic assumptions
- Actuarial cost method
- Actuarial value of assets
- Annual required contributions
- Contribution deficiencies or excess contributions

Benefits to be included Pension plan benefits should be based on the "actuarial present value of total projected benefits," which is defined as follows (GASB-27, pars. 9–10):

> All benefits estimated to be payable to plan members (retirees and beneficiaries, terminated employees entitled to benefits but not yet receiving them, and current active members) as a result of their service through the valuation date and their expected future service. The actuarial present value of total projected benefits as of the valuation date is the present value of the cost to finance benefits payable in the future, discounted to reflect the expected effects of the time value (present value) of money and the probabilities of payment.

> Expressed another way, it is the amount that would have to be invested on the valuation date so that the amount invested plus investment earnings will provide sufficient assets to pay total projected benefits when due.

The actuarial present value of total projected benefits includes all pension benefits that have been agreed to by the governmental entity based on the terms of the pension plans and benefits (such as discretionary cost-of-living adjustments) arising from additional statutory or contractual agreements.

> **PRACTICE POINT:** Although GASB-27 provides a comprehensive and economically acceptable definition of the actuarial present value of total projected benefits, that actuarial liability is not reported in the employer's financial statements.

Pension plan benefits that have been financed through allocated insurance contracts (annuity contract purchased from an insurance company) are not part of the actuarial present value of total projected benefits. Those contracts should also be excluded from pension plan assets (GASB-27, pars. 9–10).

Actuarial assumptions GASB-27 requires that all actuarial assumptions be guided by standards established by Actuarial Standard of Practice No. 4 (Measuring Pension Obligations) or any successor standard. Actuarial measurements should be based on "actual experience of the covered group" (plan members included in the actuarial valuation) modified for expected long-term trends (GASB-27, pars. 9–10).

Economic assumptions An essential factor in calculating actuarial measurements is the establishment of an investment rate assumption (discount rate). The investment rate assumption is used to determine the present value of expected future payments under the pension plan. The investment rate used in the computation should be based on the estimated long-term investment yield related to the pension plan (current and expected) assets. Thus, the interest rate used should reflect the types of pension plan investments (both current investments and anticipated investments) and the investment portfolio mix. Although the investment strategies for governmental pension plans vary, in most instances the investment rate assumption will be an estimate of long-term returns.

Another economic assumption that is critical to the computation of actuarial values is the "projected salary increase assumption," which the GASB defines as follows:

> An actuarial assumption with respect to future increases in the individual salaries and wages of active plan members;

> used in determining the actuarial present value of total projected benefits. The expected increases commonly include amounts for inflation, enhanced productivity, and employee merit and seniority.

GASB-27 requires that all economic assumptions (investment rate assumption, projected salary increase assumption, and other assumptions) be consistent. For example, if it is assumed that the rate of inflation will significantly increase, it would be inappropriate to increase the interest rate assumption but reduce the salary increase assumption (GASB-27, pars. 9–10).

Actuarial cost methods In general, there are two broad classes of actuarial cost methods: benefit-allocation methods and cost-allocation methods. In benefit-allocation methods, funding requirements generally increase over time. In cost-allocation methods, funding requirements remain level (either in relation to dollar amounts or as a percentage of compensation). GASB-27 specifies that all of the following actuarial cost methods can be used to compute the actuarial present value of total projected benefits (GASB-27, pars. 9–10):

> *Aggregate Actuarial Cost Method*—Amethod under which the excess of the Actuarial Present Value of Projected Benefits of the group included in an Actuarial Valuation over the Actuarial Value of Assets is allocated on a level basis over the earnings or service of the group between the valuation date and assumed exit. This allocation is performed for the group as a whole, not as a sum of individual allocations. That portion of the Actuarial Present Value allocated to a valuation year is called the Normal Cost. The Actuarial Accrued Liability is equal to the Actuarial Value of Assets.

> *Entry Age Actuarial Cost Method*—Amethod under which the Actuarial Present Value of the Projected Benefits of each individual included in an Actuarial Valuation is allocated on a level basis over the earnings or service of the individual between entry age and assumed exit age(s). The portion of this Actuarial Present Value allocated to a valuation year is called the Normal Cost. The portion of this Actuarial Present Value not provided for at a valuation date by the Actuarial Present Value of future Normal Costs is called the Actuarial Accrued Liability.

> *Frozen Entry Age Actuarial Cost Method*—A method under which the excess of the Actuarial Present Value of Projected Benefits of the group included in an Actuarial Valuation, over the sum of the Actuarial Value of Assets plus the Unfunded Frozen Actuarial Accrued Liability, is allocated on a level basis over the earnings or service of the group between the valuation date and assumed exit. This allocation is performed

for the group as a whole, not as a sum of individual allocations. The Frozen Actuarial Accrued Liability is determined using the Entry Age Actuarial Cost Method. The portion of this Actuarial Present Value allocated to a valuation year is called the Normal Cost.

Attained Age Actuarial Cost Method—Amethod under which the excess of the Actuarial Present Value of Projected Benefits over the Actuarial Accrued Liability in respect of each individual included in an Actuarial Valuation is allocated on a level basis over the earnings or service of the individual between the valuation date and assumed exit. The portion of this Actuarial Present Value which is allocated to a valuation year is called the Normal Cost. The Actuarial Accrued Liability is determined using the Unit Credit Actuarial Cost Method.

Frozen Attained Age Actuarial Cost Method—Amethod under which the excess of the Actuarial Present Value of Projected Benefits of the group included in an Actuarial Valuation, over the sum of the Actuarial Value of Assets plus the Unfunded Frozen Actuarial Accrued Liability, is allocated on a level basis over the earnings or service of the group between the valuation date and assumed exit. This allocation is performed for the group as a whole, not as a sum of individual allocations. The Unfunded Frozen Actuarial Accrued Liability is determined using the Unit Credit Actuarial Cost Method. The portion of this Actuarial Present Value allocated to a valuation year is called the Normal Cost.

[Projected] Unit Credit Actuarial Cost Method—A method under which the benefits (projected . . .) of each individual included in an Actuarial Valuation are allocated by a consistent formula to valuation years. The Actuarial Present Value of benefits allocated to a valuation year is called the Normal Cost. The Actuarial Present Value of benefits allocated to all periods prior to a valuation year is called the Actuarial Accrued Liability.

PRACTICE POINT: GASB-27 notes that the projected unit credit method is an acceptable actuarial method "for plans in which benefits already accumulated for years of service are not affected by future salary levels."

Actuarial value of assets GASB-27 states that generally the value of assets included in a pension plan should be based on "market-related value," which is defined as

A term used with reference to the actuarial value of assets. A market-related value may be market value (or estimated

> market value) or a calculated value that recognizes changes in market value over a period of, for example, three to five years.

Thus, market-related value is not always the same as fair value. "Fair value" refers to the price a willing buyer and a willing seller agree to in an arm's-length transaction. For example, the fair value of a marketable security is based on the market quotation, and the fair value of real estate could be determined by an appraisal. Although market-related values are based on fair values, the approach attempts to smooth out changes in values over a number of years. For example, the market-related value of a security expected to be held for a significant number of years may be based on a rolling fiveyear average, rather than on a single year-end quotation. The GASB states that because pension investment strategies and obligations are generally long-term in nature, it is inappropriate to reflect valuation fluctuations that may be short-term in nature.

GASB-27 does not specifically endorse particular smoothing techniques or smoothing periods. Procedures to be used to value plan assets are included in Actuarial Standard of Practice No. 4.

Annual required contributions The ARC is based on (1) the employer's normal costs and (2) a provision that amortizes the unfunded actuarial accrued liability.

"Normal cost" is defined as "that portion of the actuarial present value of pension plan benefits and expenses which is allocated to a valuation year by the actuarial cost method." The specific amount of normal cost allocated to a particular year is in part based on the actuarial cost method adopted by the governmental entity.

In addition to a provision for normal cost, the ARC includes a portion (amortization) of the total unfunded actuarial accrued liability. The components that comprise the unfunded actuarial liability are presented as follows, along with GASB-27 definitions of the components:

Actuarial Value of Assets	$X
Less: Actuarial Accrued Liability	–X
Unfunded Actuarial Accrued Liability	$X

> *Actuarial Value of Assets*—The value of cash, investments and other property belonging to a pension plan, as used by the actuary for the purpose of an Actuarial Valuation.
>
> *Actuarial Accrued Liability*—That portion, as determined by a particular Actuarial Cost Method, of the Actuarial Present Value of pension plan benefits and expenses which is not provided for by future Normal Costs.
>
> *Unfunded Actuarial Accrued Liability*—The excess of the Actuarial Accrued Liability over the Actuarial Value of Assets.

The unfunded actuarial liability may be positive ("unfunded actuarial liability" means that the actuarial accrued liability is greater than the actuarial value of the plans assets) or negative ("funding excess" means that the actuarial accrued liability is less than the actuarial value of the plan's assets) (GASB-27, pars. 9–10). (For purposes of subsequent discussions, GASB-27 refers to the unfunded actuarial liability, but the guidance also applies when there is a funding excess.)

> **OBSERVATION:** The unfunded actuarial liability is not a measure of the economic funding status of the pension plan because it does not equal the difference between the projected benefits obligation (actuarial present value of total projected benefits) and the fair value of plan assets. The actuarial accrued liability is composed of unrecognized prior service costs (pension benefits that were incurred when the plan was adopted and the benefits formula includes credit for years of service before the plan was adopted and additional benefits that were granted by plan amendments retroactive to prior years), and actuarial gains and losses. Netting this amount (actuarial accrued liability) by the actuarial value of assets will generally result in a significant understatement of the economic pension liability or a significant overstatement of the excess funding status of the pension plan.

> **PRACTICE POINT:** When the aggregate actuarial cost method is used, there should be no separate measurement or amortization of the unfunded actuarial liability.

The period over which the unfunded actuarial liability may be amortized is 30 years, although a maximum 40-year transition period is allowed by GASB-27. That is, a maximum 40-year amortization period may be used for 10 years from the effective date of the Statement. After the ten-year period elapses, a maximum 30-year period is to be used.

> **PRACTICE POINT:** The GASB identified a maximum period of 30 or 40 years, but did not establish a minimum amortization period (except for certain actuarial changes discussed later, for which a 10-year minimum amortization period applies). Thus, governmental entities are allowed significant flexibility (from 1 year to 40 years) in establishing an amortization period.

The unfunded actuarial liability may be amortized as a single amount or its components may be individually amortized. If the individual components are amortized over different amortization periods, the total amortization for all components must satisfy the maximum amortization period criterion. GASB-27 refers to this criterion as the "equivalent single amortization period," which it defines as follows:

> The weighted average of all amortization periods used when components of the total unfunded actuarial accrued liability are separately amortized and the average is calculated in accordance with the parameters.

Changes in the balance of the unfunded actuarial accrued liability may arise from (1) a change from one acceptable actuarial method to another acceptable method or (2) a change from one acceptable method to another acceptable method for determining the actuarial value of plan assets. Adjustments in the value of the unfunded actuarial accrued liability arising from these changes are to be amortized over a period of not less than 10 years.

The unfunded actuarial liability may be amortized using either a closed or an open amortization method. Under a closed amortization method, the unfunded actuarial liability is amortized over a fixed number of years, and at the end of that period of time, the amount is fully amortized. When the open amortization method is used, the amortization period may be changed at each new actuarial valuation date and the previously unamortized amount is then amortized over the newly established amortization period. Generally, the closed amortization method will produce more volatile measures of the actuarial accrued liability than the open amortization method.

The unfunded actuarial accrued liability should be amortized using one of two methods, which are defined in GASB-27 as follows (GASB-27, pars. 9–10):

> *Level dollar amortization method*—The amount to be amortized is divided into equal dollar amounts to be paid over a given number of years; part of each payment is interest and part is principal (similar to a mortgage payment on a building). Because payroll can be expected to increase as a result of inflation, level dollar payments generally represent a decreasing percentage of payroll; in dollars adjusted for inflation, the payments can be expected to decrease over time.
>
> *Level percentage of projected payroll amortization method*—Amortization payments are calculated so that they are a constant percentage of the projected payroll of active plan members over a given number of years. The dollar amount of the payments generally will increase over time as payroll increases due to inflation; in dollars adjusted for inflation, the payments can be expected to remain level.

When the level percentage of the projected payroll amortization method is used, the assumed payroll growth rate should not reflect an assumed increase in the number of active plan members. The assumed payroll growth rate refers to "an actuarial assumption with respect to future increases in total covered payroll attributable to inflation." Any projected decreases in covered payroll should be reflected in the amortization method if no new members are allowed to join the pension plan (GASB-27, pars. 9–10).

Contribution deficiencies or excess contributions Although GASB-27 requires that a governmental employer determine the amount of the ARC for each year, it cannot require that the amount be funded. If the required contribution is not funded, the resulting contribution deficiency (or excess contribution) is amortized beginning with the next actuarial valuation date. However, no amortization is required if it is expected that the deficiency or excess is to be settled within one year of its occurrence. When the expected settlement does not take place within the allowed period, amortization of the deficiency (or excess) should begin at the next actuarial valuation date (GASB-27, pars. 9–10).

Calculation of interest on the NPO and the adjustment to the ARC A net pension obligation (NPO) arises when there is a cumulative difference between the annual pension cost and the cumulative contributions made to the pension plan (GASB-27, pars. 11–13).

> **PRACTICE POINT:** The employer's contributions do not include contributions from employees. Likewise, the measurement of the NPO should not include contributions that are required to be paid by employees.

The cumulative differences are measured from the effective date of GASB-27 and the current date of a governmental entity's financial statements. The NPO is computed as follows:

Pension liability (or asset) that existed at the transition date	$ X
Add: Cumulative contribution deficiencies (or excess contributions) from the effective date of the statement	X
Less: Short-term differences	–X
Less: Unpaid contributions converted to pension-related debt	–X
NPO	$ X

Note: For simplicity, the above format assumes that the governmental entity has a transition pension liability (not an asset) and a cumulative contribution deficiency (not excess contributions). If these circumstances do not exist, the computation would be modified accordingly.

Short-term differences are differences expected to be settled (1) by the first actuarial valuation date after the difference arose or (2) within one year after the difference arose if the first actuarial valuation is to be made within a year. (Pension-related debt was defined earlier.)

When an entity has an NPO, annual pension cost includes interest on the NPO and an adjustment to the ARC. The interest on the NPO is based on the balance of the NPO at the beginning of the year and the assumed interest rate (which was discussed earlier). The adjustment of the ARC is needed to remove any interest and/or principal that is already included in the ARC arising from the amortization of past contribution deficiencies (or excess contributions) (GASB-27, pars. 11–13).

The adjustment to the ARC is an estimate and should be made using the following guidelines (GASB-27, pars. 11–13):

- Use the same amortization method (level dollar method or level percentage of projected payroll method) that was used to calculate the ARC.
- Use the same actuarial assumptions that were used to calculate the ARC.
- Use the same amortization period that was used to calculate the ARC.

The adjustment to the ARC must be recalculated for each year for which the governmental employer has an NPO.

PRACTICE POINT: When the ARC is calculated using more than one period, the period used to determine the ARC adjustment should be the same as that used to amortize net actuarial experience gains and losses. "Actuarial experience gains and losses" are defined as "a measure of the difference between actuarial experience and that expected based upon a set of actuarial assumptions, during the period between two actuarial valuation dates, as determined in accordance with a particular actuarial cost method." The effects of actuarial gains and losses on the measurement of future normal cost computations depend on the specific actuarial cost method used by the governmental employer. GASB-27 notes that when the ARC is calculated based on the frozen entry age method, frozen attained age method, or aggregate actuarial cost method, the calculation of the ARC adjustment should be based on the average remaining service life of active plan members.

Cost-Sharing Employers

GASB-27 defines a "cost-sharing multiple-employer pension plan" as follows (GASB-27, par. 19):

> A single plan with pooling (cost-sharing) arrangements for the participating employers. All risksrewards, and costs, including benefit costs, are shared and are not attributed individually to the employers. A single actuarial valuation covers all plan members and the same contribution rate(s) applies for each employer.

Unlike a sole employer plan and an agent employer plan, in a cost-sharing arrangement an employer's pension obligation under the pension plan is not determined based on the characteristics (age, years of service, etc.) of its employees. For this reason, the amount of the recorded pension expenditures/expense should simply be based on the contractually required contributions determined under the terms of the cost-sharing arrangement.

Any difference between the required contribution and the actual contribution made should be recorded as an asset or as a liability. The pension liability or asset position of one plan should not be netted against a different plan that has an opposite position (liability or asset position) (GASB-27, par. 19).

PRACTICE POINT: With the issuance of GASB Technical Bulletin 2004-2 (Recognition of Pension and Other Postemployment Benefit Expenditures/Expenses and Liabilities by Cost-Sharing Employers), the GASB clarified certain accounting and reporting issues related to cost-sharing plans, as follows: (1) Contractually required contributions to cost-sharing plans are attributable to the periods of time (month, quarter, or year) for which the contributions are assessed by the plan and (2) in governmental funds, expenditures should be recognized for the sum of the amount contributed and any amount contractually required but unpaid during the period.

Notes to the Financial Statements

GASB-27 requires that the following be disclosed by a governmental employer for each defined benefit pension plan in which it participates (GASB-27, pars. 20–21).

PRACTICE ALERT: GASB-50, issued in May 2007, brings current government pension disclosure requirements in line with the disclosures recently required for other postemployment benefits (OPEB). GASB-50 amends the disclosure requirements of GASB-25 and GASB-27 by requiring the following:

- Disclosure of the current funded status of the plan (the degree to which the actuarial accrued liabilities for benefits are covered by assets that have been set aside to pay for such benefits) as of the most recent actuarial valuation date in the notes to the financial statements of pension plans and certain employer governments to be presented in addition to funded status data currently presented as required supplementary information (RSI).

- Disclosure by governments that use the aggregate actuarial cost method of the funded status and present a multiyear schedule of funding progress using the entry age actuarial cost method as a surrogate; these governments currently are not required to provide this information.
- Disclosure by governments participating in multi-employer cost-sharing pension plans of how the contractually required contribution rate is determined.
- Presentation by governments in cost-sharing plans of the required schedule of funding progress if the plan does not issue a GAAP-compliant report that includes the funding progress RSI schedules or if the plan is not included in a publicly available financial report of another entity.

GASB-50 is generally effective for periods beginning after June 15, 2007, with early implementation encouraged.

Plan Description

- The plan name, the administrator of the plan, and the type of plan (single-employer, agent multiple-employer, or cost-sharing multiple-employer)
- The name of the PERS or other entity that administers the plan
- The authority on which the plan was organized and the basis for amending the plan
- The benefits provided by the plan
- Whether the plan issues separate financial statements (stand-alone financial statements) or includes its financial statements in the financial reports of a PERS or another entity, and if so, how to obtain those financial reports

Funding Policy

- The authority on which the plan's required contributions by plan members, the employer(s), and other contributing parties is based
- The required contribution rate for active plan members
- The required contribution rate for the employer expressed in dollars or as a percentage of current-year covered payroll

(When the plan is a single-employer or agent plan and the contribution rate is significantly different from the ARC, the method by which the contribution rate is determined must be disclosed. When the plan is a cost-sharing plan, the disclosure must include the required contribution and the actual percentage contributed for the current and the previous two years.)

OBSERVATION: Although the disclosures should be made for each plan, the disclosures may be formatted to eliminate duplicate information.

In addition to the information presented above, sole and agent employers must disclose the following (GASB-27, pars. 20–21):

- Current pension cost and dollar amount contributed
- For employers with an NPO, the components of the annual pension costs (specifically the ARC, interest on the NPO, and the ARC adjustment)
- For employers with an NPO, the year-end balance in the NPO and the increase or decrease in the NPO for the year
- Annual pension cost, percentage funded, and year-end balance in the NPO, if any, for the current and two previous years
- Information concerning the actuarial valuation, including:
  - Actuarial valuation date
  - Actuarial cost methods and assumptions used for the current year and for the most current information presented in the required supplementary information (see the analysis in the following section)
- Valuation method used to determine actuarial value of plan assets
- Inflation rate assumption
- Investment return assumption
- Projected salary increase assumption
- Increases in postretirement benefit assumption
- Amortization method used (level dollar method or level percentage of projected payroll method)
- Amortization period used (for plans that use more than one period, the equivalent single amortization period must be disclosed) for the most recent actuarial valuation date and whether the amortization is based on a closed or open period assumption (If the aggregate actuarial cost method is used, note that the method does not identify or separately amortize the unfunded actuarial liability.)

PRACTICE POINT: When a defined benefit pension plan is presented in the governmental employer's financial statements (pension trust fund), the requirements established by GASB-25 must be observed. (See Chapter 22, "Pension, Postemployment, and Other Benefit Plans.") Some of those disclosures are the same or similar to the requirements listed above. The disclosures made by the governmental employer must satisfy both Statements, but they should be formatted in a manner that eliminates duplication of information. GASB-27 defines a "pension trust fund" as "a fund held by a governmental entity in a trustee capacity for pension plan members; used to account for the accumulation of assets for the purpose of paying benefits when they become due in accordance with the terms of the plan; a pension plan included in the financial reporting entity of the plan sponsor or a participating employer."

Required Supplementary Information

GASB-27 requires that sole and agent employers present the following required supplementary information for defined-benefit pension plans for the most recent actuarial valuation and the previous two valuations (unless the aggregate actuarial cost method is used) (GASB-27, par. 22):

- Actuarial valuation date
- Actuarial value of plan assets
- Actuarial accrued liability
- Total unfunded actuarial liability (or overfunding)
- Funded ratio (actuarial value of assets as a percentage of the actuarial accrued liability)
- Annual covered payroll
- Ratio of the unfunded actuarial liability (or overfunding) to annual covered payroll
- Factors that significantly affect trend analysis (such as changes in actuarial assumptions)

The disclosures must be based on the parameters established by GASB-27 and should be presented, as noted earlier, for the most current actuarial valuation and for the two previous actuarial valuations.

PRACTICE POINT: Rather than present the information as required supplementary information, the governmental employer may make the disclosure in a note to the financial statements. Using this approach, the government does not need to present the required supplementary information if nformation based on all three actuarial valuation dates is presented. If not, all of the disclosures for all three actuarial valuation dates must be presented as required supplementary information.

PRACTICE POINT: GASB-25 mandates the same required supplementary information disclosures as GASB-27. When a sole employer presents the financial statements of the plan in its financial report (pension trust fund) and meets the disclosure requirements established by GASB-25, there is no need to repeat the required supplementary disclosures established by GASB-27. However, for an agent multiple-employer plan, the requirements established by GASB-27 regarding required supplementary information must be satisfied for the employer's individual pension plan disclosures. This guidance applies to an agent multiple-employer plan even when the financial statements (on an aggregate basis) are presented in the financial report of the employer government (pension trust fund).

Illustrated Disclosures (Including Required Supplementary Information)

Exhibit 13-4, an example taken from Appendix D of GASB-27, presents an illustration of a note for a governmental employer that contributes to a single-employer defined benefit pension plan.

Exhibit 13-5, an example taken from Appendix D of GASB-27, presents an illustration of a note for a governmental employer that contributes to an agent multiple-employer defined benefit pension plan.

EXHIBIT 13-4
NOTES TO THE FINANCIAL STATEMENTS FOR AN EMPLOYER CONTRIBUTING TO A SINGLE-EMPLOYER DEFINED BENEFIT PENSION PLAN

Note: This example assumes that the plan is included as a pension trust fund in the employer's financial reporting entity.Therefore, the requirement of

EXHIBIT 13-4 (*continued*)

paragraph 22 of Statement 27 to present a schedule of funding progress covering at least three actuarial valuations would be met by complying with paragraphs 33–40 of Statement 25. If the plan was not included in the employer's financial reporting entity, the employer would be required to present a schedule of funding progress.

State of Columbine Notes to the Financial Statements for the Year Ended December 31, 20X2

Note X. Pension Plan

Plan Description. State Employees Pension Plan (SEPP) is a single-employer defined benefit pension plan administered by the Columbine Retirement System. SEPP provides retirement, disability, and death benefits to plan members and beneficiaries. Cost-of-living adjustments are provided to members and beneficiaries at the discretion of the State legislature. Article 29 of the Regulations of the State of Columbine assigns the authority to establish and amend benefit provisions to the State legislature. The Columbine Retirement System issues a publicly available financial report that includes financial statements and required supplementary information for SEPP. That report may be obtained by writing to Columbine Retirement System, State Government Lane, Anytown, USA 01000, or by calling 1-800-555-PLAN.

Funding Policy. The contribution requirements of plan members and the State are established and may be amended by the State legislature. Plan members are required to contribute 7.8% of their annual covered salary.The State is required to contribute at an actuarially determined rate; the current rate is 11.9% of annual covered payroll.

Annual Pension Cost and Net Pension Obligation. The State's annual pension cost and net pension obligation to SEPP for the current year were as follows:

(Dollar amounts in thousands)	
Annual required contribution	$ 137,916
Interest on net pension obligation	2,867
Adjustment to annual required contribution	(2,089)
Annual pension cost	138,694
Contributions made	(137,916)
Increase (decrease) in net pension obligation	778
Net pension obligation beginning of year	38,221
Net pension obligation end of year	$ 38,999

The annual required contribution for the current year was determined as part of the December 31, 20X1, actuarial valuation using the entry age actuarial cost

EXHIBIT 13-4 *(continued)*

method. The actuarial assumptions included (a) 7.5% investment rate of return (net of administrative expenses) and (b) projected salary increases ranging from 5.5% to 9.5% per year. Both (a) and (b) included an inflation component of 5.5%. The assumptions did not include postretirement benefit increases, which are funded by State appropriation when granted. The actuarial value of assets was determined using techniques that smooth the effects of short-term volatility in the market value of investments over a four-year period. The unfunded actuarial accrued liability is being amortized as a level percentage of projected payroll on an open basis. The remaining amortization period at December 31, 20X1, was 23 years.

Three-Year Trend Information

(Dollar amounts in thousands)

Fiscal Year Ending	*Annual Pension Cost (APC)*	*Percentage of APC Contributed*	*Net Pension Obligation*
6/30/X0	$119,757	99.1%	$37,458
6/30/X1	125,039	99.4	38,221
6/30/X2	138,694	99.4	38,999

EXHIBIT 13-5
NOTES TO THE FINANCIAL STATEMENTS FOR AN EMPLOYER CONTRIBUTING TO AN AGENT MULTIPLE-EMPLOYER DEFINED BENEFIT PENSION PLAN

City of Dill Notes to the Financial Statements for the Year Ended December 31, 20X2

Note X. Pension Plan

Plan Description. The City's defined benefit pension plan, Dill Employees Pension Plan (DEPP), provides retirement and disability benefits, annual cost-of-living adjustments, and death benefits to plan members and beneficiaries. DEPP is affiliated with the Municipal Employees Pension Plan (MEPP), an agent multiple-employer pension plan administered by the Columbine Retirement System. Article 39 of the Regulations of the State of

EXHIBIT 13-5 *(continued)*

Columbine assigns the authority to establish and amend the benefit provisions of the plans that participate in MEPP to the respective employer entities; for DEPP, that authority rests with the City of Dill. The Columbine Retirement System issues a publicly available financial report that includes financial statements and required supplementary information for MEPP. That report may be obtained by writing to Columbine Retirement System, State Government Lane, Anytown, USA 01000, or by calling 1-800-555-PLAN.

Funding Policy. DEPP members are required to contribute 8% of their annual covered salary. The City is required to contribute at an actuarially determined rate; the current rate is 11% of annual covered payroll. The contribution requirements of plan members and the City are established and may be amended by the MEPP Board of Trustees.

Annual Pension Cost. For 20X2, the City's annual pension cost of $2,590,000 for DEPP was equal to the City's required and actual contributions. The required contribution was determined as part of the December 31, 20X1, actuarial valuation using the entry age actuarial cost method. The actuarial assumptions included (a) 7.5% investment rate of return (net of administrative expenses), (b) projected salary increases ranging from 5.5% to 11.5% per year, and (c) 2% per year cost-of-living adjustments. Both (a) and (b) included an inflation component of 5.5%. The actuarial value of DEPP assets was determined using techniques that smooth the effects of short-term volatility in the market value of investments over a four-year period. DEPP's unfunded actuarial accrued liability is being amortized as a level percentage of projected payroll on a closed basis. The remaining amortization period at December 31, 20X1, was 14 years.

Three-Year Trend Information for DEPP

(Dollar amounts in thousands)

Fiscal Year Funding	*Annual Pension Cost (APC)*	*Percentage of APC Contributed*	*Net Pension Obligation*
6/30/X0	$ 2,409	100%	$ 0
6/30/X1	2,511	100	0
6/30/X2	2,590	100	0

EXHIBIT 13-5 *(continued)*

REQUIRED SUPPLEMENTARY INFORMATION
Schedule of Funding Progress for DEPP

(Dollar amounts in thousands)

Actuarial Valuation Date	*Actuarial Value of Assets (a)*	*Actuarial Accrued Liability (AAL)— Entry Age (b)*	*Unfunded AAL (UAAL) b − a*	*Funded Ratio (a/b)*	*Covered Payroll (c)*	*UAAL as a Percentage of Covered Payroll ((b − a)/c)*
12/31/W9*	$ 49,629	$ 52,838	$ 3,209	93.9%	$ 21,367	15.0%
12/31/X0	55,088	57,615	2,527	95.6	22,276	11.3
12/31/X1	59,262	62,817	3,555	94.3	23,551	15.1

*Revised economic and noneconomic assumptions due to experience review.

Insured Plans

GASB-27 defines an "insured plan" as follows (GASB-27, par. 23):

> A pension financing arrangement whereby an employer accumulates funds with an insurance company, while employees are in active service, in return for which the insurance company unconditionally undertakes a legal obligation to pay the pension benefits of those employees or their beneficiaries, as defined in the employer's plan.

When a pension plan satisfies the criteria established in the above definition, that insured plan does not have to follow the (parameters) standards established by GASB-27. Thus, pension expenditures/expense for a particular year is the premium amount that must be paid to the insurance company.

Although a governmental entity is not required to follow the parameters established by GASB-27 when an insured plan exists, the following disclosures must be made (GASB-27, par. 23):

- The authority on which the insured plan was organized (and the basis for amendment) and a brief description of the benefits provided by the plan
- Statement that the responsibility for the payment of benefits under the plan has been effectively transferred to an insurance company

- Whether the governmental employer has guaranteed the pension payments in the event the insurance company is unable to pay the benefits
- The current-year pension expenditures/expense recognized and the amount of contributions or premiums paid during the year

Employers with Defined Contribution Plans

Although GASB-27 focuses on defined benefit plans, the Statement briefly addresses the measurement of pension expenditures/expense for defined contribution plans. Pension expenditures/expense for a defined contribution plan is recognized based on the required contribution under the terms of the plan and the basis of accounting (modified accrual for governmental fund types and accrual for proprietary fund types), depending on which type of fund is used to account for the employer's pension contribution (GASB-27, pars. 25–27).

Any difference between the required contribution and actual contributions should be recognized as an asset or liability in the employer's financial statements, depending on whether the modified accrual or accrual basis of accounting is used. An asset related to one defined contribution plan should not be offset against a liability related to another defined contribution plan. In addition, the following disclosures should be made for each defined contribution pension plan for which the government must contribute:

- The plan name, the administrator of the plan, and a statement that the plan is a defined contribution plan
- The authority on which the plan was organized (or may be amended) and a brief description of the plan provisions
- The contribution required (in dollars or as a percentage of salary) for employees, the employer, and others (such as a state government's portion) and the authority on which the contribution requirements are established (or may be amended)
- Amounts contributed by the employer and the employees

PRACTICE POINT: When a defined contribution plan is presented in a governmental employer's financial statements (pension trust fund), the disclosure requirements established by GASB-25 must be observed. Some of those disclosures are the same or similar to the requirements listed above. The disclosures made by the governmental employer must satisfy both Statements, but they should be formatted in a manner that eliminates duplication of information.

PRACTICE POINT: When a pension plan has characteristics of both a defined benefit pension plan and a defined contribution plan, the characteristics of the plan should be evaluated to determine "if the substance of the plan is to provide a defined pension benefit in some form." If the plan does provide defined pension benefits, GASB-27 requires the plan to observe the standards that apply to defined benefit pension plans.

Special Funding Situations

One governmental entity may be responsible for contributing to a pension plan that covers employees of another governmental entity. This situation often arises when state governments provide funding for pension plans for public school teachers and police officers. Under this circumstance, the governmental entity that is legally responsible for the contributions must follow the applicable standards (measurement, recognition, note disclosure, and required supplementary information standards) established by GASB-27, depending on whether the plan is a defined benefit pension plan or a defined contribution plan (GASB-27, par. 28).

When a governmental entity is legally responsible for contributions to a defined benefit pension plan and is the only contributing entity, the standards for a sole employer as established by GASB-27 must be observed, even if two or more governmental entities are covered by the pension plan.

PRACTICE POINT: Accounting and reporting standards established by GASB-24 (Accounting and Financial Reporting for Certain Grants and Other Financial Assistance) should be observed to determine how on-behalf payments should be accounted for and reported in the financial statements of the recipient governmental entity.

ACCOUNTING AND REPORTING

Recognition of Pension Expenditures/Expense, Liabilities, and Assets

A governmental employer that has more than one defined benefit pension plan should apply the measurement criteria established by GASB-27 to each plan separately; however, the pension information can generally be combined when preparing the employer's financial statements (GASB-27, pars. 14–15).

The calculation of pension expenditures/expense is based on the following:

- Contributions made based on the computation of the ARC

- Payments, if any, for pension-related debt not included as part of the ARC or the NPO

The amount of the ARC-related liability (asset) reported at the end of the year must be adjusted so that it is equal to the employer's NPO.

In addition, pension-related debt should be accounted for, taking into consideration any payments that are recorded as pension expenditures/expense as described above.

A governmental employer may make payments of ARC-related contributions to the same defined benefit pension plan from more than one fund. Under this circumstance, the employer must use its discretion to determine how to allocate the ARC to each fund.

When a governmental employer has an NPO that must be allocated to more than one fund, the allocation of the interest and ARC adjustment of the annual pension cost to each liability should be based on the proportionate share of the NPO reported in each fund as of the beginning of the year(GASB-27, pars. 14–15).

The accounting standards that are used to determine how a pension obligation should be accounted for depends to some degree on whether the liability is presented in a (1) governmental fund, (2) proprietary or fiduciary fund, or (3) the government-wide financial statements.

Governmental funds Employer pension obligation expenditures and liabilities of governmental funds should be recognized in accordance with the modified accrual basis of accounting and the current financial resources measurement focus. As a result, annual pension cost and net pension obligation would be recognized to the extent they are normally required to be liquidated with current financial resources.

Cost-sharing employers Pension expenditure and the related liability recorded for cost-sharing employers should be based on the contractually required contributions determined under the terms of the cost-sharing arrangement due and payable from current financial resources.

Insured plans When a pension plan satisfies the criteria discussed earlier in this chapter, that insured plan does not have to follow the (parameters) standards established by GASB-27. The pension expenditure presented in the governmental fund financial statements is based on the premium amount that must be paid to the insurance company from current financial resources.

Defined contribution plans Pension expenditure for a defined contribution plan is recognized in the governmental fund financial statements based on the required contribution under the terms of the plan normally payable from current financial resources.

Proprietary and fiduciary funds The recording of pension expense for proprietary and fiduciary funds (as well as other funds that use proprietary fund accounting) is based on accrual accounting and economic resources measurement focus. The expense is based on the computation of the annual pension cost as required by the standards established by GASB-27. Any difference between the amount of the accrual and the amount funded should be subtracted or added to the NPO. If the pension plan is underfunded, the amount of the liability should be reported on the proprietary fund's balance sheet. If, however, the pension plan is overfunded, the amount should be reported as a fund asset. If there are two or more pension funds with a different funding status (one underfunded and one overfunded), the balances in each fund should not be netted for financial reporting purposes (GASB-27, par. 17, as amended by GASB-34).

Cost-sharing employers As noted earlier, in a cost-sharing arrangement an employer's pension obligation under the pension plan is not determined based on the characteristics (age, years of service, etc.) of its employees. For this reason, the amount of the recorded pension expense should be based on the contractually required contributions determined under the terms of the cost-sharing arrangement. The accrual basis of accounting should be used to determine the amount of the liability to be presented in the proprietary fund (GASB-27, par. 19, and GASB-34, pars. 6 and 69).

Insured plans When a pension plan satisfies the criteria discussed earlier in this chapter, that insured plan does not have to follow the (parameters) standards established by GASB-27. The pension expense presented in the proprietary fund is the premium amount that must be paid to the insurance company. The accrual basis of accounting should be used to determine the amount of the liability to be presented in the proprietary fund (GASB-27, par. 23, and GASB-34, pars. 6 and 69).

Defined contribution plans As suggested earlier, GASB-27 briefly addresses the measurement of pension expense for defined contribution plans that relate to proprietary funds. Pension expense for a defined contribution plan is recognized based on the required contribution under the terms of the plan. The accrual basis of accounting should be used to determine the amount of the liability to be presented in the proprietary fund (GASB-27, pars. 25–27, and GASB-34, par. 6).

Government-wide financial statements The standards established by GASB-27 should be used to determine how pension expense and the related liability should be reported in a governmental employer's government-wide financial statements. Those standards are applied based on the accrual basis of accounting and economic resources measurement focus (GASB-34).

Cost-sharing employers Pension expense and the related liability recorded for cost-sharing employers should be based on the contractually required contributions determined under the terms of the cost-sharing arrangement. The accrual basis of accounting should be used to determine the amount of the liability to be presented in the entity's statement of net assets (GASB-27, par. 23, and GASB-34, pars. 6 and 69).

Insured plans When a pension plan satisfies the criteria discussed earlier in this chapter, that insured plan does not have to follow the (parameters) standards established by GASB-27. The pension expense presented in the government-wide financial statements is based on the premium amount that must be paid to the insurance company. The accrual basis of accounting should be used to determine the amount of the liability to be presented in the government-wide financial statements (GASB-27, par. 19, and GASB-34, pars. 6 and 69).

Defined contribution plans Pension expense for a defined contribution plan is recognized in the government-wide financial statements based on the required contribution under the terms of the plan. The accrual basis of accounting should be used to determine the amount of the liability to be presented in the statement of net assets (GASB-27, pars. 25-27, and GASB-34, par. 6).

> **PRACTICE POINT:** Fiduciary funds are not reported in the government-wide financial statements; however, the government's contributions to or costs associated with their participation in the fiduciary funds are reported as an expenditure/expense in the government-wide financial statements on the accrual basis of accounting.

OTHER POSTEMPLOYMENT BENEFITS: EMPLOYER REPORTING (PRE-GASB-45 IMPLEMENTATION)

In addition to pension benefits, postemployment benefits may include payments to retirees or their beneficiaries for life insurance benefits, health insurance benefits, and other pension-related benefits. The obligation related to these postemployment benefits in many cases is significant and may exceed the amount related to an employer's pension obligation.

> **PRACTICE POINT:** Pending implementation of GASB-45 (see the appendix to this chapter for a summary), governments should follow the provisions of GASB-12 and GASB-26.

Governmental accounting and reporting standards (prior to implementing GASB-45) for certain postemployment benefits are based on the following pronouncements:

- GASB-12 (Disclosure of Information on Postemployment Benefits Other Than Pension Benefits by State and Local Governmental Employers)
- GASB-26 (Financial Reporting for Postemployment Health Care Plans Administered by Defined Benefit Pension Plans)

In governmental funds, when a governmental employer's obligation related to postemployment benefits is long term, the liability should not be presented in a government fund but should be presented as part of the general liabilities in the entity's government-wide financial statements. On the other hand, if the obligation or a portion of the obligation is to be extinguished by using current expendable resources, the obligation (or portion of the obligation) should be classified as a liability of the fund responsible for the payment, and a current expenditure should be reflected in the fund's operating statement (NCGA-1, pars. 33 and 42).

GASB-12 establishes disclosure requirements for postemployment benefits, including health care, but it does not address the financial accounting and reporting that should be used to account for postemployment health-care benefits.

> **PRACTICE POINT:** GASB-26 addresses only the financial reporting standards that must be followed by governmental entities that administer postemployment health-care plans in a defined benefit pension plan prior to the implementation or effective date of GASB-43.

Disclosures for Certain Postemployment Benefits

Although the GASB has not addressed the accounting for certain postemployment benefits, GASB-12 attempts to provide minimum disclosure standards for these postemployment retirement benefits.

Definition The definition of "pension-related benefits" established in GASB-12 is based on *how* benefits are provided rather than the specific nature of those benefits. A commonsense definition of pension benefits would include benefits that provide retirement income to an individual, while the definition of pension-related benefits (referred to in GASB-12 as other postemployment benefits [OPEB]) would include all other pension benefits. GASB-12, however, states that "the term *pension benefits* refers principally to retirement income but also includes other pension-related benefits, *except postemployment health care,* when they are provided to plan participants or their beneficiaries through a public employee retirement system (PERS), pension plan, or other arrangement *to provide retirement income."* Thus, what would normally be considered a pensionrelated benefit would be a pension benefit for accounting purposes under GASB-12 if the pension-related benefit is provided through a pension fund (GASB-12, par 20).

Thus, for the purposes of GASB-12, OPEB are (1) pension-related benefits provided through a benefit plan that is separate from a retirement income plan (that is, a pension plan) and (2) postemployment health-care benefits provided through either a separate benefits plan or a retirement income plan. Therefore, postemployment health-care benefits are always considered OPEB. Possible benefits that should be evaluated to determine if they meet the definition of OPEB as established by GASB-12 include life insurance premiums, disability income payments, and tuition subsidies. Examples of health-care benefits include hospitalization, vision, and dental plans.

To properly classify what appears to be an OPEB, the method used to provide a benefit must be evaluated. For example, disability income provided through a separate benefit plan would be classified as OPEB; however, those same benefits provided through a PERS, a pension plan, or any similar arrangement to provide retirement income would be considered a pension benefit. Postemployment health-care benefits are always classified as OPEB by GASB-12 (GASB-12, pars. 20–21).

> **NOTE:** GASB-12 is not applicable to pension benefits or termination benefits.

Scope The standards established by GASB-12 apply to all governmental units that pay, either partially or fully, for postemployment benefits other than pension benefits (OPEB). The governmental entities covered include public benefit corporations and authorities, public employee retirement systems, and governmental utilities, hospitals, colleges, and universities (GASB-12, par. 9).

The reporting standards should be observed irrespective of the fund type the governmental entity uses to account for OPEB activity. For example, the standards would apply to OPEB activity accounted for in the General Fund or in an Enterprise Fund (GASB-12, par. 9).

> **PRACTICE POINT:** GASB-12 refers to postemployment rather than postretirement benefits. Postemployment is the broader of the two terms because it covers the period from termination to actual retirement.

Minimum disclosures GASB-12 provides only disclosure standards for governmental entities. During the interim period prior to implementation of GASB-45, the following disclosures, at a minimum, should be made (either for each type of benefit or for combined types of benefits) (GASB-12, par. 10):

- Describe the OPEB provided [including groups covered, eligibility requirements, and the (quantified) contribution requirements by the employer and employees].
- Disclose the basis for OPEB provided (such as the specific law or contract).
- Disclose accounting and financing or funding policies (such as cash basis or actuarial basis used to determine the amount of the expenditure/expense and to fund the plan).
- If benefits are advance-funded on an actuarial basis, disclose actuarial cost method and significant actuarial assumptions (including assumptions applicable to interest rate, rate of salary increases, and health-care inflation) and method used to value plan assets.
- If benefits are financed on a pay-as-you-go basis, or if financing is not based on an advance-funding approach, even when assets are provided for future payments, disclose the following:
  - — The amount of OPEB expenditures/expenses for the period (Reasonable methods may be used to separate pay-as-you-go OPEB expenditures/expenses from health care and other similar benefits related to active employees. If a reasonable method cannot be identified, then the disclosure should state that OPEB expenditures/expenses cannot be reasonably estimated.)
  - — The number of participants (retirees, terminated employees, and beneficiaries) eligible to receive benefits (Dependents of a participant should be counted as a single unit if participant is deceased and should not be counted if the participant is alive.)
  - — The net assets available for future payments (if assets are being set aside to finance future payments but the strategy does not constitute an advance-funded approach)
- If benefits are advance-funded on an actuarially determined basis, disclose the following:
  - — Number of active plan participants
  - — Governmental entity's actuarially required contribution and actual contribution for the period (net of employees' contributions)
  - — Net assets available for future payments

— Actuarially accrued liability and unfunded actuarial accrued liability based on the actuarial cost method used

- Disclose effect (in dollars, if measurable) of significant matters that distort the comparability of minimum disclosures required from period to period.
- Disclose any additional matters that are considered helpful to users in assessing the nature and cost of OPEB commitments.

> **OBSERVATION:** Based on research conducted by the GASB, it is apparent that many governmental entities have significant OPEB commitments, that accounting methods used to measure OPEB costs are inconsistent, and, in many instances, that disclosures are inadequate was GASB-12 was viewed as an interim step in addressing OPEB accounting and reporting deficiencies. For these reasons, the GASB emphasized that the disclosure requirements of paragraph 10 should be viewed as *minimum* disclosures. Paragraph 10(f) encourages governmental entities to provide additional disclosures that may better satisfy the standard of "fairly stated."

The following example, excerpted from Appendix B of GASB-12, illustrates footnote disclosures for OPEB:

> In addition to the pension benefits described in Note X, the State provides postretirement health care benefits, in accordance with State statutes, to all employees who retire from the State on or after attaining age 60 with at least 15 years of service. Currently, 25,000 retirees meet those eligibility requirements. The State reimburses 75 percent of the amount of validated claims for medical, dental, and hospitalization costs incurred by pre-Medicare retirees and their dependents. The State also reimburses a fixed amount of $25 per month for a Medicare supplement for each retiree eligible for Medicare. Expenditures for postretirement healthcare benefits are recognized as retirees report claims and include a provision for estimated claims incurred but not yet reported to the State. During the year, expenditures of $30 million were recognized for postretirement health care. Approximately $500,000 of the $3 million increase in expenditures over the previous year was caused by the addition of dental benefits, effective July 1, 19XX.

Focus of disclosures The disclosures related to postemployment benefits discussed in GASB-12 should differentiate between the primary government and its discretely presented component units. The focus of the disclosures should be on the primary government, which includes (1) governmental activities and business-type activities as presented in the government-wide financial statements, (2) major funds and aggregated nonmajor funds as presented in the fund financial statements, and (3) blended component units. The financial statements need only make those disclosures related to discretely presented component units that "are essential to the fair presentation of the financial reporting entity's basic financial statements." When disclosures related to discretely presented component units are made, they should be distinguished from those that relate to the primary government.

Disclosures may be made on an aggregated basis unless such presentation is misleading. If it is concluded that aggregated disclosures are not appropriate for the postemployment benefits other than pension benefits, separate disclosures for a fund(s) or a component unit(s) should be made (GASB-12, par. 12, and GASB-34, pars. 6 and 113).

Medicare Part D Payments

GASB Technical Bulletin No. 2006-1 (Accounting and Financial Reporting by Employers and OPEB Plans for Payments from the Federal Government Pursuant to the Retiree Drug Subsidy Provisions of Medicare Part D) clarifies the proper reporting of payments that an employer or a defined benefit other postemployment benefit (OPEB) plan receives from the federal government under Medicare Part D. Medicare Part D is a federal program that provides prescription drug benefits to eligible Medicare recipients.

A Medicare Part D payment from the federal government to the employer is a "voluntary nonexchange transaction," as discussed in Chapter 17, "Revenues: Nonexchange and Exchange Transactions." Accordingly, the employer should recognize an asset and revenue for the payment received following the applicable recognition requirements for voluntary nonexchange transactions. The payment is a transaction that is separate from the exchange of services for salaries and benefits (including postemployment prescription drug benefits) between employer and employees, for which the accounting is addressed in GASB-45. Therefore, a sole or agent employer should apply the measurement requirements of GASB-45 to determine the actuarial accrued liabilities, the annual required contribution of the employer (ARC), and the annual OPEB cost *without reduction* for Medicare Part D payments. In addition, the nonexchange transaction does not affect accounting for employer contributions or the financial reporting presentation by a defined benefit OPEB plan in which an employer participates. A defined benefit OPEB plan administered by a qualifying trust should apply the measurement requirements of GASB-43, as discussed in this chapter, to determine the actuarial accrued liabilities, the ARC, and the annual OPEB cost without reduction for Medicare Part D payments.

A Medicare Part D payment from the federal government to the plan is considered an on-behalf payment for fringe benefits, as discussed in Chapter 17, "Revenues: Nonexchange and Exchange Transactions." The employer should recognize revenue and expense or expenditures for the payment in accordance with the recognition and measurement requirements for such on-behalf payments, pertaining to an employer that is legally responsible for contributions to the OPEB plan. That is, the employer "should follow accounting standards for that type of transaction to recognize expenditures or expenses and related liabilities or assets."

In the statement of changes in plan net assets, the OPEB plan should separately display contributions from the employer(s) and the on-behalf payment from the federal government. In the schedule of employer contributions, the OPEB plan should include the Medicare Part D payment as on-behalf contributions from the federal government and titling the schedule as the schedule of contributions from the employer(s) and other contributing entities. The plan should present the ARC without reduction for the Medicare Part D payment.

APPENDIX
GASB-45 ACCOUNTING AND FINANCIAL REPORTING BY EMPLOYERS FOR POSTEMPLOYMENT BENEFITS OTHER THAN PENSIONS

EFFECTIVE DATE

The GASB provides for phasing in implementation of GASB-45 over a period of three years. The required implementation date for a governmental entity depends on its total annual revenues in the first fiscal year beginning after December 15, 2006. Total annual revenues for this purpose includes all revenues of the primary government's governmental and enterprise funds but not other financing sources and extraordinary gains. The following schedule identifies the required implementation date for a particular governmental entity:

The Amount of the Primary Government's Annual Revenues:	*The Required Implementation Date for the Standards:*
• Are equal to or greater than $100 million (Phase 1 Government)	For periods beginning after December 15, 2006
• Fall between $10 million and $100 million (Phase 2 Government)	For periods beginning after December 15, 2007
• Are less than $10 million (Phase 3 Government)	For periods beginning after December 15, 2008

OVERVIEW

In June 2004 the GASB issued GASB-45 (Accounting and Financial Reporting by Employers for Postemployment Benefits Other Than Pensions), which addresses other postemployment benefits (OPEB), defined as "postemployment health-care benefits, regardless of the type of plan that provides them and all postemployment benefits provided separately from a pension plan, excluding benefits defined as termination offers and benefits" provided as a defined benefit OPEB plan. Postemployment health-care benefits include "medical, dental, vision, and other health-related benefits provided to terminated or retired employees and their dependents and beneficiaries."

> **PRACTICE POINT:** GASB-45 facilitates more complete and comparable governmental financial statements because employer contributions are to be accounted for as OPEB on an accrual basis, without regard to the form—explicit or implicit—in which the contributions are made. In a press release the GASB offered the following example: "If each retiree pays a blended rate of $240 per month, but the rate attributable to those retirees based on expected claims costs for their age is $400 per month per retiree, the employer is actually providing a $160 per month benefit (or subsidy) per retiree that the GASB believes should be incorporated in the OPEB calculation. The revised proposals generally would require all employers to project future benefit payments based on retiree claims costs or on age-adjusted premiums approximating claims costs."

GASB-45 provides guidance for determining the OPEB expense/expenditures, the related liability or asset that might arise from the accrual and funding of OPEB expense/expenditures, note disclosures, and required supplementary information (RSI) for all state and local governmental employers.

GASB-45 adopts the general measurement and presentation standards established for pension benefits in GASB-27 (Accounting for Pensions by State and Local Governmental Employers). This appendix summarizes the standards in GASB-45.

> **PRACTICE POINT:** The standards proposed for expenditure/expense recognition for employers that participate in an OPEB plan are essentially the same as those established by GASB-27 for expenditure/expense recognition for employers that participate in pension plans.

> **PRACTICE POINT:** The GASB has also issued a companion statement, GASB-43 (Financial Reporting for Postemployment Benefit Plans Other Than Pension Plans), to address measurement and display issues related to OPEB plans presented as a trust fund in an employer's financial statements or stand-alone financial statements prepared by an entity that administers the plan. (See Chapter 22, "Pension, Postemployment, and Other Benefit Plans.")

A governmental employer may provide OPEB through a defined benefit OPEB plan whereby the employer participates in either a (1) sole (single) employer plan, (2) agent multiple-employer plan (agent plan), or (3) cost-sharing multiple-employer plan. These OPEB plans are defined as follows:

- *Sole-employer plan* A plan that covers the current and former employees, including beneficiaries, of only one employer
- *Agent multiple-employer plan* An aggregation of single-employer plans, with pooled administrative and investment functions. Separate accounts are maintained for each employer so that the employer's contributions provide benefits only for its employees. A separate actuarial valuation is performed for each individual employer's plan to determine the employer's period contribution rate and other information for the individual plan, based on the benefit formula selected by the employer and the individual plan's proportionate share of the pooled assets. The results of the individual valuations are aggregated at the administrative level.
- *Cost-sharing multiple-employer plan* A single plan with pooling (cost-sharing) arrangements for the participating employers. All risks, rewards, and costs, including benefit costs are shared and are not attributed individually to the employers. A single actuarial valuation covers all plan members, and the same contribution rate(s) applies for each employer.

DEFINED BENEFIT OPEB PLANS FOR SOLE AND AGENT EMPLOYERS

OPEB Cost and the Related Obligation

Governmental employers whose defined OPEB plans are administered as single-employer or agent multiple-employer plans determine the amount of pension cost by calculating their annual required contribution (ARC). The "ARC" is defined in GASB-45 as "the employer's period required contributions to a defined benefit OPEB plan, calculated in accordance with the parameters." The "parameters" are defined as "the set of requirements for calculating actuarially determined OPEB information included in financial reports." If an employer has a net OPEB obligation, the ARC must be adjusted to reflect a possible amortization of that obligation. Both the ARC and the net OPEB obligation are discussed in this appendix.

> **OBSERVATION:** The net OPEB obligation may be either positive (reflecting a liability position) or negative (reflecting an asset position). For simplicity, GASB-45 refers to a net OPEB obligation even though it could be an asset or a liability.

The "annual OPEB cost" and "net OPEB obligation" (measured amount) are not necessarily the amounts reflected in the financial statements (recognized amount). GASB-45 defines the terms in the context of the measurement of the cost and the obligation, although the actual amount recognized as an expense/expenditure and as a liability depends upon the basis of accounting used to prepare a particular financial statement. That is, the expenditure and liability recognized in the financial statements of government funds must be reported in a manner consistent with the modified accrual basis of accounting, while the expense and liability recognized in proprietary funds and government-wide financial statements must be recognized based on accrual accounting.

The ARC and the required employer contribution should be based on the same covered payroll amount. The covered payroll amount (which, as discussed later in this appendix, is the basis for determining the ARC and the employer's contribution) may be based on projected payroll, budgeted covered payroll, or actual covered payroll, as long as the measurement is consistently applied from year to year. The ARC is the basis for computing the annual OPEB cost and the net OPEB obligation, if any. Any comparison of the ARC with the required employer contribution must be based on the same definition of covered payroll. Also, the ARC does not include OPEB-related debt, which is defined by GASB-45 as follows:

> All long-term liabilities of an employer to an OPEB plan, the payment of which is not included in the annual required contributions of a sole or agent employer (ARC) or the actuarially determined required contributions of a cost-sharing employer. Payments generally are made in accordance with installment contracts that usually include interest. Examples include contractually deferred contributions and amounts assessed to an employer upon joining a multiple-employer plan.

The ARC (Parameters)

The measurement of OPEB information should be based on an actuarial valuation but the valuation date does not have to be the governmental employer's balance sheet date, although it should be on the same date for each year it is performed. The valuation must be made at least biennially for plans with total membership of 200 or more and at least triennially for plans with fewer than 200 members. Because the actuarial valuation is not required to be conducted annually or as of the employer's balance sheet date, GASB-45 provides the following guidance concerning the "age" of the actuarial information used to compute the ARC:

> The ARC reported for the employer's current fiscal year should be based on the results of an actuarial valuation performed in accordance with the parameters as of a date not

> more than twenty-four months before the beginning of that year, if valuations are annual, or before the beginning of the first year of the two-year or three-year period for which that valuation provides the ARC, if valuations are biennial or triennial.

> **PRACTICE POINT:** When a plan has experienced significant changes related to the computation of the OPEB cost, a new actuarial valuation should be performed on a current basis rather than waiting for the next scheduled valuation date.

Ideally, all actuarial computations (including the ARC) reflected in the governmental employer's financial statements should be based on the same methods and assumptions used by the employer to determine the employer's required funding amount; however, although the GASB can establish standards for financial reporting standards, it cannot require a governmental entity to fund a plan in a particular way.

The computation of the parameters is based on the following components:

- Benefits included
- Actuarial assumptions made
- Economic assumptions made
- Actuarial cost method used
- Actuarial value of assets
- Annual required contribution
- Contribution deficiency or excess contribution

Benefits included OPEB plan benefits should be based on the "actuarial present value of total projected benefits," which GASB-45 defines as follows:

> Total projected benefits include all benefits estimated to be payable to plan members (retirees and beneficiaries, terminated employees, entitled to benefits but not yet receiving them, and current active members) as a result of their service through the valuation date and their expected future service. The actuarial present value of total projected benefits as of the valuation date is the present value of the cost to finance benefits payable in the future, discounted to reflect the expected effects of the time value (present value) of money and the probabilities of payment. Expressed another way, it is the amount that would have to be invested on the valuation date so that the amount invested plus investment earnings will provide sufficient assets to pay total projected benefits when due.

The basis of what benefits should be included in the total projected benefits is the substantive plan, which is defined as "the terms of an OPEB plan as understood by the employer and plan members." That understanding is usually expressed in a written plan, but other sources of plan benefits may include communications between the employer and plan members and past practices with respect to the funding of the plan between the employer and employees.

OPEB plan benefits that have been financed through allocated insurance contracts (annuity contracts purchased from an insurance company) are not part of the actuarial present value of total projected benefits. Those contracts should also be excluded from the OPEB plan assets.

Actuarial assumptions made The ARC is based on the selection of a variety of actuarial assumptions, including the "health care cost trend rate," which is defined as follows:

> The rate of change in per capita health claims costs over time as a result of factors such as medical inflation, utilization of health-care services, plan design, and technological developments.

GASB-45 states that all actuarial assumptions are to be based on standards established by Actuarial Standard of Practice No. 6 (Measuring Retiree Group Benefit Obligations) or any successor standard. In general, these assumptions should be based on the longterm actual experience of the members covered by the OPEB plan.

Economic assumptions made An essential factor in calculating actuarial measurements is the investment rate assumption (discount rate). The investment rate assumption is used to determine the present value of expected future payments under the OPEB plan. The investment rate used in the computation should be based on the estimated long-term investment yield related to the OPEB plan (current and expected) assets, assuming that the plan benefits are paid out of the plan assets. If the plan benefits are paid on a pay-as-you-go basis, the investment return assumption should be based on the assets held by the employer. If plan benefits are expected to be funded partially by fund assets and partially by employer assets, a composite investment rate should be used, reflecting the expected mixture of the two sources of assets.

GASB-45 requires that all economic assumptions (including the investment return assumption) be consistent with assumed inflation.

Actuarial cost method used GASB-45 requires that one of six actuarial cost methods it lists be used to compute a governmental employer's OPEB. These six actuarial cost methods are described in Chapter 22, "Pension and Other Postemployment Benefit Plans," and are not repeated here.

Actuarial value of assets In general, the actuarial value identified with assets included in an OPEB plan should reflect the following guidelines:

- Valuation methods should be relevant to the type of investment and the expected holding period.
- Asset valuation assumptions should be consistent with investment return assumptions and other assumptions related to measuring the actuarial present value of total projects benefits.
- Valuation methods should be consistent with current actuarial standards for asset valuation as endorsed by the Actuarial Standards Board.

The actuarial value of OPEB plan assets, if any, should be based on "market-related value," which is defined as

> A term used with reference to the actuarial value of assets. A market-related value may be fair value, market value (or estimated market value), or a calculated value that recognizes changes in fair value or market value over a period of, for example, three to five years.

As implied by the above definition, market-related value is not always the same as fair value. Fair value refers to the price that a willing buyer and willing seller agree on in an arm's-length transaction. Although market-related values are based on fair values, the approach attempts to smooth out changes in values over a number of years. For example, the market-related value of a security expected to be held for a significant number of years may be based on a rolling five-year average rather than on a single year-end market quotation. The GASB takes the position that because OPEB investment strategies and related obligations are generally long-term in nature, it may be, based on the judgment of the reporting entity, inappropriate to reflect valuation fluctuations that are short-term in nature.

Annual required contribution The ARC is based on (1) the employer's normal costs and (2) a provision that amortizes the unfunded actuarial accrued liability (UAAL). A governmental employer's normal cost is defined as "that portion of the actuarial present value of plan benefits and expenses which is allocated to a valuation year by the actuarial cost method." Normal cost does not include any payment related to the employer's funding of its unfunded actuarial accrued liability; however, normal cost does include both the employees' as well as the employer's required contribution. The specific amount of normal cost allocated to a particular year is in part based on the actuarial cost method adopted by the governmental entity, and for that reason the method used must be disclosed in the financial statements.

In addition to a provision for normal cost, the ARC includes a portion (amortization) of the UAAL. The components that comprise this computation are presented as follows, along with the definitions of the components:

Actuarial Value of Assets	$XXX
Less: Actuarial Accrued Liability	XXX
Unfunded Actuarial Accrued Liability (UAAL)	$XXX

- *Actuarial value of assets* The value of cash, investments, and other property belonging to a plan, as used by the actuary for the purpose of an actuarial valuation
- *Unfunded actuarial accrued liability* (Also known as "unfunded actuarial liability," "unfunded accrued liability," or "unfunded actuarial reserve") The excess of the actuarial accrued liability over the actuarial value of assets.

The actuarial accrued liability is considered (1) positive when the actuarial accrued liability is greater than the actuarial value of plan assets (unfunded actuarial liability) and (2) negative when the actuarial accrued liability is less than the actuarial value of plan assets (funding excess). (For purposes of subsequent discussions, GASB-45 refers to the "unfunded actuarial liability," but the guidance also applies to occurrences of funding excess.)

The period over which the unfunded actuarial liability may be amortized is 30 years. The unfunded actuarial liability may be amortized as a single amount or its component may be individually amortized. If the individual components are amortized over different amortization periods, the total amortization for all components must satisfy the maximum amortization period criterion. GASB-45 refers to this criterion as the "equivalent single amortization period," which it defines as follows:

> The weighted average of all amortization periods used when components of the total unfunded actuarial accrued liability are separately amortized and the average is calculated in accordance with the parameters.

Changes in the balance of the unfunded actuarial accrued liability may arise from (1) a change from one acceptable actuarial cost method to another acceptable method or (2) a change from one acceptable method to another acceptable method for determining the actuarial value of plan assets. Adjustments in the value of the unfunded actuarial accrued liability arising from these changes are to be amortized over a period of not less than ten years. The minimum amortization period rule does not apply to OPEB plans that are closed to new members, and essentially all of the plan members are retirees.

The unfunded actuarial accrued liability should be amortized using one of two methods, which are defined as follows:

1. *Level dollar amortization method* The amount to be amortized is divided into equal dollar amounts to be paid over a given number of years; part of each payment is interest and part is principal (similar to a mortgage payment on a building). Because payroll can be expected to increase as a result of inflation, level dollar payments generally represent a decreasing percentage of payrolls; in dollars adjusted for inflation, the payments can be expected to decrease over time.
2. *Level percentage of project payroll method* Amortization payments are calculated so that they are a constant percentage of the projected payroll of active plan members over a given number of years. The dollar amount of the payments will generally increase over time as payroll increases due to inflation; in dollars adjusted for inflation, the payments can be expected to remain level.

When the level percentage of the projected payroll amortization is used, the assumed payroll growth rate should not reflect an assumed increase in the number of active plan members. The assumed payroll growth rate refers to "an actuarial assumption with respect to future increases in total covered payroll attributable to inflation." Any projected decreases in covered payroll should be reflected in the amortization methods if no new members are allowed to join the OPEB plan.

Contribution deficiency or excess contribution The standards in GASB-45 are based on the assumption (but not the requirement) that the amount of the ARC and the employer's contribution to the plan will be the same. However, the GASB can mandate how OPEB expenditures/expenses and the related liability should be measured and presented in a governmental entity's financial statements, but it cannot mandate how and when a governmental entity should fund its OPEB plan. If the required contribution is not funded, the resulting contribution deficiency (or excess contribution) is amortized beginning with the next actuarial valuation date. However, no amortization is required if it is expected that the deficiency or excess is to be settled within one year of its occurrence. When the expected settlement does not take place within the allowed period, amortization of the deficiency (or excess) should begin at the next actuarial valuation date.

GASB-45 points out that an employer's contribution (which in this case does not include contributions by plan members) or funding of the plan occurs only when the following events take place:

- The employer makes payments of benefits directly to or on behalf of a retiree or beneficiary
- The employer makes premium payments to an insurer
- The employer irrevocably transfers assets to a trust or other third party acting in the role of trustee for the sole purpose of the payment of plan benefits, and creditors of the government do not have access to those assets.

Calculation of the Net OPEB Obligation and the Annual OPEB Cost

A net OPEB obligation arises when there is a cumulative difference between the annual OPEB cost and the cumulative contributions made to the OPEB plan. The cumulative differences are measured from the effective date of GASB-45 and the current date of a governmental entity's financial statements. The net OPEB obligation is computed as follows:

OPEB obligation (or assets), if any, that existed at the transition date	$XXX
Add: Cumulative contribution deficiencies (or excess contributions) from the effective date of the statement	XXX
Less: Short-term differences	(XXX)
Less: Unpaid contributions converted to OPEB-related debt	(XXX)
Net OPEB obligation	$XXX

"Short-term differences" are differences expected to be settled (1) by the first actuarial valuation date after the difference arose or (2) within one year after the difference arose if the first actuarial valuation is to be made within a year.

When an entity has a net OPEB obligation, annual pension cost includes interest on the net OPEB obligation and an adjustment to the ARC. The interest on the net OPEB obligation is based on the balance of the net OPEB obligation at the beginning of the year and the assumed investment return rate. The adjustment of the ARC is needed to remove any interest and/or principal that is already included in the ARC arising from the amortization of past contribution deficiencies (or excess contributions).

The adjustment to the ARC is an estimate and should be made using the following guidelines:

- Use the same amortization method (level dollar method or level percentage of projected payroll method) that was used to calculate the ARC.
- Use the same actuarial assumptions that were used to calculate the ARC.
- Use the same amortization period that was used to calculate the ARC.

The adjustment to the ARC must be recalculated for each year for which the governmental employer has a net OPEB obligation.

OPEB Expenses/Expenditures and Related Liabilities or Assets

A governmental employer that has more than one OPEB plan should apply the measurement criteria in GASB-45 to each plan separately; however, the information can generally be combined when preparing the employer's financial statements.

The calculation OPEB expenditures/expense is based on the following:

- Contributions made based on the computation of the ARC
- Payments, if any, for OPEB-related debt not included as part of the ARC or the net OPEB obligation.

The amount of the ARC-related liability (asset) reported at the end of the year must be adjusted so that it is equal to the employer's net OPEB obligation.

A governmental employer may make payments of ARC-related contributions to the same OPEB plan from more than one fund. Under this circumstance, the employer must use its discretion to determine how to allocate the ARC to each fund.

When a governmental employer has a net OPEB obligation that must be allocated to more than one fund, between fund(s) and general long-term liabilities, or between governmental and business-type activities in the government-wide financial statements, the allocation of the interest and the ARC adjustment of the annual OPEB cost to each liability should be based on the proportionate share of the net OPEB obligation reported in each financial statement as of the beginning of the year.

Presentation in governmental fund financial statements The recognition of the OPEB expenditure for governmental funds should be consistent with the measurement criteria in GASB-45 and the modified accrual basis of accounting. That is, the OPEB expenditure should be based on contributions made to the plan during the current year plus any accrual at the end of the year that is expected to use expendable available financial resources of the current year. If the amount of expenditures recognized during the current year is not equal to the annual OPEB cost as defined by GASB-45, the difference is added or subtracted to the net OPEB obligation. The net OPEB obligation is reported as a general long-term liability in the governmental activities column in the government-wide financial statements. (If there have been payments greater than required, the difference is reported as a prepayment in the government-wide financial statements.)

Presentation in proprietary and fiduciary fund financial statements The recognition of the OPEB expense in proprietary and fiduciary funds should be consistent with the measurement criteria in GASB-45 and the accrual basis of accounting. That is, the OPEB expense should be equal to the annual OPEB cost. Any related OPEB obligation (both current and long-term) should be reported in the financial statements of the proprietary or fiduciary fund.

Presentation in government-wide financial statements The recognition of the OPEB expense in the government-wide financial statements (for both governmental activities and business-type activities) should be based on accrual accounting concepts and therefore the OPEB expense should be equal to the amount of OPEB cost computed. Any related liability (or prepayment) should be reported accordingly in the statement of net assets. OPEB plans that have different net balances (liability position versus asset position) should not be netted in the government-wide financial statements.

DEFINED BENEFIT OPEB PLANS FOR COST-SHARING EMPLOYERS

Unlike a sole employer plan and an agent employer plan, in a cost-sharing arrangement an employer's OPEB obligation under the OPEB plan is not determined based on the characteristics of its employees. For this reason, the amount of the recorded OPEB expenditures/expense should simply be based on the contractually required contributions determined under the terms of the cost-sharing arrangement. If the governmental entity participating in the costsharing arrangement accounts for its expenditures in a governmental fund type, modified accrual concepts should be used to measure OPEB expenditures for the year. On the other hand, if the OPEB payments are accounted for in a proprietary fund type or fiduciary fund type, accrual accounting concepts should be used to determine the OPEB expense for the year.

Any difference between the required contribution and the actual contribution made should be recorded as an asset or a liability in a particular fund depending on whether the modified accrual or accrual concept is the basis of accounting for the fund. The OPEB liability or asset position of one plan should not be netted against a different plan with an opposite position (liability or asset position).

NOTES TO THE FINANCIAL STATEMENTS

GASB-45 requires that the following be disclosed by a governmental employer for each defined benefit OPEB plan it participates in:

Plan Description

- The plan name, the administrator of the plan, and the type of OPEB plan (single-employer, agent multiple-employer, or cost-sharing multiple-employer)
- The name of the entity that administers the OPEB plan
- The authority on which the OPEB plan was organized and the basis for amending the plan
- The benefits provided by the OPEB plan
- Whether the OPEB plan issues separate financial statements (stand-alone financial statements) or includes its financial statements in the financial reports of the entity and, if so, how to obtain those financial reports

Funding Policy

- The authority (for initial establishment and subsequent amendment) on which the OPEB plan's required contributions by plan members, the employer(s), and other contributing parties are based
- The required contribution rate of active plan members
- The required contribution rate for the employer expressed in dollars or as a percentage of current-year covered payroll (When the plan is a single-employer or agent plan and the contribution rate is significantly different from the ARC, the method by which the contribution rate is determined must be disclosed. When the plan is a cost-sharing plan, the disclosure

must include the required contribution and the actual percentage contributed for the current year and the two years previous.)

In addition to the foregoing information, sole and agent employers must disclose the following:

- Current OPEB cost and the dollar amount contributed
- For employers with a net OPEB obligation, the components of the annual OPEB costs (specifically the ARC, interest on the net OPEB obligation, and the ARC adjustment)
- For employers with a net OPEB obligation, the year-end balance in the obligation and the increase or decrease in the obligation for the year
- Annual OPEB costs, percentage funded, and year-end balance in the net OPEB obligation, if any, for the current and two previous years [For the first two years of implementing the proposed standards, the information should be presented for the transition year (for the first year of presentation) and for the transition year and the subsequent year (for the second year of presentation).]
- Information about funding status as of the most recent valuation date (actuarial valuation date), actuarial value of assets, the actuarial accrued liability, the total unfunded actuarial liability (or funding excess), the actuarial value of assets as a percentage of the actuarial accrued liability (funded ratio), the annual covered payroll, and the ratio of the unfunded actuarial liability (or funding excess) to annual covered payroll
- Disclosures concerning the actuarial valuation, including:
    - — Actuarial valuations are based on estimates that are likely to change over time
    - — The relationship of plan assets and the accrued liability for OPEB benefits over time can be found in information immediately following the notes to the financial statements
    - — Projections of benefits are based on the nature of benefits provided under the plan at the time of the actuarial valuation and the pattern of cost sharing between the employer and plan members to that point
    - — Actuarial calculations are long-term in nature, and techniques are used to reduce the short-term volatility of actuarial accrued liabilities and the actuarial valuation of assets
- Identification of actuarial methods and significant assumptions including:

— The actuarial cost method
— Methods used to compute the actuarial value of assets
— Assumptions used including inflation rate, investment return, postretirement benefit increases, and projected salary increases
— Amortization period (level dollar or level percentage of projected payroll) and the amortization period

When an employer participates in a health-care plan that includes an "implicit rate subsidy" (that is, the difference between a premium rate charged to retirees for a particular benefit and the estimated rate that would be applicable to those retirees if that benefit was acquired for them as a separate group), the following disclosures should be made:

- Retirees are permitted to participate with active employees in the health-care plan but retirees must pay all premiums assigned to them (the method used to determine the premiums that must be paid by retirees)

Required Supplementary Information

GASB-45 requires that sole and agent employers present the following required supplementary information for the most recent actuarial valuation and the previous two valuations:

- Funding progress of the OPEB plan, including the following:
  — Actuarial valuation date
  — Actuarial value of OPEB plan assets
  — Actuarial accrued liability
  — Total unfunded actuarial liability (or overfunding)
  — Funded ratio (actuarial value of assets as a percentage of the actuarial accrued liability)
  — Annual covered payroll
  — Ratio of the unfunded actuarial liability (or overfunded) to annual covered payroll
  — Factors that significantly affect trend analysis (such as changes in actuarial assumptions)

The disclosures must be based on the parameters in GASB-45 and presented as required supplementary information.

PRACTICE POINT: When an employer uses the aggregate actuarial cost method, the disclosure should be based on the entry-age actuarial cost method, and that fact should be disclosed. Also, the disclosure should point out that the presentation is an approximation of the OPEB plan's funding progress.

The disclosures described above apply to sole and agent employers; however, the disclosures should also be made by a governmental employer that participates in a cost-sharing plan if the plan does not make its financial statements publicly available.

Insured Plans

GASB-45 defines an "insured plan" as follows:

> An OPEB financing arrangement whereby an employer accumulates funds with an insurance company, while employees are in active service, in return for which the insurance company unconditionally undertakes a legal obligation to pay the benefits of those employees or their beneficiaries, as defined in the employer's plan.

When an OPEB plan satisfies the criteria established in the above definition, that insured plan does not have to follow the (parameters) standards in GASB-45. Under this circumstance, pension expenditures/expense for a particular year are based on the premium amount that must be paid to the insurance company.

Although a governmental entity is not required to follow the parameters in GASB-45 when an insured OPEB plan exists, the following disclosures must be made:

- The authority on which the insured OPEB plan was organized (and the basis for amendments) and a brief description of the benefits provided by the plan
- A statement that the responsibility for the payment of benefits under the OPEB plan has been effectively transferred to one or more insurance companies
- A statement as to whether the governmental employer has guaranteed OPEB payments in the event the insurance company is unable to pay the benefits when due
- The current-year OPEB expenditures/expense recognized and the amount of contributions or premiums paid during the year.

EMPLOYER DEFINED CONTRIBUTION OPEB PLANS

Although GASB-45 focuses on defined benefit plans, it also briefly addresses the measurement of OPEB expenditures/expense for defined contribution plans. OPEB expenditures/expense for a defined contribution plan is recognized based on the required contribution under the terms of the OPEB plan and the basis of accounting (modified accrual for governmental fund types; accrual for proprietary or fiduciary fund types and government-wide financial statements), depending on which type of fund is used to account for the employer's OPEB contribution.

Any difference between the required contribution and actual contribution should be recognized as an asset or liability in the employer's financial statements, depending on whether the modified accrual or accrual basis of accounting is used. An asset related to one defined contribution plan should not be offset against a liability related to another defined contribution plan. In addition, the following disclosures should be made for each defined contribution OPEB plan that the governmental employer must contribute to:

- The OPEB plan's name, the administrator of the plan, and a statement that the plan is a defined contribution plan
- The authority on which the OPEB plan was organized (or may be amended) and a brief description of the plan provisions
- The contribution required (in dollars or as a percentage of salary) for employees, the employer, and others (such as a state government's portion), and the authority on which the contribution requirements are established (or may be amended)
- Amounts contributed by the employer and the employees

SPECIAL FUNDING SITUATIONS

One governmental entity may be responsible for contributing to an OPEB plan that covers employees of another governmental entity. This situation often arises when state governments provide funding for OPEB plans for public schoolteachers and public safety officers. Under this circumstance, the governmental entity that is legally responsible for the contributions must follow the standards (measurement, recognition, note disclosure, and required supplementary information) in GASB-45, depending on whether the OPEB plan is a defined benefit plan or a defined contribution plan.

When a governmental entity is legally responsible for contributions to a defined benefit plan and is the only contributing entity, the standards for a sole employer must be observed, even if two or more governmental entities are covered by the OPEB plan.

ALTERNATIVE MEASUREMENT METHOD (FEWER THAN 100 PLAN MEMBERS)

In general, the measurement standards in GASB-45 apply to all sole and agent employers; however, the GASB did attempt to simplify the implementation of the proposed standards for a sole employer that has fewer than 100 plan members in its OPEB defined benefit plan. For such plans, the employer may (1) apply all of the measurement standards without modification or (2) apply the measurement standards with one or more of the following modifications:

- *Assumptions in general* In general, assumptions should be based on actual past experience; however, grouping techniques may be used whereby assumptions are based on combined experience data for similar plans, as explained below (see "use of grouping").
- *Expected point in time at which benefits will begin to be provided* This assumption may be based on a single assumed retirement age or that all employees will retire at a particular age.
- *Health-care cost trend rate* This assumption should be based on an objective source.
- *Marital and dependency status* This assumption may be based on the current marital status of employees or historical demographic data for the covered group.
- *Mortality* This assumption should reflect current published mortality tables.
- *Plans with coverage options* Employers with postemployment benefit plans whereby the employee has coverage options should base the coverage option on past experience but also take into consideration the choices of pre- and post-Medicare-eligible members.
- *Qualification for benefits assumption* This assumption, when past experience data are not available, may be based on the simplifying assumption that the longer an employee works, the greater the probability he or she will work long enough to qualify for benefits. For example, if an employee must work for ten years to qualify for benefits, then the probability of qualification increases 10% for each year the employee works.
- *Use of grouping* Rather than consider each participant, participants may be grouped into categories based on such factors as an age range or length of service range.
- *Use of health insurance premiums* Employers with postemployment health-care plans whereby the employer makes premium payments to an insurer may use the current premium structure in order to project future health-care benefit payments.

TRANSITION GUIDANCE FOR DEFINED BENEFIT OPEB PLANS

Sole and Agent Employers

When sole or agent employers implement the standards in GASB-45, they might assume that their net OPEB obligation is zero at the beginning of the year in which the standards are implemented. However, a sole or agent employer may, if the actuarial information is available, record a net OPEB obligation (asset) at the transition date by applying the proposed standards on a retroactive basis. If a transition entry is made, the previous periods used to compute the transition adjustment should be disclosed.

Cost-Sharing Employers

When a cost-sharing employer implements the proposed standards, the OPEB liability at the beginning of the year of implementation should be equal to the sum of (1) contractually required contributions that are due at the implementation date and (2) OPEB-related debt, if any. Any other liability carried forward related to OPEB plans should be removed.

Disclosure

The following disclosures should be made for each single-employer, agent, and cost-sharing plan for the year that the proposed standards are implemented:

- That the standards were implemented prospectively (that is, no net OPEB obligation existed at the transition date) or that the standards were implemented retroactively (that is, a net OPEB obligation (asset) existed at the transition date)
- The amount of the OPEB obligation (asset) at transition, if any, and the difference, if any, between that amount and the related liability reported in the previous year's financial statements.

CHAPTER 14
LEASES

CONTENTS

INTRODUCTION

A governmental entity, like business enterprises, may enter into lease agreements whereby it acquires property rights (lessee) through a lease agreement or is obligated to provide property rights (lessor) to another party. The accounting standards that are used to account for lease transactions vary to some degree depending on whether the liability is presented in a (1) governmental fund, (2) proprietary fund or fiduciary fund, or (3) the government-wide financial statements. Governmental accounting and reporting standards for lease agreements are based on the following pronouncements:

- National Council on Governmental Accounting (NCGA) Statement No. 5 (NCGA-5) (Accounting and Financial Reporting Principles for Lease Agreements of State and Local Governments)
- GASB-13 (Accounting for Operating Leases with Scheduled Rent Increases)
- FAS-13 (Accounting for Leases)

LESSEE ACCOUNTING

A lease agreement conveys property rights to the lessee for a specific period of time. Although actual title to the property is not transferred to the lessee, a lease agreement must be evaluated to determine whether the transaction should be treated as an in-substance purchase. From the lessee's perspective, the lease may be classified as a capital lease or as an operating lease.

Capital Leases

A lease agreement is classified as a capital lease (in-substance purchase) when substantially all of the risks and benefits of ownership are assumed by the lessee. A capital lease is, for the most part, viewed as an installment purchase of property rather than the rental of property (NCGA-5, par. 12).

FAS-13 requires that a lease be capitalized if any one of the following four criteria is a characteristic of the lease transaction (FAS-13, par. 7):

Criterion #

I The lease transfers ownership of the property to the lessee by the end of the lease term.

II The lease contains a bargain purchase option.

III The lease term is equal to 75% or more of the estimated economic life of the leased property.

IV The present value of the minimum lease payments at the inception of the lease, excluding executory costs, equals at least 90% of the fair value of the leased property.

A bargain purchase option exists when the lessee can exercise a provision in the lease and buy the property sometime during the term of the lease at an amount substantially less than the estimated fair value of the property. Judgment must be used in determining whether the purchase option price will be a bargain price at the option date. If there is reasonable assurance at the inception of the lease that the purchase option will be exercised, the option is considered a bargain purchase option (FAS-13, pars. 5–7).

Lease payments include the minimum rental payments based on the term of the lease, exclusive of executory costs, such as payments for insurance and property taxes. Contingent rental payments are not included as part of the lease payments unless they are based on an existing index or rate, such as the prime interest rate. The lease payments include any residual value guaranteed by the lessee (or related party) at the end of the term of the lease. Also, any penalty payment that must be made because of a failure to renew or extend the lease is considered a lease payment (FAS-29, par. 11).

> **PRACTICE POINT:** When the lease contains a bargain purchase option, the minimum lease payments include only (1) the minimum rental payments over the term of the lease and (2) the bargain purchase option.

FAS-13 defines "lease term" as the fixed noncancelable term of the lease plus the following periods, if applicable (FAS-13, Glossary):

- Periods for which failure to renew the lease imposes a penalty on the lessee in an amount such that at the inception of the lease renewal appears to be reasonably assured
- Periods covered by a bargain renewal option
- Periods covered by ordinary renewal options during which a guarantee by the lessee of the lessor's debt related to the leased property is expected to be in effect
- Periods covered by ordinary renewal options preceding the date as of which a bargain purchase is exercisable
- Periods that represent renewals or extensions of the lease at the lessor's option (however, the lease term cannot extend beyond the date of a bargain purchase option)

When determining the present value of the lease payments, the lessee should use its incremental borrowing rate. However, the lessee should use the lessor's implicit interest rate to determine the present value of the lease payments if (FAS-13, par. 7):

1. The lessee can determine the lessor's implicit interest rate and
2. The lessor's implicit interest rate is less than the lessee's incremental borrowing rate.

The lessee's incremental borrowing rate is the estimated interest rate the lessee would have had to pay if the leased property had been purchased by the lessee and financed over the period covered by the lease (FAS-13, Glossary).

Operating Leases

When a lease does not satisfy any one of the four capitalization criteria, the agreement is classified as an operating lease. An operating lease does not require the capitalization of minimum lease payments. Therefore, neither an asset nor a liability is recorded at the inception of the lease in the government's financial statements. The rental expenditures are recognized as they become payable (NCGA-5, par. 11).

Fiscal Funding Clauses

Noncancellation is a precondition to the capitalization of a lease. In general, a lease subject to cancellation cannot be capitalized; however, if the lease is subject to cancellation based on the occurrence of a *remote* event, the lease may be capitalized if one of the four capitalization criteria is met (NCGA-5, pars. 18 and 20).

A lease with a governmental unit may contain a clause stating that the lease is cancelable if the governmental unit does not appropriate the funds necessary to make the required lease payments during the budgeting period. FASB Technical Bulletin 79-10 (FTB 79-10) (Fiscal Funding Clauses in Lease Agreements) draws the following conclusion with respect to the existence of fiscal funding clauses in lease agreements (FTB 79-10, par. 3):

> The existence of a fiscal funding clause in a lease agreement would necessitate an assessment of the likelihood of lease cancellation through exercise of the fiscal funding clause. If the likelihood of exercise of the fiscal funding clause is assessed as being remote, a lease agreement containing such a clause would be considered a noncancelable lease; otherwise, the lease would be considered cancelable and thus classified as an operating lease.

LESSOR ACCOUNTING

When a governmental unit is the lessor in a lease agreement, the agreement must be reviewed to determine whether the transaction should be treated as an in-substance sale of the property. From the lessor's perspective, the lease may be classified as a direct financing lease or an operating lease.

Direct Financing Lease

A direct financing lease transfers substantially all of the risks and benefits of ownership from the lessor to the lessee. In a direct financing lease, the lessor finances the in-substance purchase of the property by the lessee (NCGA-5, par. 15).

FAS-13 requires that a lease be classified as a direct financing lease (1) when any one of the four capitalization criteria used to define a capital lease for the lessee is met and (2) when both of the following criteria are satisfied (FAS-13, par. 8, and FAS-98, par. 22):

- Collectibility of the minimum lease payments is reasonably predictable.
- No important uncertainties surround the amount of the unreimbursable costs yet to be incurred by the lessor under the lease.

Minimum lease payments are considered collectible even though it may be necessary to estimate them based on past experience with uncollectible amounts from specific groupings of similar receivables (FAS-13, par. 8).

An important uncertainty with respect to unreimbursed future costs is an indication that the risks of ownership have not been transferred to the lessee. For example, if the lessor guarantees to replace obsolete property, the lease should not be treated as a direct financing lease. On the other hand, if the lessor is responsible for executory costs that may vary in future periods, this uncertainty alone does not preclude classifying the lease as a direct financing lease (FAS-13, par. 8).

The lessor's minimum lease payments are the same as the lessee's minimum lease payments plus any (1) residual values or (2) rental payments guaranteed by a third party not related to the lessor or lessee. In determining the present value of the minimum lease payments, the lessor should use its implicit interest rate. FAS-13 defines "implicit interest" as follows (FAS-13, Glossary):

> The discount rate that, when applied to (a) the minimum lease payments, excluding that portion of the payments

representing executory costs to be paid by the lessor, together with any profit thereon, and (b) the unguaranteed residual value accruing to the benefit of the lessor causes the aggregate present value of the beginning of the lease term to be equal to the fair value of the leased property to the lessor at the inception of the lease, minus any investment tax credit retained by the lessor and expected to be realized.

Operating Leases

When a lease agreement does not satisfy at least one of the four criteria (common to both lessee and lessor accounting) and both of the criteria for a lessor (collectibility and no uncertain reimbursable costs), the lease is classified as an operating lease. In an operating lease there is no simulated sale and the lessor simply records rent revenues as they become measurable and available. In addition, the leased property is not removed from the General Fixed Assets Account Group (FAS-13, par. 15).

OPERATING LEASES WITH SCHEDULED RENT INCREASES

Governmental entities may enter into operating lease agreements that include scheduled rent increases. Although the FASB has addressed the accounting for operating leases with scheduled rent increases, the GASB concluded that the FASB guidance was inappropriate for governmental entities and therefore issued GASB-13.

The reporting standards established by GASB-13 apply to all governmental units, including state and local governments, public benefit corporations and authorities, public employee retirement systems, and governmental utilities, hospitals, colleges, and universities (GASB-13, par. 4).

The criteria that should be used to identify an operating lease for a governmental entity are established in FAS-13. Criteria applicable to a governmental entity that is a lessee are covered in paragraph 7 of FAS-13, and criteria applicable to a lessor governmental entity are covered in paragraphs 7–8 of FAS-13.

Measurement and Recognition Criteria

An operating lease contract may include scheduled rent increases. For example, the prescribed rental payments may be $50,000 per year for the first three years and $70,000 per year for the final two years of the contract. If the rental increases are considered to be systematic and rational, rental expenditure/expense (for the lessee) or rental revenue (for the lessor) should be recognized in accordance with the operating lease contract. Thus, in the previous example, the amounts recognized would be $50,000 in each of the first three years and $70,000 in the last two years of the lease contract (GASB-13, par. 5).

> **OBSERVATION:** The accounting for scheduled rent increases established by GASB-13 is different from the method established by FAS-13 and FTB 85-3 (Accounting for Operating Leases with Scheduled Rent Increases). The FASB requires that the straight-line method be used to account for operating leases with scheduled rent increases if the increased payments are not related to the use benefit of the property. Thus, in the previous example, the amount of rental expense or rental income that would be recognized each year based on the FASB position would be $58,000 [($50,000 + $50,000 + $50,000 + $70,000 + $70,000)/5 years].

What constitutes "systematic and rational" is a matter of judgment. Although the GASB does not attempt to provide a general definition of systematic and rational, the following examples are offered as illustrations (GASB-13, par. 5):

- Scheduled rent increases are established to reflect the anticipated increase in the value of the property rented or the expected cost increases caused by inflation.
- Lease payments are structured to reflect the time pattern of the availability of the property to the lessee (such as the anticipated increase in the use of the property in later periods or the increase in the amount of property available to the lessee in later periods).

Although GASB-13 establishes the basic standard that an operating lease with scheduled rent increases should be measured consistent with the terms of the lease contract, there is an exception. This exception arises when lease payments for a year(s) are considered artificially low in relationship to other lease payments that must be made during the course of the lease agreement. Although "artificially low" is not defined in GASB-13, the term implies that the lessee is making payments during a particular time period that are substantially less than the rental value of the property being leased. GASB-13 provides the following examples as illustrations of artificially low lease payments (GASB-13, par. 6):

- The lessor reduces or eliminates lease payments for a period of time based on the strategy that subsequent lease payments are not equal to the rental value of the property and the transaction is in effect a financial arrangement between the two parties (for example, the lessor may require no lease payments for the first year but the remaining lease payments are increased accordingly to allow for the repayment of the loan to the lessee and an interest factor related to the loan).

- The lessor reduces or eliminates lease payments during the first part of the lease agreement to entice the lessee to enter into the lease agreement.

When an operating lease with scheduled rent increases is evaluated as having artificially low payments in a particular year(s), the rental expenditure/expense (for the lessee) and rental income (for the lessor) should be measured using either one of the following methods (GASB-13, par. 6):

- The straight-line method
- The estimated fair rental method

Straight-line method Under the straight-line method of accounting for operating leases with scheduled rent increases, the periodic rental expenditure/expense and rental revenue are equal to the total lease payments divided by the number of periods covered by the agreement. During the periods when lease payments are not equal to the amount of rental expenditure/expense or rental revenue, an accrual account (either a payable or a receivable) should be used to record the transaction. For example, if the amount of the rental payment is $110,000 and the amount of the rental revenue is $120,000, the following entry should be made (GASB-13, par. 5):

Cash	110,000	
Lease Payments Receivable	10,000	
Rental Revenue		120,000

PRACTICE POINT: A governmental fund would accrue the lease payment of $10,000 only if it is both measurable and available. If the revenue recognition criteria are not satisfied, the "revenue" should be reported as deferred rental revenue. Rental income would be recorded in proprietary funds, government-wide financial statements, and fiduciary funds without regard to the availability criterion.

Estimated fair rental method Under the estimated fair rental method, the periodic rental expenditure/expense and rental revenue are recorded based on the estimated fair rental value of the property. The difference between the fair rental value of the property and the lease payments should be accounted for using the interest method, whereby interest (interest expense/expenditure or interest revenue) is recorded at a constant rate based on the amount of the outstanding accrued lease receivable or payable (GASB-13, par. 7).

If a reasonable estimate of the fair rental value of the leased property cannot be made, the straight-line method should be used to account for an operating lease with scheduled rent increases (GASB-13, par. 6).

GOVERNMENTAL FUNDS

Liabilities and assets of a long-term nature that are not specifically related to proprietary funds or fiduciary funds are not recorded in a governmental fund, but rather are reported in the governmental activities column of the government-wide financial statements.

Recording a Capital Lease by the Lessor

A state or local government should record a capital lease at an amount equal to the present value of the minimum lease payments; however, the amount recorded cannot exceed the fair value of the leased property. Because general capital assets do not represent current financial resources available for appropriation and expenditure, the property rights capitalized should not be reported in a government fund but instead should be reported in the entity's government-wide financial statements. Likewise, the long-term obligation created by the capitalized lease does not require the use of current financial resources, and therefore should be reported only in the government-wide financial statements. In addition, NCGA-5 states that when the capitalized lease represents the purchase or construction of general capital assets, the transaction should be shown as an expenditure and other financing sources in a governmental fund. It is not necessary to account for the capital lease in a separately created Debt Service Fund or Capital Projects Fund unless these funds are legally mandated. A Debt Service Fund would be used when resources are being accumulated for payment of the lease payments in future periods (NCGA-5, pars. 13–14).

To illustrate the accounting for a capital lease, assume that equipment is leased for a five-year period, which is the economic life of the equipment. The lease is signed on June 30, 20X1, and beginning on this date, five annual payments of $50,000 will be made, including the first $50,000 at signing. The governmental unit's incremental borrowing rate, and the lessor's implicit interest rate, is 10%, and the fair value of the property is $208,493 at the inception of the lease. The present value of the minimum lease payments is also $208,493, as shown in the following illustration:

Annual lease payments	$ 50,000
Present value of an annuity due, interest rate is 10% and the number of periods is five	×4.16986
Present value of minimum lease payments	$208,493

The capitalized lease would be recorded as follows in the General Fund, assuming no separate Debt Service Fund or Capital Projects Fund is used to account for the transaction:

General Fund

Expenditures—Capital Outlay	208,493	
Other Financing Sources—Capitalized Leases		208,493
Expenditures—Capital Lease Principal Payment	50,000	
Cash (Vouchers Payable)		50,000

Note: The capital assets ($208,493) would be reported in the government activities column of the government-wide financial statements.

Note: A net liability of $158,493 ($208,493 – $50,000) would be reported in the government activities column of the government-wide financial statements.

In subsequent periods, the lease payments are recorded as expenditures of the fund that makes the lease payment (assumed in this example to be the General Fund). If the expenditure is recorded by object class (as described in NCGA-1 [Governmental Accounting and Financial Reporting Principles], page 17, paragraph 116), an amortization schedule must be prepared to distinguish the principal and interest portions of the lease payment. An amortization schedule based on the example discussed above is presented in the following illustration:

Amortization Schedule

Date	*Lease payment*	*Interest expenditure @10%*	*Principal expenditure*	*Amount of general long-term debt*
6/30/X1	-0-	-0-	-0-	$208,493
6/30/X1	$50,000	-0-	$50,000	158,493
6/30/X2	50,000	$15,849	34,151	124,342
6/30/X3	50,000	12,434	37,566	86,776
6/30/X4	50,000	8,678	41,322	45,454
6/30/X5	50,000	4,546	45,454	-0-

The second lease payment (6/30/X2) would be recorded in the following manner:

GENERAL FUND

Expenditures—Capital Lease Principal	34,151	
Expenditures—Capital Lease Interest	15,849	
Cash		50,000

Note: The amount of the lease liability presented in the government-wide financial statements would be reduced by $34,151 and interest expense of $15,849 would also be reported.

If the lease payments are to be paid from a Debt Service Fund, any transfers from the General Fund to the Debt Service Fund are treated as transfers and not as expenditures of the General Fund (NCGA-5, pars. 13–14).

Depreciation NCGA-1 precludes the recognition of depreciation as an expense in a governmental fund because depreciation is neither a source nor a use of financial resources of the governmental unit. However, depreciation expense would be recognized in the government-wide financial statements (NCGA-1, par. 54, as modified by GASB-34).

Contingent rentals In general, contingent rental amounts are not used to determine minimum lease payments that are to be capitalized. For example, the following amounts are not part of minimum lease payments (FAS-29, par. 11):

- Escalation of minimum lease payments because of increases in construction or acquisition cost of leased property
- Escalation of minimum lease payments because of increases in some measure of cost or value during the construction or pre-construction period
- Lease payments that are based on future use of the property (such as number of machine hours)

When the lease payments are based on an existing index or rate (such as the consumer price index), the estimated future lease payments should be included in the minimum lease payments using the position of the index or rate at the inception of the lease. Subsequent changes in the rental payments are contingent rentals and should be accrued as the index or rate changes (FAS-29, par. 11).

Increases or decreases in lease payments caused by the passage of time are not contingent rental payments and must be included as part of the minimum lease payments (FAS-29, par. 11).

To illustrate the accounting for contingent rentals, assume a governmental unit signs a 10-year lease agreement for which annual payments are to be $300,000 plus or minus $5,000 for each percentage point that the average prime interest rate exceeds or is less than 6%. If the prime interest rate is 7% at the inception of the lease, the minimum lease payments to be capitalized are $305,000

($300,000 + $5,000). If the actual prime interest rate is 10% during the second year of the lease, the additional $15,000 is treated as an expenditure of the second period, assuming the payment will be made from current available financial resources.

Recording a Direct Financing Lease by the Lessor

A governmental unit should normally record as a lease receivable (or gross investment) the total minimum lease payments plus the unguaranteed residual value of the leased property. NCGA-5 states that "only the portion of the lease receivable that represents revenue/other financing sources that are measurable and available" is to be reflected in the current statement of revenues and expenditures as revenue/other financing sources. "Measurable" refers to the ability to estimate the amount of the lease payment that will actually be collected from the lessee. "Available" means that the cash flow must be collected during the current accounting period or shortly after the end of the period but in time to pay liabilities of the current period (NCGA-5, par. 15).

The carrying value of the leased property should be removed from the government-wide financial statements and the total lease payments receivable should be reported in both the governmental fund and the government-wide financial statements. In a direct financing lease, the difference between the total lease receivable and the carrying value of the leased property represents unearned interest income. The unearned interest income is amortized over the lease term using the effective interest method. The unearned interest income is recognized only when the measurable and available criteria are satisfied (NCGA-5, par. 14).

Accounting for a direct financing lease can be illustrated by referring to the earlier example used to demonstrate the accounting for a lessee's capital lease. The total amount of the lease receivable is recorded as follows, assuming the payments under the lease will be available to the General Fund:

General Fund

Lease Payments Receivable ($50,000 × 4 years)	200,000	
Cash	50,000	
Deferred Revenue—Lease Principal Payments		158,493
Deferred Revenue—Lease Interest Payments		41,507
Revenue—Lease Principal Payments		50,000

Note: In the government-wide financial statements, the gross amount of the lease payments receivable ($200,000) would be recorded and the equipment account would be reduced ($158,493). The balance ($41,507) would be recorded as deferred revenue.

In the governmental fund, the amount of the last four lease payments ($200,000) is deferred because it is not an available financial resource. The four remaining payments, based on the original amortization schedule, are summarized in the following illustration:

	Lease payments applicable to		
Date	*Interest*	*Principal*	*Total*
6/30/X2	$15,849	$ 34,151	$ 50,000
6/30/X3	12,434	37,566	50,000
6/30/X4	8,678	41,322	50,000
6/30/X5	4,546	45,454	50,000
	$41,507	$158,493	$200,000

As payments are collected, the receivable account is reduced and the appropriate revenue and other financing sources amounts are recognized. For example, the following entries would be made to record the second lease payment on June 30, 20X2:

GENERAL FUND

Cash	50,000	
Lease Payments Receivable		50,000
Deferred Revenue—Lease Principal Payments	34,151	
Deferred Revenue—Lease Interest Payments	15,849	
Revenue—Lease Principal Payments		34,151
Interest Revenue		15,849

Bad debts If a state or local government executes several leases that are accounted for as direct financing leases, it may be necessary to provide an estimate for uncollectible payments. Because the governmental accounting model is based on the modified accrual basis, the use of a bad debts expense account is inappropriate; however, an allowance account can be established by reducing the amount of deferred revenue initially recognized when the direct financing lease was recorded. If a portion of the lease receivable has been recognized as earned at the end of the period based on the measurable and available criteria, revenue would be debited instead of deferred revenue. To return to the original illustration, assume that it is estimated that 5% of the total lease payments receivable will not be paid. To implicitly recognize the bad debts element of the transaction, the following entry would be made (NCGA-1, pars. 71–72):

GENERAL FUND

Deferred Revenue—Lease Principal Payments	10,000	
Allowance For Doubtful Accounts—Lease Payment Receivable ($200,000 × 5%)		10,000

The allowance amount is a contra asset amount presented as a reduction to the lease payments receivable amount.

Initial direct costs Costs directly related to the negotiation and consummation of the lease are referred to as initial direct costs and include expenditures such as legal fees, costs of credit investigations, and commissions. A provision for bad debts related to lease payments is not considered an initial direct cost. Initial direct costs should be recognized as expenditures when incurred, and an equal amount of unearned revenue should be recognized in the same period. For example, in the previous illustration, if the initial direct costs were $6,500, the following entries would be made (FAS-17, par. 6):

GENERAL FUND

Expenditures—Initial Direct Cost of Leases	6,500	
Cash (Vouchers Payable)		6,500
Deferred Revenue—Lease Interest Payments	6,500	
Revenue—Lease Payments		6,500

The implicit interest rate used by the lessor should be computed after deducting the amount of initial direct costs. Thus, in the current example, the implicit interest rate would be less than 10%.

Contingent rentals Contingent rentals are generally not included in the lessee's minimum lease payments. Contingent rentals are recognized by the lessor as revenue when they become measurable and available (FAS-29, par. 13).

Recording an Operating Lease by the Lessor

To illustrate the accounting for an operating lease by a lessor in a governmental fund, assume that the lease agreement requires monthly rental payments of $5,000 and is classified as an operating lease. At the time the payment is due, the lease would be recorded as follows:

GENERAL FUND

	Debit	Credit
Cash	5,000	
Revenue—Rent		5,000

FAS-13 states that rent revenue receipts that vary in amount over the life of the lease should be recognized on a straight-line basis, unless "another systematic and rational basis is more representative of the time pattern in which use benefit from the leased property is diminished." If the rent payments are greater in the earlier life of the lease, part of the payment must be deferred. To illustrate, assume that a three-year lease agreement provides for rent payments of $15,000, $13,000, and $8,000 over the three-year period. The operating lease would be accounted for in the following manner (FAS-13, par. 15):

	Debit	Credit
Year 1:		
Cash	15,000	
Revenue—Rent		12,000
Deferred Revenue—Rent		3,000
Year 2:		
Cash	13,000	
Revenue—Rent		12,000
Deferred Revenue—Rent		1,000
Year 3:		
Cash	8,000	
Deferred Revenue—Rent	4,000	
Revenue—Rent		12,000

OBSERVATION: In most instances, uneven lease payments will be characterized by higher payments in the early part of the lease. However, if the payments in the early part of the lease are not smaller, the straight-line revenue recognition method cannot be used because the accrued rent does not meet the availability criterion.

For operating leases, initial direct costs should be recognized as expenditures when incurred. Unlike similar costs for commercial enterprises, these costs cannot be capitalized and amortized over the life of the lease (FAS-13, par. 19).

Recording an Operating Lease by the Lessee

To illustrate the accounting for an operating lease by the lessee, assume that the lease agreement requires monthly rental payments of $5,000 and is classified as an operating lease. At the time the payment is due, the lease would be recorded as follows:

GENERAL FUND

Expenditures—Rent	50,000	
Cash (Vouchers Payable)		50,000

PROPRIETARY FUNDS, FIDUCIARY FUNDS, AND THE GOVERNMENT-WIDE FINANCIAL STATEMENTS

The accrual basis of accounting and the economic resources measurement focus should be used to determine how lease transactions should be reported in government-wide financial statements. That is, lease transactions are reported in proprietary and fiduciary funds and the government-wide financial statements in a manner similar to how commercial enterprises report lease transactions, which is based on the guidance established by FAS-13, as amended (NCGA-5, par. 16; GASB-34, par. 17).

Capital assets and the related obligations arising from capital lease transactions should be reported in proprietary and fiduciary funds, and the governmental entity's government-wide financial statements based on the guidance established by FAS-13, as amended (NCGA-5, pars. 16–17; GASB34, pars. 92–93 and 107).

RELATED-PARTY TRANSACTIONS

FAS-13 states that leases between related parties should be evaluated in the same manner as leases between unrelated parties. Specifically, the common criteria (for lessees and lessors) and the unique criteria (for lessor only) should be used to determine whether a lease transaction should be treated as an in-substance purchase or sale of the leased property. However, if it is obvious that the relationship of the parties has significantly affected the terms of the agreement, the accounting treatment must be modified to reflect the substance, rather than the form, of the agreement (FAS-13, par. 29).

A governmental related party transaction may arise between a state or local government and a public authority. A public authority is created to raise funds through the issuance of debt, the proceeds of which will be used to purchase or construct fixed assets. These assets may be leased by the public authority to the state or local government with title passing to the governmental entity at the end of the lease term (NCGA-5, par. 22).

The accounting treatment of a lease between a state or local government and a public authority is dependent on whether the public authority is part of the overall governmental reporting entity. GASB-14 (The Financial Reporting Entity) defines the "reporting entity" as the primary government and all related component units (GASB-14). For a more thorough discussion of the financial reporting entity, see Chapter 4, "Governmental Reporting Entity."

If the public authority is considered part of the primary government of the reporting entity, the lease classification criteria established by FAS-13 are not applied. The capital assets and long-term obligations arising from a capital lease transaction would not be reported by the primary government (NCGA-5, par. 24, as modified by GASB-34, pars. 80 and 82).

On the other hand, when the public authority is *not* considered part of the overall reporting entity, FAS-13 must be used to classify the lease. Specifically, the criteria are applied to determine if the state or local government should capitalize the lease and if the public authority should treat the lease as a direct financing lease (NCGA-5, par. 25).

Finally, as generally required by FAS-13, the nature and extent of the leasing agreement between a state or local government and a public authority should be disclosed in the financial statements of the parties involved in the lease (NCGA-5, par. 26).

DISCLOSURE REQUIREMENTS

Disclosures: Capital Leases

NCGA-5 requires that the disclosure standards established by FAS-13 be observed with respect to lease agreements. Accordingly, the following information for capital leases must be disclosed in a state or local government's financial statements (NCGA-5, par. 27):

- The gross amount of assets recorded under capital leases as of the date of each balance sheet presented by major classes according to nature or function. This information may be combined with the comparable information for owned assets.
- Future minimum lease payments as of the date of the latest balance sheet presented, in the aggregate and for each of the five succeeding fiscal years, with separate deductions from the total for the amount representing executory costs, including any profit thereon, included in the minimum lease payments

and for the amount of the imputed interest necessary to reduce the net minimum lease payments to present value.

- The total of minimum sublease rentals to be received in the future under noncancelable subleases as of the date of the latest balance sheet presented.
- Total contingent rentals actually incurred for each period for which an operating statement is presented.

In addition to these disclosures, the financial statements should include a general description of the lease agreement, including items such as the existence of renewal or purchase options, and restrictions imposed by the lease agreement (FAS-13, pars. 13 and 16).

NCGAI-6 requires that a governmental entity disclose debt service requirements to maturity but does not specify the detail information that should be included in the disclosure. GASB-38 (Certain Financial Statement Note Disclosures) requires that the disclosure be continued but with separate presentations for each of the five years following the date of the balance sheet and in five-year increments thereafter through the last year of the lease agreement. The disclosure must identify the principal and interest components of the lease payments:

NOTE—Obligations under capital leases:

Year Ended June 30	*Governmental Activities*	*Business-Type Activities*
20X1	$1,200,000	$250,000
20X2	820,000	130,000
20X3	750,000	120,000
20X4	600,000	100,000
20X5	580,000	100,000
20X6–X0	500,000	350,000
20Y1–Y5	200,000	250,000
20Y6–Z0	75,000	190,000
Total minimum lease payments	4,725,000	1,490,000
Less: Amount representing executory costs	(300,000)	(120,000)
Less: Amount representing imputed interest costs	(1,500,000)	(450,000)
Present value of minimum lease payments	$2,925,000	$920,000

Disclosures: Direct Financing Leases

State and local governments should make the following disclosures in their financial statements with respect to direct financing leases (NCGA-5, par. 27):

- The components of the net investment in direct financing leases as of the date of each balance sheet presented:
  - — Future minimum lease payments to be received, with separate deductions for (1) amounts representing executory costs, including any profit thereon, included in the minimum lease payments, and (2) the accumulated allowance for uncollectible minimum lease payments receivable
  - — The unguaranteed residual values accruing to the benefit of the lessor
  - — Unearned income
- Future minimum lease payments to be received for each of the five succeeding fiscal years as of the date of the latest balance sheet presented
- The amount of unearned income included in the activity statement to offset initial direct costs charged against revenue for each period for which an activity statement is presented
- Total contingent rentals included in revenue for each period for which an activity statement is presented

In addition, there should be a general description of the direct financing lease agreements (FAS-13, par. 23).

Exhibit 14-1 is an example of a note to the financial statements describing a governmental unit's direct financing lease operations.

EXHIBIT 14-1
EXAMPLE NOTE DESCRIBING DIRECT FINANCING LEASE OPERATIONS

The City's leasing operations consist exclusively of leasing various computer units and support equipment that were purchased in previous years but are no longer used. These leases are classified as direct financing leases and expire at various intervals over the next seven years.

The following lists the components of the net investment in direct financing leases as of June 30:

	20X2	20X1
Total minimum lease payments to be received	$450,000	$520,000
Less: Amounts representing estimated executory costs	(5,000)	(7,000)
Minimum lease payments receivable	445,000	513,000
Less: Allowance for uncollectibles	(40,000)	(43,000)
Net minimum lease payments receivable	405,000	470,000
Estimated residual values of leased property	15,000	20,000
	420,000	490,000
Less: Unearned income	(105,000)	(125,000)
Net investment in direct financing leases	$315,000	$365,000

Minimum lease payments do not include contingent rentals which may be received as stipulated in the lease contracts. These contingent rental payments occur only if the use of the equipment exceeds a certain level of activity each year. Contingent rentals amounted to $12,000 in 20X2 and $18,000 in 20X1. At June 30, 20X2, minimum lease payments for each of the five succeeding fiscal years are as follows:

Year	*Amount*
20X3	$80,000
20X4	$80,000
20X5	$75,000
20X6	$70,000
20X7	$65,000

OBSERVATION: In most in-substance sale lease agreements, a governmental unit would account for the transaction as a direct financing lease because the governmental unit is seldom involved in a lease agreement that gives rise to a manufacturer's or dealer's profit. However, a sales-type lease may occur even when the lessor is not a manufacturer or dealer. FAS-13 notes that a sales-type lease arises when the lessor realizes a profit or loss on the lease transaction. This would occur when the fair value of the lease property at the inception of the lease is greater or less than the carrying value of the property. For a governmental unit, the accounting for a sales-type lease is essentially the same as the accounting for a direct financing lease because no operating profit or loss is recognized when the lease is recorded.

Disclosures: Operating Leases

When a governmental unit has operating leases, there must be a disclosure in the financial statements describing the general characteristics of the lease agreements. In addition, the following disclosures must be made (NCGA-5, par. 27):

- The cost and carrying amount, if different, of property on lease or held for leasing organized by major classes of property according to nature or function and the amount of accumulated depreciation in total as of the date of the latest balance sheet presented
- Minimum future rentals on noncancelable leases as of the date of the latest balance sheet presented, in the aggregate and for each of the five succeeding fiscal years
- Total contingent rentals included in income for each period for which an activity statement is presented

CHAPTER 15
RISK MANAGEMENT, CLAIMS, AND JUDGMENTS

CONTENTS

INTRODUCTION

State and local governments encounter essentially the same accounting and reporting issues as commercial enterprises that purchase insurance coverage (insured). GASB-10 (Accounting and Financial Reporting for Risk Financing and Related Insurance Issues) was issued to provide guidance for governmental entities that assume the role of the insurer and the role of the insured.

> **NOTE:** For a discussion of the accounting standards established by GASB-10 that apply to governmental entities that assume the role of an insurer and pool resources of other governments, see Chapter 23, "Public Entity Risk Pools."

Most governmental entities are exposed to a variety of risks that may result in losses. These risks include possible loss from acts of God, injury to employees, or breach of contract. GASB-10 addresses risk of loss that arises from events such as the following:

- Torts (wrongful acts, injuries, or damages—not involving breach of contract—for which a civil action can be brought)
- Theft of, damage to, or destruction of assets
- Business interruptions
- Errors and omissions (such as the publication of incorrect data or the failure to disclose required information)
- Job-related illnesses or injuries to employees
- Acts of God (events beyond human origin or control—natural disasters such as lightning, windstorms, and earthquakes)
- Losses resulting from providing accident, health, dental, and other medical benefits to employees and retirees and their dependents and beneficiaries (but excluding all postemployment benefits)

A governmental entity must decide how to finance losses that may arise from these and other events. From an accounting perspective, potential losses related to these events require that a governmental entity consider whether an accrual for possible losses should be recognized at the end of an accounting period. Again, the consideration for a possible accrual for losses by a governmental entity is no different from the evaluation that a commercial enterprise must make. For this reason, GASB-10 has adopted many of the standards established in FAS-5 (Accounting for Contingencies) to provide guidance to state and local governments for the accrual of losses related to risk activities.

The accounting standards that are used to determine the amount of the liability that should be presented in a governmental entity's financial statements vary depending on whether a liability is presented in a (1) governmental fund, (2) proprietary and fiduciary funds, or (3) the government-wide financial statements.

ACCOUNTING FOR RISK MANAGEMENT LIABILITIES

General Principles of Liability Recognition

With the exception of the situation described later (when a state or local governmental entity has not transferred the risk of loss related to the events listed above to an unrelated third party), an accrual for a claim should be recognized if the following conditions exist (GASB-10, par. 53):

- On the basis of information available before the financial statements are issued, it is probable (likely to occur) that an asset has been impaired or a liability has been incurred as of the date of the financial statements.
- The loss can be reasonably estimated.

GASB-10 identifies the date of the financial statements as "the end of the most recent accounting period for which financial statements are being presented" (GASB-10, par. 53).

To determine whether a loss is probable, all relevant information available prior to the issuance of the financial statements should be evaluated. An accrual for a loss is made only if the loss was based on an event or a condition that existed on or before the date of the balance sheet (GASB-10, par. 54).

The accrual of a loss in a current period implies that an event will occur in a subsequent period that will substantiate the recognition of the accrual. The accrual of a loss due to an event that suggests that the governmental entity will be held liable for the loss will eventually be confirmed when the entity agrees (or is forced) to pay the injured party. Of course, an accrual of a loss is based on a prediction that the future event will in fact occur. GASB-10 uses the following definitions to describe the various probabilities of whether a loss will eventually be confirmed by a future event (GASB-10, par. 55):

Probable—The future event or events confirming the fact that a loss has occurred are likely to occur.

Reasonably possible—The chance of the future event or events occurring is more than remote but less than likely.

Remote—The change of the future event or event occuring is slight.

OBSERVATION: The criteria used to determine when a loss should be recorded and the discussion of this section of GASB-10 are based on standards established by FAS-5, as amended by FAS-16 (Prior Period Adjustments) and FAS-71 (Accounting for the Effects of Certain Types of Regulation), and by FASB Interpretation No. 14 (FIN-14) (Reasonable Estimation of the Amount of a Loss). The GASB used the standards established by these FASB promulgations without modification.

There are innumerable examples of loss contingencies for governmental entities. The AICPA's *State and Local Governments* Guide lists the following as examples of loss contingencies that should be evaluated for possible accrual:

- Contractual actions (such as claims for delays or inadequate specifications on contracts)
- Guarantees of other entities' debt
- Unemployment compensation claims
- Property tax appeals
- Tax refund claims
- Refunds of nonexchange revenues when the recipient government does not satisfy a provider's requirements

PRACTICE POINT: The last three items listed above (property tax appeals, tax refund claims, and other refunds) should be evaluated in the context of GASB-33 (Accounting and Financial Reporting for Nonexchange Transactions).

GASB-10 does not address the method(s) that may be used to allocate a loss among funds once the amount of the loss is determined. A governmental entity is free to allocate (or not allocate) the loss in any manner it deems appropriate (GASB-10, pars. 53–57).

The criterion that the loss must be subject to reasonable estimation before an accrual is appropriate does not imply that there must be only a single amount that is likely to be incurred. A reasonable amount can be expressed in terms of a range of possible losses. If one specific amount within the range is the most likely to occur, that amount should be accrued as a loss and the excess (the maximum amount in the range minus the amount accrued), as discussed later, should be disclosed in the financial statements.

When no single amount within the range of possible losses is most likely to occur, the minimum amount in the range should be accrued as a loss and the excess should be disclosed in the financial statements.

Incurred But Not Reported Claims

A governmental entity must evaluate its exposure to incurred but not reported (IBNR) conditions. IBNR claims are claims that have not yet been asserted, as of the financial statements issuance date, even though they may have occurred before the date of the balance sheet. If the governmental entity concludes that it is not probable that IBNR claims will be asserted, the loss should not be accrued or disclosed in the financial statements. On the other hand, if the entity concludes that it is probable that an IBNR claim will be asserted by another party, the loss should be accrued if a reasonable estimate of the loss can be made (GASB-10, par. 56).

Governmental entities must evaluate their exposure to liabilities related to unpaid claims costs, which includes both (1) claims that have been reported and (2) claims incurred but not reported. GASB-30 requires that the liability for unpaid claims costs should be based on the following factors (GASB-30, pars. 8–9):

- Total ultimate costs of settling a claim, including provisions for inflation and other societal and economic factors
- Past experience of settling claims
- Factors needed to make past experience trends consistent with current conditions

Valuation of Claims Cost Liabilities

The estimated liability for claims costs should include all costs related to the ultimate settlement of claims. In addition to an estimate for actual payments to claimants, the estimated liability for claims costs should include specific, incremental claims adjustment expenditures/expenses. Specific claims adjustment expenditures/expenses represent costs that are incurred by a governmental entity only because it is attempting to dispose of a specific claim. For example, a claim may require the governmental entity to hire an individual with a certain type of expertise to evaluate the government's legal responsibility as it relates to the claim. On the other hand, claims costs that would otherwise be incurred—for example, salaries of administrative personnel in the department that processes claims and other similar overhead costs—would generally not be considered incremental. Other allocated or unallocated claim adjustment expenditures/expenses may be included in the estimated liability for claims costs, but GASB-30 does not require their inclusion.

> **OBSERVATION:** The estimated liability for claims costs for a public entity risk pool must include a provision for other allocated or unallocated claim adjustment expenditures/expenses. The GASB implied that such expenditures/expenses are conceptually part of the estimated liability for claims costs for entities other than pools. GASB-30 includes a provision for allocated or unallocated claim adjustment expenditures/expenses in the accrual for claims costs to be optional. The composition of the accrual must be disclosed in the financial statements.

The estimated liability for claims costs should be reduced by estimated recoveries that may arise from unsettled claims. GASB-30 refers to two broad categories of recoveries, "salvage" and "subrogation," and GASB-10 provides the following definitions of these terms (the definitions have been slightly modified to reflect the discussion of governmental entities other than public entity risk pools):

> *Salvage*—The amount received by a governmental entity other than a pool from the sale of property (usually damaged) on which the entity has paid a total claim to the claimant and has obtained title to the property.
>
> *Subrogation*—The right of a governmental entity other than a pool to pursue any course of recovery of damages, in its name, against a third party who is liable for costs of an event that have been paid by the governmental entity.

In addition to claims that have not been settled, the governmental entity may also anticipate recoveries from claims that have already been settled. Anticipated recoveries on settled claims should be netted (reduced) against the estimated liability for claims costs.

The accrual for claims costs may be based on a case-by-case review, an overall approach of applying historical experience to all claims outstanding, or a combination of both approaches. GASB-30 notes that the accrual for IBNR losses must be based on historical experience. When historical experience is used to estimate the accrual, claims should be appropriately categorized by amount and type of claim to ensure that relevant historical experience is applied to similar claims.

Discounting

The GASB does not specify whether the accrual of claims liabilities should be discounted. Thus, it is acceptable to report the accrual at either a gross amount or a discounted amount, with one exception:

structured settlements should be discounted if the amount to be paid to the claimant is fixed by contract and the payment dates are fixed or determinable (GASB-10, par. 59).

When claims liabilities are presented in the financial statements at discounted amounts, the rate selected to compute the discounted amounts should take into consideration factors such as the following (GASB-10, par. 60):

- Settlement rate (the rate at which a monetary liability with uncertain terms can be settled or a monetary asset [receivable] with uncertain terms can be sold)
- Investment yield rate (the expected rate of return on investments held by the governmental entity during the period in which the expected payments to the claimant will occur)

Entities Participating in Public Entity Risk Pools with Transfer or Pooling of Risk

Premiums (or required contributions) paid by a governmental entity to a public entity risk pool that result in the transfer or sharing of risk should be reported as an expenditure/expense by the governmental entity (GASB-10, pars. 69–70, and GASB-34, par. 6).

If the governmental entity is subject to supplemental premium assessment by the public entity risk pool, consideration should be given to whether an additional expenditure or expense should be accrued or disclosed in the financial statements. An accrual for the supplemental premium assessment should be made if the following conditions exist (GASB-10, par. 69):

- A supplemental premium assessment will probably be made.
- A reasonable estimate of the supplemental premium assessment can be made.

When a possible supplemental premium assessment, including a supplemental assessment in excess of an accrued supplemental assessment, does not satisfy the criteria for accrual (probable and subject to reasonable estimation), the potential supplemental premium assessment should be evaluated to determine whether it should be disclosed in the governmental entity's financial statements. Any potential supplemental premium assessment that can be classified in one of the following categories should be disclosed (GASB-10, par. 69):

- The occurrence of assessment is probable but no reasonable estimate (or estimate range) of the assessment can be made.
- The likelihood of assessment is reasonably possible.

When a possible supplemental premium assessment is disclosed in the financial statements, the following should be part of the disclosure (GASB-10, par. 69):

- A description of the possible supplemental premium assessment
- An estimate (or estimate range) of the assessment (If no estimate can be made, disclosure of this fact is required.)

When a public entity risk pool does not have the authority to assess additional premiums and the pool has incurred a deficit, the economic viability of the pool should be evaluated. The governmental entity must be concerned with the possibility that the public entity risk pool will not be able to pay claims as they are settled. If the following conditions exist, the governmental entity should record a liability for estimated claims costs (GASB-10, par. 70):

- The public entity risk pool appears not to be able to pay the claims related to the governmental entity as they become due.
- It is probable that the governmental entity will be required to pay its own claims.
- A reasonable estimate of the amount of claims that will be paid by the governmental entity can be made.

When the likelihood of payment of claims that cannot be paid by a public entity risk pool, including any payment in excess of an accrued amount, does not satisfy the criteria for accrual (probable and subject to reasonable estimation), the potential payment should be evaluated to determine whether disclosure is appropriate. Any potential payments that can be classified in one of the following categories should be disclosed (GASB-10, par. 70):

- Potential payment is probable but no reasonable estimate (or estimate range) of the payment can be made.
- Potential payment is reasonably possible.

When a potential payment is disclosed in the financial statements, the following should be disclosed (GASB-10, par. 70):

- Nature of the potential payment
- Estimate (or estimate range) of the potential payment (If no estimate can be made, disclosure of this fact is required.)

Capitalization Contributions Made to Public Entity Risk Pools with Transfer or Pooling of Risk

When a governmental entity makes a capital contribution to a public entity risk pool whereby risk has been transferred or pooled, a determination must be made regarding whether to record the contribution as an asset or as an expenditure/expense. The contribution may be accounted for as an asset if "it is probable that the contribution will be returned to the entity upon either the dissolution of or the approved withdrawal from the pool." The judgment as to whether an asset exists should be based on the written contract that governs the relationship between the governmental entity and the public entity risk pool. In addition, an asset exists only if the public entity risk pool has the financial capacity to return the capital contribution to the governmental entity (GASBI-4, pars. 4–8).

> **PRACTICE POINT:** The assessment of whether to recognize an asset when a governmental entity makes a capital contribution to a public entity risk pool should not occur only at the date of contribution. If the public entity risk pool's financial condition changes in a period subsequent to the contribution, it may be necessary to remove the asset from the governmental entity's financial statements and recognize an expenditure/expense.

When the capital contribution made to a public entity risk pool is accounted for as an asset in a governmental fund, the entity's fund balance must be reserved to disclose that the asset is not available for expenditure in the following budgetary period.

If management concludes that it is probable that the contribution to the public entity risk pool will not be returned and the contribution is made by a governmental fund, the contribution may be accounted for using either the allocation method or the nonallocation method. When the allocation method is used, a prepayment is established at the date of the contribution and is subsequently amortized over the period for which it is expected the contribution will be used to determine the amount of premiums the contributor must pay. Again, if the period is not readily determinable, the amortization period should not exceed 10 years. Because the prepayment is not a current financial resource, the fund's fund balance account should be reserved by the amount presented for prepaid insurance.

When the nonallocation method of accounting is used in a government fund, the capital contribution is reported immediately as an expenditure. Under this approach no asset is created, and thus there is no need to establish a fund balance reserve at the end of the accounting period.

Entities Participating in Public Entity Risk Pools without Transfer or Pooling of Risk

A governmental entity may participate in a public entity risk pool when the relationship is not characterized by a transfer or pooling of risk. For example, there is no transfer or pooling of risk in a banking pool or a claims-servicing (account) pool (GASB-10, par. 71).

When there is no transfer or pooling of risk in the relationship with the public entity risk pool, the governmental entity must evaluate and recognize losses from incurred claims as if there were no participation in the public entity risk pool. Specifically, standards discussed earlier, in the section titled "General Principles of Liability Recognition," must be observed (GASB-10, par. 71).

Payments made to a public entity risk pool (including capitalization contributions) to which there has been no transfer or pooling of risk should be accounted for as either a deposit or a reduction of the claims liabilities account. A deposit should be recorded when the payment is not expected to be used to pay claims. A reduction of the claims liabilities account should be made when payments to the pool are to be used to pay claims as they are incurred (GASB-10, par. 71, and GASBI-4, par. 9).

Insurance Related Transactions

Claims-made policies A governmental entity may purchase a claims-made policy. GASB-10 defines a "claims-made policy" as follows (GASB-10, par. 72, and Glossary):

> *Claims-made policy or contract*—A type of policy that covers losses from claims asserted (reported or filed) against the policyholder during the policy period, regardless of whether the liability-imposing events occurred during the current or any previous period in which the policyholder was insured under the claims-made contract or other specified period before the policy period (the policy retroactive date).

In a claims-made policy, the risk of loss to which the governmental entity is exposed is not entirely transferred. Specifically, the governmental entity is liable for claims that have occurred but were not reported nor filed during the period covered by the claims-made policy. The exposure to loss resulting from a claims-made policy should be evaluated using the standards discussed in the previous section titled "General Principles of Liability Recognition" to determine whether such exposure requires an accrual or disclosure in the financial statements.

The risk exposure related to a claims-made policy can be avoided by acquiring a tail-coverage insurance policy. GASB-10 defines "tail coverage" as follows (GASB-10, par. 72, and Glossary):

> *Tail coverage*—A type of insurance policy designed to cover claims incurred before, but reported after, cancellation or expiration of a claims-made policy. (The term "extended discovery coverage" is used in the commercial insurance industry.)

When tail coverage is acquired, a governmental entity does not have to evaluate the possible accrual or disclosure of losses arising from claims-made policies (GASB-10, par. 72).

Retrospective-rated policies and contracts A governmental entity may purchase a retrospective-rated policy (or contract). GASB-10 defines a "retrospective (experience) rating" as follows (GASB-10, par. 73, and Glossary):

> *Retrospective (experience) rating*—A method of determining the final amount of an insurance premium by which the initial premium is adjusted based on actual experience during the period of coverage (sometimes subject to maximum and minimum limits). It is designed to encourage safety by the insured and to compensate the insurer if larger-than-expected losses are incurred.

When a retrospective-rated policy is acquired, the minimum premium should be recognized as an expenditure or expense over the period covered by the contract. In addition, the standards discussed in the section titled "General Principles of Liability Recognition" should be used to accrue for reported and unreported claims in excess of the minimum premium. If there is a maximum premium identified in the contract, the accrual should not exceed the amount of the maximum premium (GASB-10, par. 73).

In some circumstances, the conditions for recognizing a loss contingency may not exist. If this is the case, no accrual for additional premium payments should be made. However, the governmental entity should refer to the standards discussed in the section titled "Disclosure of Loss Contingencies" to determine whether the possibility of additional premiums being charged under the retrospective-rated policy should be disclosed in the notes to the financial statements (GASB-10, par. 74).

Some governmental entities purchase retrospective-rated policies that are based on the experience of a group of policyholders. When a retrospective-rated policy is based on group experience, the initial premium should be amortized as an expenditure or expense over the period of time covered by the contract. The governmental entity should accrue supplemental premiums or refunds that arise from the experience of the group to date. The accrual should be based on the ultimate cost of reported and unreported claims as of the date of the financial statements. In addition, the following disclosures should be made (GASB-10, par. 74):

- Insurance coverage is based on retrospective-rated policies.
- Premiums are accrued on the basis of the experience to date of the ultimate claims cost of the group of which the governmental entity is a participant.

> **OBSERVATION:** The governmental entity will have to rely on the insurer entity to provide the information necessary to accrue additional premiums or refunds as of the date of the balance sheet.

When an entity cannot accrue estimated losses from reported or unreported claims related to a retrospective-rated policy using group experience because the accrual criteria are not satisfied, the disclosure criteria should be used to determine whether disclosure is appropriate (GASB-10, par. 74).

Policyholder or Pool Dividends

A governmental entity may be entitled to a policyholder dividend (or return of contribution) based on the terms of its insurance contract or its participation in a public entity risk pool. GASB-10 provides the following definition of "policyholder dividends" (GASB-10, par. 75, and Glossary):

> *Policyholder dividends*—Payments made or credits extended to the insured by the insurer, usually at the end of a policy year, that result in reducing the net insurance cost to the policyholder. These dividends may be paid in cash to the insured or applied by the insured to reduce premiums due for the next policy year.

A policyholder dividend should be recorded by the governmental entity as a reduction of expenditures or expenses as of the date the dividend is declared by the insurer.

Entities Providing Claims Servicing or Insurance Coverage to Others

Governmental entities may provide insurance or risk-management coverage to individuals or entities that are not part of the governmental reporting entity (primary government and all related component units). For example, a governmental entity may provide insurance coverage under a workers' compensation plan. If there is a material transfer or pooling of risk and the activities are separate from its own risk-management activities, the governmental entity should account for these activities in a public entity risk pool by following the standards discussed in Chapter 23, "Public Entity Risk Pools" (GASB-10, par. 76).

On the other hand, a governmental entity may provide insurance or risk-management coverage to individuals or entities that are not part of the governmental reporting entity, but these services may be part of its own risk-management activities. Under this circumstance and assuming the governmental entity is the predominant participant in the fund, all of the activities should be accounted for in either the General Fund or an Internal Service Fund, and the standards discussed in this chapter should be followed. If the governmental entity is not the predominant participant, the activities should be accounted for in an Enterprise Fund, and the standards discussed in Chapter 23, "Public Entity Risk Pools" should be followed (GASB-10, par. 76).

> **OBSERVATION:** Although the General Fund can be used to account for the risk-management activities when the governmental entity is the predominant participant, the author believes it is probably preferable to account for such activities in an Internal Service Fund to limit the activities reported in the General Fund to revenues and expenses related to routine governmental transactions.

Finally, some governmental entities may service claims and provide no insurance coverage to individuals or entities that are not part of the governmental reporting entities. Under this arrangement, amounts collected or due from, and amounts paid or due to the individuals or other entities should be netted and reported as a net asset or liability determined on the accrual basis. Operating revenue and administrative costs arising from the claims-servicing activities should be accounted for consistently with the standards discussed in Chapter 23, "Public Entity Risk Pools" (see the section titled "Pools Not Involving Transfer or Pooling of Risk") (GASB-10, par. 76).

Annuity Contracts

A governmental entity may satisfy its obligation to a claimant by purchasing an annuity in the claimant's name. If the possibility of making additional payments to the claimant is remote, the claim should be removed as a liability. Under this circumstance, the claim would not be presented as a liability and the purchase of the annuity contract would not be presented as an asset (GASB-10, par. 61).

When claims have been removed from the claims liability account because of the purchase of an annuity contract, the amount removed should be disclosed as a contingent liability. The disclosure should continue as long as there is a legal possibility that the claimant could demand payment from the governmental entity. Disclosure is not required for annuity contracts purchased if both of the following conditions exist (GASB-10, par. 61):

- The claimant has signed an agreement releasing the governmental entity from further obligation.
- The likelihood of future payments to the claimant is remote.

If a claim had been removed from the claims liability account because an annuity contract was purchased in a previous period, but in the current period it was determined that the governmental entity is now primarily liable for the claim, the claim should be reestablished as a claims liability.

GOVERNMENTAL FUNDS

The modified accrual basis of accounting and current financial resources measurement focus should be applied to accounting for claims and judgments in governmental funds.

For example, assume that an entity identifies a probable loss and that a reasonable estimate of the loss ranges from $100,000 to $400,000. Assume that the most likely amount of the loss is $150,000. The amount of the claims liability that should be accrued in a governmental fund is based on the application of the modified accrual basis of accounting. If none of the $150,000 estimate is expected to use expendable available financial resources, no claims expenditure (liability) would be accrued, but the full amount ($150,000) would be presented in the government-wide financial statements (GASB-34, pars. 6, 79, and 92).

Use of a Single Fund

When a governmental entity uses a single fund to account for its risk financing activities, either the General Fund or an Internal Service Fund should be used (GASB-10, par. 63).

OBSERVATION: It would appear that the more logical fund to account for an entity's risk financing activities is an Internal Service Fund, because an Internal Service Fund and the Enterprise Fund required by the GASB to account for a public entity risk pool have the same measurement focus and basis of accounting. The GASB allowed the use of the General Fund to account for risk financing activities to be consistent with the general concept that a governmental entity should use the minimum number of funds appropriate for its operations. The following discussion assumes the risk financing activities are accounted for in the entity's General Fund.

Risk Retention

When the General Fund is used to account for a governmental entity's risk financing activities, claims liabilities and the related expenditure or expense should be recognized on the basis of standards discussed in the earlier section entitled "General Principles of Liability Recognition." These standards require that the standards established in FAS-5 related to the accrual of loss contingencies be applied to claims arising from risk financing activities. Any accrual of claims liabilities should be reduced by amounts expected to be paid through excess insurance (GASB-10, par. 64).

PRACTICE POINT: This section refers to the recognition of expenditures when the General Fund is used. In the General

Fund, only expenditures can be recorded; however, as discussed later, the total amount of the liability can be determined in the General Fund and then allocated to other funds, including those that record expenses rather than expenditures.

If it is concluded that a loss related to risk financing activities should not be accrued because the occurrence of the loss is not probable or the amount of the loss is not subject to reasonable estimation, the loss should be evaluated to determine whether disclosure in the financial statements is necessary. The standards discussed in the earlier section titled "Disclosure of Loss Contingencies" should be applied when deciding whether to disclose the loss (GASB-10, par. 64).

When the General Fund is used to account for a governmental entity's risk financing activities, the amount of the loss may be allocated to other funds in any appropriate manner. For example, assume a loss of $500,000 is computed and the loss is allocated to an Enterprise Fund, Capital Projects Fund, and General Fund, in the amounts of $50,000, $70,000, and $380,000, respectively. To record the recognition and allocation of the loss, the following entries would be made in the affected funds (GASB-10, par. 64):

GENERAL FUND		
Expenditures—Claims Costs	380,000	
Due from Enterprise Fund	50,000	
Due from Capital Projects Fund	70,000	
Estimated Claims Costs Payable		500,000
ENTERPRISE FUND		
Expenses—Claims Costs	50,000	
Due to General Fund		50,000
CAPITAL PROJECTS FUND		
Expenses—Claims Costs	70,000	
Due to General Fund		70,000

When the General Fund allocates the loss expenditure or expense to other funds and the total allocation, including the amount allocated to the General Fund, exceeds the accrual computed using the guidelines discussed in the section titled "General Principles of Liability Recognition," the excess amount should be treated as a transfer. To illustrate this requirement, assume the same facts as the previous example except assume that the Enterprise Fund and Capital Projects Fund are allocated an additional cost of $10,000 each. To record the allocation, the following entries are made (GASB-10, par. 64, and GASB-34, pars. 79 and 112):

GENERAL FUND		
Expenditures—Claims Costs	380,000	
Due from Enterprise Fund	60,000	

Due from Capital Projects Fund	80,000	
Estimated Claims Costs Payable		500,000
Transfers in—Enterprise Fund		10,000
Transfers in—Capital Projects Fund		10,000

ENTERPRISE FUND

Expenses—Claims Costs	50,000	
Transfers Out—General Fund	10,000	
Due to General Fund		60,000

CAPITAL PROJECTS FUND

Expenditures—Claims Costs	70,000	
Transfers Out—General Fund	10,000	
Due to General Fund		80,000

If one fund reimburses another fund for expenditures or expenses paid, the reimbursement should be recorded as a reduction of expenditures or expenses by the reimbursed fund and as an expenditure or expense by the reimbursing fund. This classification problem most often occurs when (1) the General Fund does not allocate loss expenditures or expenses to other funds (or the amount allocated is too small) and another fund reimburses the General Fund for the payment of a claim related to the activities of the other fund or (2) the General Fund pays insurance premiums for another fund and, at a later date, the other fund reimburses the General Fund for a portion of the premiums paid (GASB-10, par. 64).

PROPRIETARY AND FIDUCIARY FUNDS

The accrual basis of accounting and the economic resources measurement focus should be used to determine which claims should be presented in a proprietary or fiduciary fund. That is, the guidance established by FAS-5 (as discussed earlier in the section titled "General Principles of Liability Recognition") should be followed to determine the amount of the claim. If a claims liability is considered to be incurred, the liability should be presented both in the proprietary or fiduciary fund and in its business activities columns of the statement of net assets.

If a single fund is used to account for the governmental entity's claims and assessments, the entity must use either the General Fund or and Internal Service Fund (GASB-10, par. 63, and GASB-34, pars. 79, 92, and 107).

> **PRACTICE POINT:** A governmental entity that reports its operating activities in a proprietary or trust fund may participate in a risk-financing Internal Service Fund if the proprietary or trust fund is a component unit of the governmental entity that has established the Internal Service Fund. On the other hand, a

proprietary or trust fund should not account for its risk financing activities in an Internal Service Fund if the proprietary or trust fund is not a component unit of the governmental entity (GASB-10, par. 63, footnote 8).

Internal Service Fund

When an Internal Service Fund is used to account for a governmental entity's risk financing activities, claims liabilities and the related expenses should be recognized on the basis of the standards discussed in the section titled "General Principles of Liability Recognition." That discussion states that the standards established in FAS-5 related to the accrual of loss contingencies should be applied to claims arising from risk financing activities. Any accrual of claims liabilities should be reduced by amounts expected to be paid through excess insurance (GASB-10, par. 65, and GASB-34, par. 6).

If it is concluded that a loss related to risk financing activities should not be accrued because the occurrence of the loss is not probable or the amount of the loss is not subject to reasonable estimation, the loss should be evaluated to determine whether disclosure in the financial statement is necessary. The standards discussed in the section titled "Disclosure of Loss Contingencies" should be applied to make the decision of whether to disclose (GASB-10, par. 65).

NCGA-1 states that the purpose of an Internal Service Fund is "to account for the financing of goods or services provided by one department or agency to other departments or agencies of the governmental unit, or to other governmental units, on a cost-reimbursement basis." Thus, the risk financing services provided by an Internal Service Fund should be billed to those funds for those services provided. GASB-10 states that an Internal Service Fund may use any method it considers appropriate to determine the amounts charged to the various other funds as long as the following guidelines are satisfied (GASB-10, par. 66):

- The total amount for service charges to other funds is equal to the amount of liability computed in complying with the standards discussed in the previous section titled "General Principles of Liability Recognition," or
- The total amount for service charges to other funds is computed using an actuarial method or historical cost information, and that amount is adjusted over time so that the expenses and revenues of the Internal Service Fund are approximately the same.
- If the second approach is used (actuarial method or historical cost information method), an additional charge may be made to other funds that represents a reasonable provision for expected future catastrophic losses.

GASB-10 defines "actuarial method" as follows:

> *Actuarial method*—Any of several techniques that actuaries use to determine the amounts and timing of contributions needed to finance claims liabilities so that the total contributions plus compounded earnings on them will equal the amounts needed to satisfy claims liabilities. It may or may not include a provision for anticipated catastrophe losses.

The first method (based on standards discussed in the section titled "General Principles of Liability Recognition") requires that the amount billed to other funds by the Internal Service Fund be equal to the amount of liability recognized under the accrual concepts established in FAS-5. Thus, under the first method, the amount of billings must be based on the incurrence of liabilities based on specific events.

The second method (actuarial method or historical cost information method) is not based on the evaluation of events that have actually occurred. Under the second method, the amount billed can be based on projected claims that may occur (GASB-10, par. 66).

> **OBSERVATION:** The concepts established by FAS-5 do not allow for "smoothing" of expenses or expenditures as allowed by the second method. A loss contingency is accrued based on the incurrence of a liability as of the date of the balance sheet. If FAS-5 is followed, it is arguable that the concept of interperiod equity cannot be achieved because FAS-5 does not allow for the "averaging of losses" so that any one period would not have a significantly larger amount of recognized expenditures than any other period. The GASB provided a solution to the interperiod equity problem by allowing governmental entities to use an actuarial method that results in level charges and to charge an optional amount for expected future catastrophic losses.

The amount billed by the Internal Service Fund to the other funds should be recognized as revenue, and each fund should recognize either an expenditure or an expense based on the amount of the billing. For example, if an Internal Service Fund charged the General Fund and an Enterprise Fund $400,000 and $50,000, respectively, the following entries would be made (GASB-10, par. 66):

INTERNAL SERVICE FUND		
Due from General Fund	400,000	
Due from Enterprise Fund	50,000	
Revenues—Charges for Services		450,000
GENERAL FUND		
Expenditures—Payments In Lieu of Insurance Premiums	400,000	
Due to Internal Service Fund		400,000

ENTERPRISE FUND		
Expenses—Payments in Lieu of Insurance Premiums	50,000	
Due to Internal Service Fund		50,000

GASB-10 recognizes that when an actuarial method or historical cost information method is used (with or without an additional charge for expected future catastrophic losses), in any one period, the amount of the claims costs expense recognized and the amount of billings to the other funds may not be the same. The difference between the cumulative claims costs recognized and the cumulative billings does not have to be charged back to the other funds if adjustments are made over a reasonable period of time to reduce the difference. When a fund balance deficit arises, the deficit should be disclosed in the notes to the governmental entity's financial statements. Any amount in the Internal Service Fund's net assets that arose from an optional additional charge for catastrophic losses should be reported as a designated net assets (equity) for future catastrophic losses in notes to the financial statements (GASB-10, par. 67).

If the Internal Service Fund bills other funds for a total amount that is greater than the total amount as discussed earlier in this section, the excess should be accounted for as interfund transfers by the Internal Service Fund and the other funds. The Internal Service Fund would report a transfer in and the other funds would report a transfer out (GASB-10, par. 68).

The amounts billed over time and the amounts of expenses recognized by the Internal Service Fund should be approximately the same over a reasonable period. If the Internal Service Fund incurs a deficit that is not eliminated over a reasonable period of time, the deficit should be billed to the participating funds to cover the full costs of claims recognized as expenses. When a chargeback occurs, the Internal Service Fund should recognize revenue and the other funds should record either an expenditure or an expense (GASB-10, par. 68).

GOVERNMENT-WIDE FINANCIAL STATEMENTS

The accrual basis of accounting and the economic resources measurement focus should be used to determine which claims and assessments should be presented in a governmental entity's statement of net assets. That is, the guidance established by FAS-5 (as discussed earlier in the section titled "General Principles of Liability Recognition") should be followed to determine the amount of the claim. If a claims liability is considered to be incurred, the liability should be presented as a debt obligation of the governmental entity in its governmental and business activities columns of the statement of net assets. As required by GASB-34, liabilities that have an average maturity greater than one year must be reported in two components, namely, the amount due within one year and the amount due in more than one year (GASB-34, pars. 16 and 31).

When a claims expense is recorded, the expense must be evaluated to determine how the expense should be presented in the statement of activities. That is, a determination should be made as to whether the claims expense is a direct expense (expenses that are specifically associated with a service, program, or department). In some instances a claims expense may be an extraordinary item (unusual and infrequent) and therefore should be presented in the lower section of the statement of activities. When a claims expense is either unusual or infrequent, but not both, the item should be disclosed in a note to the financial statements (GASB-34, par. 31).

Reporting Risk Financing Internal Service Fund Balances and Activity

If an Internal Service Fund is used to account for risk management activities, such activities should be eliminated to avoid "doubling-up" expenses and revenues in the government activities column of the statement of activities. The effect of this approach is to adjust activities in an Internal Service Fund to a break-even balance. That is, if the Internal Service Fund had a "net profit" for the year, there should be a pro rata reduction in the charges made to the funds that used the Internal Service Fund's services for the year. Likewise, a net loss would require a pro rata adjustment that would increase the charges made to the various participating funds. After making these eliminations any residual balances related to the Internal Service Fund's assets and liabilities should be reported in the government activities column in the statement of net assets (GASB-34, pars. 59 and 62).

DISCLOSURES

Disclosure of Loss Contingencies

When a possible future loss, including any loss in excess of an accrued amount, does not satisfy the criteria for accrual (probable and subject to reasonable estimation), the loss should be evaluated to determine whether it should be disclosed in the governmental entity's financial statements. Any loss that can be classified in one of the following categories should be disclosed (GASB-10, par. 58):

- Loss is probable but no reasonable estimate (or estimate range) of the loss can be made.
- Loss is reasonably possible.

When a loss is disclosed in the financial statements, the following should be disclosed (GASB-10, par. 58):

- Nature of the loss
- Estimate (or estimate range) of the loss (If no estimate can be made, the disclosure should state so.)

Possible losses arising from unreported claims or unreported asassessments do not have to be disclosed unless the following conditions exist (GASB-10, par. 58):

- It is probable that a claim will be asserted or an assessment will be made.
- It is reasonably possible that a loss will arise from the asserted claim or assessment.

> **PRACTICE POINT:** When a loss is based on a future event whose likelihood of occurring is remote, the loss should not be accrued or disclosed in the financial statements.

Risk Management Disclosures

The following disclosures should be made in the financial statements of entities that are not public entity risk pools (GASB-10, par. 77, and GASB-30, par. 10):

- Describe the types of risk to which the governmental entity is exposed.
- Identify the methods used for risk financing (such as self-insurance, transfer of risk by purchasing insurance from a commercial enterprise, or transfer to or pooling of risk in a public entity risk pool). If the governmental entity has acquired commercial insurance that is insignificant in relation to the risk exposure, the governmental entity has in substance retained the risk of loss.
- Describe significant reductions in insurance coverage from the previous year, arranged by major category of risk, and indicate whether settlements exceeded insurance coverage for each of the past three years.
- Disclose whether the entity participates in a public entity risk pool and the nature of participation, if any, including rights and obligations of the governmental entity and the pool.
- Disclose whether the governmental entity has retained the risk of loss (risk is not transferred when activities are accounted for in an Internal Service Fund), and describe the following:
  - — Basis of estimating liabilities for unpaid claims including the effects of specific, incremental claim adjustment

expenditures/expenses, and recoveries related to salvage and subrogation, as well as the effects of other components of the estimated amount, and whether the accrual includes a provision for other allocated or unallocated claim adjustment expenditures/expenses

— Carrying amount of unpaid claims liabilities that have been computed on a present-value basis and the range of discount rates used to make the computation

— Total amount of outstanding liabilities that have been removed from the balance sheet because of the purchase of annuity contracts from third parties in the name of claimants (amount should not include amounts related to settlements for which claimants have signed an agreement releasing the entity from further obligation and the chance of further payment is remote)

- Present a total claims liabilities reconciliation, including changes in aggregate liabilities for claims in the current year and prior year using the following tabular format:
  — Beginning balance of claims liabilities
  — Provision for incurred claims expenses for the year and increases or decreases in the provision for events that were incurred in prior years
  — Payments made for claims arising during the current year and prior fiscal years
  — Explanation of other material reconciling items
  — Ending balance of claims liabilities

Level of Disclosure

Professional judgment must be exercised to determine the most appropriate level of disclosure. The notes to the financial statements should focus on the primary government (which includes its blended component units) and support the information included in the government-wide financial statements and the fund financial statements (GASB-10, par. 78, and GASB-34, par. 113).

> **PRACTICE POINT:** Note disclosures related to discretely presented component units should be presented based on the requirements established by GASB-14, paragraph 63.

In some situations, it may be appropriate for the governmental entity to make disclosures for the entity as a whole. Separate or additional disclosures by individual major funds may be appropriate in other situations (GASB-10, par. 78).

When the financial statements of a public entity risk pool are presented separately and also included in a primary government's financial report, disclosures in the primary government's financial statements should emphasize the nature of the primary government's participation in the pool. The primary government's financial report should note that the public entity risk pool presents separate financial statements (GASB-10, par. 78).

Subsequent Events

To ensure that the financial statements are not misleading, the governmental entity should consider the need to disclose subsequent events, which are events or transactions related to risk management that occur after the date of the balance sheet. Disclosure should be made for material items that have one of the following characteristics (GASB-10, par. 80):

- The subsequent event resulted in the impairment of an asset or the incurrence of a liability (actual loss, such as damage from an earthquake).
- A reasonable possibility exists that a subsequent event resulted in the impairment of an asset or the incurrence of a liability (contingent loss, such as the personal injury claims to parties in which it has been alleged that the governmental entity's negligence contributed to the injuries).

If a governmental entity concludes that a subsequent event should be disclosed, the following information should be presented in the disclosure (GASB-10, par. 80):

- The nature of the actual loss or loss contingency
- An estimate (or range of estimates) of the actual loss or contingent loss (if no estimate can be made, disclose appropriately)

In unusual circumstances, a subsequent event may result in the presentation of pro forma financial statements to supplement the historical financial statements. This should be limited to the occurrence of an actual loss that is subject to reasonable estimation. Pro forma statements are prepared by modifying the historical financial statements as if the loss had occurred on the last day of the fiscal year. Usually, only a pro forma balance sheet is presented and may be most informative if the pro forma and historical financial statements are presented on a comparative (columnar) basis (GASB-10, par. 80).

Component Unit Disclosures

The following disclosures should be made by a component unit that issues separate financial statements and participates in its primary government's risk-management Internal Service Fund (GASB-10, par. 79):

- Describe the risks of loss to which the entity is exposed and the way(s) in which those risks of loss are handled (for example, purchase of commercial insurance, participation in a public entity risk pool, risk retention).
- Describe significant reductions in insurance coverage from coverage in the prior year by major categories of risk. Also indicate whether the amount of settlements exceeded insurance coverage for each of the past three fiscal years.
- Disclose that the component unit participates in the Internal Service Fund.
- Describe the nature of the participation.
- Describe the rights and responsibilities of both the component unit and the primary government.

CHAPTER 16
OTHER LIABILITIES

CONTENTS

INTRODUCTION

The accounting standards that are used to determine which liabilities should be presented in a governmental entity's financial statements vary depending on whether a liability is presented in (1) governmental funds, (2) proprietary funds or fiduciary funds, or (3) the government-wide financial statements.

Note: Certain liabilities incurred by state and local governments are specifically addressed in other chapters as follows:

- Liabilities arising from long-term debt transactions (see Chapter 12, "Long-Term Debt")
- Liabilities arising from pension and employee benefit transactions (see Chapter 13, "Pension, Post Employment, and Other Employee Benefit Liabilities")
- Liabilities arising from lease transactions (see Chapter 14, "Leases")
- Liabilities arising from risk management activities (see Chapter 15, "Risk Management, Claims and Judgments")

This chapter discusses other liabilities of governmental funds, such as payables and accruals unique to the modified accrual basis of accounting and current financial resources measurement focus. In addition, the chapter discusses the accounting and reporting of liabilities arising from operation or responsibility for a municipal solid waste landfill, state lottery obligations, and pollution remediation obligations.

GOVERNMENTAL FUNDS

The measurement focus for governmental funds is the flow of current financial resources. Liabilities that will consume current financial resources of the fund responsible for payment during the fiscal period are presented in that fund's balance sheet. No explicit current liability classification exists on a fund's balance sheet (the financial statement is unclassified). However, the mere presentation of the liability in the balance sheet of the government's fund implies that the debt is current and will require the use of expendable financial resources (NCGA par. 18).

OBSERVATION: The definition of "current liabilities" differs significantly between a governmental fund and a commercial enterprise. ARB-43 (Restatement and Revision of Accounting Research Bulletins) describes "current liabilities" as those items that will be liquidated through the use of current assets. "Current assets" are defined as resources expected to be realized or consumed within the entity's operating cycle. Thus, the term to maturity of a current liability of a commercial enterprise could be a year or longer, depending on the entity's operating cycle. A liability of a governmental fund is considered current when it is expected to be liquidated with current financial resources. The term to maturity for a government's current liability is much shorter than that for a commercial enterprise.

General long-term liabilities (those liabilities not accounted for in proprietary or fiduciary funds) of a governmental reporting entity are presented in the entity's government-wide financial statements (NCGA-1, pars. 32–33, as amended by GASB-34).

Recording Fund Liabilities and Expenditures

As described earlier, governmental funds generally record a liability when it is expected that the liability will be paid from revenues recognized during the current period. Liabilities that are normally expected to be paid with current financial resources should be presented as a fund liability, and liabilities that have been incurred but that are not normally expected to be paid with current financial resources should be considered "general long-term liabilities." General long-term liabilities are presented in the government-wide financial statements (statement of net assets) and not in a fund balance sheet.

OBSERVATION: For many years accountants have criticized the definitions of governmental revenues/assets and expenditures/liabilities because the definitions are based on circular reasoning. That is, revenue can only be accrued at the end of a period if the revenue will be collected in time to pay accrued liabilities; however, liabilities can be accrued at year-end only when they are paid from revenues recognized during the current period. In March 2000, GASB Interpretation No. 6 (GASBI-6) (Recognition and Measurement of Certain Liabilities and Expenditures in Governmental Fund Financial Statements) was issued to provide guidance for determining when liabilities should be accrued in governmental funds.

To address the accrual of fund liabilities, GASBI-6 categorizes governmental fund liabilities as follows (GASBI-6, par. 5):

- Liabilities that are generally recognized when due

- Liabilities that are recognized when they are "normally expected to be liquidated with expendable available financial resources"
- Liabilities that have no specific accrual modification

The Interpretation does not apply to the following situations (GASBI-6, par. 7):

- Operating leases that include scheduled rent increases (the standards established by GASB-13 [Accounting for Operating Leases with Scheduled Rent Increases] should be followed)
- Employer contributions to pension plans (the standards established by GASB-27 [Accounting for Pensions by State and Local Governmental Employers] should be followed)
- Employer contributions to postemployment health-care or other postemployment benefit plans, when the entity elects to follow the standards established in GASB-27 or GASB-43

Liabilities recognized when due The basic guidance for determining when a governmental fund should accrue an expenditure/liability is found in NCGA-1 (Governmental Accounting and Financial Reporting Principles), paragraph 70, which states that "most expenditures and transfers out are measurable and should be recorded when the related liability is incurred." GASBI-6 expands on this general guidance by noting the following (GASBI-6, par. 12):

> Governmental fund liabilities and expenditures that should be accrued include liabilities that, once incurred, normally are paid in a timely manner and in full from current financial resources—for example, salaries, professional services, supplies, utilities, and travel.

These transactions give rise to fund liabilities that are considered mature liabilities because they are "normally due and payable in full when incurred." However, GASBI-6 points out that there are several significant exceptions to this general guidance established in NCGA-1. Specifically, NCGA-1 states that "unmatured long-term indebtedness" should not be reported as a fund liability (except for debts that are related to proprietary and trust funds). "Unmatured long-term indebtedness" is defined as "the portion of general long-term indebtedness that is not yet due for payment," and includes debts such as the following (GASBI-6, pars. 9–11):

- Formal debt agreements such as bonds and notes
- Liabilities "normally expected to be liquidated with expendable available financial resources"
- Other commitments that are not current liabilities properly recorded in governmental funds

GASBI-6 points out that the three specified categories listed above are exceptions to the general rule that a liability is recorded as a fund liability and "in the absence of an explicit requirement to do otherwise, a government should accrue a governmental fund liability and expenditure in the period in which the government incurs the liability" (GASBI-6, par. 12).

Formal debt agreements such as bonds and notes NCGA-1 notes that most expenditures are measurable and should be recorded when the related fund liability is incurred. An exception to this generalization is the treatment of interest and principal payments for general longterm indebtedness. Interest and principal on long-term debt are not recorded as expenditures as they accrue, but when they become due and payable. For example, if a governmental entity issues a 30-year bond, the liabilities would not be reported as fund liability until the debt is actually due and payable, which would be thirty years after issuance (GASBI-6, pars. 9 and 13).

NCGA-1 exception Current accounting standards provide for an exception to the basic concept that general long-term indebtedness is not reported as an expenditure until the amount becomes due and payable. When funds have been transferred to the Debt Service Fund during the fiscal year in anticipation of making debt service payments "shortly" after the end of the period, it is acceptable to accrue interest and debt in the Debt Service Fund as an expenditure in the year the transfer is made. Prior to the issuance of GASBI-6, there was a considerable amount of confusion as to what is meant by shortly. The Interpretation states that "shortly" means "early in the following year"; however, the period of time after the end of the year cannot be greater than one month.

The NCGA-1 exception does not apply to the following situations:

- The financial resources that will be used to pay the indebtedness early in the following year are held in fund other than a Debt Service Fund.
- The financial resources represent "nondedicated financial resources" that have been transferred to a Debt Service Fund based on management discretion.

The accumulation of resources under the two strategies described above should not be reported as an expenditure but as part of the governmental fund's fund balance.

OBSERVATION: It should be emphasized that this exception applies only when a Debt Service Fund is used to account for servicing the debt.

Liabilities "normally expected to be liquidated with expendable available financial resources" Although NCGA-1 implies that a fund liability should be recorded when the obligation is incurred, one of the most important concepts that forms the basis for preparing the financial statements of a governmental fund is that liabilities are recorded only when they are normally expected to be liquidated with expendable available financial resources. As described in GASBI-6, this exception to the broad accrual assumption is based on the same guidance established for formal debt agreements as described in the previous section. That is, "governments, in general, are normally expected to liquidate liabilities with expendable available financial resources to the extent that the liabilities mature (come due for payment) each period." In order to apply this broad generalization to current practice, GASBI-6 notes that "a series of specific accrual modifications have been established pertaining to the reporting of certain forms of long-term indebtedness." These exceptions include formal debt agreements as described in the previous section as well as the following debt arrangements (GASBI-6, pars. 7 and 14):

- Capital lease agreements (see Chapter 14, "Leases")
- Debts that arise from compensated absences, pensions, other postemploment benefits, and termination benefits (see Chapter 13, "Pension, Postemployment, and Other Employee Benefit Liabilities")
- Claims and judgments (see Chapter 15, "Risk Management, Claims, and Judgments")
- Landfill closure and postclosure obligations, discussed later in this chapter.

> **OBSERVATION:** GASBI-6 uses the phrase "normally expected to be liquidated with expendable available financial resources." This phrase is interpreted to be equivalent to other similar variations, including "normally would be liquidated with expendable available financial resources" and "payable with expendable available financial resources."

Other commitments that are not current liabilities properly recorded in governmental funds The third broad exception to the basic concept that government fund liabilities are recognized on an accrual basis relates to possible new forms of debt. In a dynamic economy, new forms of debt may be created that have not been addressed by a specific governmental accounting standard. GASBI-6 points out that these "other commitments" should be reported as a fund liability when due and payable. The total amount of the debt, regardless of when due, would be reported in the government-wide financial statements (GASBI-6, par. 17).

Accumulation of Net Assets

GASBI-6 clarifies the funding strategy with respect to unmatured liabilities that are not reported as fund obligations. Some governmental entities have established the practice of budgeting these obligations on an accrual basis or otherwise funding the eventual payment of these liabilities on something other than a budgetary basis.

For example, compensated absences may be reported as a fund expenditure of $100,000 based on the concept of "normally expected to be liquidated with expendable available financial resources" but the governmental entity may fund $300,000, which is the amount of the accrual based on the standards established by GASB-16 (GASBI-6, pars. 15–16).

GASBI-6 states that the accumulation of resources that will be used eventually to pay for unmatured general long-term indebtedness cannot be reported in a government fund as an expenditure or obligation of the fund because that funding strategy does not result in the outflow of current financial resources. Thus, in the previous example the government fund would record an expenditure of $100,000 for compensated absences and the additional $200,000 ($300,000 – $100,000) should be reported as part of the unreserved fund balance of the government fund. If appropriate action has been taken by the management of the governmental entity, the unreserved fund balance may be identified as designated for the funding of compensated absences, but that designated amount does result in expenditure recognition. However, if the government is legally required to fund these obligations, a fund balance reserve would be appropriate.

> **OBSERVATION:** GASBI-6 points out that the GASB does not establish strategies for funding obligations. That is the responsibility of the governmental entity's management; however, the GASB is not unsympathetic with those governmental entities that believe that it is advantageous and appropriate to fund certain liabilities on an accrual basis rather than on a strict budgetary basis. For example, the GASB notes that "if a government wishes to report employee benefits such as compensated absences or special termination benefits on the accrual basis in fund financial statements, as well as in government-wide financial statements, it would not be precluded from reporting them through an employee benefit trust fund, if a proper trust is established."

LANDFILL CLOSURE AND POSTCLOSURE CARE COSTS

Many governmental entities are involved with the onerous task of collecting and disposing of an ever increasing volume of refuse. One method of disposing of this material is through landfill operations.

Like other entities, landfills have cash inflows and outflows during their operating lives. However, landfills are unique because when they close, their cash inflows cease but their cash outflows generally must continue to ensure that the surrounding environment is not damaged by tainted water and other residues.

Governmental accounting and reporting standards for landfill operations are provided in GASB-18 (Accounting for Municipal Solid Waste Landfill Closure and Postclosure Care Costs).

In the past, operators and owners were not mandated to provide funds to protect the environment after closing a landfill, but the environmental protection movement fostered legislation that requires such funding. Specifically, in 1991, the U.S. Environmental Protection Agency (EPA) issued a rule (Solid Waste Disposal Facility Criteria) that applies to municipal solid waste landfills (MSWLFs). The EPA ruling establishes closure requirements for MSWLFs that accept solid waste after October 9, 1991, and "location restrictions, operating criteria, design criteria, groundwater monitoring and corrective action requirements, postclosure care requirements, and financial assurance requirements" for MSWLFs that receive solid waste after October 9, 1993.

The unique character of landfills and the EPA rule raise the accounting issues of how and when costs expected to be incurred after the close of a landfill should be recorded. Based on research conducted by GASB, it is apparent that a variety of accounting practices were being used to account for closure and postclosure care costs. In August 1993, the GASB issued GASB-18 to reduce the diversity of acceptable accounting practices in this area. With the issuance of GASB-18, the GASB took the position that the EPA rule provided very specific requirements and that the time is appropriate to establish accounting standards related to solid waste landfill closure and postclosure care costs.

> **PRACTICE POINT:** While the EPA rule concerning municipal solid waste landfill closure and postclosure care costs applies to private and public owners and operators of landfills, GASB-18 does not apply to private entities. Private entities must follow generally accepted accounting principles as interpreted under the accounting hierarchy established for nongovernmental entities in SAS-69.

GASB-18 applies to all governmental MSWLFs irrespective of what type of accounting model they use to account for the activities of a landfill. The costs incurred by the governmental entity may arise from regulations established by a federal, state, or local governmental agency. The guidance established by GASB-18 applies to both closure and postclosure care costs (GASB-18, par. 3).

> **OBSERVATION:** In footnote 2 of GASB-18, the GASB defines costs to encompass "both an economic and a financial

resources perspective." Under current governmental accounting standards, a proprietary fund recognizes as expenses both economic (for example, the depreciation of a capital asset) and financial resources (for example, cash expenditures) used in operations, while a governmental fund's measurement of expenditures is limited to the consumption of financial resources. Thus, because the costing standards established by GASB-18 are somewhat different from those associated with governmental funds, the GASB used footnote 2 to clarify the cost-recognition approach established in GASB-18.

Definition of Estimated Total Current Cost of MSWLF Closure and Postclosure Care

The basic objective of GASB-18 is to recognize all landfill costs by the time a landfill is closed (no longer accepts solid waste). Of course, once it is closed, there will be expenditures associated with the landfill (postclosure care), but those costs should have been estimated by the closure date and recognized as such in the governmental entity's financial statements. The degree to which the accounting standards established by GASB-18 are satisfied is directly related to a governmental entity's ability to accurately estimate all future costs (GASB-18, par. 4). (These costs could extend over a long period of time.)

The starting point in satisfying the standards established by GASB-18 is to identify "the estimated total current cost of MSWLF closure and postclosure care." Current cost refers to the cost of buying, in the current year, capital assets and services related to closure and postclosure care, even though those costs will actually be incurred in future periods. Specifically, the estimated total current cost of MSWLF closure and postclosure care should include the current cost of (1) capital assets, (2) final cover, and (3) monitoring and maintenance activities (GASB-18, par. 4).

Capital assets Based on the current design plans of the MSWLF, capital asset costs should include expenditures related to the acquisition and installation of equipment and the construction of facilities. Such costs should be limited to capital assets that will be acquired, installed, or built (1) at or near the date the landfill ceases to accept waste and (2) after the landfill ceases to accept waste. In addition, capital asset costs should include only those assets that will be used exclusively for the MSWLF activity. However, when a capital asset is used by more than one MSWLF, the costs should be allocated between or among the MSWLFs on the basis of usage (GASB-18, par. 4).

Final cover Once the landfill is full, it will generally be necessary to cap the facility. The current cost of the capping should be included as part of the estimated total current cost of the MSWLF (GASB-18, par. 4).

Monitoring and maintenance activities Even after the landfill no longer accepts solid waste, the governmental entity will continue to incur costs related to the monitoring and maintenance of facilities and the landfill itself. Federal, state, or local regulations will mandate how long the monitoring and maintenance period must last. These ongoing (future) costs are part of the estimated total current cost of the MSWLF. GASB-18 requires that the estimate be based on the "expected usable landfill area," which is the area expected to receive the solid waste during the life of the MSWLF. However, estimation of the landfill capacity should take into consideration a number of factors such as MSWLF permit periods (including the probability of renewals) and geological factors. For example, the capacity of the landfill may decrease if, in a subsequent year, it is determined that a portion of the area has geological characteristics that make it unsuitable to accept solid waste.

Federal, state, or local laws and regulations will mandate what measures must be used to ensure that the landfill is properly closed and monitored when solid waste is no longer accepted. These laws and regulations should be the basis for estimating the total current cost of MSWLF closure and postclosure care. Furthermore, the closure and postclosure costs should be based on the laws and regulations that have been approved as of the balance sheet date, irrespective of the effective date of the guidance (GASB-18, par. 5).

> **OBSERVATION:** Under specified circumstances, the EPA rule can be modified by allowing state or local landfill requirements to apply to a landfill owner or operator. In this case, state or local requirements would dictate which equipment, facilities, and services must be acquired with respect to closure and postclosure care, and the accounting by the governmental entity should be consistent with the modified requirements.

Annual Reevaluation

At the end of each year, a governmental entity should evaluate its estimate of the total current cost related to closure and postclosure care of a MSWLF. Changes in expected cost may arise from a number of factors, including inflation or deflation, technological advancements, and modifications to legal requirements at the local, state, or national level (GASB-18, par. 6).

Reporting MSWLFs in Proprietary Funds

When MSWLF activities are accounted for in a proprietary fund, a portion of the estimated total current cost of closure and postclosure care should be recognized each year as an expense. The cost basis for determining the amount of expense to be recognized is based on the definition of "estimated total current cost" (GASB-18, par. 7).

The amortization or allocation period starts the day the landfill accepts solid waste and continues until it no longer accepts waste. The amount of annual expense recognition is based on usage (similar to the units-of-production depreciation method). If 20% of the landfill is filled during the current year, 20% of the estimated total current cost of closure and postclosure care should be reported as a current expense. If no solid waste is accepted during a period, there should be no expense recognition for that period (GASB-18, par. 7).

It is likely that cost estimates will change from year to year, and for this reason, the computation of the annual expense must take into consideration the capacity used and the amount of expense recognized in previous years. Thus, the analysis that should be used each year to determine the amount of expense to be recognized is based on the following formula (GASB-18, par. 7):

$$\frac{\text{Estimated Total Current Cost} \times \text{Cumulative Capacity Used}}{\text{Total Estimated Capacity}} - \text{Amount of Expense Previously Recognized}$$

For example, if the estimated total current cost is $1,000,000, the cumulative capacity used is 100,000 cubic yards, the total estimated capacity is 500,000 cubic yards, and the amount of expense recognized in all previous years is $125,000, the expense to be recorded in the current year is computed as follows (GASB-18, par. 7):

$$\frac{\$1,000,000 \times 100,000 \text{ cubic yards}}{500,000 \text{ cubic yards}} - \$125,000 = \begin{array}{l}\$75,000 \\ \text{(current expenses)}\end{array}$$

Since the computation is based on expected or future cost, there is no capital asset on the records of the proprietary fund that can be amortized. For this reason, the current expense related to the estimated total current cost of MSWLF closure and postclosure care is recorded by debiting an expense account and crediting a liability. For example, the expense computed in the previous paragraph would be recognized by making the following journal entry (GASB-18, par. 7):

Expenses—Landfill Closure and Postclosure Care Costs	75,000	
Estimated Liability for Landfill Closure and Postclosure Care Costs		75,000

Acquisitions of equipment and facilities that will occur near or after the date the landfill no longer accepts waste are part of the estimated total current cost of the MSWLF. When these items are purchased (at or near the end of the life of the landfill), they should not be reported as capital assets but rather should be accounted for as a reduction to the estimated liability for landfill closure and postclosure care costs (GASB-18, par. 8).

A landfill operator may acquire capital assets used exclusively for a MSWLF that do not meet the definition of "disbursements near or after the date that the MSWLF stops accepting solid waste and during the postclosure period." These capital expenditures, based on the guidance established by GASB-18, are not a component of the estimated total current cost of MSWLF closure and postclosure care and, therefore, must be capitalized and depreciated over the estimated remaining life of the landfill. The total estimated life of the landfill is the period from the date on which waste is first accepted until the date on which waste is no longer accepted. Thus, once the facility is filled, expenditures that have been capitalized must be fully depreciated (GASB-18, par. 9). See Exhibit 16-1 for a complete illustration of the costs and related liabilities.

Reporting MSWLFs in Governmental Funds

When MSWLF activities are accounted for in a governmental fund, the basic measurement approach used by a proprietary fund should also be used by the governmental fund. Aportion of the estimated total current cost of closure and postclosure care should be recognized each year using the estimated life of the landfill and the usage of the landfill for a particular period. However, due to the difference in the measurement focus and basis of accounting of a governmental fund as compared to a proprietary fund, the annual cost recognition related to estimated closure and postclosure care costs generally will not affect a governmental entity's activity statement (GASB-18, par. 10).

The basic facts used to illustrate the accounting for MSWLF activities in a proprietary fund can be used to illustrate the activity in a governmental fund. As computed earlier, the amount of closure and postclosure care costs recognized was $75,000. This amount must be analyzed to determine whether it is to be paid with current expendable resources of the governmental entity. In almost all instances, it is unlikely that any of the estimated closure and postclosure care costs will use current expendable resources because those costs are based on "disbursements near or after the date that the MSWLF stops accepting solid waste." Assuming that none of the $75,000 is due and payable from current expendable resources, the governmental entity will report the total amount of the current cost as a general long-term liability in the governmental activities of the government-wide financial statements (GASB-18, par. 10, and GASB-34, par. 82).

Capital acquisitions that are included in estimated total current cost should be reported as closure and postclosure care expenditures (GASB-18, pars. 10–11, and GASB-34, par. 119).

Reporting MSWLFs in Government-Wide Financial Statements

Account balances and transactions related to MSWLFs should be reported in government-wide financial statements, similar to proprietary funds, based on the standards established in paragraphs 7, 10, and 11 of GASB-18, as amended by GASB-34 (GASB-34, par. 31).

Reporting Changes in Estimates

Closure and postclosure care costs generally extend over a lengthy period. For this reason, it is likely that there will be a number of changes in the components used to compute the annual costs of MSWLF closure and postclosure care. For example, the estimated cost of a landfill cap, control facilities, and maintenance services will undoubtedly change from year to year. The accounting for such changes is dependent on the period in which the change takes place. If the change in estimated costs occurs before the landfill is filled, the change is a "change in accounting estimate" and should be reported on a prospective basis. The effect of the change is allocated over the remaining estimated life of the landfill. For example, in the previous illustration, if it is assumed that in the following year the estimated total current cost is $1,000,000 (no change), the cumulative capacity used is 200,000 cubic yards, the total estimated capacity is 400,000 cubic yards (a change in estimate), and the amount of expense recognized in all previous years is $200,000 ($125,000 + $75,000), the amount of costs to be recognized for the year is computed as follows (GASB-18, par. 13):

$$\frac{\$1,000,000 \times 200,000 \text{ cubic yards}}{400,000 \text{ cubic yards}} - \$200,000 = \$300,000$$

The use of the formula established by GASB-18 takes into consideration changes in accounting estimates (GASB-18, par. 13).

When changes in estimates occur after the landfill no longer accepts solid waste, the effects of the changes should be recorded as a current year cost and not allocated over the remaining life of the closed landfill (the number of years mandated by law or regulation that the governmental entity must monitor and maintain the closed landfill). These costs should be recognized when they are probable and subject to reasonable estimation (that is, they must satisfy the criteria established by FAS-5 (Accounting for Contingencies). Whether those costs are to be reported by a governmental fund as an expenditure on its activity statement depends on whether the cost is due and payable from current expendable resources (GASB-18, par. 14).

Some costs may relate to the horizontal expansion of the landfill. Because these costs arise from the expansion of the landfill capacity, they should not affect the factors used to compute the current cost of MSWLF closure and postclosure care for the original landfill. It would be necessary under this circumstance to make two separate computations for estimated total current cost for closure and postclosure care: one for the costs related to the original landfill dimensions, and one for costs related to the (new) expanded landfill area (GASB-18, par. 13).

Accounting for Assets Placed in Trust: All Fund Types and Entities

Under requirements of the EPA rule, some owners or operators of landfills will have to provide financial assurances concerning the future landfill closure and postclosure care costs. The purpose of the EPA requirement is to make sure that landfill owners or operators will have the capability to provide resources to assure that the financial burden of a filled landfill will not become the responsibility of taxpayers. The EPArule can be achieved by putting assets in various forms of trusts (GASB-18, par. 15).

When a governmental entity makes payments to the trust, those payments should not be treated as expenditures/expenses, but rather should be reported on the balance sheet as assets with an appropriate title such as "Amounts Held by Trustee." The assets should be reported in the fund that accounts for the landfill activities. Earnings on amounts held by the trustee (or otherwise set aside) should be reported as investment income and not as a reduction to the estimated total current cost of closure and postclosure care (GASB-18, par. 15).

> **OBSERVATION:** GASB-18 establishes accounting and reporting standards for MSWLFs, but the funding strategies must be established by the governmental entity's management team, and those strategies must be in compliance with applicable laws and regulations.

Responsibility for MSWLF Closure and Postclosure Care Assumed by Another Entity

Under some circumstances the financial obligation related to closure and postclosure care of a landfill may be transferred from the governmental entity to another party, such as a private enterprise. If the responsibility has been legally transferred and the private enterprise is financially capable of meeting the financial obligation imposed by the closure and postclosure care responsibilities, the governmental entity is not required to recognize the annual portion of estimated total current cost of MSWLF closure and postclosure care (GASB-18, par. 16).

When it is concluded that the financial responsibility for the landfill has been transferred to a private enterprise, the governmental entity should continue to assess the ability of the enterprise to fulfill its obligation. If federal, state, or local laws or regulations require that the governmental entity retain contingent liability for closure and postclosure care costs, and a question regarding the ability of the assuming entity to meet its obligation arises, the governmental entity should determine whether provisions should be made for the closure and postclosure care costs. When it is determined that it is *probable* that the governmental entity will have to assume the financial responsibility because of the poor financial condition of the assuming entity, the related obligation should be recognized on the governmental entity's financial statements. The liability should be computed using the guidelines discussed earlier, depending on whether the landfill activities are accounted for in a proprietary fund or in a governmental fund (GASB-18, par. 16).

Note Disclosures: All Fund Types and Entities

GASB-18 requires that the following note(s) to a governmental entity's financial statements be presented (GASB-18, par. 17):

- Describe the laws, regulations, etc., that establish requirements for landfill closure and postclosure care.
- State that the liability for landfill closure and postclosure care costs is based on the amount of landfill used to date.
- Disclose the amount of the estimated liability for landfill closure and postclosure care costs (if not presented on the face of a financial statement) and the balance to be recognized in subsequent periods.
- Disclose the percentage of landfill used to date and the estimated remaining life (years) of the landfill.
- Describe how closure and postclosure care costs are being funded (if at all).
- Disclose the amount of assets that have been restricted for the payment of closure and postclosure costs (if not presented on the face of a financial statement).
- Describe the nature of the estimates used and the potential for changes in estimates that may result from inflation, technological changes, or regulatory changes.

The following is an example of a note to the financial statements of a government that satisfies the disclosure requirements of GASB-18. The illustrative note assumes that a proprietary fund is being used to account for the landfill activities:

Note X: Landfill Closure and Postclosure Care Costs

State and federal laws and regulations require that the City of Centerville place a final cover on its landfill when closed and perform certain maintenance and monitoring functions at the landfill site for thirty years after closure. In addition to operating expenses related to current activities of the landfill, an expense provision and related liability are being recognized based on the future closure and postclosure care costs that will be incurred near or after the date the landfill no longer accepts waste. The recognition of these landfill closure and postclosure care costs is based on the amount of the landfill used during the year. The estimated liability for landfill closure and postclosure care costs has a balance of $7,200,000 as of June 30, 20X5, which is based on 60% usage (filled) of the landfill. It is estimated that an additional $4,800,000 will be recognized as closure and postclosure care expenses between the date of the balance sheet and the date the landfill is expected to be filled to capacity (20Y3). The estimated total current cost of the landfill closure and postclosure care ($12,000,000) is based on the amount that would be paid if all equipment, facilities, and services required to close, monitor, and maintain the landfill were acquired as of June 30, 20X5. However, the actual cost of closure and postclosure care may be higher due to inflation, changes in technology, or changes in landfill laws and regulations.

The City of Centerville is required by state and federal laws and regulations to make annual contributions to finance closure and postclosure care. The City is in compliance with these requirements, and at December 31, 20X5, investments of $5,100,000 ($5,700,000 market value) are held for these purposes. These investments are held and managed by a third-party trustee and are presented on the City's statement of net assets as "Amounts Held by Trustee for Landfill Closure and Postclosure Care Costs." It is anticipated that future inflation costs will be financed in part from earnings on investments held by the trustee. The remaining portion of anticipated future inflation costs (including inadequate earnings on investments, if any) and additional costs that might arise from changes in postclosure requirements (due to changes in technology or more rigorous environmental regulations, for example) may need to be covered by charges to future landfill users, taxpayers, or both.

Landfills Reported as Component Units

When landfills are considered to be component units of the primary government, the guidelines established by GASB-14 (The Financial Reporting Entity) must be followed to determine how the financial statements and related notes of the landfill should be reported. GASB-14 adopts the basic philosophy that the financial information pertaining to the primary government (which could include landfill component units that are blended) and similar information pertaining to discretely presented landfill component units should be distinguishable. This philosophy is extended to disclosures in notes and the presentation of required supplementary information in the financial statements of the financial reporting entity (GASB-18, par. 18). Determining what should be disclosed in notes to the financial statements is a question of professional judgment. A determination must be made as to which disclosures are essential to the fair presentation of the basic financial statements (GASB-18, par. 18).

EXHIBIT 16-1
ILLUSTRATION: LANDFILL CLOSURE AND POST-CLOSURE-CARE COSTS CALCULATIONS

This example is based on Appendix C of GASB-18, and is intended to illustrate the application of the standards established. Assume the following information:

According to its operating plan filed with the state, ABC Landfill will open in 20X4 and will operate on a cell basis, opening one cell at a time and installing liners and leachate collection systems before the cell receives any waste. Construction on new cells will begin before older cells reach capacity. When a cell reaches capacity, gas collection wells will be installed, and final cover, including vegetative cover, will be put in place.Water monitoring wells, erosion control systems, and a leachate treatment plant will be constructed during the first and second years of landfill operations.

Other Assumptions

- Landfill construction begins in 20X5; opens January 1, 20X6.
- Projected landfill life in years: 33.
- The landfill will be operated on a cell basis.
- Total landfill area: 150 acres.
- Initial expected usable landfill area: 100 acres/33 cells.
- Initial estimated capacity based on expected usable landfill area: 4.5 million cubic yards (capacity per cell = 136,364 cubic yards).
- Landfill usage:

Year	Cubic Yards
20X6	90,000
20X7	120,000
20X8	135,000

- The postclosure monitoring period required by current state law is 30 years after the entire landfill receives final cover.
- In 20X7, the entity opened an area of the landfill that was subsequently determined to be unusable because of its location on unstable sediment. For this reason, estimated capacity and expected usable landfill area were reduced by approximately 5% to 4,275,000 cubic yards and 31 cells, as of December 31, 20X7. (This reduction also affects expected leachate output from the landfill.)
- Estimates are based on current costs in 20X6, adjusted using the state-provided inflation rate of 1.5% in 20X7 and 1.85% in 20X8.

Estimated Total Current Cost of Closure and Postclosure Care—20X6

1. Equipment and Facilities Cost	
Near date landfill stops accepting waste	$ 0
During closure/postclosure	
Maintenance and upgrading of on-site leachate treatment facility (costs projected to be paid principally at the end of 30 years)	375,000
Expected renewals and replacements of storm water and erosion control facilities ($50,000 per year)	1,500,000
Monitoring well replacements (30 at $25,000 each)	750,000
2. Final Cover Cost	
(Final cover, including vegetative cover, installed as cells are filled)	0
3. Postclosure Care Cost	
Inspection and maintenance of final cover ($75,000 per year)	2,250,000
Groundwater monitoring ($100,000 per year)	3,000,000
Gas monitoring ($5,000 per year)	150,000
On-site leachate pretreatment cost and off site treatment (30,000,000 gallons total × $.05 per gallon)	1,500,000
Projected remediation cost based on statistical average at similarly sited landfills	250,000
Total estimated current cost of closure and postclosure care	$ 9,775,000

Estimated Total Current Cost of Closure and Postclosure Care—20X7

1. Equipment and Facilities Cost	
Near date landfill stops accepting waste	$ 0
During closure/postclosure	
Maintenance and upgrading of on-site leachate treatment facility (costs projected to be paid principally at the end of 30 years)	380,625
Expected renewals and replacements of storm water and erosion control facilities ($50,750 per year)	1,522,500
Monitoring well replacements (30 at $25,375 each)	761,250
2. Final Cover Cost	
(Final cover, including vegetative cover, installed as cells are filled)	0
3. Postclosure Care Cost	
Inspection and maintenance of final cover ($76,125 per year)	2,283,750
Groundwater monitoring ($101,500 per year)	3,045,000
Gas monitoring ($5,075 per year)	152,250
On-site leachate pretreatment cost and off-site treatment (28,500,000 gallons total × $.05075 per gallon)	1,446,375
Projected remediation cost based on statistical average at similarly sited landfills	253,750
Total estimated current cost of closure and postclosure care	$ 9,845,500

Estimated Total Current Cost of Closure and Postclosure Care—20X8

1. Equipment and Facilities Cost	
Near date landfill stops accepting waste	$ 0
During closure/postclosure	
Maintenance and upgrading of on-site leachate treatment facility (costs projected to be paid principally at the end of 30 years)	387,667
Expected renewals and replacements of storm water and erosion control facilities ($51,689 per year)	1,550,670

Monitoring well replacements (30 at $25,844 each)	775,320
2. Final Cover Cost	
(Final cover, including vegetative cover, installed as cells are filled)	0
3. Postclosure Care Cost	
Inspection and maintenance of final cover ($77,533 per year)	2,325,990
Groundwater monitoring ($103,378 per year)	3,101,340
Gas monitoring ($5,169 per year)	155,070
On-site leachate pretreatment cost and off-site treatment (28,500,000 gallons total × $.05169 per gallon)	1,473,165
Projected remediation cost based on statistical average at similarly sited landfills	258,444
Total estimated current cost of closure and postclosure care	$ 10,027,666

Proprietary Fund Assumption

If it is assumed that the MSWLF activities are accounted for in a proprietary fund, the following entries would be made:

Entry for 20X6

The following entry would be made in 20X6, the first year of operating activity for the landfill.

Expenses—Landfill Closure and Postclosure Care Costs	195,500	
Estimated Liability for Landfill Closure and Postclosure Care Costs		195,500

$$\frac{\$9,775,000 \times 90,000 \text{ cubic yards}}{4,500,000 \text{ cubic yards}} - \$0 = \$195,500$$

Entry for 20X7

The following entry would be made in 20X7. It should be noted that the computation takes into consideration two changes in estimates. One change occurs due to the increase in the estimated total current cost of MSWLF closure and postclosure care ($9,845,500), and the other change relates to a reduction in the estimated capacity of the landfill (4,275,000 cubic yards).

Expenses—Landfill Closure and Postclosure Care Costs	288,139	
Estimated Liability for Landfill Closure and Postclosure Care Costs		288,139

$$\frac{\$9,845,000 \times (90,000 + 120,000)}{4,275,000} - \$195,500 = \$288,139$$

Entry for 20X8

The following entry would be made in 20X8. At the end of 20X8, the estimated total current cost of MSWLF closure and postclosure care has been increased to $10,027,666.

Expenses—Landfill Closure and Postclosure Care Costs	325,611	
Estimated Liability for Landfill Closure and Postclosure Care Costs		325,611

$$\frac{\$10,027,666 \times (90,000 + 120,000 + 135,000)}{4,275,000} - \$483,639 = \$325,611$$

The estimated liability for landfill closure and postclosure care costs as of December 31, 20X8, would be reported as a long-term liability in the proprietary fund's statement of net assets at $809,250.

STATE LOTTERY OBLIGATIONS

State lotteries: Generally a state lottery would satisfy one or more of the three conditions listed earlier for determining whether an activity should be reported as an Enterprise Fund. In many lottery games a fixed percentage of ticket sales must be paid out as winnings. The AICPA's *State and Local Governments* Guide points out that lottery prize costs under this or similar payout arrangements are subject to accrual based on their relationship to total ticket sales and that accrual may be appropriate under conditions such as the following:

- Prizes have been won and claimed but have not been paid.
- Prizes have been won but not claimed.
- Games are in process at the end of the year.

Some lotteries allow a winner to either take an immediate lump sum payment or receive payments over a specified period of time. If the lottery winner chooses to receive the winnings over a period of time and the state purchases an annuity from an insurance company in the name of the winner, the AICPA Audit and Accounting Guide *State and Local Governments—with conforming changes as of May 1, 2006* points out that no related liability or asset should be reported on the state's financial statements.

When the state does not purchase an annuity in the name of the winner, the liability should be presented at its present value. When determining the liability to be discounted, the amount should include amounts won as well as amounts won but not yet claimed and amounts that will be won and claimed for games in progress at the end of the year.

Furthermore, the state might decide to finance the periodic payments to the winner by "purchasing U.S. Treasury securities matched in timing and amount to the future payments." Under this arrangement, the investment in securities should be reported as an asset on the state's financial statements. The lottery liability and the investment cannot be offset against one another. When the state has financed the periodic payments to the lottery winner through the purchase of an annuity from an insurance company, the state should consider whether a contingent liability should be disclosed in its financial statements.

POLLUTION REMEDIATION OBLIGATIONS

In December 2006 the GASB issued GASB-49 (Accounting and Financial Reporting for Pollution Remediation Obligations). A number of governments are faced with the responsibility of cleaning up or remediating pollution such as asbestos, brownfields, and the like. Prior to GASB-49 no authoritative accounting standard that provided specific guidance on accounting and financial reporting for such obligations.

Under GASB-49 state and local governments are required to determine whether they should report a liability in their financial statements for pollution remediation obligations if any of the following five events (triggers) has occurred:

1. Pollution poses an imminent danger to the public or environment *and* a government has little or no discretion to avoid fixing the problem
2. A government has violated a pollution-prevention permit or license

3. A regulator has identified (or evidence indicates that a regulator will identify) a government as responsible or potentially responsible for cleaning up pollution or has stated that the government must pay all or some of the cleanup costs
4. A government is named or evidence exists that it will be named in a lawsuit to compel it to address the pollution
5. A government legally obligates itself to or begins to clean up pollution or perform post-cleanup activities.

If none of the foregoing events has occurred, a government is not required to calculate or report a pollution-remediation liability. However, if one or more of the events has occurred and a range of potential outlays can be reasonably estimated, then a government is required to calculate and report a liability within the financial statements that are reported using the full accrual basis of accounting. The government is only required to estimate and report liabilities for activities that are reasonably estimable. For example, if in the early stages of pollution remediation, only legal fees and site testing costs were reasonably estimable, then only those costs would be accrued. Once any further remediation costs were reasonably estimable, then they would be accrued at that time. Similar to current landfill closure and postclosure obligation standards, the pollution-remediation liabilities would be reevaluated periodically and estimated liabilities adjusted.

GASB-49 uses an "expected cash flow" measurement technique to measure pollution-remediation liabilities using an estimate of ranges of potential outlays required to remediate the pollution.

> **Example:** Assume a school district has been notified by a regulator that it is responsible for the entire cost of cleaning up asbestos in its school buildings. Also assume the district estimates that there is a 10% chance that cleanup will cost \$1,000,000, a 50% chance the cleanup will cost \$5,000,000 and a 25% chance the costs will be \$10,000,000. The expected cash flow technique would calculate the estimated liability as follows:
>
> $$(\$1{,}000{,}000 \times 0.1) + (\$5{,}000{,}000 \times 0.5) + (\$10{,}000{,}000 \times 0.25) = \$5{,}100{,}000$$
>
> Using this expected cash flow technique, \$5,100,000 would be reported by the government as a liability in its financial statements.

In situations where the government cannot reasonably estimate the liability for all portions of the remediation effort, it would only be required to report liabilities for the amounts that can be reasonably estimated.

In addition, the GASB-49 requires certain note disclosures, including the following:

- The nature and source of the pollution-remediation obligation
- The amount of estimated liabilities for remediation if it is not separately disclosed on the face of the financial statements
- The methods and assumption used to estimate the liability
- The potential for estimate changes due to external factors
- An estimate of the amount of any expected cost recovery from insurance or other parties

If a liability was not reasonably estimable, then the government would be required to disclose only the nature of the pollution-remediation activities.

GASB-49 requires governments to measure their pollution remediation liabilities as of the start of the first fiscal year beginning after December 15, 2007.

CHAPTER 17
REVENUES: NONEXCHANGE AND EXCHANGE TRANSACTIONS

CONTENTS

INTRODUCTION

Most governmental entities are involved in a number of nonexchange and exchange (and exchange-like) transactions. This chapter discusses the basic rules that governmental entities should follow to report these sources of revenues in governmental funds, proprietary funds, fiduciary funds, and government-wide financial statements.

REVENUES: NONEXCHANGE TRANSACTIONS

"Exchange transactions" are defined as the simultaneous transfer of approximately equal goods or services between parties. On the other hand, governmental entities are involved in a number of "nonexchange transactions," which are characterized by the transfer of goods or services that are not equal between parties. For governmental entities, nonexchange transactions range from taxes raised by governmental entities (recipient of the resources) to grants made by one governmental entity (providers of the resources) to another governmental or nongovernmental entity.

In December 1998, the GASB issued GASB-33 (Accounting and Financial Reporting for Nonexchange Transactions) to provide guidance for nonexchange transactions involving financial or capital resources. The standards established by GASB-33 do not apply to food stamps or to on-behalf services for fringe benefits and salaries, which are addressed in GASB-24 (Accounting and Financial Reporting for Certain Grants and Other Financial Assistance), but the standards do apply to pass-through grants, which are defined in GASB-24. GASB-24 did not address the issue of when pass-through grants should be recognized; therefore, the standards established by GASB-33 should be observed to determine the timing of these grants (GASB-33, par. 5).

In addition, the standards established by GASB-33 supersede (in part or in their entirety) standards established in the following pronouncements (GASB-33, par. 6):

- AICPA Statement of Position No. 75-3 (SOP 75-3) (Accrual of Revenues and Expenditures by State and Local Governmental Units)
- National Council on Governmental Accounting Statement No. 2 (NCGA-2) (Grant, Entitlement, and Shared Revenue Accounting by State and Local Governments), paragraphs 1–14, 17, 19, and 20
- NCGAInterpretation No. 3 (NCGAI-3) (Revenue Recognition—Property Taxes), paragraph 9
- GASB-6 (Accounting and Financial Reporting for Special Assessments), paragraphs 14, 15, and 23
- GASB-22 (Accounting for Taxpayer-Assessed Tax Revenues in Governmental Funds)

> **PRACTICE POINT:** The standards established by GASB-33 do not apply to the acquisition of goods and services in an exchange transaction that were funded through a nonexchange transaction (GASB-33, footnote 3). For example, the standards established by GASB-33 would not apply to the acquisition of computers from a commercial enterprise (an exchange transaction) even though the governmental entity receives the resources to pay for the computers from a state grant (a nonexchange transaction). GASB-33 does not apply to nonexchange transactions involving contributed services (GASB-33, par. 5).

The standards established by GASB-33 apply to all state and local governments (GASB-33, par. 3).

The Nature of Nonexchange Transactions

The two parties in a nonexchange transaction are the provider of the resources and the receiver of the resources. The provider of the resources could be the federal government, a state or local government, or a nongovernmental entity (such as an individual or a business entity). The receiver of the resources could be a state or local government or a nongovernmental entity. As noted earlier, what distinguishes a nonexchange transaction from an exchange transaction is that in a "nonexchange transaction" a government "either gives value (benefit) to another party without directly receiving equal value in exchange or receives value (benefit) from another party without directly giving equal value in exchange" (GASB-33, par. 7).

GASB-33 provides accounting and reporting standards for the following four categories of nonexchange transactions:

- Derived tax revenues
- Imposed nonexchange revenues
- Government-mandated nonexchange transactions
- Voluntary nonexchange transactions

The standards established by GASB-33, for the most part, apply to the four categories of nonexchange transactions and not to specific types of nonexchange transactions. For example, the GASB did not specifically prescribe how sales tax revenue should be measured but rather established general standards for derived tax revenues that apply to all revenues considered to be part of the category, including sales tax revenue. For this reason, GASB-33 requires a governmental entity to evaluate each of its nonexchange transactions and decide which of the four categories should be used to classify a particular transaction (GASB-33, par. 8).

> **OBSERVATION:** The GASB established general rather than specific standards in order to provide a flexible approach that addresses current implementation problems as well as future developments in governmental activities. The GASB could not realistically establish recognition standards for every possible type of nonexchange transaction that is currently experienced by a governmental entity. By providing general standards, the GASB enables a specific governmental entity to apply them to all of its nonexchange transactions and not just to a few specific situations. Another advantage of general standards is that they apply to "new kinds of transactions that governments may encounter or establish in the future."

In determining which category is appropriate for each nonexchange transaction, a governmental entity must look at the substance of the transaction rather than at its "label." The entity should not group a nonexchange transaction in one of the four Statement categories based on whether the transaction is described as a tax, a grant, or by some other name. For example, the GASB notes that a grant provided by a governmental entity could be designated as a voluntary contribution; however, another governmental entity's grant could be designated as a government-mandated nonexchange transaction (GASB-33, par. 9).

In a similar fashion, a governmental entity's overreliance on the "label" to name a transaction may result in misclassifying a nonexchange transaction as an exchange transaction, or vice versa. For example, a source of revenue for a governmental entity may be described as a fee (implying an exchange transaction) but the transaction may have the characteristics of a tax (a nonexchange transaction).

Furthermore, from a practical point of view, classifying a transaction as a nonexchange transaction or an exchange transaction can be difficult and requires close analysis. For example, the GASB defines an "exchange-like transaction" as "an identifiable exchange between the reporting government and another party, but the values exchanged may not be quite equal or the direct benefits of the exchange may not be exclusively for the parties to the exchange." Examples of exchangelike transactions include the following (GASB-33, par. 9):

- Fees for professional licenses and permits
- Passenger facility charges
- Certain tap fees
- Certain developer contributions
- Certain grants and donations

If after careful evaluation the governmental entity determines that the items listed are exchange-like transactions, the standards established by GASB-33 do not apply. Exchange-like transactions should be accounted for in the same manner as exchange transactions.

> **OBSERVATION:** To illustrate the difficulty of distinguishing between a nonexchange transaction and an exchange transaction, the GASB uses the example of a "grant" made by a commercial enterprise to a public university. If the university has exclusive rights to any benefits that may derive from the research effort, the transaction is a nonexchange transaction. However, if the commercial enterprise retains the right of first refusal on the results of the research, it is likely that the transaction is an exchange or exchange-like transaction. In other instances, the GASB notes that the relationship between the university and the commercial enterprise may suggest that the transaction should be divided into two separate parts: an exchange transaction portion and a nonexchange transaction portion. The standards established by GASB-33 would then apply only to the nonexchange portion of the transaction (GASB-33, par. 10).

Therefore, a governmental entity must determine whether a transaction is a nonexchange transaction or an exchange transaction, and if it is a nonexchange transaction, the entity must evaluate the transaction's characteristics in order to properly classify it into one of the four categories based on the guidance established by the GASB, which is discussed later (GASB-33, pars. 9–10).

Revenue Recognition and Expenditure Criteria

The GASB takes the position that all nonexchange transactions are fundamentally controlled by either legislation or contractual requirements or both, and these factors are essential in determining when revenues from nonexchange transactions should be recognized. For example, a governmental entity should recognize derived tax revenues when the related exchange transaction has occurred as defined by the enabling legislation. On the other hand, the entity should recognize imposed nonexchange revenues when it has an enforceable legal claim to receive the revenues. That enforceable legal claim is generally based on the governmental entity's legislative authority to impose and collect the tax. In addition, enabling legislation often identifies the period in which the resources can be used by the entity and the purposes for which the resources can be expended (GASB-33, pars. 16–18).

> **PRACTICE POINT:** GASB-33 defines "enabling legislation" as legislation that "authorizes the government to assess, levy, change, or otherwise mandate payment of resources (from external resource providers) (GASB-33, footnote 4).

> **PRACTICE POINT:** GASB-46 clarifies that a legally enforceable enabling legislation restriction is one that a party external to a government—such as citizens, public interest groups, or the judiciary—can compel a government to honor. GASB-46 states that the legal enforceability of an enabling legislation restriction should be reevaluated if any of the resources raised by the enabling legislation are used for a purpose not specified by the enabling legislation or if a government has other cause for reconsideration. Although the determination that a particular restriction is not legally enforceable may cause a government to review the enforceability of other restrictions, it should not necessarily lead a government to the same conclusion for all enabling legislation restrictions.

On the other hand, the governmental entity should recognize government-mandated nonexchange transactions and voluntary nonexchange transactions when the entity, or entities involved in the transaction, satisfies all eligibility requirements. The relevant eligibility requirements in a government-mandated nonexchange transaction are generally based on enabling legislation and related regulations. Those laws and regulations often identify purpose restrictions that apply to the resources provided under the program. The relevant eligibility requirements in a voluntary nonexchange transaction may arise from enabling legislation or from contractual agreements with a nongovernmental entity. For example, a nongovernmental entity, such as a corporation or an individual, may provide resources to a governmental entity but the provisions of those resources may depend on a number of eligibility factors contained in the donor agreement (GASB-33, par. 21).

Simultaneous Expenditure Recognition

The standards established by GASB-33 generally apply to both revenue and expenditure recognition at the same time. That is, when both parties to the nonexchange transactions are governmental entities, the same standards that the recipient government used to determine whether revenue should be recognized should be used by the provider governmental entity to determine when an expense should be recognized.

This so-called symmetrical approach does not always mean that the two participating governmental parties will record the revenue and the expense/expenditure in the same period. For example, if one governmental entity uses the accrual basis of accounting and the other entity uses the modified accrual basis of accounting, the timing of the revenue and the expense/expenditure may not be the same. On the other hand, even if both parties use the same basis of accounting, the concept of conservatism may change the timing of the transaction for the recipient government. That is, conservatism may require that the provider government recognize an expense but that the recipient government not recognize revenue because there is too much uncertainty as to whether the revenue will be realized. However, in general, when both governmental entities use the same basis of accounting, they should recognize the revenue (recipient government) and the expenditure (provider government) in the same accounting period.

> **OBSERVATION:** The symmetry concept does not apply to revenue and expenditure recognition under the modified accrual basis of accounting in that the availability criterion must be satisfied for revenue recognition but that criterion is not applicable to expenditure recognition. For example, a state government may provide expenditure-driven grants to local governments and therefore the criteria for expenditure-driven grants (see a later discussion in this chapter for the criteria) must be satisfied before an expenditure can be recognized by the state government. Likewise revenue can be recognized by the local governments only if the same criteria that are used for expenditure recognition by the state government are satisfied. However, the local governments must also apply the availability criterion to the nonexchange transaction before revenue can be recorded, but the availability criterion is not relevant to determining when an expenditure is to be recorded by the state government under the modified accrual basis of accounting.

OBSERVATION: The concept of symmetrical recognition applies only to transactions between state and local governmental entities. The recognition standards can be different when one of the parties to the transaction is the federal government or a nongovernmental entity.

Time Requirements and Purpose Restrictions

To determine when nonexchange transactions should be recorded and how those transactions should be presented in the financial statements, the governmental entity needs to consider time requirements and purpose restrictions. Time requirements and purpose restrictions do not have the same effect on the timing of revenue recognition or expense recognition that arise from nonexchange transactions.

Time requirements Resources may be provided by one governmental entity or another party to a governmental entity with the requirement that the resources be used in (or begin to be used in) a specified period(s). GASB-33 notes that "time requirements specify the period or periods when resources are required to be used or when use may begin." Time requirements may be imposed by enabling legislation or by a nongovernmental party that provides the resources to governmental entities. For example, legislation may identify the period in which a recipient governmental entity can use a grant or it may require that resources be used over a specified number of years. In other instances, time requirements imposed by either the provider government or the provider nongovernmental entity may require that the resources provided may never be used (e.g., permanent endowment) or that the resources cannot be used until a specified event has occurred (GASB-33, par. 12).

When a nonexchange transaction is subject to a timing requirement, that requirement generally affects the period in which revenue is recognized by the governmental entity. Also, the effect that a timing requirement has on a nonexchange transaction is dependent on whether the transaction is (1) a government-mandated nonexchange transaction or a voluntary nonexchange transaction or (2) an imposed nonexchange revenue transaction. This is discussed later. Generally, derived tax revenues are not subject to time requirements (GASB-33, par. 13).

Purpose restrictions Purpose restrictions relate to the use of resources that arise from a nonexchange transaction. For example, gasoline taxes may be earmarked specifically and exclusively for road maintenance. Because of the nature of purpose restrictions, a governmental entity should recognize assets, liabilities, revenues, and expenses related to nonexchange transactions in its financial statements without taking into consideration purpose restrictions.

That is, a purpose restriction does not affect the timing of the recognition of a nonexchange transaction. In fact, the GASB notes that a purpose restriction cannot be met unless a nonexchange transaction has taken place (GASB-33, par. 12).

During the period between when a governmental entity records a nonexchange transaction that has purpose restrictions and when the entity uses those resources, the entity should indicate in the equity section of its statement of position the amount of resources that is restricted. Governmental funds should report the restriction as a "reserve," and funds that use proprietary fund accounting should refer to the purpose restriction as a "restriction" of their equity, net asset balance (GASB-33, par. 14).

Purpose restrictions can arise from derived tax revenues, imposed nonexchange revenues, government-mandated nonexchange transactions, and voluntary nonexchange transactions.

DERIVED TAX REVENUE

"Derived tax revenues" are revenues from taxes that are imposed on exchange transactions. Although the tax is imposed on an exchange transaction, the source of revenue is considered revenue from a nonexchange transaction because the exchange transaction is between two parties that do not include a governmental entity. A derived tax revenue has the following principal characteristics (GASB-33, par. 7a):

- A governmental entity imposes the tax on the provider (the individual or enterprise that acquires the income, goods, or services)
- The imposition of the tax is based on an exchange transaction

For example, revenue obtained from a retail sales tax is a derived tax revenue because the tax is imposed by the governmental entity on an exchange (the sale) between a retailer (provider of the tax resource) and a customer. Other examples of derived tax revenues include personal income taxes and corporate income taxes. Under a personal income tax the governmental entity imposes a tax on an exchange transaction (wages earned from an employer). Likewise, when a corporate income tax is imposed by a governmental entity, the business entity is the provider of the tax resource based on the numerous exchanges that occur with customers and vendors.

Revenue Recognition

A governmental entity should recognize derived tax revenue when (1) the exchange that the tax is based on has occurred, (2) the amount is measurable, and (3) the tax is expected to be collected (realizable). For example, when a retail sale occurs, a governmental entity should record the sales tax derived from that sale as revenue, irrespective of when the cash is expected to be received from the retailer. However, in order to recognize revenue under this concept, a governmental entity will often use estimates in order to make an appropriate revenue accrual at the end of the year. For example, certain retail merchants are required to remit sales tax collections during the month after they actually collect the tax from customers. Under this circumstance, the governmental entity will have to estimate at the end of its fiscal year the tax collections that it will receive subsequent to year-end and that were based on sales that occurred on or before the entity's year-end date. In other instances, a governmental entity will have to estimate refunds that it must make after its fiscal year-end. For example, a governmental entity that imposes a personal income tax will generally have to make some refunds (due to overpayments) to individuals who file their tax returns after the end of the governmental entity's fiscal year (GASB-33, par. 16).

A governmental entity usually cannot collect all taxes that are legally due and, therefore, it should report as revenue only the estimated tax that it expects to realize. Under this circumstance, the governmental entity will again need to use various estimation methods in order to report net revenues from derived tax sources. For example, a governmental entity that imposes a personal income tax may use historical trend information (adjusted for current economic and enforcement conditions) in order to provide an appropriate allowance for uncollectible derived tax receivables.

> **PRACTICE POINT:** GASB-33, paragraphs 16 and 18, requires that derived taxes and imposed nonexchange revenues be reported in the statement of activities, net of estimated refunds and estimated uncollectible amounts, respectively. A bad debts expense account should not be used.

Asset Recognition

A governmental entity must record an asset arising from a derived tax revenue transaction when the related exchange transaction occurs or when the entity receives resources, whichever comes first. That asset will be recorded as cash when tax receipts are collected during the accounting period, but it will take the form of a receivable when revenue is accrued at the end of the year. However, if the entity collects taxes before the conditions of revenue recognition (as described above) are satisfied, it should record the receipt of cash as deferred revenue (liability account).

Expenditure/Liability Recognition

Only one governmental entity is involved in a derived tax revenue transaction. For this reason, this type of nonexchange transaction will give rise only to governmental revenue and not governmental expenditure.

Time Restrictions

The GASB notes that generally derived tax revenues are not subject to time restrictions (GASB-33, footnote 8).

> **PRACTICE POINT:** If a derived tax revenue is subject to time restrictions, a governmental entity should use the guidance that applies to imposed nonexchange revenue transactions.

Purpose Restrictions

As noted earlier, purpose restrictions do not affect the timing of revenues related to nonexchange transactions; however, because resources are restricted the governmental entity must disclose that fact in its financial statements. This disclosure requirement may be accomplished by establishing a fund balance reservation (for governmental fund types) or a restriction of net assets (for proprietary or fiduciary fund types). For example, assume that a governmental entity recognizes $100,000 of derived tax revenues during the period (based on exchange transactions covered by the tax legislation) and that the amount is restricted for the purchase of computers for the entity's library. Such transactions would be recorded in a governmental fund in the following manner:

Cash/Taxes Receivable	100,000	
Revenues—Derived Taxes		100,000

To record the recognition of derived tax revenues.

Fund Balance—Unreserved	100,000	
Fund Balance Reserved For The Purchase of Computers		100,000

To record the reservation of fund balance.

> **OBSERVATION:** The purpose restriction does not delay the recognition of the revenue.

IMPOSED NONEXCHANGE REVENUES

"Imposed nonexchange revenues" are based on assessments imposed by a government on a nongovernmental entity (other than assessments that are based on exchange transactions). The principal characteristic of these sources of revenue is that they are "imposed by that government on an act committed or omitted by the provider (such as property ownership or the contravention of a law or regulation) that is not an exchange transaction" (GASB-33, par. 7b). GASB-33 identifies the following as imposed nonexchange revenues:

- Property (ad valorem) taxes assessed by a governmental entity
- Fines and penalties imposed by a governmental entity
- Property seized by a governmental entity
- Property that escheats to a governmental entity

Revenue Recognition

A governmental entity should recognize imposed nonexchange revenues (1) in the period when use of the resources is required or is first permitted by time requirements, (2) when the amount is measurable, and (3) when the tax is expected to be collected (realizable). However, the application of these revenue recognition criteria depends to some extent on the type of revenue source.

Property taxes (and other ad valorem taxes) Generally, the most important example of an imposed nonexchange revenue is property tax. GASB-33 notes that the date that a governmental entity has an enforceable legal claim against a property owner is usually included in the enabling legislation. The legislation may refer to the enforceable legal claim date using a variety of terms, including the lien date, assessment date, or some other descriptive term. The term used in the legislation is not the controlling factor in determining when property tax revenue should be recognized. The basic principle adopted by GASB-33 is that a "receivable should be recognized as soon as the government has a legal claim to a provider's resources that is enforceable through the eventual seizure of the property." The entity should record the revenue/receivable at that date even if the property owner has the right to appeal the assessment or has other due process rights.

The amount of the property taxes receivable is based on the assessed value of the property and the current property tax rate used by the governmental entity. Even though a governmental entity has an enforceable legal claim against property owners, all property taxes assessed will not be collected, and the entity will need to make a reasonable estimate of the amount of uncollectible property taxes and to provide an appropriate allowance.

> **OBSERVATION:** For revenue recognition, GASB-33 emphasizes that the lien date is not the important date. The critical date is the date of an enforceable legal claim. Another important factor is that the enforceable legal claim date does not require that a governmental entity formally place a lien on the property as of that date.

There is one exception to the enforceable legal claim date. In some instances a governmental entity levies property taxes for one particular period but the enforceable legal claim date or the payment due date(s) occurs in another period. Under this circumstance, GASB-33 requires the entity to record the property taxes as revenue in the period in which it levied the taxes (GASB-33, pars. 17–18).

Property taxes are assessed for a fiscal year and are expected to finance expenditures of the year of assessment. Usually on the assessment date or levy date, the property taxes become a lien against the assessed property (demand date criterion), but the actual amounts paid to the governmental unit may be made on a quarterly or monthly basis during the year covered by the assessment. Property taxes should be recorded as revenue on a modified accrual basis and, therefore, recorded when they are both measurable and available (NCGA-1, par. 62).

Measurable The amount of the property taxes receivable is based on the assessed value of the property and the current property tax rate used by the governmental unit. All property taxes assessed will not be collected, and the measurability criterion can be satisfied only if the governmental unit can make a reasonable estimate of the amount of uncollectible property taxes (NCGA-1, par. 64).

When reasonable estimates can be made, the property tax levy may be recorded as follows:

Property Taxes Receivable—Current	400,000	
Revenues—Property Taxes		370,000
Allowance For Uncollectible Property Taxes—Current		30,000

The property tax levy revenues are recorded net of the estimated amount of uncollectible property taxes. No bad debts expense account is used because only expenditures, not expenses, are recorded by governmental funds (NCGA-1, par. 65).

> **PRACTICE POINT:** For financial reporting purposes, bad debts expense should not be reported in a governmental fund type's operating statement because the measurement focus is the flow of current financial resources. The revenue is reported as a net amount because only the net amount is expected to be available during the fiscal period. Since revenues are reported net, it is not

appropriate to record a bad debts expense because the expense does not represent an actual expenditure of current financial resources during the period. Reporting revenues on a net basis does not mean that a governmental unit cannot budget for bad debts expense and monitor the expense through its financial accounting system. When this is done, however, the bad debts expense account used for budgeting or internal purposes must be netted against the related gross revenue account and reported as net revenue for financial reporting purposes. In the following illustration, bad debts expense is not recorded, but the example journal entries could easily be modified to accommodate the use of a bad debts expense account for internal reporting purposes.

During the fiscal year, the routine transactions (such as write-offs of accounts and collections on account) affecting the receivables and allowance accounts may be recorded as follows:

Allowance for Uncollectible Property Taxes—Current	20,000	
Property Taxes Receivable—Current		20,000
Cash	350,000	
Property Taxes Receivable—Current		350,000

It may be determined during the fiscal year that the allowance for uncollectible accounts was either over-provided for or under-provided for. When this conclusion is reached, the allowance account and the revenue account are appropriately adjusted to reflect the change in the accounting estimate. For example, in the current illustration, if it were decided that the allowance provision for the year should have been $27,000 and not $30,000, the following entry would be made:

Allowance for Uncollectible Property Taxes—Current	3,000	
Revenues—Property Taxes		3,000

The adjustment is made directly through the revenue account, thus avoiding the use of a bad debts expense account.

At the end of the year, it may be decided to transfer the balance in the current receivables account to a delinquent account for internal control and analysis. The transfer does not substitute for the write-off of an account when a specific account has been identified as uncollectible. In fact, for reporting purposes, the current and delinquent balances are usually combined since they both represent specific accounts that are expected to ultimately be collected. To continue with the illustration, assume that all of the remaining net receivables are considered collectible, but they are technically delinquent at the end of the fiscal year. In this case, the following entry would be made:

Property Taxes Receivable—Delinquent	30,000	
Allowance for Uncollectible Property Taxes—Current	7,000	
Property Taxes Receivable—Current		30,000
Allowance for Uncollectible Property Taxes—Delinquent		7,000

Available In general, NCGA-1 (Governmental Accounting and Financial Reporting Principles) requires that the modified accrual basis of accounting be used to recognize revenues in government funds and provides the following guidance:

> Revenues and other governmental fund financial resources increments (for example, bond issue proceeds) are recognized in the accounting period in which they become susceptible to accrual—that is, when they become both *measurable* and *available* to finance expenditures of the fiscal period. *Available* means collectible within the current period or soon enough thereafter to be used to pay liabilities of the current period. Application of the "susceptibility to accrual" criterion requires judgment, consideration of the materiality of the item in question, and due regard for the practicality of accrual, as well as consistency in application (paragraph 62).

While the above description of revenue recognition criteria applies to the major sources of governmental revenues, NCGAI-3 (Revenue Recognition—Property Taxes) provided an interpretation of the "available" criterion as it applies to property tax revenues, which is reproduced below.

> When property tax assessment is made, it is to finance the budget of a particular period, and the revenue produced from any property tax assessment should be recognized in the fiscal period for which it was levied, provided the "available" criteria are met. *Available* means then due, or past due and receivable within the current period, and collected within the current period or expected to be collected soon enough thereafter to be used to pay liabilities of the current period. Such time thereafter shall not exceed 60 days. If, because of unusual circumstances, the facts justify a period greater than 60 days, the governmental unit should disclose the period being used and the facts that justify it.

The guidance established in NCGAI-3 addressed two issues with respect to the recognition of property tax revenue. First, it provided some much needed consistency in governmental financial reporting by establishing the "60 days" limitation for determining when resources "could" be considered available to a governmental entity. In addition, the guidance established a new revenue recognition dimension, that applies only to property taxes, by introducing a "demand criterion" (due date).

The introduction of a due date criterion created a situation whereby there was an inconsistency with the basic measurement focus (flow of current financial resources) used by governmental entities. Under the flow of current financial resources, a governmental entity should record as revenues, resources that are available to pay (current) liabilities that exist as of the end of the fiscal year. The inconsistency created with the issuance of NCGAI-3 arises when a governmental entity has a property tax installment due date (for the current year) that occurs after the end of the current fiscal year but the amount is collectible within 60 days of the year end. For example, assume that a governmental entity has levied property taxes for the fiscal year ended June 30, 20X5, and the last of four quarterly installments is due and collectible on July 1, 20X5. Based on the guidance established by NCGAI-3, the property taxes from the last quarterly installment would not be recognized as of June 30, 20X5, because the amount was not *due* until after the end of the year (July 1, 20X5). However, since the property taxes will be collected within 60 days of the end of the year, the revenue should theoretically be recognized as of June 30, 20X5, based on the flow of current financial resources measurement focus.

In order to establish common criteria for the recognition of revenue under the modified accrual basis of accounting, in November 1997, the GASB issued GASBI-5 (Property Tax Revenue Recognition in Governmental Funds), which requires that the *second sentence* of paragraph 8 of NCGAI-3 (which was reproduced earlier in this discussion) be replaced with the following sentence:

> *Available* means collected within the current period or expected to be collected soon enough thereafter to be used to pay liabilities of the current period.

> **OBSERVATION:** The revised wording established by the Interpretation uses the terminology "collected or expected to be collected," whereas paragraph 62 of NCGA-1 refers to "collectible." The GASB recognizes the different phraseology but states that "modifying the terminology in paragraph 62 of NCGA Statement 1 is beyond the scope of this Interpretation." As of the end of a fiscal year, a governmental entity must estimate the amount of property taxes that are expected to be collected within no more than 60 days of the end of the period. In most instances a reasonable estimate can be made (the measurability criterion). In other circumstances, the financial statements will not have to be finalized until after the 60-day

period, so that actual collections during the "stub" period can be the basis for the year-end accrual.

The effect of the Interpretation is to eliminate the due date criterion originally established by NCGAI-3. Thus, in order for property taxes to be reported as revenue (1) the levy must apply to the current year and (2) they must be "collected within the current period or expected to be collected soon enough thereafter to be used to pay liabilities of the current period."

When it is concluded that assessed property tax revenue will not be available, the revenue cannot be recognized in the current assessment period. Continuing with the current illustration, if it is concluded that $4,000 of the property taxes receivable at the end of the fiscal year will not be collected until more than 60 days after the close of the period, the following entry would be made (NCGA-1, par. 65):

Revenues—Property Taxes	4,000	
Deferred Revenues—Property Taxes		4,000

Deferred revenues When property taxes are received in advance of the actual levy or assessment date, the receipt should be recorded as deferred revenue. Subsequently, the revenue is recognized in the period that the tax is levied, assuming the measurable and available criteria are met (NCGA-1, par. 66).

When property taxes are delinquent but are expected to be collected, they should be reported as deferred revenue if it is estimated that the taxes will not be available to pay current obligations of the governmental fund. Generally, this would mean that the delinquent property taxes are not expected to be collected within 60 days of the close of the fiscal year. For example, if it is assumed that the previously illustrated $7,000 of delinquent property taxes are not expected to be collected within 60 days of the close of the fiscal year, the following entry would be made (NCGA-1, par. 66):

Revenues—Property Taxes (30,000 – 7,000)	23,000	
Deferred Revenues—Property Taxes		23,000

Disclosures The governmental unit must disclose the important dates associated with assessed property taxes. These dates may include the lien dates, due dates, and collection dates. In addition, some units may be prohibited from recognizing property tax revenues based on the measurable and available criteria. When this circumstance exists, the nature of the prohibition should be disclosed in a note to the financial statements. Moreover, the fund balance should be reserved by the amount of the property tax revenue recognized under generally accepted accounting principles, but this is not consistent with the legal requirement that must be observed by the governmental unit (NCGAI-3, par. 11).

Other imposed nonexchange revenues All other imposed nonexchange revenues should be recorded in the governmental entity's financial statements as of the date an enforceable legal claim arises unless the enabling legislation establishes a time requirement. When a time requirement is imposed, the entity should recognize revenue when the resources are permitted to be used (GASB-33, pars. 17–18).

> **PRACTICE POINT:** GASB-33 notes that the enforceable legal claim date for other imposed nonexchange revenues can generally be determined by the enabling legislation or related regulations.

Asset Recognition

A governmental entity must record an asset from imposed nonexchange transactions when the entity has an enforceable legal claim to the asset (as explained above) or when the entity receives resources, whichever comes first. That asset will be in the form of cash from tax receipts, fines, and so on, which are collected during the accounting period, but the asset will take the form of a receivable when revenue is accrued at the end of the year. However, if the entity collects imposed nonexchange revenue before the revenue recognition criteria are satisfied, the entity should record the receipt of cash as deferred revenue. In the case of property taxes and other ad valorem taxes, it is possible for the entity to recognize a receivable before revenue is recognized. That is, it can record property taxes as a receivable/deferred revenue when the entity has an enforceable legal claim (as described earlier) even if it levies the taxes after the date of the enforceable legal claim. Under this circumstances, as the entity receives cash (before the period for which the taxes were levied), it reduces the receivable but its deferred revenue remains the same.

Expenditure/Liability Recognition

Only one governmental entity is involved in an imposed nonexchange revenue transaction. For this reason, this type of nonexchange transaction will give rise only to governmental revenue and not governmental expenditures.

Time Restrictions

A time restriction arises when a resource provider requires that a recipient governmental entity use the resources in a specific time period or requires that they not be used until a specified date or event has occurred. When a governmental entity receives resources that are subject to a time restriction, it should record the asset (cash) but recognize deferred revenue rather than revenue. Once the time restriction has occurred or been met, the entity can recognize the imposed nonexchange revenue.

Purpose Restrictions

A purpose restriction does *not* affect the recognition of imposed nonexchange revenues. A governmental entity can record those revenues when the criteria described above are satisfied; however, the entity must indicate in its financial statements that the restricted resources received from an imposed nonexchange revenue source are to be used for a specified purpose. This is accomplished by establishing a fund balance reservation (for governmental fund types) or a restriction of net assets (for proprietary or fiduciary fund types). For example, an entity recognizes $1,000,000 of property taxes during the accounting period (based on the enforceable legal claim concept) and the amount is restricted for the construction of a public school library. At the end of the accounting period the entity would have to reserve $1,000,000 of fund balance.

GOVERNMENT-MANDATED NONEXCHANGE TRANSACTIONS

Revenues from government-mandated nonexchange transactions arise when a governmental entity provides resources to a governmental entity that is at a lower level than the governmental entity that is providing the resources and the provider entity "requires [the recipient] government to use them for a specific purpose or purposes established in the provider's enabling legislation." An example of this is when the federal government (provider government) makes resources available to a state (recipient government), or a state government (provider government) makes resources available to a municipality or other local governmental entity (recipient government). GASB-33 notes that government-mandated nonexchange revenues have the following principal characteristics (GASB-33, par. 7c):

- The provider government requires that the recipient government institute a specific program (or facilitate the performance of a specific program) conducted by the recipient government or nongovernmental entity (secondary recipient entity).
- Certain performance requirements must be fulfilled (other than the provision of cash or other assets in advance).

PRACTICE POINT: A secondary recipient in a government-mandated nonexchange transaction can be a governmental entity or a nongovernmental entity. For example, the federal government mandates that states have a drug rehabilitation program and provides some funds to be used directly by the states (recipient government), and some of the funding is passed through the state to counties and certain not-for-profit organizations. In this example, the counties and not-for-profit organizations are secondary recipients.

Because the resources received by the recipient government must be used for a particular purpose, such resources always create a purpose restriction. In many instances the resources are also subject to eligibility requirements, including time restrictions. An example of a government-mandated nonexchange transaction is the federal government requiring a state government to use federal funds to provide educational counseling to certain disadvantaged groups.

OBSERVATION: Simply mandating that a lower-level governmental entity establish a specific program does *not* create a government-mandated nonexchange transaction itself. The higher-level government must fund the program. The standards established by GASB-33 do not apply to unfunded mandates established by the federal government or state governments, because these types of programs do not involve the exchange of resources (GASB-33, footnote 5).

In a government-mandated nonexchange transaction, if the two governmental entities that are involved in the transaction are state and local governments, they are both subject to GASB accounting and reporting standards. For this reason, the standards established by GASB-33 will apply to the recognition of revenue (by the recipient government) and the recognition of an expenditure (by the provider government). However, if the provider government is the federal government or if a secondary recipient of the resources is a nongovernmental entity, then these entities are not subject to the standards established by GASB-33.

Revenue Recognition

In a government-mandated nonexchange transaction, the recipient government should recognize revenue when all eligibility requirements (which include time requirements) are satisfied. The eligibility requirements are categorized as follows (GASB-33, par. 20):

- Required characteristics of recipients
- Time requirements
- Reimbursements

All eligibility requirements must be satisfied before the recipient government in a government-mandated nonexchange transaction can recognize an operating transaction. If cash or another asset is provided before the eligibility requirements are satisfied, the recipient government records the transaction as an advance rather than as an operating transaction (a transaction that affects the operating statement) (GASB-33, par. 19).

Required characteristics of recipients A government-mandated nonexchange transaction may have an eligibility requirement that stipulates that the recipient (or secondary recipient) must have specific characteristics that have been adopted by the provider government. For example, a state government passed legislation that provides resources to local school districts to make certain expenditures that were mandated in the legislation. Under this eligibility requirement, a government-mandated nonexchange transaction can occur only if the recipient government is a school district. The GASB notes that most government-mandated nonexchange transactions have an eligibility requirement that relates to the required characteristics of recipients or secondary recipients (GASB-33, par. 20a).

Time requirements Provider governments, either through enabling legislation, related regulations, or as part of the appropriations, may identify the period during which recipient governments may expend resources provided by provider governments or they may identify the period when recipient governments can begin expending the resources (and be expended in one or more periods). A recipient government should not recognize resources that it received or expects to receive as operating transactions (i.e., presented on the statement of activity) until the recipient government satisfies the time requirements (and all other eligibility requirements), except as explained in the following paragraph (GASB-33, par. 20b):

> **PRACTICE POINT:** When a recipient government receives government-mandated nonexchange transactions to finance operations or to acquire capital assets in or beginning in a specific period, the provider government should recognize an expense/liability and the recipient government should recognize revenues/receivable when the specified period begins, assuming all other eligibility requirements are satisfied.

In some instances, the time requirement may be permanent (e.g., permanent endowment) or the restriction may state that resources may not be spent until the expiration of a specified number of years or until a specified event has occurred. Examples of this would include a governmental unit of a local government receiving a permanent addition to its endowment or other trusts, or a local public museum receiving contributions of "works of art, historical treasures, and similar assets to capitalized collections." Often during the interim period, the governmental entity may derive benefits from the resources (investment income or display the artwork or historical relics). The recipient government should recognize government-mandated nonexchange transactions of this type as revenue when they are received, assuming the recipient government has satisfied all other eligibility requirements. The time requirement is considered to be satisfied when "the recipient begins to honor the provider's stipulation not to sell, disburse, or consume the resources and continues to be met for as long as the recipient honors that stipulation." However, during the time restriction period (which means indefinitely for a permanent endowment), the recipient government should note in its statement of position the fund balance reservation for a governmental fund type or net assets restriction or similar description for a proprietary or fiduciary fund type (GASB-33, par. 22 and footnotes 12 and 13).

> **OBSERVATION:** If a governmental entity receives contributions of works of art, historical treasures, or other similar assets to be added to capitalized collections, the entity should not capitalize those receipts if the collection to which the assets are being added has not previously been capitalized.

For administrative or practical purposes, a governmental entity may receive resources early from another governmental entity. The receipt of these resources under this circumstance is not considered the receipt of an endowment or other similar receipts as described in the previous paragraph. Therefore, a recipient government should *not* record this type of receipt as revenue until all eligibility requirements that apply to government-mandated nonexchange transactions are satisfied (GASB-33, par. 23).

When the provider government does not establish time requirements, the recipient of the resources and the provider of the resources should recognize the government-mandated nonexchange transaction when all other eligibility requirements are satisfied. Assuming no other eligibility requirements exist, both the recipient government and the provider government should recognize revenue/expenditure based on the first day of the fiscal year of the provider government. For example, the relevant fiscal year of the provider government is generally the first day the appropriation becomes effective. Thus, under that circumstance, both the provider government and the recipient government should record the entire amount related to the government-mandated transaction based on the first day of the provider government's fiscal year (applicable period), unless the provider government has a biennial budgetary process. When the provider government has a biennial budgetary process, each year of the biennial period should be considered a separate year (applicable period), and "the provider and the recipients should allocate one-half of the resources appropriated for the biennium to each applicable period, unless the provider specifies a different allocation" (GASB-33, par. 24).

> **PRACTICE POINT:** When a secondary recipient government is involved in a government-mandated transaction, the primary recipient government's fiscal year should be used rather than the original provider government's fiscal year. For example, the federal government provides a state government with resources and a local government also receives some of the resources. The local government would use the state government's fiscal year to determine when to recognize revenue; however, the state government would use the federal government's fiscal year to determine when it should recognize revenue under the government-mandated program (GASB-33, footnote 14).

GASB-33 notes that some grant programs may be established by a state whereby "the required period of disbursement often is specified through the appropriation of resources under the enabling legislation, rather than as part of the legislation or related regulations." In this circumstance an explicit appropriation must be made by state legislature (the existence of the program under the enabling legislation is not enough) and the period to which the appropriation applies must have begun before a local government can recognize revenue (assuming all eligibility criteria are satisfied). The *GASB Comprehensive Implementation Guide* applies this general guidance by noting that a city that receives a grant award (but not the resources) from a state cannot recognize grant revenue unless the state has appropriated resources for the grant. However, the *GASB Q&A Guide* notes that, for example, if "state law requires the state treasurer to pay the grant whether or not the legislature appropriates resources," the city should recognize the grant when it is awarded.

Reimbursements Some government-mandated nonexchange transactions are based on a reimbursement arrangement. These transactions are referred to as "reimbursement-type transactions" or "expenditure-driven grant programs." The fundamental characteristic of these types of programs is that the provider government "stipulates that a recipient cannot qualify for resources without first incurring allowable costs under the provider's program." When government-mandated nonexchange transactions are subject to a reimbursement eligibility requirement, the recipient government should not recognize revenue until the recipient has incurred eligible costs that are reimbursable under the program (GASB-33, pars. 15 and 20c).

> **PRACTICE POINT:** GASB-33 notes that a reimbursement eligibility requirement is not a purpose restriction and, therefore, is not subject to financial statement presentation requirements that apply to purpose restrictions.

The *GASB Comprehensive Implementation Guide* raises the issue of whether capital grants subject to a reimbursement requirement can be accounted for in a manner similar to the accounting for completed contracts in commercial accounting. That is, the grant revenue is not recognized until the capital project is completed. The *GASB Comprehensive Implementation Guide* states that capital grants that are expenditure-driven are no different from other expenditure-driven grants and therefore the revenue should be recognized when the criteria listed above are satisfied.

> **PRACTICE POINT:** Under the modified accrual basis of accounting, the recognition of capital grant revenue that is expenditure-driven must satisfy the availability criterion.

Asset Recognition

An asset (receivable) must be recorded by the recipient government when the revenue criteria for government-mandated nonexchange transactions described above are satisfied. If the recipient government collects the government-mandated nonexchange revenue before the revenue recognition criteria are satisfied, the recipient government should record the receipt of cash as deferred revenue.

> **PRACTICE POINT:** The recognition of revenue by the recipient government and expenditures by the provider government should not be delayed because routine administrative procedures have not been completed. GASB-33 notes that these procedures could include filing claims for reimbursements under an expenditure-driven program or completing progress reports required by the provider government (GASB-33, footnote 10).

VOLUNTARY NONEXCHANGE TRANSACTIONS

Voluntary nonexchange transactions arise from "legislative or contractual agreements, other than exchanges, entered into willingly by two or more parties." Avoluntary nonexchange transaction can be based on either a written or an oral agreement, assuming the latter is verifiable. The principal characteristics of voluntary nonexchange transactions are listed below (GASB-33, par. 7d and footnote 6):

- They are not imposed on the provider or the recipient
- Satisfaction of eligibility requirements (other than the provision of cash or other assets in advance) is necessary for a transaction to occur

In a voluntary nonexchange transaction, a governmental entity may be the recipient or the provider of the resources, and the second party of the transaction may be another governmental entity or a nongovernmental entity, such as an individual or a not-for-profit organization. Examples of voluntary nonexchange transactions include certain grants, some entitlements, and donations. Voluntary nonexchange transactions may involve purpose restrictions and/ or time requirements, and they often require that resources be returned to the provider if purpose restrictions or eligibility requirements are contravened after the voluntary nonexchange transaction has been recognized by a governmental entity.

NOTE: For convenience, in the following discussion of voluntary nonexchange transactions it is assumed that both parties to the nonexchange transaction are governmental entities. When one of the parties to the nonexchange transaction is not a governmental entity, that nongovernmental entity is not required to follow the standards established by GASB-33. The GASB established the same (with one exception) accounting standards for government-mandated nonexchange transactions and voluntary nonexchange transactions. These standards are explained in the previous section. (The accounting standard exception for voluntary nonexchange transactions is that there are four possible eligibility requirements instead of three. The additional requirement is the contingency eligibility, which is discussed later in this section.)

Revenue Recognition

In a voluntary nonexchange transaction, the provider and the recipient should recognize the nonexchange transaction when all eligibility requirements (which include time requirements) are satisfied. The eligibility requirements are categorized as follows (GASB-33, par. 20):

- Required characteristics of recipients (discussed earlier)
- Time requirements (discussed earlier)
- Reimbursements (discussed earlier)
- Contingencies (discussed below)

All eligibility requirements must be satisfied before the parties to a voluntary nonexchange transaction can record an operating transaction. If a recipient government receives cash or other assets before the eligibility requirements are satisfied, the entity must record the transaction as an advance rather than as an operating transaction (a transaction that affects the operating statement). Likewise, until all eligibility requirements are satisfied, the provider government does not have a liability to transfer resources and the recipient does not have a right (receivable) to the resources (GASB-33, par. 19).

> **PRACTICE POINT:** In some instances where the provider of the resources is a nongovernmental entity, resources may be made on an installment basis. If there is no time restriction(s) (or other eligibility requirements) that applies to the donation, the GASB requires that the recipient government recognize the full amount of the donation as revenue. If the installments are spread over more than one year, the entity should recognize the amount of revenue as the present value of the future cash flows.

Contingencies The final possible eligibility requirement for a voluntary nonexchange transaction is based on a contingency imposed by the provider. That is, the right to receive resources by the recipient can occur only if the recipient has performed the specified requirement. For example, a state university has been promised resources by a private donor if the university can persuade its alumni to match dollar-for-dollar the promised gift of the original donor. Under this circumstance, the university can recognize an operating transaction only if the university obtains the appropriate resources from its alumni.

Asset Recognition

An asset (receivable) must be recorded by the recipient when it has satisfied the revenue criteria for voluntary nonexchange transactions described above. If the recipient collects resources from a voluntary nonexchange transaction before the recipient satisfies the revenue recognition criteria, the recipient should record the receipt of cash as deferred revenue (GASB-33, par. 21).

Pledges

Voluntary nonexchange transactions often involve pledges (promises to pay) from nongovernmental entities (e.g., individuals, business enterprises, or not-for-profit organizations). Such promises may involve cash, works of art, and various other assets, and they may or may not involve purpose restrictions or time requirements. The recipient government should record pledges as revenue by the recipient government when "all eligibility requirements are met, provided that the promise is verifiable and the resources are measurable and probable of collection." The governmental entity may have to establish an allowance account before the entity can recognize pledges as revenue so that the total pledges are reported at their expected realizable value (GASB-33, par. 25).

> **PRACTICE POINT:** The standards established by GASB-33, paragraph 22, apply to pledges. The recipient government should recognize pledges of resources that *cannot* be sold, disbursed, or consumed until after a passage of a specified period of time or the occurrence of a specified event as revenue when they are received, assuming the government has satisfied all other eligibility requirements. For example, if a government receives a pledge that involves additions to the governmental entity's permanent endowment, term endowments, or contributions of works of art, historical treasures, and similar assets to be included in the entity's collection, the governmental entity should not recognize the pledge as revenue until it receives the pledged property (GASB-33, footnote 15).

Expenditure/Liability Recognition

When the provider of resources in a voluntary nonexchange transaction is a government, that government should recognize an expenditure based on the same criteria that are used by the recipient government to recognize revenues (as discussed above). If the expenditure recognition criteria are not satisfied and the provider government has made a cash payment to the recipient government, the provider government should record the payment as an advance (asset) (GASB-33, par. 21).

ACCOUNTING AND REPORTING ISSUES

Subsequent Contravention of Eligibility Requirements or Purpose Restrictions

Sometimes a recipient government records a nonexchange transaction as an operating transaction, but subsequent events indicate that resources will not be transferred in a manner originally anticipated by both parties or that resources transferred will have to be returned to the provider. This situation may arise because (1) eligibility requirements related to a government-mandated transaction or a voluntary nonexchange transaction are no longer being satisfied or (2) the recipient will not satisfy a purpose restriction within the time period specified (GASB-33, par. 26).

When it is *probable* (likely to occur) that the recipient will not receive the resources or will be required to return all or part of the resources already received, the following procedures should be observed:

- The provider government should recognize as revenue (1) the amount of resources that will not be provided to the recipient (but that have already been recognized as an expenditure by the provider) and/or (2) the amount of resources already provided to the recipient but expected to be returned
- The recipient government should recognize as an expenditure (1) the amount of resources that have been promised by the provider (and already recognized as revenue by the recipient) and/or (2) the amount or resources already received by the recipient but expected to be returned to the provider

PRACTICE POINT: The AICPA's *State and Local Governments* Guide states that a similar situation arises when grant revenues are subject to a grant audit and the possibility of an adjustment has arisen. Under this development, the recipient governmental entity should consider whether a loss contingency arises based on the standards established by FAS-5 (Accounting for Contingencies) to determine whether a liability should be reported (or netted against a related receivable) or a note disclosure should be made.

Nonexchange Revenues Administered or Collected by Another Government

A governmental entity may collect derived tax revenues or imposed nonexchange revenues on behalf of a recipient government that imposes the tax. For example, a state government administers a local sales tax (imposed by the locality) in conjunction with the state sales tax it imposes. In this circumstance, GASB-33 requires that the recipient government apply the relevant revenue recognition standards that apply to derived tax revenues and imposed nonexchange revenues. The state government would not record revenue for the portion of the tax due to the recipient governmental entity but, rather, would recognize a liability. In some instances, the recipient government may need to estimate the amount of revenue to be accrued in a particular accounting period. The GASB assumes that the recipient government, because it imposes the tax, will have sufficient information to make an appropriate accrual at the end of the year (GASB-33, par. 27).

Derived tax revenues and imposed nonexchange revenues of one governmental entity that are shared with another governmental entity (but not imposed by the recipient government) are based on two transactions, namely, (1) events or actions that give rise to the derived tax revenue or the imposed nonexchange revenue and (2) the sharing of the revenue by one governmental entity (provider government) with another governmental entity (recipient government).

In the first transaction, a governmental entity would record revenue based on the criteria established by GASB-33, depending on whether the revenue is from derived taxes or imposed nonexchange transactions. The second transaction results in both the recording of an expenditure/expense (by the provider government) and revenue (by the recipient government) and represents either a government-mandated or a voluntary nonexchange transaction. GASB-36 requires that both the provider government and the recipient government record the expenditure/expense and revenue, respectively based on the government-mandated nonexchange or voluntary nonexchange criteria. Thus, the two governments would record the sharing of the tax revenue (as an expenditure/expense and a revenue in the same period (GASB-36, par. 2).

Continuing appropriation In some instances shared nonexchange revenues may be based on a continuing appropriation. A continuing appropriation is an "appropriation that, once established, is automatically renewed without further legislative action, period after period, until altered or revoked." When shared revenues are based on continuing appropriations, the eligibility requirement (which is the basis for recording the government-mandated or voluntary nonexchange transaction) is satisfied when either (1) the underlying transaction occurs (for derived tax revenue) or (2) the period when resources were required to be used or the first period that use was permitted has occurred (for imposed nonexchange transactions). For example, GASB-36 points out that "when a state shares its sales taxes under the requirements of a continuing appropriation, the recipient should record revenues and receivables when the underlying sales occur, regardless of whether the guidance for derived tax revenues or for government-mandated and voluntary nonexchange transactions applies."

When revenue sharing occurs based on a continuing appropriation, the recipient government should make any accrual of revenue based on information supplied by the provider government. For example, in the case of shared sales taxes, the provider government should make available to the recipient governments information about sales tax revenues that have been earned in the current period but that will not be collected from merchants until the following period. GASB-36 points out "if notification by the provider government is not available in a timely manner, recipient governments should use a reasonable estimate of the amount to be accrued."

Revenue Recognition Using the Modified Accrual Basis of Accounting

The standards established by GASB-33 retain the current fundamental criterion for revenue recognition that applies to the modified accrual basis of accounting, namely that revenue be recorded when it is both available and measurable. NCGA-1 (Governmental Accounting and Financial Reporting Principles) defines "available" as "collectible within the current period or soon enough thereafter to be used to pay liabilities of the current period." Revenue is measurable when it is subject to reasonable estimation. In addition, GASB-33 specifically states that revenue should be recognized only when it is probable (likely to occur) that it will be collected. As discussed below, the same standards for the recognition of revenue under the accrual basis of accounting should be used to record revenue under the modified accrual basis of accounting, except the revenue must be available (GASB-33, pars. 29–30).

Note disclosure for availability criterion As described above, the availability criterion requires that resources only be recorded as revenue if those resources are expected to be collected or otherwise realized in time to pay liabilities reported in the governmental fund at the end of the accounting period. In practice, the period of collectibility has generally ranged from thirty days to as much as a year. GASB-38 (Certain Financial Statement Note Disclosures) does not attempt to define the availability criterion in a more restricted manner, but it does require a governmental entity to specifically disclose what period of time is used to implement the standard. For example, the disclosure requirement could be met by simply stating "the city considers receivables collected within sixty days after year-end to be available and recognizes them as revenues of the current year" (GASB-38, par. 7).

Derived tax revenues GASB-33 requires that derived tax revenues be recorded in the same period in which the exchange transaction that generates the tax revenue occurs. Thus, once the taxable transaction has occurred, the governmental entity has an enforceable legal claim to the tax resources. If the resources related to the enforceable legal claim are available to the governmental entity, then, under the modified accrual basis of accounting, the governmental entity should record revenue.

Imposed nonexchange revenues As defined earlier, an imposed nonexchange revenue is characterized by an assessment implemented by a governmental entity "on an act committed or omitted by the provider (such as property ownership or the contravention of a law or regulation) that is not an exchange transaction." For property taxes, the standards established by GASB-33 require that governmental entities continue to use the criteria established by NCGAI-3, as amended, in order to record revenues related to property taxes. For imposed nonexchange revenues that are derived from sources other than property taxes, the governmental entity should record revenue when an enforceable legal claim arises and the related resources are available to the governmental entity.

Government-mandated nonexchange transactions Under the modified accrual basis of accounting, a recipient governmental entity should record resources received from another governmental entity that are considered government-mandated nonexchange transactions as revenue when the recipient entity has satisfied all eligibility requirements and the related resources are available to the entity.

Voluntary nonexchange transactions The characteristics of a voluntary nonexchange transaction are that (1) it is not imposed on the provider or the recipient and (2) eligibility requirements (including time requirements) must be satisfied before the transaction can occur. GASB-33 requires that the governmental entity record revenues related to a voluntary nonexchange transaction when all eligibility requirements have been satisfied and the related resources are available to the entity.

Summary of Revenue/Expenditure Recognition Criteria

Exhibit 17-1 summarizes the revenue and expense regonition criteria established by GASB-33.

EXHIBIT 17-1
REVENUE AND EXPENDITURE RECOGNITION CRITERIA

	Derived Tax Revenue	*Imposed Nonexchange Revenues*	*Goverment-Mandated Nonexchange Transactions*	*Voluntary Nonexchange Transactions*
Revenue Recognition Criteria(a)	The exchange that the tax is based on has occurred.(b)	When resources are required to be used or first period that use is permitted (b)(c)	Recipient government has satisfied all applicable eligibility requirements (required characteristics of recipients, time requirements and reimbursements).(b)	Recipient party has satisfied all applicable eligibility requirements (required characteristics of recipients, time requirements reimbursements and contingencies).(b)

Expenditure Recognition Criteria	Due to the parties involved in the transaction, no expenditure can arise for a governmental entity.	Due to the parties involved in the transaction, no expenditure can arise for a governmental entity.	Recipient government has met all eligibility requirements (as described above).	Recipient party has met all eligibility requirements (as described above).
Effect of a Time Restriction	Generally not subject to time restrictions	Revenue should not be recognized until the time restriction is satisfied.	Revenue should not be recognized until the time restriction is satisfied.(d)	Revenue should not be recognized until the time restriction is satisfied.(d)
Effect of a Purpose Restriction	The restriction should be disclosed in the financial statements.	The restriction should be disclosed in the financial statements.	The restriction should be disclosed in the financial statements.	The restriction should be disclosed in the financial statements.

(a) When revenue is recognized under the modified accrual basis of accounting, the available criterion must be satisfied.

(b) In addition, revenue can be recognized only if the amount is *measurable* (subject to reasonable estimation) and *realizable* (expected to be collected). Nonexchange transactions that are not recognizable because they are not measurable must be disclosed in the governmental entity's financial statements.

(c) When property taxes are levied for one particular period but the enforceable legal claim date or the payment due date(s) occurs in another period, GASB-33 requires that property tax revenue be recorded in the period for which the property tax is levied.

(d) When the provider of the resources prohibits the sale, disbursement, or consumption of resources for a specified period of time (or indefinitely, as in permanent endowment), or until a specified event has occurred, revenue should be recorded when the asset is received but the restriction be disclosed in the entity's financial statements.

Certain Grants and Other Financial Assistance

GASB-24 (Accounting and Financial Reporting for Certain Grants and Other Financial Assistance) establishes standards for on grants and other financial assistance that are classified as (1) pass-through grants, (2) food stamps, and (3) on-behalf payments for fringe benefits and salaries (GASB-24, par. 2).

Pass-through grants Pass-through grants are "grants and other financial assistance received by a governmental entity to transfer to or spend on behalf of a secondary recipient." A secondary recipient is "the individual or organization, government or otherwise, that is the ultimate recipient of a pass-through grant, or another recipient organization that passes the grant through to the ultimate recipient." The governmental entity that receives the grant that is distributed to a secondary recipient is the recipient government (GASB-24, par. 5 and Glossary).

For example, the federal government (the grantor government) may make a grant to a state government (recipient governmental entity) that is to be distributed by the state government to certain municipal governments (secondary recipients) within the state. The secondary recipient does not have to be a governmental entity, but rather could be individuals or nongovernmental organizations.

GASB-24 requires that cash pass-through grants generally be recorded simultaneously as revenue and expenditures or expenses in a governmental fund, or proprietary fund. Only in those instances when the recipient government functions as a cash conduit should a pass-through grant be accounted for in an Agency Fund. The GASB describes cash conduit activity as transmitting grantor-supplied moneys "without having administrative or direct financial involvement in the program." Applying the standard requires that a governmental entity evaluate its administrative and financial roles in a grant program (GASB-24, par. 5).

Administrative involvement The GASB takes the position that administrative involvement is based on whether the recipient government's role in the grant program constitutes an operational responsibility for the grant program. While there is no attempt to formally define administrative involvement, the GASB notes that the following activities constitute such involvement:

- Monitoring secondary recipients for compliance with specific requirements established by the program
- Determining which secondary recipients are eligible for grant payments (even if eligibility criteria are established by the provider government)
- Exercising some discretion in determining how resources are to be allocated

Administrative involvement may occur before the receipt of the grant by the recipient government or after the grant is received. Both pre-grant activities and post-grant activities should be evaluated to determine whether the recipient government is exercising administrative involvement in the grant program (GASB-24, par. 5).

Direct financial involvement A recipient governmental entity's role in a grant program is considered more than custodial when the entity has a direct financial involvement in the program. While the GASB does not provide a definition of direct financial involvement, the following activities would suggest that the entity's role is beyond that of custodial responsibility (GASB-24, par. 5):

- The recipient government is required to provide matching funds
- The recipient government is responsible for disallowed costs

> **OBSERVATION:** The GASB does not require a recipient government to consider payments for administrative costs (an indirect financial involvement) when determining whether its role is more than custodial. However, if the indirect financial payments are more than incidental, the recipient government's participation satisfies the administrative involvement criteria described in the standard and, therefore, it would be inappropriate to account for the pass-through grant in an Agency Fund.

Finally, the standards established by GASB-24 emphasize that all cash pass-through grants must be reported in the financial statements of the recipient government. Those grant programs considered strictly custodial in nature would be accounted for in an Agency Fund. Those grant programs that are characterized by either administrative involvement or direct financial involvement would be accounted for in a governmental fund, or a proprietary fund. It is not appropriate to record grant activity by establishing an asset and a related liability account, except in an Agency Fund. Even in an Agency Fund there must be a separate statement of changes in assets and liabilities that summarizes activity for the period (GASB-24, par. 5).

The *GASB Comprehensive Implementation Guide* states that when a state receives a grant from the federal government and subsequently passes the resources to local governments for capital purposes, the state should report the receipt as an operational grant (program revenue) and not as a capital grant. A capital grant arises only "if it is restricted to the acquisition, construction, or improvement of the state's capital assets." The distributions to the localities are reported as an expenditure.

> **PRACTICE POINT:** The AICPA's *State and Local Governments* Guide states that when a governmental entity receives a fee related to the administration of pass-through grants, the fee should be recorded as revenue.

Food stamps The food stamp program is defined in GASB-24 as "a federal program [Catalog of Federal Domestic Assistance (CFDA) program number 10.551] that is intended to improve the diets of members of low-income households by increasing their ability to purchase food." Currently, food stamps are provided by the federal government and are distributed directly to recipients by agents (including local governments) of the state governments. Recipients spend food stamps at retail establishments, and the retailers in turn deposit the spent food stamps with their banks (GASB-24, par. 6).

GASB-24 requires that receipts and disbursements under the food stamp program be accounted for by the states in the General Fund or a Special Revenue Fund. An expenditure would be recognized when benefits are distributed by the state government or its agent to a lowincome recipient. Under a manual system, distribution of benefits is assumed to occur when the food stamps are physically given to the recipients. Under the electronic system, distribution is assumed to occur when an individual uses the benefits at a retail establishment.

The GASB takes the position that the food stamp program is expenditure-driven. Therefore, when an expenditure is recognized there is an equal and simultaneous recognition of revenue. Any food stamps held by the state government at the end of the period should be reported as an asset and deferred revenue. Generally, the existence of food stamps at the end of a period could occur only in a manual system. Finally, all food stamp transactions should be recorded based on the face value of the food stamps (GASB-24, par. 6).

> **OBSERVATION:** When a state government has undistributed food stamps at the end of the period (usually only possible in a manual system), the asset should not be classified as cash or a cash-equivalent item. However, the GASB does not take a position on which title should be used.

> **PRACTICE POINT:** The standards established by GASB-24 for the food stamp program apply only to state governments. Under the current manual system of food stamp distribution, localities may be involved in the distribution system. The GASB does not require a note disclosure for these local governments, stating that it is unnecessary to describe the food stamp program activity in which a local government is involved.

On-behalf payments for fringe benefits and salaries GASB defines on-behalf payments for fringe benefits and salaries as "direct payments made by one entity (the paying entity or paying government) to a third-party recipient for the employees of another, legally separate entity (the employer entity or employer government)." They include payments made by governmental entities on behalf of nongovernmental entities and payments made by nongovernmental entities on behalf of governmental entities and may be made for volunteers as well as for paid employees of the employer entity (GASB-24, par. 7 and Glossary).

Perhaps the best example of an on-behalf payment is a pension contribution made by a state government (paying government) to the state's teachers' pension fund (third-party recipient) for employees of a school district (employer government) within the state.

On-behalf payments also include payments by a governmental entity to volunteers of another governmental entity. For example, a state government may make pension payments or other fringe benefit payments for individuals who serve as volunteer firefighters for rural fire districts (GASB-24, par. 7).

The employer entity and the paying entity may be either a governmental or a nongovernmental entity. The third-party recipient may be either an individual or an organization. Therefore, on-behalf payments addressed by GASB-24 include payments by nongovernmental entities made on behalf of governmental employees and payments made by governmental entities on behalf of nongovernmental employees. An example of the latter circumstance is the payment of faculty salaries at a public college or university by a private (not-for-profit) research foundation affiliated with the educational institution.

The standards established for on-behalf payments for fringe benefits and salaries must be observed by the employer government and the paying government.

Financial reporting by the employer governmental entity GASB-24 requires that an on-behalf payment made by the paying governmental entity be recognized both as an expenditure or expense and as revenue by the employer governmental entity. The specific amount to be recorded depends on whether the employer government is legally responsible for payment of the fringe benefit or salary. "Legally responsible entity" is defined as follows (GASB-24, par. 8):

> For on-behalf payments for fringe benefits and salaries, the entity is required by legal or contractual provisions to make the payment. Legal provisions include those arising from constitutions, charters, ordinances, resolutions, governing body orders, and intergovernmental grant or contract regulations.

When the employer government is not legally responsible for the payment, the amount to be recorded is determined by the amount actually paid by the paying governmental entity. Thus, if a state government makes a $100,000 contribution to the state pension fund on behalf of a locality, the locality would simultaneously record an expenditure or expense of $100,000 and an equal amount of revenue (GASB-24, par. 8).

A measurement problem arises when the employer government is legally responsible for payment of expenditures or expenses that are being funded by the paying government. The question arises about whether the amount of the expenditure or expense should be based on the actual payment made by the paying government or whether it should be recorded using governmental GAAP that would otherwise apply to the particular transaction.

GASB-24 requires that on-behalf payments for fringe benefits and salaries be recorded as expenditures or expenses on the basis of applicable accounting standards when the employer government is legally responsible for the item. Using this approach, the employer government refers to existing accounting standards to determine the amount of the expenditure or expense and compares that amount with the on-behalf payments made by the paying governmental entity. Any difference between the two amounts is reflected in the employer government's financial statements as an asset or a liability. The amount of revenue recognized is equal to the on-behalf payments made by the paying government and any amounts receivable from the paying government at the end of the year (GASB-24, par. 8).

> **PRACTICE POINT:** When the employer government is legally responsible for the payment from a governmental fund and there is a difference between the expenditure computed under governmental GAAP and the payment made by the paying government, modified accrual accounting standards are used to determine the presentation of any resulting asset or liability. If a liability arises from the comparison, the employer government determines whether the liability will be liquidated with expendable available financial resources. An asset that arises from the comparison is reported in the entity's financial statements if the asset represents expendable financial resources that are available for appropriation and expenditure during the next accounting period.

The accounting for on-behalf fringe benefits and salaries as prescribed by GASB-24 encourages paying governmental entities to provide employer governments with information that enables the employer governments to properly record expenditures or expenses and related revenue. In some instances, paying governments will be unable to supply employer governments with the amounts of payments made specifically on their behalf. If the paying governmental entity or the third-party recipient cannot or will not provide such information, GASB-24 requires that the employer government estimate the amount of expenditure or expense and revenue that should be recorded (GASB-24, par. 9).

A cost allocation problem arises when a paying government that provides funds to cost-sharing, multiple-employer pension plans makes a single payment that relates to many employer governments. In these circumstances, GASB-24 requires that the allocation method used to apportion the total funding among the employer governments be systematic and rational and be applied on a consistent basis. More specifically, the allocation should be based on "the ratio of an individual employer's covered payroll to the entire covered payroll related to the on-behalf payments" (GASB-24, par. 9).

PRACTICE POINT: The *GASB Comprehensive Implementation Guide* states that items recognized as revenues based on the standards established by GASB-24 should be reported as program revenues.

Differing fiscal years Because an employer government's recognition of expenditures or expenses and revenue is based on the policies and actions of the paying government, a financial reporting problem arises when the two entities do not have the same fiscal year end. In these circumstances, the employer government should attempt to obtain information from the paying government (or the third-party entity, if relevant) that would coincide with the employer government's year end. If the employer government is unable to obtain such information, the employer government should base its expenditure or expense recognition on the paying government's year-end data. To make the computation, the employer government can use either (1) the paying government's year-end date that occurs during the employer government's same fiscal year or (2) the paying government's year-end date that occurs during the employer government's first quarter subsequent to its (the employer government's) current fiscal year-end date. Once the paying government's appropriate year-end date is selected, the approach should be applied consistently from year to year (GASB-24, par. 10).

Allocation among funds On-behalf payments create a potential allocation problem among an employer government's funds. A question arises about how an on-behalf payment made by a state government for a city should be allocated to the various individual funds that might benefit from the subsidy. For example, a state government may make a single payment for employees whose activities are associated with a Special Revenue Fund and an Enterprise Fund. GASB-24 states that no allocation is necessary. However, allocation is not prohibited (GASB-24, par. 11).

Generally, when on-behalf payments are reported in only one fund, the fund used should be the General Fund (GASB-24, par. 11).

OBSERVATION: Although GASB-24 recommends that the General Fund be used when a single fund is used to account for on-behalf payments, each situation should be examined to determine whether that guidance is reasonable. For example, GASB-24 notes that when all on-behalf payments for fringe benefits and salaries are related to an Enterprise Fund, the on-behalf payments should be accounted for in the Enterprise Fund and not in the reporting entity's General Fund.

Disclosures An employer government should make the following disclosures regarding on-behalf payments in the notes to its financial statements (GASB-24, par. 12):

- Amounts of expenditure or expense and revenue recognized due to on-behalf payments for fringe benefits and salaries
- If on-behalf payments for pension plans have been made and the employer government is not legally responsible for the payments, the name of the plan and the name of the paying government

Financial reporting by the paying governmental entity GASB-24 requires the governmental entity that makes on-behalf payments for fringe benefits and salaries to classify the payments in the same way as other similar cash grants made to other entities. For example, if a state government makes on-behalf pension payments for public schoolteachers, the classification of those payments depends on how the state government classifies similar educational cash grants made to public school districts. If, for example, the latter are classified as education expenditures, the on-behalf payments should also be reported as education expenditures, not as pension expenditures (GASB-24, par. 13).

The GASB states that the legal responsibility for the funding of on-behalf payments for fringe benefits and salaries has no effect on determining how the payments should be categorized on the paying government's financial statements.

Reporting entity considerations A reporting problem arises when the two parties to pass-through grants or on-behalf payments for fringe benefits and salaries are part of the same reporting entity. The standards established in GASB-24 apply to pass-through grants and on-behalf payments for entities that are combined as part of a single reporting entity. Under these circumstances, expenditures or expenses and revenues recognized must be reclassified as transfers in a manner consistent with the standards established by GASB-14 (The Financial Reporting Entity) (GASB-24, par. 14).

For example, assume that a municipal government (paying government) makes a $500,000 pension payment for a governmental component unit (employer government). To adhere to the standards established by GASB-24, each entity would make the following entries to record the on-behalf payment:

Paying Government:		
Expenditures—Pensions	500,000	
Cash		500,000
Employer Government (Component Unit):		
Expenditures—Pensions	500,000	
Revenues—On-Behalf Payments		500,000

Note: In the example it is assumed that the pension payment is made to a third party that administers the public pension system.

When the financial statements of the two entities are blended to prepare the reporting entity's financial statements, the following worksheet entries would be made:

Transfers Out	500,000	
Expenditures—Pensions		500,000
Revenues—On-Behalf Payments	500,000	
Transfers In		500,000

Recording Nonexchange Transactions in Governmental Funds

Although the standards established in GASB-33 are written in the context of the accrual basis of accounting, they provide a significant amount of general guidance for nonexchange transactions irrespective of the basis of accounting that is used by a governmental entity. For this reason, the GASB has decided that the general guidance provided in the GASB-33 applies to governmental activities (activities accounted for in such funds as the General Fund and Special Revenue Funds) except that they must be modified to observe the modified accrual basis of accounting. However, in applying the standards the availability criterion must be satisfied when revenue is recognized under the modified accrual basis of accounting. In addition, under both the accrual basis of accounting and the modified accrual basis of accounting, nonexchange transactions are recorded only when transactions are measurable (subject to reasonable estimation) and collection is probable (realizable). GASB-33 defines "probable" as likely to occur. Nonexchange transactions that are not recorded because the measurable criterion cannot be satisfied must be disclosed in a governmental entity's financial statements (GASB-33, par. 11).

Recording Nonexchange Transactions in Proprietary and Fiduciary Funds

Revenues from nonexchange transactions should be recognized in proprietary and fiduciary funds based on accrual accounting concepts and be consistent with the standards established by GASB-33.

Presenting Nonexchange Transactions in Government-Wide Financial Statements

Revenues presented in a governmental entity's statement of activities should be based on accrual accounting concepts and be consistent with the standards established by GASB-33.

REVENUES: EXCHANGE TRANSACTIONS

In an exchange transaction the governmental entity and the other party to the transaction exchange cash, goods, or services that are essentially of the same value. For example, revenue earned from providing water services to customers is an exchange transaction. Unlike nonexchange transactions, the GASB has not provided comprehensive guidance for the recognition of exchange transactions.

> **NOTE:** The GASB has provided guidance for the recognition of investment income for certain investments. This guidance is discussed in Chapter 9, "Deposits and Investments."

Recording Exchange Transactions in Governmental Funds

Like nonexchange transactions, exchange transactions should be recorded in a governmental fund when they are measurable, available, and collection is probable. For example, a governmental entity may sell a parcel of land to another party and receive a down payment and a three-year annual note for the balance of the purchase price. The down payment, because it is available to pay current expenditures, would be recorded as revenue (an other source of financial resources or a special item); however, the subsequent installments would not be recorded as revenue until the cash is received.

Recording Exchange Transactions in Proprietary and Fiduciary Funds

FASB:CS-6 (Elements of Financial Statements) defines "revenues" as "inflows or other enhancements of assets of an entity or settlements of its liabilities (or a combination of both) during a period from delivering or producing goods, rendering services, or other activities that constitute the entity's ongoing major or central operations." A proprietary or fiduciary fund should recognize revenue on an accrual basis, meaning that revenue is considered realized when (1) the earning process is complete or virtually complete and (2) an exchange has taken place.

> **PRACTICE ALERT:** In August 2006, the Governmental Accounting Standards Board (GASB) issued an exposure draft on a proposed Concepts Statement entitled "Elements of Financial Statements." This proposed Concepts Statement would be the fourth issued by the GASB, and it proposes new definitions for seven elements of historically based financial statements of state and local governments as follows:

- Elements of the statement of financial position:

  1. Assets
  2. Liabilities
  3. Deferred Outflow of Resources
  4. Deferred Inflow of Resources
  5. Net Position

- Elements of the resources flow statements:

  6. Inflow of Resources
  7. Outflow of Resources

The GASB-proposed definitions of the elements are based upon the inherent characteristics of each element and are linked by a common definition feature in that they are based on the concept of measuring and reporting *resources.* The proposed definitions of the elements apply to an entity that is a governmental unit (that is, a legal entity) and are applicable to any measurement focus under which financial statements may be prepared, for example, economic resources, current financial resources, and cash resources measurement focuses. As CCH's 2008 *Governmental GAAP Guide* went to press the GASB was redeliberating the proposed statement based on the responses to the exposure draft. However, the results of this project are likely to differ from the concepts in FASB:CS-6.

GASB-20 allows for two distinct but acceptable alternatives for the reporting of Enterprise Funds. Under Alternative 1, governmental entities using proprietary fund accounting must follow (1) all GASB pronouncements and (2) FASB Statements and Interpretations, APB Opinions, and Accounting Research Bulletins (ARBs) issued on or before November 30, 1989, except those that conflict with a GASB pronouncement (GASB-20, pars. 6–8).

Under Alternative 2, governmental entities using proprietary fund accounting must follow (1) all GASB pronouncements and (2) all FASB Statements and Interpretations, APB Opinions, and ARBs, no matter when issued, except those that conflict with a GASB pronouncement. Unlike Alternative 1, Alternative 2 has no cutoff date for determining the applicability of FASB pronouncements (GASB-20, pars. 6–8).

NOTE: The guidance established by GASB-20 is discussed in Chapter 1, "Foundation and Overview of Governmental Generally Accepted Accounting Principles." The two alternatives are not applicable to Internal Service Funds.

Recording Exchange Transactions in Government-Wide Financial Statements

Revenues related to exchange transactions in a governmental entity's statement of activities should be based on accrual accounting concepts. Governmental activities as presented in the government-wide financial statements should be accounted for and reported based on all applicable GASB pronouncements, NCGA pronouncements, and the following pronouncements issued on or before November 30, 1989, unless they conflict with GASB or NCGA pronouncements (GASB-34, par. 17):

- Financial Accounting Standards Board (FASB) Statement and Interpretations
- Accounting Principles Board (APB) Opinions
- Accounting Research Bulletins (ARBs) of the Committee on Accounting Procedure

In the past, pronouncements of the FASB, the APB, and the Committee on Accounting Procedure have not, for the most part, been applied to information presented in governmental funds. The GASB decided that government-wide financial statements must be prepared by applying these pronouncements issued on or before November 30, 1989 (unless they conflict with GASB pronouncements), on a retroactive basis (with four exceptions discussed in paragraph 146 of GASB-34). Pronouncements issued by the FASB after November 30, 1989, are not required to be followed in the preparation of government-wide financial statements.

SALES, PLEDGES, AND INTRA-ENTITY TRANSFERS OF ASSETS AND FUTURE REVENUES

GASB-48 (Sales and Pledges of Receivables and Future Revenues and Intra-Entity Transfers of Assets and Future Revenues), issued in September 2006, provides financial statement users with consistent measurement, recognition, and disclosure across governments and within individual governments relating to the accounting for sales and pledges of receivables and future revenues and intra-entity transfers of assets and future revenues. GASB-48 is effective for financial statement periods beginning after December 15, 2006; however, early application is encouraged.

Prior to GASB-48, the guidance for reporting the effects of sales and pledges of receivables and future revenues in governmental financial statements was not provided through official authoritative literature and was located across several accounting standards. Depending on whether the transaction was a governmental activity or a business-type activity, FAS-77 (Reporting by Transferors for Transfers of Receivables with Recourse), EITF Issue No. 88-18 (Sales of Future Revenues), or FAS-140 (Accounting for Transfers and Servicing of Financial Assets and Extinguishment of Liabilities) could have applied.

GASB-48 does not apply to a government's pledge of its "full faith and credit" as security whether it relates to its own debt or to the debt of a component. The GASB stated, "by backing the government's own debt with its full faith and credit, the government makes an *unconditional commitment* to pay principal and interest on that debt without specifying the resources that will be used for repayment." Because specific revenues are not specified in this situation, these full faith and credit situations should not be included in the scope of pledged revenues. However, all state and local governments are required to apply GASB-48 to their financial statements.

GASB-48 focuses specifically on financial reporting issues associated with pledges and sales of receivables and future revenues. It makes a distinction in determining whether a transaction is a sale or a collateralized borrowing. All transactions within the scope of GASB-48 should be reported as collateralized borrowings unless certain criteria are met.

Assessing a Government's Continuing Involvement in Receivables

The right to future cash flows from receivables should be reported as a sale if the government's continuing involvement with those receivables is terminated. A government no longer has continuing involvement in receivables if all of the following criteria are met:

- The receivables are not limited by constraints imposed by the transferor government, such as the transferee's ability to subsequently sell or pledge the receivables.
- The transferor has no options or abilities to unilaterally substitute for or require specific accounts from the receivables transferred. There is no violation of the criterion if there are transfers made of defective accounts.
- The sale agreement is not cancelable by either party.
- The transferor government has been isolated from the receivables and the cash resulting from their collection. GASB-48 discusses the criteria used to determine whether receivables have been isolated from the transferor government (e.g., a separate legal standing between the transferee and the transferor)

Assessing a Government's Continuing Involvement in Future Revenues

A transaction relating to cash flows from specific future revenues that are exchanged for lump-sum proceeds should be reported as a sale if the government's continuing involvement with those revenues meets all of the following criteria:

- The future generation of revenues will not be maintained by active involvement of the transferor government. Active involvement generally requires a substantive action or performance, whereas, passive involvement in the generation of future revenues generally requires no substantive actions or performance by the government.
- The transferor government has released and has no restrictions on the transferee government's ability to subsequently sell or pledge the future cash flows.
- The transferor government has been isolated from cash resulting from the collection of the future revenues.
- There is no prohibition on the transfer or assignment of the original resources contained in the contract, agreement, or arrangement between the original resource provider and the transferor government.
- The sale agreement is not cancelable by either party.

Accounting Transactions That Do Not Qualify as Sales

In general terms, when the GASB-48 criteria required for sales reporting are not met, the transaction should be reported as a collateralized borrowing by the transferor. Rather than a sale, these sales and future revenues should be considered for financial statement purposes as pledged rather than sold.

If sale criteria are not met, then collateralized borrowing occurs and the following steps are taken by both the transferor and the transferee:

- Transferor government
  —Does not derecognize receivables
  —Continues recognition of revenues pledged
  —Recognizes liability for the proceeds received
  —Payments reduce liability
- Transferee government should recognize a receivable for the amounts paid to the pledging government

Accounting for Transactions That Meet the Criteria to Be Reported as Sales

If the GASB-48 criteria required for sales reporting are met, the transaction should be reported as a sale:

- *Receivables* In the sale of receivables, the selling government should remove the individual accounts at their carrying values and no longer recognize as assets the receivables sold.
- *Future revenues* In the sale of future revenues, the proceeds should be reported by the selling government as either revenue or deferred revenue.

The transactions are handled differently for a transfer of assets within the same financial reporting entity as opposed to when the transferee is a government outside of the selling government's financial reporting entity.

If the conditions for sale treatment are met, then the following steps are taken by both the transferor and the transferee government:

- Transferor government (also known as the selling government):
  —Derecognizes receivables
  —No asset to derecognize for future revenues
  —Difference between proceeds and carrying value is as follows: (1) on sale of receivables there is revenue recognition or a gain/loss and (2) on sale of future revenues there is generally deferred revenues—this deferral depends on why revenue had not been previously recognized by the seller.
- Transferree government (also known as purchasing government):
  —Intra-entity sale treatment has purchased receivables reported at carrying value and payments to the selling government for rights to future revenues are reported as a deferred charge.
  —Outside of the reporting entity the asset (rights) are recorded at cost.

Example: Sale of Delinquent Receivables

Facts and assumptions: A city (the seller) enters into an agreement to sell delinquent taxes due to another government entity (the purchaser). The seller city received $2,500,000 in exchange for tax receivables/liens totaling $4,000,000. The city's allowance for uncollectible accounts pertaining to those tax receivables is $1,000,000, resulting in a net carrying value of $3,000,000. The sale agreement stipulates that the liens are sold without recourse except that the city has an obligation with respect to liens found to be defective. For defective liens, the city is required to (1) perfect the liens, (2) reacquire the liens from the purchaser, or (3) deliver to the purchaser substantially equivalent liens in substitution.

Conclusion: This transaction meets the criteria to be recognized as a sale.

Accounting in the year of the sale: The seller city reduces property taxes receivable by $4,000,000, reduces the allowance for uncollectible accounts by $1,000,000, and recognizes a loss on the sale of $500,000 (the carrying value of $3,000,000 less the proceeds of $2,500,000) in the government-wide statement of activities. In its governmental funds prior to the sale, the seller city was reporting a zero net carrying value for the delinquent taxes receivable because they were either deemed to be uncollectible ($1,000,000) or deferred under the availability criterion ($3,000,000). Therefore, the entire amount of the proceeds ($2,500,000) is recognized as revenue and the remaining net receivable and related deferred revenue amounts is eliminated. The seller city has determined that if any liens are found to be defective, it would first attempt to perfect the liens and, if unable to do so, provide acceptable substitutions. The city believes it is not probable that it would repurchase defective liens and therefore does not recognize a liability.

Accounting in future years: If any of the tax liens are subsequently found to be defective and it is probable that the seller city would reacquire those liens, a liability and an expenditure/expense would be recognized, provided that the amount of the repurchase obligation is measurable. At the same time, the city would add back the reacquired tax liens receivable and reduce the expense by the estimated collectible value of those liens. In the governmental funds, either the expenditure would be reduced if the receivable were considered available or a related deferred revenue would be established.

Pledges of Future Revenues and Specific Disclosures

Some governments may not receive resources in exchange for a pledge of future cash flows of specific revenues. There may be restrictions that prohibit the government entity from issuing debt or due to a charter, statute, or constitutional requirement it may be limited in the extent that it may issue debt. When primary governments are in this situation and are empowered to create separate component units or use existing component units to issue debt on their behalf, the primary government may pledge future revenue streams as security for the debt. Pledging governments should disclose revenues pledged that have been formally committed to directly collateralize or secure debt of the pledging government or directly or indirectly collateralize or secure debt of a component unit. These required disclosures do not apply to revenues that are shared by another government. The following is an example disclosure:

> **Pledged tax increment revenues** The city has pledged a portion of future sales tax revenues to repay $2.8 million in sales tax increment bonds issued in June 200X to finance the refurbishing of the Southtown business district. The bonds are payable solely from the incremental sales taxes generated by increased retail sales in the refurbished district. Incremental sales taxes were projected to produce 128 percent of the debt service requirements over the life of the bonds. Total principal and interest remaining on the bonds is $3,490,900, payable through June 20YZ. For the current year, principal and interest paid and total incremental sales tax revenues were $395,150 and $403,291, respectively.

CHAPTER 18
EXPENSES/EXPENDITURES: NONEXCHANGE AND EXCHANGE TRANSACTIONS

CONTENTS

INTRODUCTION

With the issuance of GASB-34 (Basic Financial Statements—and Managements Discussion and Analysis—for State and Local Governments), governmental entities must measure and report in their financial reports the transactions that give rise to both expenses and expenditures. Like revenues, expenses and expenditures may arise from nonexchange transactions as well as exchange transactions.

Governmental entities that provide resources that are based on nonexchange transactions must record both expenses (for proprietary and fiduciary funds, and government-wide financial statement purposes) and expenditures (for governmental fund financial statement purposes). GASB-33 (Accounting and Financial Reporting for Nonexchange Transactions) takes the position that the same-timing recognition criteria for determining an expense under the accrual basis of accounting are applicable to determining when an expenditure should be recognized under the modified accrual basis of accounting. This chapter discusses the basic rules that governmental entities should follow to report these transactions in governmental funds, proprietary and fiduciary funds, and the government-wide financial statements.

EXPENSES/EXPENDITURES: NONEXCHANGE TRANSACTIONS

The two parties in a nonexchange transaction are the provider of the resources and the receiver of the resources. The provider of the resources could be the federal governmental, a state or local government, or a nongovernmental entity (such as an individual or business entity). The receiver of the resources could be a state or local government, or a nongovernmental entity. What distinguishes a nonexchange transaction from an exchange transaction is that in a *non*exchange transaction a government "either gives value (benefit) to another party without directly receiving equal value in exchange or receives value (benefit) from another party without directly giving equal value in exchange" (GASB-33, par. 7).

GASB-33 provides accounting and reporting standards for the following four categories of nonexchange transactions:

1. Derived tax revenues
2. Imposed nonexchange revenues
3. Government-mandated nonexchange transactions
4. Voluntary nonexchange transactions

The first two categories (derived tax revenue and imposed nonexchange revenues) do not give rise to governmental expense or expenditure because the governmental entity is always the recipient of resources and never the provider of resources under these types of nonexchange transactions.

The GASB takes the position that all nonexchange transactions are fundamentally controlled by either legislation, contractual requirements, or both, and this factor is essential in determining when expense and expenditures from nonexchange transactions should be recognized. Thus, expenses and expenditures related to governmentmandated nonexchange transactions and voluntary nonexchange transactions should be recognized when all eligibility requirements established by the relevant authority has been satisfied.

The relevant eligibility requirements in a government-mandated nonexchange transaction are generally based on enabling legislation and related regulations. Those laws and regulations often identify purpose restrictions that apply to how the resources provided under the program are to be used. The relevant eligibility requirements in a voluntary nonexchange transaction may arise from enabling legislation or from contractual agreements with a nongovernmental entity. For example, a nongovernmental entity, such as a corporation or an individual, may provide resources to a governmental entity, but the provisions of those resources may depend on a number of eligibility factors contained in the donor agreement (GASB-33, par. 21).

> **PRACTICE POINT:** The standards established by GASB-33 generally apply to both revenue and expense recognition at the same time. That is, when both parties to the nonexchange transactions are governmental entities, the same standards that are used to determine whether revenue should be recognized by the recipient government are used to determine when an expense should be recognized by the provider governmental entity.

Time Requirements and Purpose Restrictions

To determine when expenses or expenditures related to nonexchange transactions should be recorded and presented in a governmental entity's financial statements, time requirements and purpose restrictions should be taken into consideration. Time requirements and purpose restrictions do not have the same effect on the recognition of expense or expenditure in a governmental entity's financial statements.

Time requirements Resources may be provided by one governmental entity to another governmental entity with the requirement that the resources be used in (or begin to be used in) a specified period(s). GASB-33 notes that "time requirements specify the period or periods when resources are required to be used or when use may begin." Time requirements may be imposed by enabling legislation. For example, legislation may identify the period in which a recipient government can use a grant or it may require that resources be used over a specified number of years. In other instances, time requirements imposed by the provider government may require that the resources provided may never be used (permanent endowment) or that the resources cannot be used until a specified event has occurred (GASB-33, par. 12).

When a nonexchange transaction is subject to a timing requirement, that requirement generally affects the period in which expenses and expenditures are recognized by the provider government. As discussed later, the effect that a timing requirement has on a non-exchange transaction is dependent on whether the transaction is (1) a government-mandated nonexchange transaction or a voluntary nonexchange transaction or (2) an imposed nonexchange revenue transactions.

Purpose restrictions Purpose restrictions relate to the use of resources that arise from a nonexchange transaction. For example, a party may receive a grant that may be used only to purchase an emergency communication system. Because of the nature of purpose restrictions, expenses and expenditures (as well as the related liability) related to nonexchange transactions should be recognized in a governmental entity's financial statements without taking into consideration purpose restrictions. That is, a purpose restriction does not affect the timing of the recognition of a nonexchange transaction. In fact, the GASB notes that a purpose restriction cannot be met unless a nonexchange transaction has taken place (GASB-33, par. 12).

> **PRACTICE POINT:** Although purpose restrictions do not affect the timing of an expense or expenditures by the provider government, a recipient government must disclose the restriction in its financial statements. For a discussion of how this is accomplished, see the discussion in Chapter 17, "Revenues: Nonexchange and Exchange Transactions."

Purpose restrictions can be related to both government-mandated nonexchange transactions and voluntary nonexchange transactions.

Government-Mandated Nonexchange Transactions

Expenditures/expenses from government-mandated nonexchange transactions arise when a governmental entity at one level provides resources to another governmental entity at a lower level, and the higher level governmental entity "requires [the other] government to use them for a specific purpose or purposes established in the provider's enabling legislation." For example, a state government (provider government) may make resources available to a county government (recipient government). GASB-33 notes that government-mandated nonexchange expense or expenditure transactions have the following principal characteristics (GASB-33, par. 7c):

- The provider government requires that the recipient government institute a specific program (or facilitate the performance of a specific program) conducted by the recipient government or nongovernmental entity (secondary recipient entity).
- Certain performance requirements must be fulfilled (other than the provision of cash or other assets in advance).

Because the resources provided by the providing government must be used for a particular purpose, resources received under a government-mandated nonexchange transaction always create a purpose restriction. In many instances the resources are also subject to eligibility requirements, including time restrictions. An example of a government-mandated nonexchange transaction would include the requirement by a state government that a local government provide educational counseling to certain disadvantaged groups.

PRACTICE POINT: Simply mandating that a lower-level government entity establish a specific program does not create a government-mandated nonexchange transaction itself. The higher-level government must fund the program. The standards established by GASB-33 do not apply to unfunded mandates established by a government because these types of programs do not involve the exchange of resources (GASB-33, footnote 5).

In a government-mandated nonexchange transaction, when the two governmental entities that are involved in the transaction are the state and a local government, they are both subject to GASB accounting and reporting standards. For this reason, the standards established by GASB-33 will apply to the recognition of revenue (by the recipient government) and the recognition of an expenditure/expense (by the provider government).

In a government-mandated nonexchange transaction, the provider government should recognize an expense or expenditure when all eligibility requirements (which includes time requirements) are satisfied. The eligibility requirements are categorized as follows (GASB-33, par. 20):

- Required characteristics of recipients
- Time requirements
- Reimbursements

These requirements are discussed in detail in Chapter 17, "Revenues: Nonexchange and Exchange Transactions."

Voluntary Nonexchange Transactions

Voluntary nonexchange transactions arise from "legislative or contractual agreements, other than exchanges, entered into willingly by two or more parties." Avoluntary nonexchange transaction can be based on either a written or oral agreement, assuming the oral agreement is verifiable. The principal characteristics of voluntary nonexchange transactions are listed below (GASB-33, par. 7d and footnote 6):

- They are not imposed on the provider or the recipient.
- Satisfaction of eligibility requirements (other than the provision of cash or other assets in advance) is necessary for a transaction to occur.

In a voluntary nonexchange transaction, a governmental entity may be the recipient or the provider of the resources, and the parties to the transaction may be another governmental entity or a nongovernmental entity, such as an individual or a not-for-profit organization. Examples of voluntary nonexchange transactions include certain grants, some entitlements, and donations. These types of nonexchange transactions may involve purpose restrictions and/or time requirements and often the arrangement requires that resources must be returned to the provider if purpose restrictions or eligibility requirements are contravened after the voluntary nonexchange transaction has been recognized by a governmental entity.

In a voluntary nonexchange transaction, the provider and the recipient should recognize the nonexchange transaction when all eligibility requirements (which includes time requirements) are satisfied. The eligibility requirements are categorized as follows (GASB-33, par. 20):

- Required characteristics of recipients
- Time requirements
- Reimbursements
- Contingencies

These requirements are discussed in detail in Chapter 17, "Revenues: Nonexchange and Exchange Transactions."

Recording Nonexchange Transactions in Governmental Funds

Although the standards established in GASB-33 are written in the context of the accrual basis of accounting, they provide a significant amount of general guidance for nonexchange transactions irrespective of the basis of accounting that is used by a governmental entity. For this reason, the GASB states that the general guidance provided in GASB-33 applies to governmental funds (activities accounted for in funds such as the General Fund and Special Revenue Funds). Expenditures of governmental funds are accounted for under the modified accrual basis of accounting.

Recording Nonexchange Transactions in Proprietary and Fiduciary Funds

Expenses from nonexchange transactions should be recognized in proprietary and fiduciary funds based on accrual accounting concepts and be consistent with the standards established by GASB-33.

Presenting Nonexchange Transactions in Government-Wide Financial Statements

Expenses related to nonexchange transaction that are presented in a governmental entity's statement of activities should be based on accrual accounting concepts and be consistent with the standards established by GASB-33.

EXPENSES/EXPENDITURES: EXCHANGE TRANSACTIONS

In an exchange transaction the governmental entity and the other party to the transaction exchange cash, goods, or services that are essentially of the same value. For example, the purchase of a vehicle by a governmental entity from a car dealer is an exchange transaction. Unlike nonexchange transactions, the GASB has not provided comprehensive guidance for the recognition of exchange transactions.

Recording Exchange Transactions in Governmental Funds

GASB-34 requires that governmental entities produce government-wide financial statements that are based on the accrual accounting basis and the flow of all economic resources; however, GASB-34 also requires that governmental fund financial statements continue to be presented based on the modified accrual accounting basis and the flow of current financial resources.

The GASB believes that retaining the modified accrual basis of accounting for governmental funds was an important aspect of satisfying financial accountability, which is one of the foundations of governmental financial reporting.

Recording Exchange Transactions in Proprietary and Fiduciary Funds

FAS: CS-6 (Elements of Financial Statements) defines "expenses" as "outflows or other using up of assets or incidences of liabilities during a period from delivering or producing goods, rendering services, or carrying out other activities that constitute the entity's ongoing major or central operations." In general, a proprietary or fiduciary fund should record an expense when incurred; however, the recognition must be consistent with any relevant standards established by the GASB.

PRACTICE ALERT: In August 2006, the Governmental Accounting Standards Board (GASB) issued an exposure draft on a proposed Concepts Statement entitled "Elements of Financial Statements." This proposed Concepts Statement would be the fourth issued by the GASB, and it proposes new definitions for seven elements of historically based financial statements of state and local governments as follows:

- Elements of the statement of financial position:

  1. Assets
  2. Liabilities
  3. Deferred Outflow of Resources
  4. Deferred Inflow of Resources
  5. Net Position

- Elements of the resources flow statements:

  6. Inflow of Resources
  7. Outflow of Resources

The GASB-proposed definitions of the elements are based upon the inherent characteristics of each element and are linked by a common definition feature in that they are based on the concept of measuring and reporting *resources*. The proposed definitions of the elements apply to an entity that is a governmental unit (that is, a legal entity) and are applicable to any measurement focus under which financial statements may be prepared, for example, economic resources, current financial resources, and cash resources measurement focuses. As CCH's 2008 *Governmental GAAP Guide* went to press the GASB was redeliberating the proposed statement based on the responses to the exposure draft. However, the results of this project are likely to differ from the concepts in FASB:CS-6.

GASB-20 allows for two distinct but acceptable alternatives for the reporting of Enterprise Funds. Under Alternative 1, governmental entities using proprietary fund accounting must follow (1) all GASB pronouncements and (2) FASB Statements and Interpretations, APB Opinions, and Accounting Research Bulletins (ARBs) issued on or before November 30, 1989, except those that conflict with a GASB pronouncement (GASB-20, pars. 6–8).

Under Alternative 2 of GASB-20, governmental entities using proprietary fund accounting must follow (1) all GASB pronouncements and (2) all FASB Statements and Interpretations, APB Opinions, and ARBs, no matter when issued, except those that conflict with a GASB pronouncement. Unlike Alternative 1, Alternative 2 has no cutoff date for determining the applicability of FASB pronouncements (GASB-20, pars. 6–8).

NOTE: The guidance established by GASB-20 is discussed in Chapter 1, "Foundation and Overview of Governmental Generally Accepted Accounting Principles." The two alternatives are not applicable to Internal Service Funds.

Recording Exchange Transactions in Government-Wide Financial Statements

Expenses related to exchange transactions in a governmental entity's statement of activities should be based on accrual accounting concepts. Governmental activities as presented in the governmentwide financial statements should be accounted for and reported based on all applicable GASB pronouncements, NCGA pronouncements, and the following pronouncements issued on or before November 30, 1989, unless they conflict with GASB or NCGA pronouncements (GASB-34, par. 17):

- Financial Accounting Standards Board (FASB) Statement and Interpretations
- Accounting Principles Board (APB) Opinions
- Accounting Research Bulletins (ARBs) of the Committee on Accounting Procedure

In the past, pronouncements of the FASB, the APB, and the Committee on Accounting Procedure have not, for the most part, been applied to information presented in governmental funds. The GASB decided that government-wide financial statements must be prepared by applying these pronouncements issued on or before November 30, 1989, unless they conflict with GASB pronouncements, on a retroactive basis (with four exceptions discussed in paragraph 146 of GASB-34). Pronouncements issued by the FASB after November 30, 1989, are not required to be followed in the preparation of government-wide financial statements.

DEPRECIATION EXPENSE IN PROPRIETARY AND FIDUCIARY FUNDS AND THE GOVERNMENT-WIDE FINANCIAL STATEMENTS

Depreciation Expense

An exchange transaction occurs when a governmental entity acquires capital assets. The expense related to that exchange transaction arises when depreciation expenses are recorded in the government-wide financial statements. In proprietary and fiduciary funds and the government-wide financial statements, the cost (net of estimated salvage value) of capital assets (except for certain infrastructure assets, which are discussed later) should be depreciated over their estimated useful lives. Inexhaustible capital assets (such as land, land improvements, and certain infrastructure assets) should not be depreciated (GASB-34, par. 21).

The *GASB Comprehensive Implementation Guide* points out that the estimated useful life of an asset is the period of time that the governmental entity believes the asset will be used in its activities. The *GASB Q&A Guide* notes that factors that are relevant to making this determination include the following:

- The asset's present state of condition
- How the asset will be used
- Maintenance policy
- Relevant service and technology demands

The *GASB Comprehensive Implementation Guide* notes that the estimated useful life relates to the expected experience of the governmental entity. The experience of other governmental entities is relevant only if the expected experience is anticipated to be the same.

The *GASB Comprehensive Implementation Guide* notes that there is not a generally accepted schedule of useful lives that can be used to determine depreciation expense for governmental entities. Although informal schedules or guidance are provided by professional organizations, it is the responsibility of management to determine the estimated useful life of a capital asset. Furthermore, the Internal Revenue Service's schedule of lives for property classes related to the Modified Accelerated Cost Recovery System is not based on the actual estimated economic lives of assets.

The *GASB Comprehensive Implementation Guide* suggests that the following may be used to estimate the useful lives of depreciable assets:

- General guidelines obtained from professional and industry organizations
- Information for comparable assets of other governments
- Internal information

These sources should be considered starting points and should be modified based on the specific characteristics and expected use of a newly acquired capital asset.

The *GASB Comprehensive Implementation Guide* notes that, in general, the lives of capital assets should be reviewed each year; however, from a practical point of view, a governmental entity reviews only those lives that may have changed because some of the following events have occurred during the current year:

- Property replacement policies have changed.
- Preventive maintenance policies have changed.
- Unexpected technological changes have occurred.

If it is concluded that the life of a capital asset should be changed, APB-20 (Accounting Changes) requires that its undepreciated cost (less the revised residual value) be allocated over the remaining life of the asset. This is a change in an accounting estimate.

As with commercial accounting, there is no specific list of acceptable depreciable method; however, the method selected must be systematic and rational. GASB-34 notes that depreciation may be applied in the following manner (GASB-34, par. 22):

- To a class of assets
- To a network of assets
- To a subsystem of a network assets
- To individual assets

> **PRACTICE POINT:** The composite depreciation method, which was illustrated in GASB-34 in the context of infrastructure assets, can also be used to compute depreciation expense for other capital assets; however, the method should not be applied across classes of assets. In grouping assets for the purpose of computing depreciation expense, the *GASB Comprehensive Implementation Guide* points out that assets should not be grouped in a manner that would not enable a governmental entity to report depreciation expense as a direct expense for particular functions as required by paragraph 44 of

GASB-34 or note disclosures required by paragraph 117d. The composite method is discussed later in this chapter.

PRACTICE POINT: The *GASB Comprehensive Implementation Guide* states that when infrastructure assets are sold or otherwise disposed of, the gain or loss reported on the statement of activities is the difference between the net book value of the capital asset (original cost or estimated cost minus accumulated depreciation) and the proceeds from the disposition. If the infrastructure is not being depreciated (as allowed under the modified method under certain conditions), the gain or loss is the difference between the original cost (or estimated cost) and the proceeds.

Depreciation expense: Modified approach The GASB does not require that infrastructure assets that are part of a network or subsystem of a network (referred to as eligible infrastructure assets) be depreciated if the following conditions are satisfied (GASB-34, par. 23):

- An asset management system is employed that:
  - Has an up-to-date inventory of eligible infrastructure assets
  - Performs condition assessments of the assets and summarizes the results using a "measurable scale"
  - Estimates, on an annual basis, the annual amount needed to "maintain and preserve the eligible infrastructure assets at the condition level established and disclosed by the government"
- The government documents that the eligible infrastructure assets are being "preserved approximately at (or above) a condition level established and disclosed by the government."

A governmental entity that adopts the modified approach may continue to use it as long as the two conditions listed above are met. The *GASB Comprehensive Implementation Guide* points out that the second criterion listed refers to the conditions of the asset, not the amount of resources expended to maintain the asset at a particular condition. For example, if a governmental entity originally estimated that a specific amount was needed to maintain the asset but did not actually expended those funds, that does not mean that the entity can no longer use the modified approach—as long as the condition of the asset does not fall below the established condition level.

OBSERVATION: The documentation of condition assessments must be carefully done so that their results can be replicated. GASB-34 describes results being subject to replication as "those that are based on sufficiently understandable and complete measurement methods such that different measurers using the same methods would reach substantially similar results."

The condition level must be established and documented by governmental policy or legislative action and the assessment itself may be made either by the governmental entity directly or by external parties. Professional judgment and good faith are the basis for determining what constitutes acceptable and accurate documentation of the condition of eligible infrastructure assets. However, GASB-34 states that governmental entities should document the following (GASB-34, par. 24):

- Complete condition assessments of eligible infrastructure assets are performed in a consistent manner at least every three years
- The results of the three most recent complete condition assessments provide reasonable assurance that the eligible infrastructure assets are being preserved approximately at (or above) the condition level established and disclosed by the government

PRACTICE POINT: GASB-34 points out that the condition level could be applied to a group of assets by using a condition index or "as the percentage of a network of infrastructure assets in good or poor condition."

PRACTICE POINT: If a governmental entity identifies a subsystem of infrastructure assets as "eligible" (and therefore the computation of depreciation is optional), the documentary requirements apply only to the subsystem and not to the entire network of infrastructure assets.

A governmental entity may perform the condition assessment annually or may use a cycle basis. If the entity uses a cyclical basis for networks or subsystems, it must assess all assets of these groups during the cycle. However, rather than apply the condition assessment to all assets, the entity may employ a statistical sample approach in the annual approach or in the cycle approach.

Because eligible infrastructure assets do not have to be depreciated, all expenditures related to their maintenance should be recognized as a current expense when incurred. Expenditures that are capital in nature (additions and improvements) should be capitalized as part of the eligible infrastructure assets because they, by definition, increase the capacity or efficiency of the related infrastructure asset (GASB-34, par. 25).

The adequate maintenance of the condition of eligible infrastructure assets is a continuous process and if the conditions established by GASB-34 are initially satisfied but subsequently are not, the infrastructure assets are not considered "eligible" and depreciation expense for them must be computed and reported in the statement of activities. The change in accounting for depreciation expense should be reported a change in an accounting estimate. APB-20 (Accounting Changes) requires that a change in estimate be accounted for on a prospective basis. That is, the balances in the infrastructure assets (net of residual values, if any) are to be depreciated over the remaining lives of the assets when the governmental entity no longer qualifies to use the modified approach (GASB-34, par. 26).

While GASB-34 provides guidance for a change from not depreciating certain infrastructure assets to the recognition of annual depreciation expense on those assets, it does not address how the reverse situation should be reported in a governmental entity's financial statements. A change from depreciating infrastructure assets to not depreciating them could arise for reasons such as the following:

- Business-type activities might decide on a nondepreciating strategy when they implement the standards established by GASB-34.
- Infrastructure networks or subsystems may be transferred from an Enterprise Fund to general capital assets.
- At a date after the implementation of the standards established by GASB-34 a governmental entity may decide to change from depreciating infrastructure assets to the modified approach because it now satisfies the requirements established by paragraph 23 of GASB-34.

GASB-37 requires that a change from the depreciating approach to the nondepreciating approach (modified approach) for certain infrastructure assets be accounted for on a prospective basis (change in an accounting estimate). Thus, when this type of change is made, the carrying amount of the asset remains the same and that amount provides the basis for computing subsequent depreciation expense.

> **OBSERVATION:** The GASB considered whether to account for this type of change as a change in an accounting principle, but rejected this approach which would have required that "the carrying amount of the asset... be restated to remove previously recorded accumulated depreciation and previously capitalized preservation costs, if any."

GASB-34 (par. 144) requires that accounting adjustments in governmental, proprietary, and fiduciary funds related to the implementation of GASB-34 be treated as adjustments of prior periods. (That is, adjust the beginning fund balance or net asset balance and adjust the asset/liability balance.) In some instances a governmental unit may change from the depreciation method to the modified approach (as a business-type activity or in an Enterprise Fund) as part of implementing GASB-34 standards. GASB-37 notes that "a change to the modified approach should be accounted for as a change in an accounting estimate and would not require restatement of prior periods." Thus, the balance in the qualifying infrastructure assets as of the first day of the year in which the standards established by GASB-34 are implemented are to be used as the amount reported for the infrastructure assets. A governmental entity is not allowed to restore the amount of depreciation expense that had previously been recognized on the infrastructure assets before the modified approach was adopted (GASB-37, par. 8).

> **PRACTICE POINT:** The nonrecognition of depreciation expense for eligible infrastructure assets is optional. A governmental entity can decide to depreciate all infrastructure assets that are exhaustible rather than carve out and identify "eligible infrastructure assets."

Maintenance and preservation costs The *GASB Comprehensive Implementation Guide* states that the treatment of maintenance costs (i.e., routine repairs) is the same for the modified approach and the traditional depreciation approach. That is, under both approaches, maintenance costs are expensed.

The treatment of preservation costs is different under the two approaches. Preservation costs are not defined in GASB-34 but are described in the GASB's *Guide* as cost that "generally are considered to be those outlays that extend the useful life of an asset beyond its original estimated useful life, but do not increase the capacity or efficiency of the asset." Some accountants refer to preservation costs as "major repairs." Under the modified approach preservation costs are expensed; under the traditional depreciation approach preservation costs are capitalized. Under both approaches additions and improvements are capitalized. Of course, differentiating among these costs (preservation, additions, and improvements) is often difficult. The governmental entity should use "any reasonable approach" to make the cost allocation.

> **OBSERVATION:** The *GASB Comprehensive Implementation Guide* demonstrates how the above guidance should be applied by raising the question of whether the cost of removing and replacing or resurfacing an existing roadway should be capitalized if the modified approach is used. The results arising from the removing and replacing or resurfacing must be evaluated to determine whether the activity is considered (1) maintenance or preservation or (2) an increase in the capacity or efficiency of the roadway. If the costs are related

to maintenance or preservation, they should be expensed under the modified approach. If the costs increase the capacity or efficiency of the roadway, they must be capitalized. Capacity is increased when a capital asset can provide more services or goods. Efficiency is increased when a capital asset can accomplish the same level of service at a lower cost.

CHAPTER 19
SPECIAL ASSESSMENTS

CONTENTS

INTRODUCTION

A governmental entity may raise resources assessing only the properties of taxpayers who would directly benefit either from the construction or improvement of a capital asset or from the provision for special services. For example, a city may assess property owners in order to improve water or sewer lines in a specific location within the city or a local government may assess businesses in a downtown area in order to provide special sanitation maintenance on an ongoing basis. These special assessment activities provided by a governmental entity are generally characterized by their narrow scope and the method by which they are financed.

Governmental accounting and reporting standards for special assessments are based on the guidance established by GASB-6 (Accounting and Financial Reporting for Special Assessments).

Before the issuance of GASB-6, Special Assessment Funds were used to account for special assessments. Generally, the use of Special Assessment Funds resulted in a deficit fund balance. Although capital outlays were recorded as expenditures, the special assessment debt was recorded as a liability of the Special Assessment Fund (rather than as an other source of financing). In addition, the special assessments levied against property owners were not recorded as revenue until the measurable and available criteria were satisfied.

GASB-6 significantly reduced the likelihood of fund balance deficits resulting from special assessments by treating special assessment debt like all other debt issued by a governmental unit. The proceeds of the special assessment debt should be recorded as an other source of financing, and the debt should be reported as part of the governmental unit's general long-term debt if the unit is directly liable or in some manner liable for the special assessment debt.

Another significant accounting standard established by GASB-6 is the prohibition of the use of Special Assessment Funds for governmental financial reporting. The rationale for the prohibition is that special assessment transactions and balances are no more unique than capital expenditures, debt service expenditures, and special levies that are accounted for in the other governmental funds or in Enterprise Funds. Special assessment transactions and balances generally will be accounted for in a number of different funds.

> **PRACTICE POINT:** If legal requirements are not satisfied because a separate Special Assessment Fund cannot be used for financial reporting purposes, it may be necessary to make additional disclosures in notes, schedules, and explanations, or perhaps by the preparation of separate special reports.

TYPES OF SPECIAL ASSESSMENTS

Services Financed by Special Assessments

Special assessments used to finance special types of service or special levels of service should be accounted for generally in the General Fund, a Special Revenue Fund, or an Enterprise Fund. The GASB states that the number of separate funds established should be kept to the minimum level that will satisfy legal and administrative requirements. Therefore, in some cases, services financed by special assessments may be accounted for in the General Fund. Assessment revenues and related expenditures/expenses should use the accounting basis that is appropriate for the fund used. The activities related to the special assessment should be reported in the government-wide financial statements, using the accrual basis of accounting, in either the governmental or business-type activities depending on the nature of the service provided (GASB-6, par. 14 and GASB-34, pars. 15–16).

> **PRACTICE POINT:** The *GASB Comprehensive Implementation Guide* notes that special assessment activities provided by a governmental entity are generally characterized by their narrow scope and the method by which they are financed. For financial reporting purposes operating special assessments revenues are not considered general revenues like property taxes. Operating special assessments are program revenues (charges for services) because they are assessed against those specific parties who are entitled to the specific service.

Capital Improvements Financed by Special Assessments

Generally, capital improvements financed by special assessments have two distinct phases: the construction phase and the debt service phase. When a governmental unit is directly liable or obligated in some manner (as defined in the section titled "Governmental Liability for Debt") for the special assessment debt, the capital construction and related debt service transactions should be accounted for in a manner similar to other governmental capital outlays and debt service payments. For this reason, special assessment transactions related to capital improvements may be accounted for in a Capital Projects Fund or Debt Service Fund. If there are no legal or administrative requirements that necessitate the use of a separate Capital Projects Fund or Debt Service Fund, the General Fund can be used (GASB-6, par. 15).

When a governmental entity is obligated in some manner to make debt repayments in the case of default by property owners, the expenditures (expenses) "should be reported in the same manner and on the same basis of accounting, as any other capital improvement and financing transaction." Revenues from special assessment capital improvement transactions should be accounted for based on the standards established by GASB-33 (Accounting and Financial Reporting for Nonexchange Transactions) (GASB-6, as amended by GASB-33).

PRACTICE POINT: The *GASB Comprehensive Implementation Guide* states that capital special assessments are program revenues (program-specific capital grants and contributions) because the property owners derive a direct beneficiary from the contributions that they make to the program.

ACCOUNTING AND REPORTING FOR SPECIAL ASSESSMENTS

Governmental Liability for Debt

Because property owners are generally obligated to finance all or part of the repayment of special assessment debt, a question arises whether the special assessment debt should be reported as debt of the governmental entity. When the governmental unit is primarily liable for the special assessment debt, the debt should be reported as debt by the governmental entity. In addition, special assessment debt should be reported as such when the governmental unit is "obligated in some manner" to repay the debt in cases where property owners default. GASB-6 states that a governmental unit is obligated in some manner to pay the special assessment debt if one of the following two circumstances exists (GASB-6, par. 16):

- The governmental unit is legally obligated to assume all or part of the special assessment debt if property owners default.
- The governmental unit, although not required to do so, may assume secondary responsibility for all or part of the special assessment debt, and the governmental unit has either taken such action in the past or indicated that it will take such action.

The following specific conditions would indicate that a governmental unit is obligated in some manner to repay the special assessment debt (GASB-6, par. 16):

1. When lien foreclosure proceeds are inadequate and the governmental unit is required to fund the deficiencies
2. When reserves, guarantees, or sinking funds must be established by a governmental unit
3. When delinquencies occur and the governmental unit is required to fund such delinquencies until proceeds are received from foreclosures
4. When properties put up for sale because of delinquencies are not sold at public auction and must be acquired by the governmental unit

5. When the governmental unit is authorized to and in fact establishes reserves, guarantees, or sinking funds (even if an authorized fund has not yet been established, the governmental unit may still be obligated in some manner with respect to the special assessment debt based on the conditions described in 7 and 8 below)
6. When the governmental unit is authorized to and in fact establishes a separate fund to be used to purchase or redeem special assessment debt (even if an authorized fund has not yet been established, the governmental unit may still be obligated in some manner with respect to the special assessment debt based on the conditions described in 7 and 8 below)
7. When it is explicitly indicated by contract that the governmental unit may finance delinquencies, although there is no legal duty to do so
8. When it is probable that the governmental unit will accept responsibility for defaults based on either legal decisions within the state or action previously taken by the governmental unit with respect to special assessment defaults

As the above conditions suggest, the GASB takes a very broad approach in identifying special assessment debt that should be reported by a governmental unit as debt. This broad approach to debt classification is further endorsed in GASB-6 when the phrase "obligated in some manner" is described as including all situations except for the following (GASB-6, par. 16):

- The governmental unit is prohibited from assuming responsibility for the special assessment debt in case of default.
- The governmental unit is not legally liable to assume the special assessment debt in case of default and has in no way indicated that it will or may assume the debt.

Classification of Special Assessment Debt

When property owners are responsible for paying all or a portion of special assessment debt issued to finance capital improvements, the accounting for the special assessment is dependent on whether (1) the debt is general obligation debt, (2) the governmental unit is obligated in some manner to repay the debt, or (3) the governmental unit is in no way obligated to repay the debt (GASB-6, par. 17).

General obligation debt General obligation debt is backed by the full faith and credit of a governmental unit. When special assessment debt is backed by a governmental unit, the debt must be reported as general long-term debt in the governmental activities column in the statement of net assets (government-wide financial statement).

Obligated in some manner A governmental unit is obligated in some manner to pay special assessment debt when (1) the governmental unit is legally obligated to assume all or part of the special assessment debt if property owners default or (2) the governmental unit may assume secondary responsibility for all or part of the debt and the unit has either taken such action in the past or indicated that it will take such action. Special assessment debt that a governmental unit is obligated for in some manner should be reported as general long-term debt in the statement of net assets, but the debt should be referred to as "Special Assessment Debt with Governmental Commitment."

Special assessment debt may be issued when the governmental unit is both (1) obligated in some manner for the debt and (2) obligated to pay part of the special assessment based on the public benefit portion of the capital improvement, or because the governmental unit owns property subject to the special assessment. Under this circumstance, the portion of the special assessment debt represented by the special assessment obligation of the governmental unit should be recorded as general long-term debt in the statement of net assets and the balance of the special assessment debt should be recorded as "Special Assessment Debt with Governmental Commitment."

The portion of special assessment debt (for which a governmental unit is somewhat obligated) that is a direct obligation of an Enterprise Fund or is to be repaid from operating revenues of an Enterprise Fund should be recorded as a liability of the Enterprise Fund and reported as debt in the business-type activities column in the statement of net assets (GASB-6, par. 17, and GASB-34, pars. 15–16 and 81).

No obligation to pay debt In some cases, special assessment debt may be issued with the governmental unit having no obligation to repay the debt. Under this circumstance, the special assessment debt would not be reported as an obligation by the governmental entity. However, if a portion of the special assessment is to be paid by the governmental unit based on the public benefit portion of the capital improvement or because the governmental unit owns property that is subject to the special assessment, this portion of the special assessment debt would be recorded as a general long-term debt in the statement of net assets.

When a governmental unit is in no way obligated for the special assessment debt, the debt is not reported in the unit's financial statements. However, transactions related to the financing and construction of the capital asset must be reported by the governmental entity. The receipt of the funds is reported in an Agency Fund (statement of fiduciary net assets). Construction expenditures should be accounted for in a Capital Projects Fund and the receipt of resources should be reported as "contribution from property owners" rather than described as "bond proceeds." The capital asset should be reported in the governmental activities column in the statement of net assets (GASB-6, par. 19, and GASB-34, pars. 80 and 106).

Special Assessment Reserve, Guarantee, or Sinking Fund

A governmental unit may be required or authorized to establish a reserve, guarantee, or sinking fund to accumulate resources in case property owners default on their special assessments. ADebt Service Fund should be used when resources are accumulated for principal and interest payments due in future years.

Financing Special Assessments with Current Resources

A capital improvement may be initially financed with currently available resources of the governmental unit rather than with proceeds from the issuance of special assessment debt. Payments that are made directly from a governmental fund (usually the General Fund) for capital improvements should be recorded as capital expenditures in the fund making the payments. Resources transferred from a governmental fund to a Capital Projects Fund should be recorded as interfund transfers, and capital outlays eventually made by the Capital Projects Fund should be recorded as capital expenditures (GASB-6, par. 22).

The levy of the special assessment against property owners should be recorded in the governmental fund that initially provided the resources used to finance the capital improvement. The portion of the special assessment that should be recorded as revenue is the amount that is both measurable and available. The balance of the special assessment should be recorded as deferred revenue (GASB-6, par. 20).

Reporting Capital Assets Financed by Special Assessment Debt in Enterprise Funds

Capital assets constructed for an Enterprise Fund and financed by special assessments should be accounted for in a manner similar to other capital improvements financed by special assessments. However, the capital asset should be recorded both by the Enterprise Fund and in the business-type activities column of the statement of net assets.

The cost of the capital asset should be capitalized, net of special assessment revenues. The special assessment debt related to the construction of the capital asset should be recorded as a liability of the Enterprise Fund only if one of the following conditions exists (GASB-6, par. 23):

- The Enterprise Fund is directly liable for the special assessment debt.
- The Enterprise Fund is not directly liable for the special assessment debt, but the debt is expected to be repaid from revenues of the Enterprise Fund.

Debt expected to be repaid by an Enterprise Fund should be reported as debt of the Enterprise Fund even though the debt may be backed by the full faith and credit of the governmental unit. The debt must also be reported in the government-wide statement of net assets (GASB-6, par. 23).

Although GASB-6 states that most capital assets constructed for an Enterprise Fund and financed by special assessments will be accounted for as described in the previous paragraph, it is acceptable to record all special assessment transactions solely in the Enterprise Fund. Under this approach, the special assessment levy would be recorded as a receivable and contributed capital revenue. Special assessment debt for which the Enterprise Fund is directly liable or expected to repay from its revenues would be accounted for in the Enterprise Fund. The accrual basis of accounting should be used to account for special assessments receivable and the related interest income, and special assessment debt and the related interest expense (GASB-6, par. 23).

> **OBSERVATION:** Although the GASB accepted two methods of accounting for special assessment capital projects that benefit Enterprise Funds, it did not suggest that one method was preferable to the other. The GASB did state that, generally, the guidance provided by paragraph 15 of GASB-6 should be followed (see section titled "Capital Improvements Financed by Special Assessment Related Debt"). The GASB stated in an appendix that "reporting all transactions and balances in an Enterprise Fund is not appropriate in many instances" (par. 42). The basic concern by the GASB is that project cash and receivables, and the special assessment debt, often do not meet the definitions of assets and liabilities. Thus, even though it is not suggested in the accounting standards paragraphs of GASB-6, the preparer of governmental financial statements must carefully review the facts related to the special assessment to determine whether there is any justification for reporting all special assessment transactions and balances in an Enterprise Fund.

Reporting Capital Assets Financed by Special Assessment Debt in Government-Wide Financial Statements

As noted earlier, capital assets or improvements financed by special assessment debt for which the entity is obligated in some manner must be reported as capital assets in either the governmental or business-type activities column in the statement of net assets. The related special assessment revenue and receivables must be accounted for on the accrual basis of accounting.

When the governmental entity is not obligated for the special assessment debt, the capital asset must be reported on the statement of net assets and an equal amount of program revenue (capital contributions) should be reported on the statement of activities (GASB-6, par. 19, and GASB-34, pars. 16 and 50).

Special Assessment Districts of Component Units

A component unit applies the criteria established by GASB-6 to determine how special assessment transactions and accounts should be reported. When the component unit's financial statements are blended with the primary government's financial statements to form the reporting entity, the component unit's special assessment debt should be reported as a liability in the reporting entity's financial statements based on GASB-6 criteria even though the primary government may not be responsible in any way for the component unit's special assessment debt (GASB-6, par. 24).

DISCLOSURES

The disclosures in the governmental unit's financial statements with respect to special assessment debt depend on whether the unit is responsible for the debt (GASB-6, pars. 20–21).

Governmental Unit Obligated for Debt

When the governmental unit is primarily obligated or obligated in some manner for the repayment of special assessment debt, the following disclosures that are applicable to all general obligation debt should be made in the unit's financial statements (GASB-6, par. 20):

- Nature of governmental unit's obligation for special assessment debt
- Description of individual special assessment debt issues
- Description of requirements or authorizations for the establishment of guarantees, reserves, or sinking funds if defaults occur

- Changes in general long-term debt (special assessment debt for which the unit is primarily responsible) and special assessment debt with governmental commitment (special assessment debt for which the unit is obligated in some manner)
- Summary of debt service requirements to maturity
- Special assessment debt authorized but unissued

In addition, the amount of the special assessments receivable that is delinquent should be disclosed on the face of the balance sheet or in a note to the financial statements (GASB-6, par. 20).

Governmental Unit Not Obligated for Debt

When the governmental unit is not obligated in any manner for repayment of the special assessment debt, the following disclosures should be made in the unit's financial statements (GASB-6, par. 21):

- Present amount of special assessment debt outstanding
- Statement that the governmental unit is in no manner obligated to repay the special assessment debt
- Statement that the governmental unit functions as an agent for the property owners by collecting assessments, forwarding collections to special assessment debt-holders, and, if appropriate, beginning foreclosure

IV. FINANCIAL REPORTING BY GENERAL-PURPOSE GOVERNMENTS

CHAPTER 20
COMPREHENSIVE ANNUAL FINANCIAL REPORT

CONTENTS

INTRODUCTION: COMPREHENSIVE ANNUAL FINANCIAL REPORT

The GASB takes the position that every governmental entity should prepare and publish a comprehensive annual financial report (CAFR) "as a matter of public record." The CAFR is a governmental entity's official annual report and should include the following sections:

- Introductory section
- Financial section
  - —Auditor's report
  - —Management's discussion and analysis (MD&A)
  - —Basic financial statements
  - —Notes to the basic financial statements
  - —Required supplementary information (other than MD&A)
  - —Combining statements and individual fund statements and schedules
- Statistical section

Although the GASB encourages the preparation of a CAFR, it identifies certain components as the minimum required presentation under generally accepted accounting principles. These minimum required components include

- Management Discussion and Analysis (MD&A)
- Basic Financial Statements
- Notes to the Basic Financial Statements
- Required Supplementary Information (other than MD&A)

INTRODUCTORY SECTION

Generally, the introductory section of the CAFR contains items such as a title page, a table of contents, a letter of transmittal, and other material deemed appropriate by management. Aletter of transmittal is a cover letter that summarizes the basis for the financial report, highlights financial activity for the period, and may refer to other significant events that have occurred during the period. The letter is usually addressed to the chief executive of the governmental unit and/or the legislative body and is generally signed by the chief financial officer of the state or local government that prepared the CAFR.

PRACTICE POINT: The *GASB Comprehensive Implementation Guide* notes that the GASB encourages governmental entities not to report information in the letter of transmittal of the CAFR that is included in the MD&A section of the basic financial statements. The *GASB Q&A Guide* notes that duplication can be minimized by making a brief reference to an item in the letter of transmittal with an appropriate reference to the further discussion of the item in the MD&A. A governmental entity has significant flexibility in determining what should be included in the letter of transmittal because there are no GAAP rules that apply to the letter.

FINANCIAL SECTION

The financial section of the CAFR includes the auditor's report, management's discussion and analysis, the basic financial statements, required supplementary information (other than the MD&A), and supplementary information (NCGA-1, par. 139, as amended by GASB-34).

Auditor's Report

Generally accepted auditing standards (GAAS) and in certain cases *Government Auditing Standards,* issued by the comptroller general of the United States of America (GAGAS), are applicable to audits of governmental entities examined by an independent auditor. The independent auditors report on the fair presentation of the reporting entity's various opinion units as defined in the AICPA's *State and Local Governments* Guide.

Management's Discussion and Analysis (MD&A)

The basic financial statements should be *preceded* by management's discussion and analysis (MD&A), which the GASB classified as required supplementary information (RSI). MD&A information should "provide an objective and easily readable analysis of the government's financial activities based on currently known facts, decisions, or conditions." This information should provide a broad overview of both the short-term and longterm analyses of the government's activities based on information presented in the financial report and fiscal policies that have been adopted by the governmental entity. Although the analysis provided by management should be directed to current-year results in comparison with the previous year's results, the emphasis should be on the current year. The

MD&A presentation should not be viewed as a public relations opportunity for the governmental entity but rather should be based on factual information and incorporate both positive and negative developments. In an attempt to make the information meaningful and understandable to constituents of the governmental entity, it may be appropriate to use graphs, multiple-color presentations, or other presentation strategies that might provide insight into the analysis (GASB-34, par. 8-9).

> **PRACTICE POINT:** The *GASB Comprehensive Implementation Guide* points out that GASB-34 does not address specifically whether MD&A should be placed before or after the letter of transmittal, rather, it simply states that it must precede the financial statements; however, the *GASB Q&A Guide* suggests that (1) MD&A should be presented as part of the financial section of the CAFR and (2) the letter of transmittal should be part of the introductory section of the CAFR. In addition, it is not advisable to place the letter of transmittal between MD&A and the audited (basic) financial statements, because there may be some confusion about whether the auditor's opinion applies to the letter of transmittal.

The MD&A information should focus on the primary government's activities (both governmental and business-type activities) and distinguish between its activities and its discretely presented component units. Professional judgment must be exercised to determine whether MD&A should include comments related to a specific discretely presented component unit. Factors that may be relevant in making that determination include the relationship between the component unit and the primary government and the significance of the component unit in comparison to all discretely presented component units. In some instances, it may be appropriate to refer readers to the separately presented financial statements of the component unit (GASB-34, par. 10).

The GASB emphasizes that management of the governmental entity should see the MD&A section of the financial report as an opportunity to communicate with interested parties, and it warns against preparing boilerplate material that adds little insight into the financial position and activity of the government. However, this emphasis on flexibility by the GASB is tempered in that, at a minimum, the following issues should be discussed (GASB-34, par. 11):

a. Brief discussion of the basic financial statements
b. Presentation of condensed financial information
c. Analysis of the overall financial position and results of operations
d. Analysis of balances and transactions of individual funds
e. Analysis of significant budget variations

f. Discussion of significant capital assets and long-term debt activity

g. Discussion of modified depreciation approach (if employed by the governmental entity)

h. Description of currently known facts, decisions, or conditions

> **PRACTICE POINT:** The *GASB Comprehensive Implementation Guide* states that a government with both governmental and business-type activities may present comparative data (for example, total reporting entity columns for the current and a previous year) in its basic financial statements. MD&A is not required for the previous year's presentation because that presentation does not constitute a complete set of financial statements (basic financial statements, notes, and RSI). On the other hand most governmental entities do not present comparative financial statements (basic financial statements, notes, and RSI for two years) because of the complexity of such presentations; however, if comparative financial statements are presented, MD&A must be presented for each year. That does not mean that there must be two completely separate MD&A presentations. For example, condensed financial information in MD&A for both years could be presented on a comparative basis but the analysis of the overall financial position and results of operations for each year could be included in the same paragraph or section. Governmental entities that might have the space to present comparative financial statements include governments that have a single program or a business-type activities only entity.

> **PRACTICE POINT:** The MD&A presentations, because they are RSI, should be limited to the eight elements listed above. For example, service efforts and accomplishments (SEA) or performance data should not be presented as a separate category (because it is not listed as such in the "a through h" listing); however, SEA or performance data could be introduced in a "listed" category if that information helps to explain the required MD&A. That is, performance data could be discussed in item c if it clarifies why certain operating results change from one year to the next. If it is concluded that it is inappropriate to include an item in MD&A, that information could be included in supplementary information or the letter of transmittal. The degree of detail related to the eight elements will vary from governmental entity to governmental entity. At a minimum, however, the specific requirements addressed in these elements, and described below, must be presented in MD&A.

> **PRACTICE POINT:** Some readers of GASB-34 interpreted this requirement to mean that MD&A had to include at least these eight components (a through h) but that a financial statement preparer was free to add other components. GASB-37 points out that the language in paragraph 11 should have been

interpreted to mean that "the information presented should be confined to the topics discussed in a through h."

Discussion of the basic financial statements The MD&A information should include a description of the basic financial statements and how the government-wide financial statements relate to the fund financial statements. This discussion should explain how fund financial statements either "reinforce information in government-wide statements or provide additional information." Topics that may be included in this section of MD&A include the following:

- The broad scope and overall perspective government-wide financial statements (statement of net assets and the statement of activities)
- The nature of major fund financial statements for governmental funds (balance sheet and statement of revenues, expenditures, and changes in fund balances) and proprietary fund activities (statement of net assets, statement of revenues, expenses, and changes in fund net assets, and statement of cash flows)
- The fiduciary role of the governmental entity and the nature of the related financial statements (statement of fiduciary net assets and statement of changes in fiduciary net assets)

PRACTICE POINT: The *GASB Comprehensive Implementation Guide* points out that the totals in the government-wide financial statements will generally not equal to the totals in the fund financial statements, because different measurement focuses and bases of accounting are used to prepare the financial statements. For this reason GASB-34 (par. 77) requires that at the bottom of the fund financial statements or in a separate schedule there be a summary reconciliation between the fund financial statements and the government-wide financial statements. Specifically, the amount shown as the "total fund balances" in the "total governmental funds" column on the fund balance sheets must be reconciled to the "net assets" for governmental activities presented on the statement of net assets. Also, the amount shown as "net changes in fund balance" in the "total governmental funds" column on the statements of revenues, expenditures, and changes in fund balances must be reconciled to the "changes in net assets" for governmental activities presented on the statement of activities. Requirement 11a focuses on the same concept as paragraph 77, but MD&A should provide only an overview of the differences, and that overview should be in a narrative form. If the totals on the government-wide financial statements and fund financial statements are essentially the same, MD&A should note that they are similar.

Presentation of condensed financial information The MD&A information should include condensed government-wide financial statements and comments on the significant changes from the previous year to the current year. The condensed presentation should include information, at a minimum, that supports the analysis of the overall financial position and results of operations (which is the next topic discussed below). The condensed information section should include the following:

- Total assets, distinguishing between capital and other assets
- Total liabilities, distinguishing between long-term debt outstanding and other liabilities
- Total net assets, distinguishing between amounts invested in capital assets (net of related debt), restricted amounts, and unrestricted amounts
- Total program revenues (by major sources)
- General revenues (by major sources)
- Total revenues
- Program expenses (by functional category, at a minimum)
- Total expenses
- Excess (deficiency) before contributions to term and permanent endowments or permanent fund principal, special and extraordinary items, and transfers
- Contributions
- Extraordinary and special items
- Transfers
- Change in net assets
- Beginning and ending net assets

> **PRACTICE POINT:** *The GASB Comprehensive Implementation Guide* notes that although paragraph 9 of GASB-34 encourages the use of charts and graphs in the MD&A, comparison of condensed financial information should not be presented as charts and graphs; however, charts and graphs may be used to elaborate on the presentation of the condensed information.

Analysis of the overall financial position and results of operations There should be an analysis of the overall improvement or deterioration of financial position and results of operations of the governmental entity based on government-wide financial statements. The analysis should focus on both governmental activities and business-type activities. The emphasis on the comments about the condensed government-wide financial statements should be analytical and not just computational. For example, percentage changes from the previous year to the current year should be supplemented with a discussion of important economic factors, such as interest rate changes and changes in regional economic activity, that affected the governmental entity's operating results for the year.

Analysis of balances and transactions of individual funds Part of MD&A should concentrate on significant changes in balances and transactions that are related to individual funds. Information concerning the availability of resources for future use should be discussed, taking into consideration restrictions, commitments, and other factors.

Analysis of significant budget variations The analysis of budgetary information should focus on significant differences between (1) the original budget and the final budget and (2) actual budgetary results and the final budget. The commentary should include analysis of currently known reasons that are expected to have a significant effect on future services or liquidity.

> **PRACTICE POINT:** The *GASB Comprehensive Implementation Guide* states that the MD&A should not merely point out the obvious. For example, stating that there was an increase from the original budget in order to "cover higher-than-expected expenditures" is not helpful. The analysis should explain what factors led to the increase in expenditures.

Discussion of significant capital assets and long-term debt activity MD&A information should describe activity that affected capital assets and long-term debt during the period. The discussion should include commitments for capital expenditures, changes in credit ratings, and whether debt limitations may affect future planned activities. In this analysis there is no need to repeat the information that is contained in the notes to the financial statements that relate to capital assets and long-term liabilities; however, the information may be presented in a summary form.

> **PRACTICE POINT:** The *GASB Comprehensive Implementation Guide* notes that MD&A does not have to include special assessment debt for which the governmental entity is not obligated in any manner (as described in GASB-6 (Accounting and Financial Reporting for Special Assessments)). However, the *GASB Q&A Guide* notes that special assessment debt may be included in the MD&A discussion "if, for example, the proceeds were used to build or acquire significant infrastructure assets for the government."

Discussion of modified depreciation approach (if employed by the governmental entity) As discussed earlier, a governmental entity may not depreciate certain "eligible" infrastructure assets but rather may use the modified depreciation approach. For governments that use the modified depreciation approach, the MD&A information should discuss the following:

- Any significant changes in the assessed level of condition of eligible infrastructure assets from previous condition assessments
- A comparison of the current level of asset condition with the condition level that the government has established
- Any significant difference between the actual amounts spent to maintain the current level and condition and the estimated annual amount needed to maintain or preserve eligible infrastructure assets at an appropriate level of condition

Description of currently known facts, decisions, or conditions MD&A should describe current known facts, decisions, or conditions that are expected to have a significant effect on the entity's financial position (net assets) and operations results (revenues, expenses, and other changes in net assets). GASB-34 emphasizes that currently known facts do not constitute prospective information, such as forecasted financial statements.

> **OBSERVATION:** *GASB Comprehensive Implementation Guide* notes that currently known facts must be based on events that have taken place. For example, the enactment of a new sales tax is a currently known fact and should be included in the MD&A. The prediction of how much tax receipts will increase if there is an economic upturn is not a known fact and such a discussion is inappropriate in MD&A. Also, the GASB'S *Guide* points out that some currently known facts that are discussed in the MD&A could also be included in the notes to the financial statements. Under this circumstance, the MD&A presentation should only highlight the information that is included in the note. The GASB'S *Guide* also states that the discussion of currently known facts, decisions, or conditions should focus on both governmental and business-type activities separately.

Basic Financial Statements

GASB-34 lists the following as the components of a governmental entity's basic financial statements (GASB-34, par. 6):

- Government-wide financial statements (basic financial statements)

- Fund financial statements (basic financial statements)
- Notes to the basic financial statements

> **OBSERVATION:** The basic financial statements established by GASB-34 replaces the general purpose financial statements currently required by NCGA-1 (Governmental Accounting and Financial Reporting Principles).

> **PRACTICE POINT:** GASB-34 provides that the required budgetary comparison schedules may be presented as a component of the basic financial statements rather than as required supplemental information. When the budgetary comparison schedules are presented as a basic financial statement, the schedules should be reported within the governmental fund financial statements.

Government-Wide Financial Statements

The focus of government-wide financial statements is on the overall financial position and activities of the government as a whole. These financial statements are constructed around the concept of a primary government as defined by GASB-14 (The Financial Reporting Entity) and therefore encompass the primary government and its component units, except for fiduciary funds of the primary government and component units that are fiduciary in nature. Financial statements of fiduciary funds are not presented in the government-wide financial statements but are included in the fund financial statements (GASB-34, par. 13).

> **PRACTICE POINT:** The financial statements of Fiduciary Funds are excluded from government-wide financial statements because resources of these funds cannot be used to finance a governmental entity's activities. The financial statements of a Fiduciary Fund are included in the entity's fund financial statements because the governmental entity is financially accountable for those resources even though they belong to other parties.

The GASB believes that government-wide financial statements will provide user groups with the following (GASB-34, par. 12):

- Present financial information about the overall government without presenting information about individual funds or fund types
- Exclude financial information about fiduciary activities

- Differentiate between financial information that applies to the primary government and that of discretely presented component units
- Differentiate between the primary government's governmental activities and business-type activities
- Measure and present all financial balances and activities based on the economic resources measurement focus and the accrual basis of accounting

> **PRACTICE POINT:** The *GASB Comprehensive Implementation Guide* states that a governmental entity cannot simply issue only government-wide financial statements or only fund financial statements. However, the reporting requirements for certain special-purpose governments are somewhat different, as described in paragraphs 138 and 139 of GASB-34. In addition, generally governments cannot combine the government-wide and fund financial statements; however, single-program governments may combine the government-wide and fund financial statements. This exception is discussed in GASB-34 (par. 136).

In order to achieve some of the objectives listed above, GASB-34 requires that government-wide financial statements be formatted following these guidelines (GASB-34, pars. 14–15):

- Separate rows and columns should be used to distinguish between the primary government's governmental activities and business-type activities.
- A total column should be used for the primary government.
- Separate rows and columns should distinguish between the total primary government (governmental activities plus business-type activities) and its discretely presented component units.
- A total column may be used for the reporting entity (primary government and discretely presented component units), but this is optional.
- A total column may be used for prior-year information, but this is optional.

> **PRACTICE POINT:** GASB-34 states that governmental activities are "generally financed through taxes, intergovernmental revenues, and other nonexchange revenues," and business-type activities are financed to some degree by charging external parties for the goods or services they acquire. Governmental activities are generally accounted for in governmental funds and Internal Service Funds. Business-type activities are usually reported in Enterprise Funds.

PRACTICE POINT: A total column should be used to combine the governmental activities and the business-type activities of a governmental entity. A separate column that combines the government and its component units (discretely presented) may or may not be used; however, if it is used, it should not be titled "memorandum only." The "memorandum only" columnar heading is appropriate only when columns with different measurement focuses and bases of accounting are added together. The government-wide financial statements are based on a single measurement focus and basis of accounting.

PRACTICE POINT: As described above, the government-wide financial statements have separate columns for governmental activities and business-type activities. *GASB Comprehensive Implementation Guide* points out that generally, governmental funds are combined to form the governmental activities column and Enterprise Funds are combined to form the business-type activities column; however, an activity and a fund are not the same. An "activity" refers to a program or service but a "fund" is an accounting and reporting vehicle. For this reason, an activity (governmental or business-type) could be performed in one or more funds, and a fund could perform one or more activities. For example, an Enterprise Fund could perform an activity that is governmental, rather than business, in nature and that activity should be presented in the governmental activities column in the government-wide financial statements. If this occurs, the activity would represent a reconciling item between the fund financial statements and the government-wide financial statements as required by GASB-34, paragraph 77.

OBSERVATION: *GASB Comprehensive Implementation Guide* points out that GASB-34 does not require that comparative prior-year data be presented but that it may be presented. For this reason, GASB-34 provides no guidelines for the presentation of prior-year data. Presenting comparative data in governmental financial statements, as opposed to corporate financial statements, is very problematic because of the complicated structure of governmental statements. For example, reporting a comparative statement of net assets for many governmental entities requires eight columns or more. Trying to format a statement of activities for many governmental entities would probably be too unwieldy. If a governmental entity is not a complex reporting entity (for example, if it has only governmental activities and no component units), presenting prior-year data might not be cumbersome. The GASB'S *Guide* points out that for more complicated reporting entities the best way to present prioryear data may be by reproducing the prior-year financial statements in the current-year's financial statements.

Governmental activities should be accounted for and reported based on all applicable GASB pronouncements, NCGA pronouncements, and the following pronouncements issued on or before November 30, 1989, unless they conflict with GASB or NCGA pronouncements (GASB-34, par. 17):

- Financial Accounting Standards Board (FASB) Statements and Interpretations
- Accounting Principles Board (APB) Opinions
- Accounting Research Bulletins (ARBs) of the Committee on Accounting Procedure

OBSERVATION: In the past, pronouncements of the FASB, the APB, and the Committee on Accounting Procedure have not, for the most part, been applied to information presented in governmental funds. The GASB decided that government-wide financial statements must be prepared by applying these pronouncements issued on or before November 30, 1989, (unless they conflict with GASB pronouncements) on a retroactive basis (with four exceptions discussed in paragraph 146 of GASB-34). Pronouncements issued by the FASB after November 30, 1989, are not followed in the preparation of financial statements for governmental activities.

Business-type activities must follow either Alternative 1 or Alternative 2 of GASB-20 (Accounting and Financial Reporting for Proprietary Funds and Other Governmental Entities That Use Proprietary Fund Accounting). Under Alternative 1, governmental entities using proprietary fund accounting must follow (1) all GASB pronouncements and (2) FASB Statements and Interpretations, APB Opinions, and Accounting Research Bulletins (ARBs) issued on or before November 30, 1989, except those that conflict with a GASB pronouncement. Under Alternative 2, governmental entities using proprietary fund accounting must follow (1) all GASB pronouncements and (2) all FASB Statements and Interpretations, APB Opinions, and ARBs, no matter when issued, except those that conflict with a GASB pronouncement. Unlike Alternative 1, Alternative 2 has no cutoff date for determining the applicability of FASB pronouncements.

OBSERVATION: Even though governmental activities are presented in the government-wide financial statements based on the same measurement focus and basis of accounting as business-type activities, the GASB does not allow governmental activities to be accounted for using the approach found in Alternative 2 of GASB-20. Enterprise Funds only are allowed to use Alternative 2 "to permit the financial reporting of state and local governments' business-type activities to more nearly parallel that of their private-sector counterparts." No similar need for comparison exits for governmental activities.

PRACTICE POINT: FAS-71 (Accounting for the Effects of Certain Types of Regulation) does not preclude the application of its standards to governmental entities. The guidance allows governmental entities to follow the standards established by FAS-71, but does not require them to do so. GASB-34 does not change the application guidance established in FAS-71. Thus, because FAS-71 was issued before November 30, 1989, the standards established by FAS-71 may be used under Alternative 1 or Alternative 2 of GASB-20 because application was made optional under FAS-7. However, GASB-34 notes that the standards established by FAS-71 apply only when (a) an Enterprise Fund is used and (b) the three criteria of FAS-71, paragraph 5, are satisfied. Also, the GASB points out that normal Medicare and Medicaid arrangements with health-care providers do not satisfy the criteria established by paragraph 5 of FAS-71.

As noted above, the flow of economic resources measurement focus and accrual accounting (which are the concepts upon which commercial enterprises prepare their financial statements) are the basis upon which government-wide financial statements are prepared. Under the flow of economic resources measurement focus and accrual basis of accounting, revenues are recognized when earned and expenses are recorded when incurred when these activities are related to exchange and exchange-like activities. In addition, longlived assets (such as buildings and equipment) are capitalized and depreciated over their estimated economic lives (GASB-34, par. 16).

Unlike commercial enterprises, much of the revenue received by governments is not based on an exchange or an exchange-like transaction (i.e., the selling of a product or service and receiving something of approximate equal value) but rather arises from the entity's taxing powers or as grants from other governmental entities or individuals (nonexchange transactions). For these nonexchange transactions, the standards established by GASB-33 (Accounting and Financial Reporting for Nonexchange Transactions) are used.

The government-wide financial statements include the following:

- Statement of net assets
- Statement of activities

NOTE: A government-wide statement of cash flows is not required.

Statement of net assets GASB-34 recommends that the statement of net assets be formatted so that the net asset amount of the reporting entity is formed by subtracting total liabilities from total assets. The category "net assets" as recommended replaces the fund equity section previously used by governmental entities (GASB-34, par. 30).

> **OBSERVATION:** Although the GASB recommends that the netasset format be adopted for the statement of net assets, the Board does not prohibit formatting the statement so that a net asset section (equity) is presented whereby total asset equals total liabilities plus the residual balance. Irrespective of how the statement of net assets is formatted, the difference between total assets and total liabilities must be referred to as "net assets" rather than "fund balances" or "equity."

Presentation of assets and liabilities Assets and liabilities should be presented in the statement of net assets based on their relative liquidity. The liquidity of assets is determined by their ability to be converted to cash and the absence of any restriction that might limit their conversion to cash. The liquidity of liabilities is based on maturity dates or expected payment dates. Because of the significant degree of aggregation used in the preparation of government-wide financial statements, the GASB notes that the liquidity of an asset or liability account presented in the statement of net assets should be determined by assessing the average liquidity of the class of assets or liabilities to which it belongs, "even though individual balances may be significantly more or less liquid than others in the same class and some items may have both current and long-term element" (GASB-34, par. 31).

Most governmental entities prepare an unclassified statement of net assets that lists assets based on their liquidity. Alternatively, GASB-34 notes that assets and liabilities may be presented in the statement of net assets using a classified financial statement format whereby accounts are grouped in current and noncurrent categories similar to the presentation used by business enterprises.

When a governmental entity presents a classified statement of net assets, the question arises as to whether the amount that represents restricted net assets (in the equity section) requires that specific assets be identified as "restricted assets" (in the asset section). In preparing financial statements, there is no general requirement that specific equity accounts be traceable to specific assets. Therefore, when a classified statement of net assets is presented, there is no need to establish a subcategory of assets identified as restricted; however, a financial statement preparer should carefully evaluate the ramifications of restrictions to determine whether they are determinant in categorizing an asset as current or noncurrent.

ARB-43 (Restatement and Revision of Accounting Research Bulletins) notes that current assets should not include "cash and claims to cash that are restricted as to withdrawal or use for other than current operations, are designated for expenditure in the acquisition or construction of noncurrent assets, or are segregated for the liquidation of long-term debt." The *GASB Comprehensive Implementation Guide* states that "resources accounted for in the General Fund, Special Revenue Funds, and Debt Service Funds are generally expected to be used in current operations or to liquidate current obligations and thus generally would be considered current assets." On the other hand, cash presented in a Capital Projects Fund or a Permanent Fund, due to the nature of each fund type, should be evaluated to determine whether the amount or a portion of the amount should be reported as a current or noncurrent asset.

The AICPA'S *State and Local Governments* Guide addresses the issue of how "assets restricted for debt retirement [that] include amounts due from other funds" should be reported in the statement of net assets. For example, the assets of a Debt Service Fund may include an amount due from the General Fund. When all governmental funds are consolidated to create the government activities column in the statement of net assets, the interfund receivable and payable are eliminated, but care must be taken that the implied restriction on cash for debt retirement is considered when a classified statement of net assets is prepared (differentiating between current and noncurrent assets) and when an unclassified statement of net assets is prepared (listing assets based on their liquidity).

Once individual liabilities are grouped into accounts titles for financial statement presentation, account groupings that have an average maturity of greater than one year must be reported in two components—the portion due within one year and the portion due beyond one year. For example, if several individual general ledger accounts have been grouped for financial statement purposes in the account titled "notes payable" and on average this grouping has an average maturity greater than one year, the presentation on the statement of net assets could appear as follows:

Notes Payable:	
Due with one year	$1,000,000
Due beyond one year	6,000,000

PRACTICE POINT: If several liability groupings, have an average maturity life beyond one year, the detail information by account title (e.g., notes payable, bonds payable) do not have to be made on the face of the statement of net assets but rather may be presented in a note to the financial statements with appropriate reference.

PRACTICE POINT: The *GASB Comprehensive Implementation Guide* states that a governmental entity must make an estimate of compensated absences that may be paid within one year based on factors such as (1) historical experience, (2) budgeted amounts, and (3) personnel policies concerning the length of accumulation.

PRACTICE POINT: The *GASB Comprehensive Implementation Guide* states that the unfunded actuarial liability is not an accounting liability. The liability or asset related to a governmental entity's pension plan should be reported based on paragraphs 11, 17, and 39 of GASB-27 (Accounting for Pension by State and Local Governmental Employers). However, the *GASB Q&A Guide* notes that if a government issues tax-supported general obligation bonds to fund the unfunded actuarial liability of its pension plan, that obligation would be reported on the statement of net assets in the governmental activities column. If any of the proceeds of the issuance remain, that amount should be reported as an asset.

OBSERVATION: The *GASB Comprehensive Implementation Guide* states that when a governmental entity accounts for its risk financing activities in its General Fund (modified accrual based accounting), the liability/expense related to claims should be reported on an accrual basis as defined in GASB-10 (Accounting and Financial Reporting for Risk Financing and Related Insurance Issues), paragraphs 53-57, in the government-wide financial statements.

Presentation of capital assets The governmental entity should report all of its capital assets in the statement of net assets, based on their original historical cost plus ancillary charges such as transportation, installation, and site preparation costs. Capital assets that have been donated to a governmental entity must be capitalized at their estimated fair value (plus any ancillary costs) at the date of receipt. Capital assets are discussed in Chapter 10, "Capital Assets."

PRACTICE POINT: Because capital assets are presented in the government-wide financial statements, the previous requirement that a governmental entity present its capital assets in a General Fixed Assets Account Group (GFAAG) was rescinded by GASB-34.

Presentation of restricted assets The liquidity of assets is determined by their ability to be converted to cash and the absence of any restriction that might limit their conversion to cash. If an asset is restricted, the nature of the restriction must be evaluated to determine the appropriate location within the asset classification. The *GASB Comprehensive Implementation Guide* provides the following examples of how restrictions would affect asset presentation:

Cash restricted for the servicing of debt If the cash is expected to be used to pay "current maturities," the cash could be reported with unrestricted cash.

Permanently restricted assets If assets are permanently restricted, they are not available to pay a governmental entity's expenses and are therefore as illiquid as capital assets.

Term restrictions The term of the restriction determines where assets subject to term restrictions are presented. If the restriction ends within a short period after the date of the financial statements, the assets would be relatively liquid. On the other hand, if the time restriction is longer than one year, the assets are as illiquid as long-term receivables that have a similar "maturity" date.

Presentation of long-term liabilities In the government-wide financial statements, both short-term and long-term liabilities of a governmental entity are presented as described earlier. Long-term liabilities may include debts such as notes, mortgages, bonds, and obligations related to capitalized lease agreements. In addition, operating liabilities related to activities such as compensated absences and claims and assessments must be reported in the statement of net assets.

PRACTICE POINT: Because all general long-term obligations are presented in the government-wide financial statements, the requirement that a governmental entity present such obligations as part of a General Long-Term Debt Account Group (GLTDAG) was rescinded by GASB-34.

Presentation of components of net assets Net assets represent the difference between a governmental entity's total assets and its total liabilities. The statement of net assets must identify the components of net assets, namely (1) invested in capital assets, net of related debt; (2) restricted net assets; and (3) unrestricted net assets (GASB-34, par. 32).

PRACTICE POINT: The *GASB Comprehensive Implementation Guide* specifically notes that other terms, such as "equity," "net worth," and "fund balance" should not be used in the statement of net assets.

The *GASB Comprehensive Implementation Guide* makes the following observations about invested in capital assets (net of related debt):

- All capital assets, regardless of any restrictions (for example, federal surplus property), must be considered in the computation of net assets invested in capital assets (net of related debt). The *GASB Comprehensive Implementation Guide* notes that the purpose of identifying net assets as restricted and unrestricted is to provide insight into the availability of *financial,* not capital, resources.

- Net assets invested in capital assets (net of related debt) is the difference between (1) capital assets net of accumulated depreciation and (2) liabilities "attributable to the acquisition, construction, or improvement of those assets." When debt has been issued to finance the acquisition, construction, or improvement of capital assets but all or part of the cash has not been spent by the end of the fiscal year, the unspent portion of the debt should not be used to determine the amount of invested capital assets (net or related debt) amount. The portion of the unspent debt "should be included in the same net assets component as the unspent proceeds—for example, *restricted for capital projects.*"
- Many governmental entities create (1) a Capital Projects Fund to account for capital debt proceeds to be used to acquire, construct, or improve infrastructure assets and buildings (including land) and (2) specific accounts in the General Fund or other funds for capital debt proceeds to be used to acquire capital assets other than infrastructure assets. When these approaches are used, it is relatively simple to identify the unspent portion of capital debt proceeds. For those governmental entities that do not use these two approaches and commingle funds, the *GASB Comprehensive Implementation Guide* states that they must "use their best estimates—in a manner that can be documented—to determine the unspent portion."
- When debt is issued to refund existing capital-related debt, the newly issued debt is considered capital-related and is used to compute the net assets invested in capital assets (net of related debt) component.
- When a governmental entity has capital assets but no related debt, the net asset component should be simply identified as "net assets invested in capital assets."
- When a general purpose government issues bonds to construct school buildings for its independent school districts and the repayment of the bonds is the responsibility of the general purpose government, because the debt was not used to acquire, construct, or improve capital assets for the governmental entity, the outstanding debt is not capital-related and is not used to compute the amount of net assets invested in capital assets (net of related debt) of the general purpose government. The effect is to reduce unrestricted net assets. The *GASB Comprehensive Implementation Guide* notes that if doing so has a significant effect on the

unrestricted net assets component, the circumstances may be further explained in a note to the financial statements.

Restricted net assets arise if either of the following conditions exists (GASB-34, par. 34):

- Externally imposed by creditor (such as through debt covenants), grantors, contributors, or laws or regulations of other governments
- Imposed by law through constitutional provisions or enabling legislation

GASB-34 points out that enabling legalization "authorizes the government to assess, levy, charge, or otherwise mandate payment of resources (from external resource providers) and includes a legally enforceable requirement that those resources be used only for the specific purposes stipulated in the legislation.

PRACTICE POINT: GASB-46 defines "legal enforceability" as meaning that a government can be compelled by an external party—citizens, public interest groups, or the judiciary—to use resources created by enabling legislation only for the purposes specified by the legislation. However, enforceability cannot ultimately be proven unless tested through the judicial process; therefore professional judgment must be exercised.

PRACTICE POINT: When a state legislature passes a law to earmark a percentage of specific tax proceeds (e.g., a percent of its sales taxes) for a specific purpose, this is not the same as enabling legislation. The enabling-legislation criterion is satisfied only when the same law creates both the tax and the resection on how the resulting resources may be used.

Restricted net assets should be identified based on major categories that make up the restricted balance. These categories could include items such as net assets restricted for capital projects and net assets restricted for debt service.

PRACTICE POINT: The *GASB Comprehensive Implementation Guide* states that GASB-34 requires that information supporting details of restricted net assets be presented in the body of the financial statements and not in the notes to the financial statements.

PRACTICE POINT: The liabilities related to restricted assets must be considered in determining restricted net assets as presented on the statement of net assets. For example, the statement of net assets would generally identify net assets restricted for capital projects. In order to determine that amount, the starting point would be to identify total net assets (total assets minus total liabilities) in all Capital Projects Funds. Additionally, because a Capital Projects Fund is on the modified accrual basis and the statement of net assets is on the accrual basis, it would be necessary to take into consideration any "conversion" adjustments that would increase or decrease the liabilities in the Capital Projects Funds. However, a negative (deficit) balance in restricted net assets cannot be displayed on the statement of net assets. Any negative amount would be used to reduce the unrestricted net asset balance.

In some instances, net assets may be restricted on a permanent basis (in perpetuity). Under this circumstance, the restricted net assets must be subdivided into expendable and nonexpendable restricted net assets (GASB-34, par. 35).

PRACTICE POINT: GASB-34 points out that, generally, the amount of net assets identified as restricted on the statement of net assets will not be the same as the amount of reserved fund balance or reserved net assets presented on the fund balance sheets/statement of net assets because (1) the financial statements are based on different measurement focuses and bases of accounting and (2) there are different definitions for restricted net assets and reserved fund balance. (Fund financial statements are discussed later.)

GASB Comprehensive Implementation Guide makes the following observations about restricted net assets:

- Paragraph 34 of GASB-34 is the starting point for determining whether net assets are restricted. In addition, the *GASB Q&A Guide* points out that in order to be considered restricted net assets, the restriction must be narrower than the "reporting unit in which it is reported." For example, if the resources are restricted to "public safety," then the resources are considered to be restricted. On the other hand, if the resources are to be used "for the benefit of the citizens," that restriction is as broad as the governmental entity and there is effectively no restriction on net assets.
- The requirements of paragraph 35 apply only to permanent endowments or permanent fund principal because restrictions imposed on term endowments will at some point be expendable.
- The liabilities related to restricted assets must be considered in determining restricted net assets.
- Earmarking an existing revenue source is not the same as enabling legislation. The enabling legislation criterion is satisfied

only when the same law creates a tax or other source of revenue and the restriction on how the resulting resources may be used.

Assets that are not classified as invested in capital assets (net of related debt) or restricted are included in the category unrestricted net assets. Portions of the entity's net assets may be identified by management to reflect tentative plans or commitments of governmental resources. The tentative plans or commitments may be related to items such as plans to retire debt at some future date or to replace infrastructure or specified capital assets. Designated amounts are not the same as restricted amounts because designations represent planned actions, not actual commitments. For this reason, designated amounts should not be classified with restricted net assets but rather should be reported as part of the unrestricted net asset component. In addition, designations cannot be disclosed as such on the face of the statement of net assets (GASB-34, pars. 36–37).

Relationship of restricted assets and equity accounts The statement of net assets illustrated in this chapter (Exhibit 20-1) is unclassified. Alternatively, GASB-34 notes that assets and liabilities may be presented in the statement of net assets using a classified financial statement format whereby accounts are grouped in current and noncurrent categories similar to the presentation used by business enterprises. When a governmental entity presents a classified statement of net assets, the question arises as to whether the amount that represents restricted net assets (in the equity section) requires that specific assets be identified as "restricted assets" (in the asset section). In preparing financial statements there is no general requirement that specific equity accounts be traceable to specific assets. Therefore, when a classified statement of net assets is presented there is no need to establish a subcategory of assets identified as restricted; however, a financial statement preparer should carefully evaluate the ramifications of restrictions to determine whether they are determinant in categorizing an asset as current or noncurrent. ARB-43 (Restatement and Revision of Accounting Research Bulletins) notes that current assets should not include "cash and claims to cash that are restricted as to withdrawal or use for other than current operations, are designated for expenditure in the acquisition or construction of noncurrent assets, or are segregated for the liquidation of long-term debt."

GASB Comprehensive Implementation Guide states that "resources accounted for in the General Fund, Special Revenue Funds, and Debt Service Funds are generally expected to be used in current operations or to liquidate current obligations and thus generally would be considered current assets." On the other hand, cash presented in a Capital Projects Fund or a Permanent Fund, due to the nature of each fund, should be evaluated to determine whether the amount or a portion of the amount should be reported as a current or noncurrent asset.

Excess restricted assets A restricted fund (for example, a Special Revenue Fund) may include an asset balance that exceeds the requirements of the related restriction. *GASB Comprehensive Implementation Guide* states that under this circumstance the excess amount should be used to compute the amount of unrestricted net assets.

General restrictions imposed by a state government on local revenue sources In some instances a state statute may exist that requires that "revenues derived from a fee or charge shall not be used for any purpose other than that for which the fee or charge was imposed." *GASB Comprehensive Implementation Guide* states that if a local government has imposed such a fee or charge (for example for the replacement of infrastructure assets) the unspent resources accumulated from the fee or charge represent a restricted net asset (the equity account component).

Subsequent legislation changing the use of specific tax revenues A state legislature may change an existing law that previously restricted the use of tax revenue to a particular type of expenditure. *GASB Comprehensive Implementation Guide* points out that although "the new restriction is not established by the original enabling legislation the net assets arising from the changed legislation are nonetheless restricted for purposes of financial statement disclosure even though the new tax revenues are to be used for a purpose different from that identified in the original legislation."

Revenue flow assumption concerning unrestricted and restricted net assets A Special Revenue Fund may include resources that are unrestricted (for example, a transfer from the General Fund) and resources that are restricted (for example, revenues from a stateshared motor fuel tax that must be used for street repair and maintenance). Because the resources (cash) are fungible, a revenue flow assumption must be made by the governmental identify to identify whether unrestricted or restricted resources are used first. *GASB Comprehensive Implementation Guide* states that either approach is acceptable; however, the financial statements must disclose the accounting policy adopted.

Capital debt and unreported capital assets Under some circumstances a governmental entity may report capital debt but not report the capital asset that was purchased with the debt proceeds. For example, so-called Phase 3 governments are encouraged but not required to report major general infrastructure assets retroactively; however, the related debt must be reported. Under this circumstance, the question arises as to whether the capital debt should be considered in determining the amount to be reported as net assets invested in capital assets (net of related debt). *GASB Comprehensive Implementation Guide* states that the capital debt must be used to compute the amount of net assets invested in capital assets (net of related debt) even though the related capital asset is not reported in the statement of net assets. Furthermore, if the total capital debt is greater than the reported capital assets, the net assets invested in capital assets (net of related debt) will have a negative (debit) balance; however that negative amount must nonetheless be reported in the governmental entity statement of net assets.

Assets restricted for the payment of capital debt In some instances a governmental entity may specifically restrict assets that are to be used to pay the current portion of bonds that were issued to finance the acquisition of capital assets. Even though the restricted assets are used to determine the amount of restricted net assets, *GASB Comprehensive Implementation Guide* states that the related current portion of the maturing debt must be used to determine the amount of net assets invested in capital assets (net of related debt) rather than restricted net assets.

Unamortized debt issuance costs and deferred amounts from refundings Costs related to the issuance of debt and gains/losses related to the refunding of debt must be amortized and, for reporting purposes, *GASB Comprehensive Implementation Guide* points out that the unamortized portion of these accounts is used to determine the amount of the related net assets based on the purpose of issuing the debt. For example, if debt was issued to finance the construction of a capital asset, any unamortized balances are used to compute the reported amount of net assets invested in capital assets (net of related debt). On the other hand, if debt was issued for a specific purpose and the proceeds have not been expended, the unamortized balances are used to determine the amount of restricted net assets. If the debt was issued and the proceeds were not restricted, the unamortized balances are used to compute unrestricted net assets.

Equity interest in a joint venture *GASB Comprehensive Implementation Guide* states that an equity interest in a joint venture is represented by unrestricted net assets because the investment does not reflect capital assets (1) held directly by the governmental entity or (2) restricted as defined in paragraph 34 of GASB-34. The unrestricted net asset category is the default category. If an item does not qualify for classification as invested in capital assets (net of related debt) or restricted net assets, then it must be classified as unrestricted net assets.

Exhibit 20-1 is an illustration of a statement of net assets consistent with the standards established by GASB-34.

Statement of activities The format for the government-wide statement of activities is significantly different from any operating statement previously used in governmental financial reporting. The focus of the statement of activities is on the net cost of various activities provided by the governmental entity. The statement begins with a column that identifies the cost of each governmental activity. Another column identifies the revenues that are specifically related to the classified governmental activities. The difference between the expenses and revenues related to specific activities computes the net cost or benefits of the activities, which "identifies the extent to which each function of the government draws from the general revenues of the government or is self-financing through fees and intergovernmental aid" (GASB-34, pars. 38–40).

OBSERVATION: The GASB established the unique presentation format for the statement of activities in part because it believes that format provides an opportunity to provide feedback on a typical budgetary question that is asked when a program is adopted; namely, "What will the program cost and how will it be financed?"

PRACTICE POINT: The *GASB Comprehensive Implementation Guide* emphasizes that expenses and revenues should be reported gross on the statement of activities.

The governmental entity must determine the level at which governmental activities are to be presented; however, the level of detail must be at least as detailed as that required in the governmental fund financial statements (which are discussed later). Generally, activities would be aggregated and presented at the functional category level; however, entities are encouraged to present activities at a more detailed level, such as by programs. Due to the size and complexities of some governmental entities it may be impractical to expand the level of detail beyond that of functional categories. (The discussion that follows assumes that the level of detail presented in the statement of activities is at the functional category level.)

PRACTICE POINT: The level of detail for expenses presented on the statement of activities is based on the minimum level of detail required for government funds (governmental activities) and proprietary funds (business-type activities). For governmental funds, the minimum level of detail, as established NCGA-1, paragraphs 111–116, is by function. For proprietary funds, the minimum level of detail, as established by GASB-34, paragraph 122, by object is function.

The level of detail for presentation on the statement of activities is the required minimum level and not the actual level of detail used to prepare the fund financial statements. That is, fund financial statements could be prepared at a more detailed level than the minimum required and the statement of activities could reflect a lesser level (e.g., the minimum level required).

EXHIBIT 20-1
STATEMENT OF NET ASSETS

City of Centerville
Statement of Net Assets
June 30, 20X5

	Primary Government			
	Governmental Activities	*Business-Type Activities*	*Total*	*Component Units*
ASSETS				
Cash and cash equivalents	$5,500,000	$5,600,000	$11,100,000	$760,000
Receivables (net)	7,804,000	13,209,000	21,013,000	750,000
Investments	13,728,000	2,500,000	16,228,000	950,000
Inventories and prepayments	230,000	723,000	953,000	502,000
Internal balances	112,000	(112,000)		
Land	5,600,000	11,000,000	16,600,000	—
Other capital assets, net (See Note X)	40,400,000	11,000,000	51,400,000	12,400,000
Total Assets	$73,374,000	$43,920,000	$117,294,000	$15,362,000
LIABILITIES				
Accounts payable	$2,800,000	$1,300,000	$4,100,000	$420,000
Deferred revenue	60,000	50,000	60,000	7,000
Other payables	150,000	300,000	500,000	100,000
Long-term debt (See Note XX)				
Due within one year	3,800,000	350,000	4,150,000	540,000
Due beyond one year	22,000,000	12,500,000	34,500,000	10,200,000
Total Liabilities	$28,810,000	$14,500,000	$43,310,000	$11,267,000
NET ASSETS				
Invested in capital assets, net of related debt	$22,428,000	$16,700,000	$39,128,000	$1,700,000
Restricted for:				
Capital projects	6,200,000	7,300,000	13,500,000	750,000
Debt service	2,100,000	2,550,000	4,650,000	120,000
Other purposes	9,404,000	1,220,000	10,624,000	75,000
Unrestricted	4,432,000	1,650,000	6,082,000	1,450,000
Total Net Assets	$44,564,000	$29,420,000	$73,984,000	$4,095,000

GASB-34 requires that business-type activities be separately reported at least by segment on the statement of activities (government-wide financial statement). Rather than define a segment in the context of the statement of activities, GASB-34 used the definition of a segment, which is reproduced as follows, established for the presentation of segment information in a note to the financial statements for Enterprise Funds:

> ... segment is considered to exist when "an identifiable activity reported as or within an Enterprise Fund or another standalone entity for which one or more revenue bonds or other revenue-backed debt instruments (such as certificates of participation) are outstanding." Asegment has a specific identifiable revenue stream pledged in support of revenue bonds or other revenue-backed debt and has related expenses, gains and losses, assets, and liabilities that can be identified.

The GASB's objective for reporting disaggregated information in the business-type activities section of the statement of activities was not to identify segment information but rather to have a separate presentation for activities that are different. In order to better achieve this objective, GASB-37 amends GASB-34 by requiring that the statement of activities present "activities accounted for in Enterprise Funds by different identifiable activities," which is described as follows (GASB-37, par. 10):

> An activity within an Enterprise Fund is identifiable if it has a specific revenue stream and related expenses and gains and losses that are accounted for separately. Determining whether an activity is different may require the use of professional judgment, but is generally based on the goods, services, or programs provided by an activity.

GASB Comprehensive Implementation Guide points out that "generally the difference between activities in the goods, services or programs provided" is obvious, but in some circumstances professional judgment must be used to determine which activities should be reported separately. For example, the *GASB Q&A Guide* states that a city that uses a single fund to account for water and electric utilities should report these two activities as separate functions or programs in the statement of activities if separate assets and liabilities can be identified for each activity. On the other hand, a city that uses four separate funds to report its four separate water districts may (but does not have to) combine the four sets of accounts and report a single separate activity or function on its statement of activities.

> **OBSERVATION:** The GASB's objective is "to present a level of detail that will provide useful information to meet the needs of users of the financial statements." For example, GASB-37 points out that an Enterprise Fund may be used to account for natural gas services and electric services. Although both of these services are considered "utility services," they are different activities and should be presented as such on the statement of activities if separate assets and liabilities can be identified for each activity. On the other hand, a public college accounted for as an Enterprise Fund would likely have revenues from residence halls, food services, and a bookstore. GASB-37 suggests that these revenue-producing functions would generally not be considered separate activities because they are all related to the single activity of providing the higher education service.

Expenses Once the level of detail is determined, the primary government's expenses for each governmental activity should be presented. It should be noted that these are expenses and not expenditures and are based on the concept of the flow of economic resources, which includes depreciation expense. As noted earlier, the minimum level of detail allowed by GASB-34 is functional program categories, such as general government, public safety, parks and recreation, and public works. At a minimum, each functional program should include "direct expenses," which are defined as "those that are specifically associated with a service, program, or department and, thus, are clearly identifiable to a particular function" (GASB-34, par. 41).

Some functional categories, namely general government and administrative support, are by their very nature indirect expenses and GASB-34 does not require that these indirect expenses be allocated to other functional categories. However, if these indirect expenses are in fact allocated (either partially allocated or fully allocated) to the other functional expense categories, the statement of activities must be expanded to include separate columns for direct and indirect expenses so that the presentation format provides a basis for comparison with other governmental entities that chose not to allocate their indirect expenses (GASB-34, par. 42).

> **PRACTICE POINT:** When a governmental entity allocates part or all of its indirect costs (and therefore presents columns for direct and indirect costs), a column that presents the total of these two columns may be presented on the statement of activities, but a total column is not required.

In some instances, a governmental entity will charge (through the General Fund or an Internal Service Fund) other funds or programs an overhead rate that is based on general administrative expenses. GASB states that under this circumstance it is not necessary to identify and eliminate these charges from the various direct program expenses presented in the statement of activities; however, the summary of significant accounting policies should state that the direct program expenses include such charges (GASB-34, par. 43).

Indirect expense allocation to business-type activities *GASB Comprehensive Implementation Guide* states that indirect expenses could be allocated to business-type activities as well as governmental activities assuming there is a reasonable basis for doing so. However, if those expenses are allocated to business-type activities, the allocation creates an additional item that has to be disclosed as a reconciling item between the fund financial statements and the government-wide financial statements.

Common support costs When a governmental entity performs a common support activity (for example, vehicle maintenance) for a variety of programs (public safety, streets, etc.), to the extent possible the common activity costs should be allocated as a direct expense of the specific programs. *GASB Comprehensive Implementation Guide* notes that any costs that cannot be allocated to a specific function should be reported as "general government or a similar indirect cost center" on the statement of activities.

Employee benefit costs GASB-34 requires that each functional program include direct expenses, which are defined as "those that are specifically associated with a service, program, or department and, thus, are clearly identifiable to a particular function." *GASB Comprehensive Implementation Guide* points out that nonenterprise fund employee benefit costs (such as pension costs, vacation pay, etc.) should be allocated to functional programs (such as public safety, streets, etc.) if the employee's wage is also considered a direct expense.

Overhead rates for indirect expenses A governmental entity may negotiate indirect costs rates under various federal governmental grants and contracts whereby those rates are used to transfer the costs (reimbursement) from the General Fund to specific governmental funds that administer the federal awards. *GASB Comprehensive Implementation Guide* states that because the rates are based on indirect costs, they cannot be reported as direct expenses of a particular function but, rather, must be reported as "general government" expenses (or an equivalent caption) on the statement of activities.

Reporting depreciation expense Generally the cost (net of estimated salvage value) of capital assets should be depreciated over their estimated useful lives. For a discussion of depreciation expense see Chapter 18, "Expenses/Expenditures: Nonexchange and Exchange Transactions." Depreciation expense should be reported as a direct expense of the specific functional category if the related capital asset can be identified with the functional category. For example, depreciation expenses related to a police vehicle should be reported, along with other direct expenses, at the appropriate functional expense category (for example, public safety). Depreciation on capital assets that are shared by two or more functions should be reported as a direct expense based on a pro rata allocation to the appropriate functional expense categories. For example, if a building houses the administrative office of the police department and the public assistance department, the depreciation expense for the office building would be allocated on an appropriate basis to the two functional expense categories (for example, public safety and health and welfare) (GASB-34, par. 44).

Depreciation expense related to capital assets that are not identified with a particular functional category (such as the depreciation of city hall) does not have to be reported as a direct expense to specific functions but rather may be presented as a separate line item in the statement of activities or included in the general government functional category. However, when unallocated depreciation expense is reported as a separate line in the statement of activities, it should be indicated on the face of the statement that the amount reported as depreciation expense represents only unallocated depreciation expense and not total depreciation expense.

> **PRACTICE POINT:** The *GASB Comprehensive Implementation Guide* points out that the notation about unallocated depreciation expense must be on the face of the statement. That can be achieved by using an appropriate description of the line item, such as "Unallocated Depreciation Expense," or by labeling the line item "Depreciation Expense" with a reference (such as an asterisk) to the bottom of the statement that states that "the amount represents only unallocated depreciation expense and not total depreciation expense."

Reporting interest expense Generally, interest expense on general long-term debt is considered an indirect expense and should not be allocated as a direct expense to specific functional categories but rather should be presented as a single line item, appropriately labeled. However, GASB-34 notes that "when borrowing is essential to the creation or continuing existence of a program and it would be misleading to exclude the interest from direct expenses of that program," the related interest expense should be reported as a direct expense with the appropriate functional classification. *GASB Comprehensive Implementation Guide* provides the following example of a financing arrangement whereby interest expense is considered a direct expense and allocated to a particular function or program:

> A state government has a program to make reduced-rate loans to school districts in the state. The initial funding for the program was provided by a large bond issue. Since the bond issue is fundamental to the school district loan program and is an integral part of the cost of providing the program to local districts, the interest expense should be allocated to this activity.

If part of interest expense is reported as a direct expense of a functional line item, it should be indicated on the face of the statement that that amount reported as interest expense represents only unallocated interest expense and not total interest expense. The amount of total interest expense must be determinable on the face of the statement of activities or it must be disclosed in a note to the financial statements.

> **OBSERVATION:** The GASB takes the position that treating interest expense as a direct expense is inconsistent with the nature of financing projects. For example, a capital asset related to one project may be purchased with existing funds, and a similar asset for another project may be financed. Under a direct allocation approach, one project would have more expenses than the other even though the determination of the interest expense is based on management discretion rather than the nature of each project.

GASB Comprehensive Implementation Guide makes the following observations about reporting interest expense on the statement of activities:

- Interest expense related to a capital lease is not a direct expense of the function that uses the capital assets subject to the lease. The use of a capital lease is just another financing option and should be evaluated like any other borrowing arrangement.
- Under most circumstances no interest on general long-term liabilities is reported as a direct expenses; therefore, using the caption "interest on long-term debt" is sufficient to indicate that all interest expense is indirect. The amount of total interest expense must be determinable on the face of the statement of activities or it must be disclosed in a note to the financial statements.

GASB Comprehensive Implementation Guide states that interest expense for Enterprise Funds and component units does not have to be reported as a separate line item in the business-type activities section of the statement of activities because the expense is considered to be a direct expense for each of these operating units.

A state's constitution might not allow for the issuance of debt except by a constitutional amendment approve by voters. Under this circumstance the debt is issued only for a specific activity; however, the *GASB Comprehensive Implementation Guide* states that the interest on the debt is still considered indirect and should not be allocated to the specific function or activity. If the state government is concerned that a functional activity should in fact include interest expense, the alternative format for the statement of activities (see paragraph 42 of GASB-34) may be used whereby indirect expenses are allocated (either partially allocated or fully allocated) to the other functional expense categories. Under this format the statement of activities must be expanded to include separate columns for direct and indirect expenses so that the presentation format provides a basis for comparison with other governmental entities that choose not to allocate their indirect expenses.

Revenues and other resource inflows A fundamental concept in the formatting of the statement of activities, as described above, is the identification of resource inflows to the governmental entities that are related to specific programs and those that are general in nature. GASB-34 notes that specific governmental activities are generally financed from the following sources of resource inflows:

- Parties who purchase, use, or directly benefit from goods and services provided through the program (*GASB Comprehensive Implementation Guide* lists as examples fees for garbage collections, transportation fares, fees for using recreational facilities, building permits and hunting permits)
- Outside parties (other governments and nongovernmental entities or individuals) who provide goods and services to the governmental entity (for example, a grant to a local government from a state government)
- The reporting government's constituencies (for example, property taxes)
- The governmental entity (for example, investment income)

The first source of resources listed above is always program revenue. The second source is program revenue if it is restricted to a specific program, otherwise the item is considered general revenue. The third source is always general revenue, even when restricted. The fourth source of resources is usually general revenue.

PRACTICE POINT: The *GASB Comprehensive Implementation Guide* notes that GASB-34 provides definitions for program

> revenues (charges for services, operating grants and contributions, and capital grants and contributions) in paragraphs 48–51, and general revenues in paragraph 52. The GASB's *Guide* notes that the definitions for the various types of revenues are mutually exclusive and therefore a particular source of revenue can only meet the definition of one type of revenue.

Using this classification scheme the governmental entity should format its statement of activities based on the following broad categories of resource inflows (GASB-34, par. 47):

- Program revenues
  —Charges for services
  —Operating grants and contributions
  —Capital grants and contributions
- General revenues
- Contributions to permanent funds
- Extraordinary items
- Special items
- Transfers

Program revenues These revenues arise because the specific program with which they are identified exists, otherwise the revenues would not flow to the governmental entity. Program revenues are presented on the statement of activities as a subtraction from the related program expense in order to identify the net cost (or benefit) of a particular program. This formatting scheme enables a reader of a governmental entity to identify those programs that are providing resources that may be used for other governmental functions or those that are being financed from general revenues and other sources of resources. Program revenues should be segregated into (1) charges for services, (2) operating grants and contributions, and (3) capital grants and contributions (GASB-34, par. 48).

During the implementation process for GASB-34, questions arose about how revenues raised by one function/activity but used by another function/activity should be classified in the statement of activities. For example, if revenue generated by a state lottery (one function/activity) must be used to finance education (an other function/activity) should the proceeds from the lottery be reported as revenue for the lottery or for education?

GASB-37 states that the following factors are to be used to determine which revenue should be related to a program (GASB-37, pars. 11–12):

- For charges for services, the determining factor is which function generates the revenue.
- For grants and contributions, the determining factor is the function to which the revenue is restricted.

Thus, in the lottery example, the proceeds from the lottery would be reported as charges for services of the lottery activity because the educational activity used the resources but did not charge for the services.

In some instances it is impractical to classify the program that should report a particular program revenue, in which case the governmental entity may establish a policy for classifying the program revenue if the policy is consistently applied.

PRACTICE POINT: The language used in GASB-34 strongly implied that only three categories could be used to identify program revenues, namely (1) charges for services, (2) operating grants and contributions, and (3) capital grants and contributions. GASB-37 states that the formatting of the statement of activities is more flexible than originally conveyed in GASB-34. For example, more than one column could be included under one of the three program revenue columns. Furthermore, the columnar heading may be modified to be more descriptive. For example, a program revenue column could be labeled "operating grants, contributions, and restricted interest."

PRACTICE POINT: Identifying revenues with a particular function does not mean that revenues must be allocated to a function. Revenues are related to a function only when they are directly related to the function. If no direct relationship is obvious, the revenue is a general revenue, not a program revenue.

A governmental entity that classifies its expenses by *function* may receive a state grant (which meets the definition of program revenue) that is to be used for specified programs. *GASB Comprehensive Implementation Guide* states that the fact that the grant is based on one classification scheme and a governmental entity's statement of activities is based on another does not change the original character of the revenue. That is, the grant is still classified as program revenue (not general revenue) even though it must be allocated to a variety of functions in the statement of activities.

GASB Comprehensive Implementation Guide provides the following to illustrate how potential program revenues should be evaluated based on the guidance established in GASB-34:

Fact Pattern	*Suggested Guidance*
State law requires that 20% of the state's lottery sales revenue are required to be used for elementary and secondary education programs in the state. Should the 20% be allocated to the education function as program revenue?	No. The proceeds from the sales of lottery tickets are related to the "lottery" program and not to the education program. Presenting the net revenues of a program on a statement of activities does not imply that those net proceeds are used for that particular program. In this instance, the net revenue from the lottery program is a "profit" that reduces the governmental entity's need to finance other programs (including educational programs) through general revenues.
State gas taxes are shared with eligible local governments. The local governments have discretion over when and how the money is spent, as long as it is for road and highway projects. Even though a high percentage of the revenue will likely be spent for capital purposes, maintenance and repair expenses are also allowable. How should the revenue (grants and contributions) be reported by the local governments—capital, operating, or some combination?	GASB-34 (par. 50) notes that if a grant or contribution can be used either for operating or capital purposes, at the discretion of the governmental entity, it should be reported as an operating contribution.
A government charges indirect expenses to its human services program through an indirect cost plan and is reimbursed by the federal and state grant agencies for the costs of the program. However, in the statement of activities, the government does not allocate the indirect expenses to the human services program, but rather, reports them in the general government function. Should the portion of the grant that reimburses the indirect expense be reported as program revenues of the human services or general government function?	In this instance there should be a "matching" of program revenues and program expenses. If the indirect expenses are allocated to the human services program, the portion of the grant that reimburses the indirect expenses should be reported as program revenues. If the indirect expenses are not allocated to the human services program, the portion of the grant that reimburses the indirect expenses should be reported as program revnues for the general government function.

GASB Comprehensive Implementation Guide states that investment revenue that qualifies as program revenues (legally restricted for a particular purpose) should be reported as program revenue. Depending on the nature of the restriction, the restricted investment revenue should be reported either as operating, or capital grants and contributions in the statement of activities.

Charges for services Revenues that are characterized as charges for services are based on exchange or exchange-like transactions and arise from charges for providing goods, services, and privileges to customers or applicants who acquire goods, services, or privileges directly from a governmental entity. Generally, these and similar charges are intended to cover, at least to some extent, the cost of goods and services provided to various parties. GASB-34 lists the following as examples of charges for services revenue (GASB-34, par. 49):

- Service charges (such as water usage fees and garbage collection fees)
- Licenses and permit fees (such as dog licenses, liquor licenses, and building permits)
- Operating special assessments (such as street-cleaning assessments or special street-lighting assessments)
- Intergovernmental charges that are based on exchange transactions (such as one county being charged by another that houses its prisoners)

With the issuance of GASB-34, some financial statement preparers were unsure about how revenues related to fines and forfeitures should be classified in the statement of activities. Paragraph 49 of GASB-34 states that "charges for services"(program revenues) "include revenues based on exchange or exchange-like transactions," which would imply that the fines and forfeitures could not be classified as program revenue. However, *GASB Comprehensive Implementation Guide* states that fines and forfeitures should be reported as charges for services "because fines and forfeitures are generated by the program, they are more like charges for services than grants and contributions."

In order to clarify the guidance established by GASB-34 and the *GASB Comprehensive Implementation Guide,* GASB-37 modifies GASB-34 by specifically stating that fines and forfeitures are to be classified as charges for services because "they result from direct charges to those who are otherwise directly affected by a program or service, even though they receive no benefit." However, GASB-37 recognizes that there is an element of confusion and arbitrariness in classifying fines and forfeitures as charges for services by noting that the statement of activities could be formatted (1) in order to present a separate column labeled "Fines and Forfeitures" under the "Charges for Services" column or (2) by retitling the column

"Charges for Services, Fees, Fines, and Forfeitures" (GASB-37, par. 13).

In some instances a state law might prohibit the use of fines for particular purposes (for example, public safety expenses and other expenses that are related to the generation of the fine revenue). Even though the uses of the fine revenues (or in general, all charges for services) are somewhat limited, *GASB Comprehensive Implementation Guide* states that they are nonetheless program revenues and not general revenues.

The size or importance of a program's revenue does not change the character of the revenue for classification purposes on the statement of activities. For example, the *GASB Comprehensive Implementation Guide* notes that a community that has a substantial amount of fines that are used to fund a variety of programs does not make the fine revenue general revenue. The *GASB Comprehensive Implementation Guide* also notes that "the net cost of a function or program is the difference between (1) expenses and (2) the charges, fees, and fines that derive directly from it and the grants and contributions that are restricted to it." A particular function may generate a "profit" that can be used in a variety of ways. That fact does not make the revenue general.

Some public schools charge tuition fees for programs such as out-of district students, vocational education, and adult educational programs whereby the fee is intended to cover the direct instructional cost of the program plus indirect administrative and support services. *GASB Comprehensive Implementation Guide* notes that the tuition revenue should be classified with the appropriate program revenue classification on the statement of activities. None of the revenue should be allocated to the indirect functional classification.

Program-specific grants and contributions (operating and capital) Governmental entities may receive mandatory and voluntary grants or contributions (nonexchange transactions) from other governments or individuals that must be used for a particular governmental activity. For example, a state government may provide grants to localities that are to be used to reimburse costs related to adult literary programs. These and other similar sources of assets should be reported as program-specific grants and contributions in the statement of activities but they must be separated into those that are for operating purposes and those that are for capital purposes. If a grant or contribution can be used either for operating or capital purposes, at the discretion of the governmental entity, it should be reported as an operating contribution (GASB-34, par. 50).

NOTE: Mandatory and voluntary nonexchange transactions are defined in GASB-33 (Accounting and Financial Reporting for Nonexchange Transactions).

Grants and contributions that are provided to finance more than one program (multipurpose grants) should be reported as program-specific grants "if the amounts restricted to each program are specifically identified in either the grant award or the grant application." (The grant application should be used in this manner only if the grant was based on the application.) If the amount of the multipurpose grants cannot be identified with particular programs, the revenue should be reported as general revenue rather than program-specific grants and contributions.

Earnings related to endowments or permanent fund investments are considered program revenues if they are restricted to a specific program use; however, the restriction must be based on either an explicit clause in the endowment agreement or contract. Likewise, earnings on investments that do not represent endowments or permanent fund arrangements are considered program revenues if they are legally restricted to a specific program. Investment earnings on endowments or permanent fund investments that are not restricted and, therefore, are available for general operating expenses are not program revenues but rather should be reported as general revenues in the "lower" section of the statement of activities.

A Permanent Fund may be managed and controlled by one function (such as the transportation function) but a portion of the investment income may be restricted for use in another function (such as the public safety function). *GASB Comprehensive Implementation Guide* points out that the portion of the investment income restricted to the other function should be reported as program revenue for the other function and not the function that is managing the Permanent Fund. That is, restricted resources are "program revenues of the function to which they are restricted."

Also, earnings on "invested accumulated resources" of a specific program that are legally restricted to the specific program should be reported as program revenues (GASB-34, par. 51).

GASB Comprehensive Implementation Guide provides the following to illustrate how potential grants and contributions should be evaluated based on the guidance established in GASB-34:

Fact Pattern	*Suggested Guidance*
A school district is awarded an operating grant from the state department of education. The grant agreement states that the department will reimburse the school district for all eligible expenses of three specific programs. The grant award, however, does not specifically identify the amounts restricted to each program, as required by	The grant should be reported by the school district as program revenue and allocated to specific functions based on the amounts of reimbursable expenses incurred for each program. Since the reimbursements are known (even though they were not known at the time of the state grant) before the financial statements are

Fact Pattern	*Suggested Guidance*
paragraph 50, because they will not be known until the school district submits its after-the-fact request for funding. Can the school district report the grant as program revenues for the three programs, or should it be reported as general revenue?	prepared, the state grants do relate to a specific program.
A local government is awarded a categorical grant that finances a large number of its programs. The grant award lists the programs covered but does not restrict any specific amounts to specific programs. Should the government allocate the grant amount to covered programs and report it as program revenue?	Grants and contributions that are provided to finance more than one program (multipurpose grants) should be reported as program-specific grants "if the amounts restricted to each program are specifically identified in either the grant award or the grant application." The grant application should be used in this manner only if the grant was based on the application. If the amount of the multipurpose grants cannot be identified with particular programs, the revenue should be reported as general revenues rather than program-specific grants and contributions. In this case the grants must be reported as general revenues.
State law allocates a percentage of the state's sales tax revenues to local governments. A portion of the local share is restricted to education. At the local level, is the sales tax allocation to education program or general revenue?	The local government should classify the shared sales tax revenue as a voluntary contribution and not as a tax, as required by GASB-36. The portion of the shared revenue for a local school district would be reported as a general revenue because the resources are available for "education" and not for a particular program within the educational activities.
A local government receives a large bequest from the estate of a wealthy benefactor. The corpus of the donation cannot be spent, but instead is required to be invested to provide earnings that are restricted to a special use. Because the principal amount can never be spent, how should it be reported?	The receipt of the gift should be accounted for in a Permanent Fund and reported as revenue in the fund's statement of revenues, expenditures, and changes in fund balances. The principal amount would be reported as reserved on the fund's balance sheet. When a governmental entity receives contributions to its term and

Fact Pattern	*Suggested Guidance*
	permanent endowments or to permanent fund principal, those contributions should be reported as separate items in the lower portion of the statement of activities. These receipts are not considered to be program revenues (such as program specific grants), because in the case of permanent contributions, the principal can never be expended. On the statement of net assets, the principal would be reported as restricted.

GASB Comprehensive Implementation Guide points out that losses related to changes in the fair value of investments subject to the standards established by GASB-31 (Accounting and Financial Reporting for Certain Investments and for External Investment Pools) should be reported as an offset to program revenues when the earnings from the investments are restricted for a specific purposes. If no restriction exists, the losses would be reported as a loss or an offset to investment income in the general revenue section of the statement of activities.

General revenues General revenues should be reported in the lower potion of the statement of activities. Such revenues include resource flows related to income taxes, sales taxes, franchise taxes, and property taxes, and they should be separately identified in the statement. Nontax sources of resources that are not reported as program revenues must be reported as general revenues. This latter group includes unrestricted grants, unrestricted contributions, and unrestricted investment income (GASB-34, par. 52).

General revenues are used to offset the net (expense) revenue amounts computed in the upper portion of the presentation, and the resulting amount is labeled as excess (deficiency) of revenues over expenses before extraordinary items and special items.

> **OBSERVATION:** All taxes, including dedicated taxes (for example, motor fuel taxes), are considered general revenues rather than program revenues. The GASB takes the position that only charges to program customers or program-specific grants and contributions should be characterized as reducing the net cost of a particular governmental activity.

Careful analysis is sometimes needed to properly classify a revenue source as either program revenue or general revenue. For example, the *GASB Comprehensive Implementation Guide* provides an illustration whereby a developer is required to make a one-time contribution to a municipality based on the assessed value of a recently completed project and those resources are to be used to help maintain the infrastructure related to the project. The *GASB Comprehensive Implementation Guide* states that the revenue source is not a program revenue but, rather, a general revenue because it "arises from an imposed nonexchange transaction that is, in substance, a tax." Therefore the contribution would be presented in the lower portion of the statement of activities and could be labeled as "restricted for infrastructure maintenance."

In some instances a governmental entity may establish a prerequisite fee or license that must be paid before a business or other party is subject to another charge or tax. The *GASB Comprehensive Implementation Guide* points out that the character of each revenue source must be evaluated independently to determine whether it is program revenue or a tax (general revenue). For example, a local governmental entity may require a business to obtain a business license and in order to maintain the license, the business must also pay a "business license tax" that is based on the entity's gross receipts. The license and any license renewal fee are program revenues (charges for services), whereas the business license tax is general revenue (gross receipts tax) even though it is related to maintaining the business license.

The *GASB Comprehensive Implementation Guide* notes that not all program revenues create restricted net assets. By their nature, grants and contributions (both operational and capital) give rise to restricted net assets, but charges for services may be unrestricted, restricted to the program that gave rise to the charge, or restricted to a program that is unrelated to the revenue generated service. On the other hand, the *GASB Comprehensive Implementation Guide* states that a tax revenue could be restricted for a particular use (for example, taxes levied specifically to pay debt service) but nonetheless reported as general revenue, perhaps under a heading that identifies it as restricted for a particular purpose.

> **PRACTICE POINT:** The *GASB Comprehensive Implementation Guide* notes that GASB-34 states that taxes imposed by another government are not a tax receipt (by the recipient government) but, rather, a nonexchange transaction as defined by GASB-33. The characteristics of the shared tax revenue must be examined to determine whether it is a program revenue (as defined by paragraph 50) or general revenue (as defined by paragraph 52).

GASB Comprehensive Implementation Guide emphasizes the point that all taxes are considered general revenues rather than program revenues with the following illustrations (in each case the tax receipt is reported as general revenue):

- A county government imposes a separate sales tax, the proceeds of which are required to be used for public safety or health and welfare programs. Because of the resections on use, these taxes are not "discretionary" revenues.
- A city levies a special tax that is restricted for use within a specific program or function (a separate property tax levied to pay debt service costs, for example).
- A county government has enacted a transient occupancy (hotel/motel) tax, a percentage of which is required to be used for "tourism" programs in the county. The county has significant tourism activity and reports it as a separate function in its statement of activities. The county maintains that the revenue comes from "those who directly benefit from the goods or services of the program," and consequently should be reported as charges for services.

PRACTICE POINT: The *GASB Comprehensive Implementation Guide* points out that GASB-33 (pars. 16 and 18) requires that derived taxes and imposed nonexchange revenues (both general revenues) be reported net of estimated refunds and estimated uncollectible amounts, respectively. The GASB *Guide* also notes that uncollectible exchange transactions revenues related to governmental activities on the statement of activities should also be recorded net of any uncollectible amounts. That is, a bad-debts expense account should not be used for presentation purposes.

Contributions to permanent funds When a governmental entity receives contributions to its term and permanent endowments or to permanent fund principal, those contributions should be reported as separate items in the lower portion of the statement of activities. These receipts are not considered to be program revenues (such as program-specific grants) because, in the case of term endowments, there is an uncertainty of the timing of the release of the resources from the term restriction and, in the case of permanent contributions, the principal can never be expended (GASB-34, par. 53).

PRACTICE POINT: The *GASB Comprehensive Implementation Guide* notes that GASB-34 points out that when the earnings of a Permanent Fund are required to be used for a specific purposes but are not distributed in the current year, those earnings (even though they are not distributed or spent) should be reported as program revenues.

Extraordinary items The next section of the statement of activities includes a category where extraordinary items (gains or losses) are to be presented. GASB-34 incorporates the definition of "extraordinary items" (unusual in nature and infrequent in occurrence) as provided in APB-30 (Reporting the Results of Operations—Reporting the Effects of Disposal of a Segment of a Business, and Extraordinary, Unusual, and Infrequently Occurring Events and Transactions) (GASB-34, par. 55).

The *GASB Comprehensive Implementation Guide* notes that an event is unusual in nature if it "possess[es] a high degree of abnormality" and therefore is not related to the entity's normal operations. An event is infrequent in occurrence if it is not expected to occur again in the foreseeable future. These concepts must be applied in the context of the characteristics of a particular entity, and their application is highly judgmental. Thus, what is considered unusual or frequent for one governmental entity may not be for another governmental entity.

There is no list of extraordinary items, because that determination must be made on a case-by-case basis using professional judgment. The *GASB Comprehensive Implementation Guide* states that the following may qualify as extraordinary items:

- Costs related to an environmental disaster caused by a large chemical spill in a train derailment in a small city.
- Significant damage to the community or destruction of government facilities by natural disaster (tornado, hurricane, flood, earthquake, and so forth) or terrorist act. Geographic location of the government may determine if a weatherrelated natural disaster is infrequent.
- A large bequest to a small government by a private citizen.

Special items Unlike APB-30, the GASB identifies a new classification, *special items,* which are described as "significant transactions or other events within the control of management that are either unusual in nature or infrequent in occurrence." Special items should be reported separately and before extraordinary items. If a significant transaction or other event occurs but is not within the control of management and that item is either unusual or infrequent, the item is not reported as a special item but the nature of the item must be described in a note to the financial statements (GASB-34, par. 56).

GASB Comprehensive Implementation Guide states that the following may qualify as special items:

- Sales of certain general governmental capital assets
- Special termination benefits resulting from workforce reductions due to sale of utility operations
- Early-retirement program offered to all employees
- Significant forgiveness of debt.

An item can only satisfy the criteria of either an extraordinary item or a special item, but not both. For example, if an item is both unusual and infrequent it must be reported as an extraordinary item regardless of whether it was subject to management control.

> **OBSERVATION:** An extraordinary or special item to one government may not be an extraordinary or special item to another government. For example, consider the following:

Question: Example County is located on the Florida coastline and has sustained significant damage to the entire county, including county government facilities, from a recent hurricane. The County has incurred approximately $110,000,000 in expenses in the current year related to recovery from the hurricane damage. Do these expenses qualify to be reported as extraordinary or special items on the County's statement of activities?

Response: These expenses do not qualify as either special items or extraordinary items. Expenses incurred resulting from natural disasters, such as hurricanes, are never considered "special items" because they are not *within the control of management*. Therefore, these hurricane recovery expenses do not qualify for special item reporting treatment. As to whether these hurricane recovery expenses qualify for reporting as "extraordinary items." Question 7.217 of the GASB *Comprehensive Implementation Guide* states that geographic location of the government may determine whether a weather-related natural disaster is infrequent. Because Example County is located on the Florida coastline and hurricanes are not infrequent at this location, these expenses would not qualify for reporting treatment as extraordinary items.

Transfers Transfers should be reported in the lower portion of the statement of activities (GASB-34, par. 53). (The standards that determine how transfers should be reported in the statement of activities are discussed later in the context of fund statements.)

Gain or loss on disposal of capital assets The *GASB Comprehensive Implementation Guide* states that gains and losses arising from the disposition of capital assets that are related to specific programs should be reported as either general revenues (gains) or general government-type expenses (losses) because they are peripheral activities and not derived directly from a program. The *GASB Comprehensive Implementation Guide* also notes that if the gains or losses are insignificant, they could be offset against depreciation expense for the period. Governmental entities that use group or composite depreciation methods would generally close disposition gains and losses to accumulated depreciation.

Eliminations and reclassifications As suggested earlier, the preparation of government-wide financial statements is based on a consolidating process (similar to corporate consolidations) rather than a combining process. Eliminations and reclassifications related to the consolidation process are based on (1) internal balances—statement of net assets, (2) internal activities—statement of activities, (3) intra-entity activity, and (4) Internal Service Fund balances (GASB-34, par. 57).

Internal balances (statement of net assets) The government-wide financial statements present the governmental entity and its blended component units as a single reporting entity. Based on this philosophy, most balances between funds that are initially recorded as interfund receivables and payables at the individual fund level should be eliminated in the preparation of the statement of net assets within each of the two major groups of the primary government (the government activities and business-type activities). The purpose of the elimination is to avoid the grossing-up effect on assets and liabilities presented on the statement of net assets.

For example, if there is an interfund receivable/payable between the General Fund and a Special Revenue Fund, those amounts would be eliminated in order to determine the balances that would appear in the governmental-activities column. Likewise, if there is an interfund receivable/payable between two proprietary funds of the primary government, those amounts would also be eliminated in the business-type activities column. However, the net residual interfund receivable/payable between governmental and business-type activities should not be eliminated but, rather, should be presented in each column (government activities and business-type activities) and labeled as "internal balances" or a similar description. These amounts will be the same and will therefore cancel out when they are combined (horizontally) in the statement of net assets in order to form the column for total primary government activities (GASB-34, par. 58).

> **PRACTICE POINT:** Generally, a governmental entity will maintain its accounting transactions using the conventional fund approach and convert this information to a government-wide basis using the flow of economic resources and accrual basis of accounting. Thus, at the fund level the internal balance between a government fund (modified accrual basis) may not equal the related balance with a proprietary fund (accrual basis); however, once the government fund is adjusted (through a worksheet) to the government-wide (accrual) basis, those adjusted amounts will equal the amounts presented in the proprietary funds.

There also may be interfund receivables/payables that arise because of transactions between the primary government and its fiduciary funds. These amounts should not be eliminated but rather should be reported on the statement of net assets as receivables from and payables to external parties (GASB-34, par. 58). (The financial statements of fiduciary funds are not consolidated as part of the government-wide financial statements.)

Internal activities (statement of activities) In order to avoid the doubling-up effect of internal activities among funds, interfund transactions should be eliminated so that expenses and revenues are recorded only once. For example, a fund (generally the General Fund or an Internal Service Fund) may charge other funds for services provided (such as insurance coverage and allocation of overhead expenses) on an internal basis. When these funds are consolidated in order to present the functional expenses of governmental activities in the statement of activities, the double counting of the expense (with an offset to revenue recorded by the provider fund) should be eliminated in a manner so that "the allocated expenses are reported only by the function to which they were allocated" (GASB-34, par. 59).

Internal activities should not be eliminated when they are classified as "interfund services provided and used." For example, when a municipal water company charges a fee for services provided to the general government, the expense and revenues related to those activities should not be eliminated (GASB-34, par. 60). (This type of internal activity is more fully discussed later in the section titled "Fund Financial Statements.")

Intra-entity activity Transactions (and related balances) between the primary government and its blended component units should be reclassified based on the guidance discussed later in the section titled "Fund Financial Statements." Transactions (and related balances) between the primary government and its discretely presented component units should not be eliminated in the government-wide perspective financial statements. That is, the two parties to the transactions should report revenue and expense accounts as originally recorded in those respective funds. Amounts payable and receivable between the primary government and its discretely presented component units should be reported as a separate line item on the statement of net assets. Likewise payables and receivables among discretely presented component units must also be reported separately (GASB-34, par. 61).

Internal Service Fund balances As described above (see "internal activities" [statement of activities]) internal service fund and similar activities should be eliminated to avoid doubling-up expenses and revenues in preparation of the government-activities column of the statement of activities. The effect of this approach is to adjust activities in an Internal Service Fund to a break-even balance. That is, if the Internal Service Fund had a "net profit" for the year there should be a pro rata reduction in the charges made to the funds that used the Internal Service Fund's services for the year. Likewise, a net loss would require a pro rata adjustment that would increase the charges made to the various participating funds. After making these eliminations any residual balances related to the Internal Service Fund's assets and liabilities should be reported in the government-activities column in the statement of net assets (GASB-34, par. 62).

PRACTICE POINT: In some instances an internal service might not be accounted for in an Internal Service Fund but, rather, is accounted for in another governmental fund (probably the General Fund or a Special Revenue Fund). Furthermore, the internal-service transaction might not cut across functional expense categories. That is, there is a "billing" between different departments but the expenses of those departments are all included in the same functional expenses. Conceptually, the same break-even approach as described earlier should be applied so as not to gross-up expenses and program revenues of a particular functional expense; however, the GASB does not require that an elimination be made (unless the amounts are material), because the result of this nonelimination is that direct expenses and program revenues are overstated by equal amounts but net (expense) revenue related to the function is not overstated.

OBSERVATION: The GASB takes the position that activities conducted with an Internal Service Fund are generally government activities rather than business-type activities even though an Internal Service Fund uses the flow of economic resources and the accrual basis of accounting. However, when Enterprise Funds account for all or the predominant activities of an Internal Service Fund, the Internal Service Fund's residual assets and liabilities should be reported in the business-type activities column of the statement of net assets.

Exhibit 20-2 provides an illustration of a statement of activities consistent with the standards established by GASB-34. Exhibit 20-3 illustrates a statement of activities in which indirect expenses have been allocated to the various functions of the governmental entity.

Alternative presentation As shown in Exhibit 20-2, the format of the statement of activities is unwieldy. When an entity has only governmental activities and a few functions, it may be possible to simplify the presentation of the statement by starting with a total column and then adding columns to the right of the total column that identify expenses and program revenues. The formatted statement could look something like the following:

EXHIBIT 20-2
STATEMENT OF ACTIVITIES
City of Centerville
Statement of Activities
For the Year Ended June 30, 20X5

		Program Revenues			Net (Expense) Revenue and Changes in Net Assets			
					Primary Government			
	Expenses	*Charges for Services*	*Operating Grants and Contributions*	*Capital Grants and Contributions*	*Governmental Activities*	*Business-Type Activities*	*Total*	*Component Units*
GOVERNMENTAL FUNCTIONS								
Primary Government								
Governmental Activities								
General government	$2,000,000	$750,000	$220,000		($1,030,000)		($1,030,000)	
Public safety	8,000,000	230,000	320,000	$30,000	(7,420,000)		(7,420,000)	
Streets	2,500,000	64,000	20,000		(2,416,000)		(2,416,000)	
Recreation and parks	1,200,000	470,000	120,000	50,000	(560,000)		(560,000)	
Health and welfare	3,000,000	1,700,000	340,000		(960,000)		(960,000)	
Education (payment to school district)	6,500,000				(6,500,000)		(6,500,000)	
Interest on long-term debt	1,100,000				(1,100,000)		(1,100,000)	
Total governmental activities	24,300,000	3,214,000	1,020,000	80,000	(19,986,000)		(19,986,000)	
Business-Type Activities								
Airport	3,500,000	3,900,000		130,000		$530,000	530,000	

Water & Sewer	2,100,000	4,300,000				2,200,000	2,200,000	
Total business-type activities	5,600,000	8,200,000		130,000		2,730,000	2,730,000	
Total primary government	$29,900,000	$11,414,000	$1,020,000	$210,000	(19,986,000)	2,730,000	(17,256,000)	
Component Units								
Public school district	$8,500,000	$120,000	$920,000	$205,000				($7,255,000)
Public transit authority	2,100,000	1,200,000	120,000	410,000				(370,000)
Total component units	$10,600,000	$1,320,000	$1,040,000	$615,000				($7,625,000)
General Revenues								
Taxes								
Property taxes					13,400,000		13,400,000	
Wage taxes					3,300,000		3,300,000	
Other					2,900,000		2,900,000	
Payment from the City of Centerville								6,500,000
Unrestricted grants and contributions					1,200,000		1,200,000	605,000
Interest and Investment income					750,000	210,000	960,000	110,000
Other					345,000	105,000	450,000	50,000
Special item—Gains from sale of real estate					430,000		430,000	
Transfers					125,000	(125,000)		
Total general revenues, special items, and transfers					22,450,000	190,0002	2,640,000	7,265,000
Change in net assets for the year					2,464,000	2,920,000	5,384,000	(360,000)
Net assets—Beginning of year					42,100,000	26,500,000	68,600,000	4,455,000
Net assets—Ending of year					$44,564,000	$29,420,000	$73,984,000	$4,095,000

EXHIBIT 20-3
STATEMENT OF ACTIVITIES (ALLOCATION OF INDIRECT EXPENSES)

City of Centerville
Statement of Activities
For the Year Ended June 30, 20X5

			Program Revenues			*Net (Expense) Revenue and Changes in Net Assets*			
						Primary Government			
	Expenses	*Indirect Expense Allocation*	*Charges for Services*	*Operating Grants and Contributions*	*Capital Grants and Contributions*	*Governmental Activities*	*Business-Type Activities*	*Total*	*Component Units*
GOVERNMENTAL FUNCTIONS:									
Primary Government:									
Governmental activities:									
General government	$2,000,000	$(1,030,000)	$750,000	$220,000					
Public safety	8,000,000	852,000	230,000	320,000	$30,000	$(8,272,000)		$(8,272,000)	
Streets	2,500,000	639,000	64,000	20,000		(3,055,000)		(3,055,000)	
Recreation and parks	1,200,000	532,500	470,000	120,000	50,000	(1,092,500)		(1,092,500)	
Health and welfare	3,000,000	106,500	1,700,000	340,000		(1,066,500)		(1,066,500)	
Education (payment to school district)	6,500,000					(6,500,000)		(6,500,000)	
Interest on long-term debt	1,100,000	(1,100,000)							
Total governmental activities	24,300,000		3,214,000	1,020,000	80,000	(19,986,000)		(19,986,000)	
Business-Type Activities:									
Airport	3,500,000		3,900,000		130,000		530,000	530,000	

Water & Sewer	2,100,000	4,300,000				2,200,000	2,200,000	
Total business-type activities	5,600,000	8,200,000		130,000		2,730,000	2,730,000	
Total primary government	$29,900,000	$11,414,000	$1,020,000	$210,000	(19,986,000)	2,730,000	(17,256,000)	
Component Units:								
Public school district	8,500,000	120,000	920,000	205,000				($7,255,000)
Public transit authority	2,100,000	1,200,000	120,000	410,000				(370,000)
Total component units	$10,600,000	$1,320,000	$1,040,000	$615,000				(7,625,000)
General Revenues:								
Taxes:								
Property taxes					13,400,000		13,400,000	
Wage taxes					3,300,000		3,300,000	
Other					2,900,000		2,900,000	
Payment from the City of Centerville								6,500,000
Unrestricted grants and contributions					1,200,000		1,200,000	605,000
Interest and investment income					750,000	210,000	960,000	110,000
Other					345,000	105,000	450,000	50,000
Special item—Gains from sale of real estate					430,000		430,000	
Transfers					125,000	(125,000)		
Total general revenues, special items, and transfers					22,450,000	190,000	22,640,000	7,265,000
Change in net assets for the year					2,464,000	2,920,000	5,384,000	(360,000)
Net assets—beginning of year					42,100,000	26,500,000	68,600,000	4,455,000
Net assets—ending of year					$44,564,000	$29,420,000	$73,984,000	$4,095,000

	Total	*Function #1*	*Function #2*	*Function #3*
Expenses:				
Details	$XXX	$XXX	$XXX	$XXX
Total expenses	XXX	XXX	XXX	XXX
Program revenues:				
Charges for services	XXX	XXX	XXX	XXX
Operating grants and contributions	XXX	XXX	XXX	XXX
Capital grants and contributions	XXX	XXX	XXX	XXX
Net Program expense	XXX	$XXX	$XXX	$XXX
General revenues:				
Taxes:	XXX			
Real estate	XXX			
Others	XXX			
Unrestricted grants and contributions	XXX			
Unrestricted investment earnings	XXX			
Total general revenues	XXX			
Change in net assets	XXX			
Net assets—beginning	XXX			
Net assets—ending	$XXX			

Fund Financial Statements

Fund-based financial statements must be included in a governmental entity's financial report in order to demonstrate that restrictions imposed by statutes, regulations, or contracts have been followed. GASB-34 identifies the following as fund types that are to be used to record a governmental entity's activities during an accounting period (GASB-34, par. 63):

- Governmental funds (emphasizing major funds)
  - —General Fund
  - —Special Revenue Funds
  - —Capital Projects Funds
  - —Debt Service Funds
  - —Permanent Funds

- Proprietary funds
  —Enterprise Funds (emphasizing major funds)
  —Internal Service Funds
- Fiduciary funds and similar component units
  —Pension (and other employee benefit) Trust Funds
  —Investment Trust Funds
  —Private-Purpose Trust Funds
  —Agency Funds

> **OBSERVATION:** The fund classification scheme described above is for external reporting. The GASB does not direct how a governmental entity should construct its internal accounting structure to fulfill legal requirements or satisfy management strategies.

See Chapters 6–8 for a detailed discussion of fund accounting by type of fund.

Governmental and proprietary fund financial statements A governmental entity should report (1) financial statements for its governmental funds and (2) proprietary funds, but the basis for reporting these funds is not by fund type but rather by major funds (GASB-34, par. 74).

Focus on major governmental and proprietary funds A significant change in the focus of reporting governmental funds and proprietary funds is that major funds are reported for these funds; however, combined financial statements for fund types are not reported.

GASB-34 requires that a governmental fund or Enterprise Fund be presented in a separate column in the fund financial statements if the fund is considered a major fund. A major fund is one that satisfies *both* of the following criteria (GASB-34, pars. 75–76, as amended by GASB-37, par. 15):

A. 10% Threshold—Total assets, liabilities, revenues, or expenditures/expenses of the governmental (enterprise) fund are equal to or greater than 10 percent of the corresponding element total (assets, liability, and so forth) for all funds that are considered governmental funds (enterprise funds).

B. 5% Threshold—The same element that met the 10 percent criterion in (a) is at least 5 percent of the corresponding element total for all governmental and Enterprise Funds combined.

OBSERVATION: In establishing major fund criteria the GASB intended that a major fund arises when a particular element (assets, for example) of a fund meets both the 10% and the 5% threshold. Some preparers read the requirement as originally stated in GASB-34 to mean that a major fund arises when one element (assets, for example) satisfies the 10% threshold and another element (revenues, for example) satisfies the 5% threshold. GASB-37 clarifies the GASB's original intent. That is, a single element must satisfy both criteria. *GASB Comprehensive Implementation Guide* states that revenue net of discounts and allowance (rather than gross revenues) should be used in applying the major fund criteria to governmental fund and Enterprise Fund activities. Also, in determining total revenues and expenditures/expenses, extraordinary items would be excluded.

PRACTICE POINT: In some instances a governmental entity may account for all of its activities in only governmental funds or, alternatively, may use only Enterprise Funds. Under either of these two circumstances, *GASB Comprehensive Implementation Guide* states that only the 10% test is relevant because if the 10% test is satisfied, obviously the 5% test will also be satisfied.

The General Fund is always considered a major fund and therefore must be presented in a separate column. Major fund reporting requirements do not apply to Internal Service Funds.

If a fund does not satisfy the conditions described above, it can still be presented as a major fund if the governmental entity believes it is important to do so. All other funds that are not considered major funds must be combined in a separate column and labeled as nonmajor funds.

OBSERVATION: Based on research conducted by the GASB, it appears that major funds represent a significant percentage of a governmental entity's account balances and transactions. However, the major fund concept is a minimum threshold. If a governmental entity believes that a fund that is not considered a major fund is, important to readers of the financial statements, the entity should present that fund in a separate column.

Consistent presentation of a fund A governmental entity must apply the major fund criteria each year to determine which funds are major funds. Thus, for example, a particular Capital Projects Fund might be reported as a major fund one year and the next year considered a nonmajor fund; however, if a fund does not satisfy the conditions for a major fund, it can still be presented as a major fund if the governmental entity believes that for consistency it is important to do so.

Internal Service Fund *GASB Comprehensive Implementation Guide* points out that Internal Service Funds cannot be presented as major funds. They should be aggregated and presented in a separate column on the face of the proprietary fund financial statements, just to the right of the total column for Enterprise Funds. If a governmental entity wants to present additional detail about Internal Service Funds, that information can be presented in combining statements, but those statements are optional and they are not considered to be part of the basic external financial statements. They are part of the CAFR.

Nonmajor funds All other funds that are not considered major funds must be aggregated in a separate column and labeled as nonmajor funds. The *GASB Comprehensive Implementation Guide* states that more than one column cannot be used to present nonmajor funds, for example, by fund type.

Eliminations for aggregated nonmajor funds GASB-34 does not require interfund balances and activities to be eliminated when nonmajor funds are aggregated; however, a governmental entity may choose to do so.

The *GASB Comprehensive Implementation Guide* provides the following illustrations for identifying major funds:

Fact Pattern	*Suggested Guidance*
A city has a component unit that meets the criteria for blending and is included with its Special Revenue Funds. Do the major fund reporting requirements apply to blended component units?	If a governmental entity chooses to report a component unit's balances and transactions as a separate fund, then the major fund reporting requirements apply to the fund.
Paragraph 76a states that governments should apply the 10% major fund criterion to all funds of that category or type. When should "category" be used and when should "type" be used?	The major fund criteria applies to the totals that represent (1) the governmental activities (a category) (General Fund, Special Revenue Funds, Capital Projects Funds, Debt Service Funds, and Permanent Funds) and (2) Enterprise Funds (a fund type). Internal Service Funds are not included in with Enterprise Funds when applying the criteria.
If an individual governmental or Enterprise Fund meets the initial	No. A fund is considered a major fund when the element satisfies

Fact Pattern	*Suggested Guidance*
10% criterion for one element (total assets, liabilities, revenues, or expenses/expenditures), and meets the 5% benchmark for a different element, is that fund required to be presented as a major fund?	both the 10% and the 5% criteria, not just one of the criteria.
In applying the major fund criteria to Enterprise Funds, should the government consider both operating and nonoperating revenues and expenses?	Yes. The application of the tests requires that both operating and nonoperating revenues and expenses be considered for an Enterprise Fund.
For determining major governmental funds, are other financing sources and uses included in the calculations?	No. In performing the criteria tests for governmental funds, other financing sources and uses would be excluded.
Can a non-GAAP budgetary basis of accounting be used to determine major funds?	No. The modified accrual basis for governmental funds and the accrual basis for Enterprise Funds must be used to apply the major funds test.
For major fund determination, should total assets, liabilities, revenues, or expenditures/expenses include the effects of the items in the reconciliation of the fund statements to the government-wide statements?	No. The importance of a particular fund is based on the basis of accounting used to report the fund in the fund financial statements, not the government-wide financial statements.
Are interfund balances and transactions required to be eliminated from the totals in the major fund test?	Interfund balances should not be eliminated to perform the major fund test. However, if there are interfund receivables and payables, a governmental entity could adopt a policy (if applied consistently) of netting receivables and payables (for the purpose of the test only). Thus the balance sheet totals for a fund and for the total fund category or fund type would be the basis for performing the test. (The question is not relevant to performing the major fund test for operating statements because

Fact Pattern	*Suggested Guidance*
	transfers in and transfers out are not used to determine revenues and expenditures/expenses. It should be noted that interfund services provided and used are considered other revenues and expenditures/expenses.)

Required reconciliation to government-wide financial statements The totals in the government-wide financial statements for governmental activities will not equal the totals in the governmental fund financial statements because different measurement focuses and bases of accounting are used to prepare the financial statements. For this reason, the GASB requires that at the bottom of the fund financial statements or in a separate schedule a summary reconciliation between the fund financial statements and the government-wide financial statements be provided. That is, the amount shown as the "total fund balances" in the column "total governmental funds" on the fund balance sheets must be reconciled to the "net assets" column for governmental activities presented on the statement of net assets. Also, the amount shown as "net changes in fund balance" in the column, "total governmental funds" on the statements of revenues, expenditures, and changes in fund balances must be reconciled to the "changes in net assets" column, for governmental activities presented on the statement of activities (GASB-34, par. 77).

In many instances the GASB believes that summary reconciliation can achieve the objective of tying the financial statements together with simple explanations that appear on the face of the fund financial statements or in an accompanying schedule. However, the GASB points out that "if the aggregated information in the summary reconciliation obscures the nature of the individual elements of a particular reconciling item, governments should provide a more detailed explanation in the notes to the financial statements." *GASB Comprehensive Implementation Guide* points out that this could occur when a reconciling item is "a combination of several similar balances or transactions, or is a net adjustment." For example, the reconciling item could be described as arising because liabilities are reported on the fund financial statements only when they are due and payable in the current period but appear on the government-wide financial statements when they are incurred. If this reconciling item includes a variety of liabilities (such as compensated absences, bonds, litigation, and accrued interest), a governmental entity may decide to further explain the nature of the reconciling item and its components in a note.

The financial statement preparer must be careful not to present lengthy explanations on the face of the financial statements or in the accompanying schedules that detract from the financial statements themselves. For this reason, it is best to present the detailed explanations in a note to the financial statements.

> **PRACTICE POINT:** Summary reconciliation provides a "crosswalk" between government-wide financial statements and fund financial statements in order to facilitate an understanding by financial statement readers who may be concerned that two different measurement approaches are reflected in a governmental entity's financial report.

The *GASB Comprehensive Implementation Guide* raised the question of whether the accounting records for governmental funds should include the adjustment necessary to report governmental activities on an accrual basis because it is usually assumed that financial statements should be derived from account balances in the accounting records. The formal accounting records should not include adjustments of this nature. Governmental funds are typically accounted for on a cash, modified accrual, or budgetary basis of accounting, and if necessary, worksheet adjustments are made to convert these balances to a GAAP-basis (modified accrual) for financial reporting purposes. The modified accrual based financial statements are the basis for preparing the fund financial statements required by GASB-34. Once the governmental funds have been converted to the modified accrual basis, they are combined for internal purposes, and various worksheet conversion adjustments are made to convert them to an accrual basis for reporting governmental activities in the government-wide financial statements.

Reporting when all but one fund in either the governmental fund category or enterprise fund category are major funds A governmental entity may apply the major fund criteria to its activities (governmental or enterprise funds) and determine that all of its funds are major funds except one. For example, it may have a single Special Revenue Fund that is a major fund, a single Capital Projects Fund that is a major fund, a General Fund (which is always a major fund) and a remaining Permanent Fund that is not a major fund. Based on the reporting requirements established by GASB-34 there will be a separate column that reports the Permanent Fund even though it is not a major fund; however, the *GASB Comprehensive Implementation Guide* states that the financial statements must "clearly distinguish between major and nonmajor funds." This could be accomplished by providing (1) a superheading labeled "Major Funds" and placing beneath it the separate columns for the General Fund, the Special Revenue Fund, and the Capital Projects Fund and (2) a superheading labeled "Other Fund" and placing beneath it a single separate column for the Permanent Fund.

Required financial statements: governmental funds The measurement focus and the basis of accounting used to prepare financial statements for governmental funds is the current financial resources measurement focus and the modified accrual basis of accounting as defined in NCGA-1 (GASB-34, par. 79).

Based on the fundamental concepts discussed above, the following financial statements must be prepared for governmental funds (GASB-34, par. 78):

- Balance sheet
- Statement of revenues, expenditures, and changes in fund balances

Balance sheet A governmental fund's balance sheet should be prepared using the "balance sheet format," whereby assets equal liabilities plus fund balances. The balance sheet should report the governmental entity's current financial resources and the claims to those resources for each major governmental fund and for the nonmajor funds. A total column should be used to combine all of the major funds and nonmajor funds (GASB-34, par. 83).

Presentation of reserved and unreserved fund balance The equity of a governmental fund (fund balance) should be identified as reserved amounts and unreserved amounts based on the standards established in NCGA-1, paragraphs 118–121. The reserved fund balances of the combined nonmajor funds must be presented in appropriate detail to inform the reader of the nature of the reservation and to identify the amount of net unreserved current financial resources that are available for future appropriation. For example, the fund balance for nonmajor Debt Service Funds may be described as reserved for debt service. In addition, unreserved fund balances for nonmajor funds must be identified by fund type on the face of the balance sheet (GASB-34, par. 84).

> **NOTE:** Reserved and unreserved fund balance accounts are discussed in Chapter 5, "Terminology and Classification."

Required reconciliation As noted earlier, there must be a summary reconciliation between the total fund balances on the balance sheet and the total net assets as presented on the statement of net assets for governmental activities (government-wide financial statement). Some of the typical items that may be needed to reconcile the two amounts are as follows (GASB-34, par. 85):

- The difference between reporting capital assets (net of accumulated depreciation) on the statement of net assets and the nonrecognition of those assets on the fund balance sheets.
- The difference between reporting long-term liabilities on the statement of net assets and the nonrecognition of those liabilities on the fund balance sheets.

- The difference between the recognition of other liabilities on the statement of net assets when they are incurred and the recognition on the fund balance sheets of only those liabilities that are payable with current financial resources.
- The difference between reporting the net asset balances of Internal Service Funds on the statement of net assets and the nonrecognition of those net assets on the fund balance sheets.

Exhibit 20-4 provides an illustration of fund balance sheets for governmental funds consistent with the standards established by GASB-34.

Statement of revenues, expenditures, and changes in fund balances This operating statement for governmental funds measures the flow of current financial resources and therefore would essentially follow the current standards used to prepare governmental financial statements. The operating statement would have columns for each major fund, one for all (combined) nonmajor funds and a total column. NCGA-1 illustrates three distinct formats that can be used to prepare the statement of revenues, expenditures, and changes in fund balances for governmental funds; however, GASB-34 mandates that the following format be observed (GASB-34, par. 86).

	Major Fund #1	*Major Fund #2*	*Nonmajor Funds*	*Total*
Revenues (detailed)	$XXX	$XXX	$XXX	$XXX
Expenditures (detailed)	XXX	XXX	XXX	XXX
Excess (deficiency) of revenues over (under) expenditures	XXX	XXX	XXX	XXX
Other financing sources and uses, including transfers (detailed)	XXX	XXX	XXX	XXX
Special and extraordinary items (detailed)	XXX	XXX	XXX	XXX
Net change in fund balance	XXX	XXX	XXX	XXX
Fund balances—Beginning of period	XXX	XXX	XXX	XXX
Fund balances—End of period	$XXX	$XXX	$XXX	$XXX

OBSERVATION: The above format is selected because the GASB believes that most readers of the financial statements focus on the (1) the excess (deficiency) of revenues over expenditures and (2) the overall change in the fund balance. Also, the GASB noted that the format is one of the formats most commonly used by governmental entities.

Classification of revenues and expenditures Revenues and expenditures presented in the statement of revenues, expenditures, and changes in fund balances are classified consistent with the standards discussed in NCGA-1, paragraphs 110 and 111-116. GASB-34 points out that debt issuance costs paid out of the proceeds of debt issuance should be reported as an expenditure rather than netted against the proceed (and presented as an other financing source). Debt issuance costs paid from resources other than debt proceeds should be recorded as an expenditure at the same time the related debt proceed is recorded (GASB-34, par. 87).

Other financing sources and uses The category "other financing sources and uses" would include items such as (1) sale of long-term debt (including the effects of premiums and discounts), (2) certain payments to escrow agents related to bond refundings, (3) proceeds from the sale of capital assets (unless these items are special items), and (4) transfers (GASB-34, par. 88).

GASB-34 originally required that the "proceeds" from the sale of longterm debt be reported as an other financing source and that any related discount or premium or debt issuance costs be separately reported. Taken literally, that cannot be accomplished, because the term "proceeds" generally means that any discount or premium and the related cost is netted against the face amount of the debt. The *GASB Q&A Guide* points out that GASB-34 should have referred to the "face amount" of the debt and to the proceeds. GASB-37 amends GASB-34 by substituting the term "proceeds" with "face amount." Thus, under the clarified language, if debt with a face amount of $1,000,000 was issued for $1,100,000, the transaction would be presented as follows in a governmental fund's operating statement (GASB-37, par. 16):

Other financing sources and uses:	
Long-term debt issued	$1,000,000
Premium on long-term debt issued	100,000

Special and extraordinary items This category includes special items and extraordinary items as defined earlier and is presented after the category titled "other financing sources and uses." If a governmental entity has both special items and extraordinary items they should be reported under the single heading labeled "special and extraordinary items." That is, there should not be separate broad headings for each item type (GASB-34, par. 89).

When a significant transaction or other event occurs that is either unusual or infrequent, but not both, and is not under the control of management, that item should be reported in one of the following ways:

EXHIBIT 20-4
FUND BALANCE SHEETS
City of Centerville
Fund Balance Sheets
Governmental Funds
June 30, 20X5

	General Fund	*Hotel & Entertainment Tax*	*Multi-Purpose Improvement Bonds*	*Other Governmental Funds (A)*	*Total Governmental Funds*
ASSETS					
Cash and cash equivalents	$4,300,000	$2,350,000	$1,350,000	$2,900,000	$10,900,000
Receivables (net)	2,130,000	270,000	250,000	2,970,000	5,620,000
Investments	2,780,000	1,600,000	2,540,000	1,340,000	8,260,000
Inventories and prepayments	125,000			47,000	172,000
Receivable from other funds		130,000			130,000
Total Assets	$9,335,000	$4,350,000	$4,140,000	$7,257,000	$25,082,000
LIABILITIES					
Accounts payable	1,470,000	$360,000	$340,000	$560,000	$2,730,000
Other payables	60,000	20,000	60,000	30,000	170,000
Payable to other governments		50,000			50,000
Deferred revenue	40,000	30,000	5,000	22,000	97,000
Total Liabilities	1,570,000	460,000	405,000	612,000	3,047,000

FUND BALANCES					
Reserved for:					
Noncurrent assets	824,000				824,000
Encumbrances	55,000	27,000	122,000	77,000	281,000
Other purposes	450,000			375,000	825,000
Unreserved, reported in:					
General fund	6,436,000				6,436,000
Special revenue fund		3,863,000			3,863,000
Capital projects funds			3,613,000		3,613,000
Other funds				6,193,000	6,193,000
Total Fund Balances	7,765,000	3,890,000	3,735,000	6,645,000	22,035,000
Total Liabilities and Fund Balances	$9,335,000	$4,350,000	$4,140,000	$7,257,000	$25,082,000
Fund Balance of Governmental Funds					$22,035,000
Amounts presented for governmental activities in the Statement of Net Assets are different because:					
Capital assets reported in the Statement of Net Assets are not financial resources					43,500,000
Other long-term assets reported in the Statement of Net Assets are not available to pay for current period expenditures					1,242,000
Assets and liabilities of Internal Service Funds reported in the Statement of Net Assets are used to charge the cost of certain activities and resources to individual funds and therefore are not reported in the fund balance sheets					740,000
Long-term liabilities are reported in the Statement of Net Assets but they are not due and payable in the current period and therefore are not reported as liabilities of fund balance sheets					(26,000,000)
Net Assets of Governmental Activities					$44,564,000

(A) Combining statements for nonmajor funds may be presented as supplementary information but there is no requirement to do so unless the entity elects to prepare a CAFR

- Presented and identified as a separate line item in either the "revenue" category or "expenditures" category.
- Presented but not identified as a separate line item in either the "revenue" category or "expenditures" category and described in a note to the financial statements.

> **PRACTICE POINT:** An extraordinary gain or loss related to the early extinguishment of debt cannot occur on a statement of revenues, expenditures, and changes in fund balances because this statement presents only the changes in current financial resources (as part of other financing sources and uses) and not gains and losses from events and transactions.

Required reconciliation As noted earlier there must be a summary reconciliation between the total net change in fund balances (total governmental funds) as shown on the statement of revenues, expenditures, and changes in fund balances and the change in net assets as presented in the governmental activities column of the statement of activities. Some of the typical items that will be needed to reconcile the two amounts are (GASB-34, par. 90):

- The difference between reporting revenues and expenses on the accrual basis on the statement of activities and the reporting of revenues and expenditures on the modified accrual basis on the statement of revenues, expenditures, and changes in fund balances
- The difference between reporting depreciation expense on the statement of activities and reporting the acquisition of capital assets as an expenditure on the statement of revenues, expenditures, and changes in fund balances
- The difference between reporting proceeds from the issuance of long-term liabilities as an other source of financing on the statement of revenues, expenditures, and changes in fund balances and the nonrecognition of those proceeds on the statement of activities
- The difference between reporting the repayment of long-term liabilities as an expenditure on the statement of revenues, expenditures, and changes in fund balances and the nonrecognition of those payments on the statement of activities
- The difference between reporting the net revenue (expenses) of Internal Service Funds on the statement of activities and the nonrecognition of those activities on the statement of revenues, expenditures, and changes in fund balances

Exhibit 20-5 provides an illustration of a statements of revenues, expenditures, and changes in fund balances for governmental funds consistent with the standards established by GASB-34.

Required financial statements: proprietary funds Financial statements for proprietary funds should be based on the flow of economic resources (measurement focus) and the accrual basis of accounting. The proprietary fund category includes Enterprise Funds and Internal Service Funds. Proprietary fund activities should be accounted for and reported based on all applicable GASB pronouncements, NCGA pronouncements, and the following pronouncements issued on or before November 30, 1989, unless they conflict with GASB or NCGA pronouncements (GASB-34, pars. 17, 92, and 93).

- Financial Accounting Standards Board (FASB) Statements and Interpretations
- Accounting Principles Board (APB) Opinions
- Accounting Research Bulletins (ARBs) of the Committee on Accounting Procedure

Enterprise Funds that qualify may follow the standards established by FAS-71 and related pronouncements issued on or before November 30, 1989 (GASB-34, par. 94).

Separate presentation of internal service funds The major fund reporting requirement does not apply to Internal Service Funds even though they are proprietary funds. However, all Internal Service Funds should be combined into a single column and presented on the face of the proprietary funds' financial statements. This column must be presented to the right of the total column for all Enterprise Funds. The Internal Service Funds column and the Enterprise Funds total column should not be added together (GASB-34, par. 96).

Based on the fundamental concepts discussed above, the following financial statements must be prepared for proprietary funds (GASB-34, par. 91):

- Statement of net assets (or balance sheet)
- Statement of revenues, expenses, and changes in fund net assets
- Statement of cash flows

Statement of net assets Assets and liabilities presented on the statement of net assets of a proprietary fund should be classified as current and long-term, based on the guidance established in Chapter 3 of ARB-43 (Restatement and Revision of Accounting Research Bulletins). The statement of net assets may be presented in either one of the following formats (GASB-34, pars. 97-98):

- Net assets format (where assets less liabilities equal net assets)
- Balance sheet format (where assets equal liabilities plus net assets)

EXHIBIT 20-5
STATEMENT OF REVENUES, EXPENDITURES, AND CHANGES IN FUND BALANCES
City of Centerville
For the Year Ended June 30, 20X5

	General Fund	*Hotel & Entertainment Tax*	*Multi-Purpose Improvement Bonds*	*Other Governmental Funds*	*Total Governmental Funds*
REVENUES					
Property taxes	$10,125,000			$2,750,000	$12,875,000
Wage taxes	2,410,000			842,000	3,252,000
Other taxes	922,000	$1,615,000		330,000	2,867,000
Fees and other nontax revenues	2,700,000			496,000	3,196,000
Grants and receipts from other governments	907,000			183,000	1,090,000
Investment income	347,000	103,000	$161,000	119,000	730,000
Other	1,365,000			167,000	1,532,000
Total Revenues	18,776,000	1,718,000	161,000	4,887,000	25,542,000
EXPENDITURES					
Current operating:					
General government	1,610,000			295,000	1,905,000
Public safety	6,950,000			877,000	7,827,000
Streets	2,175,000			293,000	2,468,000
Recreation and parks	647,000	299,000		242,000	1,188,000
Health and welfare	2,842,000			148,000	2,990,000
Education (payment to school district)	6,500,000				6,500,000
Debt service:					
Principal				3,500,000	3,500,000
Interest				1,085,000	1,085,000
Capital Expenditures			4,250,000		4,250,000

Total Expenditures	20,724,000	299,000	4,250,000	6,440,000	31,713,000
Excess (deficiency) of revenues over expenditures	(1,948,000)	1,419,000	(4,089,000)	(1,553,000)	(6,171,000)
OTHER FINANCING SOURCES (USES)					
Long-term debt issued			4,500,000	1,200,000	5,700,000
Transfers in	45,000			670,000	715,000
Transfers out	(547,000)	(115,000)		(33,000)	(695,000)
Total Other Financing Sources And Uses	(502,000)	(115,000)	4,500,000	1,837,000	5,720,000
SPECIAL ITEMS					
Proceeds from sale of real estate	1,890,000				1,890,000
Net Change in Fund Balances	(560,000)	1,304,000	411,000	284,000	1,439,000
Fund Balances—Beginning	8,325,000	2,586,000	3,324,000	6,361,000	20,596,000
Fund Balances—Ending	$7,765,000	$3,890,000	$3,735,000	$6,645,000	$22,035,000

Net Change in Fund Balances (As Presented In This Statement)	1,439,000
Amounts presented for governmental activities in the Statement of Activities are different because:	
Governmental funds report capital investments as expenditures while the Statement of Activities reports depreciation expense on capital assets. This is the difference between the two amounts for this year.	1,030,000
Revenues in the Statement of Activities that do not provide current financial resources are not reported as revenues in governmental funds.	47,000
Some expenses reported in the Statement of Activities do not require the use of current financial resources and therefore are not reported as expenditures in governmental funds.	(123,000)
Proceeds from the issuance of long-term debt are reported as providing current financial resources in governmental funds but are reported as long-term debt in the government-wide financial statements and repayments of such debt is reported as an expenditure for governmental funds but is reported as a reduction of debt in government-wide financial statements.	(2,200,000)
In the Statement of Activities only the gain on the sale of real estate is reported while in the governmental funds the proceeds from the sale increase current financial resources.	2,344,000
Activities of Internal Service Funds are reported as net revenue (expense) in the governmental activities.	(73,000)
Change in Net Assets of Governmental Activities as Reported on the Statement of Activities	$2,464,000

Net assets should be identified as (1) invested in capital assets, net of related debt; (2) restricted; and (3) unrestricted. The guidance discussed earlier (in the context of government-wide financial statements) should be used to determine what amounts should be related to these three categories of net assets. GASB-34 notes that capital contributions should not be presented as a separate component of net assets. Also, designations of net assets cannot be identified on the face of the statement of net assets.

GASB Comprehensive Implementation Guide points out that although the identification of capital contributions should not be presented in the statement of net assets, the amount of capital contributions may be disclosed in a note to the financial statements.

> **PRACTICE POINT:** A governmental entity can use either the title "statement of net assets" or "balance sheet." For simplicity purposes, the following discussion uses "statement of net assets."

Reporting restrictions on asset use In a proprietary fund it is assumed that assets (especially current assets) are unrestricted in that there are no conditions that would prevent the governmental entity from using the resources to pay existing liabilities. If the name of the asset account does not adequately explain the normally perceived availability of that asset, the item should be identified as a restricted asset on the statement of net assets. For example, an amount of cash may be restricted to a specific type of expenditure and therefore it would be misleading to report the restricted cash with all other cash (classified as current asset). Under this circumstance, the cash should be reported as restricted cash in the financial statement category labeled "noncurrent assets." On the other hand, equipment is not available to pay liabilities but the title of the account adequately describes the availability (or lack of liquidity) of the asset and therefore there is no need to identify the asset as restricted (GASB-34, par. 99).

GASB Comprehensive Implementation Guide points out that ARB-43 (chapter 3, paragraph 62) notes that current assets do not include cash and claims to cash when they are restricted under the following conditions:

- Amounts cannot be used for current operations.
- Amounts are to be used to acquire noncurrent assets.
- Amounts are to be used to pay long-term debts.

Many governmental entities have assets that are restricted to specific purposes, but if those purposes are related to current operations, they should be reported as current assets.

PRACTICE POINT: As pointed out earlier, restricted net assets arise only when assets are (1) externally imposed by a creditor (such as through debt covenants), grantors, contributors, or laws or regulations of other governments or (2) imposed by law through constitutional provisions or enabling legislation.

PRACTICE POINT: There is no requirement that there be a specific one-to-one relationship between assets and liabilities presented and the amounts presented in the three categories of net assets. In other words, a reader will not generally be able to look at the statement of net assets and identify the specific assets and liability accounts that are reported as, for example, unrestricted net assets.

Exhibit 20-6 provides an illustration of a statements of net assets for proprietary funds consistent with the standards established by GASB-34.

EXHIBIT 20-6
STATEMENT OF NET ASSETS:
PROPRIETARY FUNDS
City of Centerville
For the Year Ended June 30, 20X5

	Airport	*Water and Sewer*	*Totals*	*Governmental Activities— Internal Service (See Note X)*
ASSETS				
Current Assets:				
Cash and cash equivalents	$1,200,000	$3,100,000	$4,300,000	$430,000
Receivables (net)	2,100,000	11,109,000	13,209,000	1,209,000
Investments	1,300,000	1,200,000	2,500,000	35,000
Inventories and prepayments	45,000	678,000	723,000	108,000
Total Current Assets	4,645,000	16,087,000	20,732,000	1,782,000
Noncurrent Assets:				
Restricted cash and cash equivalents	300,000	1,000,000	1,300,000	23,000
Capital Assets:				
Land	7,450,000	3,550,000	11,000,000	
Buildings	19,188,000	3,212,000	22,400,000	
Equipment	2,100,000	1,200,000	3,300,000	1,422,000
Less accumulated depreciation	(7,450,000)	(7,250,000)	(14,700,000)	(345,000)
Capital assets, net	21,288,000	712,000	22,000,000	1,077,000
Total Assets	$26,233,000	$17,799,000	$44,032,000	$2,882,000
LIABILITIES				
Current Liabilities:				
Accounts payable	$275,000	$1,025,000	$1,300,000	$375,000

Deferred revenue	45,000	5,000	50,000	32,000
Claims and judgments	3,000	67,000	70,000	41,000
Due to other funds		112,000	112,000	
Current portion of long-term debt	120,000	230,000	350,000	
Other	20,000	210,000	230,000	18,000
Total Current Liabilities	463,000	1,649,000	2,112,000	466,000
Noncurrent Liabilities:				
Claims and judgments	200,000	1,100,000	1,300,000	42,000
Bonds, notes, and loans payable	4,200,000	7,000,000	11,200,000	
Total Noncurrent Liabilities	4,400,000	8,100,000	12,500,000	42,000
Total Liabilities	4,863,000	9,749,000	14,612,000	508,000
NET ASSETS				
Invested in capital assets, net of related debt	12,900,000	3,800,000	16,700,000	1,077,000
Restricted	7,070,000	4,000,000	11,070,000	623,000
Unrestricted	1,400,000	250,000	1,650,000	674,000
Total Net Assets	$21,370,000	$8,050,000	$29,420,000	$2,374,000

Statement of revenues, expenses, and changes in fund net assets The operating statement of a proprietary fund is the statement of revenues, expenses, and changes in fund net assets. In preparing this statement, the following standards should be observed (GASB-34, par. 100):

- Revenues should be reported by major source.
- Revenues that are restricted for the payment of revenue bonds should be identified.
- Operating and nonoperating revenues should be reported separately.
- Operating and nonoperating expenses should be reported separately.
- Separate subtotals should be presented for operating revenues, operating expenses, and operating income.
- Nonoperating revenues and expenses should be reported after operating income.
- Capital contributions and additions to term and permanent endowments should be reported separately.
- Special and extraordinary items should be reported separately.
- Transfers should be reported separately.

OBSERVATION: Revenues should be reported net of related discounts or allowances. The amount of the discounts or allowances must be presented on the operating statement (either parenthetically or as a subtraction from gross revenues) or in a note to the financial statements.

GASB-34 requires that the statement of revenues, expenses, and changes in fund net assets should be presented in the following sequence (GASB-34, par. 101):

	Major Fund #1	*Major Fund #2*	*Nonmajor Funds*	*Total*
Operating revenues (detailed)	$XXX	$XXX	$XXX	$XXX
Total operating revenues	XXX	XXX	XXX	XXX
Operating expenses (detailed)	XXX	XXX	XXX	XXX
Total operating expenses	XXX	XXX	XXX	XXX
Operating income (loss)	XXX	XXX	XXX	XXX
Nonoperating revenues and expenses (detailed)	XXX	XXX	XXX	XXX
Income before other revenues, expenses, gains, losses, and transfers	XXX	XXX	XXX	XXX
Capital contributions, additions to permanent and term endowments, special and extraordinary items (detailed), and transfers	XXX	XXX	XXX	XXX
Change in net assets	XXX	XXX	XXX	XXX
Net assets—Beginning of period	XXX	XXX	XXX	XXX
Net assets—End of period	$XXX	$XXX	$XXX	$XXX

Defining operating revenues and expenses An important element of the statement of revenues, expenses, and changes in fund net assets is that there must be a differentiation between operating revenues and nonoperating revenues, and operating expenses and nonoperating expenses based on policies established by the governmental entity. Those policies should be disclosed in the entity's summary of significant accounting policies and must be applied consistently from period to period. GASB-34 states that, in general, differentiations between operating and nonoperating transactions should follow the broad guidance established by GASB-9 (Reporting Cash Flows of Proprietary and Nonexpendable Trust Funds and Governmental Entities That Use Proprietary Fund Accounting). For example, transactions related to (1) capital and related financing activities, (2) noncapital financing activities, (3) investing activities, and (4) nonexchange revenues, such as tax revenues, generally would be considered nonoperating transactions for purposes of preparing the statement of revenues, expenses, and changes in net assets (GASB-34, par. 102).

In addition, GASB-34 provides the following guidance:

> Revenue and expense transactions normally classified as other operating cash flows from operations in most proprietary funds should be classified as operating revenues and expenses if those transactions constitute the reporting proprietary fund's principal ongoing operations. For example, interest revenue and expense transactions should be reported as operating revenue and expenses by a proprietary fund established to provide loans to first-time homeowners.

PRACTICE POINT: The *GASB Comprehensive Implementation Guide* emphasizes that a governmental entity must decide how to define its operating and nonoperating activities for proprietary funds. The reference in GASB-34 to the guidance provided in GASB-9 (pars. 17–19) simply provides general concepts but they should not be viewed as requirements.

Reporting capital contributions and additions to permanent and term endowments Based on the standards established by GASB-34 the statement of revenues, expenses, and changes in fund net assets must reflect the "all-inclusive" concept. That is, except for prior period adjustments and the effects of certain changes in accounting principles, all resources inflows (except for liabilities) must be reported on a proprietary fund's operating statement. Thus, additions to permanent and term endowments can no longer be shown as direct additions to a fund capital. The guidance for determining when these items should be recognized is based on GASB-33 (GASB-34, par. 103).

PRACTICE POINT: The fact that capital contributions are reported on a proprietary fund's operating statement does not mean that the contribution results in an increase in unrestricted net assets. The transactions must be evaluated to determine whether the amount is appropriately presented as part of net assets invested in capital assets (net of related debt).

Required reconciliations As described earlier, there must be a reconciliation between the government-wide financial statements and the governmental fund financial statements. Generally, there is no need for a similar reconciliation between the government-wide financial statements and proprietary fund financial statements because both sets of financial statements are based on the same measurement focus and basis of accounting (GASB-34, par. 104).

Typically there are no reconciling items between business-type activities as they appear on the government-wide financial statements and the fund financial statements because both statements are prepared on the accrual basis of accounting and economic resources measurement focus. However *GASB Comprehensive Implementation Guide* states that generally only the following could arise as reconciling items:

- When Enterprise Funds are the only or predominant participants in an Internal Service Fund, the balances related to the Internal Service Fund must be included in the business-type activities column (not the governmental activities column, which is the typical presentation). Because Internal Service Funds are not included in the totals of the Enterprise Funds (but rather, are presented in a column to the right of those funds) in the fund financial statements, a reconciling item arises.
- When Enterprise Funds participate in an Internal Service Fund and the Internal Service Fund is not at a "break even" position, a look-back adjustment must modify the expenses in the business-type activities column. This creates a difference between the expenses as presented in the fund financial statements and the expenses presented in the government-wide financial statements.
- When a governmental activity is performed in an Enterprise Fund (or vice versa), the results of the activity are presented in an Enterprise Fund financial statement, but those same results are also presented in the governmental activity column of the government-wide financial statements. This creates a difference between the two financial statements.

Exhibit 20-7 provides an illustration of a statements of revenues, expenses, and changes in net assets for proprietary funds consistent with the standards established by GASB-34.

Statement of cash flows Proprietary funds should prepare a statement of cash flows based on the guidance established by GASB-9, except the statement of cash flows should be formatted based on the direct method in computing cash flows from operating activities. The statement of cash flows would be supplemented with a reconciliation of operating cash flows and operating income (GASB-34, par. 105).

EXHIBIT 20-7
STATEMENT OF REVENUES, EXPENSES, AND CHANGES IN NET ASSETS: PROPRIETARY FUNDS

City of Centerville
For the Year Ended June 30, 20X5

	Enterprise Funds			*Governmental Activities—Internal Service (See Note X)*
	Airport	*Water and Sewer*	*Totals*	
Operating Revenues:				
Charges for services	$3,900,000	$4,300,000	$8,200,000	$1,600,000
Other	90,000	15,000	105,000	320,000
Total Operating Revenues	3,990,000	4,315,000	8,305,000	1,920,000
Operating Expenses:				
Personal services	1,305,000	1,270,000	2,575,000	1,477,000
Purchase of services	400,000	58,000	458,000	222,000
Materials and supplies	225,000	112,000	337,000	122,000
Depreciation	1,100,000	210,000	1,310,000	82,000
Other	250,000	20,000	270,000	26,000
Total Operating Expenses	3,280,000	1,670,000	4,950,000	1,929,000
Operating Income (Loss)	710,000	2,645,000	3,355,000	(9,000)
Nonoperating Revenues (Expenses)				
Interest and investment income	140,000	70,000	210,000	4,000
Interest Expense	(200,000)	(400,000)	(600,000)	(2,000)
Miscellaneous Expenses	(20,000)	(30,000)	(50,000)	(5,000)
Total Nonoperating Revenue (Expenses)	(80,000)	(360,000)	(440,000)	(3,000)
Net Income (Loss) Before Contributions and Transfers	630,000	2,285,000	2,915,000	(12,000)
Capital contributions	130,000		130,000	46,000
Transfers out	(125,000)		(125,000)	(107,000)
Change in net assets	635,000	2,285,000	2,920,000	(73,000)
Net assets—Beginning	11,500,000	15,000,000	26,500,000	2,447,000
Net assets—Ending	$12,135,000	$17,285,000	$29,420,000	$2,374,000

Exhibit 20-8 provides an illustration of a statement of cash flows for proprietary funds consistent with the standards established by GASB-34.

EXHIBIT 20-8
STATEMENT OF CASH FLOWS: PROPRIETARY FUNDS

City of Centerville
For the Year Ended June 30, 20X5

	Enterprise Funds			*Governmental Activities—Internal Service (See Note X)*
	Airport	*Water and Sewer*	*Totals*	
CASH FLOWS FROM OPERATING ACTIVITIES:				
Receipts from customers	$3,400,000	$4,450,000	$7,850,000	$1,910,000
Payments to suppliers	(609,000)	(162,000)	(771,000)	(347,000)
Payments to employees	(1,310,000)	(1,245,000)	(2,555,000)	(1,420,000)
Other receipts (payments)	(197,000)	(18,000)	(215,000)	(17,000)
Net Cash Provided (Used) By Operating Activities	1,284,000	3,025,000	4,309,000	126,000
CASH FLOWS FROM NONCAPITAL FINANCING ACTIVITIES:				
Operating grants/transfers	(125,000)		(125,000)	(107,000)
CASH FLOWS FROM CAPITAL AND RELATED FINANCING ACTIVITIES:				
Proceeds from issuance of debt	1,500,000	850,000	2,350,000	
Capital contributions	130,000		130,000	46,000
Purchases of capital assets	(1,350,000)	(800,000)	(2,150,000)	(85,000)
Principal paid on capital debt	(1,200,000)	(900,000)	(2,100,000)	
Interest paid on debt	(210,000)	(380,000)	(590,000)	(2,000)
Other receipts (payments)	(40,000)	(22,000)	(62,000)	
Net Cash Provided (Used) By Capital And Related Financing Activities:	(1,170,000)	(1,252,000)	(2,422,000)	(41,000)
CASH FLOWS FROM INVESTING ACTIVITIES:				
Proceeds from sales and maturities of investments	220,000	135,000	355,000	34,000
Interest and dividends	40,000	25,000	65,000	2,000
Net Cash Provided (Used) By Investing Activities	260,000	160,000	420,000	36,000
Net Increase (Decrease) In Cash And Cash Equivalents	249,000	1,933,000	2,182,000	14,000
Balances—Beginning of the year	1,251,000	2,167,000	3,418,000	439,000
Balances—End of the year	$1,500,000	$4,100,000	$5,600,000	$453,000
RECONCILIATION OF OPERATING INCOME (LOSS) TO NET CASH PROVIDED (USED) BY OPERATING ACTIVITIES:				
Operating income (loss)	$710,000	$2,645,000	$3,355,000	($9,000)

Adjustments to reconcile operating income to net cash provided (used) by operating activities:				
Depreciation expenses	1,100,000	210,000	1,310,000	82,000
Changes in net assets and liabilities:				
Receivables, net	(420,000)	205,000	(215,000)	(13,000)
Inventories	(125,000)	(33,000)	(158,000)	42,000
Accounts payable	10,000	(29,000)	(19,000)	8,000
Other	9,000	27,000	36,000	16,000
Net Cash Provided By Operating Activities	$1,284,000	$3,025,000	$4,309,000	$126,000

Required financial statements: Fiduciary funds and similar component units Assets held by a governmental entity for other parties (either as a trustee or as an agent) and that cannot be used to finance the governmental entity's own operating programs should be reported in the entity's fiduciary fund financial statement category. The financial statements for fiduciary funds should be based on the flow of economic resources measurement focus and the accrual basis of accounting (with the exception of certain liabilities of defined benefit pension plans and certain postemployment healthcare plans). Fiduciary fund financial statements are not reported by major fund (which is required for governmental funds and proprietary funds) but must be reported based on the following fund types (GASB-34, pars. 106-107):

- Pension (and other employee benefit) Trust Funds
- Private-Purpose Trust Funds
- Investment Trust Funds
- Agency Funds

The financial statements of a fiduciary component unit should be included in one of the four fund types listed above. *GASB Comprehensive Implementation Guide* emphasizes that a fiduciary fund that a governmental entity believes is particularly important cannot be presented in a separate column in the fund financial statements. If a governmental entity wants to present additional detail about its fiduciary funds, that information can be presented in combining statements; however, those statements are optional and are not considered to be part of the basic external financial statements. They are part of the CAFR.

PRACTICE POINT: The financial statements for individual pension plans and postemployment health-care plans are presented in the notes to the financial statements when separate GAAP-based financial statements are not prepared by the plans. If separate financial statements are prepared it is only necessary to explain how the separate financial statements of the plan can be obtained. Guidance for preparing these disclosures are established in GASB-25 (par. 19) and GASB-26 (par. 7).

The following financial statements should be included for fiduciary funds:

- Statement of fiduciary net assets
- Statement of changes in fiduciary net assets

PRACTICE POINT: Only a statement of fiduciary net assets is prepared for an Agency Fund.

Statement of fiduciary net assets The assets, liabilities, and net assets of fiduciary funds should be presented in the statement of fiduciary net assets. There is no need to divide net assets into the three categories (invested in capital assets (net of related debt), restricted net assets, and unrestricted net assets) that must be used in the government-wide financial statements (GASB-34, par. 108).

Statement of changes in fiduciary net assets The statement of changes in fiduciary net assets should summarize the additions to, deductions from, and net increase or decrease in net assets for the year. GASB-34 also requires the statement to provide information "about significant year-to-year changes in net assets" (GASB-34, par. 109).

Exhibit 20-9 is a statement of fiduciary net assets and Exhibit 20-10 is a statement of changes in fiduciary net assets.

Reporting agency funds Because an Agency Fund is established to account for assets of another party, only a statement of fiduciary net assets should be reported for these funds. Furthermore, since the governmental entity has no equity in an Agency Fund, a statement of fiduciary net assets should report only assets and liabilities (no amount for net assets) (GASB-34, par. 110).

EXHIBIT 20-9
STATEMENT OF FIDUCIARY NET ASSETS

City of Centerville
June 30, 20X5

	Pension and Benefits Trust Funds	*Private-Purpose Trust Funds*	*Agency Funds*
ASSETS			
Cash	$750,000	$625,000	$134,000
Receivables	340,000	2,000	
Investments	10,700,000		
Other assets	122,000		746,000
Due from other funds	87,000		
Total Assets	11,999,000	627,000	$880,000
LIABILITIES			
Accounts payable	9,000	1,000	
Other liabilities			880,000
Total Liabilities	9,000	1,000	$880,000
NET ASSETS			
Held in trust for pension benefits and other purposes	$11,990,000	$626,000	

EXHIBIT 20-10
STATEMENT OF CHANGES IN FIDUCIARY NET ASSETS

City of Centerville
For the Year Ended June 30, 20X5

	Pension and Benefits Trust Funds	*Private-Purpose Trust Funds*
ADDITIONS		
Contributions:		
Employer	$1,200,000	
Plan members	720,000	
Total Contributions	1,920,000	
Investment Income:		
Net appreciation (depreciation) in fair value of investments	1,400,000	
Interest	100,000	

Dividends	140,000	$6,000
Total Investment Income	1,640,000	6,000
Less investment expense	103,000	
Net Investment Income	1,537,000	6,000
Total Additions	3,457,000	6,000
DEDUCTIONS		
Benefits	1,220,000	4,000
Refunds of contributions	194,000	
Administrative expenses	87,000	1,000
Total Deductions	1,501,000	5,000
Net increase	1,956,000	1,000
Net assets—Beginning of the year	10,034,000	625,000
Net assets—End of the year	$11,990,000	$626,000

GASB-34 notes that an Agency Fund may be used as a clearing account when one governmental entity collects or receives financial resources that are to be distributed to other funds and other governmental entities. For example, a county government may collect property taxes that are to be allocated to the county government and to school districts, fire districts, or other governmental entities that are not part of the county government. Under this circumstance, the portion of the assets that belong to the county government (the reporting entity) should not be reported in an Agency Fund but rather should be reported as assets of the appropriate county governmental fund (GASB-34, par. 111).

Reporting Interfund Activity

In order to determine how intergovernmental transfers within and among governmental funds, proprietary funds, and fiduciary funds should be presented in the government-wide and fund financial statements, transfers must be categorized as follows (GASB-34, par. 112):

- Reciprocal interfund activity
  —Interfund loans
  —Interfund services provided and used
- Nonreciprocal interfund activity
  —Interfund transfers
  —Interfund reimbursements

Reciprocal interfund activities are internal fund activities that have many of the same characteristics of exchange and exchange-like transactions that occur with external parties. Nonreciprocal interfund activities are internal fund activities that have many of the same characteristics of nonexchange transactions that occur with external parties.

Interfund loans (reciprocal interfund activity) The concept of a loan as envisioned by GASB-34 is based on the expectation that the loan will be repaid at some point. Loans should be reported as interfund receivables by the lender fund and interfund payables by the borrower fund. That is, the interfund loan should not be eliminated in the preparation of financial statements at the fund level. Thus, the proceeds from interfund loans should not be reported as "other financing sources or uses" in the operating statements in the fund financial statements. If a loan or a portion of a loan is not expected to be repaid "within a reasonable time," the interfund receivable/payable should be reduced by the amount not expected to be repaid, and that amount should be reported as an interfund transfer by both funds that are a party to the transfer.

GASB Comprehensive Implementation Guide points out that professional judgment must be used to determine what constitutes "expected within a reasonable time." For example, the past history of repayment or lack of history can be relevant in making the determination. In other circumstances, the ability of a fund to make repayment could help make the determination.

Interfund service provided and used (reciprocal interfund activity) Interfund receivables/payables may arise from an operating activity (that is, the sale of goods and services) between funds rather than in the form of a loan arrangement. If the interfund operating activity is recorded at an amount that approximates the fair value of the goods or services exchanged, the provider/seller fund should record the activity as revenue and the user/purchaser fund should record an expenditure/expense. Any unpaid balance at the end of the period should be reported as an interfund receivable/payable in the fund statements.

PRACTICE POINT: GASB-34 points out that GASB-10 (Accounting and Financial Reporting for Risk Financing and Related Insurance Issues), paragraph 64, requires that when the General Fund is used to account for risk-financing activities, interfund charges to other funds must be accounted for as reimbursements.

Interfund transfers (nonreciprocal interfund activity) This type of nonreciprocal transaction represents interfund activities whereby the two parties to the events do not receive equivalent cash, goods, or services. Governmental funds should report transfers of this nature in their activity statements as other financing uses and other financial sources of funds. Proprietary funds should report this type of transfer in their activity statements after nonoperating revenues and nonoperating expenses.

> **PRACTICE POINT:** Based on the standards established by GASB-34, there is no differentiation between operating transfers and residual equity transfers. Thus, no transfers can be reported as adjustments to a fund's beginning equity balance.

> **PRACTICE POINT:** GASB-34 points out that most payments "in lieu of taxes" should be reported as interfund transfers, unless the payments and services received are equivalent in value based on the exchange of specific services or goods. If the two are equivalent in value, the disbursing fund may treat the payment as an expenditure (expense) and the receiving fund may record revenue. It is unlikely that current *in lieu of tax* arrangements involve the payments for identifiable services that are based on the value of services rendered.
>
> *GASB Comprehensive Implementation Guide* raises the question of how a governmental entity should report a "payment in lieu of taxes" from an Enterprise Utility Fund to its General Fund. The nature of the payment must be examined to determine whether it approximates a fair value exchange. If the interfund operating activity is recorded at an amount that approximates the fair value of the goods or services exchanged, the General Fund (provider/seller fund) should record the activity as revenue and the Enterprise Utility Fund (user/purchaser fund) should record an expenditure/expense. It is unlikely that this type of transaction would involve an exchange of services of equivalent value because of the indirect nature of the services provided through the General Fund. For this reason, it is probable that the payment would be treated as a transfer-out by the Enterprise Utility Fund and transfer-in by the General Fund.

Interfund reimbursements (nonreciprocal interfund activity) A fund may incur an expenditure or expense that will subsequently be reimbursed by another fund. Reimbursements should not be reported in the governmental entity's financial statements in order to avoid "double counting" revenues and expense/expenditure items.

Notes to the Basic Financial Statements

The notes to the financial statements should focus on the primary government (which includes it blended component units) and support the information included in the government-wide financial statements and the fund financial statements (GASB-34, par. 113).

> **PRACTICE POINT:** Note disclosures related to discretely blended component units should be presented based on the requirements established by GASB-14, paragraph 63.

> **NOTE:** Appendix 20B provides a governmental entity presentation and disclosure checklist.

Note disclosures established by GASB-34 as amended by GASB-38 do not replace the disclosures required by NCGAI-6 (Notes to the Financial Statements Disclosure), as amended. NCGAI-6 lists the following as notes that are essential to the fair presentation of the basic financial statements:

A. Summary of significant accounting policies

1. A description of the government-wide financial statements, noting that neither fiduciary funds nor component units that are fiduciary in nature are included.
2. A brief description of the component units of the financial reporting entity and their relationships to the primary government. This should include a discussion of the criteria for including component units in the financial reporting entity and how the component units are reported. Also include information about how the separate financial statements for the individual component units may be obtained.
3. A description of the activities accounted for in each of the following columns—major funds, Internal Service Funds, and fiduciary funds types—presented in the basic financial statements.
4. The measurement focus and basis of accounting used in the government-wide statements, and the revenue recognition policies used in fund financial statements.
5. The length of time used to define "available" for purposes of revenue recognition in the governmental fund financial statements.
6. The policy for eliminating internal activity in the government-wide statement of activities.

7. A description of the types of transactions included in program revenues and the policy for allocating indirect expenses to functions in the statement of activities.
8. The policy for defining operating and nonoperating revenues of proprietary funds.
9. The policy for applying FASB pronouncements issued after November 30, 1989 to business-type activities and to Enterprise Funds of the primary government.
10. The definition of cash equivalents used in the statement of cash flows for proprietary fund types.
11. The government's policy regarding whether to first apply restricted or unrestricted resources when an expense is incurred for purposes for which both restricted and unrestricted net assets are available.

B. Cash deposits with financial institutions
C. Investments
D. Significant contingent liabilities
E. Encumbrances outstanding
F. Significant effects of subsequent events
G. Annual pension cost and net pension obligations
H. Significant violations of finance-related legal or contractual provisions and actions taken to address such violations
I. Debt service requirement to maturity
J. Construction and other significant commitments
K. Required disclosures about capital assets
L. Required disclosures about long-term liabilities
M. Deficit fund balance or net assets of individual funds
N. Interfund balances and transfers
O. Significant transactions between discretely presented component units and with the primary government
P. Disclosures about donor-restricted endowments

In addition, NCGAI-6 points out that the above notes to the financial statements are not the only disclosures required and that additional disclosures, such as the following, should be made:

A. Entity risk management activities
B. Property taxes
C. Segment information for Enterprise Funds

D. Condensed financial statements for major discretely presented component units
E. Budget basis of accounting and budget/GAAP reporting differences not otherwise reconciled in the financial statements
F. Short-term debt instruments and liquidity
G. Related party transactions
H. The nature of the primary government's accountability for related organizations
I. Capital leases
J. Joint ventures and jointly governed organizations
K. Debt refundings
L. Grants, entitlements, and shared revenues
M. Methods of estimation of fixed asset costs
N. Fund balance designations
O. Interfund eliminations in fund financial statements not apparent from headings
P. Pension plans—in both separately issued plan financial statements and employer statements
Q. Bond, tax, or revenue anticipation notes excluded from fund or current liabilities (proprietary funds)
R. Nature and amount of inconsistencies in financial statements caused by transactions between component units having different fiscal year-ends or changes in component unit fiscal year-ends
S. In component unit separate reports, identification of the primary government in whose financial report the component unit is included and a description of its relationship to the primary government
T. Reverse repurchase and dollar reverse repurchase agreements
U. Securities lending transactions
V. Special assessment debt and related activities
W. Demand bonds
X. Postemployment benefits other than pension benefits
Y. Landfill closure and postclosure care
AA. On-behalf payments for fringe benefits and salaries
BB. Entity involvement in conduit debt obligations
CC. Sponsoring government disclosures about external investment pools reported as Investment Trust Funds
DD. The amount of interest expense included in direct expenses
EE. Disaggregation of receivable and payable balances

The disclosures listed above are not all-inclusive. Professional judgment must be used to determine whether additional disclosures should be made in the financial statements.

> **PRACTICE POINT:** Paragraph 11a of GASB-34 requires that the MD&A provide a brief discussion of the basic financial statements; paragraph 115a requires a description of the government-wide financial statements in the summary of significant accounting policies. *GASB Comprehensive Implementation Guide* notes that the difference between these two requirements is that paragraph 115a focuses on a description and scope of the government-wide financial statements and paragraph 11a requires a discussion of both government-wide and fund financial statements.

> **PRACTICE POINT:** *GASB Comprehensive Implementation Guide* states that the disclosure related to the policy regarding the use of restricted resources (paragraph 115h) requires the governmental entity to explain when restricted resources are used. That is, are restricted resources used only after unrestricted resources have been spent for a particular purpose or are restricted resources assumed to be spent first?

Required note disclosures about fund types and activities of funds The appendix to NCGAI-6 originally recommended that the financial statements include a description of fund categories and generic fund types; however, in practice there is some question about whether these descriptions provide an adequate explanation of the activities performed by a governmental entity. In addition, GASB-34 requires, for the most part, that the focus of fund financial statements be directed away from fund types to major funds, aggregated nonmajor governmental and proprietary funds, the internal service fund type, and fiduciary fund types. With the implementation of the standards established by GASB-34, it is likely that the disclosure requirements recommended by NCGAI-6 will be even less useful to those readers of the financial statements who want a clear understanding of the activities provided by a particular governmental entity.

In order to address this issue, GASB-38 requires that the summary of significant accounting policies include a description of the activities accounted for in the following columns of fund financial statements presented in the basic financial statements, assuming the columnar titles used in the fund financial statements are not sufficiently descriptive of the activities accounted for in a specific fund or fund type (GASB-38, par. 6):

- Major funds (governmental and proprietary funds)

- Internal Service Funds
- Fiduciary Fund Types (Pension [and other employee benefit] Trust Funds, Investment Trust Funds, Private-Purpose Trust Funds, and Agency Funds).

The description should not focus on the definition of the fund type used to account for the activity but, rather, should describe the nature of the activities specifically accounted for in the fund. For example, if a restricted grant is accounted for in a Special Revenues Fund, the description should not simply present the definition of a Special Revenue Fund as provided by NCGA-1 but, rather, should describe the source, purpose, and the restrictive nature of the grant. Because the Internal Service Fund column and the columns for each of the four fiduciary fund types could be made up of two or more separate funds, the description should include the major activities combined in each of these financial statement columns.

The followings are examples of fund titles and related descriptions that more fully describe the activities of a fund:

Fund Title	Disclosure (description of fund activity)
Roads and Bridges Tax Fund	This fund accounts for the City's portion of the state gasoline tax that is used solely for the maintenance of City streets and bridges.
Roads and Bridges Bond Fund	This fund accounts for proceeds from bonds issued by the City that are used exclusively for safety improvements to streets and bridges.
Toll Bridge Fund	This fund collects tolls to finance the maintenance and preservation of the Centerville Toll Bridge and approximately 10 miles of access ramps.
Lottery Fund	This fund accounts for the state's various lottery games. The net proceeds from this activity are used to finance prescription drugs for elderly citizens.
Route 30 Construction Fund	This fund accounts for state grants and bonds proceeds that are used for the improvement of Route 30.
Cemetery Fund	This fund is used to help preserve and maintain the Centerville Cemetery. Only the investment earnings from the permanent endowment can be used by the fund.

PRACTICE POINT: Based on the standards established by GASB-34, the General Fund is always considered a major fund. Because of the nature of a General Fund, its description could be limited to a general statement such as "this fund is the municipality's primary operating fund and it is used to account for all financial resources of the general government except those required to be accounted for in another fund." However, in some instances a governmental entity may decide the title (General Fund) is sufficiently descriptive and provide no description of the fund in the summary of significant accounting policies.

Required note disclosures about capital assets and long-term liabilities In order to support information included in a governmental entity's statement of net assets prepared on a government-wide basis, disclosures related to capital assets and long-term liabilities should be included in the governmental entity's notes. The disclosures should observe the following guidance (GASB-34, par. 116):

- The presentations should be based on major classes of capital assets and long-term liabilities.
- Capital assets and long-term liabilities should be segregated into governmental activities and business-type activities.
- Nondepreciable capital assets, such as land, must be presented separately from depreciable capital assets.

Capital asset disclosures Disclosures that relate to capital assets should include the following information (GASB-34, par. 117):

- Beginning and year-end balances (regardless of whether prior-year data are presented on the face of the government-wide financial statements), with accumulated depreciation separately identified
- Capital acquisitions for the period
- Sales or other dispositions for the period
- Current-period depreciation expense, supported by identifying amounts allocated to each functional expense presented in the statement of activities

If a governmental entity chooses not to capitalize collection items (as discussed earlier), the following disclosures should be made (GASB-34, par. 118):

- A description of the capital assets not capitalized
- The reason the assets are not capitalized

PRACTICE POINT: If collections are capitalized, the disclosures that apply to all other capital assets must be observed.

Exhibit 20-11 illustrates a note that incorporates the disclosure requirements for capital assets established by GASB-34.

EXHIBIT 20-11
CAPITAL ASSET DISCLOSURES

City of Centerville
For the Year Ended June 30, 20X5

NOTE X: The following summarizes activity in capital assets for the year ended June 30, 20X5.

	Primary Government			
	Beginning Balance	*Additions*	*Retirements*	*Ending Balance*
GOVERNMENTAL ACTIVITIES				
Land	$8,300,000	$74,000	$2,774,000	$5,600,000
Depreciable capital assets:				
Buildings	12,675,000	1,220,000	145,000	13,750,000
Equipment	9,100,000	760,000	710,000	9,150,000
Infrastructure	27,304,000	2,196,000		29,500,000
Totals	57,379,000	4,250,000	3,629,000	58,000,000
Less accumulated depreciation				
Buildings	2,970,000	850,000	420,000	3,400,000
Equipment	3,089,000	756,000	645,000	3,200,000
Infrastructure	4,036,000	1,364,000		5,400,000
Total accumulated depreciation	10,095,000	2,970,000(a)	1,065,000	12,000,000
Governmental Activities Capital Assets (Net)	$47,284,000	$1,280,000	$2,564,000	$46,000,000
BUSINESS-TYPE ACTIVITIES				
Land	$11,770,000	$450,000	$1,220,000	$11,000,000
Depreciable capital assets:				
Buildings	20,600,000	2,400,000	600,000	22,400,000
Equipment	2,790,000	675,000	165,000	3,300,000
Totals	35,160,000	3,525,000	1,985,000	36,700,000
Less accumulated depreciation				
Buildings	12,870,000	1,050,000	470,000	13,450,000
Equipment	1,055,000	305,000	110,000	1,250,000
Total accumulated depreciation	13,925,000	1,355,000	580,000	14,700,000
Business-Type Capital Assets (Net)	$21,235,000	$2,170,000	$1,405,000	$22,000,000

(a) Depreciation expense was charged to governmental activities as follows:

General government	$237,600
Public safety	267,300

Streets	1,009,800
Recreation and parks	326,700
Health and welfare	475,200
Internal Service Fund	653,400
Total depreciation expense	$2,970,000

Long-term liabilities disclosures The disclosures related to long-term debt should encompass both long-term debt instruments (such as bonds, loans, and capitalized leases) and other long-term liabilities (such as estimated liabilities related to compensated absences and claims and judgments). These disclosures should include the following information (GASB-34, par. 119):

- Beginning and year-end balances (regardless of whether prior-year data are presented on the face of the government-wide perspective financial statements)
- Increases and decreases (separately presented) for the period
- The part of each liability that is due within one year
- The governmental fund that has been generally used to pay other long-term liabilities (that is, items such as compensated absences and claims and judgments)

PRACTICE POINT: The *GASB Comprehensive Implementation Guide* states that if a governmental entity has changed its policy concerning which governmental fund has been used in the past to liquidate certain long-term liabilities, that change should be disclosed in the financial statements.

PRACTICE POINT: Information related to net pension obligations must be reported in a separate note and must satisfy the disclosure requirements established by GASB-27 (Accounting for Pensions by State and Local Governments).

Exhibit 20-12 illustrates a note that incorporates the disclosure requirements for long-term liabilities established by GASB-34.

Professional judgment must be used to determine the degree to which, if any, disclosures related to capital assets and long-term liabilities of discretely presented component units should be made (GASB-34, par. 120).

Disclosures about interfund balances and transfers Various interfund transfers occur within most governmental reporting entities. For example, an interfund balance may arise from the sale of goods or services, the reimbursement of expenditures or expenses, or the

EXHIBIT 20-12
LONG-TERM DEBT DISCLOSURES
City of Centerville
For the Year Ended June 30, 20X5

NOTE X: The following summarizes activity in long-term debt for the year ended June 30, 20X5.

	Beginning Balance	*Additions*	*Reductions*	*Ending Balance*	*Amount Due Within One Year*
GOVERNMENTAL ACTIVITIES					
Bonds and Notes Payable:					
General obligation debt	$4,000,000	$2,000,000	$1,000,000	$5,000,000	$2,500,000
Revenue bonds	7,900,000	2,300,000	1,200,000	9,000,000	500,000
Special assessment bonds	500,000	500,000		1,000,000	
Equipment notes	2,400,000	900,000	1,300,000	2,000,000	50,000
Total Bonds and Notes Payable	14,800,000	5,700,000	3,500,000	17,000,000	3,050,000
Other Liabilities:					
Compensated absences	3,400,000	550,000	450,000	3,500,000	650,000
Claims and judgments	1,320,000	400,000	220,000	1,500,000	100,000
Total Other Liabilities	4,720,000	950,000	670,000	5,000,000	750,000
Total Long-Term Debt—Governmental Activities	$19,520,000	$6,650,000	$4,170,000	$22,000,000	$3,800,000
BUSINESS-TYPE ACTIVITIES					
Bonds and Notes Payable:					
Airport debt	$3,900,000	$1,500,000	$1,200,000	$4,200,000	$120,000
Water and sewer systems debt	7,050,000	850,000	900,000	7,000,000	230,000
Total Bonds and Notes Payable	10,950,000	2,350,000	2,100,000	11,200,000	350,000
Other Liabilities:					
Compensated absences	956,000	74,000	30,000	1,000,000	20,000
Claims and judgments	280,000	210,000	190,000	300,000	205,000
Total Other Liabilities	1,236,000	284,000	220,000	1,300,000	230,000
Total Long-Term Debt—Business-Type Activities	$12,186,000	$2,634,000	$2,320,000	$12,500,000	$580,000

provision of operating capital. These transfers can be an important resource for governmental services performed, and for this reason an analysis of interfund balances and transfers can provide insight into the viability of a particular governmental activity. GASB-38 requires that the following information for interfund balances included in fund financial statements be disclosed in a note to the financial statements:

- Identification of the amounts due from other funds by (1) individual major funds, (2) aggregated nonmajor governmental funds, (3) aggregated nonmajor Enterprise Funds, (4) aggregated Internal Service Funds, and (5) fiduciary fund types.
- The purpose for interfund balances.
- Interfund balances that are not expected to be repaid within one year of the date of the balance sheet.

The presentation should include interfund balances that are considered material. Those that are immaterial should be aggregated and presented as a single amount. However, the total of all balances should agree with the total interfund balances presented in the statements of net assets/balance sheet for governmental funds and proprietary funds.

The focus of the aforementioned analysis is on the debtor fund rather than the creditor fund because the GASB believes that it is important for readers to be able to assess the likelihood that a particular interfund loan can be repaid. On the other hand, the explanations for interfund balances that are not expected to be paid within a year can alert readers of the financial statements to loan arrangements that are more or less long-term in nature, recurring, or unusual.

An example of the disclosures that would be made in a note related to interfund balances is presented as follows:

NOTE—Analysis of Interfund Balances

Interfund balances as of June 30, 20X5 were made up of the following:

	Due From					
	General Fund	**Internal Service Funds**	**Enterprise Funds**	**Capital Projects Funds**	**All Others**	**Total**
General Fund		$1,500,000	$3,400,000	$325,000	$750,000	$5,975,000
Route 30 Construction Fund	$1,400,000			150,000		1,550,000
Gas Tax Fund	750,000			500,000	45,000	1,295,000
Parking Authority	1,200,000				27,000	1,227,000
Municipal Airport	4,000,000					4,000,000
Nonmajor governmental funds	230,000	220,000	140,000		75,000	665,000
Nonmajor Enterprise Funds		65,000			22,000	87,000
Internal Service Funds	720,000		35,000	22,000	420,000	1,197,000
All others	120,000	45,000			105,000	270,000
Total	$8,420,000	$1,830,000	$3,575,000	$997,000	$1,444,000	$16,266,000

The General Fund has amounts due from Internal Service Funds ($1,500,000) and Enterprise Funds ($3,400,000) that arose when the funds were initially created. None of those balances are expected to be collected in the subsequent year.

All remaining balances resulted from the time lag between the dates that (1) interfund goods and services are provided or reimbursable expenditures occur, (2) transactions are recorded in the accounting system, and (3) payments between funds are made.

GASB-38 also requires that interfund activity for the year be summarized in a note to the financial statements that includes the following:

- Disclosure of amounts transferred from other funds by (1) individual major funds, (2) aggregated nonmajor governmental funds, (3) aggregated nonmajor Enterprise Funds, (4) aggregated Internal Service Funds, and (5) fiduciary fund types.

- General description of the principal reasons for the government's interfund transfers.
- The purpose and amount of significant transfers that satisfy either or both of the following criteria:
  —Do not occur on a routine basis
  —Are inconsistent with the activities of the fund making the transfer

The focus of the disclosure of interfund transfers for the period is on the fund that provides the resources to another fund. The GASB believes that this focus is justified because it will help readers to determine whether the provider fund has the ability to continue to make subsidies to the recipient fund. However, the scope of the disclosure is limited in that there is no requirement to disclose the nature of *all* interfund transfers except in general terms. For example, the principal reasons for interfund transfers could include subsidy strategies, debt service requirements, and the need to match grants received from other governmental entities. However, if during the year there has been an interfund transfer that is not routine, financial statements readers should be informed of the size and nature of the transfer. In a similar fashion, when an interfund transfer is not consistent with the nature of the provider fund, readers should also be informed of that matter. For example, if a Debt Service Fund makes a transfer to an Enterprise Fund, that interfund transfer generally must be explained.

The presentation should include transfers that are considered material. Those that are immaterial should be aggregated and presented as a single amount. However, the total of all transfers should agree with the total transfers presented in the financial statements of governmental funds and proprietary funds.

An example of the disclosures that would be made in a note related to interfund transfers for the period is presented as follows:

NOTE—Analysis of Interfund Transfers

Interfund transfers for the year ended June 30, 20X5 were made up of the following amounts:

	Transfers From					
	General Fund	Route 30 Construction Fund	Nonmajor Governmental Funds	Municipal Airport	All Others	Total
General Fund			$30,000		$220,000	$250,000
Debt Service	$1,350,000	$475,000				1,825,000
Enterprise Funds	250,000					250,000

	Transfers From					
	General Fund	Route 30 Construction Fund	Nonmajor Governmental Funds	Municipal Airport	All Others	Total
Internal Service Funds	400,000					400,000
Capital Projects Funds	1,700,000			$50,000		1,750,000
All others	350,000					350,000
Total	$4,050,000	$475,000	$30,000	$50,000	$220,000	$4,825,000

The City's routine transfers include transfers made to move (1) unrestricted revenues or balances that have been collected or accumulated in the General Fund to other funds based on budgetary authorization, and (2) revenues from a fund that by statute or budgetary authority must collect them to funds that are required by statute or budgetary authority to expend them.

During the year, the City made a transfer of $475,000 from the Route 30 Construction Fund to a Debt Service Fund. The amount transferred represented unanticipated cost savings on the project and those savings must be used to service the related debt issued to finance the construction of the project. Also, $50,000 was transfers from the Municipal Airport to a capital project to help finance certain road improvements on airport access highways and ramps.

Disclosures about donor-restricted endowments The following disclosures must be made for donor-restricted endowments (GASB-34, par. 121):

- The amount of net appreciation on investments related to donor-restricted endowments that are available for expenditure and how that appreciation is reported in net assets
- The state law that establishes how net appreciation may be spent by the governmental entity
- The investment-spending policy (that is, the rate of endowment investments that may be authorized for expenditure)

Segment information Segment disclosures must be made by governmental entities that report Enterprise Funds or that use enterprise fund accounting and reporting standards to report activities. Segment information is discussed in Chapter 7, "Proprietary Funds."

Commitments National Council of Governmental Accounting Interpretation No. 6 (NCGAI-6) (Notes to the Financial Statements Disclosure), paragraph 4, requires that construction and other significant commitments by governmental entities be disclosed in a note. The AICPA's *State and Local Governments* Guide defines "commitments" as "existing arrangements to enter into future transactions or events, such as long-term contractual obligations with suppliers for future purchases at specified prices and sometimes at specified quantities."

> **PRACTICE POINT:** Commitments should be evaluated to determine whether they give rise to encumbrances that must be reported as reserves by governmental funds.

Fund balance or net assets deficit Generally, a governmental entity's general purpose external financial statements may include an aggregation of nonmajor funds. For this reason the reporting entity may not be able, without reference to the CAFR, to identify those individual funds that have a fund balance deficit or a net assets deficit. NCGAI-6 suggests that entities disclose fund balance deficits and net assets deficits in a note to the financial statements. The note may include an explanation for the deficit and remedial action planned or required to deal with the deficit (NCGAI-6, Appendix, as amended).

Reporting Component Units

The reporting of component units in a primary government's basic external financial statements is discussed in Chapter 4, "Governmental Reporting Entity."

Required Supplementary Information Other Than MD&A

Required supplementary information (RSI) is not part of the basic financial statements, but the GASB considers RSI to be an important part of a governmental entity's financial report. All RSI (with the exception of MD&A information) must be presented immediately after the notes to the basic financial statements. Currently, the GASB has established the following RSI standards in various GASB statements:

- MD&A(see earlier discussion in this chapter)
- Budgetary comparison schedules (see the following discussion)
- Reporting infrastructure assets under the modified approach (see Chapter 10, "Capital Assets")
- Employee benefit related information (see Chapter 13, "Pension, Postemployment, and Other Employee Benefit Liabilities")

Budgetary comparison schedules GASB-34 requires that the budgetary comparison schedules for the General Fund and each major

Special Revenue Fund that has a legally adopted annual budget be presented as RSI. The schedule should include columns for the following (GASB-34, par. 130):

- The original budget
- The final appropriated budget
- Actual results (presented on the government's budgetary basis as defined in NCGA-1, paragraph 154)

PRACTICE POINT: The *GASB Comprehensive Implementation Guide* states that governments that budget on a biennial basis must report the budgetary comparison information required by GASB-34.

PRACTICE POINT: The *GASB Comprehensive Implementation Guide* states that neither (1) nonmajor Special Revenue Funds nor (2) Capital Projects and Debt Service Funds can be presented in the budgetary information, because GASB-34 specifically limits the presentation to the General Fund and major Special Revenue Funds.

The following budgetary descriptions are established by GASB-34:

Original budget—The first complete appropriated budget. The original budget may be adjusted by reserves, transfers, allocations, supplemental appropriations, and other legally authorized legislative and executive changes before the beginning of the fiscal year. The original budget should also include actual appropriation amounts automatically carried over from prior years by law.

Final budget—The original budget adjusted by all reseves, transfers, allocations, supplemental appropriations, and other legally authorized legislative and executive changes applicable to the fiscal year, whenever signed into law or otherwise legally authorized.

Appropriated budget—The expenditure authority created by the appropriation bills or ordinances which are signed into law and related estimated revenues.

The GASB encourages (but does not require) governmental entities to present an additional column that reflects the differences between the final budget and the actual amounts. An additional column may present the differences between the original budget and the final budget.

OBSERVATION: The comparative budgetary information described above can be presented as a basic financial statement

> rather than as RSI (schedule presentation). When the information is presented as a basic financial statement, the *GASB Comprehensive Implementation Guide* states that the information should be reported with fund financial statements after the statement of changes in revenues, expenditures, and changes in fund balances. The GASB's *Guide* also states that all of the budgetary information must be presented in one place. That is, a governmental entity may not present budgetary comparison information for its General Fund as a basic financial statement and present similar information related to its major Special Revenue Funds as RSI. In some instances, a governmental entity might not be required to legally adopt an annual budget for its General Fund or a Special Revenue Fund that is a major fund and therefore there is no requirement to present the budgetary comparison information. If that is the case, GASB-34 requires that the fact that budgetary comparison information is not presented for a particular fund be included in the notes to RSI. However, the AICPA's *State and Local Governments* Guide points out that "if the government chooses to present its required budgetary comparison information in the basic financial statements, that disclosure should be made in the notes to the financial statements."

The comparative budgetary information may be presented "using the same format, terminology, and classifications as the budget document, or using the format, terminology, and classifications in a statement of revenues, expenditures, and changes in fund balances." In either case, there must be a reconciliation (presented in a separate schedule or in notes to RSI) between the budgetary information to GAAP information (as required by NCGAI-10 and discussed later in this chapter). Any excess of expenditures over appropriations in an individual fund must be disclosed in a note to the RSI as required by NCGAI-6, paragraph 4, and discussed later in this chapter. If the governmental entity presents the comparative budgetary information as a basic financial statement, the note related to the excess of expenditures over appropriations must be reported as a note to the financial statements rather than as a note to RSI (GASB-34, par. 131).

The *GASB Comprehensive Implementation Guide* provides the following guidance for original and final budgets:

- Some governmental entities initially use an interim budget (for example, three months) that provides temporary spending authority. The original budget (as described above) must cover the entire fiscal period.
- GASB-34, paragraph 130a, specifically states that "the original budget includes actual appropriation amounts automatically

carried over from prior years by law." If prior-year encumbrances are rolled forward by law, the current (original) budget includes those items. The amount of the encumbrances will be known or a reasonable estimate of them can be made in time to prepare the financial information.

- GASB-34, paragraph 130b, specifically states that amendments (such as transfers of appropriations between line items) must be included in the final budget, regardless of when they are "signed into law or otherwise legally authorized."

> **PRACTICE POINT:** In some instances, a governmental entity is, for budgetary purposes, required to account for an activity in a particular fund type but based on the definitions established by GASB-34 must report that activity in another fund type. The *GASB Comprehensive Implementation Guide* states that the reporting and disclosure requirements established by GASB-34 apply to the fund type that is actually used to report the activity and not to the fund type required for internal budgetary purposes.

Disclosure of budgetary policies The appendix to NCGAI-6 recommends that the financial statements include a description of general budgetary policies. To comply with this recommendation, some governmental entities disclose their budgetary calendar and the legal level of budgetary control. According to GASB-38 general budget policies are not to be included as part of the appendix to NCGAI-6.

> **OBSERVATION:** The GASB believes that sufficient presentation of budgetary information is achieved by the requirements established previously by NCGA pronouncements and GASB-34. These presentation requirements include (1) budgetary comparison schedules, (2) reconciliation of budgetary information to GAAP information, (3) disclosure of the budgetary basis of accounting, and (4) disclosure of violations of legal provisions.

Budgetary comparison schedules for other funds Some governmental entities may include in the financial section of their CAFR budgetary comparisons for debt service, capital projects, nonmajor special revenue funds, and other funds that have legally adopted budgets. However, the *GASB Comprehensive Implementation Guide* points out that GASB-34 establishes standards for the basic financial statements, MD&A, and certain RSI, but that its scope does not cover other components of the CAFR. If a governmental entity decides to present budgetary comparison schedules for debt service, capital projects, nonmajor special revenues funds, and other funds, the guidance established by GASB-34 (pars. 130–131) may but does not have to be followed.

Excess of expenditures over appropriations GASB-34 requires that budgetary comparison schedules be presented only for the General Fund and each major Special Revenue Fund that has a legally adopted annual budget. Additionally, paragraph 131 of GASB-34 establishes disclosure requirements for budgetary comparison schedules. One of the requirements states that any excess of expenditures over appropriations in an individual fund must be disclosed. The question has arisen regarding whether the required disclosure applies to only those funds that are presented in the budgetary comparison schedule. GASB-37 clarifies the standards established by GASB-34 by limiting the disclosures related to budgetary comparison schedules to the funds that are part of the required supplementary information. However, the *GASB Comprehensive Implementation Guide* points out that paragraph 4g of NCGAI-6 requires governmental entity to disclose material violations of finance-related legal and contractual provisions. GASB-38 requires this requirement to be expanded to include actions taken by the governmental entity to remedy the violations.

> **PRACTICE POINT:** Any excess of expenditures over appropriations must be disclosed in the notes to the RSI; however, if the amount is considered a "material violation of finance-related legal provisions," the violations must also be disclosed in a note to the basic financial statements.

Reconciling budget and GAAP information Budgetary comparison schedules should be accompanied by information that reconciles GAAP information and budgetary information. These differences may arise because of (1) entity differences, (2) perspective differences, (3) basis differences, (4) timing differences, or (5) other differences (NCGAI-10, par. 15; NCGAI-6, par. 5; and GASB-34, par. 131).

Entity differences The reporting entity may include component units whose activities are not part of the appropriated budget. For example, a component unit may be subject to a legal nonappropriated budget and, thus, be excluded from the appropriated budget. But based on the criteria established in GASB-14 (The Financial Reporting Entity), the component may be part of the overall reporting entity (NCGAI-10, pars. 23–24).

Perspective differences The structure of the budget itself determines its perspective. The financial information contained in the budget may be constructed to reflect various points of view including the governmental unit's organizational structure, fund structure, or program structure. For example, budgetary information may be prepared on a program basis whereby all expenditures associated with a particular objective may be grouped irrespective of which organizational unit or fund makes the expenditure (NCGAI-10, pars. 12–14).

> **OBSERVATION:** When there is a difference between the perspective for budgeting purposes and for financial reporting purposes, it is often difficult to reconcile the two sets of financial information. For example, if the budgetary system uses a program basis and the financial reporting system uses the fund basis, it is unlikely that a meaningful reconciliation can be prepared. In this case, the reconciliation between the GAAP-basis financial statements and the budgeted financial statements would be limited to entity, basis, and timing differences.

In most instances perspective differences are minor and can easily be isolated in order to prepare the necessary reconciliation between the budgetary and GAAP information. However, GASB-41 points out that some governmental entities have "budgetary structures that prevent them from associating the estimated revenues and appropriations from their legally adopted budget to the major revenue sources and functional expenditures that they report in their General Fund and major Special Revenue Funds" and therefore are not able to prepare budgetary comparison schedules (or statements) required by GASB-34. For example, assume that a governmental entity's budgetary focus is referred to as the "Comprehensive Statutory Budget" and its budget is as follows:

	(in thousands of dollars) *Budgeted per Statutory Ordinance*
REVENUES:	
Property taxes	$1,000,000
Fees and other nontax revenues	770,000
Grants and receipts from other governments	730,000
Other taxes	120,000
Total Revenues	2,620,000
EXPENDITURES:	
General government	500,000
Public safety	400,000
Streets	330,000
Health and welfare	210,000
Principal repayments	400,000
Interest	150,000
Capital outlays	620,000
Total Expenditures	2,610,000
Estimated Surplus (Deficit)	$ 10,000

However, many of the revenues and expenditures are not reported in the General Fund for financial reporting purposes but rather are distributed as follows:

(in thousands of dollars)

	Budgeted per Statutory Ordinance	*General Fund*	*Special Revenue Fund*	*Debt Service Fund*	*Capital Projects Fund*
REVENUES:					
Property taxes	$1,000,000	$700,000	$300,000		
Fees and other nontax revenues	770,000	600,000	170,000		
Grants and receipts from other governments	730,000	80,000			$650,000
Other taxes	120,000	30,000	90,000		
Total Revenues	2,620,000				
EXPENDITURES:					
General government	500,000	450,000	50,000		
Public safety	400,000	250,000	150,000		
Streets	330,000	330,000			
Health and welfare	210,000	30,000	180,000		
Principal repayments	400,000			$400,000	
Interest	150,000	1,000		145,000	4,000
Capital outlays	620,000				620,000
Total Expenditures	2,610,000				
Estimated Surplus (Deficit)	$10,000				

If a budgetary comparison schedule is prepared that compares the Comprehensive Statutory Budget to a statement of revenues, expenditures, and change in fund balance, a number of reconciling items are needed to explain the differences between budgetary inflows and outflows on an actual basis and those amounts reported in the General Fund on a GAAP basis.

The standards established by GASB-41 require (as was required previously) a comparative schedule for the General Fund and for each major Special Revenue Fund that has a legally adopted annual budget but allows one exception: A governmental entity that has perspective differences of the nature described above may prepare a budgetary comparison schedule as RSI based on the fund organization, or program structure that the entity uses as a basis for the legally adopted budget. The foundation for this exception is that the focus of the comparison schedule will be based on activities that are reported in the entity's General Fund or in a Special Revenue Fund. That is, when an activity (or collection of activities) is not presented as part of the General Fund or a Special Revenue Fund, the budgetary unit that includes various activities cannot be the focus for presenting budgetary comparison schedules.

> **PRACTICE POINT:** The exception perspective that is allowed for comparative budgetary information can only be in the form of budgetary comparison schedules presented as RSI and not as financial statements.

Under the alternative comparison schedule focus approach, most of the items on the reconciliation would be similar to other reconciliations, but the following two items (based on the example presented above) would be used to remove the budgetary amounts for the various other funds (it is assumed in this example that the Special Revenue Fund is not a major fund and therefore does not require a separate budgetary comparison schedule) from the actual amounts reported on the budgetary comparison schedule. These two reconciling items could be described as follows:

Revenues for a Special Revenue Fund ($560,000) and a Capital Projects Fund ($650,000) are reclassified to their respective funds.	(1,210,000)
Expenditures for a Special Revenue Fund ($380,000), Debt Service Fund ($545,000), and a Capital Projects Fund ($624,000) are reclassified to their respective funds.	(1,549,000)

Basis differences The budgeting basis may differ from the accounting basis. For example, the governmental unit may be required by law to use the cash basis for budgeting purposes, but may be required by financial reporting purposes to use the modified accrual basis (GAAP basis) (NCGAI-10, pars. 16–17).

Timing differences There may be differences between the budgetary amounts and the GAAP basis amounts due to the different treatment of items such as continuing appropriations and biennial budgeting. For example, a governmental unit may treat encumbrances that are outstanding at the end of the year as expenditures of the current period for budgetary purposes, but, for reporting purposes, they cannot be classified as expenditures of the current period (NCGAI-10, par. 18).

Other differences NCGAI-10 notes that differences not classified in the previous four categories also should be included in the reconciliation between the entity's budgetary practices and GAAP practices.

Additional reporting The prior discussion has been concerned exclusively with budgetary reporting on a comparative basis with actual results for funds that adopt an annual appropriated budget. NCGA-1 recognizes that governmental units may be subject to control through the implementation of other types of budgets. For example, NCGAI-10 defines a "nonappropriated budget" as follows (NCGAI-10, par. 11):

> A financial plan for an organization, program, activity, or function approved in a manner authorized by constitution, charter, statute, or ordinance but not subject to appropriation and therefore outside the boundaries of the definition of "appropriated budget."

The NCGA takes the position that "more comprehensive budget presentations are generally to be preferred over the minimum standards." Thus, the existence of the minimum presentation requirements should not inhibit a reporting entity from presenting additional budgetary information. Even if additional budgetary disclosures are not made, there should be a disclosure in notes to the financial statements describing budgetary controls, including appropriated budgets and other budget or financial control plans used by the reporting entity (NCGAI-10, par. 13).

Some governmental entities establish various levels of budgetary control through multiple appropriation bills and ordinances. When budgetary comparison schedules required by GASB-34 are presented, the budgetary control classification scheme can be aggregated based on functional or program costs and "sources" of revenue (such as taxes, licenses and permits, intergovernmental revenues, charges for services, fines and forfeits, and miscellaneous items). However, when reporting individual funds on a budgetary basis at the CAFR level, the presentation generally requires a level of account detail that is consistent with actual budgetary control within the entity. NCGAI-10 states that in an "extreme" circumstance, the reporting entity may need to prepare a separate report in order to present revenues and expenditures in enough detail that is consistent with the budgetary control. When the entity must present a separate report, the notes to the RSI should refer to the separate report (NCGAI-10, par. 14, and GASB-34, pars. 6 and 131).

> **PRACTICE POINT:** The level of detail included in the separate report cannot be greater than that used to present the budgetary information included in the RSI.

Exhibit 20-13 illustrates a budget-to-actual comparison schedule in a format allowed by GASB-34.

Exhibit 20-14 illustrates a budget-to-GAAP reconciliation required by GASB-34.

EXHIBIT 20-13
BUDGET-TO-ACTUAL COMPARISON SCHEDULE

General Fund
City of Centerville
For the Year Ended June 30, 20X5

	Budgeted Amounts		Actual Amounts (Budgetary Basis See Note X)	Variance with Final Budget Positive (Negative)
	Original	*Final*		
Budgetary Fund Balance, June 30, 20X4	$8,100,000	$7,920,000	$7,920,000	
Resources (Inflows):				
Property taxes	10,200,000	10,098,000	$10,125,000	$27,000
Wages taxes	2,300,000	2,277,000	2,410,000	133,000
Other taxes	940,000	930,600	922,000	(8,600)
Fees and other nontax revenues	2,720,000	2,692,800	2,700,000	7,200
Grants and receipts from other governments	900,000	891,000	907,000	16,000
Investment income	300,000	297,000	347,000	50,000
Other	1,420,000	1,405,800	1,365,000	(40,800)
Transfers in	50,000	49,500	45,000	(4,500)
Special items	2,000,000	1,980,000	1,890,000	(90,000)
Amounts Available for Appropriation	28,930,000	28,541,700	28,631,000	89,300
Charges to Appropriations (Outflows):				
General government	1,590,000	1,574,100	1,610,000	(35,900)
Public safety	7,000,000	6,930,000	6,950,000	(20,000)
Streets	2,200,000	2,178,000	2,175,000	3,000
Recreation and parks	640,000	633,600	647,000	(13,400)
Health and welfare	2,900,000	2,871,000	2,842,000	29,000
Education (payment to school district)	6,400,000	6,336,000	6,500,000	(164,000)
Transfers out	600,000	594,000	547,000	47,000
Total Charges to Appropriations	21,330,000	21,116,700	21,271,000	(154,300)
Budgetary Fund Balance, June 30, 20X5	$7,600,000	$7,425,000	$7,360,000	$65,000

EXHIBIT 20-14
BUDGET TO GAAP RECONCILIATION

General Fund
City of Centerville
For the Year Ended June 30, 20X5

NOTE X: Explanation of differences between budget and GAAP.

	General Fund
SOURCES/INFLOWS OF RESOURCES	
Actual amounts (budgetary basis) available for appropriation from the Budget to Actual Comparison Schedule	$28,631,000
Differences—budget to GAAP:	
The fund balance at the beginning of the year is a budgetary resource but is not a current year revenue for financial reporting purposes	(7,920,000)
Transfers from other funds are inflows of budgetary resources but are not revenues for financial reporting purposes	(45,000)
The proceeds from the sale of real estate are budgetary resources but are considered a special item, rather than revenue, for financial reporting purposes	(1,890,000)
Total revenues as reported on the Statement of Revenues, Expenditures, and Changes in Fund Balance—Governmental Funds	$18,776,000
USES/OUTFLOWS OF RESOURCES	
Actual amounts (budgetary basis) for total charges to appropriations from the Budget to Actual Comparison Schedule	$21,271,000
Difference—budget to GAAP:	
Transfers to other funds are outflows of budgetary resources but are not expenditures for financial reporting purposes	($547,000)
Total expenditures as reported on the Statement of Revenues, Expenditures, and Changes in Fund Balances—Governmental Funds	$20,724,000

SUPPLEMENTARY INFORMATION

Combining Financial Statements

Although it is not required in the minimum presentation in order to be in accordance with GAAP, a CAFR should include combining statements for the following situations:

- Combining financial statements by fund type for the primary government when there is more than one nonmajor fund
- Combining financial statements for discretely presented component units when the reporting entity has more than one nonmajor component unit (fund financial statements for individual component units are required if the financial information is not available to readers in separately issued reports)

More than one nonmajor fund The focus of the fund statements included in the general purpose external financial statements is on the major funds. As noted earlier, each major fund is presented in the fund statements in a separate column. Nonmajor funds are aggregated and presented in a single column. There is no requirement to present combining statements for nonmajor funds in the basic external financial statements but the information may be presented as supplementary information to the financial statements. If the nonmajor funds are not presented as supplementary information they must be presented as part of the CAFR in combining financial statements by fund type for the primary government.

The combining statements could have a section for all Special Revenue Funds, Capital Projects Funds, and so on. For instance, a governmental unit may have five nonmajor Special Revenue Funds and three nonmajor Capital Projects Funds. The combining financial statements would include a separate column for each of the eight nonmajor funds and a total column that can be traced into the fund financial statements that present major funds and aggregated nonmajor funds. In addition, the overall format and terminology used in the fund financial statements and the combining financial statements should be similar to provide a basis for easy cross-reference between the two sets of information.

The concept of a major fund does not apply to an Internal Service Fund. For this reason, all Internal Service Funds are presented in combining financial statements as part of the CAFR rather than as part of the basic external financial statements in a manner similar to the presentation described in the previous paragraph.

PRACTICE POINT: If a governmental entity has only a single Internal Service Fund, it is presented in the fund financial statements as a separate column and there would be no need to present its financial information in a combining financial statement.

More than one nonmajor discretely presented component unit GASB-34 was written in a manner that satisfies the financial reporting entity standards originally established by GASB-14 (The Financial Reporting Entity) with respect to component units. Relevant guidance established by GASB-14 is as follows:

> The financial statements of the reporting entity should allow users to distinguish between the primary government and its component units by communicating information about the component units and their relationships with the primary government rather than creating the perception that the primary government and all of its component units are one legal entity [GASB-14, par. 42].

In addition, paragraph 51 of GASB-14 requires that information related to each major component unit be presented in the reporting entity's basic financial statements. To satisfy this standard, any one of the following approaches can be used:

- Present each major component unit in a separate column in the government-wide financial statements
- Present combining statements (with a separate column for each major unit and a single column for the aggregated nonmajor units)
- Present condensed financial statements in a note to the financial statements (with a separate column for each major unit and a single column for the aggregated nonmajor units)

PRACTICE POINT: The requirement for major component unit information does not apply to component units that are fiduciary in nature.

Each of these three presentation methods creates information that is part of the basic external financial statements; however, if there is more than one nonmajor component unit, the information concerning these nonmajor units must be presented in combining financial statements.

Individual Fund Financial Statements

The CAFR should include individual fund statements for the following situations:

- When the primary government has a single nonmajor fund of a given fund type

- When it is necessary to present comparative budgetary information about the previous year and the current year, if it is not presented in RSI

Content of Combining Statements and Individual Fund Statements

GASB-34 requires that a primary government present its major governmental and proprietary funds on the face of the fund financial statements. In addition, the following combining and individual fund statements must be included in the financial section of the CAFR (NCGA-1, par. 143; GASB-9, par. 67; GASB-34, par. 70):

- Nonmajor governmental funds
  - —Combining balance sheets
  - —Combining statements of revenues, expenditures, and changes in fund balances
  - —Individual fund balance sheets and statements of revenues, expenditures, and changes in fund balances and schedules necessary to demonstrate compliance with finance-related legal and contractual provision of governmental funds
- Internal Service Funds and Nonmajor Enterprise Funds
  - —Combining statements of net assets/balance sheets
  - —Combining statements of revenues, expenses, and changes in fund net assets/equity
  - —Combining statements of cash flows
  - —Individual statements of revenues, expenses, and changes in fund net assets/equity and individual statements of cash flows and schedules necessary to demonstrate compliance with finance-related legal and contractual provisions
- Fiduciary Funds
  - —A combining statement of fiduciary net assets
  - —A combining statement of changes in fiduciary net assets

Other Supplementary Schedules

The CAFR should include other schedules for the following situations:

- When it is necessary to demonstrate compliance with finance-related legal and contractual provisions

- When it is useful to bring together information that is spread throughout the financial statements and present the information in more detail
- When it is useful to present more detail for a line item that is presented in a financial statement

PRACTICE POINT: Narrative descriptions that facilitate the understanding of information in combining financial statements, individual fund and component unit financial statements, and schedules may be included directly on divider pages, the financial statements or schedules, or in an accompanying section appropriately labeled.

STATISTICAL SECTION

Information included in the statistical tables section is not part of the governmental unit's basic financial statements even though the material is part of the CAFR. Statistical tables may include nonaccounting information and often cover more than two fiscal years. In general, the purpose of presenting statistical tables is to give the user a historical perspective that will enhance the analysis of the governmental unit's financial condition (NCGA-1, pars. 160 and 161).

PRACTICE POINT: GASB-44 (Economic Condition Reporting—The Statistical Section) establishes new reporting requirements for the statistical section of governments' annual reports when a CAFR is presented. The provisions of GASB-44 are effective for periods beginning after June 15, 2005. Governments that prepare a statistical section for the first time in response to GASB-44, or that previously prepared a statistical section but did not present certain information, are encouraged but not required to report all required years of information retroactively. Governments are also encouraged but not required to implement the government-wide information required by GASB-44 retroactively to the year they implemented GASB-34.

GASB-44 defines the objectives of reporting statistical section information as follows:

> To provide financial statement users with additional historical perspective, context, and detail to assist in using the information in the financial statements, notes to financial statements, and required supplementary information to understand and assess a government's economic condition.

GASB-44 separates the statistical information into five categories:

1. *Financial trends information* is intended to assist users in understanding and assessing how a government's financial position has changed over time. Examples for general purpose governments are
   - Net assets by component and changes in net assets by component for the last 10 fiscal years
   - Fund balances for governmental funds and changes in fund balances for governmental funds for the last 10 fiscal years
2. *Revenue capacity information* is intended to assist users in understanding and assessing the factors that affect a government's ability to generate its own revenues. Examples for general purpose governments are
   - Assessed and actual values of taxable property for the last 10 fiscal years
   - Direct and overlapping property tax rates for the last 10 fiscal years
   - Principal property taxpayers for the current year and nine years ago
   - Property tax levies and collections for the last 10 fiscal years
3. *Debt capacity information* is intended to assist users in understanding and assessing a government's debt burden and its ability to issue additional debt. Examples for general purpose governments are
   - Ratios of outstanding debt by type for the last 10 fiscal years
   - Ratios of general bonded debt outstanding for the last 10 fiscal years
   - Direct and overlapping governmental activities debt as of current year-end
   - Legal debt margin for the last 10 fiscal years
   - Pledged revenue coverage for the last 10 fiscal years
4. *Demographic and economic information* is intended to assist users in understanding the socioeconomic environment that a government operates within, and it provides information that facilitates comparisons betweens governments over time. Examples for general purpose governments are
   - Demographic and economic statistics for the last 10 calendar years
   - Principal employers for the current year and nine years ago

5. *Operating information* is intended to provide contextual information about a government's operations and resources in order for users to understand and assess its economic condition. Examples for general purpose governments are
   - Full-time equivalent employees by function/program for the last 10 fiscal years
   - Operating indicators by function/program for the last 10 fiscal years
   - Capital asset statistics by function/program for the last 10 fiscal years

   PRACTICE POINT: Appendix C to GASB-44 provides comprehensive illustrated examples of statistical schedules for both general purpose governments and special purpose governments.

Professional judgment should be used to determine whether statistical tables other than the ones listed should be presented in the CAFR.

The statistical tables should include information for blended component units by combining the primary governmental statistics and the component units' statistics. Professional judgment should be used to determine whether statistical data related to discretely presented component units should be presented.

BASIC FINANCIAL STATEMENTS REQUIRED FOR SPECIAL-PURPOSE GOVERNMENTS

The standards established by GASB-34 are written in the context of general purpose governmental entities, such as state and local governments. However, these standards also apply, with some modification, to special-purpose governments that are "legally separate entities and may be component units or other stand-alone governments." GASB-14 provides the following definitions of these entities (GASB-34, par. 134):

> Component units are legally separate organizations for which elected officials of the primary government are financially accountable. In addition, a component unit can be another organization for which the nature and significance of its relationship with a primary government are such that exclusion would cause the reporting entity's financial statements to be misleading or incomplete.
>
> An other stand-alone government is a legally separate governmental organization that (a) does not have a separately

elected governing body and (b) does not meet the definition of a component unit. Other stand-alone governments include some special-purpose governments, joint ventures, jointly governed organizations, and pools.

PRACTICE POINT: GASB-34 does not provide a definition of special-purpose governments; however the *GASB Comprehensive Implementation Guide* notes that such governments "generally provide a limited (or sometimes a single) set of services or programs, for example, fire protection, library services, mosquito abatement, and drainage." It is important to distinguish between a general government and a special-purpose government because under certain circumstances identified in GASB-34 not all of the reporting standards established by GASB-34 must be observed by special-purpose governments.

See Chapter 21, "Public Colleges and Universities"; Chapter 22, "Pension and Other Postemployment Benefit Plans"; and Chapter 23, "Public Entity Risk Pools," for further discussion and examples of financial statements for special-purpose governments.

APPENDIX 20A CONVERTING FROM FUND FINANCIAL STATEMENTS TO GOVERNMENT-WIDE STATEMENTS UNDER GASB-34

Perhaps the most complex task facing those who prepare governmental financial statements based on the standards established by GASB-34 is the development of system procedures that facilitate the presentation of the two levels of financial statements. Most governmental entities solve this problem by maintaining accounting systems necessary to prepare the fund financial statements, and then use a worksheet approach to convert the fund financial statements' basis of accounting and measurement focus as needed in order to prepare the government-wide financial statements.

The purpose of this appendix is to demonstrate how fund financial statement information can be converted to government-wide financial statement information through the use of worksheet conversion entries. The following conversion issues are addressed:

- Issuance of debt
- Debt service transactions
- Capital expenditures
- Lease agreements
- Accrual of certain operating expenses
- Nonexchange transactions
- Previous years' transactions

NOTE: The emphasis of this appendix is governmental funds (General Fund, Special Revenue Funds, Capital Projects Funds, Debt Service Funds, and Permanent Funds) rather than proprietary funds because the presentation basis for the proprietary fund category is already accrual accounting and economic resources focus. Fiduciary funds are not discussed, because they are presented in the fund financial statements but are not incorporated into the government-wide financial statements.

ISSUANCE OF DEBT

Generally liabilities that do not consume the current financial resources of a governmental fund are not reported at the fund financial statement level. However, the proceeds from the issuance of debt are recorded as an other financing source in a governmental fund. On the other hand, in the government-wide financial statements, both short-term and long-term liabilities of a governmental entity are presented. Long-term liabilities may include such debts as notes, mortgages, bonds, and obligations related to capitalized lease agreements (discussed later).

In order to illustrate the worksheet entries necessary to convert the issuance of debt from the fund-financial statements to the government-wide financial statements, assume that on October 1, 20X0, a governmental entity issued bonds with a maturity value of $10,000,000 for $9,328,956. The bonds carry a stated interest rate of 7% and were sold at an effective interest rate of 8%. Interest is paid annually. That transaction is recorded as follows in a governmental fund:

Cash	9,328,956	
Discount on Long-Term Debt Issued (Other Uses of Financial Resources)	671,044	
Long-Term Debt Issued (Other Sources of Financial Resources)		10,000,000

In the governmental fund financial statements the issuance of the debt is presented on the statement of revenues, expenditures, and changes in fund balances as an other financing source, but the amount is not presented in the balance sheet at the fund statement level. In order to convert the transaction from a fund perspective to a government-wide perspective, the following worksheet entry is made:

Long-Term Debt Issued (Other Sources of Financial Resources)	10,000,000	
Discount on Long-Term Debt Issued (Other Uses of Financial Resources)		671,044
Long-Term Liabilities		9,328,956

PRACTICE POINT: The above entry records the net proceeds as a long-term liability. It would also be acceptable to create a separate discount account (contra liability account) and record the maturity value of the debt in a separate account.

The effect of the worksheet entry is to report the transaction as a long-term general obligation in the government-wide financial statements (governmental activities column).

DEBT SERVICE TRANSACTIONS

NCGA-1 points out that most expenditures are measurable and should be recorded when the related governmental fund liability is incurred. An exception to this generalization is the treatment of interest and principal payments for general long-term indebtedness. Interest and principal on governmental fund long-term debt are not recorded as expenditures as they accrue but, rather, when they become due and payable. However, for the government-wide financial statements, interest expense is subject to accrual.

For example, the following bond discount amortization schedule would be prepared for the $10,000,000 bonds that were issued at a discount in the previous section:

Date	*Cash*	*Interest*	*Amortization*	*Book Value*
10/1/X1				9,328,956
10/1/X2	700,000	746,316	−46,316	9,375,272
10/1/X3	700,000	750,022	−50,022	9,425,294
10/1/X4	700,000	754,024	−54,024	9,479,318
10/1/X5	700,000	758,345	−58,345	9,537,663
10/1/X6	700,000	763,013	−63,013	9,600,676
10/1/X7	700,000	768,054	−68,054	9,668,730
10/1/X8	700,000	773,498	−73,498	9,742,229
10/1/X9	700,000	779,378	−79,378	9,821,607
10/1/Y0	700,000	785,729	−85,729	9,907,336
10/1/Y1	700,000	792,664R	−92,664	10,000,000

R = rounded

Based on the above amortization schedule, no interest is recorded during the fiscal year ended June 30, 20X2. However, in order to convert the transaction to an accrual basis the following worksheet entry is made:

Interest Expense ($746,316 × 9/12)	559,737	
Interest Payable ($700,000 × 9/12)		525,000
Long-Term Liabilities		34,737

The credit to the account "Long-Term Liabilities" represents the amortization of the discount for the partial year.

PRACTICE POINT: If a separate discount is created, the credit is to the discount account.

If long-term debt has been repaid during the year, the principal repayment is recorded as an expenditure in the fund financial statements, but a worksheet entry is necessary to convert the principal payment from an expenditure to a reduction to the governmental entity's general debt.

CAPITAL EXPENDITURES

When capital assets are acquired by a governmental funds, payments related to acquisitions are recorded as expenditures at the fund statement level. In order to convert the fund financial statements from a fund perspective to a government-wide perspective, the expenditure must be capitalized and any related depreciation expense recorded.

To illustrate the conversion of capital expenditures the government-wide perspective, assume that on November 1, 20X1, a purchase order for $900,000 for various vehicles for the following governmental programs was signed to be paid from the General Fund (the vehicles have estimated useful lives of three years and no residual values):

General government	$100,000
Police activities	300,000
Streets department	400,000
Parks department	100,000
Total payments	$900,000

Further assume that the vehicles ordered on November 1 were received on December 1, and that the vendor was paid on December 15. These transactions are recorded in the appropriate governmental fund in the following manner:

11/1/X1	Encumbrances	900,000	
	Reserve for Encumbrances		900,000
12/1/X1	Reserve for Encumbrances	900,000	
	Encumbrances		900,000
	Expenditures—General Government	100,000	
	Expenditures—Public Safety	300,000	

	Expenditures—Streets	400,000	
	Expenditures—Recreation and Parks	100,000	
	Accounts Payable		900,000
12/15/X1	Accounts Payable	900,000	
	Cash		900,000

In order to report the capital assets (vehicles) illustrated in this example as required by GASB-34, in the government-wide financial statements, the following worksheet entry is made to the amounts reported in the fund financial statements:

6/30/X2	Vehicles—Capital Asset	900,000	
	Expenditures—General Government		100,000
	Expenditures—Public Safety		300,000
	Expenditures—Streets		400,000
	Expenditures—Recreation and Parks		100,000

Depreciation expense should be reported as a direct expense of the specific functional categories if the related capital asset can be identified with the functional category. For example, depreciation expense related to police vehicles should be reported (along with other direct expenses) as part of the appropriate functional expense category (for example, public safety). Depreciation on capital assets that are shared by two or more functions should be reported as a direct expense based on a pro rata allocation to the appropriate functional expense categories. Depreciation expense related to capital assets that are not identified with a particular functional category does not have to be reported as a direct expense to specific functions but, rather, may be presented as a separate line item in the statement of activities or included in the general governmental functional category.

In the current example, the depreciation expense on the various vehicles to be reported in the government-wide financial statements is directly related to specific governmental programs. In order to reflect the relevant costs of these programs, the following worksheet entry is made:

Expenses—General Government (1/9)	19,445	
Expenses—Public Safety (3/9)	58,333	
Expenses—Streets (4/9)	77,778	
Expenses—Recreation and Parks (1/9)	19,444	
Accumulated Depreciation— Vehicles ($900,000 × 1/3 × 7/12)		175,000

LEASE AGREEMENTS

Rather than purchase a capital asset directly from a vendor, a governmental entity might lease the item. If the agreement is considered a capitalized lease as defined in NCGA-5 (Accounting and Financial Reporting Principles for Lease Agreements of State and Local Governments), the transaction is accounted for in a governmental fund as both a resource from the issuance of debt and a capital expenditure (both of which are discussed earlier in this Appendix). Thus, in order to convert the fund financial statements to the government-wide statements, the expenditure must be capitalized, any related depreciation expense must be recorded, and the debt must be recognized along with the accrual of any related interest expense.

To illustrate the capitalization of a lease, assume a governmental entity, a city, leases office equipment that has an economic life of five years and no residual value. Lease payments of $100,000 to be paid from a government fund are to be made in five annual installments beginning on August 1, 20X1. The city's incremental borrowing rate is 8%. The capitalized value of the lease is computed as follows:

$100,000 × ($n = 4; i = 8\%$) 3.31213	=	$331,213
First payment on first day of contract	=	100,000
Total present value		$431,213

The following amortization schedule applies to the lease.

Date	*Cash*	*Interest*	*Amortization*	*Book Value*
8/1/X1				431,213
8/1/X1	100,000			331,213
8/1/X2	100,000	26,497	73,503	257,710
8/1/X3	100,000	20,617	79,383	178,327
8/1/X4	100,000	14,266	85,734	92,593
8/1/X5	100,000	7,407	92,593	-0-

The equipment is part of the general government overhead costs.

The execution of the lease is recorded on August 1, 20X1, in the governmental fund as follows:

Capital Expenditures—General Government	431,213	
Other Financing Sources—Capitalized Leases		431,213

In the governmental fund financial statements the issuance of the debt component of the lease is presented on the statement of revenues, expenditures, and changes in fund balances as an other financing source, but the amount is not presented in the balance sheet as a liability at the fund statement level. Likewise, the capital expenditure component of the lease is presented as an expenditure.

In order to convert the transaction from a fund financial statement perspective to the government-wide perspective, the following worksheet entries are prepared:

Account	Debit	Credit
Other Financing Sources—Capitalized Leases	431,213	
Capital Expenditures—General Government		431,213
Equipment—Capital Assets	431,213	
Lease Obligation Payable—due within one year		73,503
Lease Obligation Payable—due beyond one year		357,710
Lease Obligation Payable	100,000	
Debt Service Expenditures—General Government		100,000
Expenses—General Government (60%)	47,434	
Expenses—Public Safety (20%)	15,812	
Expenses—Streets (10%)	7,906	
Expenses—Recreation and Parks (5%)	3,953	
Expenses—Health and Welfare (5%)	3,953	
Accumulated Depreciation—Capitalized Leases (431,213 × 1/5 × 11/12)		79,058
Interest Expenses	24,290	
Interest Payable (26,497 × 11/12)		24,290

The entries above reflect the allocation (which is assumed) for depreciation expenses to various governmental programs (general, public safety, streets, etc.).

ACCRUAL OF CERTAIN OPERATING EXPENSES

The basic guidance for determining when a governmental fund should accrue an expenditure/liability is found in NCGA-1, paragraph 70, which states that "most expenditures and transfers out are measurable and should be recorded when the related liability is incurred." GASBI-6 (Recognition and Measurement of Certain Liabilities and Expenditures in Governmental Fund Financial Statements) expands on this general guidance by noting the following:

> Governmental fund liabilities and expenditures that should be accrued include liabilities that, once incurred, normally are paid in a timely manner and in full from current financial resources—for example, salaries, professional services, supplies, utilities, and travel. These transactions give rise to fund liabilities that are considered mature liabilities because they are "normally due and payable in full when incurred."

To illustrate this approach, assume that a governmental entity's legal department evaluates a $5,000,000 claim that has been raised by an individual based on alleged property damages caused by an emergency vehicle. It is probable that the claim will have to be paid, and the estimate of the loss is about $300,000. It is also believed that the claim will probably be settled in approximately 24 months. This event represents a loss contingency of $300,000, but because the loss will not use current expendable financial resources it is not accrued in the governmental fund. However, the long-term liability amount ($300,000) is reported in the governmental activities column of the government-wide financial statements.

NONEXCHANGE TRANSACTIONS

GASB-33 (Accounting and Financial Reporting for Nonexchange Transactions) provides accounting and reporting standards for the following four categories of nonexchange transactions:

1. Derived tax revenues
2. Imposed nonexchange revenues
3. Government-mandated nonexchange transactions
4. Voluntary nonexchange transactions

The standards established by GASB-33 retained the current fundamental criteria for revenue recognition that applies to the modified accrual basis of accounting, namely, that revenue is to be recorded when it is both available and measurable. NCGA-1 defines available as "collectible within the current period or soon enough thereafter to be used to pay liabilities of the current period." Revenue is measurable when it is subject to reasonable estimation.

In preparing government-wide financial statements the same standards established by GASB-33 (Accounting and Financial Reporting for Nonexchange Transactions) should be used to determine when revenue related to nonexchange transactions should be recognized except that the available criterion does not have to be satisfied. Thus nonexchange transactions need to be analyzed at the end of the accounting period to identify those that would require a worksheet adjustment to convert from the modified accrual to the accrual basis of accounting. For example, assume that a state government approved unrestricted operating grants for various localities for the fiscal year ended June 30, 20X2, and that a particular municipality's share of the grant is $24,000,000, to be paid in four equal installments with no further eligibility requirements. If the last installment ($6,000,000) does not meet the definition of "available" but the terms of the grant satisfy the accrual standards as established by GASB-33, only $18,000,000 of the grant would be reported in the governmental fund financial statements. However, at the end of the period a worksheet entry is made for the $6,000,000 (fourth installment) as shown below, in order to convert the information to an accrual basis:

Intergovernmental Grants Receivable	6,000,000	
General Revenues—Unrestricted Grants		6,000,000

PREVIOUS YEARS' BALANCES

In addition to current year transactions, previous years' balances are analyzed to determine how permanent balances (balance sheet accounts) that appeared on last year's government-wide financial statements affect the current year's government-wide financial statements. Worksheet entries arising from this analysis are made through the beginning balance of net assets.

For example, assume that a governmental entity had the following general long-term debt items outstanding as of the beginning of the current year:

Bonds Payable	$10,000,000
Notes Payable	1,000,000
Compensated absences obligation	750,000
Claims and judgments obligation	220,000
Total	$11,970,000

Based on the above obligations the following worksheet entry is made to establish the beginning balances related to the governmental activities column in the statement of net assets:

Net Assets—Beginning	11,970,000	
Bonds Payable		10,000,000
Notes Payable		1,000,000
Compensated Absences Obligation		750,000
Claims and Judgments Obligation		220,000

In addition, a governmental entity will generally have to analyze its capital assets at the beginning of the year in a similar manner. For example, assume that a governmental entity had the following capital assets at the beginning of the year:

	Cost	*Accumulated Depreciation*
Land	$100,000,000	
Buildings (60% depreciated)	400,000,000	$240,000,000
Equipment (70% depreciated)	200,000,000	140,000,000
Total	$700,000,000	$380,000,000

Based on the above analysis the following worksheet entry is made to establish the beginning balances related to the governmental activities column in the statement of net assets:

Land	100,000,000	
Buildings	400,000,000	
Equipment	200,000,000	
Accumulated Depreciation—Buildings		240,000,000
Accumulated Depreciation—Equipment		140,000,000
Net Assets—Beginning		320,000,000

APPENDIX 20B GOVERNMENTAL ENTITY PRESENTATION AND DISCLOSURE CHECKLIST

INTRODUCTION

The 2008 *Governmental GAAP Guide* provides a listing of the common presentation and disclosure requirements for financial statements of general purpose governmental units as required by generally accepted accounting principles (GAAP) that have been adopted by GASB-34 (Basic Financial Statements—and Management's Discussion and Analysis—for State and Local Governments). Note that this is a disclosure checklist, not a GAAP application checklist; accordingly, GAAP measurement and presentation questions are not included.

The checklist presented here includes occasional references to Statements on Auditing Standards (SAS) published by the AICPA. For example, subsequent events disclosure requirements are included in the auditing pronouncements. The financial statement preparer would normally include these auditing type note disclosures. This is considered an acceptable practice whether the financial statements are audited or unaudited.

PRACTICE POINT: The financial statement preparer should be aware that this governmental disclosure checklist will not include specific disclosures relating to legal or regulatory requirements specific to each state of jurisdiction. Also, this governmental disclosure checklist may only give the generic disclosure required by GAAP. For details about disclosure requirements see the references that accompany the generic disclosures in the following checklist. For disclosures relating to a specific situation you should review the examples provided within the appropriate professional standards.

PRACTICE POINT: Note disclosure requirements, like all other GAAP requirements, apply only to material items. To determine whether a note would be considered material, consider whether the omission would be important to certain financial statement users, either by financial significance or inherent interest.

NOTE: This checklist is not intended to be a complete disclosures checklist for special-purpose governments. The unique disclosures applicable to such entities also need to be considered.

Governmental Entity Presentation and Disclosure Checklist	Disclosure Required? Yes	No	N/A
Financial Statement Presentations			
If the presentation is intended to meet the minimum requirements for general purpose external financial reporting (i.e., not a single financial statement presentation or limited reporting engagement financial statements), does the presentation include the following, where applicable? (GASB sec. 2200.102)			
1. Management's discussion and analysis			
a. Precedes the basic financial statements as required supplementary information? (GASB-34, par. 8)	_____	_____	_____
b. Discusses current-year results in comparison with the prior year, placing emphasis on the current year? (GASB-34, par. 9)	_____	_____	_____
c. Focuses on the primary government, distinguishing between information for the primary government and that of its component units? (GASB-34, par. 10)	_____	_____	_____
d. Includes all required items for MD&A (GASB-37, par. 4):			
i. A brief discussion of the basic financial statements, including the relationship of the statements to each other?	_____	_____	_____
ii. Condensed financial information from the government-wide statements comparing current year to prior year (when two years of data is available)?	_____	_____	_____
iii. An analysis of the government's overall financial position and results of operations?	_____	_____	_____
iv. An analysis of balances and transaction of individual funds, including reasons for changes in fund balances or net assets?	_____	_____	_____

Governmental Entity Presentation and Disclosure Checklist	Disclosure Required? Yes	No	N/A
v. An analysis of significant variations between originals and final budget amounts and between final budget amounts and actual results for the General Fund?	____	____	____
vi. A description of significant capital asset and long-term debt activity for the year?	____	____	____
vii. A description of assessed condition information for governments that use the modified approach for reporting infrastructure assets?	____	____	____
viii. A description of currently known facts, decisions, or conditions that are expected to have a significant effect on financial position or results of operations?	____	____	____
2. Basic financial statements include			
a. Government-wide financial statements of net assets and activities?	____	____	____
b. Appropriate fund financial statements?	____	____	____
c. Appropriate presentations related to major funds?	____	____	____
d. Reconciliations between government-wide and fund financial statements, where appropriate?	____	____	____
e. Cash flow statements for proprietary funds (using the direct method)?	____	____	____
f. Budgetary comparison schedules within the basic financial statements when such reporting option as a basic financial statement is elected?	____	____	____
g. Notes to the financial statements?	____	____	____
3. Required supplementary information other than the MD&A, where applicable, including:			
a. Budgetary comparison schedules when not reported within the basic financial statements? (GASB secs. 2200.179-.180 and 2400.102-.103; GASB-41)	____	____	____

Governmental Entity Presentation and Disclosure Checklist	Disclosure Required?		
	Yes	No	N/A
b. For entities participating in a sole or agent defined benefit pension or OPEB plan, schedules of funding progress and employer contributions? (GASB sec. Pe5.125.132)	____	____	____
c. Asset condition schedules for governmental entities using the modified approach for infrastructure assets? (GASB sec. 1400.118–.119)	____	____	____
4. If the financial statements are intended to be a presentation in accordance with regulatory requirements, other comprehensive basis of accounting or are intended to be limited reporting engagement financial statements, do the financial statements contain the appropriate contents for such a presentation, including the applicable note disclosures? (AU Secs. 623, 508.33 and .34)	____	____	____
5. If the financial statements are intended to be a complete presentation for a special-purpose government, do the financial statements contain the appropriate contents for such presentation? (GASB sec. Sp20)	____	____	____
6. If the report is a Comprehensive Annual Financial Report (CAFR), are the appropriate combining and individual financial statements and schedules included and does the report include a statistical section consistent with GASB-44? (GASB sec. 2200)	____	____	____
7. Are the financial statements suitably titled? (AU Sec. 623.07, .24 and GASB sec. 2200.105)	____	____	____
8. Presentation of internal balances and internal service funds.			
a. Are internal balances eliminated in the statement of net assets to minimize the grossing up of internal balances, leaving a net amount due between the governmental and business-type activities that is eliminated in the total primary government column? (Balances of fiduciary activities are not considered to be internal balances.) (GASB-34, par. 58)	____	____	____

Governmental Entity Presentation and Disclosure Checklist	Disclosure Required?		
	Yes	**No**	**N/A**
b. Are eliminations made in the statement of activities to remove the duplication of internal service fund activity, leaving the expenses reported in the function to which they were allocated? (GASB-34, par. 59)	____	____	____
c. Are transactions between the primary government and discretely presented component units are reported as external transactions, and are receivable/payables reported on a separate line? (GASB-34, par. 61)	____	____	____
d. Unless dominated by enterprise funds, are internal service fund balances reported in the governmental activities column of the statement of net assets? (GASB-34, par. 62)	____	____	____
Possible Supplemental Schedules Required			
9. Does the presentation include the following budgetary information where applicable? (GASB secs. 2200.179 and 2400.102)			
a. Budgetary comparisons for the General Fund and each major Special Revenue fund that has a legally adopted annual budget? (GASB secs. 2200.179 and 2400.102)	____	____	____
b. The original budget, final budget and actual balances for the audit period? (GASB secs. 2200.179 and 2400.102)	____	____	____
c. If the budgetary basis is different from GAAP or the basis of presentation in the basic financial statements, is there accompanying information (either in a schedule or in the notes to RSI) that reconciles budgetary information to GAAP/OCBOAinformation? (GASB secs. 2200.180, 2400.103, and .119)	____	____	____
10. Does the presentation include the following RSI schedules when modified approach on eligible infrastructure assets is elected? (GASB sec. 1400.118)			

Governmental Entity Presentation and Disclosure Checklist	Disclosure Required? Yes	No	N/A
a. Assessed condition of the infrastructure assets, performed at least every three years, for the three most recent complete condition assessments.	____	____	____
b. For each of the past five reporting periods, the estimated annual amount calculated and actual amounts expensed to preserve and maintain the condition level established for the assets.	____	____	____

Comparative Financial Statements

11. Does the prior period's information contain sufficient detail to constitute fair presentation in conformity generally accepted accounting principles? (AU Sec. 508.65, fn. 23; AAG-SLV, pars. 14.33–.38)	____	____	____

Component Units

12. If the governmental entity presentation includes component units, do the presentations meet the following requirements, where applicable? (GASB sec. 2600)			
a. If the governmental entity presentation includes component units, did the component units also implement GASB-34/GASB-35? (GASB sec. 2600)	____	____	____
b. Component units that are fiduciary in nature have been properly excluded from the government-wide presentation and are only included in the fund financial statements. (GASB sec. 2600.107)	____	____	____
c. If separate financial statements of a component unit are issued, the relationship of the component unit to the reporting or oversight entity is disclosed. (GASB sec. 2600.128)	____	____	____
d. In the reporting entity financial statements of the primary government, the component units are properly reported as blended or discrete. (GASB sec. 2600.107–.113 and .115–.117)	____	____	____

Governmental Entity Presentation and Disclosure Checklist	Disclosure Required? Yes	No	N/A
e. All other nonfiduciary discretely presented component units have been reported in a separate column or columns to the right of the total column for the primary government statements. (GASB sec. 2600.107)	____	____	____
f. The governmental entity reported as a component unit those organizations that raise and hold economic resources for the direct benefit of the governmental unit as required by GASB-39 (Determining Whether Certain Organizations Are Component Units, An Amendment of GASB Statement No. 14.)	____	____	____
Summary of Significant Accounting Policies			
Are the required disclosures regarding the following significant accounting policies adequate?			
1. Description of the government-wide financial statements and exclusion of fiduciary activities and similar component units (GASB secs. 2300.106a(1) and 2200.111).	____	____	____
2. Definition of the primary government and component units that make up the governmental reporting entity and the criteria used to determine the scope of the reporting entity (GASB secs. 2300.106a(2) and 2600.120).	____	____	____
3. A brief description of the included component units, their relationship to the primary government, and how the separate financial statements for the individual component units may be obtained (GASB secs. 2300.106a(2) and 2600.120).	____	____	____
4. Nature of the primary government's accountability for related organizations and joint ventures, if any, including joint venture disclosures, including description of ongoing financial interest or responsibility and guidance on how to get joint venture financial information (GASB secs. 2300.107g, I, and J50.109–.111).	____	____	____

Governmental Entity Presentation and Disclosure Checklist	Disclosure Required?		
	Yes	**No**	**N/A**
5. A description of the activities accounted for in the columns for major funds, internal service funds, and fiduciary fund types presented in the basic financial statements (GASB secs. 2300.106a(3) and 1300.125).	____	____	____
6. Measurement focus and basis of accounting applied to the government-wide presentations and the fund financial statements (GASB secs. 1600 and 2300).	____	____	____
7. Revenue recognition policies in the fund financial statements, including the length of time used to define "available" for the purposes of revenue recognition under the modified accrual base of accounting (GASB secs. 2300.106a(5), 1600.106, .115, .130, and .134).	____	____	____
8. Policy for elimination of internal activity in the government-wide financial statements (GASB secs. 2300.106a(6) and 2200.128).	____	____	____
9. Policies for capitalizing assets and for estimating the useful lives of those assets and, if applicable, a description of the modified approach for infrastructure (GASB secs. 2300.106a(7), 1400.102, and .104).	____	____	____
10. Types of transactions included in program revenues (GASB secs. 2300.106a(8) and 2200.132–.136).	____	____	____
11. If applicable, policies for allocating indirect expenses to functions in the statement of activities (GASB secs. 2300.106a(8) and 2200.126–.131).	____	____	____
12. The policy for defining operating and nonoperating revenues of proprietary funds (GASB secs. 2300.106a(9) and P80.118).	____	____	____
13. Policy regarding application of FASB pronouncements for business-type activities and enterprise funds of the primary government (GASB secs. 2300.106a(10) and P80.103).	____	____	____
14. The definition of cash and cash equivalents used in the statement of cash flows (GASB secs. 2300.106a(11) and 2450.106–.108).	____	____	____

Governmental Entity Presentation and Disclosure Checklist	Disclosure Required?		
	Yes	**No**	**N/A**
15. Policy regarding whether to first apply restricted or unrestricted resources when an expense is incurred for purposes for which both restricted and unrestricted net assets are available (GASB secs. 2300.106a(12) and 1800.134).	_____	_____	_____

Compliance and Accountability Disclosures

Are the disclosures adequate regarding the following compliance and accountability issues, if applicable?

	Yes	No	N/A
1. Deficit fund balances or net assets of individual nonmajor funds (GASB sec. 2300.106n).	_____	_____	_____
2. Significant violations of finance-related legal or contractual provisions (GASB secs. 2300.106h and 1200.112).	_____	_____	_____
3. Actions taken to address such violations (GASB secs. 2300.106h and 1200.112).	_____	_____	_____

Deposits and Investments Disclosures

Are the following disclosures adequate regarding deposits and investments, if applicable?

	Yes	No	N/A
1. Legal or contractual provisions affecting deposits or investments (GASB-40, par. 6, GASB sec. I50.120).	_____	_____	_____
2. Investments made during the year but not owned at period end (GASB sec. I50.120).	_____	_____	_____
3. Restricted cash (e.g., compensating balances) (AC secs. B05.107 and C59.120).	_____	_____	_____
4. For financial statements issued for periods after June 15, 2003, for derivatives and similar debt and investment transactions the objective, significant terms, fair value, associated debt, and risks (i.e., credit, interest rate, basis, termination, rollover, and market access risks) (GASB:TB 2003-1).	_____	_____	_____
5. Terms or circumstances concerning repurchase or reverse repurchase agreements (GASB secs. 2300.106c, .107r, I50, and I55).	_____	_____	_____
6. Securities lending transactions (GASB secs. 2300.107s and I60.109–.114).	_____	_____	_____

Governmental Entity Presentation and Disclosure Checklist	Disclosure Required? Yes	No	N/A
7. The methods and significant assumptions used to estimate fair value of investments if the fair value is based on other than quoted market prices (GASB sec. I50.119).	____	____	____
8. The policy for determining which investments, if any, are reported at amortized cost (GASB sec. I50.119).	____	____	____
9. For investments in external investment pools that are not SEC-registered, a brief description of any regulatory oversight for the pool and whether the fair value of the position in the pool is the same as the value of the pool shares.	____	____	____
10. Any involuntary participation in an external investment pool.	____	____	____
11. If any entity cannot obtain information from a pool sponsor to allow it to determine the fair value of its investment in the pool, the methods used and significant assumptions made in determining that fair value and the reasons for having had to make such an estimate.	____	____	____
12. Any income from investments associated with one fund that is assigned to another fund.	____	____	____
13. For governmental entities that disclose realized gains/losses on investments, do the notes disclose (GASB sec. I50.119) the following:			
a. The calculation of realized gains or losses is independent of a calculation of the net change in the fair value of investments.	____	____	____
b. Realized gains or losses on investments that had been held in more than one fiscal year and sold in the current year were included as a net change in the fair value of investments reported in the prior year(s) and the current year.	____	____	____
c. Pooled cash and investment accounts (GASB sec. 1800.601).	____	____	____
d. Investment risk disclosures by investment type, including the following (GASB-40):			

Governmental Entity Presentation and Disclosure Checklist	Disclosure Required?		
	Yes	**No**	**N/A**
• Credit quality ratings of investments, where applicable.	_____	_____	_____
• Custodial credit risk for certain deposits and investments.	_____	_____	_____
• Concentration (5% or more) risk of certain investments.	_____	_____	_____
• Interest rate risk of debt instruments.	_____	_____	_____
• Foreign currency risk of investments.	_____	_____	_____

Capital Assets Disclosures

Are the following disclosures adequate regarding capital assets, if applicable?

	Yes	No	N/A
1. Disclosures divided into major classes of capital assets (GASB sec. 2300.111).	_____	_____	_____
2. Disclosures divided between capital assets of governmental activities and business-type activities (GASB sec. 2300.111).	_____	_____	_____
3. Beginning and end-of-year balances separated between historical cost and accumulated depreciation (GASB sec. 2300.112).	_____	_____	_____
4. Reporting period additions and sales or dispositions (GASB sec. 2300.112).	_____	_____	_____
5. Reporting-period depreciation expense, with disclosure of the amounts charged to each of the functions in the statement of activities (GASB sec. 2300.112).	_____	_____	_____
6. For collections of works of art and historical treasures not capitalized, a description of the collection and the reasons the assets are not capitalized (GASB sec. 2300.106).	_____	_____	_____
7. A general description of any capital asset impairment loss, including any insurance recoveries, if not apparent from the face of the financial statements (GASB-42, par.17).	_____	_____	_____
8. Carrying amount of any capital assets that are idle at year-end (GASB-42, par. 20).	_____	_____	_____

Governmental Entity Presentation and Disclosure Checklist	Disclosure Required? Yes	No	N/A

Long-Term Debt Disclosures

Are the following disclosures adequate regarding notes payable, bonds payable, revenue or bond anticipation notes, capital leases payable, and other debt, if applicable?

1. Debt descriptions including maturities and rates (AC sec. C32.104 and .105). _____ _____ _____
2. Other significant terms and covenants (AC sec. C59.120). _____ _____ _____
3. Effect of interest rates that do not reflect market rates (AC sec. I69). _____ _____ _____
4. Effect of troubled debt restructurings (AC sec. D22.121). _____ _____ _____
5. Beginning and end-of-year balances by type of debt (GASB sec. 2300.114a). _____ _____ _____
6. Increases and decreases separately presented (GASB sec. 2300.114b). _____ _____ _____
7. The portions of each type of debt that are due within one year of the statement date (GASB sec. 2300.114c). _____ _____ _____
8. The governmental funds that have typically been used to liquidate other long-term liabilities in prior years (GASB sec. 2300.114d). _____ _____ _____
9. Debt-service requirements to maturity, including the following (GASB secs. 2300.106i and 1500.118):
   a. Principal and interest requirements to maturity, presented separately for each of the five subsequent years and in five-year increments thereafter. _____ _____ _____
   b. The terms by which interest rates change for any variable-rate debt. _____ _____ _____
10. Debt refunding resulting in defeasance of debt (GASB secs. 2300.107j and D20.111–.115). _____ _____ _____
11. Unpaid debt outstanding at period end that has been defeased (GASB sec. D20.111–.114). _____ _____ _____
12. Nature of any significant restrictions on assets related to debt (AAG-SLV, Ch. 11, par. 11.31). _____ _____ _____

Governmental Entity Presentation and Disclosure Checklist	Disclosure Required?		
	Yes	**No**	**N/A**
13. Demand bonds (GASB secs. 2300.107u and D30.111–.112).	____	____	____
14. Conduit debt obligations (GASB secs. 2300.107y and C65.102).	____	____	____
15. Landfill closure and post-closure-care costs and liabilities (GASB sec. L10.115–.116).	____	____	____
16. Claims and judgments (GASB sec. 2300.106d).	____	____	____
17. Capital-lease obligations (GASB sec. 2300.107h).	____	____	____
18. Special-assessment debt and related activities (GASB secs. 2300.107t and S40.126–.127).	____	____	____
19. The amount of interest expense included in direct expenses in the statement of activities (GASB secs. 2300.107 and 2200.131).	____	____	____
20. Pollution remediation obligation (GASB-49).	____	____	____

Short-Term Debt Disclosures

Are the following disclosures adequate regarding short-term debt obligations and activity?

1. Schedule of changes in short-term debt balances (GASB sec. 2300.118a).	____	____	____
2. The purpose for which the short-term debt was issued (GASB sec. 2300.118b).	____	____	____

Interfund Balances and Disclosures of Transfers

Are the following disclosures adequate regarding interfund balances and activity, if applicable?

1. Amounts due from other funds by individual major fund, nonmajor governmental funds in the aggregate, nonmajor enterprise funds in the aggregate, internal service funds in the aggregate, and fiduciary fund type (GASB sec. 2300.120a).			
2. The purpose of interfund balances (GASB sec. 2300.120b).	____	____	____

Governmental Entity Presentation and Disclosure Checklist	Disclosure Required?		
	Yes	**No**	**N/A**
3. Interfund balances that are not expected to be repaid within one year from the date of the financial statements (GASB sec. 2300.120c).	____	____	____
4. Amounts transferred from other funds by individual major fund, nonmajor governmental funds in the aggregate, nonmajor enterprise funds in the aggregate, internal service funds in the aggregate, and fiduciary fund type (GASB sec. 2300.121a).	____	____	____
5. A general description of the principle purposes of the interfund transfers (GASB sec. 2300.121b).	____	____	____
6. The intended purpose and amount of significant transfers that either do not occur on a routine basis or are inconsistent with the activities of the transferring fund (GASB sec. 2300.121c).	____	____	____
7. For each major component unit, the nature and amount of any significant transactions with other discretely presented component units or with the primary government (GASB sec. 2300.106p).	____	____	____
8. Transfers of receivables or other assets or the pledge of future revenues intra-entity (GASB-49).	____	____	____
Pension and Other Postemployment Benefit Plan Disclosure Requirements			
1. For defined benefit plans (GASB-27, pars. 16–21, GASB-45, pars. 24–25):			
a. Plan identification, description, name, type, and who administers the plan.	____	____	____
b. Funding-policy disclosures such as required contribution rates, authority for contributions, and amounts of required contributions.	____	____	____
c. For single-employer and agent multiple-employer plans, the annual pension/OPEB cost and its components, any net pension/OPEB obligation, and actuarial information such as assumptions, methods, and dates.	____	____	____

Governmental Entity Presentation and Disclosure Checklist	Disclosure Required?		
	Yes	**No**	**N/A**
d. For single-employer and agent multiple-employer plans, if the aggregate actuarial cost method is not used, disclosures of actuarial liabilities and funded status, and factors affecting funded status trends.	_____	_____	_____
e. For insured plans, a description of the plan, discussion of the obligation transfer, any employer guarantees, current-year pension/OPEB expenditures and contributions.	_____	_____	_____
2. For defined contribution plans (GASB-27, par. 27; GASB-45, par. 31):			
a. Plan identification, description, name, type, and who administers the plan.	_____	_____	_____
b. Brief description of the plan provisions and authority to contribute.	_____	_____	_____
c. Contribution requirements and actual contributions made by the plan members and employer.	_____	_____	_____
Other Disclosure Requirements			
If material, are the presentations appropriate and are disclosures adequate regarding the following other disclosure requirements?			
1. Condensed financial statements for major component units in the component units column(s) [major component units may be presented in one of the following three manners: (1) separate columns in the entity-wide statements, (2) combining statements after the basic fund statements before the footnotes, or (3) condensed financial statements in the footnotes] (GASB secs. 2300.107d and 2600.108–.109).	_____	_____	_____
2. Accounting changes (AC sec. A06).	_____	_____	_____
3. Related-party transactions (GASB sec. 2300.107f).	_____	_____	_____
4. Nonmonetary transactions (GASB secs. 2300.107c and 2500).	_____	_____	_____
5. Detail of the government's property-tax calendar, including the lien, levy, due, and collection dates (GASB sec. P70.109).	_____	_____	_____

Governmental Entity Presentation and Disclosure Checklist	Disclosure Required?		
	Yes	**No**	**N/A**
6. On-behalf payments for fringe benefits and salaries (GASB secs. 2300.107x and N50.134).	____	____	____
7. Discounts and allowances that reduce gross revenues, when not reported on the face of the financial statements (GASB secs. 2300.107 and 2200, fn. 30).	____	____	____
8. Other assets, including intangible assets and deferred charges, if applicable (AC secs. I08 and I60).	____	____	____
9. Sold or pledged receivables, other assets, or future revenues (GASB-48).	____	____	____
10. Disaggregation of receivable and payable balances and receivable balances not expected to be collected within one year (GASB Sec. 2300.119).	____	____	____
11. Designations, reservations, or other restrictions of fund balances or net assets, including separate disclosure of net assets restricted by enabling legislation, if not disclosed on the face of the financial statements (GASB sec. 1800.123–.127; AAG-SLV 10.08–10.18, GASB-46).	____	____	____
12. Disclosures about donor-restricted endowments (GASB sec. 2300.117).	____	____	____
13. Risk management and related financing activities, including types of risks and how they are managed, any significant reduction in coverages, and whether any settlements have exceeded insurance coverages in the past three years (GASB secs. 2300.107a, C50.101, and .109–.141)?	____	____	____
14. Are the nature and amount of inconsistencies in the financial statements caused by transactions between component units having different year-ends properly disclosed (GASB sec. 2300.107p).	____	____	____
15. Significant transactions or other events that are either unusual or infrequent but not within the control of management (GASB secs. 2300.107, 2200.141, and .159).	____	____	____

Governmental Entity Presentation and Disclosure Checklist	Disclosure Required? **Yes**	**No**	**N/A**
16. Nature of individual elements of a particular reconciling item, if obscured in any aggregated information in the reconciliation between the fund and government-wide statements (GASB secs. 2300.107 and 2200.151).	_____	_____	_____
17. Any significant economic dependence on one or more major taxpayers, customers, or suppliers if the government entity has publicly traded debt (FAS-21, par. 9).	_____	_____	_____
18. Segment disclosures for activities associated with enterprise funds and stand-alone business-type activities (GASB-34, pars. 48, 122, and 123).	_____	_____	_____
Contingencies and Commitments Disclosures			
The following disclosures regarding contingencies and commitments, if applicable:			
1. Loss contingencies (GASB secs. C50.110–.115, 1500.110, and 1600.118; AC sec. C59.104–.116 and .120).	_____	_____	_____
2. Construction and other significant commitments (GASB sec. 2300.106k).	_____	_____	_____
3. Commitments under operating leases (GASB secs. 2300.106j, L20.124, and .125).	_____	_____	_____
Subsequent Event Disclosures			
1. Significant subsequent events and whether or not adjustments were made to the financial statements (GASB secs. 2300.106f, C50.140; AU sec. 560.03–.07).	_____	_____	_____

V. STAND-ALONE FINANCIAL REPORTING BY SPECIAL-PURPOSE GOVERNMENTS

CHAPTER 21
PUBLIC COLLEGES AND UNIVERSITIES

CONTENTS

INTRODUCTION

As originally issued, the standards established by GASB-34 did not apply to public colleges and universities (PCUs). GASB-35 amends GASB-34, footnote 3, by requiring PCUs to report as special-purpose governments when they are legally separate entities as defined by GASB-14 (The Financial Reporting Entity). Special-purpose entities may be a component unit of a primary government or may be a stand-alone government.

The standards established by GASB-35 supersede the following previous standards established by the GASB:

- GASB-8—Applicability of FASB Statement No. 93, "Recognition of Depreciation by Not-for-Profit Organizations," to Certain State Local Governmental Entities — The Statement is superseded. GASB-8 addressed which governmental not-for-profit entities could follow the standards established by and FAS-93.
- GASB-14—The Financial Reporting Entity — Paragraph 48 is superseded. The paragraph established presentation formats in a primary

	government's financial statements for PCUs that use the AICPA College Guide model.
• GASB-15—Governmental College and University Accounting and Financial Reporting Models	The Statement is superseded. GASB-15 clarified the application of accounting standards that could be used by PCUs.
• GASB-16—Accounting for Compensated Absences	Footnote 2 is superseded. The footnote provided guidance for presenting compensated absences information for PCUs that used the AICPA College Guide model.
• GASB-18—Accounting for Municipal Solid Waste Landfill Closure and Post-closure Care Costs	Paragraph 12 and footnote 5 are superseded. These standards required a PCU that uses the AICPA's College Guide model and that owned or operated alandfill to report the activity in the entity's unrestricted current fund.
• GASB-19—Governmental College and University Omnibus Statement	The Statement is superseded. GASB-19 required a PCU that uses the AICPA's College Guide model to report Pell grants in a restricted current fund and provided guidance for the reporting of risk financing activities in a single fund.
• GASB-23—Accounting and Financial Reporting for Refundings of Debt Reported by Proprietary	Footnote 2 is superseded. The footnote required a PCU that uses the governmental model to follow the standards established Activities by GASB-23.
• GASB-27—Accounting for Pensions by State and Local Governmental Employers	Paragraph 18 is superseded. The paragraph provides guidance for measuring and reporting pension expenditures of a PCU that uses the AICPA's College Guide model.
• GASBI-4—Accounting and Financial Reporting foot Capitalization of Contributions to Public Entity Risk Pools	Paragraphs 8 and 17 and footnote 7 are superseded. These standards provided guidance for accounting for premium payments to public entity risk-pools by a PCU that uses the AICPA's College Guide model.

• GASB: TB 92-1—Display of Governmental College University Compensated Absences Liabilities	The Technical Bulletin is superseded. GASB: TB 92-1 and provided guidance for the presentation of compensated absences liabilities for a PCU that uses the AICPA's College Guide model.

In addition to the standards that GASB-35 superseded, GASB-35 also amended the following standards:

• GASB-14—The Financial Reporting Entity	Paragraphs 19 and 44 and footnote 6 are amended. These standards established presentation formats in a primary government's financial statements for a PCU that uses the AICPA College Guide model or the governmental model.
• GASB-16—Accounting for Compensated Absences	Paragraph 2 is amended. The paragraph discussed the applicability of standards established by FAS-43 (Accounting for Compensated Absences) to a PCU that uses the AICPA College Guide model.
• GASB-18—Accounting for The Municipal Solid Waste Landfill Closure and Post-closure Care Costs	Paragraph 16 is amended. paragraph provided a cross-reference to material now superseded by GASB-35.
• GASB-24—Accounting and Financial Reporting for Certain Grants and Other Financial Assistance	Paragraph 4 is amended. The paragraph provided an exemption for the accounting for pass-through grants of a PCU that uses the AICPA College Guide model.
• GASB-31—Accounting and The Financial Reporting for Certain Investments and for External Investment Pools	Paragraph 14 is amended. paragraph provided an exemption for the assignment of investment income of a PCU that uses the AICPA College Guide model.
• GASB-33—Accounting and The Financial Reporting for Nonexchange Transactions	Paragraph 11 is amended. paragraph provided an exemption for expenditure recognition for a PCU that uses the AICPA College Guide model.

• GASB-9—Reporting Cash Flows of Proprietary and Nonexpendable Trust Funds and Governmental Entities That Use Proprietary Fund Accounting	Paragraph 5 is amended. That paragraph provided an exemption for the preparation of a statement of cash flows for a PCU that uses the AICPA College Guide model.
• GASB-23—Accounting and Financial Reporting for Refundings of Debt Reported by Proprietary Activities	Paragraph 3 is amended. That paragraph provided an exemption for current refundings and an advance in proprietary activities for a PCU that uses the governmental model.

BASIC REPORTING MODELS

GASB-35 requires that, in general, PCUs use the same accounting and financial reporting standards that will be used by all other governmental entities once the standards established by GASB-34 become effective. Specifically, PCUs that issue separate financial reports should observe the guidance established in GASB-34 for special-purpose governmental entities (paragraphs 134–138), depending on which of the following reporting environments is appropriate:

- Reporting only business-type activities (Enterprise Fund Model)
- Reporting both business-type and governmental activities
- Reporting only governmental activities

Professional judgment must be used to determine the nature of the activities conducted by a PCU. GASB-34 states that governmental activities are "generally financed through taxes, intergovernmental revenues, and other nonexchange revenues," and business-type activities are financed to some degree by charging external parties for the goods or services they acquire. Governmental activities are generally accounted for in governmental funds and Internal Service Funds. Business-type activities are usually reported in Enterprise Funds.

REPORTING ONLY BUSINESS-TYPE ACTIVITIES (ENTERPRISE FUND MODEL)

GASB-34 states that an Enterprise Fund must be used to account for an activity if any one of the following criteria is satisfied:

- The activity is financed with debt that is secured solely by a pledge of the net revenues from fees and charges of the activity.
- Laws or regulations require that the activity's costs of providing services, including capital costs (such as depreciation or

capital debt service), be recovered with fees and charges rather than with taxes or similar revenues.

- The pricing policies of the activity establish fees and charges designed to recover its costs, including capital costs (such as depreciation or debt service).

The first condition refers to debt secured solely by fees and charges. If that debt is secured by a pledge of fees and charges from the activity and the full faith and credit of the PCU or the component unit, this arrangement does not satisfy the "sole source of debt security" criterion and the activity does not have to be accounted for (assuming the other two criteria are not satisfied) in an Enterprise Fund. This conclusion is not changed even if it is anticipated that the PCU or the component unit is not expected to make debt payments under the arrangement. On the other hand, debt that is secured partially by a portion of its own proceeds does satisfy the "sole source of debt security" criterion.

Although the criteria established above identify those conditions under which an activity must be accounted for in an Enterprise Fund, GASB-34 also states that an Enterprise Fund may be used to "report any activity for which a fee is charged to external users for goods or services." The GASB believes that many PCUs can report as an Enterprise Fund because they generally charge tuition fees and various other fees for their educational services.

A PCU that reports only business-type activities must follow either Alternative 1 or Alternative 2 of GASB-20 (Accounting and Financial Reporting for Proprietary Funds and Other Governmental Entities That Use Proprietary Fund Accounting). Under Alternative 1, a PCU must observe (a) all GASB pronouncements and (b) FASB Statements and Interpretations, APB Opinions, and Accounting Research Bulletins (ARBs) issued on or before November 30, 1989, except those that conflict with a GASB pronouncement. Under Alternative 2, a PCU reporting only business-type activities must follow (a) all GASB pronouncements and (b) all FASB Statements and Interpretations, APB Opinions, and ARBs, no matter when issued, except those that conflict with a GASB pronouncement. Unlike Alternative 1, Alternative 2 has no cutoff date for determining the applicability of FASB pronouncements.

OBSERVATION: Alternative 2 of GASB-20 allows Enterprise Funds to adopt all FASB pronouncements, including those issued after November 30, 1989, as long as those standards do not conflict with a GASB pronouncement. With the issuance of FAS-116 (Accounting for Contributions Received and Contributions Made) and FAS-117 (Financial Statements of Not-for-Profit Organizations), which were directed to not-for-profit accounting and reporting issues, there was uncertainty about whether proprietary funds should incorporate the standards established by these two Statements. GASB-20 states that Alternative 2 should be interpreted to include only those

FASB Statements and Interpretations that apply to commercial enterprises. Thus, the standards established by FAS-116 and FAS-117 are not incorporated into Alternative 2.

> **OBSERVATION:** One of the advantages of a PCU reporting only business-type activities is that the resulting financial statements are to some degree similar to those required by not-forprofit colleges and universities that must observe the standards established by FAS-117. However, there are some differences, including the structure of the net asset section of the statement of net assets. As noted earlier, a PCU's net assets must be categorized as (1) invested in capital assets, net of related debt; (2) restricted; or (3) unrestricted, and a not-for-profit college or university must label its net asset section as (1) temporarily restricted, (2) permanently restricted, or (3) unrestricted. Also, there are significant differences in the structure of the activity statements under the two reporting models.

When a PCU is engaged in only business-type activities, it must observe only some of the standards established by GASB-34. Specifically, a PCU under this circumstance must observe the standards established by the following paragraphs of GASB-34:

GASB-34 *Paragraphs*	*Topic*
91–105	Enterprise Fund financial statements
113–123	Notes to the financial statements
8–11 (as appropriate)	MD&A information
132–133 (if applicable)	RSI (other than MD&A)

Enterprise Fund Model Financial Statements (GASB-34, pars. 91–105)

The financial statements of a PCU that is engaged only in business-type activities should include the following statements:

- Statement of net assets (balance sheet)
- Statement of revenues, expenses, and changes in fund net assets
- Statement of cash flows

Statement of net assets Assets and liabilities presented in the statement of net assets of a PCU reported as an Enterprise Fund should be classified as current and long-term, based on the guidance established in Chapter 3 of ARB-43 (Restatement and Revision of Accounting Research Bulletins).

Exhibit 21-1 is an illustration of a statement of net assets for a PCU consistent with the standards required by GASB-35.

EXHIBIT 21-1
STATEMENT OF NET ASSETS

Centerville University
Statement of Net Assets
June 30, 20X5

	Centerville University	*University Medical Center*
ASSETS		
Current Assets:		
Cash and cash equivalents	$ 3,175,000	$ 750,000
Other receivables, net	18,000,000	6,500,000
Contributions receivable, net	7,800,000	1,800,000
Student loans, net	15,600,000	
Deposits with bond trustees	5,000,000	
Other	1,450,000	2,700,000
Total Current Assets	$ 51,025,000	$ 11,750,000
Noncurrent Assets:		
Restricted cash and cash equivalents	720,000	1,400,000
Investments in securities	17,800,000	3,500,000
Investments in real estate	4,500,000	
Capital assets, net (see Note 1)	32,171,000	7,600,000
Total Noncurrent Assets	55,191,000	12,500,000
Total Assets	$106,216,000	$ 24,250,000
LIABILITIES		
Current Liabilities:		
Accounts payable and accrued liabilities	$ 650,000	$ 210,000
Deferred revenue	170,000	25,000
Current portion of long-term debt (Note 2)	450,000	200,000
Total Current Liabilities	1,270,000	435,000
Noncurrent Liabilities:		
Deferred revenues	1,900,000	32,000
Long-term debt (Note 2)	21,050,000	1,400,000
Total Noncurrent Liabilities	22,950,000	1,432,000
Total Liabilities	$ 24,220,000	$ 1,867,000
NET ASSETS		
Invested in capital assets, net of related debt	$ 7,500,000	$ 5,000,000

Restricted for:		
Nonexpendable:		
Scholarships	18,330,000	
Research	14,100,000	10,800,000
Expendable:		
Scholarships	2,300,000	
Research	4,700,000	4,200,000
Training	2,550,000	720,000
Loans	5,100,000	
Capital projects	6,500,000	340,000
Debt service	1,100,000	100,000
Unrestricted	19,816,000	1,223,000
Total Net Assets	$ 81,996,000	$ 22,383,000

Statement of revenues, expenses, and changes in fund net assets The operating or change statement of an Enterprise Fund is the statement of revenues, expenses, and changes in fund net assets.

When a PCU has only business-type activities, the formatting of its statement of revenues, expenses, and changes in fund net assets must differentiate between operating and nonoperating transactions and events.

Exhibit 21-2 is an illustration of a statement of revenues, expenses, and changes in fund net assets for a PCU consistent with the standards established by GASB-35.

EXHIBIT 21-2
STATEMENT OF REVENUES, EXPENSES, AND CHANGES IN NET ASSETS

Centerville University
Statement of Revenues, Expenses, and Change in Net Assets
For the Year Ended June 30, 20X5

	Centerville University	*University Medical Center*
OPERATING REVENUES		
Student tuition and fees (net of scholarship allowance of $4,500,000)	$28,000,000	

	Centerville University	University Medical Center
Patient services (net of charity care of $500,000)		$12,500,000
Grants and contracts	8,500,000	1,300,000
Gifts	2,500,000	770,000
Investment income (net of expense of $5,000 for the primary institution and $2,000 for the medical center)	300,000	35,000
Auxiliary activities:		
Residential halls (net of scholarship allowance of $220,000)	18,500,000	
Bookstore (net of scholarship allowance of $45,000)	7,250,000	
Other	1,200,000	345,000
Total Operating Revenues	66,250,000	14,950,000
OPERATING EXPENSES		
Salaries:		
Faculty (physicians for the medical center)	23,500,000	7,450,000
Exempt staff	28,700,000	4,550,000
Nonexempt wages	5,500,000	1,700,000
Fringe benefits	12,500,000	3,700,000
Scholarships and fellowships	3,400,000	
Depreciation	2,400,000	850,000
Other	3,750,000	2,300,000
Total Operating Expenses	79,750,000	20,550,000
Net Operating Income (Loss)	(13,500,000)	(5,600,000)
NONOPERATING REVENUES (EXPENSES)		
State appropriations	6,200,000	3,200,000
Investment income (net of expense of $42,000 for the primary institution and $9,000 for the medical center)	2,300,000	420,000
Interest expense	(1,400,000)	(92,000)
Gifts and grants for noncapital purposes	4,500,000	230,000
Other	135,000	77,000
Total Nonoperating Revenues	11,735,000	3,835,000

	Centerville University	University Medical Center
OTHER REVENUES		
Capital gifts and grants	7,200,000	230,000
Additions to permanent endowments	300,000	300,000
Total Other Revenues	7,500,000	530,000
Changes In Net Assets	5,735,000	(1,235,000)
Net Assets—July 01, 20X4	76,261,000	23,618,000
Net Assets—June 30, 20X5	$ 81,996,000	$ 22,383,000

The *GASB Comprehensive Implementation Guide* states that a PCU that reports as a specialpurpose government engaged only in business-type activities may report its expenses using either natural or functional classifications, noting that neither GASB-34 nor GASB-35 specifies which classification scheme should be used. It should be noted that GASB-34 requires that the basic financial statements be preceded by MD&A (which is discussed later in this chapter). Paragraph 11 of GASB-34 lists the specific components that should comprise MD&A, and one of the components relates to condensed institution-wide financial statements and comments on the significant changes from the prior year to the current year. Furthermore, the condensed presentation should include information that, at a minimum, supports the analysis of the overall financial position and results of operations. One of the specific items that must be presented as condensed financial information is "program expenses, at a minimum by function." Thus, it may appear that there is a conflict between the requirements of GASB-34 (reporting program expenses) and the statement that a PCU could report its expenses using a natural rather than a functional classification. The *GASB Comprehensive Implementation Guide* points out that GASB-34 states that special-purpose governments engaged only in business-type activities should follow the requirements for MD&A (paragraphs 8–11) only as appropriate. Thus, a PCU could report its expenses on a natural basis, but if it does so, the MD&A related to condensed expenses should also be based on a natural classification discussion rather than on a program basis.

Statement of cash flows A PCU should prepare a statement of cash flows based on the guidance established by GASB-9, except the statement of cash flows should be formatted based on the direct method in computing cash flows from operating activities. The statement of cash flows would be supplemented with a reconciliation of operating cash flows and operating income (the indirect method).

Exhibit 21-3 provides an illustration of a statement of cash flows consistent with the standards established by GASB-35.

EXHIBIT 21-3
STATEMENT OF CASH FLOWS

Centerville University
Statement of Cash Flows
For the Year Ended June 30, 20X5

	Centerville University	*University Medical Center*
CASH FLOWS FROM OPERATING ACTIVITIES		
Tuition and fees	$ 27,800,000	
Gifts	700,000	$ 755,000
Grants and contracts	8,550,000	
Medicaid and medicare reimbursements		9,400,000
Payments from patients and insurance reimbursements		4,380,000
Residence Halls	18,400,000	
Bookstore	7,230,000	
Employee and related payments	(70,150,000)	(17,361,000)
Supplier and vendor payments	(3,500,000)	
Loans to students	(3,400,000)	(2,310,000)
Collection of student loans	2,800,000	
Other	(2,940,000)	
Net Cash Provided (Used) by Operating Activities	(14,510,000)	(5,136,000)
CASH FLOWS FROM NONCAPITAL FINANCING ACTIVITIES		
State appropriations	6,010,000	3,148,000
Gifts and grants	4,600,000	240,000
Other	125,000	97,000
Private gifts—endowments	400,000	50,000
Net Cash Flows Provided (Used) by Noncapital Financing Activities	11,135,000	3,535,000
CASH FLOWS FROM CAPITAL AND RELATED FINANCING ACTIVITIES		
Capital gifts and grants	8,000,000	500,000

	Centerville University	University Medical Center
Proceeds from sale of capital assets	1,000,000	400,000
Purchases of capital assets	(6,900,000)	(600,000)
Principal repayments	(400,000)	(200,000)
Interest payments	(1,380,000)	(89,000)
Deposit with bond trustees	(500,000)	
Net Cash Provided (Used) by Capital and Related Financing Activities	(180,000)	11,000
CASH FLOWS FROM INVESTING ACTIVITIES		
Proceeds from sales of investments	4,200,000	100,000
Interest and other income	1,350,000	495,000
Purchases of securities investments	(4,000,000)	(120,000)
Purchase of real estate investment	(3,600,000)	
Net Cash Provided (Used) by Investing Activities	(2,050,000)	475,000
Net Increase (Decrease)	(5,605,000)	(1,115,000)
Cash and cash equivalents—July 1, 20X4	9,500,000	1,865,000
Cash and cash equivalents—June 30, 20X5	$3,895,000	$750,000

NONCASH CAPITAL AND FINANCING ACTIVITIES

During the year the University had a significant noncash transaction that resulted in the acquisition of capital assets of $500,000 which was financed by the issuance of mortgages.

RECONCILIATION OF NET OPERATING INCOME

Reconciliation of net operating income (loss) to net cash provided (used) by operating activities:

Net operating income (loss)	($13,500,000)	($5,600,000)
Adjustments to reconcile net operating income (loss) to net cash provided (used) by operating activities:		
Depreciation expenses	2,400,000	850,000
Changes in assets and liabilities:		
Receivables, net	(300,000)	(30,000)
Contribution receivables, net	(1,800,000)	(15,000)

	Centerville University	University Medical Center
Student loans	(600,000)	
Accounts payable and accrued liabilities	60,000	7,000
Other liabilities	700,000	22,000
Deferred revenue	30,000	10,000
Cash flows reported in other categories:		
Interest	(300,000)	(35,000)
Other	(1,200,000)	(345,000)
Net Cash Provided (Used) by Operating Activities	($14,510,000)	($5,136,000)

Notes to the Financial Statements (GASB-34, pars. 113–123)

GASB-35 does not change the general note disclosures required of PCUs from those of other governmental entities. See Chapter 20, "Comprehensive Annual Financial Report," for details on required notes to the financial statements.

Required Supplementary Information

A PCU should present the following RSI:

- Management's discussion and analysis information
- Infrastructure assets (if the modified approach is used)
- Pension plan schedules (if applicable)

> **OBSERVATION:** GASB-34 requires that certain funds disclose budgetary comparison schedules as RSI; however, it would generally be inappropriate for a PCU that reports as an Enterprise Fund to do so.

See Chapter 20, "Comprehensive Annual Financial Report," for a detailed discussion of RSI.

REPORTING BOTH BUSINESS-TYPE AND GOVERNMENTAL ACTIVITIES

When a PCU that is engaged in both business-type and governmental activities, it must essentially follow all of the standards established by GASB-34. Specifically, a PCU under these circumstances must observe the standards established by paragraphs 8–131 of GASB-34. The paragraph topics are summarized as follows:

GASB-34 Paragraphs	*Topic*
12–62	Institutional-wide financial statements
63–112	Fund financial statements
113–123	Notes to the financial statements
8–11	MD&A information
123–128	Reporting component units
129–131	RSI (other than MD&A)

NOTE: Only the first two topics (institutional-wide financial statements and fund financial statements) and budgetary information that is considered RSI are discussed in this section. The other four topics were discussed in the previous section.

Professional judgment must be exercised to determine the nature of the activities conducted by a PCU. GASB-34 states that governmental activities are "generally financed through taxes, intergovernmental revenues, and other nonexchange revenues," while business-type activities are financed to some degree by charging external parties for the goods are services they acquire. Governmental activities are generally accounted for in governmental funds and Internal Service Funds. Business-type activities are usually reported in Enterprise Funds.

Institutional-Wide Financial Statements

The financial statements of a PCU that is engaged in both governmental and business-type activities should include the following institutional-wide financial statements:

- Statement of net assets
- Statement of activities

See Chapter 20, "Comprehensive Annual Financial Report," for a detailed discussion of the statements of net assets and activities.

Exhibit 21-4 illustrates a PCU's statement of net assets that is consistent with the standards established by GASB-34.

EXHIBIT 21-4
STATEMENT OF NET ASSETS

Centerville Community College
Statement of Net Assets
June 30, 20X5

	Governmental Activities	*Business-Type Activities*	*Total*
ASSETS			
Cash	$16,500,000	$2,800,000	$19,300,000
Property taxes and other receivables (net)	23,412,000	6,604,500	30,016,500
Investments	41,184,000	1,250,000	42,434,000
Inventories and prepayments	690,000	361,500	1,051,500
Internal balances	336,000	(56,000)	280,000
Capital assets, net (See Note X)	138,000,000	11,000,000	149,000,000
Total Assets	220,122,000	21,960,000	242,082,000
LIABILITIES			
Accounts payable	8,400,000	650,000	9,050,000
Deferred tuition revenue	180,000	25,000	205,000
Other payables	450,000	150,000	600,000
Long-term debt (See Note XX)			
Due within one year	11,400,000	175,000	11,575,000
Due beyond one year	66,000,000	6,250,000	72,250,000
Total Liabilities	86,430,000	7,250,000	93,680,000
NET ASSETS			
Invested in capital assets, net of related debt	67,284,000	8,350,000	75,634,000
Unrestricted	66,408,000	6,360,000	72,768,000
Total Net Assets	$133,692,000	$14,710,000	$148,402,000

Exhibit 21-5 illustrates a PCU's statement of activities that is consistent with the standards established by GASB-34.

Fund Financial Statements

The financial statements of a PCU that is engaged in both governmental and business-type activities should include the following fund-based financial statements:

- Balance sheet (governmental funds)
- Statement of revenues, expenditures, and changes in fund balances (governmental funds)
- Statement of net assets (proprietary funds)
- Statement of revenues, expenses, and changes in net assets (proprietary funds)
- Statement of cash flows (proprietary funds)

See Chapter 20, "Comprehensive Annual Financial Report," for a detailed discussion of the fund financial statements.

Governmental funds A governmental funds' financial statements have a short-term emphasis and generally measure and account for cash and "other assets that can easily be converted to cash." A significant change in the focus of reporting governmental funds and business-type funds is that major funds are reported for these funds; however, combined financial statements for fund types are not reported.

Exhibit 21-6 is an illustration of fund balance sheets for governmental funds and Exhibit 21-7 is an illustration of a Statements of Revenues, Expenditures, and Changes in Fund Balances for governmental funds of a PCU consistent with the standards established by GASB-34.

Proprietary funds Financial statements for proprietary funds should be based on the flow of economic resources (measurement focus) and the accrual basis of accounting. However, unlike current PCU financial reporting standards, GASB-34 requires fund reporting be restricted to a PCU's "major" funds.

Exhibit 21-8 is an illustration of a statement of net assets for proprietary funds of a PCU consistent with the standards established by GASB-34.

Exhibit 21-9 is an illustration of a statement of revenues, expenses, and changes in net assets for a PCU proprietary funds consistent with the standards established by GASB-34.

EXHIBIT 21-5
STATEMENT OF ACTIVITIES
Centerville Community College
Statement of Activities
For the Year Ended June 30, 20X5

		Program Revenues			*Net (Expense) Revenue & Changes in Net Assets*		
	Expenses	*Tuitions & Fees*	*Services & Other Revenues*	*Capital Grants & Contributions*	*Governmental Activities*	*Business-Type Activities*	*Total*
GOVERNMENTAL FUNCTIONS:							
Primary Institution:							
Governmental activities:							
Instruction	$ 24,000,000	$ 8,760,000	$ 1,680,000		$ (13,560,000)		$(13,560,000)
Academic support	6,000,000	690,000	960,000		(4,350,000)		(4,350,000)
Student activities	7,500,000	192,000	420,000	$240,000	(6,648,000)		(6,648,000)
Administrative	3,600,000				(3,600,000)		(3,600,000)
Institutional support	9,000,000				(9,000,000)		(9,000,000)
Maintenance and other	19,500,000				(19,500,000)		(19,500,000)
Interest on long-term debt	3,300,000				(3,300,000)		(3,300,000)
Total governmental activities	72,900,000	9,642,000	3,060,000	240,000	(59,958,000)		(59,958,000)

Business-Type Activities:							
Bookstore	1,750,000	1,950,000		65,000		265,000	265,000
Food services	1,050,000	2,150,000				1,100,000	1,100,000
Total business-type activities	2,800,000	4,100,000		65,000		1,365,000	1,365,000
Total primary government	$75,700,000	$13,742,000	$3,060,000	$305,000	(59,958,000)	1,365,000	(58,593,000)
General Revenues:							
State appropriations					22,200,000		22,200,000
Property taxes					40,200,000		40,200,000
Interest and investment income					2,250,000	105,000	2,355,000
Other					1,035,000	52,500	1,087,500
Special item—Gains from sale of real estate					1,290,000		1,290,000
Transfers					375,000	(375,000)	
Total general revenues, special items, and transfers					67,350,000	(217,500)	67,132,500
Change in net assets for the year					7,392,000	1,147,500	8,539,500
Net assets—beginning of year					37,172,000	28,272,500	65,444,500
Net assets—ending of year					$44,564,000	$29,420,000	$73,984,000

EXHIBIT 21-6
FUND BALANCE SHEETS
Centerville Community College
Fund Balance Sheets
Governmental Funds June 30, 20X5

	General Fund	*Grants and Contracts Funds*	*Multi-Purpose State Improvement Bonds*	*Other Governmental Funds (A)*	*Total Governmental Funds*
ASSETS					
Cash	$12,900,000	$ 7,050,000	$ 4,050,000	$ 8,700,000	$ 32,700,000
Property taxes and other receivables (net)	6,390,000	810,000	750,000	8,910,000	16,860,000
Investments	8,340,000	4,800,000	7,620,000	4,020,000	24,780,000
Inventories and prepayments	375,000			141,000	516,000
Receivable from other funds		390,000			390,000
Total Assets	28,005,000	13,050,000	12,420,000	21,771,000	75,246,000
LIABILITIES					
Accounts payable	4,410,000	1,080,000	1,020,000	1,680,000	8,190,000
Deferred tuition revenue	180,000	60,000	180,000	90,000	510,000
Payable to other governments		150,000			150,000
Other deferred revenue	120,000	90,000	15,000	66,000	291,000
Total Liabilities	4,710,000	1,380,000	1,215,000	1,836,000	9,141,000

FUND BALANCES					
Reserved for:					
Noncurrent assets	2,472,000				2,472,000
Encumbrances	165,000	81,000	366,000	231,000	843,000
Other purposes	1,350,000			1,125,000	2,475,000
Unreserved, reported in:					
General fund	19,308,000				19,308,000
Special revenue fund		11,589,000			11,589,000
Capital projects funds			10,839,000		10,839,000
Other funds				18,579,000	18,579,000
Total Fund Balances	23,295,000	11,670,000	11,205,000	19,935,000	66,105,000
Total Liabilities and Fund Balances	$28,005,000	$13,050,000	$12,420,000	$21,771,000	$75,246,000

Amounts presented for governmental activities in the Statement of Net Assets are different because:	
Capital assets reported in the Statement of Net Assets are not financial resources	130,500,000
Other long-term assets reported in the Statement of Net Assets are not available to pay for current period expenditures	3,726,000
Assets and liabilities of Internal Service Funds reported in the Statement of Net Assets are used to charge the cost of certain activities and resources to individual funds and therefore are not reported in the fund balance sheets	2,220,000
Long-term liabilities are reported in the Statement of Net Assets but they are not due and payable in the current period and therefore are not reported as liabilities of fund balance sheets	(78,000,000)
Net Assets of Governmental Activities	$133,692,000

(A) Combining statements for nonmajor funds may be presented as supplementary information but there is no requirement to do so, unless the PCU elect to prepare a CAFR.

EXHIBIT 21-7

STATEMENT OF REVENUES, EXPENDITURES, AND CHANGES IN FUND BALANCES

Centerville Community College
Statement of Revenues, Expenditures, and Changes in Fund Balances
Governmental Funds
June 30, 20X5

	General Fund	*Grants and Contracts Funds*	*Multi-Purpose State Improvement Bonds*	*Other Governmental Funds (A)*	*Total Governmental Funds*
REVENUES					
Tuition and fees	$ 2,400,000			$ 8,260,000	$ 10,660,000
Property taxes	33,530,000			3,426,000	36,956,000
State appropriations	16,115,000	$ 4,845,000		995,000	21,955,000
Grants and receipts from other governments	223,000			749,000	972,000
Investment income	1,500,000	309,000	$ 483,000	330,000	2,622,000
Other	2,560,000			901,000	3,461,000
Total Revenues	56,328,000	5,154,000	483,000	14,661,000	76,626,000
EXPENDITURES					
Current operating:					
Instruction	4,830,000			885,000	5,715,000
Academic support	20,850,000			2,631,000	23,481,000
Student activities	6,525,000			879,000	7,404,000
Administrative	1,941,000	897,000		726,000	3,564,000
Institutional support	8,526,000			444,000	8,970,000
Maintenance and other	19,500,000				19,500,000
Debt service:					
Principal				10,500,000	10,500,000
Interest				3,255,000	3,255,000
Capital Expenditures			12,750,000		12,750,000
Total Expenditures	62,172,000	897,000	12,750,000	19,320,000	95,139,000

Excess (deficiency) of revenues over expenditures	(5,844,000)	4,257,000	(12,267,000)	(4,659,000)	(18,513,000)
OTHER FINANCING SOURCES (USES)					
Proceeds from issuance of long-term debt			13,500,000	3,600,000	17,100,000
Transfers in	135,000			2,010,000	2,145,000
Transfers out	(1,641,000)	(345,000)		(99,000)	(2,085,000)
Total Other Financing Sources and Uses	(1,506,000)	(345,000)	13,500,000	5,511,000	17,160,000
SPECIAL ITEMS					
Proceeds from sale of real estate	5,670,000				5,670,000
Net Change In Fund Balances	(1,680,000)	3,912,000	1,233,000	852,000	4,317,000
Fund Balances—Beginning	24,975,000	7,758,000	9,972,000	19,083,000	61,788,000
Fund Balances—Ending	$ 23,295,000	$ 11,670,000	$ 11,205,000	$ 19,935,000	$ 66,105,000

Net Change in Fund Balances (As Presented In This Statement)	$ 4,317,000
Amounts presented for governmental activities in the Statement of Activities are different because:	
Governmental funds report capital investments as expenditures while the Statement of Activities reports depreciation expense on capital assets. This is the difference between the two amounts for this year.	3,090,000
Revenues in the Statement of Activities that do not provide current financial resources are not reported as revenues in governmental funds.	141,000
Some expenses reported in the Statement of Activities do not require the use of current financial resources and therefore are not reported as expenditures in governmental funds.	(369,000)
Proceeds from the issuance of long-term debt are reported as providing current financial resources in governmental funds but are reported as long-term debt in the government-wide financial statements and repayments of such debt is reported as an expenditure for governmental funds but is reported as a reduction of debt in government-wide financial statements.	(6,600,000)
In the Statement of Activities only the gain on the sale of real estate is reported while in the governmental funds the proceeds from the sale increase current financial resources.	7,032,000
Activities of Internal Service Funds are reported as net revenue (expense) are reported in the governmental activities.	(219,000)
Change in Net Assets of Governmental Activities as Reported on the Statement of Activities.	$ 7,392,000

EXHIBIT 21-8
STATEMENT OF NET ASSETS: PROPRIETARY FUNDS

Centerville Community College
Statement of Net Assets Proprietary Funds
June 30, 20X5

	Enterprise Funds			*Governmental Activities—Internal Service (See Note X)*
	Bookstore	*Food Services*	*Totals*	
ASSETS				
Current Assets:				
Cash	$600,000	$1,550,000	$2,150,000	$1,290,000
Property taxes and other receivables (net)	1,050,000	5,554,500	6,604,500	3,627,000
Investments	650,000	600,000	1,250,000	105,000
Inventories and prepayments	22,500	339,000	361,500	324,000
Total Current Assets	2,322,500	8,043,500	10,366,000	5,346,000
Noncurrent Assets:				
Restricted cash	150,000	500,000	650,000	69,000
Capital Assets:				
Land	3,725,000		3,725,000	
Buildings	9,594,000		9,594,000	
Equipment	1,050,000	600,000	1,650,000	4,266,000
Less accumulated depreciation	(3,725,000)	(244,000)	(3,969,000)	(1,035,000)
Capital assets, net	10,644,000	356,000	11,000,000	3,231,000
Total Assets	$13,116,500	$8,899,500	$22,016,000	$8,646,000
LIABILITIES				
Current Liabilities:				
Accounts payable	$137,500	$512,500	$650,000	$1,125,000
Deferred tuition revenue	22,500	2,500	25,000	96,000
Claims and judgments	1,500	33,500	35,000	123,000
Due to other funds		56,000	56,000	
Current portion of long-term debt	60,000	115,000	175,000	
Other	10,000	105,000	115,000	54,000
Total Current Liabilities	231,500	824,500	1,056,000	1,398,000
Noncurrent Liabilities:				
Claims and judgments	100,000	550,000	650,000	126,000
Bonds, notes and loans payable	2,100,000	3,500,000	5,600,000	
Total Noncurrent Liabilities	2,200,000	4,050,000	6,250,000	126,000

Total Liabilities	$2,431,500	$4,874,500	$7,306,000	$1,524,000
NET ASSETS				
Invested in capital assets, net of related debt	$6,450,000	$1,900,000	$8,350,000	$3,231,000
Unrestricted	4,235,000	2,125,000	6,360,000	3,891,000
Total Net Assets	$ 10,685,000	$4,025,000	$14,710,000	$7,122,000

EXHIBIT 21-9
STATEMENT OF REVENUES, EXPENSES, AND CHANGES IN NET ASSETS: PROPRIETARY FUNDS

Centerville Community College
Statement of Revenues, Expenses, and
Changes in Net Assets—Proprietary Funds
For the Year Ended June 30, 20X5

	Enterprise Funds			*Governmental Activities—Internal Service (See Note X)*
	Bookstore	*Food Services*	*Totals*	
Operating Revenues:				
Charges for services	$1,950,000	$2,150,000	$4,100,000	$4,800,000
Other	45,000	7,500	52,500	960,000
Total Operating Revenues	1,995,000	2,157,500	4,152,500	5,760,000
Operating Expenses:				
Personal services	652,500	635,000	1,287,500	4,431,000
Purchase of services	200,000	29,000	229,000	666,000
Materials and supplies	112,500	56,000	168,500	366,000
Depreciation	550,000	105,000	655,000	246,000
Other	125,000	10,000	135,000	78,000
Total Operating Expenses	1,640,000	835,000	2,475,000	5,787,000
Operating Income (Loss)	355,000	1,322,500	1,677,500	(27,000)
Nonoperating Revenues (Expenses)				
Interest and investment income	70,000	35,000	105,000	12,000

	Enterprise Funds			*Governmental Activities—Internal Service (See Note X)*
	Bookstore	*Food Services*	*Totals*	
Interest Expense	(100,000)	(200,000)	(300,000)	(6,000)
Miscellaneous Expenses	(10,000)	(15,000)	(25,000)	(15,000)
Total Nonoperating Revenue (Expenses)	(40,000)	(180,000)	(220,000)	(9,000)
Net Income (Loss) Before Contributions and Transfers	315,000	1,142,500	1,457,500	(36,000)
Capital contributions	65,000		65,000	138,000
Transfers out	(62,500)		(62,500)	(321,000)
Change in net assets	317,500	1,142,500	1,460,000	(219,000)
Net assets—beginning	10,367,500	2,882,500	13,250,000	7,341,000
Net assets—ending	$10,685,000	$4,025,000	$14,710,000	$7,122,000

Exhibit 21-10 is an illustration of a Statement of Cash Flows for a PCU's proprietary funds consistent with the standards established by GASB-34.

Budgetary Comparison Schedules

A PCU that has governmental activities must prepare budgetary comparison schedules for its General Fund and each major Special Revenue Fund that has a legally adopted annual budget. These schedules should be reported as RSI and include the following columns:

- The original budget
- The final appropriated budget
- Actual results (presented on the PCU's budgetary basis as defined in NCGA-1, paragraph 154)

REPORTING ONLY GOVERNMENTAL ACTIVITIES

A PCU involved only in governmental activities should present both institutional-wide and fund financial statements (for governmental activities) and therefore must observe essentially all of the standards established in paragraphs 8–131 of GASB-34 (as illustrated in the previous section).

EXHIBIT 21-10
STATEMENT OF CASH FLOWS: PROPRIETARY FUNDS

Centerville Community College
Statement of Cash Flows
For the Year Ended June 30, 20X5

	Enterprise Funds			*Governmental Activities—Internal Service (See Note X)*
	Bookstore	*Food Services*	*Totals*	
Cash Flows from Operating Activities:				
Receipts from customers	$1,700,000	$2,225,000	$3,925,000	$5,730,000
Payments to suppliers	(304,500)	(81,000)	(385,500)	(1,041,000)
Payments to employees	(655,000)	(622,500)	(1,277,500)	(4,260,000)
Other receipts (payments)	(98,500)	(9,000)	(107,500)	(51,000)
Net Cash Provided (Used) By Operating Activities	642,000	1,512,500	2,154,500	378,000
Cash Flows from Noncapital Financing Activities:				
Operating grants/transfers	(62,500)		(62,500)	(321,000)
Cash Flows from Capital and Related Financing Activities:				
Proceeds from issuance of debt	750,000	425,000	1,175,000	
Capital contributions	65,000		65,000	138,000
Purchases of capital assets	(675,000)	(400,000)	(1,075,000)	(255,000)
Principal paid on capital debt	(600,000)	(450,000)	(1,050,000)	
Interest paid on debt	(105,000)	(190,000)	(295,000)	(6,000)
Other receipts (payments)	(20,000)	(11,000)	(31,000)	
Net Cash Provided (Used) By Capital and Related Financing Activities:	(585,000)	(626,000)	(1,211,000)	(123,000)
Cash Flows from Investing Activities:				
Proceeds from sales and maturities of investments	110,000	67,500	177,500	102,000
Interest and dividends	20,000	12,500	32,500	6,000
Net Cash Provided (Used) By Investing Activities	130,000	80,000	210,000	108,000

	Enterprise Funds			Governmental Activities—Internal Service (See Note X)
	Bookstore	Food Services	Totals	
Net Increase (Decrease) in Cash and Cash Equivalents	124,500	966,500	1,091,000	42,000
Balances—beginning of the year	1,251,000	2,167,000	3,418,000	439,000
Balances—end of the year	$1,375,500	$3,133,500	$4,509,000	$481,000
Reconciliation of Operating Income (Loss) to Net Cash Provided (Used) by Operating Activities				
Operating income (loss)	$355,000	$1,322,500	$1,677,500	($27,000)
Adjustments to reconcile operating income to net cash provided (used) by operating activities:				
Depreciation expenses	550,000	105,000	655,000	246,000
Changes in net assets and liabilities:				
Receivables, net	(210,000)	102,500	(107,500)	(39,000)
Inventories	(62,500)	(16,500)	(79,000)	126,000
Accounts payable	5,000	(14,500)	(9,500)	24,000
Other	4,500	13,500	18,000	48,000
Net Cash Provided by Operating Activities	$642,000	$1,512,500	$2,154,500	$378,000

If a PCU is engaged in only a single governmental program, the PCU can combine the institutional-wide and fund financial statements by using a columnar format that reconciles individual line items of the institutional-wide data to the fund financial data. A description of the reconciling items may be presented on the face of the financial statements, in a note, or in an accompanying schedule. Rather than placing the institutional-wide and fund financial statements on the same page, the PCU can present separate institutional-wide and fund financial statements, but under this approach GASB-34 allows a PCU to use an alternative format for the statement of activities. The alternative format (single-column presentation) described in GASB-34 is presented as follows:

Expenses	$ XXX
Revenues (by major source)	XXX
Net revenue (expense)	XXX
Contributions to permanent and term endowments	XXX
Special and extraordinary items	XXX
Transfer	XXX
Net change in net assets	XXX
Net assets—beginning	XXX
Net assets—ending	$ XXX

PRACTICE POINT: A PCU is not considered a single-program entity as described in the previous paragraph if it "budgets, manages, or accounts for its activities as multiple programs." For example, a PCU in general has a single purpose (education), but it is likely that it has multiple programs.

COMPONENT UNITS

Reporting Component Units

GASB-34 was written in a manner that satisfies the financial reporting entity standards originally established by GASB-14 with respect to component units. Relevant guidance established by GASB-14 in this regard is as follows:

> The financial statements of the reporting entity should allow users to distinguish between the primary government and its component units by communicating information about the component units and their relationships with the primary government rather than creating the perception that the primary government and all of its component units are one legal entity. To accomplish this goal, *the reporting entity's financial statements should present the fund types* and account groups *of the primary government (including its blended component units, which are, in substance, part of the primary government) and provide an overview of the discretely presented component units* (GASB-14, par. 11). *Financial statements of the reporting entity should provide an overview of the entity based on financial accountability, yet allow users to distinguish between the primary government and its component units* (GASB-14, par. 42). (emphasis added)

NOTE: GASB-34 amends GASB-14 in order to eliminate the reference to account groups.

This general guidance established by GASB-14 is incorporated in GASB-35 and therefore applies to PCUs. The financial reporting concepts expressed in GASB-14 are accomplished by the display of discretely presented component units in the institutional-wide financial statements. Blended component units will continue to be folded into the financial statements of the primary institution as required by GASB-14, paragraphs 52–54.

In addition, GASB-14, paragraph 51, requires that information related to each major component unit be presented in the reporting entity's basic financial statements. To satisfy this standard, any one of the following approaches can be done:

- Present each major component unit in a separate column in the basic financial statements
- Present combining statements of the major component units (separate columns) and a single column for all nonmajor component units
- Present condensed financial statements in a note to the financial statements

> **PRACTICE POINT:** The requirement for major component unit information does not apply to component units that are fiduciary in nature.

> **PRACTICE POINT:** If the combining statement method is used, the totals in the combining statements should be consistent with the information presented in the component unit column in the institution-wide financial statements. Also, if this approach is used, a combining statement for nonmajor component units may be presented as supplementary information (but this is not a requirement).

If the note disclosure method is used, the following disclosures must be made:

- Condensed statement of net assets
  - — Total assets, distinguishing between capital assets and other assets (Amounts receivable from the primary institution or from other component units of the same reporting entity should be reported separately.)
  - — Total liabilities, distinguishing between long-term debt outstanding and other liabilities (Amounts payable to the primary institution or to other component units of the same reporting entity should be reported separately.)
  - — Total net assets, distinguishing between restricted, unrestricted, and amounts invested in capital assets, net of related debt
- Condensed statement of revenues, expenses, and changes in fund net assets

— Expenses, with separate identification of depreciation expense and amortization of long-lived assets
— Other nontax general revenues
— Contributions to endowments and permanent fund principal
— Extraordinary and special items
— Change in net assets
— Beginning and ending net assets

The notes to the financial statements should also describe the nature and amount of significant transactions between major component units and the primary government and other component units.

Exhibits 21-1 through 21-3 illustrate a component unit (University Hospital) using a discrete presentation format. The *GASB Comprehensive Implementation Guide* raises the issue of whether component units' financial information that is presented in combining financial statements (the second reporting approach) or notes to the financial statements (the third reporting approach) must be presented on a PCU's basic financial statements. If the second or third reporting approach is used, the PCU must nonetheless report all of its PCUs in a single column in the basic financial statements.

PRACTICE POINT: The requirement for major component unit information does not apply to component units that are fiduciary in nature.

Nongovernmental Component Units

The *GASB Comprehensive Implementation Guide* raises the issue of how a PCU should report a component unit's financial statements for a component unit that uses a nongovernmental GAAP reporting model. Based on the guidance established by GASB-39 (Determining Whether Certain Organizations Are Component Units), many organizations classified as component units under GASB-39 are expected to be organizations that prepare their financial statements based on the not-for-profit reporting model described in FAS-117 (Financial Statements of Not-for-Profit Organizations). This not-for-profit reporting model is not the same as the reporting model used by primary governments to prepare their government-wide financial statements. Although both models are based on accrual accounting concepts (component units are presented only in the government-wide financial statements), there are differences. GASB-39 states that these reporting model incompatibilities can be addressed in the following ways:

- Present the not-for-profit organization's financial statements separately from the primary government's statement of net assets and statement of activities

- Directly integrate the not-for-profit organization's financial statements into the primary government's statement of net assets and statement of activities

If the primary government decides that the accounting and reporting model for a not-for-profit organization is too dissimilar from the governmental accounting and reporting model, the not-for-profit organization's financial statements should be presented separately from the primary government's government-wide financial statements. This alternative is supported by the Chapter 4 of the *GASB Comprehensive Implementation Guide* in its discussion of the financial reporting entity, which states the following:

> Any noncompatible or additional statements required by the component unit's reporting model would not be *integrated into the reporting entity's government-wide financial statements,* but instead would be presented as separate statements in the *general purpose external financial statements.* (The language in italics has been changed to conform to language consistent with the GASB-34 reporting model.)

Under this approach, the (not-for-profit) component unit's financial statements would not be presented in the primary government's statement of net assets or statement of activities, but rather would be presented immediately after those financial statements using the accounting standards and reporting format for a not-for-profit organization.

GASB-39 points out that the primary government might decide that the financial statements of the (not-for-profit) component unit are not "completely incompatible" with the governmental financial reporting model. Under this circumstance, the component unit's financial statements could be "reconfigured to allow for a side-by-side columnar presentation" with the primary government.

OTHER MEASUREMENT AND REPORTING ISSUES

Eliminations and Reclassifications in Institutional-Wide Financial Statements

A PCU may use a variety of funds to account for transactions during an accounting period. The preparation of institution-wide financial statements is based on a consolidating process (similar to corporate consolidations) rather than a combining process, whereby the PCU is reported as a single operating entity. These eliminations and reclassifications related to the consolidation process are based on (1) internal balances (statement of net assets), (2) internal activities (operating statement), and (3) intra-entity activity.

Internal balances (statement of net assets) The institution-wide financial statements present the primary institution and its blended component units, if any, as a single reporting entity. Based on this philosophy, most balances between funds that are initially recorded as interfund receivables and payables at the individual fund level should be eliminated when preparing the statement of net assets. The balances are eliminated to avoid the "grossing-up" effect on assets and liabilities presented on the statement of net assets. For example, if there is an interfund receivable/payable between two proprietary funds of the primary institution, those amounts would be eliminated.

There also may be interfund receivables/payables that arise because of transactions between the primary institution and its fiduciary funds. These amounts should not be eliminated but rather should be reported on the statement of net assets as receivables from and payables to external parties.

Internal activities (operating statement) In order to avoid the "doubling-up" effect of internal activities among funds, interfund transactions should be eliminated so that expenses and revenues are recorded only once. For example, a fund may charge other funds for services provided (such as insurance coverage and allocation of overhead expenses) on an internal basis. When these funds are consolidated in order to present the operating expenses of institutional activities, the double counting of the expense (with an offset to revenue recorded by the provider fund) should be eliminated in a manner so that "the allocated expenses are reported only by the function to which they were allocated."

Interfund activities between a PCU and its auxiliary enterprises The reporting of interfund activities between a PCU and its auxiliary enterprises is dependent upon which reporting model is used by the PCU. A PCU that is engaged in both business-type and governmental activities essentially must follow all of the standards established by GASB-34. The *GASB Comprehensive Implementation Guide* notes that, under this reporting model, interfund activities between the PCU and its auxiliary enterprises should be accounted for based on the guidance established by paragraphs 59, 60, and 112. Paragraph 59 requires that the doubling-up effect of Internal Service Fund activities and similar internal events be eliminated in the institution-wide financial statements. However, paragraph 60 requires that transactions based on "interfund services provided and used" between functions not be eliminated. Paragraph 112 provides guidance for reporting (1) interfund loans, (2) interfund services provided and used, (3) interfund transfers, and (4) interfund reimbursements in the proprietary funds.

The *GASB Comprehensive Implementation Guide* notes that a PCU that is engaged in only business-type activities and reports as single-column business-type activity should eliminate internal transactions between the PCU and its auxiliary enterprises.

Intra-entity activity Transactions (and related balances) between the primary institution and its discretely presented component units should not be eliminated in the institutional-wide perspective financial statements. That is, the two parties to the transactions should report revenue and expense accounts as originally recorded in those respective funds. Amounts payable and receivable between the primary government and its discretely presented component units should be reported as separate line items on the statement of net assets. Likewise payables and receivables between discretely presented component units must also be reported separately.

Pell Grants

GASB-24 (Accounting and Financial Reporting for Certain Grants and Other Financial Assistance) establishes standards for pass-through grants, which includes Pell Grants. In addition, GASB-19 (Governmental College and University Omnibus Statement) required Pell Grants to be accounted for as restricted current fund revenues. GASB-35 supersedes GASB-19, and the *GASB Comprehensive Implementation Guide* raises the question of whether Pell Grants can be reported in an Agency Fund.

GASB-24 describes pass-through grants as "grants and other financial assistance received by a governmental entity to transfer to or spend on behalf of a secondary recipient." GASB-24 requires that cash pass-through grants generally be recorded simultaneously as revenue and expenditures or expenses in a governmental fund or proprietary fund. Only in those instances when the recipient government functions as a cash conduit should a pass-through grant be accounted for in an Agency Fund. The GASB describes cash conduit activity as transmitting grantor-supplied moneys "without having administrative or direct financial involvement in the program."

Administrative involvement is based on whether the recipient government's role in the grant program constitutes an operational responsibility for the grant program, such as the following:

- Monitoring secondary recipients for compliance with specific requirements established by the program
- Determining which secondary recipients are eligible for grant payments (even if eligibility criteria are established by the provider government)
- Exercising some discretion in determining how resources are to be allocated

The *GASB Comprehensive Implementation Guide* states that because of the administrative involvement under the current Pell Grant program, "public institutions should record Pell Grant receipts as revenue in their financial statements, and any amounts applied to student receivable accounts should be recorded as scholarship discounts or allowances."

Split-Interest Agreements

A PCU may receive a gift from a donor structured as a split-interest agreement, whereby the PCU acts as the trustee. Generally, a split-interest agreement takes one of two forms: (1) an annuity trust or (2) a unitrust. Under an annuity trust, the donor receives an annual fixed payment during the period covered by the trust agreement. Under a unitrust, the donor receives an annual payment based on a specified percentage of the fair value of the market value of the trust's assets. The *GASB Comprehensive Implementation Guide* raises the issue of how split-interest agreements should be reported in a PCU's financial statements.

At the date the assets are received under the trust agreement, the PCU records the assets based on their fair value, and an estimated liability is recorded based on the present value of the distributions expected to be made to the donor or other beneficiary. The difference is recorded as gift revenue. For example, the following entry would be made by a PCU that receives trust assets (securities) with a market value of $1,000,000 whereby the beneficiary's interest in those assets is estimated to be $700,000:

Accounts	*Debit*	*Credit*
Investments in Marketable Securities	1,000,000	
Obligation to Beneficiaries under Trust Agreements		700,000
Gift Revenue		300,000

As payments to beneficiaries are made on an annual basis the beneficiary obligation is reduced; however, during the term of trust agreement the obligation may be changed based on other conditions such as changes in the actuarial assumptions made to initially record the donor transaction. These changes should be reported in the PCU's statement of revenues, expenses, and changes in net assets or the statement of activities, depending upon the reporting model used by the PCU. For example, if the market securities are investments in bonds and the market value of the investment is greater than the carrying value, the difference is recorded as investment income.

The trust agreement terminates after a specified number of years or at the death of the beneficiary, at which point the beneficiary obligation is removed and any balance is reflected in the PCU's operating statement. For example, if a beneficiary dies prematurely, when the carrying amount of the beneficiary obligation is $250,000, the following entry is made:

Accounts	*Debit*	*Credit*
Obligation to Beneficiaries under Trust Agreements	250,000	
Miscellaneous Revenue		250,000

Investment Income Restricted to Permanent or Term Endowments

One of the classifications established by GASB-34 (and therefore incorporated into GASB-35) was "additions to permanent and term endowments." When a PCU receives contributions to its term and permanent endowments or to permanent fund principal, those contributions should be reported as separate items in the lower portion of the statement of activities or statement of revenues, expenses, and changes in fund net assets (depending upon which reporting model is used by the PCU). These receipts are not considered to be program revenues (such as program-specific grants) because, in the case of term endowments, there is an uncertainty of the timing of the release of the resources from the term restriction and, in the case of permanent contributions the principal can never be expended.

The question arises as to whether investment income that is restricted to permanent or term endowments could be reported as additions to permanent and term endowments. The *GASB Comprehensive Implementation Guide* states that investment income of this nature should not be reported as additions to permanent and term endowments. If the PCU reports as a special-purpose governmental entity and reports only business-type activities (Enterprise Fund Model), investment income restricted to permanent or term endowments should be reported as nonoperating revenue. If the PCU reports governmental activities and therefore prepares a statement of activities, the income should be reported as general revenues in the lower portion of the financial statement.

Accrual of Tuition and Fees Revenue

PCUs often receive revenues for tuition and fees in one year for services that must be delivered across more than one fiscal year. The *GASB Comprehensive Implementation Guide* states that tuition and fees should be reported as revenue in the period they are earned.

CHAPTER 22
PENSION AND OTHER POSTEMPLOYMENT BENEFIT PLANS

CONTENTS

INTRODUCTION

State and local governments often administer and/or account for pension and other employee benefit plans and report such plans in stand-alone special-purpose reports or as fiduciary funds within the financial statements of the sponsoring government. The employee benefit plans addressed in this chapter are follows:

- Public employee retirement systems
- IRC 457 deferred compensation plans
- Postemployment benefit plans other than pensions

PUBLIC EMPLOYEE RETIREMENT SYSTEMS

GASB-25 notes that a PERS is a separate legal entity that administers a public employee pension plan(s). However, the Statement emphasizes that the PERS is the administrator of the plan and is not itself the plan (GASB-25, pars. 14–17).

For example, a PERS in a particular state may administer numerous defined benefit pension plans as well as defined contribution plans, deferred compensation plans, and postemployment healthcare plans.

The standards established by GASB-25 apply to a particular pension plan and not to a particular PERS. However, when a PERS presents the separate financial statements of a defined pension plan in its financial report, the standards established by GASB-25 must be observed. If the financial statements of more than one defined benefit pension plan are included in the PERS report, the standards must be applied separately to each plan. The financial statements for each plan should be presented separately in the combining financial statements of the PERS along with appropriate schedules and other disclosures required by GASB-25.

> **OBSERVATION:** GASB-25 notes that when the terms "agent multiple-employer plan" and "agent plan" are used, the requirements apply to the plan and not to individual employers that make up the multiple-employer plan. Thus, when a PERS administers an agent multiple-employer plan, the standards established by GASB-25 apply to the financial statements of the plan and not to the financial statements of each single-employer plan in the agent multiple-employer plan.

To determine whether a PERS is administering a single pension plan or two or more pension plans (thus requiring separate reporting), the custody of the assets held must be analyzed to determine whether they are (1) available to pay benefits for all of the members of the plan or (2) available to pay benefits only for certain plan members.

Assets Available to All Plan Members

If assets held by the PERS are legally available to pay benefits (including refunds of member contributions) for all of the plan members, the pension plan is a single plan, and only a single set of financial statements needs to be prepared. Plan members generally include "employees in active service, terminated employees who have accumulated benefits but are not yet receiving them, and retired employees and beneficiaries currently receiving benefits." GASB-25 notes that a plan is a sole plan even if the following circumstances exist:

- Legally or because of administrative policy, the plan must maintain separate accounts based on such factors as specified groups, specific employers, or benefits provided by the plan.
- Separate actuarial valuations are made for classes or groups of covered employees.

Assets Available Only to Certain Plan Members

If any portion of the assets held by the PERS legally can be paid only to certain classes of employees (for example, only to public safety officers) or employees of certain employers (for example, only to state governmental employees), more than one plan is being administered and separate financial statements must be prepared for each plan.

The asset availability criterion also must be applied to a governmental employer's CAFR. Separate reporting is required in the governmental employer's CAFR when more than one defined benefit pension plan is presented in the CAFR.

Defined Benefit Financial Reporting

GASB-25 states that the financial reporting objectives of a defined benefit pension plan are to provide information that helps assess (GASB-25, pars. 18–19):

1. The stewardship of plan resources and the ability of the plan to pay pension benefits as they arise

2. The financial demands on plan members, employers, and other contributors imposed by the plan
3. Compliance with financial-related pension laws, regulations, and contractual commitments

To satisfy these three objectives, GASB-25 states that the plan should present the following information (supported with appropriate notes):

- Financial Statements
  — Statement of plan net assets
  — Statement of changes in plan net assets
- Required Supplementary Information
  — Schedule of funding progress
  — Schedule of employer contributions

Statement of plan net assets The statement of plan net assets is prepared on an accrual basis and reports the plan's assets, liabilities, and net assets. For the most part, the plan's net assets are reported on a fair value basis and certain plan liabilities (but not all economic liabilities) are presented (GASB-25, pars. 20–21).

The statement of plan net assets should identify the major assets of the plan (for example, cash, receivables, investments, and operating assets), and the receivables and investments categories should be further divided into their significant components. Reported liabilities should be subtracted from total assets, and the difference reported as "net assets held in trust for pension benefits."

The example of a statement of plan net assets shown in GASB-25 is reproduced in Exhibit 22-1.

Statement of changes in plan net assets A pension plan should prepare an operating statement that reports the net increase or decrease in net plan assets from the beginning of the year until the end of the year. The statement of changes in plan net assets should be prepared on the same basis of accounting used to prepare the pension plan's statement of plan net assets. The two financial statements are inter related (in a manner similar to an income statement and a balance sheet) in that (1) the net increase as reported on the statement of changes in plan net assets, when added to (2) the beginning balance of plan net assets on the statement of plan net assets, is equal to (3) the net plan assets as reported at the end of the year on the statement of net plan assets (GASB-25, par. 28).

The statement of changes in plan net assets should present separate categories for additions and deductions in net assets for the year.

EXHIBIT 22-1
COLUMBINE RETIREMENT SYSTEM: STATEMENT OF PLAN NET ASSETS
as of June 30, 20X2, and 20X1

(Dollar amounts in thousands)

	State Employees	*School Districts*	*Municipal Employees*	*20X2 Total*	*20X1 Total*
Assets					
Cash and short-term investments	$ 66,129	$ 116,988	$ 27,014	$ 210,131	$ 440,146
Receivables					
Employer	16,451	18,501	2,958	37,910	45,770
Employer—long-term		986		986	1,088
Interest and dividends	33,495	48,299	4,951	86,745	81,183
Total receivables	49,946	67,786	7,909	125,641	128,041
Investments, at fair value					
U.S. Government obligations	541,289	780,541	80,001	1,401,831	1,571,404
Municipal bonds	33,585	48,416	4,969	86,970	86,417
Domestic corporate bonds	892,295	1,217,251	191,801	2,301,347	1,961,288
Domestic stocks	1,276,533	1,784,054	183,893	3,244,480	3,230,446
International stocks	461,350	665,269	68,187	1,194,806	1,187,703
Mortgages	149,100	209,099	24,453	382,652	319,745

Real estate	184,984	266,748	27,350	479,082	420,806
Venture capital	26,795	38,638	3,960	69,393	37,120
Total investments	3,565,931	5,010,016	584,614	9,160,561	8,814,929
Properties, at cost, net of accumulated depreciation of $5,164 and $4,430, respectively	6,351	8,924	1,040	16,315	16,093
Total assets	3,688,357	5,203,714	620,577	9,512,648	9,399,209
Liabilities					
Refunds payable and other	4,212	1,849	429	6,490	37,211
Net assets held in trust for pension benefits (A schedule of funding progress for each plan is presented on page ____.*)	$3,684,145	$5,201,865	$620,148	$9,506,158	$9,361,998

* The preparer should cite the page number of the plan's or system's report.

Additions to net assets GASB-25 requires that the additions section of the statement of changes in plan net assets include the following components (GASB-25, par. 29):

- Contributions received from employer(s)
- Contributions received from employees (including those received via the employer)
- Contributions received from those other than employer(s) and employees
- Net investment income for the year (includes the net appreciation or depreciation of the fair value of the plan assets) and investment income and other increases not reported as net appreciation or depreciation (these two components of investment income may be separately reported or reported as a single amount)
- Total investment expense (including investment fees, custodial fees, and "all other significant investment-related costs")

PRACTICE POINT: Investment income includes interest income, dividend income, income from real estate investments, realized gains and losses arising from the disposition of investments during the period, and unrealized gains and losses. Unrealized gains and losses must be recorded because fair value is the basis for measuring investments held by the pension plan. When debt securities are held by the pension plan, any related discount or premium should not be amortized as part of investment income, and interest income should be based on the stated interest rate.

GASB-25 establishes the following guidance for measuring additions to the pension plan's assets for the period:

- The net appreciation (or depreciation) of the fair value of the plan assets for the year should include realized gains and losses on investments bought and sold during the current year.
- Realized gains and losses, and unrealized gains and losses, should not be presented separately in the statement of changes in plan net assets. However, all realized gains and losses may be presented separately in a note to the financial statements (assuming that realized gains and losses are based on the difference between the sale price and the original cost of the investment).
- If realized gains and losses are separately presented in a note to the financial statements, the disclosure must state that (1) the measurement of realized gains and losses is independent of the measurement of the net appreciation (depreciation) in the fair value of plan assets and (2) investments purchased in a previous year and sold in the current year resulted in their realized gains and losses being reported in the current year and their net appreciation (depreciation) in

plan assets being reported in both the current year and the previous year(s).

- Investment-related costs need not be reported if those costs are not readily distinguishable from investment income (thus, the expense may be offset against investment income) or general administrative expenses of the plan.
- Premiums and discounts on debt securities should not be amortized as part of investment income.

Deductions from net assets Deductions on the statement of changes in plan net assets should include pension benefit payments to retirees and beneficiaries and administrative expenses. These items should not be combined but rather separately presented on the statement (GASB-25, pars. 30–31).

Deductions should not include payments made by an insurance company based on allocated insurance contracts, but the original acquisition of allocated insurance contracts should be reported as benefits paid. The amount paid for such contracts may be reported net of any income earned on the excluded contract for the year.

Administrative expenses, such as depreciation expense and operating expenses, should be measured using accrual accounting.

> **PRACTICE POINT:** While administrative expenses are reported on an accrual basis, pension benefits paid are based on actual payments made and the accrual for benefits that satisfy the concept of due and payable.

The example of a statement of changes in plan net assets shown in GASB-25 is reproduced in Exhibit 22-2.

Notes to the financial statements GASB-25 requires that the following be disclosed by a defined benefit pension plan when the plan's financial statements are presented in a stand-alone financial report or when those financial statements are presented only in an employer financial report (GASB-25, par. 32):

Plan Description

- Type of pension plan (single-employer, agent multiple-employer, or cost-sharing multiple-employer)*
- Number of governmental employers participating in the plan and other entities contributing to the plan*

---

* Only these items need to be disclosed in a governmental employer's financial statements when the pension plan is presented as part of the employer's financial report and (1) the pension plan also separately presents its financial statements (which include all disclosures established by GASB-25) in a stand-alone financial report and (2) the governmental employer states in its financial statements how the stand-alone financial statements may be obtained.

EXHIBIT 22-2
COLUMBINE RETIREMENT SYSTEM: STATEMENTS OF CHANGES IN PLAN NET ASSETS
for the Years Ended June 30, 20X2, and 20X1

(Dollar amounts in thousands)

	State Employees	*School Districts*	*Municipal Employees*	*20X2 Total*	*20X1 Total*
Additions					
Contributions					
Employer	$ 137,916	$ 157,783	$ 19,199	$ 314,898	$ 284,568
Employer—long-term		102		102	102
Plan member	90,971	117,852	16,828	225,651	216,106
Total contributions	228,887	275,737	36,027	540,651	500,776
Investment income					
Net appreciation (depreciation) in fair value of investments	(241,408)	(344,429)	(35,280)	(621,117)	788,913
Interest	157,371	225,446	23,098	405,915	422,644
Dividends	123,953	177,654	18,191	319,798	560,848
Real estate operating income, net	10,733	15,383	1,575	27,691	25,296
	50,649	74,054	7,584	132,287	1,797,701
Less investment expense	54,081	61,872	7,529	123,482	500,674

Net investment income	(3,432)	12,182	55	8,805	1,297,027
Total additions	225,455	287,919	36,082	549,456	1,797,803
Deductions					
Benefits	170,434	172,787	18,073	361,294	325,881
Refunds of contributions	15,750	13,200	3,671	32,621	38,406
Administrative expense	4,984	5,703	694	11,381	12,681
Total deductions	191,168	191,690	22,438	405,296	376,968
Net increase	34,287	96,229	13,644	144,160	1,420,835
Net assets held in trust for pension benefits					
Beginning of year	3,649,858	5,105,636	606,504	9,361,998	7,941,163
End of year	$3,684,145	$ 5,201,865	$ 620,148	$ 9,506,158	$ 9,361,998

- Type of governmental employees covered by the plan and their plan status (such as active members, retirees and beneficiaries receiving benefits, and terminated employees not yet receiving benefits) (When the plan is closed to new entrants, that fact should be disclosed.)
- Description of plan provisions [such as types of benefits provided and policies concerning cost-of-living adjustments (automatic or discretionary)]
- Authority under which benefits are provided or may be amended

Summary of Significant Accounting Policies

- Basis of accounting (accounting methods used to recognize contributions, benefits, and refunds and depreciation methods related to administrative assets)*
- Methods used to determine the fair value of plan investments*

Contributions and Reserves

- Authority under which pension plan funding sources are established and may be amended
- Funding policies (including description of how required payments by various contributors are determined, the authority under which those payments are established, and the manner in which administrative costs are funded)
- Required contribution rate for active plan members
- Description of long-term commitments for contributions to the plan and related amounts outstanding as of the reporting date*
- Balances reported as legally required reserves at the reporting dates, their purposes, and whether they are fully funded (Balances reported as "designations," as defined in NCGA-1, also may be reported but should not be reported as reserves.)

Concentration of Credit Risk

- Identification, by amount and issuer, of investments in any one issuer that represent 5% or more of plan net assets. (Investments issued or explicitly guaranteed by the U.S. government and investments in mutual funds, external investment pools, and other pooled investments are excluded from this requirement.)*

---

* Only these items need to be disclosed in a governmental employer's financial statements when the pension plan is presented as part of the employer's financial report and (1) the pension plan also separately presents its financial statements (which include all disclosures established by GASB-25) in a stand-alone financial report and (2) the governmental employer states in its financial statements how the stand-alone financial statements may be obtained.

Exhibit 22-3 contains note disclosures as shown in GASB-25.

EXHIBIT 22-3
COLUMBINE RETIREMENT SYSTEM:
NOTES TO THE FINANCIAL STATEMENTS
for the Fiscal Year Ended June 30, 20X2

The Columbine Retirement System (CRS) administers three defined benefit pension plans—State Employees Pension Plan (SEPP), School District Employees Pension Plan (SDEPP), and Municipal Employees Pension Plan (MEPP). Although the assets of the plans are commingled for investment purposes, each plan's assets may be used only for the payment of benefits to the members of that plan, in accordance with the terms of the plan.

A. Summary of Significant Accounting Policies

Basis of Accounting. CRS's financial statements are prepared using the accrual basis of accounting. Plan member contributions are recognized in the period in which the contributions are due. Employer contributions to each plan are recognized when due and the employer has made a formal commitment to provide the contributions. Benefits and refunds are recognized when due and payable in accordance with the terms of each plan.

Method Used to Value Investments. Investments are reported at fair value. Short-term investments are reported at cost, which approximates fair value. Securities traded on a national or international exchange are valued at the last reported sales price at current exchange rates. Mortgages are valued on the basis of future principal and interest payments, and are discounted at prevailing interest rates for similar instruments. The fair value of real estate investments is based on independent appraisals. Investments that do not have an established market are reported at estimated fair value.

B. Plan Descriptions and Contribution Information

Membership of each plan consisted of the following at December 31, 20X1, the date of the latest actuarial valuation:

	SEPP	*SDEPP*	*MEPP*
Retirees and beneficiaries receiving benefits	15,274	17,337	1,857
Terminated plan members entitled to but not yet receiving benefits	1,328	1,508	162
Active plan members	38,292	61,004	3,481
Total	54,894	79,849	5,500
Number of participating employers	1	203	53

State Employees Pension Plan

Plan Description. SEPP is a single-employer defined benefit pension plan that covers the employees of the State including all departments and agencies. SEPP provides retirement, disability, and death benefits to plan members and their beneficiaries. Cost-of-living adjustments (COLA) are provided at the discretion of the State legislature. Article 29 of the Regulations of the State of Columbine assigns the authority to establish and amend the benefit provisions of the plan to the State legislature.

Contributions. Plan members are required to contribute 7.8% of their annual covered salary. The State is required to contribute at an actuarially determined rate. Per Article 29, contribution requirements of the plan members and the State are established and may be amended by the State legislature. Administrative costs of SEPP are financed through investment earnings.

School District Employees Pension Plan

Plan Description. SDEPP is a cost-sharing multiple-employer defined benefit pension plan that covers teaching-certified employees of participating school districts. SDEPP provides retirement, disability, and death benefits to plan members as well as an annual COLA. Article 30 of the Regulations of the State of Columbine assigns the authority to establish and amend benefit provisions to the SDEPP Board of Trustees.

Contributions. Plan members are required to contribute 7.6% of their annual covered salary. Participating school districts are required to contribute at actuarially determined rates. Per Article 30, contribution requirements of the plan members and the participating employers are established and may be amended by the SDEPP Board of Trustees. Administrative costs of SDEPP are financed through investment earnings and an assessment of 0.18% of covered payroll for each participating school district.

Long-Term Receivables. In addition to actuarially determined contributions, certain employers also make semi-annual installment payments, including interest at 8% per year, for the cost of service credit granted retroactively to employees when the employers initially joined SDEPP. As of June 30, 20X2 and 20X1, the outstanding balances were $986 and $1,088, respectively. These payments are due over various time periods not exceeding ten years at June 30, 20X2, and 11 years at June 30, 20X1.

Municipal Employees Pension Plan

Plan Description. MEPP is an agent multiple-employer defined benefit pension plan that covers general and public safety employees of political subdivisions of the State of Columbine that have elected to participate in

MEPP. Benefit provisions are established by each participating employer when the employer elects to participate in MEPP. Benefit provisions may be amended by the individual participating employers. MEPP provides retirement, disability, and death benefits to plan members and beneficiaries. An annual COLA is provided to benefit recipients of employers that contract for this option. At December 31, 20X1, the date of the most recent actuarial valuation, there were 53 participating employers consisting of:

Cities	16
Townships	15
Counties	10
Special Districts	12
Total	53

Contributions. Contribution rates for each participating employer and its covered employees are established and may be amended by the MEPP Board of Trustees. The contribution rates are determined based on the benefit structure established by each employer. Plan members are required to contribute between 4 and 12% of their annual covered salary. Participating employers are required to contribute the remaining amounts necessary to finance the coverage of their employees through periodic contributions at actuarially determined rates. Administrative costs of MEPP are financed through investment earnings and an assessment of $20 per participating active plan member per year.

Note: In this illustration, there are no legally required reserve accounts, no investment concentrations, and no differences between required and actual contributions.

NOTE: These disclosure requirements relate to defined pension benefit plans. Pension expenditures/expense disclosures are established in GASB-27, as discussed in Chapter 13, "Pension, Postemployment, and Other Employee Benefit Liabilities."

PRACTICE ALERT: GASB-50, issued in May 2007, brings current government pension disclosure requirements in line with the disclosures recently required for other postemployment benefits (OPEB). GASB-50 amends the disclosure requirements of GASB-25 and GASB-27 by requiring the following:

- Disclosure of the current funded status of the plan (the degree to which the actuarial accrued liabilities for benefits are covered by assets that have been set aside to pay for such benefits) as of the most recent actuarial valuation date in the notes to the financial statements of pension plans and certain employer governments to be presented in addition to funded status data currently presented as required supplementary information (RSI).

- Disclosure by governments that use the aggregate actuarial cost method of the funded status and present a multiyear schedule of funding progress using the entry age actuarial cost method as a surrogate; these governments currently are not required to provide this information.
- Disclosure by governments participating in multi-employer cost-sharing pension plans of how the contractually required contribution rate is determined.
- Presentation by governments in cost-sharing plans of the required schedule of funding progress if the plan does not issue a GAAP-compliant report that includes the funding progress RSI schedules or if the plan is not included in a publicly available financial report of another entity.

GASB-50 is generally effective for periods beginning after June 15, 2007, with early implementation encouraged.

Required supplementary information Except as noted in the following paragraph, GASB-25 requires that a schedule of funding progress, a schedule of employer contributions, and notes to support the two schedules be presented in the financial statements of a defined benefit pension plan. This required supplementary information should be presented immediately after the notes to the financial statements (GASB-25, pars. 33–34).

OBSERVATION: When a pension plan uses the aggregate cost method, GASB-25 requires that only a schedule of employer contributions be presented. However, the plan must disclose the fact that the aggregate cost method is used.

Required supplementary information is not required when the financial statements of a cost-sharing plan or an agent plan are included in the governmental employer's financial report if both of the following conditions are satisfied:

1. The pension plan also separately presents its financial statements (which include the required supplementary information) in a publicly available, stand-alone financial report.

2. The governmental employer states in a note to its financial statements how the stand-alone financial statements may be obtained.

When the financial statements of a single-employer pension plan are included in the governmental employer's financial report, that financial report should include only the schedule of funding progress for the three most recent actuarial valuations; the schedule of employer contributions should not be presented. Also, the employer government should disclose the availability of the standalone pension plan report.

When a pension plan's financial statements are not publicly available in a stand-alone financial report, the governmental employer's financial report should include both the schedule of funding progress and the schedule of employer contributions for all years required by the standards established by GASB-25.

Alternative reporting format GASB-25 states that some or all of the required supplementary information may be presented in either of, or in a combination of, the following two alternative formats:

1. A separate financial statement(s) (statement of funding progress and/or a statement of employer contributions)
2. A note to the financial statements

When an alternative format is used, the information must be presented for, at a minimum, the most recent year (latest actuarial valuation date). If all of the required information is not presented either in a separate financial statement or in a note, all of the required information must also be presented as required supplementary information.

> **PRACTICE POINT:** GASB-27 establishes the required supplementary information for pension expenditures/expense that must be disclosed in an employer's financial statements. (See Chapter 13, "Pension, Postemployment, and Other Employee Benefit Liabilities.")

Schedule of funding progress The schedule of funding progress should contain the following information for at least the preceding six years (GASB-25, par. 37):

- Actuarial valuation date
- Actuarial value of plan assets
- Actuarial accrued liability
- Total unfunded actuarial liability

- Actuarial value of assets as a percentage of the actuarial accrued liability (funded ratio)
- Annual covered payroll (all elements included in compensation paid to active employees on which contributions to the pension plan are based)
- Ratio of unfunded actuarial liability to annual covered payroll

The actuarial information should be presented as of the actuarial valuation date and should be measured in accordance with the standards established by GASB-25. However, pension plans that obtain biennial valuations do not have to repeat duplicate information.

> **PRACTICE POINT:** When a funding excess exists, the ratios should be computed in the same manner as when a funding deficiency exists.

The example of a schedule of funding progress shown in GASB-25 is reproduced in Exhibit 22-4.

Schedule of employer contributions The schedule of employer contributions should contain the following information for at least the past six years (GASB-25, pars. 38–39):

- Dollar amount of annual required contributions (ARC) of the employer(s)
- Percentage of ARC recognized as an employer contribution in the pension plan's statement of changes in plan net assets
- Dollar amount of required contributions (if any) from other than employers and plan members

EXHIBIT 22-4
REQUIRED SUPPLEMENTARY INFORMATION: SCHEDULES OF FUNDING PROGRESS

(Dollar amounts in thousands)

Actuarial Valuation Date	*Actuarial Value of Assets (a)*	*Actuarial Accrued Liability (AAL) —Entry Age (b)*	*Unfunded AAL (UAAL) (b – a)*	*Funded Ratio (a/b)*	*Covered Payroll (c)*	*UAAL as a Percentage of Covered Payroll [(b – a)/c]*
SEPP						
12/31/W6	$ 2,005,238	$ 2,626,296	$ 621,058	76.4%	$ 901,566	68.9%
12/31/W7	2,411,610	2,902,399	490,789	83.1	956,525	51.3
12/31/W8	2,709,432	3,331,872	622,440	81.3	1,004,949	61.9
12/31/W9*	3,001,314	3,604,297	602,983	83.3	1,049,138	57.5
12/31/X0	3,366,946	3,930,112	563,166	85.7	1,093,780	51.5
12/31/X1	3,658,323	4,284,961	626,638	85.4	1,156,346	54.2
SDEPP						
12/31/W6	$ 2,888,374	$ 3,499,572	$ 611,198	82.5%	$ 1,205,873	50.7%
12/31/W7	3,473,718	3,867,483	393,765	89.8	1,279,383	30.8
12/31/W8	3,902,705	4,439,761	537,056	87.9	1,344,151	40.0
12/31/W9*	4,323,137	4,802,700	479,563	90.0	1,403,255	34.2
12/31/X0	4,849,798	5,236,922	387,124	92.6	1,462,965	26.5
12/31/X1	5,269,502	5,709,764	440,262	92.3	1,546,650	28.5*
MEPP						
12/31/W6	$ 301,305	$ 342,842	$ 41,537	87.9%	$ 163,508	25.4%
12/31/W7	362,366	378,885	16,519	95.6	173,476	9.5
12/31/W8	407,117	434,949	27,832	93.6	182,258	15.3
12/31/W9*	450,975	470,512	19,537	95.8	190,272	10.3
12/31/X0	505,714	513,044	7,330	98.6	198,368	3.7
12/31/X1	549,696	559,367	9,671	98.3	209,715	4.6

*Revised economic and noneconomic assumptions due to experience review.

- Percentage of required contributions (if any) from other than employers and plan members recognized in the pension plan's statement of changes in plan net assets

> **PRACTICE POINT:** If contributions are made by parties other than employers and plan members, the schedule should be titled "Schedule of Contributions from the Employer(s) and Other Contributing Entities."

> **PRACTICE POINT:** The comparison of the ARC and the required employer contribution (percentage of ARC recognized as an employer contribution in the pension plan's statement of changes in plan net assets) should be based on the same covered payroll amount. The covered payroll amount (which is the basis for measuring the ARC and the employer's contribution) may be based on projected payroll, budgeted payroll, or actual covered payroll, as long as the measurement is consistently applied from period to period.

The example of a schedule of employer contributions shown in GASB-25 is reproduced in Exhibit 22-5.

Notes to the required schedules The schedule of funding progress and schedule of employer contributions should be supported by the following disclosures (GASB-25, par. 40):

- The actuarial methods and significant assumptions used for the most recent year presented in the schedules (including actuarial cost method, methods used to measure the actuarial value of plan assets, and assumptions concerning the inflation rate, investment return, projected salary increases, and postretirement benefit increase)
- The amortization method (dollar or level percentage of projected payroll) and the amortization period (equivalent single amortization period when multiple periods are used for amortization computation) for the most recent actuarial valuation date, and whether the amortization period is closed or open
- If a pension plan uses the aggregate actuarial cost method, statement that the method does not "identify or separately amortize unfunded actuarial liabilities"
- Any significant factors that would distort the evaluation of trends for amounts presented in the two schedules (examples include change in benefits and actuarial methods used) (However, previous information should not be restated.)

EXHIBIT 22-5
SCHEDULES OF EMPLOYER CONTRIBUTIONS

(Dollar amounts in thousands)

	Employer Contributions					
	SEPP		*SDEPP*		*MEPP*	
Year Ended June 30	*Annual Required Contribution*	*Percentage Contributed*	*Annual Required Contribution*	*Percentage Contributed*	*Annual Required Contribution*	*Percentage Contributed*
20W7	$ 100,729	100%	$ 115,935	100%	$ 15,042	100%
20W8	106,030	100	122,682	100	15,959	100
20W9	112,798	100	129,822	100	16,768	100
20X0	118,735	100	137,378	100	17,505	100
20X1	124,276	100	142,347	100	18,049	100
20X2	137,916	100	157,783	100	18,653	100

The example of a note to the required schedules shown in GASB-25 is reproduced in Exhibit 22-6.

EXHIBIT 22-6
NOTE TO THE SCHEDULE OF FUNDING PROGRESS AND SCHEDULE OF EMPLOYER CONTRIBUTIONS

The information presented in the required supplementary schedules was determined as part of the actuarial valuations at the dates indicated. Additional information as of the latest actuarial valuation follows.

	SEPP	*SDEPP*	*MEPP*
Valuation date	12/31/X1	12/31/X1	12/31/X1
Actuarial cost method	Entry age	Entry age	Entry age
Amortization method	Level percent open	Level percent closed	Level percent closed
Remaining amortization period	23 years	15 years	Weighted average of 25 years
Asset valuation method	4-year smoothed market	4-year smoothed market	4-year smoothed market
Actuarial assumptions:			
Investment rate of return*	7.5%	7.5%	7.5%
Projected salary increases*	5.5–9.5%	5.5–11.5%	5.5–11.5%
*Includes inflation at	5.5%	5.5%	5.5%
Cost-of-living adjustments	None	1/2 CPI increase, maximum of 3%	1–3%

Defined Contribution Plans

Although GASB-25 primarily focuses on accounting and reporting issues related to defined benefit pension plans, it does mandate

* Only these items need to be disclosed in a governmental employer's financial statements when the pension plan is presented as part of the employer's financial report and (1) the pension plan also separately presents its financial statements (which include all disclosures established by GASB-25) in a stand-alone financial report and (2) the governmental employer states in its financial statements how the stand-alone financial statements may be obtained.

some disclosures for defined contribution plans. A defined contribution plan should disclose the following when the plan's financial statements are presented in a stand-alone financial report or when those financial statements are presented only in an employer financial report (GASB-25, par. 41):

Plan description

- Statement that the pension plan is a defined contribution plan and disclosure of the number of participating employers (and other contributing entities)*
- Number of current members in the plan and type of employees covered
- Description of plan provisions and authority on which the plan is based
- Contribution rate required for members, employer(s), and other contributing entities
- Authority on which required contribution rates are based

Summary of Significant Accounting Policies

- Basis of accounting, fair value of plan assets (unless those assets are presented at fair value), and description of methods used to determine fair value of plant investments

Concentration of Credit Risk

- Identification, by amount and issuer, of investments in any one issuer that represent 5% or more of the plan net assets. (Investments issued or explicitly guaranteed by the U.S. government and investments in mutual funds, external pools, and other pooled investments are excluded from this requirement.)*

> **PRACTICE POINT:** GASB-27 establishes standards for governmental employer's measurement and presentation of pension expenditure/expense. (See Chapter 13, "Pension, Postemployment, and Other Employee Benefit Liabilities.")

---

* Only these items need to be disclosed in a governmental employer's financial statements when the pension plan is presented as part of the employer's financial report and (1) the pension plan also separately presents its financial statements (which include all disclosures established by GASB-25) in a stand-alone financial report and (2) the governmental employer states in its financial statements how the stand-alone financial statements may be obtained.

IRC SECTION 457 DEFERRED COMPENSATION PLANS

GASB-2 (Financial Reporting of Deferred Compensation Plans Adopted under the Provisions of Internal Revenue Code Section 457) was issued in 1986 to address IRC Section 457 deferred compensation plans. The objective of an IRC Section 457 plan is similar to the objectives related to 403(b) and 401(k) deferred compensation plans. However, deferred compensation plans created to satisfy the requirements established by IRC Section 457 presented a somewhat unique financial reporting problem because although the governmental employer had an obligation to pay beneficiaries at various future dates based on contributions to the plan and plan earnings, those same assets and earnings were accessible by the governmental entity and by its general creditors. In fact, if the resources of the plan were placed in a trust or otherwise insulated so that the governmental entity or its general creditors could not gain access to the resources, the deferred compensation amounts and related earnings were considered to be taxable income to participating employees. On the other hand, compensation deferred under 403(b) and 401(k) arrangements does not create a similar financial reporting problem because the assets held under these plans belong (with certain withdrawal restrictions) to the individuals (not accessible by the governmental employer's general creditors) that participate in the deferred compensation plan. Based on the characteristics of an IRC Section 457 plan, GASB-2 required that balances and transactions related to such plans should be accounted for in an Agency Fund.

In order to treat assets and income related to IRC Section 457 plans similar to other employee deferred compensation plans, Congress passed legislation in 1996 that governs IRC Section 457 plans. Specifically, the legislation states that a plan "shall not be treated as an eligible deferred compensation plan unless all assets and income of the plan described in subsection (b)(6) are held in trust for the exclusive benefit of participants and their beneficiaries." The federal law applies to all newly formed deferred compensation plans created as of August 20, 1996. In addition, existing IRC Section 457 plans were required to be modified to comply with the legislative requirements by January 1, 1999. In October 1997, the GASB issued GASB-32 (Accounting and Financial Reporting for Internal Revenue Code Section 457 Deferred Compensation Plans) in order to address the financial reporting ramifications of the new federal legislation.

GASB-32 superseded standards established by GASB-2 and in so doing eliminated all financial accounting and reporting guidance related to IRC Section 457 plans. The GASB takes the position that IRC Section 457 plans are no different (from a financial reporting perspective) from other deferred compensation plans. (There are no specific GASB standards that apply to 403(b) and 401(k) deferred compensation plans.) In addition, GASB-32 also amended GASB-31

(Accounting and Financial Reporting for Certain Investments and for External Investment Pools). Thus, governmental entities that report IRC Section 457 plan must observe the valuation and disclosure standards established by the following GASB pronouncements:

- GASB-3 (Deposits with Financial Institutions, Investment (Including Repurchase Agreements), and Reverse Repurchase Agreements)
- GASB-14 (The Financial Reporting Entity)
- GASBI-3 (Financial Reporting for Reverse Repurchase Agreements)
- GASB-28 (Accounting and Financial Reporting for Securities Lending Transactions)
- GASB-31 (Accounting and Financial Reporting for Certain Investments and for External Investment Pools)

Fund Reporting

Depending on how a deferred compensation plan, under the new statute, is administered, its creation may place a governmental employer in a fiduciary role. GASB-32 points out that NCGA-1, paragraph 26(3)(8), provides the following definition of a "fiduciary fund" (Trust Funds and Agency Funds):

> Fiduciary Funds are used to account for assets held by a governmental unit in a trustee capacity or as an agent for individuals, private organizations, other governmental units, and/or other funds.

The governmental entity must exercise judgment to determine whether a fiduciary relationship exists between the entity and the IRC Section 457 deferred compensation pension plan.

> **OBSERVATION:** Factors that may be considered in determining whether a fiduciary relationship exists include the presence of a formal trust agreement between the governmental entity and the Section 457 plan (trustees), the provision of investment advice, and governmental involvement in the administration of the plan. The GASB notes that, based on its research, most governmental entities that have established Section 457 plans neither provide administrative services to the plan nor investment advice for the plans. While, the GASB does not provide specific guidance as to what constitutes a fiduciary relationship between the governmental entity and the Section 457 plan, it notes that determining a fiduciary relationship applies to all trust fund arrangements, not just to Section 457 plans.

If such a fiduciary relationship does exist, the standards established by GASB-32 require that the balances and transactions related to the plan be accounted for in an Other Employee Benefit Trust Fund. If no fiduciary relationship exists, the balances and activities of the Section 457 plan would not be reported in the governmental entity's financial statements.

Generally, a valuation report should be obtained from the plan administrator and ideally the administrator's valuation date should coincide with the governmental entity's reporting date. When it is impractical to obtain a report that measures plan assets as of the governmental entity's reporting date, the most recent report should be used and adjusted for contributions and withdrawals subsequent to the date of the valuation report.

Financial Statements

When an IRC Section 457 plan is reported in an Other Employee Benefit Trust Fund or stand-alone report, the following financial statements should be presented:

- Statement of fiduciary net assets
- Statement of changes in fiduciary net assets

Fiduciary financial statements are presented in the fund financial statement section of the governmental entity's financial report. Fiduciary fund financial statements are not presented in the government-wide financial statements.

POSTEMPLOYMENT BENEFIT PLANS OTHER THAN PENSION PLANS (PRE-GASB-43 IMPLEMENTATION)

In addition to pension and deferred compensation benefits, postemployment benefits may include payments to retirees or their beneficiaries for life insurance benefits, health insurance benefits, and other pension-related benefits. The obligation related to these postemployment benefits in many cases is significant and may exceed the amount related to an employer's pension obligation.

> **PRACTICE POINT:** In April 2004, the GASB issued GASB-43 (Financial Reporting for Postemployment Benefit Plans Other Than Pension (OPEB) Plans), which establishes uniform financial reporting standards for OPEB plans and supersedes the interim guidance in GASB-26. These standards apply for OPEB trust funds of a plan sponsor or governmental unit employer as well as for stand-alone reports of OPEB plans. For

single-employer OPEB plans, GASB-43 is effective one year prior to the effective date of the related financial statement (see the appendix to Chapter 13, "Pension, Postemployment, and Other Employee Benefit Liabilities") for the employer. For multipleemployer OPEB plans, GASB-43 is effective one year prior to the effective date of the related financial statement for the largest participating employer in the plan. The required implementation is phased in over a three-year period, similar to the GASB-34 phase-in, beginning with the periods beginning after December 15, 2005. Early implementation is encouraged by the GASB.

Until GASB-43 is implemented or is effective, OPEB plans are to continue following the interim guidance in GASB-26. Governments that are implementing GASB-43 early should follow the guidance in GASB-43 (see the appendix to this chapter) rather than the guidance in GASB-26.

Historically, governmental accounting and reporting standards for certain postemployment benefits were based on the following pronouncements:

- GASB-12 (Disclosure of Information on Postemployment Benefits Other Than Pension Benefits by State and Local Governmental Employers)
- GASB-26 (Financial Reporting for Postemployment Healthcare Plans Administered by Defined Benefit Pension Plans)

NOTE: The standards established by GASB-12 are discussed in Chapter 13, "Pension, Postemployment, and Other Employee Benefit Liabilities")

GASB-26 addresses only the financial reporting standards that governmental entities that administer postemployment health care plans in a defined benefit pension plan must follow.

PRACTICE POINT: GASB-26 provides interim guidance for postemployment benefits other than pension benefits upon implementation of GASB-43, this interim guidance GASB-26 will be superseded.

The standards established by GASB-26 apply to all state and local governmental entities that administer postemployment health-care plans in a defined benefit pension plan. A "defined benefit pension plan" is defined as follows (GASB-26, pars. 3–6):

A pension plan having terms that specify the amount of pension benefits to be provided at a future date or after a certain period of time; the amount specified usually is a function of one or more factors such as age, years of service, and compensation.

GASB-26 addresses financial reporting issues related to postemployment health-care benefits, which include "medical, dental, vision, and other health-related benefits provided to terminated employees, retired employees, dependents, and beneficiaries."

> **PRACTICE POINT:** GASB-25 (Financial Reporting for Defined Benefit Pension Plans and Note Disclosures for Defined Contribution Plans) addresses financial accounting and reporting issues related to defined benefit pension plans; however, that Statement did not establish standards for the portion, if any, of a defined benefit pension plan that provides postemployment health care benefits. GASB-25 states that postemployment health care benefits "provided through a defined benefit pension plan, and the assets accumulated by the plan for the payment of postemployment health-care benefits, are considered, in substance, a postemployment health-care plan administered by but not part of the pension plan."

The standards established by GASB-26 apply to defined pension benefit plans irrespective of how they are funded. The following defined benefit pension plans are included (GASB-26, pars. 3–6):

> *Single-employer plan*—A plan that covers the current and former employees, including beneficiaries, of only one employer.
>
> *Agent multiple-employer plan*—An aggregation of single-employer plans, with pooled administrative and investment functions. Separate accounts are maintained for each employer so that the employer's contributions provide benefits only for employees of that employer. A separate actuarial valuation is performed for each individual employer's plan to determine the employer's periodic contribution rate and other information for the individual plan, based on the benefit formula selected by the employer and the individual plan's proportionate share of the pooled assets. The results of the individual valuations are aggregated at the administrative level.
>
> *Cost-sharing multiple-employer plan*—A single plan with pooling (cost-sharing) arrangements for the participating employers. All risks, rewards, and costs, including benefit costs, are shared and are not attributed individually to the employers. A single actuarial valuation covers all plan members and the same contribution rate(s) applies for each employer.

> **PRACTICE POINT:** When the defined benefit pension plan is an agent multiple-employer plan or a public employee retirement system (PERS), the standards established by GASB-26 apply to the overall plan, not to the individual plans. For example, a PERS must present information related to postemployment health-care benefits on an aggregate basis and not for *each* health care benefit plan it administers.

The standards established by GASB-26 apply to the reporting of postemployment health-care plans administered by pension plans and include the following presentations:

- Stand-alone financial statements for the plan are presented (that is, the plan's financial statements are presented as separate reports by the plan or PERS).
- Pension Trust Fund or a fiduciary component unit in the statement of fiduciary net assets and statement of changes in fiduciary net assets are presented by the plan sponsor or employer.

GASB-26 defines a "pension trust fund" as "a fund held by a governmental entity in a trustee capacity for pension plan members; used to account for the accumulation of assets for the purpose of paying benefits when they become due in accordance with the terms of the plan; a pension plan included in the financial reporting entity of the plan sponsor or a participating employer." A defined benefit pension plan may provide a variety of benefits other than postemployment health-care benefits, which are classified and defined by GASB-26 as follows (GASB-26, pars. 3–6):

> *Pension benefits*—Retirement income and all other benefits, including disability benefits, death benefits, life insurance, and other ancillary benefits, *except health-care benefits*, that are provided through a *defined benefit* pension plan to plan members and beneficiaries after termination of employment or after retirement. Postemployment health-care benefits are considered other postemployment benefits, whether they are provided through a defined benefit pension plan or another type of plan.
>
> *Postemployment*—The period between termination of employment and retirement as well as the period after retirement.
>
> *Other postemployment benefits*—Postemployment benefits other than pension benefits; other postemployment benefits include postemployment health care benefits, regardless of the type of plan that provides them, and all postemployment benefits provided through a plan that does not provide retirement income, except benefits defined as special termination benefits in NCGA Interpretation 8, *Certain Pension Matters*, as amended.

For the purposes of GASB-26, pension plan benefits are considered retirement income and all other benefits except postemployment health-care benefits. GASB-25 establishes financial accounting and reporting standards for pension plan benefits administered in a defined benefit pension plan (referred to in GASB-26 as "pension plan reporting standards"), and GASB-26 establishes financial reporting standards for health-care benefits administered by a defined benefit pension plan. Thus, health-care benefits provided and the assets accumulated to pay for those benefits, if any, are characterized by GASB-26 as being administered by a defined benefit pension plan but in substance not part of the defined benefit pension plan for financial reporting purposes.

Financial Statements and Disclosures

GASB-26 requires that the following financial statements be presented by defined benefit pension plans for the portion of their activities administered as postemployment health-care plans (GASB-26, par. 7):

- Statement of postemployment health-care plan net assets
- Statement of changes in postemployment health-care plan net assets
- Notes to the financial statements

> **OBSERVATION:** When a defined benefit pension plan that administers a postemployment health-care plan is included in the employer's or sponsor's financial report as a pension or other employee benefit trust fund, there is no need to present combining statements of fiduciary net assets and changes in fiduciary net assets; however, care must be taken to differentiate the amount of net assets held in trust for employees' pension benefits and those related to employees' postemployment health-care benefits. Also, the net increase or decrease in net assets (as shown in the statement of changes in fiduciary net assets) must be subdivided into amounts related to the pension benefits and the postemployment health-care benefits. Finally, the financial statements of individual postemployment health-care plans should be presented in the primary government's financial statements as a note if separate financial reports for the plan have not been issued. If separate (GAAP-based) financial statements have been issued, the note should simply state how the financial statements might be obtained.

The postemployment health-care plan's set of financial statements should be prepared using the standards established by GASB-25. In addition to the guidance provided in GASB-25, the notes should include the following:

- Description of the eligibility requirements
- Required employer contribution rate(s)

> **PRACTICE POINT:** GASB-12 establishes note disclosures for governmental employers that incur other postemployment benefits expenditures/expense. When the financial statements of a post-employment health-care plan are included in the

governmental entity's financial statements (they would be presented in a pension trust fund), the required disclosures (as established by GASB-26 and GASB-12) may be combined to eliminate duplicate information.

When preparing its financial statements, the defined benefit pension plan should be careful to separate the financial statements of the pension plan and the postemployment health-care plan into separate columns in the combining financial statements (GASB-26, par. 7).

Supplementary Schedules

GASB-25 requires that defined benefit pension plans present certain supplementary schedules (schedule of funding progress, schedule of employer contributions, and related notes). GASB-26 does not require postemployment health-care plans to make similar presentations.

If a postemployment health-care plan decides to present the supplementary schedules required by GASB-25 (which is strictly voluntary), then all of the standards established by GASB-25 must be observed. In addition, the supplementary information for the defined benefit pension plan and the postemployment health-care plan must be separately presented. That is, (1) if the information is presented in schedules, separate schedules for the pension plan and the postemployment health-care plan must be presented, (2) if the information is presented in separate statements, separate columns must be presented in the combining financial statements, or (3) if the information is presented in notes to the financial statements, separate notes must be presented for each plan (GASB-26, pars. 8–9).

If a postemployment health-care plan decides to present supplementary schedules, GASB-26 does not require it to measure the funding and pension obligation in a manner that satisfies the parameters established by GASB-25. However, the methods and assumptions used to develop the information must be internally consistent, consistently applied, and disclosed similarly to the information (notes to supplementary information) required by GASB-25. In addition, the health-care inflation assumption for the most recent year presented in the schedules must be disclosed.

GASB-26 requires that the same methods and assumptions be used by both the postemployment health-care plan and the employer, when both the plan and the employer include in their financial reports similar or related information about the plan's funded status or the employer's required contributions (GASB-26, pars. 8–9). (A similar requirement is established by GASB-27 [Accounting for Pensions by State and Local Governmental Employers], which is addressed in Chapter 13, "Pension, Postemployment, and Other Employee Benefit Liabilities.")

APPENDIX FINANCIAL REPORTING FOR POSTEMPLOYMENT BENEFIT PLANS OTHER THAN PENSION PLANS (GASB-43)

Overview

GASB-43 (Financial Reporting for Postemployment Benefit Plans Other Than Pension Plans) addresses other postemployment benefits (OPEB) that are defined as "postemployment healthcare benefits, regardless of the type of plan that provides them and all postemployment benefits provided separately from a pension plan, excluding benefits defined as termination offers and benefits" and are provided as a defined benefit OPEB plan.

Postemployment health-care benefits include "medical, dental, vision, and other health-related benefits provided to terminated or retried employees and their dependents and beneficiaries."

> **PRACTICE POINT:** OPEB may be provided in a defined benefit OPEB plan or a defined contribution plan. A defined benefit OPEB plan has "terms that specify the amount of benefits to be provided at a future date or after a certain period of time. The amount specified usually is a function of one or more factors such as age, years of service, and compensation." A defined contribution plan is an OPEB plan that has "terms that specify how contributions to a plan member's account are to be determined, rather than the amount of benefit the member is to receive. The amounts received by a member will depend only on the amount contributed to the member's account, earnings on investments of those contributions, and forfeitures of contributions made for other members that may be allocated to the member's account."

Specifically, GASB-43 provides guidance for determining the assets, liabilities, net assets, and changes in net assets that are held in trust for the payment of OPEB and actuarial information concerning the funded status of the plan. The plan, which functions as a trustee, holds and manages the plan assets exclusively for plan members and their beneficiaries, and its activities may be reported as an Employee Benefit Trust Fund (fiduciary fund), a fiduciary component unit of the related governmental employer (or plan sponsor), or a Public Employee Retirement System (PERS).

The GASB-43 standards adopt the general measurement and presentation standards established for pension plans in GASB-25 (Financial Reporting for Defined Benefit Pension Plans and Note Disclosures for Defined Contribution Plans). This appendix summarizes the standards in GASB-43.

> **NOTE:** The GASB has also issued a companion statement, GASB-45 (Accounting and Financial Reporting by Employers for Postemployment Benefits Other Than Pensions) that addresses measurement and display issues related to employers that provide postemployment benefits other than pensions. (See the appendix to Chapter 13, "Pension, Postemployment, and Other Employee Benefit Liabilities.")

Some OPEB plans have characteristics of both defined benefit OPEB plans and defined contributions plans. GASB-43 states that "if the substance of the plan is to provide a defined benefit in some form—that is, if the benefit to be provided is a function of factors other than the amounts contributed and amounts earned on contributed assets—the provisions of this Statement for defined benefit plans apply." Also, the standards proposed apply to single-employer, agent multiple-employer, and cost-sharing multiple-employer plans, which are defined as follows:

- *Sole-employer plan* A plan that covers the current and former employees, including beneficiaries, of only one employer
- *Agent multiple-employer plan* An aggregation of single-employer plans, with pooled administrative and investment functions. Separate accounts are maintained for each employer so that the employer's contributions provide benefits only for its employees. A separate actuarial valuation is performed for each individual employer's plan to determine the employer's period contribution rate and other information for the individual plan, based on the benefit formula selected by the employer and the individual plan's proportionate share of the pooled assets. The results of the individual valuations are aggregated at the administrative level.
- *Cost-sharing multiple-employer plan* A single plan with pooling (cost-sharing) arrangements for the participating employers. All risks, rewards, and costs, including benefit costs, are shared and are not attributed individually to the employers. A single actuarial valuation covers all plan members, and the same contribution rate(s) applies for each employer.

Administering Public Employee Retirement Systems

The GASB points out that a PERS is a separate legal entity that administers a public employee OPEB plan(s). However, GASB-43 emphasizes that the PERS is the administrator of the plan and is not the plan itself. For example, a PERS in a particular state may administer numerous defined benefit pension plans, defined contribution plans, deferred compensation plans, as well as OPEB plans. The standards in GASB-43 apply to a particular OPEB plan and not to a particular PERS. However, when a PERS presents the separate financial statements of a defined OPEB plan in its financial report, the standards in GASB-43 must be observed for that particular plan.

If the financial statements of more than one defined OPEB are included in the PERS report, the standards must be applied separately to each plan. The financial statements for each plan should be presented separately in the combining financial statements of the PERS along with appropriate schedules and other required disclosures. Thus, the standards apply to the individual plans administered by the PERS but the PERS itself must follow the standards established by GASB-34 (Basic Financial Statements—and Management's Discussion and Analysis—for State and Local Governments) in order to prepare its financial statements. Specifically, the PERS would report as a special-purpose government engaged only in fiduciary activities as defined by GASB-34.

To determine whether a PERS is administering a single OPEB plan or two or more OPEB plans (thus requiring separate reporting), the custody of the assets held must be analyzed to determine whether they are (1) available to pay benefits for all of the members of the OPEB plans or (2) available to pay benefits only to certain plan members.

Assets available to all plan members If assets held by the PERS are legally available to pay benefits for all of the plan members, the OPEB plan is a single plan, and only a single set of financial statements needs to be prepared. GASB-43 notes that an OPEB plan is a sole plan even if the following circumstances exist:

- Legally or because of administrative policy, the OPEB plan must maintain separate accounts based on such factors as specified groups, specific employers, or benefits provided by the plan.
- Separate actuarial valuations are made for classes or groups of covered employees.

Assets available only to certain plan members If any portion of the assets held by the PERS can be paid legally only to certain classes of employees (for example, public safety officers) or employees of certain employers (for example, only to state government employees), more than one plan is being administered and separate financial statements must be prepared for each plan.

The assets availability criterion must also be applied to a governmental employer's CAFR. Separate reporting is required in the governmental employer's (or sponsor's) CAFR when more than one OPEB plan is being presented in the CAFR.

Financial Reporting

GASB-43 requires that the following financial statements be presented by a defined benefit OPEB plan:

- Statement of plan net assets
- Statement of changes in plan net assets
- Notes to financial statements

Statement of Plan Net Assets

The statement of plan net assets is prepared on an accrual basis and reports the plan's assets, liabilities, and net assets. The statement should identify the major assets of the OPEB plan (for example, cash, receivables, investments, and operating assets), and the receivables and investments categories should be further divided into their significant components. Reported liabilities should be subtracted from total assets and the difference reported as "net assets held in trust for OPEB."

Exhibit 22-7 is an illustration of a statement of plan net assets.

EXHIBIT 22-7
FINANCIAL STATEMENTS AND NOTE DISCLOSURES FOR A POSTEMPLOYMENT PLAN ADMINISTERED BY A QUALIFYING TRUST

Cinnabar Employees Postemployment Benefit Plan

Statements of Plan Net Assets as of June 30, 20X9, and 20X8

	20X9	*20X8*
Assets		
Cash and short-term investments	$ 307,724	$485,692
Receivables:		
Employer	9,939	8,762
Plan member	3,313	2,540
Interest and dividends	557,093	575,841
Total receivables	570,345	587,143

	20X9	20X8
Investments, at fair value:		
U.S. Government obligations	1,202,224	1,127,564
Domestic corporate bonds	1,322,057	1,210,398
Domestic stocks	2,971,217	2,469,533
International stocks	1,062,635	972,466
Mortgages	557,093	510,042
Other	565,408	517,654
Total investments	7,680,634	6,807,657
Total assets	8,558,703	7,880,492
Liabilities		
Accounts payable and other	243,878	267,929
Net assets held in trust for postemployment benefits	$8,314,825	$7,612,563

Statement of Changes in Plan Net Assets

An OPEB plan should prepare an operating statement that reports the net increase or decrease in net plan assets from the beginning of the year until the end of the year. The statement of changes in plan net assets should be prepared on the same basis of accounting used to prepare the OPEB plan's statement of plan net assets. The two financial statements are interrelated in that (1) the net increase as reported on the statement of changes in plan net assets when added to (2) the beginning balance of plan net assets on the statement of plan net assets is equal to (3) the net plan assets as reported at the end of the year on the statement of net plan assets.

The statement of changes in plan net assets should present separate categories for additions and deductions in net assets for the year.

Additions to net assets The additions section of the statement of changes in plan net assets should include the following components:

- Contributions received from an employer(s)
- Contributions received from employees (including those received via the employer)
- Contributions received from those other than employer(s) and employees
- Net investment income for the year (includes the net appreciation or depreciation of the fair value of the plan assets) and investment income and other increases not reported as net appreciation or depreciation (these two components of invest-

ment income may be separately reported or reported as a single amount)

- Total investment expenses (including investment fees, custodial fees, and "all other significant investment-related costs")

Medicare Part D Payments

GASB Technical Bulletin No. 2006-1 (Accounting and Financial Reporting by Employers and OPEB Plans for Payments from the Federal Government Pursuant to the Retiree Drug Subsidy Provisions of Medicare Part D) clarifies the proper reporting of payments that an employer or a defined benefit other postemployment benefit (OPEB) plan receives from the federal government under Medicare Part D. Medicare Part D is a federal program that provides prescription drug benefits to eligible Medicare recipients.

A Medicare Part D payment from the federal government to the employer is a "voluntary nonexchange transaction," as discussed in Chapter 17, "Revenues: Nonexchange and Exchange Transactions." Accordingly, the employer should recognize an asset and revenue for the payment received following the applicable recognition requirements for voluntary nonexchange transactions. The payment is a transaction that is separate from the exchange of services for salaries and benefits (including postemployment prescription drug benefits) between employer and employees, for which the accounting is addressed in GASB-45. Therefore, a sole or agent employer should apply the measurement requirements of GASB-45 to determine the actuarial accrued liabilities, the annual required contribution of the employer (ARC), and the annual OPEB cost *without reduction* for Medicare Part D payments. In addition, the nonexchange transaction does not affect accounting for employer contributions or the financial reporting presentation by a defined benefit OPEB plan in which an employer participates. A defined benefit OPEB plan administered by a qualifying trust should apply the measurement requirements of GASB-43, as discussed in this chapter, to determine the actuarial accrued liabilities, the ARC, and the annual OPEB cost without reduction for Medicare Part D payments.

A Medicare Part D payment from the federal government to the plan is considered an on-behalf payment for fringe benefits, as discussed in Chapter 17, "Revenues: Nonexchange and Exchange Transactions." The employer should recognize revenue and expense or expenditures for the payment in accordance with the recognition and measurement requirements for such on-behalf payments, pertaining to an employer that is legally responsible for contributions to the OPEB plan. That is, the employer "should follow accounting standards for that type of transaction to recognize expenditures or expenses and related liabilities or assets."

In the statement of changes in plan net assets, the OPEB plan should separately display contributions from the employer(s) and the on-behalf payment from the federal government. In the schedule of employer contributions, the OPEB plan should include the Medicare Part D payment as on-behalf contributions from the federal government and titling the schedule as the schedule of contributions from the employer(s) and other contributing entities. The plan should present the ARC without reduction for the Medicare Part D payment.

Deductions from net assets Deductions on the statement of changes in plan net assets should include OPEB payments to retirees and beneficiaries, and administrative expenses. These items should not be combined but rather separately presented on the statement. Deductions should not include payments made by an insurance company based on allocated insurance contracts, but the original acquisition of allocated insurance contracts should be reported as benefits paid. The amount paid for such contracts may be reported net of any income earned on the excluded contract for the year. Administrative expenses, such as depreciation expense and operating expenses, should be measured using accrual accounting and reported as deductions from net assets.

Exhibit 22-8 is an illustration of a statement of changes in plan net assets.

EXHIBIT 22-8
FINANCIAL STATEMENTS AND NOTE DISCLOSURES FOR A POSTEMPLOYMENT PLAN ADMINISTERED BY A QUALIFYING TRUST

Cinnabar Employees Postemployment Benefit Plan

Statements of Changes in Plan Net Assets for the years ended June 30, 20X9 and 20X2

	20X9	*20X8*
Additions		
Contributions:		
Employer	$399,761	$379,772
Plan member	133,253	126,591
Total contributions	533,014	506,363
Investment income:		
Net appreciation (depreciation) in fair value of investments	297,239	277,321

	20X9	20X8
Interest	173,993	162,334
Dividends	224,742	209,681
Other income	28,999	27,056
	724,973	676,392
Less investment expense	39,842	35,693
Net investment income	685,131	640,699
Total additions	1,218,145	1,147,062
Deductions		
Benefits	511,827	511,043
Administrative expense	4,056	3,982
Total deductions	515,883	515,025
Net increase	702,262	632,037
Net assets held in trust for postemployment benefits		
Beginning of year	7,612,563	6,980,526
End of year	$8,314,825	$7,612,563

Notes to the Financial Statements

GASB-43 requires that the following be disclosed by an OPEB plan when the plan's financial statements are presented in a stand-alone financial report or when those financial statements are presented in an employer's financial statements as an OPEB Trust Fund.

Plan Description

- Type of OPEB plan (single-employer, agent multiple-employer, or cost-sharing multiple-employer)*
- Number and classes of governmental employers participating in the plan and other entities contributing to the plan*
- Type of governmental employees covered by the OPEB plan and the plan status (such as active members, retirees, and beneficiaries receiving benefits and terminated employees not yet receiving benefits) (When the plan is closed to new entrants, that fact should be disclosed.)
- Description of plan provisions (such as types of benefits provided and policies concerning automatic or ad hoc increases in benefits)

- Authority under which benefits are provided or may be amended

Summary of Significant Accounting Policies

- Basis of accounting (accounting methods used to recognize contributions, benefits, and refunds)*
- Methods used to determine the fair value of plan investments, including significant assumptions*

Contributions and Reserves

- Authority under which OPEB plan funding sources are established and may be amended
- Funding policies (including description of how required payments by various contributors are determined, the authority under which those payments are established, and the manner in which administrative costs are funded)
- Required contribution rates for active plan members or retired plan members expressed as an amount per member or a percentage of covered payroll
- Description of long-term commitments for contributions to the plan and related amounts outstanding as of the reporting date*
- Balances reported as legally required reserves at the reporting dates, their purposes, and whether they are fully funded.

Funded Status and Funding Progress

- Information about the funded status of the plan as of the most recent valuation date (including actuarial value of assets, actuarial accrued liability, total unfunded actuarial accrued liability, funded rate, annual covered payroll, and ratio of unfunded actuarial liability to annual covered payroll)
- Information concerning actuarial methods and assumptions used

---

* Only asterisked items need to be disclosed in a governmental employer's financial statements when the OPEB plan is presented as a trust fund and (1) the OPEB plan also separately presents its financial statements (which include all disclosures established by the proposed companion statement) in a stand-alone financial report and (2) the governmental employer states in its financial statements how the stand-alone financial statements may be obtained.

- Identification of the actuarial methods and significant assumptions used to determine the ARC

Required Supplementary Information

Except as noted in the following paragraph, GASB-43 requires that a schedule of funding progress, a schedule of employer contributions, and notes to support the two schedules be presented in the financial statements of the OPEB plan. This required supplementary information (RSI) should be presented immediately after the notes to the financial statements.

RSI is not required when the financial statements of a cost-sharing OPEB plan or an agent plan are included in the governmental employer's financial report if both of the following two conditions are satisfied:

1. The OPEB plan also separately presents its financial statements (which include the required supplementary information) in a publicly available, stand-alone financial report.
2. The governmental employer states in a note to its financial statements how the stand-alone financial statements may be obtained.

When the financial statements of a single-employer OPEB plan are included in the governmental employer's financial report, that financial report should include only the schedule of funding progress for the three most recent actuarial valuations; the schedule of employer contributions should not be presented. Also, the employer government should disclose the availability of the standalone OPEB plan report.

When an OPEB plan's financial statements are not publicly available in a stand-alone financial report, the governmental employer's financial report should include both the schedule of funding progress and the schedule of employer contributions for all years required by the standards.

Schedule of Funding Progress

The schedule of funding progress should include the following information for at least the most recent valuation and the two preceding valuations:

- Actuarial valuation date
- Actuarial value of OPEB plan assets
- Actuarial accrued liability
- Total unfunded actuarial liability

- Actuarial value of assets as a percentage of the actuarial accrued liability (funded ratio)
- Annual covered payroll
- Ratio of unfunded actuarial liability to annual covered payroll

The actuarial information should be presented as of the actuarial valuation date and measured in accordance with the standards in GASB-43.

> **PRACTICE POINT:** OPEB plans that use the aggregate actuarial cost method should use the entry age actuarial cost method for presentation purposes. That fact should be disclosed and it should be noted that the "the purpose of the disclosure is to provide information that approximates the funding progress of the plan based on the use of the aggregate actuarial cost method."

Schedule of Employer Contributions

The schedule of employer contributions should include the following information for at least the most recent valuation and the two preceding valuation dates:

- Dollar amount of annual required contributions (ARC)
- Percentage of ARC recognized as an employer contribution in the OPEB plans' statement of changes in plan net assets
- Dollar amount of required contributions (if any) from other than employers and plan members
- Percentage of required contributions (if any) from other than employers and plan members recognized in the OPEB plan's statement of changes in plan net assets

> **OBSERVATION:** If contributions are made by parties other than employers and plan members, the schedule should be titled "Schedule of Contributions from the Employer(s) and Other Contributing Entities."

For the years of transition (the year the standards in GASB-43 are implemented by the OPEB plan and until three actuarial valuations have been performed) the required information for the schedules of funding progress and employer contributions should include the current year (that is, the transition year) and as many of the previous years for which acceptable information is available. The information is acceptable only if it was developed (or can be developed) to satisfy the parameters required by GASB-43. Noncompliance information should not be presented in the schedules.

Notes to the Required Schedules

The schedule of funding progress and schedule of employer contributions should be supported by disclosures that provide insight into trends that are reflected in the schedules. These disclosures include changes in actuarial methods and/or assumptions, and benefit provisions.

Alternative Measurement Method: Small Plans

In general, the measurement standards required by GASB-43 apply to all OPEB plans; however, the GASB did attempt to simplify the implementation of the proposed standards for a sole-employer plan that has fewer than 100 plan members. For such plans, the OPEB plan may (1) apply all of the measurement standards without modification or (2) apply the measurement standards with one or more of the following modifications:

- *Assumptions in general* In general, assumptions should be based on actual past experience, but grouping techniques may be used whereby assumptions may be based on combined experience data for similar plans as explained below (see "use of grouping")
- *Expected point in time at which benefits will begin to be provided* This assumption may be based on a single assumed retirement age or that all employees will retire at a particular age.
- *Health-care cost trend rate* This assumption should be based on an objective source.
- *Marital and dependency status* This assumption may be based on the current marital status of employees or historical demographic data for the covered group.
- *Mortality* This assumption should reflect current published mortality tables.
- *Plans with coverage options* Employers with postemployment benefit plans whereby the employee has coverage options should base the coverage option on past experience but also take into consideration the choices of pre- and post-Medicare-eligible members.
- *Qualification for benefits assumption* This assumption, when past experience data are not available, may be based on the simplifying assumption that the longer an employee works, the greater the probability he or she will work long enough to qualify for benefits. For example, if an employee must work for 10 years to qualify for benefits, then the probability

of qualification increases 10% for each year the employee works.

- *Use of grouping* Rather than consider each participant, participants may be grouped into categories based on such factors as an age range or length of service range.
- *Use of health insurance premiums* Employers that have postemployment health-care plans whereby the employer makes premium payments to an insurer may use the current premium structure in order to project future health-care benefit payments.

Defined Contribution Plans

When an OPEB is a defined contribution plan, it should prepare its financial statements based on the general guidance for fiduciary funds as required by GASB-34. In addition, the disclosure requirements established by GASB-25 (paragraph 41) for defined-contribution pension plans should also be observed.

CHAPTER 23
PUBLIC ENTITY RISK POOLS

CONTENTS

***Exhibit 23-3:** Required Supplementary Information for Reconciliation of Claims Liabilities by Type of Contract* **23.28**

PUBLIC ENTITY RISK POOLS

State and local governments encounter essentially the same accounting and reporting issues as commercial enterprises that provide insurance coverage (insurer) and that purchase insurance coverage (insured). GASB-10 (Accounting and Financial Reporting for Risk Financing and Related Insurance Issues) was issued to provide guidance for governmental entities that assume the role of the insurer and the role of the insured.

When a governmental entity is organized as a public entity risk pool, it may take on many of the characteristics of an insurer.

GASB-10 defines a public entity risk pool as follows (GASB-10, par. 17):

> *Public entity risk pool*—A cooperative group of governmental entities joining together to finance an exposure, liability, or risk. Risk may include property and liability, workers' compensation, and employee health care. A pool may be a stand-alone entity or be included as part of a larger governmental entity that acts as the pool's sponsor.

The activities of a public entity risk pool vary, but in general they can be classified as follows:

- *Risk-sharing pool* Governmental entities join together to share in the cost of losses.
- *Insurance-purchasing pool (risk-purchasing group)* Governmental entities join together to acquire commercial insurance coverage.
- *Banking pool* Governmental entities are allowed to borrow funds from a pool to pay losses.
- *Claims-servicing or account pool* Governmental entities join together to administer the separate account of each entity in the payment of losses.

An individual public entity risk pool can perform one or more of the above activities, but the latter two activities (banking pool and claims-servicing or account pool) do not result in the transfer of risk from the participating governmental entity to the public entity risk pool (GASB-10, par. 17).

A public entity risk pool must be evaluated to determine the rights and responsibilities of the pool and the governmental entities that participate in the pool. The agreement between a public entity risk pool and the governmental entity may transfer part or all of the risk of loss to the risk pool or may retain all of the risk (GASB-10, par. 17).

In addition to the agreement between the pool and the participants, the laws of a particular jurisdiction and the economic resources of the ultimate insurer should be taken into consideration when determining to what extent, if any, there has been a transfer of risk to the public entity risk pool from a governmental entity. For example, if a public entity risk pool has insufficient resources to pay claims as incurred, the risk of loss is retained by the individual governmental entity, irrespective of the agreement between the two parties. On the other hand, if an agreement has a deductible amount clause per claim, only the risk related to the amount of the loss in excess of the deductible amount is transferred to the public entity risk pool (GASB-10, par. 17).

> **PRACTICE POINT:** The accounting and reporting standards established for public entity risk pools are essentially the same as the standards established in FAS-60 as amended by FAS-97 (Accounting and Reporting by Insurance Enterprises for Certain Long-Duration Contracts and for Realized Gains and Losses from the Sale of Investments). The GASB states that the accounting and reporting of risk activities are essentially the same regardless of whether the entity related to the activities is a public entity or a commercial enterprise.

Irrespective of whether a public entity risk pool is involved in risk-sharing activities or insurance-purchasing activities, those activities should be accounted for in an Enterprise Fund (GASB-10, par. 18).

> **PRACTICE POINT:** Because the accounting and reporting standards applicable to public entity risk pools are derived from FAS-60, an Enterprise Fund, which has a measurement focus and a basis of accounting similar to a commercial enterprise, is the appropriate fund to account for such entities.

ACCOUNTING AND REPORTING

Premium Revenue

A public entity risk pool should recognize premium revenue (or required contributions) over the contract period based on the amount of risk protection provided to the insured entity. In those instances where the risk protection for each period is the same, premium revenue should be recognized on a straight-line basis. For example, if a public entity risk pool charges $110,000 to a participating governmental entity for $5,000,000 of coverage for losses over a two-year period, the amount of premium revenue recognized each year is $55,000. On the other hand, if coverage for losses is $5,000,000 in year 1 and $6,000,000 in year 2, premium revenue is computed as follows (GASB-10, par. 19):

	Premium Revenue	
	Year 1	*Year 2*
($110,000 × $5,000,000)/$11,000,000	$50,000	
($110,000 × $6,000,000)/$11,000,000		$60,000

In most instances, the period of risk and the contract period are the same; however, when they are significantly different, the premium revenue should be recognized over the period of risk (GASB-10, par. 19).

It may not be possible to determine the exact amount of the premium until after the end of the contract period. For example, a premium may be based on the amount of actual claims incurred during a period. An example of an experience-based premium contract is a contract that uses "retrospective rating," which GASB-10 defines as follows (GASB-10, par. 20 and Glossary):

> *Retrospective (experience) rating*—A method of determining the final amount of an insurance premium by which the initial premium is adjusted based on actual experience during the period of coverage (sometimes subject to maximum and minimum limits). It is designed to encourage safety by the insured and to compensate the insurer if larger-than-expected losses are incurred.

In other instances, the premium may be based on the value of property covered during a contract period. An example of a value-based contract is a "reporting-form contract," which is defined as follows (GASB-10, par. 20 and Glossary):

> *Reporting-form contract*—A contract or policy in which the policyholder is required to report the value of property insured to the insurer at certain intervals. The final premium on the contract is determined by applying the contract rate to the average of the values reported.

In most instances of experience-based or valuation-based premiums, the public entity risk pool should be able to determine a reasonable estimate of the total premium. In this case, the premium revenue should be recognized over the contract period, based on the amount of risk protection provided. Estimates of the total premium should be revised as the public entity risk pool accumulates experience statistics from participants or receives revised property valuation reports from participants.

In accordance with APB-20 (Accounting Changes), changes in accounting estimates should be treated in a prospective manner. Thus, any adjustment to estimated total premiums would be reflected in any current and future financial statements in which the premium revenue is recognized. For example, assume that a premium of $150,000 for fire insurance is charged for a three-year period, given that the amount of property covered by the contract is expected to be $20,000,000 in year 1, $25,000,000 in year 2, and $30,000,000 in the final year (year 3) of the contract. The amount of premium revenue to be recognized in each of the three years under a reporting-form contract that is retrospectively rated is computed as follows:

	Premium Revenue		
	Year 1	*Year 2*	*Year 3*
($150,000 × $20,000,000)/$75,000,000	$40,000		
($150,000 × $25,000,000)/$75,000,000		$50,000	
($150,000 × $30,000,000)/$75,000,000			$60,000

During year 2, assume that the estimated amounts of property covered in years 2 and 3 increase to $28,000,000 and $33,000,000, respectively, and that the total premium is estimated to be $172,000. In this circumstance, the amount of premium revenue to be recognized in years 2 and 3 would be as follows:

	Premium Revenue	
	Year 1	*Year 2*
([$172,000 – $40,000] × $28,000,000)/$61,000,000	$60,590	
([$172,000 – $40,000] × $33,000,000)/$61,000,000		$71,410

If the public entity risk pool cannot reasonably estimate the total premium, premium revenue should be recognized using either the cost-recovery method or the deposit method. GASB-10 describes these two methods as follows (GASB-10, par. 20 and Glossary):

> *Cost recovery method*—Under the cost recovery method, premiums are recognized as revenue in an amount equal to estimated claims costs as insured events occur until the ultimate premium is reasonably estimable, and recognition of income is postponed until that time.

> *Deposit method*—Under the deposit method, premiums are not recognized as revenue and claims costs are not charged to expense until the ultimate premium is reasonably estimable; recognition of revenue is postponed until that time.

To illustrate the cost-recovery method and the deposit method, assume that a public entity risk pool decides to bill a governmental entity the following amounts, but the billings are tentative because the total premium is based on retrospective rating and is not subject to reasonable estimation at the end of year 1:

Year 1	$100,000
Year 2	110,000
Year 3	130,000
	$340,000

If estimated claims costs are $90,000 at the end of year 1, the following entries would be made by the risk pool under each of the two revenue recognition methods:

Cost-Recovery Method (Year 1):		
Premiums Receivable	100,000	
Premium Revenue		90,000
Unearned Revenue		10,000
Expenses—Claims Costs	90,000	
Estimated Claims Costs Payable		90,000
Deposit Method (Year 1):		
Premiums Receivable	100,000	
Unearned Revenue		100,000
Deferred Claims Costs	90,000	
Estimated Claims Costs Payable		90,000

Assume that during year 2, the following reasonable estimates of premium revenue are made:

Year 1	$130,000
Year 2	150,000
Year 3	170,000
	$450,000

Based on the fact that the public entity risk pool can reasonably estimate premium revenues, the following entries would be made in year 2:

Cost-Recovery Method (Year 2):		
Premiums Receivable	180,000	
Unearned Revenue	10,000	
Premium Revenue		190,000

(A) ($130,000 + $150,000 – $100,000)

Deposit Method (Year 2):

Unearned Revenue	100,000	
Premiums Receivable	180,000	
Premium Revenue ($130,000 + $150,000)		280,000
Claims Costs	90,000	
Deferred Claims Costs		90,000

A public entity risk pool may collect a premium (or required contribution) that is specifically identified for coverage of future catastrophic losses. GASB-10 defines "catastrophe" as follows (GASB-10, par. 21 and Glossary):

> *Catastrophe*—A conflagration, earthquake, windstorm, explosion, or similar event resulting in substantial losses *or* an unusually large number of unrelated and unexpected losses occurring in a single period.

The accounting problem with respect to premiums related to catastrophic loss protection is that it is difficult to match the recognition of premium revenues and the recognition of losses that arise from future catastrophic losses. Specifically, should the premium related to catastrophic losses be recorded as deferred revenue until the actual loss occurs? The GASB states that premiums specifically related to future catastrophic losses should be recognized as premium revenue over the period covered by the contract. However, premium revenue related to catastrophic losses should be separately reported in the balance sheet as a reservation of equity if either one of the following conditions exists:

- The premium is contractually restricted for catastrophic losses
- The premium is legally restricted for catastrophic losses by an outside organization or individual (for instance, by pool participants)

> **PRACTICE POINT:** Although GASB-10 refers specifically to the conditions necessary for the identification of a reservation of public entity risk pool equity, in the absence of such conditions, a pool could designate a portion of its equity for future catastrophic losses.

Claims Costs

Claims costs to be paid by a public entity risk pool should be evaluated using the fundamental criteria established by FAS-5. Thus, claims costs should be accrued at the end of the accounting period if the following conditions exist (GASB-10, par. 22):

- Information available prior to issuance of the financial statements indicates that it is probable (the likely occurrence of the future event(s) that confirms that a loss has occurred) that a liability has been incurred at the date of the financial statements.
- The amount of the loss can be reasonably estimated.

Estimated claims costs become liabilities for the public entity risk pool when the covered event occurs. The occurrence of a fire or the injury of an individual covered by an agreement with the pool represents the critical date for determining a liability. In addition, some coverage (and therefore the recognition of a liability) is based on claims-made policies. This type of policy is defined as follows (GASB-10, par. 22 and Glossary):

> *Claims-made policy or contract*—A type of policy that covers losses from claims asserted (reported or filed) against the policyholder during the policy period, regardless of whether the liability-imposing events occurred during the current or any previous period in which the policyholder was insured under the claims-made contract or other specified period before the policy period (the policy retroactive date).

Using the criteria established in FAS-5 and the critical event (date of occurrence or claims-made policy criterion) for liability recognition, the public entity risk pool must estimate a liability for unpaid claims costs. GASB-10 defines "liability for unpaid claims costs" in the following manner (GASB-10, par. 22 and Glossary):

> *Liability for unpaid claims costs*—The amount needed to provide for the estimated ultimate cost of settling claims for events that have occurred on or before a particular date (ordinarily, the balance sheet date). The estimated liability includes the amount of money that will be needed for future payments on both (a) claims that have been reported and (b) incurred but not reported (IBNR) claims.

The above definition includes estimates for costs related to filed claims as well as incurred but not reported (IBNR) claims. "IBNR claims" are defined as follows (GASB-10, par. 22 and Glossary):

> *Incurred but not reported (IBNR) claims*—Claims for insured events that have occurred but have not yet been reported to the governmental entity, public entity risk pool, insurer, or reinsurer as of the date of the financial statements. IBNR

> claims include (a) known loss events that are expected to later be presented as claims, (b) unknown loss events that are expected to become claims, and (c) expected future development on claims already reported.

The estimated liability for unpaid claims costs must be evaluated periodically to determine whether current factors make it necessary to adjust the liability for unpaid claims costs. For example, recent settlements may suggest that claims that have not been settled are understated. Adjustments of this nature are considered to be a change in an accounting estimate and, therefore, the resulting adjustment should be accounted for as an increase (or decrease) to current expenses of the public entity risk pool.

The estimated liability for unpaid claims costs should be reduced by estimated recoveries that may arise from unsettled claims. GASB-10 provides the following examples of recoveries (GASB-10, par. 22 and Glossary):

> *Salvage*—The amount received by a public entity risk pool from the sale of property (usually damaged) on which the pool has paid a total claim to the insured and has obtained title to the property.
>
> *Subrogation*—The right of an insurer to pursue any course of recovery of damages, in its name or in the name of the policyholder, against a third party who is liable for costs of an insured event that have been paid by the insurer.

When a liability for unpaid claims is recognized, a related accrual should also be made for claim adjustment expenses. Claim adjustment expenses should include an estimate for all future adjustment expenses that arise in connection with the settlement of unpaid claims. Both allocated and unallocated claim adjustment expenses should be part of the accrual (GASB-10, par. 23).

Allocated claim adjustment expenses are directly related to the settlement or processing of specific claims, and include expenses such as fees paid to adjusters and legal fees. Unallocated claim adjustment expenses are related to the settlement and processing of claims but are not traceable to a specific claim. Overhead costs of the public entity risk pool's claims department, such as administrative personnel salaries, allocations of depreciation, and utilities costs, are examples of unallocated claim adjustment expenses (GASB-10, par. 23).

> **PRACTICE POINT:** The requirement to include unallocated expenses in the accrual for claim adjustment expenses presents a difficult allocation problem for most public entity risk pools. For example, what portion of the forthcoming year's overhead costs for the claims department should be included in the

accrual? In addition, should only the future unallocated expenses of a single year be considered if it is likely that it may take years to settle some claims? A practical solution to the allocation problem is to estimate the percentage of claims identified and settled in one year and consider the balance to be the basis for the portion of overhead costs to be included in the year-end accrual. To illustrate, assume that a public entity risk pool has budgeted $500,000 for its overhead costs during the forthcoming year and it is estimated that about 80% of the claims processed are identified and settled in the same year. In this illustration, the liability for claim adjustment expenses should include an accrual of $100,000 ($500,000 × 20%) for unallocated claim adjustment expenses. Other more sophisticated allocation schemes are possible, but it is unlikely that the difference in amounts accrued between another allocation scheme and the one described here would have a material effect on the entity's financial statements.

In part, the accrual for claims liabilities represents estimates of cash flows that may occur several months or years into the future. The existence of such deferred payments raises the question of whether future cash flows related to the settlement of claims should be reported at gross value or at a discounted amount. The GASB does not take a position of whether future cash flows should be discounted. Thus, the accrual for claims liabilities can be reported either at a gross amount or at a discounted value (GASB-10, par. 24).

PRACTICE POINT: The public entity risk pool should disclose the method (gross method or discounting method) used to measure the accrual for claims liabilities.

The GASB provides one exception to its neutral position with respect to discounting. Structured settlements should be discounted if the payout amounts and payment dates are fixed by contract. The GASB provides the following definition for "structured settlement" (GASB-10, par. 24):

Structured settlement—A means of satisfying a claim liability, consisting of an initial cash payment to meet specific present financial needs combined with a stream of future payments designed to meet future financial needs, generally funded by annuity contracts.

To illustrate a structured settlement, assume that a public entity risk pool agrees in a written settlement to pay $100,000 immediately and to purchase three annuities of $200,000 (representing various payments to the claimant spread over a period of years) at the end of year 2, year 4, and year 5. If a 10% discount rate is assumed, the claims liability should be recorded for $526,000 as follows:

Year	*Future Cash Flows As Required By Contract*	*10% Present Value Factor*	*Present Value*
1	$100,000	1.000	$100,000
2	200,000	.826	165,200
4	200,000	.683	136,600
5	200,000	.621	124,200
			$526,000

The following entry would be made to record the structured settlement:

Expenses—Claims Costs	526,000	
Estimated Claims Costs Payable		526,000

At the end of each year, it would be necessary to record the amount of increase in the estimated liability due to the effects of discounting. For example, at the end of year 1, the following entry would be made:

Expenses—Claims Costs	42,600	
Estimated Claims Costs Payable (A)		42,600

(A) ($526,000 – $100,000) × 10%

If the public entity risk pool uses the discounting technique to measure claims liabilities, the GASB recommends that factors such as the pool's settlement rate and its investment yield rate be considered in establishing a discount rate. The "settlement rate" is defined as follows (GASB-10, par. 25 and Glossary):

> *Settlement rate*—The rate at which a monetary liability with uncertain terms can be settled or a monetary asset (receivable) with uncertain terms can be sold.

The investment yield rate is the rate that the public entity risk pool is earning or expects to earn on its portfolio of investments over the period covered by the structured settlement.

Some claims against the public entity risk pool may be settled by the purchase of an annuity contract. GASB-10 defines "annuity contract" as "a contract that provides fixed or variable periodic payments made from a stated or contingent date and continuing for a specified period, such as for a number of years or for life" (GASB-10, par. 26).

When a claim is settled by the purchase of an annuity contract, the claim should be removed from the accrued liability account if the possibility of additional payments to the claimant are remote (likelihood of future payment is slight). Thus, neither the claim nor the investment in the annuity contract is reported in the public entity risk pool's balance sheet. Under this arrangement, the claim is accounted for as an in-substance defeasance of the debt. Thus, the responsibility for payment of the claim has been met, although the claim is still legally an outstanding obligation (GASB-10, par. 26).

To illustrate the in-substance payment of a claim through the purchase of an annuity contract, assume that a claim with a recorded value of $250,000 is settled with the purchase of an annuity contract at a cost of $260,000. To record the purchase of the annuity contract, the following entry would be made:

Estimated Claims Costs Payable	250,000	
Expenses—Claims Costs	10,000	
Cash		260,000

PRACTICE POINT: It is unlikely that the cost of purchasing an annuity will equal the recorded value of the claim. For example, a difference will arise if the public entity risk pool does not use discounting to measure its claims. Even when discounting is used (for example in a structured settlement), the rate used to discount a claim is not likely to be the rate that will be charged by the commercial enterprise from which the annuity is acquired. Any difference should be accounted for as an increase (decrease) in the claims costs expense for the year.

When claims have been removed from the claims liability account due to settlement by the purchase of an annuity contract, there is still a contingent liability. If the commercial enterprise could not fulfill its contractual requirements, the responsibility for payment would revert to the public entity risk pool. For this reason, GASB-10 requires the disclosure of the amount of claims removed from the claims liability account due to settlement by the purchase of annuity contracts, and that this disclosure continue for as long as the pool's contingent liability exists. Disclosure is not required if both of the following conditions exist (GASB-10, par. 26):

- The claimant has signed an agreement releasing the public entity risk pool from further obligation.
- The likelihood of future payments to the claimant is remote.

Loss Contingencies

The conditions for recording a claim are that it is probable (likely to occur) that a liability has been incurred and a reasonable estimate of the liability can be made. If either of these conditions does not exist and there is at least a reasonable possibility (more than remote but less than probable) that a loss or an additional loss may have been incurred, the claim must be disclosed. The disclosure should include the following (GASB-10, par. 27):

- Nature of the claim
- Estimate of the possible loss or range of loss (or state that an estimate cannot be made)

Similar disclosures should be made for any excess over amounts of claims accrued, if there is a reasonable possibility that an amount in excess of the accrued amount may have to be paid by the public entity risk pool (GASB-10, par. 27).

Acquisition Costs

Acquisition costs represent costs that arise from the acquisition of new contracts or the renewal of new contracts, including commissions, inspection fees, and salaries of employees involved in the underwriting process (process of selecting, classifying, evaluating, rating, and assuming risks) (GASB-10, par. 28 and Glossary).

Acquisition costs should be capitalized as an asset and amortized as an expense over the life of the contract, in proportion to the amount of premium revenues recognized. To simplify the amortization of acquisition costs, contracts with similar characteristics should be grouped together. The groupings should be based on common characteristics such as the manner of (1) acquiring contracts, (2) servicing those contracts, and (3) determining the revenue and other expenses related to the contracts. GASB-10 provides the following definition of "type of contract" (GASB-10, par. 29 and Glossary):

> *Type of contract*—Classification of policies or participation contracts based on the nature of the coverages provided that distinguishes them as an identifiable class of contract. For example, types of contracts may include general liability, property, automobile liability, automobile physical damage, multi-peril, and workers' compensation.

Rather than track the acquisition costs of a specific contract, a public entity risk pool may develop an overall percentage based on the relationship between costs incurred and premiums from new and renewed contracts for a specific period. If such a percentage is developed and used, that percentage should be used throughout the periods represented by the new and renewed contracts used to originally compute the percentage (GASB-10, par. 30).

Other Costs

Costs that are not capitalized as acquisition costs for new contracts or renewed contracts should be expensed as incurred. Costs subject to immediate expense include gains or losses related to the management of the pool's portfolios of investments, administrative costs, and policy maintenance. "Policy maintenance costs" are "costs associated with maintaining records relating to insurance contracts and with the processing of premium collections and commissions" (GASB-10, par. 31 and Glossary).

Policyholder Dividends and Experience Refunds

A public entity risk pool may return a portion of the original premium paid based on the experience of the pool or a class of policies issued by the pool. The amount of the policyholder dividend (or return of contribution) is based on the overall experience of the covered group, not the experience of a particular policyholder or pool participant (GASB-10, par. 30).

Amounts of policyholder dividends should be accounted for as a dividends expense. At the end of the accounting period, an estimate of the amount to be distributed should be accrued (GASB-10, par. 30).

In some circumstances, the public entity risk pool may simply credit the amount of the policyholder dividend to the amount due from the policyholder for the next premium payment. The issuance of a premium credit should be recorded as both a dividends expense and premium revenue. For example, assume that $500,000 of policyholder dividends was accrued, of which $150,000 will be used by the policyholder as credit toward the next premium payment. The accrual would be recorded as follows:

Policyholder Dividends Expense	500,000	
Policyholder Dividends Payable		350,000
Premium Revenue		150,000

Policyholder dividends that arise from the return of excess premiums related to future catastrophic losses should be accounted for as policyholder dividends expense (GASB-10, par. 32).

Experience refunds are related to the specific experience of a policyholder or pool participant. Thus, the more claims a governmental entity incurs, the lower the refund. If the policy contract includes an experience refund clause, a separate liability for the estimated experience refunds should be created. The amount of the accrual should be based on the terms of the contract and the claims paid and incurred for the specific policyholder or pool participant. When the accrual is made, the offset should be to premium revenue (GASB-10, par. 33).

For example, assume that an experience refund of $5,000 for a particular policyholder is estimated. To record the estimate, the following entry would be made:

Premium Revenue	5,000	
Estimated Liability for Experience Refunds		5,000

Premium Deficiency

GASB-10 requires that a net realizable value test be made to determine whether there is a loss on existing contracts. If future expenses, plus any unamortized acquisition costs, exceed future premiums, then a loss or expense should be recognized (GASB-10, par. 34).

Contracts should be grouped and evaluated to determine whether the public entity risk pool has incurred a premium deficiency. The contracts should be grouped on the basis of common characteristics, such as the manner of acquisition, policy servicing, and measuring the revenue and expense related to the contracts. Once the contracts are grouped, a premium deficiency will exist if unearned (future) premiums related to the group are less than the sum of (1) expected claims costs (including IBNR claims), (2) expected claim adjustment expenses, (3) expected dividends to policyholders or pool participants, and (4) unamortized acquisition costs (GASB-10, par. 35, and GASB-30, par. 3.)

When a group of contracts has a premium deficiency, the deficiency should be charged to any existing unamortized acquisition costs. If the premium deficiency is greater than the unamortized acquisition costs, the excess should be accrued as an expense. To illustrate, assume that a public entity risk pool has made the following analysis for a group of contracts (GASB-10, pars. 35–36):

Expected claims costs (including IBNR)	$ 600,000
Expected claim adjustment expenses	150,000
Expected dividends to policyholders	20,000
Unamortized acquisition costs	10,000
	780,000
Unearned (future) premiums	(765,000)
Premium deficiency	$ 15,000

To record the premium deficiency computed, the following entry would be made:

Premium Deficiency Expenses	15,000	
Unamortized Acquisition Costs		10,000
Liability Related to Premium Deficiency		5,000

GASB-10 does not provide guidance as to whether expected investment income related to the grouping of contracts should be used to determine a premium deficiency. In the previous illustration, for example, if expected investment income is $30,000, there would be no premium deficiency. If expected investment income is used as part of the determination of a premium deficiency, that fact should be disclosed (GASB-10, par. 35).

GASB-10 did not address the recognition of a premium deficiency beyond the write-off of the unamortized acquisition costs. If the premium deficiency were $100,000 and the unamortized cost (an asset) equaled $70,000, should the remaining portion of the premium deficiency ($30,000) be recorded as a liability? GASB-30 amended GASB-10 by specifically stating that the "deficiencies in excess of unamortized acquisition costs should be recognized as a premium deficiency liability as of the balance sheet date and as a premium deficiency expense."

> **PRACTICE POINT:** While GASB-10 did not specifically address the recognition of a premium deficiency that exceeds unamortized acquisition costs, Chapter 3 of *GASB Comprehensive Implementation Guide* states that any premium deficiency that exceeds unamortized acquisition costs should be reported as a liability. In addition, FAS-60 (Accounting and Reporting by Insurance Enterprises [as amended]), which was the basis for GASB-10, requires the recognition of a premium deficiency that exceeds unamortized acquisition costs.

The premium deficiency computation should be made for contracts that represent a risk-sharing arrangement, whereby participants must make additional contributions for all or part of the deficiency. For this type of arrangement, the public entity risk pool should simultaneously record assessments receivable and revenue for the premium deficiency if all of the following conditions are satisfied (GASB-10, par. 36):

- A reasonable estimate of the additional contributions due can be made.
- The public entity risk pool has a legally enforceable claim to additional contributions.
- The collectibility of the additional contributions is probable.

Reinsurance

A public entity risk pool may enter into reinsurance contracts. The GASB defines "reinsurance" as follows (GASB-10, Glossary):

> *Reinsurance (reinsurer)*—A transaction in which an assuming enterprise (reinsurer), for a consideration (premium),

> assumes all or part of a risk undertaken originally by another insurer (ceding enterprise). However, the legal rights of the insured are not affected by the reinsurance transaction, and the ceding enterprise issuing the original insurance contract remains liable to the insured for payment of policy benefits.

The purpose of reinsurance is to spread the risk of loss, especially unusual losses that may occur, to more than one insurer.

The public entity risk pool must evaluate the terms of the reinsurance contract to determine how certain accounts should be presented in its financial statements (GASB-10, pars. 37–39).

When the public entity risk pool (ceding enterprise) can recover amounts from reinsurers (or excess insurers) based on paid claims and claim adjustment expenses, a receivable should be recorded and claims costs expense should be reduced. If it is expected that the total amount due from reinsurers will not be collected, an allowance for estimated uncollectible amounts should be established (GASB-10, par. 37).

When amounts due from reinsurers are related to unpaid claims and claim adjustment expenses, the estimated amount due should be netted against the estimated claims costs liability and the claims costs expense should be reduced (GASB-10, par. 37).

To account for the premium given by the public entity risk pool to the reinsurer, the portion (or all) of the unearned ceded premiums should be offset against the unearned premiums received from policyholders or pool participants. For example, assume a public entity risk pool receives unearned premiums of $700,000 from policyholders and 40% of these premiums are due to the reinsurer. These two transactions would be recorded as follows:

Cash	700,000	
Unearned Premium Revenue		700,000

To record premiums received from policyholder.

Unearned Premium Revenue Ceded	280,000	
Ceded Premiums Payable ($700,000 × 40%)		280,000

To record ceded premiums due to reinsurer.

For financial reporting purposes, receivables due from and payables due to the same reinsurer should be netted. In addition, (1) reinsurance premiums paid and related earned premiums and (2) reinsurance recoveries on claims and incurred claims costs may be netted on the public entity risk pool's operating statements (GASB-10, par. 37).

Amounts received from reinsurance transactions that represent the recovery of acquisition costs incurred by the public entity risk pool should be netted against the unamortized acquisition costs.

The net amount of acquisition costs (original acquisition costs "recoveries related to reinsurance transactions) should be amortized in a manner proportional to the amount of net revenue recognized (GASB-10, par. 38).

The public entity risk pool may agree to service all of the ceded insurance contracts while being reasonably compensated by the reinsurer. Under this circumstance, an accrual should be made for the estimated future (excess) maintenance costs related to the ceded contracts (GASB-10, par. 38).

Some agreements may be a reinsurance transaction in form but not in substance. The risk of economic loss may not be shifted from the public entity risk pool to the reinsurer. In this case, amounts paid to the reinsurer should be treated as a deposit. If the amount received from a reinsurer exceeds the amount of the deposit, a net liability should be presented on the public entity risk pool's balance sheet (GASB-10, par. 39).

Capitalization Contributions Made to Other Public Entity Risk Pools

A public entity risk pool may have a relationship with another public entity risk pool that is similar to the relationship between a governmental entity and a public entity risk pool (as described earlier). For example, a public entity risk pool (the participant pool) may share a portion of its risk with another public entity risk pool (the excess pool). When this arrangement exists, and the participant pool makes a capitalization contribution to the excess pool, the participant pool should observe the accounting standards established in paragraphs 3–6 of GASBI-4. In addition, the participant pool must also observe the accounting standards that relate to reinsurance contracts (as established by paragraphs 37–39 of GASB-10) (GASBI-4, pars. 10 and 18).

The guidance related to reinsurance may require the participant pool to net some balances related to the excess pool, or to treat certain payments to the excess pool as a deposit.

Capitalization Contributions Received

If it is probable that a capitalization contribution made to a public entity risk pool will be returned to the participant in the pool. The public entity risk pool (with transfer or pooling of risk) should account for the receipt of the contribution as a liability. If it is as probable that the contribution will *not* be returned, the receipt of the contribution should be reported as unearned premiums (a liability). The unearned premiums should be amortized and reported as premium revenue over the period for which it is expected that the capital contribution will be used to determine the amount of premiums the contributor must pay. However, if the period for which it is expected that the capital contribution will be used to determine the amount of premiums is not readily determinable, the amortization period cannot exceed 10 years (GASBI-4, pars. 11–12).

> **PRACTICE POINT:** The standards established by GASBI-4 require that all capitalization contributions received by a public entity risk pool that had previously been recorded as a component of capital be reclassified as a liability. Any capitalization contribution that had previously been recorded as revenue should be accounted for as a prior-period adjustment, with the restatement of the beginning balance of retained earnings for each period reported on a comparative basis.

Investments

Public entity risk pools, like commercial insurance companies, acquire a variety of investments to partially finance their costs of operations. A discussion of the method of accounting for these investments and other related issues is provided in Chapter 9, "Deposits and Investments."

Pools Not Involving Transfer or Pooling of Risks

Because of the arrangement between the public entity risk pool and participants, there may be no risk transfer or risk pooling among the participants. Under this arrangement, the public entity risk pool does not assume the role of an insurer but rather takes on the role of an agent for participants by performing the administrative duties of a claims servicer. Furthermore, under this arrangement, each participant is responsible for its own incurred claims (GASB-10, par. 51).

When there is no transfer or pooling of risks, standards established in the previous section do not apply. Although the transactions and events related to the public entity risk pool (claims-servicing pool) are accounted for in an Enterprise Fund, no liability for incurred claims costs is reported. The pool's balance sheet would reflect amounts due from participants as receivables and amounts due to participants as payables. In addition, GASBI-4 states that the receipt of a capitalization contribution should be netted against any related amount and a single asset or liability should be reported. That is, the pool's balance sheet would reflect amounts due from participants as receivables and amounts due to participants as payables, after the amount of the capitalization contribution is taken into consideration. On the income statement, revenue from performing claims-servicing activities and related administrative expenses would be reported (GASB-10, par. 51, and GASBI-4, par. 13).

FINANCIAL STATEMENTS

Because public entity risk pools are accounted for as Enterprise Funds, the financial statement requirements applicable to Enterprise Funds are applicable to governmental public entity risk pools. See Chapter 8, "Proprietary Funds," for a discussion of these required financial statements.

DISCLOSURES

The following additional information should be disclosed in the public entity risk pool's financial statements (GASB-10, par. 49, and GASB-30, par. 6):

- A description of the nature of risk transfer or the pooling agreement, including the rights and responsibilities assumed by both the public entity risk pool and its participants
- A description of the number and types of participants
- An explanation of the basis used to estimate the liabilities for unpaid claims and claim adjustment expenses, and an explicit statement that the estimate of the liabilities is based on the ultimate cost of settling the claims and includes the effects of inflation and other societal and economic factors
- A description of the nature of acquisition costs that are capitalized, the method used to amortize such costs, and the amount of acquisition costs amortized for the period
- Disclosure of the face (gross) amounts and carrying amounts of liabilities for unpaid claims and claim adjustment expenses presented on a present-value basis and the range of annual interest rates used to determine their present value
- A statement of whether the public entity risk pool takes into consideration estimated investment income when determining if premium deficiencies exist
- A description of the importance of excess insurance or reinsurance transactions to the public entity risk pool, including the following:
  - — Type of coverage
  - — Reinsurance premiums ceded
  - — Estimated amounts recoverable from excess insurers and reinsurers as of the balance sheet date that reduce the unpaid claims and claim adjustments expenses
- A presentation of a total claims liabilities reconciliation, including changes in aggregate liabilities for claims and claim adjustment expenses from the prior year to the current year using the following tabular format (see the example in Exhibit 23-2):

- — Beginning balance of liabilities for unpaid claims and claim adjustment expenses
- — Incurred claims and claim adjustment expenses for the year (with separate disclosure for the provision for insured events related to the current year and increases or decreases in the provision for events that were incurred in prior years)
- — Payments made (with separate disclosure for payments of claims and claim adjustment expenses related to insured events of the current year and payments of claims and claim adjustment expenses related to incurred events of prior years)
- — Explanation for other material reconciling items
- — Ending balance of liabilities for unpaid claims and claim adjustment expenses

- Disclosure of the total amount of outstanding liabilities that have been settled by purchasing annuity contracts from third parties in the name of claimants and the amount of liabilities that have been omitted from the balance sheet (The disclosure should not include amounts related to settlements in which claimants have signed agreements releasing the pool from further obligation and the chance of further payment is remote.)

REQUIRED SUPPLEMENTARY INFORMATION

GASB-30 establishes standards for reporting premium or required contribution revenue and claims development information (GASB-30, par. 7).

When a public entity risk pool presents separate financial statements, the revenue and claims development information should be presented as required supplementary information immediately after the notes to the financial statements. Required supplementary information is not considered to be part of the basic financial statements, because such information is not deemed essential to achieving the objective of adequate disclosure as required by governmental generally accepting accounting principles. On the other hand, required supplementary information is considered to be useful to various interested parties that must make assessments about a reporting entity.

PRACTICE POINT: When a public entity risk pool presents separate financial statements, the revenue and claims development information should be presented as required supplementary information immediately after the notes to the financial statements. When a public entity risk pool does not present separate financial statements, but rather presents its statements as part of another general governmental reporting entity's financial report, the revenue and claims development information may be presented as statistical information in the combined entity's comprehensive annual financial report (CAFR).

The standards established by GASB-30 supersede paragraph 50 of GASB-10, which described the format for required supplementary information for revenue and claims development information. The purpose of the presentation is to provide a basis for interested parties to identify and track trends related to current claims and developments in prior years' claims. In addition, the presentation provides a basis for determining the success of a pool's underwriting function and its ability to estimate its loss reserve over time.

Claims Development Information

The required supplementary information should be presented in a 10-year schedule (including the latest fiscal year) and include seven components (seven separate lines). The seven components are discussed in the following section and are cross-referenced to Exhibit 23-1, which is part of the illustration in Appendix D of GASB-30.

Line 1 The first line of the schedule of required supplementary information for revenue and claims development information focuses on revenues. Apublic entity risk pool should present (1) the amount of gross premium (or required contributions) revenue and reported investment revenue, (2) the amount of premium (or required contributions) revenue ceded, and (3) the amount of net reported premium (or required contributions) revenues (net of excess insurance or reinsurance) and reported investment revenue.

Line 2 The second line in the required supplementary information schedule discloses the amount of reported unallocated claim adjustment expenses and other costs.

PRACTICE POINT: Allocated claim adjustment expenses are directly related to the settlement or processing of specific claims, and they include expenses such as fees paid to adjusters and legal fees. Unallocated claim adjustment expenses are related to the settlement and processing of claims, but are not traceable to a specific claim. Overhead costs of the public entity risk pool's claims department, such as administrative personnel salaries, allocations of depreciation, and utilities costs, are examples of unallocated claim adjustment expenses.

PRACTICE POINT: Other costs that are not capitalized as acquisition costs for new contracts or renewed contracts should be expensed as incurred. Costs subject to immediate expense include gains or losses related to the management of the pool's portfolios of investments, administrative costs, and policy maintenance costs. "Policy maintenance costs" are "costs associated with maintaining records relating to insurance contracts and with the processing of premium collections and commissions."

Line 3 The third line in the schedule should present (1) the gross amount of incurred claims and allocated claim adjustment expenses, (2) the loss assumed by excess insurers or reinsurers, and (3) the net amount of incurred claims and allocated claim adjustment expenses. These three disclosures should include both paid and accrued amounts.

Incurred claims and allocated claim adjustment expenses may be internally developed by a public entity risk pool using various reporting methods. GASB-30 allows a public entity risk pool to present its claims information on an accident-year basis for occurrence-based policies, and a report-year basis for claims-made policies. Alternatively, the information may be presented on a policy-year basis. These alternatives are given the following definitions in GASB-10:

> *Claims-made policy*—A type of policy that covers losses from claims asserted (reported or filed) against the policyholder during the policy period, regardless of whether the liability-imposing events occurred during the current or any previous period in which the policyholder was insured under the claims-made contract or other specified period before the policy period (the policy retroactive date).
>
> *Policy-year basis*—For disclosure purpose as used in this Statement, a method that assigns incurred loses and claim adjustment expenses to the year in which the event that triggered coverage under the pool insurance policy or participation contract occurred. For occurrence-based coverage for which all members have a common contract renewal date, the policy year basis is the same as the accident-year basis. For claims-made coverage, policy year basis is the same as the report-year basis.

Amounts included in incurred claims and allocated claim adjustment expenses for a particular year should result only from events that triggered coverage under the policy or participation contract.

Once a method of developing the incurred claims and allocated claim adjustment expenses is adopted by a public entity risk pool, the method should be used consistently throughout each period.

OBSERVATION: The acceptability of more than one reporting basis (accident-year basis, report-year basis, and policy-year basis) raises the question of whether required supplementary

EXHIBIT 23-1
TEN-YEAR CLAIMS DEVELOPMENT INFORMATION

Fiscal and Policy Year Ended (In Thousands of Dollars)

	20W9	20X0	20X1	20X2	20X3	20X4	20X5	20X6	20X7	20X8
1. Required contribution and investment revenue:										
Earned	$908	$957	$1,357	$1,493	$1,479	$1,595	$1,811	$1,993	$2,192	$2,411
Ceded	366	387	559	615	624	686	754	830	913	1,004
Net earned	542	570	798	878	855	909	1,057	1,163	1,279	1,407
2. Unallocated expenses	64	68	81	91	70	81	92	110	123	131
3. Estimated claims and expenses, end of policy year:										
Incurred	287	303	453	503	569	651	780	909	1,092	1,512
Ceded	52	54	96	111	129	148	168	186	210	251
Net incurred	235	249	357	392	440	503	612	723	882	1,261
4. Net paid (cumulative) as of:										
End of policy year	118	124	179	196	220	251	306	361	450	641
One year later	177	186	268	294	330	377	459	542	675	
Two years later	254	268	385	422	474	542	660	779		
Three years later	304	321	461	506	568	649	790			
Four years later	359	379	545	597	671	766				
Five years later	404	427	614	673	756					

EXHIBIT 23-1 *(continued)*
TEN-YEAR CLAIMS DEVELOPMENT INFORMATION

Six years later	445	469	674	740						
Seven years later	473	499	717							
Eight years later	473	499								
Nine years later	473									
5. Reestimated ceded claims and expenses	104	109	160	174	184	195	211	217	234	251
6. Reestimated net incurred claims and expenses:										
End of policy year	235	249	357	392	440	503	612	723	882	1,261
One year later	294	311	447	490	550	628	765	898	1,102	
Two years later	338	357	513	563	632	722	874	1,028		
Three years later	380	401	577	632	710	811	982			
Four years later	422	446	641	703	789	902				
Five years later	449	474	682	748	840					
Six years later	468	494	710	779						
Seven years later	473	499	717							
Eight years later	473	499								
Nine years later	473									
7. Increase in estimated net incurred claims and expenses from end of policy year	238	250	360	387	400	399	370	305	220	0

information presented by public entity risk pools will be comparable. The GASB states that since the information is presented on a 10-year basis, trends for one public entity risk pool can be identified and compared to trends for other public entity risk pools. Furthermore, the GASB noted that some public entity risk pools have already developed trend information on an accident-year basis for statutory reporting, and therefore it is not necessary to require these pools to develop the information on another basis.

Line 4 The fourth line in the 10-year trend schedule relates the amount of incurred claims and allocated expense amounts recognized for a year and actual subsequent payments related to those amounts. The amounts should be presented on a cumulative basis from year to year, and should extend out for up to ten years. For example, in Exhibit 23-1 the net amount that was originally estimated in 20W9 ($287,000) resulted in actual cash payments in 20W9 of $118,000, and actual cash payments over the ten-year period of $473,000.

Line 5 The fifth line in the schedule discloses the reestimated amount for losses assumed by excess insurers or reinsurers based on the information available as of the end of the most current year. For example, in Exhibit 23-1 the original estimated ceded claims and expenses made in 20W9 was $52,000, but the most recent estimate of that amount (as of 20X8) is $104,000.

Line 6 The sixth line in the schedule presents the reestimated net incurred claims and expenses based on the information available as of the end of the most current year. For example, in Exhibit 23-1 the original estimate of net incurred claims and expenses made in 20W9 was $235,000; however, the estimates change in subsequent years as the public entity risk pool gains more experience (settlement of actual claims) with the policies. By the seventh year of experience, the reestimated net incurred claims and expenses are equal to the net amount paid ($473,000), which suggests that the public entity risk pool follows that no additional liability exists related to policy claims initiated in 20W9.

Line 7 The seventh line in the ten-year schedule provides insight into the public entity risk pool's ability to estimate claims and expenses by relating the original estimate of claims and expenses to the most recent estimate. For example, in Exhibit 23-1 the original estimate of estimated claims and expenses was $235,000 (Line 3) for 20W9, but the most recent reestimated amount as of 20X8 was $473,000 (Line 6). The difference of $238,000 ($473,000 " $235,000) is presented in Line 7 and labeled as the "increase in estimated net incurred claims and expenses from end of policy year."

PRACTICE POINT: The information developed for Line 4, Line 5, Line 6, and Line 7 should be based on the same reporting method(s) used in Line 3 (accident year, report year, or policy year).

The dollar amounts presented in the ten-year required supplementary information by public entity risk pools may be supplemented by the presentation of the same information on a percentage basis, although the latter presentation is not required. Also, percentage presentations cannot be substituted for dollar amount presentations (dollar amounts are illustrated only in Exhibit 23-1). GASB-10 notes that the presentation of percentage information "should not obscure or distort required elements of the table."

See Exhibits 23-2 and 23-3.

EXHIBIT 23-2
NOTE DISCLOSURE FOR UNPAID CLAIMS LIABILITIES

Unpaid Claims Liabilities

As discussed in Note A, the Fund establishes a liability for both reported and unreported insured events, which includes estimates of both future payments of losses and related claim adjustment expenses, both allocated and unallocated. The following represents changes in those aggregate liabilities for the Fund during the past two years (in thousands):

	20X8	20X7
Unpaid claims and claim adjustment expenses at beginning of year	$1,421	$1,189
Incurred claims and claim adjustment expenses:		
Provision for insured events of current year	1,282	900
Increases in provision for insured events of prior years	649	540
Total incurred claims and claim adjustment expenses	1,931	1,440
Payments:		
Claims and claim adjustment expenses attributable to insured events of current year	641	450
Claims and claim adjustment expenses attributable to insured events of prior years	904	758
Total payments	1,545	1,208
Total unpaid claims and claim adjustment expenses at end of year	$1,807	$1,421

At year-end 20X8, $718,000 of unpaid claims and claim adjustment expenses are presented at their net present value of $576,000. These claims are discounted at annual rates ranging from 8 1/2% to 11%. Unpaid claims expenses of $249,000 are not reported in the 20X8 year-end balances because the Fund has purchased annuities in claimants' names to settle those claims.

EXHIBIT 23-3
REQUIRED SUPPLEMENTARY INFORMATION FOR RECONCILIATION OF CLAIMS LIABILITIES BY TYPE OF CONTRACT

Reconciliation of Claims Liabilities by Type of Contract

The schedule below presents (in thousands) the changes in claims liabilities for the past two years for the Fund's two types of contracts: property and casualty and employee health and accident benefits.

	Property and Casualty		*Employee Health and Accident*		*Totals*	
	20X8	*20X7*	*20X8*	*20X7*	*20X8*	*20X7*
Unpaid claims and claim adjustment expenses at beginning of year	$762	$716	$659	$476	$1421	$1192
Incurred claims and claim adjustment expenses:						
Provision for insured events of current year	513	360	769	540	1282	900
Increases in provision for insured events of prior fiscal years	389	324	260	216	649	540
Total incurred claims and claim adjustment expenses	902	684	1029	756	1931	1440
Payments:						
Claims and claim adjustment expenses attributable to insured events of current fiscal year	256	180	385	270	641	450

	Property and Casualty		*Employee Health and Accident*		*Totals*	
	20X8	*20X7*	*20X8*	*20X7*	*20X8*	*20X7*
Claims and claim adjustment expenses attributable to insured events of prior fiscal years	542	455	362	303	904	758
Total payments	798	635	747	573	1545	1208
Total unpaid claims and claim adjustment expenses at end of fiscal year	$866	$765	$941	$659	$1807	$1424

ACCOUNTING RESOURCES ON THE WEB

Presented here are World Wide Web URLs of interest to industry accountants. Because of the constantly changing nature of the Internet, addresses change and new resources become available every day. To find additional resources, use search engines such as Google (http://www.google.com/), and Yahoo! (http://search.yahoo.com).

AICPA http://www.aicpa.org

Accounting Research Manager
http://www.accountingresearchmanager.com/

American Accounting Association http://aaahq.org/raw/aaa/

CCH INCORPORATED http://tax.cchgroup.com/

Code of Federal Regulations
http://www.gpoaccess.gov/cfr/index.html

FASB http://accounting.rutgers.edu/raw/fasb/

Federal Register http://www.gpoaccess.gov/fr/

Federal Tax Code Search http://www.gpoaccess.gov/cfr/

Fedworld http://www.fedworld.gov/

GASB http://www.gasb.org

Government Accountability Office http://www.gao.gov/

Government Printing Office http://www.gpoaccess.gov/

International Accounting Standards Board [formerly International Accounting Standards Committee (IASC)]
http://www.iasb.org.uk/

IRS Digital Daily http://www.irs.gov/

The Library of Congress http://www.loc.gov/

Loislaw http://www.loislaw.com/

Office of Management and Budget
http://www.whitehouse.gov/omb

Thomas: Legislative Information http://thomas.loc.gov/

U.S. Government's Official Web Portal
http://www.firstgov.gov/

U.S. House of Representatives http://www.house.gov/

U.S. Senate http://www.senate.gov/

The White House http://www.whitehouse.gov/

CROSS-REFERENCE

ORIGINAL PRONOUNCEMENTS TO COMPREHENSIVE GOVERNMENTAL GAAP GUIDE CHAPTERS

This locator provides instant cross-reference between an original pronouncement and the chapter(s) in this publication where such pronouncement appears. Original pronouncements are listed chronologically on the left and the chapter(s) in which the pronouncement appears in CCH's *Governmental GAAP Guide* on the right. Primary Codification section references are in parentheses.

GOVERNMENTAL ACCOUNTING STANDARDS BOARD STATEMENTS

GASB Statements are issued by the Governmental Accounting Standards Board under the authority of Rule 203 of the AICPA's Code of Professional Conduct. Rule 203 states in part that an AICPA member shall not express an opinion or state affirmatively that financial statements are presented in conformity with generally accepted accounting principles if such statements contain any departure from an accounting principle promulgated by bodies designated by the AICPACouncil. Members of the AICPAshould be prepared to justify any departures from the Rules of Conduct of the Code of Professional Conduct. Unless otherwise specified, GASB Statements apply to financial reports of all state and local governmental entities, including public benefit corporations and authorities, public employee retirement systems, and governmental utilities, hospitals, colleges, and universities.

ORIGINAL PRONOUNCEMENT	GOVT GAAP GUIDE REFERENCE
GASB Statement No. 1 (1984) Authoritative Status of NCGA Pronouncements and AICPA Industry Audit Guide (throughout)	Foundation and Overview of Governmental Generally Accepted Accounting Principles, Chapter **1**
GASB Statement No. 2 (1986) Financial Reporting of Deferred Compensation Plans Adopted under the Provisions of Internal Revenue Code Section 457 (D25)	Superseded by GASB-32
GASB Statement No. 3 (1986) Deposits with Financial Institutions, Investments (Including Repurchase Agreements), and Reverse Repurchase Agreements (C20; I50; R10)	Deposits and Investments, Chapter **9**

GASB Statement No. 4 (1986) Applicability of FASB Statement No. 87, "Employers' Accounting for Pensions," to State and Local Governmental Employers	Superseded by GASB-25 and GASB-27
GASB Statement No. 5 (1986) Disclosure of Pension Information by Public Employee Retirement Systems and State and Local Governmental Employers	Superseded by GASB-25 and GASB-27
GASB Statement No. 6 (1987) Accounting and Financial Reporting for Special Assessments (S40)	Special Assessments, Chapter **19**
GASB Statement No. 7 (1987) Advance Refundings Resulting in Debt Defeased Debt (D20)	Long-Term Debt, Chapter **12**
GASB Statement No. 8 (1988) Applicability of FASB Statement No. 93, "Recognition of Depreciation by Not-for-Profit Organizations," to Certain State and Local Governmental Entities (Co5; Pu5)	Superseded by GASB-35
GASB Statement No. 9 (1989) Reporting Cash Flows of Proprietary and Nonexpendable Trust Funds and Governmental Entities That Use Proprietary Fund Accounting (2450)	Proprietary Funds, Chapter **7**
GASB Statement No. 10 (1989) Accounting and Financial Reporting for Risk Financing and Related Insurance Issues (Po20; C50)	Public Entity Risk Pools, Chapter **23**
GASB Statement No. 11 (1990) Measurement Focus and Basis of Accounting—Governmental Fund Operating Statements	Rescinded
GASB Statement No. 12 (1990) Disclosure of Information on Post-employment Benefits Other Than Pension Benefits by State and Local Governmental Employers (P50)	Pension, Postemployment, and other Employee Benefit Liabilities, Chapter **13**

GASB Statement No. 13 (1990) Accounting for Operating Leases with Scheduled Rent Increases (L20)	Leases, Chapter **14**
GASB Statement No. 14 (1991) The Financial Reporting Entity (2300; 2600)	Governmental Reporting Entity, Chapter **4**
GASB Statement No. 15 (1991) Governmental College and University Accounting and Financial Reporting Models (Co5)	Superseded by GASB-35
GASB Statement No. 16 (1992) Accounting for Compensated Absences (C60)	Pension, Postemployment, and other Employee Benefit Liabilities, Chapter **13**
GASB Statement No. 17 (1993) Measurement Focus and Basis of Accounting—Governmental Fund Operating Statements: Amendment of the Effective Dates of GASB Statement No. 11 and Related Statements	Rescinded
GASB Statement No. 18 (1993) Accounting for Municipal Solid WasteLandfill Closure and Postclosure Care Costs (L10)	Other Liabilities, Chapter **16**
GASB Statement No. 19 (1993) Governmental College and University Omnibus Statement (Co5)	Superseded by GASB-35
GASB Statement No. 20 (1993) Accounting and Financial Reporting for Proprietary Funds and Other Governmental Entities That Use Proprietary Fund Accounting (P80)	Foundation and Overview of Government Generally Accepted Accounting Principles, Chapter **1**
GASB Statement No. 21 (1993) Accounting for Escheat Property (E70)	Other Assets, Chapter **11**
GASB Statement No. 22 (1993) Accounting for Taxpayer-Assessed Tax Revenues in Governmental Funds (1600)	Superseded by GASB-33
GASB Statement No. 23 (1993) Accounting and Financial Reporting for Refundings of Debt Reported by Proprietary Activities (D20)	Long-Term Debt, Chapter **12**

GASB Statement No. 24 (1994) Accounting and Financial Reporting Certain Grants and Other Financial Assistance (G60)	Revenues: Nonexchange and Exchange Transactions, Chapter **17**
GASB Statement No. 25 (1994) Financial Reporting for Defined Benefit Pension Plans and Note Disclosures for Defined Contribution Plans (Pe5)	Pension and Other Postretirement Benefit Plans, Chapter **22**
GASB Statement No. 26 (1994) Financial Reporting for Postemployment Healthcare Plans Administered by Defined Benefit Pension Plans (Po50)	Pension and Other Postretirement Benefit Plans, Chapter **22**
GASB Statement No. 27 (1994) Accounting for Pensions by State and Local Governmental Employers (P20)	Pension, Postemployment, and Other, Employee Benefit Liabilities Chapter **13**
GASB Statement No. 28 (1995) Accounting and Financial Reporting for Securities Lending Transactions (I60)	Deposits and Investments, Chapter **9**
GASB Statement No. 29 (1995) The Use of Not-for-Profit Accounting and Financial Reporting Principles by Governmental Entities (N80)	Superseded by GASB-34
GASB Statement No. 30 (1996) Risk Financing Omnibus (C50 and Po20)	Risk Management Claims and Judgments, Chapter **15** Public Entity Risk Pools, Chapter **23**
GASB Statement No. 31 (1997) Accounting and Financial Reporting for Certain Investments and for External Investment Pools (I5O)	Deposits and Investments, Chapter **9**
GASB Statement No. 32 (1997) Accounting and Financial Reporting for Internal Revenue Code Section 457 Deferred Compensation Plans	Pension and Other Postretirement Benefit Plans, Chapter **22**
GASB Statement No. 33 (1998) Accounting and Financial Reporting for Nonexchange Transactions	Revenues: Nonexchange and Exchange Transactions, Chapter **17**

GASB Statement No. 34 (1999) Basic Financial Statements—and Managreement's Discussion and Analysis—for State and Local Governments	Comprehensive Annual Financial Report, Chapter **20**
GASB Statement No. 35 (1999) Basic Financial Statements—and Management's Discussion and Analysis—for Public Colleges and Universities	Public Colleges and Universities, Chapter **21**
GASB Statement No. 36 (2000) Recipient Reporting for Certain Shared Nonexchange Revenues	Revenues: Nonexchange and Exchange Transactions, Chapter **17**
GASB Statement No. 37 (2001) Basic Financial Statements—and Management's Discussion and Analysis—for State and Local Governments: Omnibus	Comprehensive Annual Financial Report, Chapter **20**
GASB Statement No. 38 (2001) Certain Financial Statement Note Disclosures	Budgetary Accounting and Reporting, Chapter **2** Revenues: Non-exchange and Exchange Transactions, Chapter **17** Other Assets, Chapter **11** Other Liabilities, Chapter **16** Leases, Chapter **14** Special Assessments, Chapter **19**
GASB Statement No. 39 (2002) Determining Whether Certain Organizations Are Component Units	Governmental Reporting Entity, Chapter **4**
GASB Statement No. 40 (2003) Deposit and Investment Risk Disclosures	Deposits and Investments, Chapter **9**
GASB Statement No. 41 (2003) Budgetary Comparison Schedules—Perspective Difference—and amendment of GASB Statement No. 34	Budgetary Accounting and Reporting, Chapter **2**
GASB Statement No. 42 (2003) Accounting and Financial Reporting for Impairment of Capital Assets and for Insurance Recoveries	Capital Assets, Chapter **10**

GASB Statement No. 43 (2004)	
Financial Reporting for Postemployment Benefit Plans Other Than Pension Plans	Pension and Other Postemployment Benefit Plans, Chapter **22**
GASB Statement No. 44 (2004)	
Economic Condition Reporting: The Statistical Section—an amendment of NCGA Statement	Comprehensive Annual Financial Report, Chapter **20**
GASB Statement No. 45 (2004)	
Accounting and Financial Reporting by Employers for Postemployment Benefits Other Than Pensions	Pension, Postemployment, and Other Employee Benefit Liabilities, Chapter **13**
GASB Statement No. 46 (2004)	
Net Assets Restricted by Enabling Legislation—an amendment of GASB Statement No. 34	Terminology and Classification, Chapter **5**
GASB Statement No. 47 (2005)	
Accounting for Termination Benefits	Pension, Postemployment, and Other Employee Benefit Liabilities, Chapter **13**
GASB Statement No. 48 (2006)	
Sales and Pledges of Receivables and Future Revenues and Intra-Entity Transfers of Assets and Future Revenues	Revenues: Nonexchange and Exchange Transactions, Chapter **17**
GASB Statement No. 49 (2006)	
Accounting and Reporting of Pollution Remediation Obligations	Other Liabilities, Chapter **16**
GASB Statement No. 50 (2007)	
Pension Disclosures	Pension, Postemployment, and Other Employee Benefit Liabilities, Chapter **13** Pension and Other Postemployment Benefit Plans, Chapter **22**

GOVERNMENTAL ACCOUNTING STANDARDS BOARD INTERPRETATIONS

GASB Interpretations are issued by the Governmental Accounting Standards Board under the authority of Rule 203 of the AICPA's Code of Professional Conduct. Rule 203 states in part that an AICPA member shall not express an opinion or state affirmatively that financial statements are presented in conformity with generally accepted accounting principles if such statements contain any departure from an accounting principle promulgated by bodies designated by the AICPACouncil. Members of the AICPA should be prepared to justify any departures from the Rules of Conduct of the Code of Professional Conduct. Unless otherwise specified, GASB Interpretations apply to financial reports of all state and local governmental entities, including public benefit corporations and authorities, public employee retirement systems, and governmental utilities, hospitals, colleges, and universities.

ORIGINAL PRONOUNCEMENT	GOVT GAAP GUIDE REFERENCE
GASB Interpretation No. 1 (1984) Demand Bonds Issued by State and Local Governmental Entities (D30)	Long-Term Debt, Chapter **12**
GASB Interpretation No. 2 (1995) Disclosure of Conduit Debt Obligations (C65)	Other Liabilities, Chapter **16**
GASB Interpretation No. 3 (1996) Financial Reporting for Reverse Repurchase Agreements (I55)	Deposits and Investments, Chapter **9**
GASB Interpretation No. 4 (1996) Accounting and Financial Reporting for Capitalization Contributions to Public Entity Risk Pools (C50 and Po20)	Public Entity Risk Pools, Chapter **23**
GASB Interpretation No. 5 (1997) Property Tax Revenue Recognition in Governmental Funds (an interpretation of NCGA Statement 1 and an amendment of NCGA Interpretation 3)	Revenues: Nonexchange and Exchange Transactions, Chapter **17**
GASB Interpretation No. 6 (2000) Recognition and Measurement of Certain Liabilities and Expenditures in Governmental Fund Financial Statements	Other Liabilities, Chapter **16**

GOVERNMENTAL ACCOUNTING STANDARDS BOARD TECHNICAL BULLETINS

GASB Technical Bulletins are issued by the Governmental Accounting Standards Board but are not issued under the authority of Rule 203 of the AICPA's Code of Professional Conduct. The GASB has authorized its staff to prepare Technical Bulletins to respond to governmental accounting issues on a timely basis. Technical Bulletins are not voted on formally by the GASB; however, a Technical Bulletin will not be issued if a majority of the members of the GASB object to its issuance.

ORIGINAL PRONOUNCEMENT	GOVT GAAP GUIDE REFERENCE
GASB Technical Bulletin 84-1 (1984) Purpose and Scope of GASB Technical Bulletins and Procedures for Issuance	Foundation and Overview of Governmental GenerallyAccepted Accounting Principles, Chapter **1**
GASB Technical Bulletin 87-1 (1987) Applying Paragraph 68 of GASB Statement 3 (I50)	Deposits and Investments, Chapter **9**
GASB Technical Bulletin 92-1 (1992) Display of Governmental College and University Compensated Absences Liabilities (Co5)	Superseded by GASB-35
GASB Technical Bulletin 94-1 (1994) Disclosures About Derivatives and Similar Debt and Investment Transactions (2300)	Superseded by GASB TB 2003-1
GASB Technical Bulletin 96-1 (1996) Application of Certain Pension Disclosure Requirements for Employers Pending Implementation GASB Statement 27 (P20)	Superseded by GASB-27
GASB Technical Bulletin 97-1 (1997) Classification of Deposits and Investments into Custodial Credit Risk Categories for Certain Bank Holding Company Transactions	Deposits and Investments, Chapter **9**
GASB Technical Bulletin 98-1 (1998) Disclosures about Year 2000 Issues	Rescinded
GASB Technical Bulletin 99-1 (1999) Disclosures about Year 2000 Issues—An Amendment of Technical Bulletin 98-1	Rescinded

GASB Technical Bulletin 2000-1 (2000)	
Disclosures about Year 2000 Issues—A Recission of GASB Technical Bulletins 98-1 and 99-1	No reference
GASB Technical Bulletin 2003-1 (2003)	
Disclosure Requirements for Derivatives Not Reported at Fair Value on the Statement of Net Assets	Deposits and Investments, Chapter **9**
GASB Technical Bulletin 2004-1 (2004)	
Tobacco Settlement Recognition and Financial Reporting Entity Issues	No reference
GASB Technical Bulletin 2006-1 (2006)	
Accounting and Financial Reporting by Employers and OPEB Plans for Payments from the Federal Government Pursuant to the Retiree Drug Subsidy Provisions of Medicare Part D	Pension, Postemployment, and Other Employee Benefit Liabilities, Chapter **13** Pension and Other Postemployment Benefit Plans, Chapter **22**

GOVERNMENTAL ACCOUNTING STANDARDS BOARD CONCEPTS STATEMENTS

GASB Concepts Statements are issued by the Governmental Accounting Standards Board; however, Concepts Statements do not establish generally accepted accounting principles for state and local governmental entities. Concepts Statements identify concepts that will be used by the GASB in establishing future governmental accounting and reporting standards.

ORIGINAL PRONOUNCEMENT	GOVT GAAP GUIDE REFERENCE
GASB Concepts Statement No. 1 (1987)	
Objectives of Financial Reporting (100)	Foundation and Overview of Governmental Generally Accepted Accounting Principles, Chapter **1**
GASB Concepts Statement No. 2 (1994)	
Service Efforts and Accomplishments Reporting (100)	Foundation and Overview of Governmental Generally Accepted Accounting Principles, Chapter **1**
GASB Concepts Statement No. 3 (2005)	
Communication Methods in General Purpose External Financial Reports That Contain Basic Financial Statements	Foundation and Overview of Governmental Generally Accepted Accounting Principles, Chapter **1**

NATIONAL COUNCIL ON GOVERNMENTAL ACCOUNTING STATEMENTS

NCGA Statements were issued by the National Council on Governmental Accounting until 1984, when the GASB assumed the role of promulgating accounting principles for state and local governments. GASB Statement No.1 states that NCGA Statements not otherwise superseded are considered authoritative support for determining generally accepted accounting principles for state and local governments.

ORIGINAL PRONOUNCEMENT	GOVT GAAP GUIDE REFERENCE

NCGA Statement No. 1 (1979)
Governmental Accounting and Financial Reporting Principles (throughout)

• Accounting and Reporting Capabilities	Foundation and Overview of Governmental Generally Accepted Accounting Principles, Chapter **1**
• Fund Accounting Systems	Foundation and Overview of Governmental Generally Accepted Accounting Principles, Chapter **1**
• Fund Types	Comprehensive Annual Financial Report, Chapter **20**
• Number of Funds	Foundation and Overview of Governmental Generally Accepted Accounting Principles, Chapter **1**
• Reporting Capital Assets	Capital Assets, Chapter **10**
• Valuation of Capital Assets	Capital Assets, Chapter **10**
• Depreciation of Capital Assets	Capital Assets, Chapter **10**
• Reporting Long-Term Liabilities	Other Liabilities, Chapter **16**
• Measurement Focus and Basis of Accounting in the Basic Financial Statements	Basis of Accounting and Measurement Focus, Chapter **3**
• Budgeting, Budgetary, Control, and Budgetary Reporting	Budgetary Accounting and Reporting, Chapter **2**
• Transfer, Revenue, Expenditure, and Expense Account Classification	Terminology and Classification, Chapter **5**
• Common Terminology and Classification	Terminology and Classification, Chapter **5**
• Annual Financial Reports	Foundation and Overview of Governmental Generally Accepted Accounting Principles, Chapter **1**

NCGA Statement No. 2 (1980) Grant, Entitlement, and Shared Revenue Accounting by State and Local Governments (G60)	Superseded by GASB-33 and GASB-34
NCGA Statement No. 3 (1981) Defining the Governmental Reporting Entity (no reference)	Superseded by GASB-14
NCGA Statement No. 4 (1982) Accounting and Financial Reporting Principles for Claims and Judgments and Compensated Absences (C50; C60)	Risk Management, Claims and Judgments, Chapter **15** Governmental Funds, Chapter **6**
NCGA Statement No. 5 (1983) Accounting and Financial Reporting Principles for Lease Agreements of State and Local Governments (L20)	Leases, Chapter **14**
NCGA Statement No. 6 (1983) Pension Accounting and Financial Reporting: Public Employee Retirement Systems and State and Local Government Employers (P20; Pe5)	Superseded by GASB-25 and GASB-27
NCGA Statement No. 7 (1984) Financial Reporting for Component Units within the Governmental Reporting Entity (no reference)	Superseded by GASB-14

NATIONAL COUNCIL ON GOVERNMENTAL ACCOUNTING INTERPRETATIONS

NCGA Interpretations were issued by the National Council on Governmental Accounting until 1984, when the GASB assumed the role of promulgating accounting principles for state and local governments. GASB-1 states that NCGA Interpretations not otherwise superseded are considered authoritative support for determining generally accepted accounting principles for state and local governments.

ORIGINAL PRONOUNCEMENT	GOVT GAAP GUIDE REFERENCE
NCGA Interpretation No. 1 (1976) GAAFR and the AICPA Audit Guide (no reference)	Superseded by NCGA-1
NCGA Interpretation No. 2 (1980) Segment Information for Enterprise Funds (2500)	Superseded by GASB-34

NCGA Interpretation No. 3 (1981) Revenue Recognition—Property Taxes (P70)	Revenues: Nonexchange and Exchange Transaction, Chapter **17**
NCGA Interpretation No. 4 (1981) Accounting and Financial Reporting for Public Employee Retirement Systems and Pension Trust Funds (no reference)	Superseded by NCGA-6
NCGA Interpretation No. 5 (1982) Authoritative Status of Governmental Accounting, Auditing, and Financial Reporting (1968) (1100)	Superseded by GASB-34
NCGA Interpretation No. 6 (1982) Notes to the Financial Statements Disclosure (2300)	Comprehensive Annual Financial Reports, Chapter **20**
NCGA Interpretation No. 7 (1983) Clarification as to the Application of the Criteria in NCGA Statement 3, "Defining the Governmental Reporting Entity" (no reference)	Superseded by GASB-14
NCGA Interpretation No. 8 (1983) Certain Pension Matters (P20; T25)	Risk Management, Claims and Judgments, Chapter **15**
NCGA Interpretation No. 9 (1984) Certain Fund Classifications and Balance Sheet Accounts (B50; D20; E70; U50)	Capital Assets, Chapter **10** Long-Term Debt, Chapter **12**
NCGA Interpretation No. 10 (1984) State and Local Government Budgetary Reporting (2400)	Budgetary Accounting and Reporting, Chapter **2**
NCGA Interpretation No. 11 (1984) Claim and Judgment Transactions for Governmental Funds (C50)	Risk Management, Claims and Judgments, Chapter **15**

AICPA AUDIT AND ACCOUNTING GUIDE: STATE AND LOCAL GOVERNMENTS—WITH CONFORMING CHANGES AS OF MAY 1, 2006

SAS-69 (The Meaning of Present Fairly in Conformity with Generally Accepted Accounting Principles) establishes a public-sector accounting hierarchy for determining the applicability of specific accounting and reporting standards for state and local governments. The accounting hierarchy has five levels, each of which is subordinate to the levels directly above it. The second level in the hierarchy (Level B) includes AICPA Audit and Accounting Guide made applicable by the AICPAand cleared by the GASB. In September 2002, the AICPA issued an audit and accounting guide titled "Audits of State and Local Governments (ASLG)," which is considered to be Level B guidance.

ORIGINAL PRONOUNCEMENT	GOVT GAAP GUIDE REFERENCE
Definition of a governmental entity (par. 1.01)	Foundation and Overview of Governmental Generally Accepted Accounting Principles, Chapter **1**
Restricted net assets (par. 2.56)	Terminology and Classification, Chapter **5** Comprehensive Annual Financial Report, Chapter **20**
Arbitrage liability (par. 5.07)	Other Liabilities, Chapter **16**
Investments not subject to GASB-31 (par. 5.21)	Deposits and Investments, Chapter **9**
Overdrafts in internal investment pools (par. 5.27)	Other Assets, Chapter **11**
Negative cash positions or excess liabilities in Agency Funds (par. 5.29)	Fiduciary Funds, Chapter **8**
Loss contingencies related to the audit intergovernmental grants (par. 6.34)	Revenues: Nonexchange and Exchange Transactions, Chapter **17**
Reporting nonoperating revenues for proprietary funds (par. 6.73)	Proprietary Funds, Chapter **7**
Timing the recording of the proceeds from the issuance of debt (par. 8.16)	Governmental Funds, Chapter **6**
Fees related to pass-through grants (par. 8.34)	Revenues: Nonexchange and Exchange Transactions, Chapter **17**
Loss contingencies (par. 8.48)	Risk Managements, Claims and Judgments, Chapter **15**
Customer deposits for utility services (par. 8.55)	Proprietary Funds, Chapter **7**
Inventories/supplies in governmental funds (par. 8.57)	Other Assets, Chapter **11**
Commitments (par. 8.83)	Comprehensive Annual Financial Report, Chapter **20**
Fund balance reserves (par. 10.10)	Terminology and Classification, Chapter **5**
Designations in governmental funds (par. 10.17)	Terminology and Classification, Chapter **5**
Reporting budgetary information (pars. 11.16 and 14.57)	Budgetary Accounting and Reporting, Chapter **2**
Public finance authorities (par. 12.31)	Long Term Debt, Chapter **12**

Nonoperating revenues (par. 12.68)	Public Colleges and Universities, Chapter **21**
Lottery prize costs (par. 12.103)	Proprietary Funds, Chapter **7**
Lottery prize liabilities and related assets (pars. 12.104)	Proprietary Funds, Chapter **7**

NATIONAL COUNCIL ON GOVERNMENTAL ACCOUNTING CONCEPTS STATEMENTS

NCGA Concepts Statements were issued by the National Council on Governmental Accounting until 1984, when the GASB assumed the role of promulgating accounting principles for state and local governments. NCGA Concepts Statement No. 1 was superseded by GASB Concepts Statement No. 1; however, the GASB concluded that NCGA Concepts Statement No. 1 is nonetheless a useful source for understanding the role of financial reporting by governmental entities.

ORIGINAL PRONOUNCEMENT	GOVT GAAP GUIDE REFERENCE
NCGA Concepts Statement No. 1 (1982)	
Objectives of Accounting and Finan- Reporting for Governmental Units (Appendix B)	Foundation and Overview of Governmental Generally Accepted Accounting Principles, Chapter **1**

INDEX